GREAT
AMERICAN
COOPERATORS

Biographical Sketches of
101 Major Pioneers
in Cooperative Development

by
JOSEPH G. KNAPP AND ASSOCIATES

American Institute of Cooperation
Washington, D.C.

TO THE ARCHITECTS
AND THE BUILDERS
OF COOPERATION'S FUTURE

"There are pioneer souls that blaze their paths where highways never ran."—Sam W. Foss, *The House by the Side of the Road.*

Foreword

I AM GRATEFUL TO DR. KNAPP and all of the authors who made this book possible. Too little of our cooperative history has been accurately and completely recorded. This collection of profiles is fascinating reading. It will be most interesting to those of us who are older and knew many, if not most of those included here, but I hope it will inform and inspire "new students" and challenge them to greater things.

We could use to good advantage today a lot of the enthusiasm, the optimism, the courage, the persistence, and the willingness to make personal sacrifices that characterized most of these pioneers.

J. Kenneth Stern

President,
American Institute of Cooperation

Editor's Preface

THIS VOLUME HAS GROWN out of a remark by Orion Ulrey of Michigan State University following a research and teaching conference on agricultural cooperation held in Washington, D. C., in the spring of 1965. Dr. Ulrey expressed the view that there is a need for a book of brief biographies on the pioneers who helped bring our present cooperatives into existence. He suggested that a book of this type could be prepared as a joint effort by those interested in the history of cooperative development, and he urged that I take the lead in getting the job done.

The idea appealed to me and I began to consider how the project might be carried through. In December, 1965, I therefore wrote to several friends to enlist their help in selecting the names of cooperative pioneers who might be portrayed in such a volume and persons who might best prepare profiles of those selected.

The following generously helped me in this way, and I am greatly indebted to them for their advice and counsel: Martin A. Abrahamsen, Deputy Administrator, Farmer Cooperative Service, U.S.D.A.; Henry E. Erdman, Emeritus Professor, University of California; Kelsey B. Gardner, Cooperative Consultant, Washington, D. C.; Harold Hamil, Senior Vice-President, Farmland Industries, Kansas City, Missouri; Kenneth Hinshaw, Editor, *Agway Co-operator*, Syracuse, New York; Adlowe L. Larson, Director, International Cooperative Training Center, Madison, Wisconsin; E. P. Roy, Professor, Department of Agricultural Economics, The Louisiana State University; Marvin A. Schaars, Professor, Department of Agricultural Economics, University of Wisconsin; Claud L. Scroggs, Director, Economic Research Department, Southern States Cooperative, Inc., Richmond, Virginia; J. Kenneth Stern, President, American Institute of Cooperation; and Orion Ulrey, Associate Professor, Department of Agricultural Economics, Michigan State University.

It was understood from the beginning that all of the work in preparing this volume would be given freely as a labor of love, and that any proceeds from its sale would be contributed to the Awards Funds of the American Institute of Cooperation to encourage research and education relating to cooperatives. Under this general understanding, J. Kenneth Stern, President of the American Institute of Cooperation, agreed that the A.I.C. would publish the book in an attractive manner.

There is one aim that we hope this book will achieve—make cooperation as a form of business enterprise more alive to many who know little of those who built the cooperative highways on which we now travel. The great development of cooperatives in this country did not come entirely as an automatic response to felt needs. Although economic opportunity was of fundamental importance, cooperative advancement called for the intelligent and dedicated efforts of many persons—as these essays will make clear.

One cannot study the lives of great cooperators without realizing that they have been men and women motivated by ideals of service. Moreover, it becomes self-evident that those portrayed here are only samples of many others. The number of great cooperators is legion when one thinks of the thousands of cooperatives that have come into existence and thrived because of certain imaginative and inventive individuals who gave unstintingly of their time and energies to make them successful. In saluting the leaders included in this volume we also must remember the troops as well as the officers. Every state could well have a volume devoted to the cooperative leaders who have helped make cooperation successful in their states, and it is hoped that this book will stimulate the preparation of such volumes.

In planning this book it was agreed that emphasis should be focused on those who made their contributions in the years from 1900 to 1950 when cooperative enterprise was gaining national significance. Although some of them are still active they are included primarily because of their important contributions prior to 1950.

It will be seen from the contents of this book that great cooperators do not fall into any pattern. Some have made their mark by being great executives or leaders of men. Others have been theorists, lawyers, economists, sociologists, and educators. It takes all kinds of people to make a world, and likewise it takes people with many talents to give life and meaning to any great movement. One thing is clear from this group of essays—there has been no one dominating cooperator. A corollary for this statement is that great cooperators create and stimulate other great cooperators. They seem to come in clusters.

In preparing a book of this kind it is inevitable that some will feel that important persons have been left out. Although about 100 persons are honored here with vignettes or profiles, there are many others who qualify for inclusion. I regret that space and available time has forced their omission.

All of those portrayed in this book have made their cooperative contribution as Americans. There is one person who would have been included if he were not so well known as an Irishman—Sir Horace Plunkett. However, his interests were so close to this country that his biographer, Margaret Digby, called him "an Anglo-American Irishman." His name crops up in several of the American profiles for he had a pervasive influence on the development of agricultural cooperation in the United States. President Theodore Roosevelt recognized our debt to him in a letter to the British Ambassador:

> I have been interested for many years in farm life . . . But my interest did not reach the point of action until I began to follow what was being accomplished through the farmers' cooperative movement in Ireland. My old friend, Horace Plunkett, whom I saw on his periodical journeys to America, kept me informed of the Irish agricultural situation and of the movement for better living on the farms of Ireland. We Americans owe much to Ireland and to Plunkett in the work we have been trying to do in the United States, and before I leave the Presidency I want to acknowledge our debt and to send through you, my thanks for the help we have had . . .

A primary object of this book is to help present-day cooperators—and those of tomorrow—better understand and appreciate the efforts of men and women who have contributed so much to cooperative enterprise as it exists in the United States today.

While the pioneers of modern-type cooperative enterprise are mostly a product of the first half of the present century they were preceded by a number of important "forerunners." A volume could well be devoted to them, but here we are only selecting a few for brief treatment as an introduction to the main group which are designated "the builders."

Since several persons helped build the Federal Land Banks they are brought together in one general essay by Robert B. Tootell under the heading, "The Pioneers of Cooperative Credit." This forms Part III of this book.

All of the profiles were written as independent biographies. The authors were given a free hand to develop their sketches as they deemed appropriate. Thus each essay stands on its own merit and may be read in whatever order a reader may prefer. The profiles of "the builders" are arranged alphabetically rather than in any chronological order, as their cooperative contributions overlapped.

I have never worked on a project where I have received more generous cooperation. All the authors who have contributed have expressed pleasure in doing so.

Also, there have been many who have greatly helped with advice and suggestions. Here I would like to mention Martin A. Abrahamsen, Henry E. Erdman, Kelsey B. Gardner, Kenneth Hinshaw, Edwin G. Nourse, Theodore Saloutos, Marvin Schaars, and Orion Ulrey.

I wish to thank also my wife, Carol, for many useful suggestions on the profiles I have written, and Mrs. Jeanne Franklin for painstaking secretarial assistance.

Appreciation is expressed to William L. Robinson of Travilah, Md., for his perceptive help on format and production details, in final editing, and for the index which is a very valuable part of this particular book.

As I have worked with the other authors in preparing this volume, one fact has impressed me—pioneers keep on coming. As stages of development pass, new leaders are needed to meet new conditions. The pioneering job is never done in a world of constant change.

Joseph G. Knapp

CONTENTS

Part I

The Forerunners

Xerxes Addison Willard

by H. E. Erdman

DURING THE SECOND QUARTER of the 19th Century the grasslands area of central New York had gradually changed from grain farming to dairying. In a few counties, notably Herkimer and Oneida, the emphasis was on cheese; in Orange it was on butter. Such cheese and butter had always been made in the family kitchen or a milkhouse of the farm on which the milk was produced. Then, in 1851, began a revolutionary change to a system in which the milk from groups of farms was hauled to centrally located community factories, first for the manufacture of cheese, then, after 1861, butter also. By 1866 there were over 600 such factories in New York alone and about 200 in other states. These were popularly called "associated dairies," and as a group were referred to as "the factory system" as contrasted with the "family system."

At first, these were in no formal sense cooperative in nature. Within a decade, however, a number of cooperative features developed which were later to become common in various farmers' organizations, namely, ownership of the facilities by the patrons, with investment and voting related to patronage, and with proceeds allocated on the base of milk deliveries. An effort to learn more about the cooperative features which had developed among these factories led to the writing of my article on "The Associated Dairies of New York as Precursors of American Agricultural Cooperatives" (*Agricultural History*, vol. 36, no. 2, April 1962, pp. 82–90).

The leading contemporary writer on the new system and easily the most popular speaker at dairy meetings was a young "cheese dairyman," Xerxes Addison Willard. He was born in Herkimer County, New York, in 1820, the son of Nathan S. Willard, a physician. Upon graduation from Hamilton College in 1845, he returned to Little Falls where he studied law for three years. In 1848 he married Miss Harriet L. Hallet, gave up law, bought a farm, and by 1850 was engaged in "cheese dairying." He found so much difficulty in getting and keeping good dairymaids that he personally learned and took over the job of cheese making for a time. Although he continued his dairying, he found much time for writing, travel, and other activity.

Prolific Writer

Except for about three years when he was collector for the Canal Company at Little Falls, he was successively connected with the *Herkimer County Journal* (editor, 1858–1860), the *Utica Herald* (one of the editors, 1864–1869), the *Rural New Yorker* (dairy editor, 1869–1877), and free-lance writer to the time of his death in 1882.

Willard's early writings dealt mainly with various aspects of dairy farming. In March of 1857 he helped organize the Little Falls Farmers' Club. For about a dozen years he acted as secretary and, as such, edited the formal papers presented there and discussions of them for publication in local newspapers. In mid-1859 he published those of the first two years in a volume of some 250 pages, *Essays and Discussions on Agriculture* (D. Ayer, Little Falls).

After 1860 his writing dealt more largely with the new factory system which began to spread rapidly from that time. The rapidity of the spread to new communities raised many problems because of its departures from the past. Thus it involved changes in buildings, equipment, management, milking habits, and the relationship between the farmers of a community. Much of this material was later brought together in an organized fashion in his *Practical Dairy Husbandry* (D. D. T. Moore, 1871, 546 pp.) and *Practical Butter Book* (Rural Publishing Co., New York, 1875, p. 171). Both were standard authorities for a number of years.

Willard's descriptions of the business operations of cheese factories were usually quite sketchy and were tucked away in articles covering numerous other aspects. The best statement I have found is that in a three-column letter to the Secretary of the Royal Agricultural Society of England as published in *Moore's Rural New Yorker*, April 17, 1869 ("The American Dairy System," *Moore's Rural New Yorker*, vol. 20, April, 1869, p. 251). Generally, in the early factories the operators had purchased the milk. By the time Willard began to write about them, a pooling system had evolved. Two general types of organization had emerged:

1. An individual, a partnership, or a corporation owned buildings and facilities, and contracted with the patrons to manufacture the milk from their cows at a "price" per hundredweight. The patrons, as an informal association, then owned the cheese, sold it, and prorated the proceeds on the basis of milk deliveries.

2. The producers formed a "joint stock company" which acquired building and facilities, hired the cheese maker and assistants, paid all expenses, and prorated the proceeds to the patrons as in Plan 1.

In his occasional suggestions on how to start a factory he did not discuss the process of incorporation, nor did he use the term "cooperation." Instead, he recommended the "joint-stock company" or "joint-stock association"—advisedly, we may assume, since he had studied law in the mid-forties when that term was applied to an unincorporated organization in which a sort of "constitution" was accepted as the legal compact binding on the participants. (See Joseph Stancliffe Davis, *Essays in the Earlier History of American Corporations*, [vol. 2, Cambridge: Harvard University Press, 1917], pp. 33, 256, 258). Incidentally, something similar was reported in 1924 as the typical form of Danish cooperative (See Chris L. Christensen, *Agricultural Cooperation in Denmark*, U. S. Department of Agriculture Bulletin 1266, 1924, p. 10, lines 13–21).

Often Defended "Cooperative" Principle

Willard frequently found it necessary to defend the factory system and to explain the advantages of "associated capital and labor" as compared with individual effort. Thus in 1864 he stated that the dairyman, standing alone, is at the mercy of corporations and speculators, but "when associated with others, in neighborhoods, in towns, in counties, and in the State, he becomes formidable. . ." Later on he discussed marketing. On the one hand, he explained the services rendered by the marketing agencies, and on the other hand he wrote that "Too many middlemen intervene between the farmer and the consumer" (X. A. Willard, "The Marketing of Dairy Products," *Rural New Yorker*, May 27, 1871, p. 334). Again he referred to the "loose and unskillful manner of marketing dairy produce" (Transactions, *New York State Agricultural Society, 1871*, p. 376). One step toward remedying the bad situation was the establishment of the Cheese Boards which brought the bidding and offerings out into the open and left on the blackboard the record of sales by specific lots and prices. Willard took an active part in the establishment of that at Little Falls, long one of the more importantly quoted markets.

In 1865, Willard had studied the growing demand for cheese as reflected in English literature, and read a long report on it. The next year the American Dairymen's Association sent him to Europe to study the industry at first-hand. Upon his return he reported in detail.

He emphasized that the best American cheese was well received but warned strongly that too much inferior cheese was being sent and that the introduction of the factory system in Europe was improving the quality of competing European cheese.

Willard was not an innovator. He could perhaps best be called a catalyst—when he spoke to an audience or published a paper he centered interest on points of recognized importance and thus pointed the way toward profitable discussion and toward progress.

Founder

of the Grange

Oliver Hudson Kelley

by Theodore Saloutos

OLIVER HUDSON KELLEY, a farm organizer and founder of the National Grange, was born in Boston, Mass., on January 7, 1826, where he worked as a newspaper reporter and telegraph operator before settling on a farm near Itasca, Minn., in 1849. Little is known about his activities in Minnesota other than what he relates in the *Origin and Progress of the Order of the Patrons of Husbandry in the United States* (1875). In this Kelley tells of the hardships of the Minnesota farmers, the excessive drought of 1862 and 1863, his contributions to the newspapers which he said were favorably received, and of Senator Alexander Ramsey of Minnesota who helped him obtain a clerkship in the United States Department of Agriculture in 1864.

During the fall of 1865, Kelley was informed by Isaac Newton, the Commissioner of Agriculture, that he was assigned to go into the Southern States that winter "on special business." After a series of delays and a meeting with President Andrew Johnson, who at the time was having his problems with Congress, Kelley left on his long cherished trip on January 13, 1866. His task was to gather reliable information on the mineral and agricultural resources of the South, submit this to the department for publication, keep a daily record of his trip and observations, and communicate regularly with the Commissioner of Agriculture. These experiences had a profound effect on him and influenced the organization of the Grange.

Fraternal Order of Farmers Conceived

Kelley, while traveling in the South, sensed the bitterness toward the North, but discovered that being a Mason was "no disadvantage." These sad experiences also convinced him that peace between the sections would be restored only through a fraternity that would enable the people of the North and South to know each other as members of a big family. From then on his thoughts were dominated by the idea of building a fraternal body of agriculturalists transcending sectional lines.

After being unable to persuade his superiors of the wisdom of forming "a Secret Society of Agriculturalists" and failing to receive an appointment from President Johnson, he took a position in the Post Office Department in 1867. Later that same year Kelley and six other government employees, following some discouraging preliminary experiences, organized the National Grange of the Patrons of Husbandry of which he became the first national secretary.

Before long the earlier enthusiasm for an organization concerned chiefly with healing the scars of war gave way to demands for a broader organization that provided for the social and cultural uplift of the farmers; then came the economic crisis of 1873 and the depression. For the time being, the Grange cast aside its social and cultural cloak, and launched a double-barreled crusade for reform along political and economic lines.

Kelley realized that for the Grange to grow he had to cater to the economic needs of the farmers, and one of these was the establishment of cooperative enterprises. At first Kelley seemed indifferent to such activities, but then he seems to have become more receptive. His first effort was to keep a record of reputable and disreputable dealers. He kept two sets of books: one, the red book contained the names of the honest dealers; the second, the blue book, the names of the dishonest dealers. He hoped to expand this program into a national secret and protective association. Another plan was to appoint a local agent for each Grange who was to record the needs of the customer and the supplies of the farmers on hand.

The Minnesota Grange was a pioneer in these cooperative endeavors. In 1869 the advice was that local Granges "have flouring mills, flour their own wheat and keep the bran and shorts for feed, and not send any raw material into the eastern market, but, instead, appoint a business agent at St. Paul, who should receive the flour and send it on commission." Kelley wrote to Francis M. McDowell, the financier of the Order, about this proposal who disapproved of it on the grounds that it was fraught with financial dangers. But after the Minnesota Grange persisted and threatened to bolt the Order, Kelley advised the Minnesotans to proceed on a local basis and that the National Grange had not approved it as part of its program. The Minnesotans responded by appointing the first agent for the buying of supplies and farm implements. Meanwhile, it had become clear that the National Grange had no intention of fathering cooperatives.

Grange Incorporates Principle of Cooperation in "Purposes"

By 1874 the pressure for cooperatives had become so great that the Grange had to capitulate to the wishes of the members. The principle of cooperative enterprise was incorporated into the *Declaration of Purposes* and became one of the leading objects of the Order. The Declaration proposed "buying together, selling together, and in general, acting together for mutual protection, as occasion may require." It also proposed "to bring producers and consumers, farmers and manufacturers, into the most direct and friendly relations possible." As a consequence, the Granges entered the field of cooperation on an extensive and varied scale. Cooperative stores sought to lessen the retail margin. Short-lived cooperative grain elevators, livestock shipping associations and cheese factories tried to decrease marketing costs. More permanent and prosperous were the farmers' mutual insurance companies which enjoyed remarkable success from the start. Less successful were the Granger efforts to manufacture farm machinery and implements, sewing machines, wagons and other needs on a cooperative basis.

By 1880 nearly all ventures except fire insurance, exchanges, and such cooperative plans that called for the pooling of orders, had failed. This hurt the reputation of the Order, especially in the West where it had a large following.

Although Kelley's role as a pioneer in the field of cooperatives was not as positive as it might have been, his success in organizing the farmers contributed to the pioneering phases of the movement. He helped charter local and state Granges which furthered the growth of cooperatives. Without the enthusiasm of Kelley the Grange might never have been organized and the cooperatives never have received the early support they obtained from the Grange.

Kelley resigned his position as national secretary in November, 1878, because of the pressures of private business. He had become involved in a large development in Florida where he wanted to locate the office of secretary as a matter of convenience to him. The executive committee opposed this and he became estranged from the Order for many years. In 1905, when Kelley was almost 80 years old and the only surviving founder of the Order, the Grange adopted a resolution expressing its gratitude to him for the part he played in founding the Order and voted him a monthly sum of $100 to be paid for the remainder of his life. Kelley died in 1913 at the age of 87.

Large-Scale
Cooperative Advocate

3

Charles W. Macune

by Theodore Saloutos

CHARLES W. MACUNE, an early advocate of cooperative marketing and selling, was born on May 20, 1851, in Kenosha, Wis. His Scotch-Irish father, a blacksmith by trade and a Methodist preacher by avocation, migrated to the United States from Canada; while his mother Mary Almira (McAfee) Macune sprang from a family of early Kentucky settlers. Charles' father died when he was an infant and his widowed mother moved to Freeport, Ill. where young Macune attended elementary school until he was 10 years old and then went to work as a farm laborer to support his mother.

Macune had a rather checkered career. After the Civil War he left for California where he ranched briefly, headed for Kansas where he joined a circus, and then became a cattle driver. In 1874 he settled in Barnett, Tex., where he made an unsuccessful attempt to publish a newspaper and the following year married Sally Vickery. After trying his hand at operating a hotel, he moved west to San Saba, a growing agricultural center, where he supported his family by painting houses and studying medicine with a local doctor. He passed his medical examination before moving eastward to Milam County, Tex. Meanwhile, he also found time to study law.

Macune must have been a very persuasive person for he became chairman of the executive committee and acting president of the Texas Farmers Alliance in 1886, the same year he joined the organization. This spectacular rise of his may be attributed to his skill as an organizer and speaker, and the lack of leadership among the farmers who, in turn, were swayed, by persons with powers of oratory.

Favored Regional Associations to Aid Farmers

He believed that the farmers should concentrate their efforts on "buying and selling, producing and consuming," and avoid political action. He favored business associations that encompassed entire regions on the theory that this would bring greater economies, as against state associations. In launching this program he suggested that the local, county, and state Farmers Alliances appoint representatives to sit on a board representing their respective units, where they could devise a system for collecting information to assist the farmers in producing and selling their cotton. If this proposal failed to bring the farmers higher prices, then they might consider a plan for gradually reducing the size of the cotton crop.

Macune believed that the business future of the Farmers Alliance was contingent on the construction of central agencies that were owned by patrons who had money to invest and products to sell. A strong central business organization would enable the local stores to withstand the attacks of the hostile merchants, and the mushrooming of helpless unaffiliated stores.

It was midst some such atmosphere that Macune was chosen as business manager of the Texas Exchange which began business in Dallas in 1887. The methods used in selecting its personnel and organizing its affiliates were questionable, to say the least. Macune, despite his forensic powers, was a poor choice. Nothing in his background, training or experience suggested that he was remotely qualified to become the business manager. He lacked managerial experience in a day when opposition to cooperatives was very strong.

Financial Difficulties Beset Exchange

The Exchange was in trouble early. One of its publicized purposes was to abolish the credit system that burdened the farmers. Alliance lecturers, newspapers, and leaders kept the credit issue and the Exchange topic "red hot," leaving the members and the general public in a general state of expectancy. They predicted that the day was near at hand when the farmers would own their own cotton and woolen mills, implement and wagon factories, and a huge printing press. Once the marketing program was announced, the debt-ridden farmers began pressing for money advances. By March, 1888, the board had approved advances of $128,000 in goods despite the fact that only $17,000 worth of capital stock had been sold. Shortly thereafter the board signed a contract for a building that increased the liabilities of the Exchange by another $35,000. More difficulties were in store when the Exchange failed to obtain a loan on the mortgage notes it had accepted.

The Exchange failed after being in business only 20 months because of poor business management and the lack of capital. It had only a fraction of the $500,000 it needed to carry on its business and this was poorly managed. It borrowed to build and acquire houses, purchase goods, and transact business. It sold goods at about 10 percent above cost which was barely enough to meet unavoidable and incidental expenses, leaving little, if anything, to defray general expenses. Peace was restored when Macune resigned as business manager, and a change occurred in the editorship of the *Southern Mercury* which had been critical of Macune and the business policies of the Exchange. But it was too late. The damage had been done.

Macune also advocated a subtreasury plan that would authorize the federal government to establish warehouses in every county that offered $500,000 or more of certain non-perishable commodities for sale each year. As part of this plan, the government would issue treasury notes up to 80 percent of the current value of the stored goods. The farmer after depositing his goods would receive a warehouse receipt he could exchange for treasury notes or sell. The holder of the receipt who claimed the goods from the warehouse would have to pay the equivalent of the original advance, the interest, storage, and insurance charges.

After stepping down as manager of the Texas Exchange, Macune became the editor of the *National Economist*, the weekly newspaper of the Southern Alliance, with headquarters in Washington, D.C. This enabled him to lobby in behalf of the subtreasury plan until the opposition to it became very strong. When the Populist Party came into being Macune, as editor of the *National Economist*, gave it outward support. But after the campaign of 1892 he was accused of having helped publish a pamphlet urging Alliancemen to vote for Cleveland. These charges undermined the confidence of the members in him and he was defeated in his bid for the presidency by H. L. Loucks of South Dakota, a strong Populist. In 1893, Macune dropped out of the Alliance.

After leaving the Alliance, Macune made another unsuccessful effort to publish a newspaper in Cameron, Tex., then practiced law, and finally in 1900 he asked the Central Methodist Conference to appoint him "a supply preacher." He preached in a series of small Texas towns and following his retirement in 1918 he did volunteer medical work among the poor with his son, the Reverend Dennis Macune. He died on November 3, 1940, at the age of 89 in Fort Worth, Tex. where he had been living since 1921.

Father of the
Cooperative Creameries

C. L. Haecker

by John W. Dysart

THEOPHILUS L. HAECKER is known as the father of dairying and of the cooperative creamery system in the State of Minnesota.

Born at Liverpool, Ohio, May 4, 1846, Haecker grew up in Dane County, Wis., where he received his initial training in the line of agriculture to which he contributed so much.

He served in the Civil War, later entering the University of Wisconsin, where he was enrolled as a student for two years. In 1874, he was appointed Executive Clerk to the Governor of Wisconsin, and served six different governors until 1891. While clerk he operated his own dairy farm.

In 1891, Haecker was invited to be an instructor in dairying at the new University of Minnesota Short Course for a period of six months. At the end of this period he received the appointment of Professor, and remained at the University for 27 years. He retired in 1918 to become professor emeritus.

Haecker's work has left a permanent impression on the state along two lines: the establishment of the cooperative creamery system, and the nutrition of dairy cattle.

Haecker unquestionably did more than any other man to establish the cooperative creamery movement in Minnesota. Traveling by horse and buggy, he spent the greater part of 1892 in surveying the situation with respect to dairying in the state. He found conditions discouraging.

In the course of his travels he happened across a local cooperative creamery at Clarks Grove, Minn. After a careful study of the possibilities of the cooperative creamery, Haecker became convinced that it offered the solution for many of the serious problems of the dairy industry in Minnesota.

In 1894, the Minnesota Agricultural Experiment Station issued a bulletin by Haecker, *Organizing Cooperative Creameries*. It described how to organize, number of cows required, and had model articles and bylaws.

Haecker's contemporaries describe him as a fighter and a man of indefatigable energy. It is said that he stumped the state more thoroughly than a would-be senator. He did not wait for invitations— he invited himself. Wherever he could find an audience he would speak. He kept up this incessant barrage over the decade of 1892–1902. The number of cooperative creameries increased from the original four to 542 during this period. When he retired in 1918 there were 630 cooperative creameries in the state.

It was one of Haecker's star pupils, A. J. McGuire, who along with others joined many of these cooperatives together to form the large cooperative dairy marketing organization, Land O'Lakes Creameries, Inc., of Minneapolis, Minn.

Haecker's other great work was the research which led to the issuing of the *Haecker Feeding Standard.* It is safe to say that he exerted an influence upon practical dairy feeding practices equal to or greater than any man in his time.

Charles Orrin Drayton

by Theodore Saloutos

CHARLES ORRIN DRAYTON, a rural organizer, the founder and President of the Farmers Equity Union, was born on December 16, 1851, on a farm in Highland, Madison County, Ill., the son of Robert I. and Margaret Ann (Gracy) Drayton. He was educated at the State Normal University which he attended from 1870 to 1874, and where as a college student he gained recognition as a speaker and debater. These forensic experiences were to serve him well in his organizing and speaking activities. He taught in the country schools of Illinois for about 20 years, and farmed 240 acres for many years.

Drayton probably was greatly influenced by the activities of the Grangers, the Farmers Mutual Benefit Association, the Farmers Alliance, and other lesser known groups, and became prominent in local agricultural circles. However, his name does not forge into the limelight until March, 1903, when he joined the American Society of Equity and became an organizer. The Equity had been founded in Indianapolis, Ind. on December 24, 1902, for the purpose of helping the farmers obtain higher prices for their products. His experiences with the American Society of Equity were to serve as a testing ground for his later activities with the Farmers Equity Union. His abilities as an organizer became known early and, as a consequence, he rose high in the echelons of the Equity.

Differences soon broke out within the American Society of Equity over the policies of the organization. Drayton believed in a more centralized organization, which was different from the prevailing Equity administration. While a member of the Equity he temporarily favored the formation of local, county, state, and district unions, as well as a national union, but he opposed the department union which he believed invited trouble. He argued that since the department unions were based on specific commodities such as livestock, grain, and tobacco, they would eventually shift for themselves, and provide no financial support for the parent organization.

He further maintained that the district unions, exchanges, and

15

terminal market associations should be chartered and placed under the control of the national union; and a fraction of one percent of the gross sales of all Equity pools and net earnings of the exchanges should be paid the national union. He also believed that the national union should be authorized to enter into contracts with reliable commission firms and handle the products of its members.

Founded Farmers Equity Union in 1910

These views of Drayton, and his disapproval of the structure and practices of the American Society of Equity, eventually led to his resignation as an officer and member of the parent organization and the forming of the Farmers Equity Union of which he is recognized as the founder. The new organization, chartered on December 10, 1910, reflected the philosophy of organization and cooperation that he believed in.

Unlike the American Society of Equity, the Farmers Equity Union was organized solely for the purpose of establishing farmers' cooperative associations. The relations between the local unions and the business enterprises were very close. Units of the Farmers Equity Union were organized in Ohio, Indiana, Illinois, Texas, Kansas, Nebraska, and other states. The commitment to cooperative business enterprises did not deter the Farmers Equity Union from lobbying in Congress for legislation favorable to the farmers.

The structure of the Farmers Equity Union and its affiliates account for much of the success it enjoyed. The local union and the local exchange were one and the same organization; while the township, county, and state units were discarded. The locals and the national union constituted the Farmers Equity Union, but the locals were designed to engage in business. The locals were established in towns where business facilities were available, while the central exchanges were set up in large cities where they could best serve the needs of the locals. These units, however, maintained their separate identities.

The establishment of the local exchanges was governed by local needs and organized to conduct the business of grain elevators, stores, creameries, and other commodity groups. Each member was obligated to subscribe to two shares of stock which were paid for according to a pre-arranged plan. Products of nonmembers were also handled, but the nonmembers did not share in the cooperative profits.

On the other hand, the centralized exchanges or companies were organized in the large cities where they served as buying and selling agencies of the local exchanges. The stockholders in the centralized companies were the local exchanges, not the individual members. The excellent reports circulating about the local and centralized exchanges left little doubt that the Farmers Equity Union was one of the foremost farmer organizations in the country dedicated to cooperative marketing and buying.

Success Attributed to Leadership, Business Abilities

The success of the Farmers Equity from the very outset must be attributed to the leadership and good business judgment of Drayton. By the time he stepped down from the presidency of the Farmers Equity Union in 1922, and after serving as its head for 12 years, he had organized 560 locals—a masterful achievement. Most of his organizing work was done at a time when the hostility of the traditional business agencies to cooperatives was very strong and legislation to encourage them was still in its infancy. Later, Drayton became the national president of the Wheat Growers Association, which again was a tribute to his qualities as a leader. However, his reputation as a pioneer in the cooperative field rests largely on his achievements as head of the Farmers Equity Union. In private life he was a Prohibitionist, a Presbyterian, and a Mason. Death came to him in his home in Greenville, Ill. at the age of 76.

Part II

The Builders

A. C. "Doc" Adams

by Paul T. DeVore and Don H. Phipps

FARMERS IN THE PACIFIC NORTHWEST were groping uncertainly but hopefully during the first two decades of this century with cooperative ideas and techniques to protect their vulnerability in the market place.

Cooperative-oriented grain elevators and fruit warehouses and Grange stores were being established rapidly in response to the individual farmer's need to command more reasonable prices for the goods he offered to the market and the goods he bought from the market. Social needs also influenced the development of cooperatives in the early 1900's, but economic necessity was the primary motivation for the cooperative movement which was developing in most rural communities of the United States.

Instinctively, farmers reacted to their difficult economic environment by cooperating and by 1920 cooperative-type warehouses and stores were beginning to take on a more definite shape. No federal laws then existed to promote or guide the development of cooperatives, and state cooperative laws in the Pacific Northwest states were still to come.

Yet the cooperatives grew in number and importance. Wheat farmers in Washington and Idaho, for example, were spurred into action because they feared a complete collapse of wheat prices after World War I. In 1920, the wheat farmers organized the first two regional wheat marketing cooperatives in the Pacific Northwest—the Washington Wheat Growers Association, incorporated August 8, 1920, and the Idaho Wheat Growers Association, incorporated a month later. These organizations were known as wheat pools, for they pooled the wheat of the members for marketing.

The wheat pool directors in both states picked A. C. "Doc" Adams, a young 28-year-old accountant just recently returned from the war, to serve as their secretary-treasurer and young Adams broke a lot of cooperative marketing ground before the pools dissolved about 1925. Though short-lived, the Idaho and Washington wheat marketing cooperatives laid the foundation for future wheat cooperatives such as the North Pacific Grain Growers.

Adams not only shaped the early cooperative wheat movement in the Pacific Northwest but he went on to contribute to the development of farmer cooperatives and cooperative farm credit institutions both in the Pacific Northwest and throughout the United States as President of the Spokane Bank for Cooperatives.

Despite his young years in 1920, it is not surprising that Adams was asked by the wheat farmers of Washington and Idaho to manage the pioneering wheat pools. Adams had grown up with one of the first farmer-owned grain warehouses in Washington and before and after the war had done many bookkeeping jobs for a number of small warehouses. His father helped organize the Waterville (Wash.) Grain Warehouse Company in 1908. Young Adams worked in the warehouse stacking wheat sacks after school. He studied all of the accounting courses his small high school had to offer and when he graduated in 1910, the grain warehouse hired him as its bookkeeper.

Farmers Had Been at Mercy of Buyers

The Waterville grain warehouse, founded in 1908, was one of the first in the country. Before the Farmers Educational Cooperative Union of America (Farmers' Union) movement, which started in Texas in 1902, swept across the Great Plains and into the Pacific Northwest, the wheat farmers took what they could get from the old line traders. The millers and exporters knew a farmer holding only several thousand sacks of wheat in and around his grain shed was in no position to haggle much over the price, particularly if he had bills to pay—and it seemed that the buyer always timed his visit with the coming of bills.

The Grange stores, which had been in Washington and Idaho since 1873, were of little help to the wheat farmer in the bargaining with the old line traders. The stores saved many pennies in the purchase of store goods. But the Granges couldn't bargain for the wheat farmer and most of the wheat families lived too far apart to organize retail stores.

The first two grain warehouses sponsored and partially financed by the Farmers Union were started in Waitsburg and Prescott. Warmly received by the grain farmers, such warehouses spread like stubble fire over the wheat growing areas of the Pacific Northwest with farmers providing much of the $4,000 to $10,000 capital needed to build a warehouse in those days.

Adams grew up with this cooperative development and he came to appreciate its significance while only a youth.

Adams was probably the youngest county clerk in the State of Washington in the early 1900's. In 1913, he left the Waterville warehouse and accepted a job in the Douglas County auditor's office and a year later he was elected county clerk. He was 21 at the time. Adams was re-elected again in 1916.

A Douglas County judge observed the young clerk's ability around the court house at Waterville. He urged Adams to study all he could of law and accounting, which Adams did, mostly through correspondence courses.

World War I compelled Adams to resign as county clerk early in 1917. Just before he was shipped overseas he married Harriette Elizabeth Hagaman, and following the war he and his wife moved to Spokane where he managed to provide a reasonably good living as a free-lance bookkeeper for a number of grain warehouses.

Adams worked hard at the bookkeeping jobs—12 to 18 hours a day. He did a good job and the farmers who sat on the small warehouse boards took notice of this competent young man.

End of War Conditions Leads to Agitation for State Pools

While moving from warehouse to warehouse, Adams heard talk that the farmers might build a central warehouse and sales agency at Spokane. Farmers were deeply concerned about mounting surpluses and rumors that the government was going to take the price controls off wheat now that the war was over. The small wheat warehouses had done well in bargaining for good prices before and during the war for Europe needed all of the soft white wheat it could get. But now that the war was over the demand for Pacific Northwest soft white wheat dropped sharply.

Although the fear of low prices motivated the action for the creation of the Washington and Idaho wheat pools, the need had been developing for years. Warehouses just couldn't bargain to the best advantage for their members if they operated independently. So, on August 1, 1919, wheat farmers met in Spokane to discuss the possibility of organizing state wheat pools.

When the Washington and Idaho Wheat Growers Associations were incorporated in the summer of 1920 no cooperative laws yet existed, so they were incorporated under state laws governing fraternal organizations.

Adams accepted the job as secretary of both pools, with headquarters at Spokane, for $350.00 per month.

Shortly after they organized the pools in 1920, the wheat farmers sent Adams to Washington, D. C., to see if he could obtain a commitment from the War Finance Corporation. Adams conferred with WFC Head Eugene Meyer, later to become FICB Commissioner and later publisher of the *Washington Post*. A $10 million loan was arranged. While in Washington, Adams also participated in the deliberation of three bills that eventually were combined to make one bill creating the Federal Intermediate Credit Banks in 1923.

The pools sold several million bushels of wheat for their members during the first year of operation. One year the pools exported one-third of the Pacific Northwest wheat sold at Liverpool, England.

But the wheat farmers encountered a number of problems. One was developing a sales contract between the wheat farmer and the pool that would be honored by both parties and the commercial bank in which the individual was doing his personal financing. A standard contract was developed to the satisfaction of the banks. Another was grading and accounting procedure for accurately identifying amounts and grades of wheat to each individual farmer so that the farmer got paid for exactly the kind and amount of wheat he delivered to the pools. Possibly the problem of delivering as promised could have been solved with more intensive educational efforts. But there wasn't time to do the necessary educating.

Dissolving of Pools Leads to Better Cooperative

So in 1925 the pools started to dissolve, a gradual process that took about 10 years. The pools had accomplished several important things, however. They established the right of a body of this kind to organize. They created a workable grading and accounting program for marketing wheat. They left $100,000 in trust in the event another wheat cooperative marketing organization would start up again. And that happened.

In 1929 Congress created the Federal Farm Board. One of its chief purposes was to encourage and assist—with loans—the farmer cooperatives now springing up rapidly throughout the country. The wheat men, after the dissolution of the wheat pools, were in the same poor bargaining position they were in before 1920. So a group of them got their heads together and, with the help of the Federal Farm

Board, founded the North Pacific Grain Growers, modeling it in many respects after the wheat pools.

Naturally they looked to Adams as the most capable man to manage the new cooperative. Adams was reluctant to accept after the failure of the wheat pools. He was doing well with a Spokane bank as assistant trust officer, but the main reason he refused was skepticism about the wheat farmers themselves. Would they continue to break contracts when an old line trader enticed them as in the days of the wheat pool? The president of the bank encouraged Adams to take the demanding job, appealing to his idealistic instincts. In one talk between Adams and the president, the banker said to him, "As a member of the community you owe something to this committee, even your mistakes. Your experience will help these farmers. You try it and if you don't like it, you'll have your job waiting for you here."

"Doc" consented and did a brilliant job of organizing the North Pacific Grain Growers which serves the wheat farmers of the Pacific Northwest in an admirable fashion today.

North Pacific Export Organized; Wheat Up 15¢ a Bushel

Wheat prices dropped as low as 35 cents per bushel in the Pacific Northwest in the early 1930's just about the time the North Pacific Grain Growers was getting well established. The board of directors suggested that Adams go to Washington and see if something could be done. What they had in mind was getting authorization to create a wheat export corporation. Secretary of Agriculture Henry Wallace thought it was a good idea and assigned an assistant to discuss the matter more fully with Adams. As a result, the North Pacific Export came into being in 1933 and within a few months the price of wheat jumped from 35 to 50 cents a bushel.

While in Washington on the export matter, Adams was asked to sit in on some intensive planning for a new farm credit bill. He worked closely with the late Albert Goss, the chairman of the National Grange's legislative committee. Goss was working hard for a new farm credit bill. Adams contributed much to the bill and, in fact, was the author of section 6b of the Farm Credit Act of 1933, which allowed the Production Credit Corporation to buy stock in a cooperative.

Adams' thoughtful contributions to this important piece of legislation resulted in his appointment as general agent of the Farm Credit Administration of Spokane in 1933. He became President of the Spokane Bank for Cooperatives in 1935, which provided a good opportunity for him to influence the trends of cooperative development in the four Northwest States.

One of Doc's greatest assets was his warm sense of humor. He enjoyed life and imparted a joy of living to those with whom he came in contact. He could laugh at himself and enjoy an amusing situation. He loved expressive words and once wrote to a Washington official to modestly turn down a request for a forecast of what might happen in the next 10 years:

> Your invitation to blueprint a capital structure for farmer cooperatives 10 years from now deserves to be better dealt with by those who are endowed with a high degree of clairvoyant discernment in their ability to plot the trend of current prices and to pinpoint the moments when they will explode into compelling action.

A. C. "Doc" Adams, as he was intimately known throughout the cooperatives of the Pacific Northwest, was a man of high integrity, firm policy, and deepseated philosophy. This not only related to cooperatives, but to many other facets of the total society that "Doc" Adams influenced and worked into and out of during his active days.

Always Found a Way to Aid Farmers, Growers

Some of his aggressive achievements during his term as President of the Spokane Bank for Cooperatives could be summed up as "when there was a need that would benefit the producer, 'Doc' Adams seemed to find a way to fulfill this need." Sometimes it would take special twists and efforts, as well as on occasion changing regulations or legislation, but such stumbling blocks never inhibited his progress to serve.

Perhaps one of his most significant contributions was in the fruit industry of the Pacific Northwest and the cooperative corporation development during the distressed times of the late 1930's and 1940's, in the early development of the cooperative bank system. It was during these trying days with shortages of funds and extremely stressing conditions throughout the production area that "Doc" Adams and his persistent personality expressed its finest traits. Incident after incident for special consideration brought forth a thriving cooperative within the fruit community. This was only one of the examples of the many turns of events throughout all of the agriculture industry on the Pacific Northwest that retains the footprints and handiwork of a great cooperative leader—A. C. "Doc" Adams.

"Doc" retired in 1962, and passed away after a short illness in 1965—to the end, full of good nature and interest in his fellowman.

Champion of Cooperative Neutrality

V. S. Alanne

by Erick Kendall

V. S. (VIENO SEVERI) ALANNE, who has been called by many of his contemporaries "the dean of cooperative educators in America," was born in Finland in 1878. He graduated from the University of Helsinki as a chemical engineer, and was in charge of the Chemical Department of the Helsinki Vocational School for two years, 1905–07. At that time, Finland was under Russian rule and V. S. became a militant Finnish nationalist. For his efforts in behalf of Finnish independence he became one of the objects of Czarist Russian persecution. Alanne migrated to Canada in 1907 as a political refugee. The following year he came to the U.S., where he was naturalized in 1915.

In Canada, Alanne was one of the founders and the editor of a Finnish language newspaper. In the U.S., he worked as a newspaper editor for brief periods at three different times—1908, 1914–15 and 1919–20. During his early years here Alanne also managed a coal mine in Wyoming for two years, was a research chemist in Massachusetts, and worked for five years compiling the largest and most comprehensive Finnish-English dictionary ever published. He was fond of calling himself "a jack of all trades."

Alanne's interest in cooperatives, and particularly their ideological and social improvement implications, dates back to his early youth in Finland. He became a professional cooperative educator in 1920 as the Educational Director of Cooperative Central Exchange, Superior, Wis., which was a regional wholesale of food and general merchandise cooperatives owned and operated by Finnish-American immigrants in the northern North Central states.

At that time most of these cooperatives, and the regional itself, were controlled by the overtly communistic Finnish Workers Federation, and many of their top leaders were openly declaring that cooperatives were a "part of the working class movement. . . . In the class struggle the cooperative movement is a mighty weapon in the hands of the workers. . . . The cooperative movement, if its aim is a better system of society and not dividend checks, must be a labor movement. It must work hand in hand with labor in all its struggles, be they on the economic or the political field." (From an official 1925 policy statement by the management of Cooperative Central Exchange).

Firmly Supported Rochdale Principle of Neutrality

Alanne was a firm believer in the Rochdale principle of political neutrality and refused to be associated with this policy. He resigned in 1925, four years before an open factional fight broke out in the C.C.E. cooperatives, that struggle eventually resulting in an ouster of the Communists and their sympathizers from these cooperatives.

Alanne's resignation and his resultant freedom to speak and write freely on the subject of cooperative political neutrality played a great role in the victory of the pro-democracy forces in that struggle in the C.C.E. member cooperatives and their regional wholesale. From Superior he moved to Minneapolis, becoming the educational director of the Franklin Cooperative Creamery (1925–26), and the organizer and full-time director of the Northern States Cooperative League (1926–38). In 1928, he wrote in the Fourth Yearbook of the Northern States Cooperative League:

> On one hand we have those cooperators who urge that our movement must be considered a part of the labor movement and that it should, in its activities, assume the class struggle attitude.
> On the other hand, there are those cooperators—and the undersigned is in sympathy with them—who do not believe in the wisdom of tying our movement too closely with any political movement . . . we must strive to build our movement on the broadest possible basis and not let it become divided by any class or party lines . . ."

Alanne's fellow Finnish-Americans up north read, and believed, as testified to by the successful anti-Communist house-cleaning that broke out one year later.

Alanne resigned from the secretaryship of the Northern States Cooperative League in 1938 to devote his time to writing and to the development of the Cooperative Correspondence School. He served as the full-time director of that school for five years.

Authored Important, Widely-Used Textbooks

Alanne authored several pamphlets and books, in English and Finnish. The most noteworthy of these is his *Fundamentals of Con-*

sumers Cooperation, which went through eight editions (8th revised edition, 1946) in English, and has been translated into several other languages. It is still considered a standard text at cooperative schools and institutes in various parts of the world. Another important work was the *Manual for Co-op Directors* (1938). The English language editions of both books are now out of print.

Alanne edited four *Northern States Cooperative League Yearbooks*, two *Cooperative League of the U.S.A. Yearbooks* and prepared eight correspondence courses on cooperative management and other subjects. He was instructor, over a period of 27 years, at cooperative training schools for managers and other functionaries at Minneapolis, Minn.; Superior, Wis.; and Kansas City, Mo. In the years immediately preceding World War II he conducted classes for cooperative directors and members in scores of localities in the North Central states, and classes and home study courses for the employees of Midland Cooperatives, Inc. He served on the board of directors of the Cooperative League of the U.S.A. from 1923 to 1940.

Allane returned to Finland in 1951 as a full-time employee of a large publishing house, commissioned to bring out a revised edition of his Finnish-English dictionary. Alanne finished that project, and was working on an equally comprehensive English-Finnish dictionary when he died in 1960.

Paul S. Armstrong

by Joseph G. Knapp

I CAME FIRST TO KNOW PAUL ARMSTRONG in 1930 when I was a young professor at North Carolina State University. At that time I was gathering information on the workings of our major cooperative marketing associations, and I had written to Sunkist, then the California Fruit Growers Exchange, for information. My request was answered by Paul Armstrong who was then the Exchange's Assistant General Manager. What impressed me was the fullness of the information provided me. He was apparently proud of the Exchange, and anxious that I be completely informed on its organization and operations. I have come to know Paul Armstrong intimately since my first contact with him through correspondence, and my first impression of his open-mindedness and deep belief in the principles of agricultural cooperation have been amplified and strengthened.

Paul Stuart Armstrong was born in Worcester, Mass., May 8, 1892. His father was a graduate in mechanical engineering who, after some difficult times during the great money panic of 1893, entered government service in the United States Patent Office. He remained in that service until his retirement as Examiner-in-Chief at the age of 71.

The family moved to Washington, D. C. and settled in Kensington, Md., so Paul was reared in a suburban environment which was then more "country" than it is now. After the seventh grade, he attended Washington schools, graduating from Central High School in 1911. When the time came to go away to college, Paul was influenced in selecting Michigan Agricultural College by Dr. W. A. Taylor, then Chief of the Bureau of Plant Industry, U.S.D.A., and himself a graduate of that institution in the 80's.

Armstrong entered there, intending to study forestry but switched to horticulture as a result of his contacts with Professor Harry J. Eustace, head of that department. This contact and this decision were to profoundly influence his life.

Paul told me he often reflected on the circumstances that cause a person to follow a certain career—circumstances which are more often

than not unrecognized at the time. His was a case in point as he
related it:

> Mr. G. Harold Powell, who was at the time chief of the Bureau of
> Plant Industry, U.S.D.A., came to California about 1907 or 1908
> as I recall, as the head of a scientific task force to ascertain the
> cause or causes of the serious decay of navel oranges in transit.
> This task force found the answer and influenced by this achieve-
> ment, as well as his other qualities, Mr. Powell was invited to
> become general manager of California Fruit Growers Exchange
> about 1912—a position he occupied for 10 years or until his death
> in 1922.
>
> One of the members of this task force was Harry J. Eustace, who
> later became head of the department of horticulture, Michigan
> State University, then known as Michigan Agricultural College.
> It was not the usual practice then, as it is today, for business
> corporations to recruit personnel from universities but Mr. Powell,
> desiring to recruit some likely young men for the Exchange organi-
> zation, asked his friend, Professor Eustace, to recommend some
> to him. This was done and about a half a dozen members of the
> horticulture class of 1914 were employed by the Exchange and
> assigned to various starting positions in the organization. They
> worked out so well that more recommendations were requested
> from the next class of 1915 and I was one of those recommended
> by Professor Eustace. That is how my career in Sunkist started
> and I wish I could say I planned it that way, but I didn't.
>
> At that particular time, jobs were hard to come by and it was a
> close question whether you could line up one at all upon gradua-
> tion. I was glad to get the job at the starting salary of $60 a
> month and my career unfolded from there and I never worked for
> anyone else in the 41 years of my business career.
>
> I go into this much detail to make the point that little do we know
> what chance circumstances causes us to follow a particular line
> of work and with a particular company. If I had not attended
> Michigan State and been there at the time Professor Eustace was
> requested to recommend recruits I might have ended up in an
> entirely different line of work and in another part of the country,
> as I had not the remotest idea of coming to California.

While in college, Armstrong became a close friend of Don Francisco
and was associated with him in a number of student activities. This,
too, was to have a marked effect on Paul's career because Francisco
was responsible for organizing the dealer service work in the Exchange
and the one who selected the men to staff it. He selected Paul as
one of them.

How Pioneer "Merchandising" of Oranges Began

Dealer Service was something of an innovation for sales organizations when the Exchange started it in 1915. They wanted to learn more about how fruit was handled and sold by the retailer. They learned a good deal and soon the dozen men engaged in this new work were bringing the box of oranges out from under the counter, making colorful window displays of the fruit and urging sales at special prices to increase volume and profit.

Armstrong recalls that retail grocers were unaccustomed to have men call on them except to sell them something and were a bit suspicious of "our motives at first but as we became acquainted and the sales results showed up, our work was welcomed by the dealers and appreciated. Today it is a general practice and is called 'merchandising.'"

In 1916, motor transportation was still not general and Armstrong further recalls lugging Sunkist display material on foot until he was provided with a Model T Ford Roadster, equipped with clincher tires and a hand crank to start it. The open car was air-conditioned by nature in the cold New England winter.

In 1917, Armstrong was made Manager of the Sunkist Dealer Service Division and transferred to the California headquarters in Los Angeles. Soon afterwards he was promoted to Assistant Advertising Manager under Don Francisco, and when Francisco resigned to become local manager of the advertising agency handling the Sunkist account in 1921, Armstrong became the Advertising Manager. He was 29.

Francisco and Armstrong worked together on a number of sales promotion programs of which the most fruitful was the "Drink an Orange" program. At that time, it was usual to eat half an orange with a spoon as we now eat a grapefruit. With orange juice, it required the juice from two oranges to make a respectable serving.

It has been claimed, with reason, that this "Drink an Orange" campaign changed one of our national eating habits and, in time, Sunkist pioneered in developing electric juice extractors and dispensers to further expand orange juice consumption. The orange industry would be not over one-fourth its present size if it were not for orange juice.

In 1925, Armstrong was promoted to Assistant General Manager and in this position he led Sunkist to its second giant step in increasing sales—the "Vitamin C" campaign.

Through research undertaken by chemists on oranges, it was found that oranges were a ready source of Vitamin C, just as people were becoming vitamin conscious. As a result, oranges became a health item and sales spurted.

When Armstrong became General Manager in 1931, in the middle of the depression, he was broadly informed on all phases of Sunkist operations. His first job was to build confidence in the growers, many of whom were "barely hanging on to their groves." A real crisis came in 1933 with the closing of the banks, for 1,000 or more carloads of Sunkist fruit were rolling eastward with a payment-on-receipt draft attached to each car. He had two choices: Either to divert the shipments to already supplied auction markets which would have ruined the price, or to relax the payment requirement.

On his own, he released every car on open account to the buyers who had contracted for the oranges.

"We didn't lose a dime," Armstrong later recalled, "it taught me a great lesson in the fundamental honesty of people."

Cooperative Purpose of Sunkist Always Kept Paramount

Although Armstrong has always been marketing-minded, he has equally been cooperative-minded. The cooperative marketing system developed by Sunkist has always seemed to him to be the logical method of marketing agricultural products. In all of his relationships he never forgot that the purpose of Sunkist was to efficiently market the products of its members.

I once asked him, "What is your important problem?" He answered that it was to keep control of the organization in the hands of the producers. He said that there was always a tendency for growers to look to their local or central organization for decisions that they should make themselves. He pointed out that this tendency could result in a strong central organization out of touch with its members. He said the time may come when some industry program needs full grower support and it would be unfortunate if the growers were then divorced from a feeling of ownership and responsibility for their organization. Under Paul Armstrong the employees knew who they were working for —the growers. And the members knew that Sunkist was their organization and that they were, in the long run, responsible for its maintenance.

On another occasion Paul Armstrong pointed out to me that Sunkist was set up to help citrus growers market their crop. It couldn't control their operations as farmers. All that it could do was help them market most efficiently the crop as produced. Of course, Sunkist has always taken a great interest in encouraging them to follow recommended cultural practices to produce high-quality fruit for marketing. In its marketing operations it has always reflected back to growers better prices for high-quality fruit which has been a great incentive to high-quality production.

Armstrong, representing Sunkist's philosophy, has felt that the problem of orderly shipment control required federal agricultural marketing programs which came into being when enabling legislation was first passed in 1933. In fact, Sunkist gave encouragement to such programs and its support has enabled them to operate effectively in adjusting supply to demand, maintaining a stable market, and in improving returns to all citrus growers.

It is generally recognized by well-informed agricultural marketing authorities that a strong cooperative like Sunkist Growers, which represents a large number of growers, is essential and even a prerequisite to the successful operation of a marketing agreement.

Armstrong Built Strong Sunkist Export Sales

Armstrong has long been a vigorous exponent of selling Sunkist fruit in foreign countries. This program goes back a long way, for a gift package of oranges was sent to Queen Victoria in the Gay Nineties. By the late 20's exports of oranges to Europe had become quite significant on a consignment basis and through the auctions, so a representative from the Los Angeles office was sent over to help the London brokerage office which arranged shipments and orders to European customers. From then on, export sales became increasingly important and the Sunkist name has become known throughout the world.

Armstrong himself never ceased to be a Sunkist salesman. In the spring of 1951 he was in Chicago when the board of directors asked him to make a quick trip to Europe to see what might be done to stimulate orange exports. As soon as he could get passage and passport he sailed on the New Amsterdam, taking with him in his stateroom a wooden box of regular Sunkist lemons, weighing 80 pounds, then "completely unfamiliar" in Europe. He carried a few in his pockets and when he called on distributors he would place one in his hand and start looking at it. This aroused curiosity and led to trial shipments, with the result that export sales of lemons now amount to 30 percent of Sunkist's fresh lemon business.

Shortly after Armstrong's retirement in January, 1957, U.S. Secretary of Agriculture Ezra T. Benson requested him to review the work and program of the Farmer Cooperative Service in order to suggest how the service of the U.S.D.A. to cooperatives might be strengthened and made more effective.

His work in this capacity gave me many opportunities to discuss with him cooperative programs and problems. I was especially impressed with the way he interviewed all members of our staff to find out what they were doing, and why and how they were doing it. The entire staff had respect for his thorough methods of inquiry and his apparent fairness. We later found that he had given the Farmer Cooperative Service a clean bill of health although he had offered a few critical suggestions to help us improve our procedures. This review came at an important time, and I am sure that it helped us maintain and improve our program of work.

Paul Armstrong is a man who has never lost the common touch. He was and is at home among all classes of people and interested in their lives and welfare.

Although he received many honors, such as the Honorary Degree of Doctor of Agriculture, conferred upon him in 1946 by his alma mater—Michigan State University—it never impaired his basic modesty. In a recent letter to me he said, "An individual's career is greatly influenced by being in the right place at the right time and getting the breaks along the way and I never forget that there are people equally qualified who do not happen to get the breaks." Any breaks that came to Paul Armstrong he deserved.

The Molder of the
Production Credit System

Carl Raymond Arnold

by Homer G. Smith

CARL RAYMOND ("CAP") ARNOLD, has been referred to by many as "the father of the production credit system." His background and experience fitted him for his professional career.

"Cap" was born on a farm in the Willamette Valley in Oregon in 1891, where his father operated a livestock ranch. At the age of 16 he moved with his family to Darke County, Ohio, where he completed his high school education at Arcanum, Ohio. He was active as a debater and as a captain of many of the school's sports teams.

Following his high school graduation, "Cap" taught in the rural schools of that state for three years. He then entered Ohio State University where, after a year in the Chemical Warfare Service of the United States Army, he graduated in 1920. He then became an extension worker at Ohio State University. He was granted a leave of absence for the academic year 1925–26 to do work at the University of Minnesota, where he received an M.A. Degree in Economics. He also was given a leave of absence for seven months in 1931 to help organize extension work in the Bureau of Agricultural Economics, U. S. D. A.

"Cap" gained a national reputation at Ohio State as an extension worker in farm management. Following his graduation from the University of Minnesota, he also taught courses in Agricultural Economics, Farm Management, and Prices. While at Ohio State, he did pioneer work in preparing outlook materials on various Ohio farm products.

"Cap" joined the Farm Credit Administration in 1933. He helped organize the first Production Credit Corporation in the St. Louis District in 1933—the first of 12 such corporations throughout the country. He also helped organize the first Production Credit Association at Champaign, Ill.

"Cap" continued his affiliation with the Farm Credit Administration until he retired in 1951. He was made Deputy Production Credit Commissioner in 1933. From 1941 to 1951 he served as Production Credit Commissioner.

Following his initial retirement, he was persuaded to again join the Farm Credit System as Governor in 1953 to serve out the unexpired term of Governor I. W. Duggan. He retired from this position in 1954.

Following his retirement in 1954, "Cap" actively operated his 60-acre farm in Ohio, 50 acres of which were devoted to apple production. He also went to Greece for the International Cooperative Administration to study and make recommendations on the farmers' credit problems of that country. In 1963 he was honored by Ohio State University when it bestowed on him an Honorary Doctor of Humane Letters Degree.

Rural Credit Contributions in Four Areas

"Cap's" outstanding contributions in rural credit were in four areas:

1. He was one of the influential early leaders to foresee and emphasize the key role to be played by farmers and stockmen. He was sure that if groups of farmers had full information, they generally would come to sound conclusions. This faith had a profound effect on the direction of the Production Credit System. It resulted in early emphasis on good business meetings of the farmer membership, and on group meetings of managers and farmer directors emphasizing training and educational aspects. As farmer directors, association and district management gained in knowledge and experience, "Cap" became one of the principal early proponents of decentralization from Washington to the districts and from the districts to the associations.

2. He stressed the farm management approach in extending credit. Loans should be constructive and serve to increase the farmer's income. His views in this regard resulted in including many people with farm management backgrounds in the staffing at the local, district, and national levels. This led to early special attention to loan purpose determination of funds needed and income available for loan repayment—i.e., the budgeted loan with loan advances as funds were needed and with repayments as income was received.

3. He was one of the early leaders in the Production Credit System with a vision of the feasibility and importance of full ownership of the associations by farmers and stockmen. His leadership was instrumental in the great progress toward this objective. His views on this subject are well expressed in an FCA Circular, *Farmers Build Their Own Production Credit System.*

4. Through the years preceding the Farm Credit Act of 1953 and until the Federal Farm Credit Board was settled in its responsibilities, "Cap" was a tower of strength as an enthusiastic, articulate, and courageous leader who stood for farmer ownership and control, constructive credit tailored to the farm operations, and decentralization. His influence during this period was of great significance and had a definite effect on the direction taken by the whole Farm Credit System.

Through his close connections with farming "Cap" maintained a practical approach to the problems of agriculture. Probably more than any other person he helped farmers build the production credit system in this country that has served as a model for other countries.

Mary Ellicott Arnold

by Leslie Woodcock

THE COOPERATIVE PIONEERS OF ROCHDALE had their Ann Tweedale, and the consumer cooperatives of the United States have their Mary Arnold, who was born in Staten Island, N. Y., in 1876. It is not as a woman, however, but as a dynamic organizer and leader that cooperators in the United States regard Miss Arnold.

To summarize Miss Arnold's early life: Deciding on a business career she took a business course at Drexel Institute, started work at $5 a week with a county newspaper; owned and operated a 55-acre farm from 1901 to 1906 with Mabel Reed on which they "went broke;" served as a field matron of the U. S. Indian Bureau in Northern California 1908 to 1910; was a dietician and cafeteria operator at Cornell University, 1914 to 1917, where she also enrolled in the School of Nutrition; and an executive of the U. S. Employment Service in New York during World War I (4 years). A remarkable book, *In the Land of the Grasshopper Song* (Vintage Press) tells the story of two years she spent as representative of "The Great White Father" among the Karok Indians.

Starts Cafeteria to Prove Consumer Co-op Principle

In 1919, after consulting a group largely made up of "middle class" social workers, she started a little cafeteria at 52 East 25th Street in New York City. But this was not to be a private business. It was to be a consumers' cooperative in which the customers were to be the members and owners. So, in 1920, the little business was incorporated under the Cooperative Law, and Miss Arnold was elected general manager, a position which she held until 1937. The business was successful, and the membership grew. After only one year, a second branch was established. Within 10 years, there were 10 branches, a 67-family co-op apartment house, and around 6,000 members. Its name is Consumers' Cooperative Services, Inc.

The idea which dominated Miss Arnold's creative leadership was the soundness of consumer ownership as an economic principle. Certainly the food served in the cooperative cafeterias was outstanding in both quality and price.

Between 1926 and 1931, as a representative of Consumers' Cooperative Services, she was a driving force in the establishment of the Eastern Cooperative League and the Eastern Cooperative Wholesale as the regional educational and wholesale federation serving cooperatives from Washington to Boston. She was a director from 1926 to 1938, and from 1944 to 1950.

Miss Arnold also had an important place on the national scene. As early as 1919 she became a close friend of Dr. and Mrs. Warbasse of the Cooperative League, and attended many congresses of the League, starting at the second congress at Cincinnati in 1920. An effective public speaker, she concentrated on changing the League from a contribution supported (largely by the Warbasses) to a dues supported organization. She served as its treasurer for the nine years (1929–1938) during which the transformation took place. She was a League director from 1927–1938, and again from 1945–1950.

Goes on to Other Urban Co-op Developments

Miss Arnold loved adventure and change, so, after 17 years at CCS, she left New York in 1937 to work as co-op organizer and student of adult education for three years in the Extension Department of St. Francis Xavier University in Nova Scotia under the direction of Father M. McCoady. A major accomplishment there was advising (in the fields of architecture, finance, building construction, and co-op theory) in the creation of a co-op housing community of union miners in what became Tompkinsville, Nova Scotia. Later, she published *The Story of Tompkinsville* in book form.

After Nova Scotia, she spent a year as co-op organizer in Newfoundland. Then, in 1941, she organized credit unions and other co-ops among the Maine lobster fishermen and was promoter and producer of a documentary film with an all lobster-fisherman cast and a co-op story.

Miss Arnold would not feel this account complete without mention of her life-long friend and co-worker, Miss Mabel Reed. Their friendship began as children and continued in all of the above activities from the farming experience (flowers), down to Miss Reed's death a few years ago. In a real sense, Miss Reed, too, was a cooperative pioneer.

Since 1942, Miss Arnold has lived near Philadelphia. For some years she directed the Philadelphia Area Cooperative Federation, helped a local housing group, and from this constituency served again on the boards of both the Cooperative League and the Eastern Cooperative Wholesale. In 1949, she served for a period in an administrative capacity without salary for Eastern Cooperative Wholesale.

During this period she has been active with several Friends' Committees, served for a time as treasurer of the Women's League for Peace and Freedom, served as treasurer of a local theater group (The Hedgerow Theater), served on a committee interested in the American Indian and another on race relations. She is still actively interested in the cooperative movement and world affairs.

Howard Edward Babcock

by Warren A. Ranney

H OWARD EDWARD BABCOCK was 37 years old when I first met
him in December, 1926. It was not in his office; I was to learn
that he never spent a great deal of time there. He did most of his
real work elsewhere—in other people's offices, in the little office in
the back of his home at Sunnygables Farm, located a few miles south
of Ithaca, and most especially while he was doing chores around the
farm.

He was 37, with what seemed to be a lifetime's experience already
behind him. I was 20, a sophomore at Cornell, and had just started
to work for GLF, on a part-time basis, to help prepare advertising
and membership material.

He was in a hurry that day—as he was all his life—but he gave
me and the moment his full attention. His outgoing warmth, good
humor, personal interest in my interests, and evidence of his own
inward excitement about building useful institutions for farmers—all
of these things came through to me, fast and clear.

I was certainly no exception. Every individual was important to
Babcock. He never wasted a personal encounter. When it came to
people, he was never half-attentive or preoccupied with other matters.
This was perhaps his greatest quality. With it, he inspired friendship
and confidence, and at the same time transmitted to others his own
sense of adventure and lively commitment to constructive objectives.
With a host of friends who believed in him—and most of them were
farm people—he built his record and carried out his strongest conviction: That farm people themselves, through self-reliance coupled
with intelligent cooperation, could and should determine their own
future.

Along with this great quality of his to inspire people to make unusual efforts and accomplish so much, there was another equally great
quality: His frequent and sincere acknowledgment of the value and
indispensability of every man and woman who worked with him
over the years on what seemed to be an endless stream of new ideas,

new projects, new visions, new ways to adapt to the pressing demands
of a fast-changing world.

Of course, all of this was not obvious to me at our first meeting—
nor for a long time. But it was fascinating to encounter a man who
was so friendly and exciting. After a few more encounters, and opportunities to work on some assignments that fitted into his plans, my
own thoughts were: How did he get this way? Where is he going?

In 1926, when we first met, his already seasoned judgment and
maturity reflected his background and the constructive activities that
he had already packed into those 37 years.

Deeply Aware of Frustrations Common to Farm Life

Always sensitive and perceptive, Babcock early developed a deep
awareness of the frustrating circumstances under which the farmers
of that era lived. These circumstances seemed to be the most memorable part of his boyhood experiences, and a growing awareness of
their ultimate consequences began to shape his sense of values and
his objectives as he was growing up on his father's and mother's farm
near Gilbertsville, N.Y., where he was born on February 23, 1889.
He saw the same unhappy conditions prevailing among the neighbors,
the farm people of that valley and the surrounding uplands.

Then, as a young man, after he graduated from college (Syracuse
University, B.A., 1911), he saw the same circumstances duplicated in
other regions of his native state.

I guess he never forgot that era of frustrations and the prevailing
sense of hopelessness among farm people, because he often talked
about it—but, characteristically, those circumstances didn't engender
bitterness in Babcock; instead, they constantly challenged him to
examine the problems, piece by piece, and to figure out the key solutions, step by step. In this orderly, systematic way, he could arrive
at actions that would be practical, possible, and productive. This was
how his mind worked.

Probably everyone who had a chance to work with Babcock soon
took for granted his special talent for dealing with people, his natural
way of enlisting their support, and his always graceful acknowledgment of everyone's efforts. He could say "thank you" more effectively
than anyone I have ever known. He made each person really feel
a part of whatever was being accomplished. And one could always
sense that, to Babcock, service to one's fellow-men came first. True,
Babcock earned much praise and respect, but these were inescapable
by-products; I'm sure his real satisfaction was in seeing progress and

growth and development in the things he valued most—his family, his farm, his associates, his conviction that new concepts must evolve to deal with the emerging new social order, and his personal commitment to help better the life of all who lived on America's farms and enhance their personal dignity in the eyes of all Americans.

Special Traits Were Rare Perspective, Critical Review

But one of Babcock's qualities—or habits of work—was not so easy to take for granted. This was his mental processes which were always guided by his sense of perspective—to him, people were always more important than things or machines or methods or institutions or traditions that needed to be changed—and, what is still more rare, his dominant capacity to examine and re-examine a viewpoint, a course of action, a decision, a set of values. He constantly used this critical capacity to judge the merits of people, the validity of viewpoints, the consequences of events, the soundness of plans.

This quality can be called intellectual honesty. He practiced it in his dealings with all men; he used it most often on himself—to test and correct his own thinking and beliefs.

For me, as I worked with Babcock through my college years, on through my twenties and thirties, and into my early forties, it was this self-imposed practice of intellectual honesty that fascinated me most. I was especially aware of it because we often talked so frankly about so many things and events. It's fairly easy to understand how a man can acquire and improve his skills in dealing with people, in writing, in speaking, in organizing, in using influence adroitly. It is not quite so easy to comprehend fully the spirit and drive and determination of a man, like Babcock, who insistently practices a very high order of intellectual honesty—and who relentlessly practices it on himself. Most men, after a certain point, seem willing to enjoy the luxury of a little self-deception now and then.

And then there was his talent for reducing the complex problems and the involved issues to their essential elements, keeping cause and effect differentiated, and then seeking the most simple and workable answers—always making allowances in his plans for two of Everyman's dominant characteristics, his reluctance to do things differently and his compulsion to gain a fair advantage.

This habit of seeking simple and workable answers to sticky problems must have started pretty early in Babcock's life. It was a useful habit to have when he took a job, at 22, to plan and start one of the state's first high school courses in agriculture. This was at Albion, in 1911.

He also coached the track team there and met a young lady whom he greatly admired—a Miss Butler. Then he moved to the Elmira Free Academy to teach biology for six months until he had the chance, in 1913, to become one of the state's first Farm Bureau managers, serving in Cattaraugus and Tompkins counties.

Now it was that Miss Hilda Wall Butler of Albion and Howard Edward Babcock decided to get married, and to set up their home in Ithaca. As soon as possible, they acquired a fine farm. It was known as Sunnygables. It came by its name naturally; the old house was big, comfortable, bright, and carried its eight American gothic gables, gingerbread, finial posts and all, with real distinction. Here at Sunnygables, Hilda and Ed reared their three children: Howard, John, and Barbara, who is the wife of Doctor John Hirshfeld.

This family and this farm were always the central core of Ed Babcock's life. Certainly Mrs. Babcock's character and her achievements, as a wife and mother, have always had the utmost admiration from all who knew them. Her nature is strong, she quietly emphasizes the positive, she has the gift of understanding people. Her never failing encouragement, her sound common sense, and her calm, orderly, friendly personality contributed always to Ed's successes and to the character of the children, who are now all married and enjoying children of their own.

Brief Farm Bureau Work Led to Key Positions

This 1913 was to be a memorable year and a starting point in Babcock's life. With a new wife, plans for their new home, some brief but intensive work as Farm Bureau manager in two counties, he was asked to be assistant state leader of the county Farm Bureaus. Then, successively, during the next five years or so, he became state leader of the Farm Bureaus, helped organize the county units into a new State Federation of County Farm Bureaus and became a leader in founding the Agricultural Conference Board (now known as the New York State Conference Board of Farm Organizations). He served as secretary of both these organizations, and was also state leader of the county agents.

And so, in these several key positions of agricultural leadership, Babcock's gift for finding simple and workable answers to the ever-increasing and more complex problems of the day was a priceless gift as the impacts of World War I, with its urgent demands for more food and manpower, swept in on farmers and triggered the great revolution in all of America's rural ways of life.

Some 20-odd years later, Babcock wrote of those days to a friend, and said, "My first experience with the real meaning of food and nutrition for both animals and humans came during the First World War when I was put in charge of food conservation for the state by the Federal Food Administration under Herbert Hoover . . . I carried on this responsibility along with my Farm Bureau duties." And he continued, "I now realize that it was the conditioning I got then in dealing with food . . . that established my ongoing interest in what farmers might do for themselves through a cooperative like GLF." Then he continued in his letter:

It is interesting to look back now and see how circumstances shaped my life before I was able to do much shaping myself.

The teaching of agriculture in high school, the county agent work, the participation in the organization of the State Federation of Farm Bureaus and the New York Conference Board of Farm Organizations, the experience of calling and attending the first meetings that developed the American Farm Bureau Federation moved me up over a period of five years from the community level of thinking to a state and national level.

With this background, I had to deal with the food shortages of World War I. . . . then came the period of opportunity for organizing GLF, during which I unconsciously drew on my knowledge of farm activities and needs at the community, county, state and national levels.

I became an employee of GLF on June 1, 1920. During that June, I was one of the incorporators of GLF and, when the certificate of incorporation was granted, became a director and the first secretary of the organization.

"Professorship Most Prized Post"

Babcock, as secretary of the new GLF, organized and conducted the stock-selling campaign which provided the initial financing. By Fall, the job was done, and he resigned his brief post as secretary to become a professor. In the letter, Babcock went on to say:

"With GLF launched, there came the appointment, offered by Dr. George F. Warren, as full Professor of Marketing . . . which remains in my memory as the most prized post I have ever filled."

This appraisal of his two years as a professor at Cornell was written more than 20 years later—after he had gone back to GLF to serve as its general manager (1922–36), had served as GLF's first director of research (1936–45), had become a recognized writer for several regional and national periodicals (*American Agriculturist,*

Cooperative Digest, Country Gentlemen, Readers Digest, Saturday Evening Post, etc.), had become known nationally as an outstanding speaker on the issues of the day, had served as a member and then as chairman of the board of trustees of Cornell University, had been called on for counsel by governors and Presidents, had served as co-president of the National Cooperative Council (now known as the National Council of Farmer Cooperatives) and chairman of the American Institute of Cooperation, had served on the Federal Farm Board and on the board of the Central Bank for Cooperatives, along with active involvement in many other public services such as membership on President Roosevelt's Agricultural Advisory Commission.

It's against this background—and much more could be added to this brief summary—that Babcock looked back on his job as a professor and called it "the most prized post I have ever filled."

Of that job at Cornell, Babcock further wrote that it "left me in a position where I could observe and study the new organization (GLF) and, as a teacher, contribute to the training of its future general manager, James A. McConnell . . . and a dozen other fellows who were to become leaders of agricultural thought during the next quarter century." At heart, Babcock was really a great teacher.

His successes in so many other fields, and with so many of the ideas and projects he promoted, were simply extensions of his talents as a teacher—the kind of teacher who somehow creates self-motivations in others, and inspires them to seek sound goals, and set higher than usual standards of performance for themselves.

Co-op to Babcock Was "Means to an End"

Babcock, because he did so much to build GLF as an effective farmer cooperative, was and is generally regarded as a cooperative pioneer. But the term "cooperative pioneer" needs some examination when applied to Babcock. His zeal was not based on his philosophical acceptance of the classic principles of cooperation; rather his zeal was for getting needed things done by giving his friends—the farm people he knew so well—the hope, the vision, the will, and the means to shape their own future. To Babcock, the cooperative was "not an end in itself, but a means to an end . . ." as he, himself, wrote in August of 1935. In fact, he often said to me and others that any form of business organization could accomplish what needed doing, but the cooperative corporation—with all its limitations—offered the only form of legal entity that would assure continuing farmers-determination and farmer-control.

His years at the helm of a growing cooperative—first as its secretary and chief fund-raiser in 1920, and next as its General Manager for 14 years (1920–36)—were a prelude to still another chapter in his life. This was started in 1937, with Jim McConnell as GLF's new General Manager, and with himself standing by as a counselor and innovator. In this role, he continued until 1945—the 25th anniversary of GLF's incorporation—and in these nine years was active as the cooperative's first Director of Research, developed the cooperative's original body of thinking on marketing, and started a systematic program for training employees.

It was during this same period that he was called on more and more to help guide Cornell University—as chairman of its board of trustees—through its substantial wartime and post-war expansion, to serve on many state and national committees, to speak more widely, to write articles for more and more periodicals. And all of these activities—whenever they could enhance the position and future of farmers—he pursued with determination until just a few weeks before he died on July 12, 1950. Death came as the result of a heart attack he suffered while recovering from a minor operation.

Babcock's Versatility Praised by Dean Myers

His close friend, Bill Myers, Dean of the College of Agriculture at Cornell, nicely characterized Babcock when he said, after Babcock's death:

> Ed was great because he was versatile. He could do almost any essential job as well or better than recognized experts in a given field. As a writer, speaker, teacher, salesman, cattle judge, Yankee trader, planner, organizer, executive or advertiser, his achievements ranked with the best in quality, originality, vigor, and effectiveness. . . . The organizations and activities which he initiated and carried on successfully arc ample proof of the enormous range of his interests and abilities.

This praise rings true to all who knew Babcock well and worked with him on countless projects. Yet all that Babcock did was almost exclusively focused on the basic goals he had adopted years before. He could state those goals in a few words, as he did on New Year's Day of 1947 when he typed on a little piece of paper:

Lifetime Objectives

I. Perpetuate the family farm economy in America.
II. Focus research, education, and cooperative action on family-farm problems.

    III. Upgrade the American diet as the most practical means by which family-farm operators may protect their way of life and serve human welfare.

Then, before he slipped that piece of paper under the glass on his desk at Sunnygables, he wrote by hand the three catchwords of his life's purpose: *Grass—Livestock—Nutrition.*

Later, when I saw and read this piece of paper on his desk, his habit of self-criticism prompted him to remark that in using the term "family farm," he was not being strictly accurate; that really he was more interested in the future of the "farm family" than in what happened to the "family farm."

Certainly, his record and accomplishments merited the respect he won among his fellowmen; his monument is in the organizations he built and the men he inspired.

Where does the drive, the sense of purpose and the qualities of a man such as Babcock come from? Maybe he licked them off the grass. Maybe they were a measure of his own self-discipline, acquired progressively as he moved from one set of demanding challenges to the next. Maybe some of both. At any rate, he grew in wisdom and effectiveness all his life.

In the sense that he comprehended the needs of his day, worked for a better and more promising tomorrow, put the interests of people first, and practiced intellectual honesty, Babcock was clearly what the classic historians call a Renaissance Man. As such, his interests were broad, his skills many, his sense of values stable and enduring, his objectives simple and geared to the needs of others.

Charles F. Baker

by James Hill, Jr.

SEPTEMBER 19, 1894 on a 1500-acre wheat ranch 10 miles south of Ione, Ore., Charles F. Baker entered this world, the first son in a family of five girls and ultimately five boys.

Charles received his early education at the "Little Red School House" some three miles from the ranch. He walked to and from school each day—a feat that either developed his physical stamina early or else attested to the strong physical make-up he inherited.

Being the oldest boy, Charles began to help his father on the farm at an early age. When he was six years old he drove a six-horse plow team and would go to school the four winter months and work on the ranch the balance of the year—a combination of "Book Learnin'" and application in the field.

When Charles was 11 years old, his father sold the wheat ranch and bought an irrigated ranch near Walla Walla, Wash. Charles completed his grade school education at a country school there— skipping the entire sixth grade, then on to Walla Walla High School where he was on the debating term and graduated with honors. These early years indicated and developed talents Charles would effectively use in his later years—great physical stamina, hard work, intelligence, and ability to speak and move people.

After high school graduation, Charles worked two years as a ranch hired hand. In the slack winter periods he bought alfalfa hay and sold it to add to his savings. In the two and one-half years of hired hand and traveling hay salesman he saved $1,000. In telling the story Charlie laughs and says, "Why, later in my life I spent more money in one night than I would spend in a year when I was trying to get started."

In November, 1915, he married an attractive French girl, Mona Compau. Shortly after marriage, Charles leased a 50-acre dairy farm in the Walla Walla valley for three years, and then bought a 140-acre irrigated farm just outside Walla Walla. He has kept this farm to this day and this is where he presently lives and has always lived even at the height of his cooperative business career.

Early Ability as Competent Organizer Recognized

After World War I, wheat dropped from $2.40 per bushel to 80¢ per bushel between late fall and early spring. In the same short time, butter fat went from 80¢ to 13¢. Charles saw and experienced the serious economic problems of the farm people and responded to the Farm Bureau organization drive of that period by helping to organize the Walla Walla County Farm Bureau and establishing some 600 memberships at $10 each. They hired a young fellow as secretary and in three months all the money was gone. The group then asked Charles to come in from his dairy farm three days a week to serve as acting secretary at $10 per day for time spent. He did this job for several years, keeping the organization active and growing.

When the local creamery went broke in 1923, Charles helped organize the Walla Walla Dairymen's Association, served as a director, and after three years was made president to serve in this capacity for 27 years.

Also, in 1923, the South Eastern Washington County Fair stock company went broke. The Farm Bureau felt a fair was needed and in 1926 Charles Baker accepted the job as secretary of a new county fair organization. Under his leadership, the group put on a fair with no money. This first fair made money and it has been successful ever since and now ranks as one of the best in the state of Washington.

From 1925 to 1933, Charles served as state legislative representative for the Washington State Farm Bureau and, in addition, served as secretary of the State Farm Bureau and as vice president.

In 1929–30, when wheat growers were being encouraged by the Hoover Administration to form farm cooperatives, "Co-op" Baker helped organize the Walla Walla Grain Growers, which is today a highly successful growers' cooperative.

In 1932, there was great interest in the Walla Walla Wheat Plan. Charles was one of the local leaders sent to Washington, D. C. to appear before Congressional Committees on this plan. Since that time, Charles has appeared many times on the Washington scene particularly in connection with the Inland Empire Waterways, which he helped found in 1933. Purpose of this organization was to promote the full development of the water resources of the Pacific Northwest. Baker was elected its first president and has served in this capacity to this day. The organization has been of tremendous significance in the development of the water resources of the Pacific Northwest.

In 1933, Organizer Baker helped start the Walla Walla Production Credit Association, where he served as a director and as president for a period of 10 years.

Best Known for Creation of Pacific Supply Cooperative

For all of the many successful organizations which Charles helped to organize and spearhead through their early years, he is probably best known for his creation of Pacific Supply Cooperative. So to that story.

Back in the beginning of the great depression—1930–31—Charles was working with the Farm Bureau which had concerned itself with several cooperative purchasing programs in the neophyte stage. Sacks and twine purchases and petroleum products were the major items in the beginning. Charles, as a Farm Bureau secretary, first dealt in grain bags. One year when the contract market seemed cheap, he contracted the purchase of 700,000 grain bags—enough to handle 1½ million bushels of grain. When it became necessary to dig up some money on these contracts, Charles and his organization had no net worth. However, he went to a banker anyway and told him his story. He got the $15,000 needed to cinch the deal. As Charles tells the story, "He borrowed $15,000 when he wasn't worth 15¢." This lesson indicated to him that if people believe in you and you are honest, you can get most anything done.

Through his experiences with farm supply purchasing he learned that there had to be better organization and cooperation. Charles got in touch with Homer Young of the Cooperative Union Oil Company at Kansas City, and he had Homer come out to Oregon for meetings at Portland, to which all cooperatives were invited. As a result of these meetings, a small group in November, 1933, decided to form a purchasing cooperative and named it Pacific Supply Cooperative. There were 10 charter members who contributed $100 per member. Most of this money was spent on preparing articles of incorporation and bylaws. The first annual meeting was held in January, 1934, and Baker was elected secretary and manager.

From this inauspicious start of 10 local cooperatives joining together under Baker's leadership, Pacific Supply Cooperative grew from a $1,000 company to become one of the main federated regionals in the Pacific Northwest country, and one of the key regionals in cooperative circles of this nation.

Pacific Supply Cooperative originally got its start in petroleum, then in tires, batteries, and accessories, and then in fertilizer and seeds. Built by earnings, the company now boasts a net worth of some $12 million, sales volume over $40 million, and membership of over 100 local organizations.

Baker's Aggressive Leadership Left Heritage

Consistently in the growth of Pacific Supply Cooperative there has been the aggressive and compelling leadership of Charles Baker, who from early times felt there was an urgency to induce farm people to organize along co-op lines to solve their own problems. Charles is a strong believer in commodity groups as the best way of doing the job and he feels that in the future commodity groups must better organize to do the job. Supply co-ops, in Charles' opinion, face a very real problem of being large enough and strong enough to attract the management and capital necessary to do the job.

Charles Baker, retired as general manager of Pacific Supply Cooperative in 1962, now spends his time actively on his diversified ranch near Walla Walla. There he has 70 acres in asparagus—his major crop—plus corn and sugar beets and some wheat. His long-range plan—"looking down the road"—is to have all 140 acres in asparagus. He processes and markets most of his asparagus as a fresh product under his own brand, "Baker Ranch Asparagus." At the time this article is written Charles Baker is 72 years old and you can find him active on his farm putting in 9–10 hours a day in the field—irrigating, driving a tractor, supervising the asparagus harvest when he has a 25-man crew working in the fields—all of which keeps him fit, healthy, and in excellent physical condition—almost beyond comprehension. As an indication of his ability to think ahead and plan, he made arrangements several years back to take the entire manure output of a close-by cattle feeder from which he spreads 4,000 to 5,000 tons of manure a year on his 140 acres of land resulting in constantly improved production results.

Besides his cooperative organization efforts in dairy, wheat, credit, and supply developments, Charles is probably most proud of his very constructive work in the development of Pacific Northwest water resources. To this day he works tirelessly on this project and can expound and dramatize the great future involved in this subject.

Charles Baker, farmer, organizer, and cooperator early learned that he had the ability to lead people—to direct them into channels of effort that would be beneficial to them. In so doing he has led a successful business life with many rewards—most of which involved the satisfaction of helping people to help themselves.

Charles Baker has enjoyed a full life and still keeps on going strong. He loves people—he loves to sing but is probably a better fisherman than a singer. However, he has sung his favorite rendition of "Paper Doll" on several famous bandstands across this nation. Charles Baker, a better fisherman than singer, but he certainly enjoys both! Last summer, when asparagus cutters were in short supply, Charles took his shift in the field cutting asparagus—stoop labor that few owners will still do, but Charles put in his six hours a day earning $2.50 per hour, and he did this for 10 days in a row at 72 years of age. His blood pressure went up a little bit—quite a little bit—but the point is, that he had the ability to do what he was asking others to do.

Therein lies the success story of a very remarkable man—whether in the field, the business office, Washington, D. C., or on the bandstand singing "Paper Doll."

Charles F. Baker, in his active business lifetime accomplished many things in behalf of agriculture and the Pacific Northwest. The organizations he helped start, the results they obtained, and the continuity of their growth account for a record of achievement of which any man can rightly be proud. Charles is proud of these achievements and the farm and cooperative people of this Pacific Northwest deeply appreciate his lifetime of service.

Harry J. Beernink

by Harry B. Carroll

THE NAME OF HARRY J. BEERNINK has been closely associated with the cooperative marketing of eggs and poultry in the state of Washington since 1917. As a young poultryman he was drawn by necessity to the cooperative method of marketing his products. Since then, until his retirement in 1964, his life was devoted to the expansion of cooperative procedures to help the poultrymen and other farm families of the Northwest. It can be said that he went every step of the way from pioneer to modern—for when he retired he was General Manager of an organization that embraced over 50,000 poultrymen and other farmers in the states of Washington, Oregon, and Idaho, with a volume of business of $80 million and total assets of $34 million. The career of Harry Beernink is also the career of Western Farmers, Inc., for neither can leave out the other.

Harry Beernink was born on May 10, 1899 in Wisconsin, but his parents moved West a year later to settle at Lynden, Whatcom County, Wash., a rough, undeveloped area in the northwest corner of the United States, full of opportunity for the courageous.

Harry's father worked in lumber mills and logging camps until he could raise enough money to buy a small farm. While his father and two brothers raised livestock, Harry got started raising chickens. He had his first flock of White Leghorns while attending school. He early found that just ordinary birds didn't lay enough eggs so he built up a breeder-hatchery enterprise which included trapnesting, an unusual practice then. He thus developed a superior strain of White Leghorn chickens, some of which held state laying records.

Harry soon learned that to prosper he would have to advertise his products so, in partnership with another poultry fancier, he learned how to display his birds on the show circuit, with the result that he won laurels in many places. Thus as a young man still in his teens he became well known in the state's growing poultry industry. At about this time he learned that he couldn't make progress all alone, so late in 1916 he married a neighboring farm girl, Ella Mueller, in whom he found a perfect partner and homemaker. They raised two sons and a daughter.

Crisis Leads to Thoughts of Cooperation

In 1917, with poultry raising in western Washington hitting full stride, local markets for eggs became saturated and prices fell rapidly. Poultrymen throughout the state were demoralized and were ripe for any plan that would stabilize their industry.

For several years poultrymen in western Washington had been experimenting with cooperative methods on a local basis but the general situation now called for a broader approach. Through the good offices of Professor W. A. Linklater, supervisor of the Western Washington Experiment Station at Puyallup, a statewide meeting of poultrymen was called for February 15, 1917, at Seattle.

Among the 114 who responded to the invitation to be present was Harry Beernink. The group was unanimously in favor of forming a statewide organization and a committee was formed to draft its constitution and bylaws. At a second meeting on February 24, 1917, the constitution and bylaws were adopted with few changes and the Washington Cooperative Egg and Poultry Association came into being.

The Association made modest progress during its first year and was well on its way when the first annual meeting was held in Seattle on January 29, 1918. At that time Harry Beernink, although but 19 years of age, was named one of the Trustees and in this capacity he served on the finance committee comprised of five Trustees—later designated as Directors.

At this time Harry was interested in the association as a member and not as an employee. On his farm he worked to make cooperation practical. With two neighbors he bought a carload of corn, and they prepared a "mixed formula" by stirring ingredients with a scoop shovel on a warehouse floor. They saved $35 a ton and this experience had a profound influence on Harry by impressing on him the importance of working and purchasing together as well as of marketing together.

When the office of the Extension Service was opened in Whatcom County on May 1, 1917, as the first County Agent, I soon came to know and rely on Harry as one of the most progressive young men in the county. Harry's poultry farm was always available for use in conducting various types of demonstration meetings. I found that he was always ready to work with others, and we held many meetings to explain how the Washington Co-op, as the state association was called, could serve the needs of poultry farmers.

In the early days, the directors of the Washington Co-op spent every possible hour they could spare away from their own homes canvassing poultrymen for new members and in 1920, partly as a result of Harry's efforts, two branch stations were opened for business in Whatcom County.

For the first three years the Washington Co-op operated without a general manager—the function being performed by the Secretary-Treasurer. In 1921, H. E. Wills, the Manager of the Lynden Station, became the first fulltime manager and Harry, who was then Vice-President, resigned to accept the appointment of Manager of the Lynden Station. It is of interest that Samuel D. Sanders, who later made such a prominent record as General Manager, succeeded Harry as Vice-President later in this year.

Harry's favorable experience in buying and mixing feed led him to propose that the Washington Co-op set up a feed department, and in 1922 this department got underway and then grew phenomenally.

In January, 1923, S. D. Sanders was elected General Manager of the Association and he held this position until 1937 when he resigned to serve as Cooperative Bank Commissioner of the Farm Credit Administration in Washington, D. C. Under his leadership the Washington Co-op had grown to become one of the nation's most progressive cooperatives both in cooperative marketing and purchasing.

Becomes General Manager in 1937

When Sanders gave up the post of General Manager, Harry Beernink, who had been serving as his Assistant Manager since 1928, was unanimously chosen to succeed him, and he continued in this position until his retirement in 1964.

Harry knew the organization from inside out and there was no slacking in its pace under his management. Almost immediately the Association greatly broadened its operations in the purchasing field to include petroleum products, seeds, fertilizers, and other farm supplies.

As the Association widened its field of operations to serve all types of farmers it changed its name to Washington Co-operative Farmers Association in 1945, and then, as it expanded into Oregon and Idaho, it changed its name again to Western Farmers Association in February, 1960.

When Harry Beernink gave up the post of General Manager, he

was head of one of the great business enterprises of the Northwest. He made his dreams come true.

Harry Beernink has long been known as one of the nation's influential cooperative leaders, and his abilities have been recognized in many ways.

From 1943 until his retirement he served on the board of directors and executive committee of the National Council of Farmer Cooperatives, and in 1957 and 1959 he served as its President after serving two terms as its Vice-President He was the National Council's first representative at the International Food and Agricultural Producers meeting in Paris in 1948, and he represented the Council at other meetings of this international organization.

For two 3-year terms he served on President Eisenhower's Agricultural Advisory Commission, and for many years he served as a Trustee and Vice-Chairman of the American Institute of Cooperation.

He helped organize the Washington State Council of Farmer Cooperatives in September, 1936, and served five years as its President. He was a director or officer of that organization until he retired from the Western Farmers Association in 1964. He also was closely associated for many years with the Seattle Chamber of Commerce, serving both as director and as Vice-President. He was also a member and a director of the executive committee of the Association of Washington Industries.

To Harry Beernink agricultural cooperation was not a religion but just good common sense. However, Harry became so identified with the merits and the practice of cooperation that not only in the Northwest but throughout the land the name of Beernink is almost a synonym for cooperation in the best sense of this word.

Roland N. Benjamin

by *John B. Jones*

"A LEADER OF MEN."

His personal magnetism is generated by his home-spun Abe Lincoln characteristics.

His greatest contribution to cooperative development in Pennsylvania was his sincere and profound belief that cooperative self-help organizations could be the answer to the economic plight of what he termed "the little people." He liked to build people. To Pennsylvania farmers, "R. N." always stood forth as a man of integrity—with the welfare of the farmer uppermost in his mind.

In looking back over the years, I am convinced that any success we may have had in building Pennsylvania Farm Bureau Cooperative Association was greatly influenced by the confidence engendered in the minds of both the farmer members and the employees of the organization by R. N.

R. N. is undoubtedly the most influential cooperative leader in Pennsylvania during the last three decades. He not only helped build Pennsylvania Farm Bureau Cooperative Association, but every other co-op which asked for his help.

These are typical of the plaudits of the men who have worked and hunted and fished with Roland N. Benjamin, the first President and during many subsequent years the Executive Secretary of Pennsylvania Farm Bureau Cooperative Association, now a part of Agway, Inc.

This author first saw "The Chief," as he was affectionately called by his associates in Farm Bureau, during his first visit to the Harrisburg headquarters of PFBCA in 1943. Noticeable at that time was the unique relationship that existed between the two members of the famous "Agster-Benjamin" team that supplied the management leadership of that successful cooperative during its first 20 years.

The relationship was unique in that it was at variance with a cardinal principle of sound management structure—yet successful. As one of the founders, the first President, and subsequently Executive Secretary of PFBCA, Mr. Benjamin had in 1934 journeyed to the Midwest in search of a general manager for the embryonic farm supply wholesale. He was successful in weaning away from Indiana Farm Bureau Cooperative Association an "action-operator" in the person of H. S. Agster, a well-known farm leader in his own right and the other member of "the team" mentioned above—first as General Manager and later as Executive Vice President and General Manager.

Benjamin-Agster in Unusual 22-Year "Partnership"

"In our very first conversation," Mr. Agster has recalled, "before I had agreed to accept the job, R. N. made it plain to me that we were always to be equals—I to attend to the operating and he to membership and public relations along with his duties for the insurance company. For the next 22 years we worked side by side, and in all that time we never had one disagreement or a cross word. We did not always see things just alike, but when we came to that kind of thing we argued it out until we were of one mind."

Mr. Benjamin confirms the understanding they had, adding, "Ag told me there was 'one thing to be thoroughly understood—anytime we disagree, you've got to make the decision.' It never happened. Not one time did we disagree. We talked it out and reached an agreement. When we encountered any kind of office rumors or intrigue, or any indication of folks trying to play one of us against the other, we always compared notes and met it head-on as one."

Unusual? Yes, but in this instance it worked—a tribute to the intelligence and integrity of the two men. Under their leadership, the organization grew in 22 years from a lowly beginning in a rented room, with $1,000 in capital and a small volume of purchases for three local cooperatives, to a financially strong organization providing some 70,000 farmers with $27 million in farm supplies services annually through their 31 local cooperatives and 20 service agents. During those formative years, these two men traveled thousands of miles throughout the state supplying the leadership that made it all possible.

This leadership was not confined to the family of Farm Bureau Cooperatives in Pennsylvania. It played a part in the developing scene of "cooperation among cooperatives"—joint ownership by large regionals of feed mills, fertilizer plants, refineries, research facilities, and other joint sources of supplies and services.

And it was always available to any group, large or small, when wanted; which calls to mind an incident during the early Depression years. Mr. Benjamin was attending a meeting of apple growers who were dissatisfied with the extremely low prices being received by them. He had noticed that the only apples to be found at the stores in the area were those attractively graded and packaged Northwestern apples—no local apples. He had bought a couple of them at a nickel apiece. He had also picked up a couple of apples in a nearby Pennsylvania city from a large and attractive display which he happened to know had been purchased in that very county, graded, packaged, and sold at a good profit by a man he knew.

"The Chief" held up the 4 apples to see if his audience could notice any difference in them. They couldn't. All four were beautiful Delicious apples. He knew that the local apples were more flavorful. Then he told them what he had done.

"Now don't blame the government," he admonished them. "Don't blame anybody but yourselves. You know how to grow them, all right. But you're like the Irishman who came to this country and got a job as a hod-carrier. He had someone write a letter for him to his brother back in Ireland and said, 'Come to America quick, it's a fine country—all you have to do is carry the brick and mortar up to the second story and the man there does all the laying of the brick!' "

"Now you fellows," Benjamin continued, "are carrying the brick and mortar up there and the man up there does all the layin'—and the fellow up there gets the money!"

"If you want to know who's most to blame for the low prices you get—don't try to find someone else—go get a mirror and look right straight in it!"

That group of apple growers organized themselves into a cooperative the following year, built a small packing house, and began packing and marketing their crop as a group. They also handled farm supplies. Not too much was accomplished the first years, except to gain some experience and a foothold. But today this group is one of the largest and most successful fruit marketing groups in the East.

Benjamin's Ability to "Plant the Idea" Cited

The above story is indicative of the Benjamin philosophy, as is a favorite quotation of his that "He who chops his own wood warms himself twice." It is also indicative of his leadership. He didn't organize the apple co-op. But he planted the seed. And many similar tales could be recounted, in every part of the state, and in every commodity group.

While championing the farmer's ability to help himself, and his right and his obligation to do so, Benjamin has been outspoken against handouts and government doles. "They weaken the very fabric of our people," he asserts. "If we continue to accept Government aid whenever a cloud appears in the sky, we must expect to have Government dictation to the end of our days."

When you scan the background of this rugged leader you begin to understand why he is the way he is. And at 78 (3-8-66) he is still rugged. Well over six feet, lean—a man who still literally "chops his own wood," grows his own vegetables, hunts deer and bear each year with a few of his old cronies who are still around, and still likes to have that occasional stroll on a wooded mountain top "alone with his thoughts."

Mr. Benjamin was born in the rugged confines of Bradford County, Pa., on March 8, 1888, in Asylum Township (where Queen Antoinette of France was scheduled to live out her time instead of keeping her date with the guillotine), 6 miles from the County Seat of Towanda. His father was Guy C. Benjamin, his mother Cassie Neiley (formerly McNeiley) Benjamin. He had four Scotch grandparents. His Benjamin forebears came to Connecticut from England and migrated to Northern Pennsylvania when that area was thought to be a part of the Connecticut grant.

His grandfather Benjamin cut the first tree that was ever cut on the land on which R. N. was born and reared, and which he farmed until he moved to Harrisburg in 1930 to become State Agent for Ohio Farm Bureau Insurance Company (now Nationwide). "It was covered mostly in big white pine," relates Mr. Benjamin, "and today it would be worth a million dollars. Except for what was needed for a cabin, it was cut down and burned. He built a dam, and set up a sawmill. Later owned five farms on down the creek—and a sawmill at every place. Floated lumber down to Harrisburg."

Mr. Benjamin likes to think that possibly some of the white pine timbers in his 150-year-old stone home in New Cumberland (a suburb of Harrisburg) came off the land on which he was reared. And the big wood pile, noticeable even on the 4½ acres surrounding the big stone house, is reminiscent of his logging, woodcutting, farming background in Bradford County. The wood pile fits into his physical fitness routine and supplies fuel for at least one fireplace still in use. There are eight in the house, including two in the long living room and one in the kitchen in which even Benjamin can stand upright.

He still "grows his own potatoes," too, along with other garden stuff. This, too, is reminiscent of his younger days on the farm. He "grew the first field of 400 bushels-per-acre of potatoes known in Pennsylvania." He and one other farmer in Bradford County had agreed to work with Dr. Nixon of Penn State to demonstrate to other farmers what could be accomplished with good seed and improved cultural practices. "I got the first spraying machine in the county, and we had a good demonstration. Good year, and good seed potatoes from Michigan. One hundred people there at digging time. Where the rows were not sprayed, we got 75 bushels of good potatoes. The rest of the field went over 400 bushels per acre. It cost, at that time, about $8. or $9. an acre to spray. Had 325 extra bushels at an additional cost of only $8. or $9.—cheapest potatoes I ever raised."

The above experience propelled Benjamin into the business of growing seed potatoes and seed grains which he shipped all over the state for the next 10 years.

That and similar evidences of leadership and progressive thinking were doubtless the reason that he became Master of the Pomona Grange and later Overseer of the Pennsylvania State Grange for a maximum of three terms. He was also sought out by the State Chamber of Commerce in the early 'teens to serve as its Agricultural Director and served in that capacity for 15 years. He was sought out in these capacities while a relatively young man—despite the fact that his formal education was limited to that available in a one-room country school!

Interested Only in "Action" Programs

All of this transpired prior to 1930, when he left the farm and Bradford County for Harrisburg at 42 years of age. This time he was sought out by the leadership of Pennsylvania Farm Bureau Federation to help increase the effectiveness of its program in the state. R. N. was not interested in promoting another "membership organization" in the state. He preferred "action" programs designed to "help farmers help themselves" as farm business operators.

Accordingly, PFBF sponsored Farm Bureau Insurance Company of Ohio in the state, and Mr. Benjamin became State Agent. Within a short time PFBF's debts were paid and the Insurance Company was firmly established in Pennsylvania—eventually to become the largest single insurer of automobiles in the state. In 1938, R. N. became the first Director of the insurance company from outside Ohio.

Meanwhile, in 1934, Pennsylvania Farm Bureau Cooperative Association came into being, as previously related, as a business "action" program—in line with R. N.'s philosophy. Local leaders of both the Grange and Farm Bureau were on the incorporating and subsequent boards of directors of PFBCA and its county affiliates. R. N. supplied the leadership which made this possible.

Mr. Benjamin has been a Director of the now Nationwide group of insurance companies for 22 years and was recently elected for another three-year term, a total of 25 years. He says this will be the last term; that age 81 is long enough to shoulder such responsibilities. He served six years as Chairman of the Board of the life company, and continues as a Director of seven other Nationwide affiliates.

This busy man also found the time to serve nine years (1954–1962) as a member (elected by farmer cooperatives) of the Farm Credit Board of Baltimore, and four years (1961–1964) as a Director of the Central Bank for Cooperatives, in Washington, D.C. He served as a director, as Vice Chairman, and as Chairman of the Baltimore Board.

And recently he became a Texan in his spare time—big hat and all —as a member of the boards of directors of the Commercial Standard group of insurance companies headquartered in Ft. Worth (life, casualty, fire, and title insurance).

So it is seen that "The Chief" has been kept quite busy since his "retirement" at age 65 from Pennsylvania Farm Bureau Cooperative Association—and is still fairly busy as a "co-op pioneer" at age 78!

Roy F. Bergengren

by *John E. Eidam*

ROY F. BERGENGREN was a man of action. Had it not been for him, it is doubtful that credit unions, discovered by Edward A. Filene of Boston, while traveling in Europe and Asia, would have been propagated across the United States as they have been.

Edward A. Filene was a businessman and a philanthropist. It was he who saw that unless credit was made available to people of ordinary means at reasonable rates, they would be unable to purchase the goods coming off the mass production lines. The American economy needed credit unions in order to make it spin.

Credit unions accomplished several things. They mobilized credit for the use of the ordinary man. They established guide lines and competition in interest rates. And perhaps more importantly, they established control by the membership over their own assets and, similarly, established their own policies with respect to lending.

Edward A. Filene needed someone to do the intricate work of mobilizing dedicated people, contacting legislatures, convincing banking supervisory officials and organizing a self-perpetuating institution that would provide the funds, the know-how, the inspiration, and the leadership to carry forward credit union and cooperative philosophy.

Such a man was Roy F. Bergengren (1879–1955).

Being a lawyer, he was very cognizant of organization structural problems. He was familiar with legislation. He had the status to command respect in state capitols and legislative halls. Despite his technical training and educational background he was not primarily a technician. He was a crusader! He agreed with Mr. Filene to use a million dollars to develop the credit union idea in the United States.

Roy Bergengren worked closely with Edward A. Filene, first in the establishment of the Credit Union Extension Bureau. This activity began in 1921.

Being a person with an orderly mind, unusual for one who was also a promoter and crusader, he set down the goals and objectives which were to occupy much of his time for the next 13 years.

The first of these five was, "Get the Laws." This engaged most of his time. Obtaining 48 (later 50) state laws and a federal law was no small assignment.

Bergengren was a prodigious worker. He wrote four textbooks on credit unions, the first one in 1923.

Realizing the magnitude of the task before him, Bergengren early began looking for, and mobilizing the talents of liberal-minded persons over the United States. He taught them about credit unions and inspired them with visions of what could be accomplished if ordinary people were able to have something to say about the use of their own money.

He became interested very early in definitions that were developed to describe a credit union. One from the *Southern Agriculturist* was "A credit union is based on the principle of self-help, and the financial strength of the community is mobilized for the use of those who live in it."

Traveling over the United States, carrying on a voluminous correspondence, he virtually ran a one-man show until Agnes Gartland appeared on the scene in 1928, to act as his secretary and assistant.

It became apparent to Bergengren that he must truly democratize the structure that needed to be formulated to succeed the Credit Union Extension Bureau, which had been financed by Filene.

Bergengren's Pioneering Leads to CUNA Organization

This led to the famous Estes Park Conference in 1934. About 70 persons were invited to this meeting. Of the 50 who came, most came at their own expense. They met in the YMCA camp. Articles of Association and bylaws were adopted. This was the beginning of CUNA-Credit Union National Association.

Roy F. Bergengren was a dedicated man. With his roots in Boston and the East, when the decision was reached to move CUNA to Madison, Wis., he left his homeland and moved there to head the organization. This must have been a most trying yet rewarding time for so energetic a person. His goals then were:

1. To organize credit unions.
2. To obtain the balance of the state laws.
3. To obtain a federal law.
4. To formalize the organization structure he headed, and to democratize it.

5. To obtain adequate financial support from the state leagues in order to replace the subsidy provided by Edward A. Filene.
6. To establish a national credit union publication.
7. To write copiously and clearly, texts, and inspirational books.
8. To continually inspire leaders in the various states to carry on the organizational and operational effort necessary to make the program work.
9. To travel widely in order to carry on his crusade.
10. To furnish leadership and guidance so as to coordinate varying ideas that were bound to arise from the various parts of the country.

All of those things he did. He did them well.

That he considered his activity to be a form of cooperative action for the handling of money can be gained from the titles of two of his books: *Cooperative Banking—A Credit Union Book,* is one of his early texts. Another is: *Credit Union—A Cooperative Banking Book.*

Later in writing *I Speak for Joe Doakes,* Bergengren said, "I wrote this book because I feel that through the more than four million members (1945) of cooperative banks and credit unions which I have helped to organize in the last 25 years, I have been in unusually close contact with the ordinary worker. I feel that I have always been working for him. He needs someone to speak for him. I believe I have been able to consider economic problems in a way that interests him and shows his stake in their outcome."

Bergengren knew about, visited, organized, and spoke before little credit unions as well as large ones.

He was a religious man, and he attracted leaders to his cause who were strong in their own religious beliefs. These people came from all faiths—Protestant, Catholic, and Jewish.

In speaking of one small community that had a cooperative and a credit union, he said, "It is my proof that God has committed to us potentialities of service and that cooperation is one key that will unlock the door."

Bergengren was emphatic in his belief that capitalism, in order to survive, must be geared to the common man. This was not a cliche, or a "political trick." He described best what he believed in this field by the following paragraph:

> If there is a message for capitalism in this book it is that captains of industry and captains of banking should stop thinking in terms of the officers of their ships and begin to give thought to the *crew* and the *passengers*—in other words, to all of us who are the victims or the beneficiaries of capitalism."

The Credit Union National Association has been the only organization of its kind that has ignored national boundary lines. CUNA was CUNA for the United States and Canada almost from the beginning. The executive committee consisted of leaders from both countries.

Later CUNA became international and has membership from South American, African, and Asian countries. Also Australia and New Zealand, as well as Canada and the United States.

His Genius, Compassion Conceive Loan Insurance Plan

To illustrate how Cuna Mutual Insurance Society came into existence is at once a portrayal of Bergengren's genius and the compassion of ordinary people. The idea for such an insurance society to insure the payment of a loan if the maker died or became permanently disabled was in the minds of some people for a considerable time. The incident that brought the matter into focus was the death of a lineman for a power company. He had just negotiated a loan through his credit union. As was usual in the early 30's, some of his fellow employees had co-signed on the loan and were responsible for its repayment. The question was asked, why?

Why couldn't there be an insurance company to repay such loans? Why not, indeed!

This incident became a cause celebre. As a result of the discussion, Cuna Mutual was organized. It needed a net worth of $25,000 as a starter. Edward A. Filene furnished the money. It was later repaid.

Earl Rentfro of Missouri was enlisted by Bergengren to aid in forming Cuna Mutual. Rentfro was the first general manager.

Various plans for group insurance had been in existence in one way or another through leagues and in some cases through the credit union treasurer, before Cuna Mutual was organized; but until Cuna Mutual was formed, no company had offered direct insurance to the credit unions at an attractive rate for which the credit union itself would pay the premium.

Cuna Mutual has always had an "A-Plus-Excellent" rating by Dunne's Insurance Reports and now has coverage of $9.7 billion as of December 31, 1965; and assets of $56.6 million. It holds sixth place in comparative coverage in the United States.

The operation of this company as an affiliate of CUNA and the leagues has caused credit unions who carry this coverage to say that the "debt dies with the debtor."

Many credit unions also carry life savings insurance which insures the savers' accounts up to $2,000 with some declining amounts when the saver reaches an older age.

Bergengren retired in 1946, as managing director but was later designated Managing Director Emeritus and continued quite active in that capacity.

Taught Members That Money Is Man's Servant, Not Master

Roy Bergengren was a real capitalist and an ardent advocate of our democratic society. He wrote:

> We, in Credit Unions, probably would compose the strongest group in the United States opposed to communism, if there ever was a real danger of communism in this country. Why? Simply because, as the most elementary economist knows, communism stands for common ownership of property to which we are diametrically opposed. All we are trying to do is to get some property for our members to own by stopping the wastes which now take our earnings—without equivalent return in goods. . .We are teaching our members that there is nothing basically wrong about money so long as money becomes the servant of man and ceases to be his master.

In 1952, Bergengren wrote his greatest book, *Crusade*. I treasure the copy which he presented to me with his friendly comment that I, too, had contributed to the credit union movement.

He said that one of his greatest satisfactions was that he had found that in credit union work people became increasingly aware of the dignity and integrity of the average man. A realization came that quite literally the people can do 10 times what they think they can do.

He was heartened that businessmen found the theory of the brotherhood of man does work better than the dog-eat-dog philosophy of the survival of the least scrupulous; and, in sober fact, there can be no true political democracy without economic democracy as well.

That he was a genius, an organizer, an innovator, and a doer goes without saying. He was one of the greatest leaders in the field of cooperative credit since Frederick William Raiffeisen (1818–83) of Germany.

Bergengren not only knew the facts and the philosophy, taught it to hundreds and thousands but crusaded by every means at hand to implement his ideas.

Bergengren felt that credit unions were cooperatives whose product was money. He said:

> The cooperative idea has a sound ancestry to back it up. The centennial of the famous Rochdale Cooperative was celebrated

in various parts of the world in 1944. From the little shop in Toad Lane, organized by the weavers of Rochdale in 1844, developed the great consumer-cooperative system of Great Britain. In 1948 the cooperative-credit associations, which have come to be known as "credit unions" celebrated their one-hundredth birthday. If there be virtue in ancient lineage, the cooperative movement can offer an adequate family tree and a century of progress.

That he was deeply religious and injected his mind, heart, and spirit into his crusade is evidenced by his statement as he approached the end of his service:

—In such surroundings was my crusade to continue; in the end, I think, I found my Holy Grail.

One of the great tributes paid him after 20 years of service by his associates was expressed by Tom Doig:

It has been said the life of man shall be measured by three score years and ten, but I say to you the life of man shall be measured, not in years, but in the service he renders his fellowman.

Surely such a man was Roy F. Bergengren. Now passed to his final reward, he lives in the hearts and minds of credit union folks over many lands.

Robert Worth Bingham

by Theodore Saloutos

ROBERT WORTH BINGHAM was influential in encouraging the growth of cooperative marketing of tobacco, even though he was better known as a newspaper publisher and a United States Ambassador to the Court of St. James. His background was unusual and atypical of the pioneers in the cooperative movement. Born in Orange, N.C., on November 8, 1871, he was the fourth of five children born to Robert and Delphine Louise (Worth) Bingham and descended from a family of clergymen and educators. His father, head of the Bingham School from 1873 to 1923, was a captain in the North Carolina infantry throughout the Civil War.

His early career revolved around law, the holding of public office, and service as a judge rather than farming. He attended the University of North Carolina, the University of Virginia, and the University of Louisville, from which he received his law degree in 1897. He served as the county attorney of Jefferson County, Ky., from 1903 until 1907, when Governor J.C.W. Beckham appointed him to serve as interim Mayor of Louisville. In 1911 he was appointed Chancellor of the Circuit Court of Jefferson County, but declined the nomination to succeed himself.

Bingham commenced his newspaper career as a publisher when he bought a two-thirds interest in the *Louisville Courier-Journal* and the *Louisville Times*. The newspapers under his ownership continued to exert the influential role they exerted when Henry Watterson owned them, but they also underwent changes. Under Bingham the papers became devoted to the public interest; they supported the League of Nations, prohibition, woman suffrage, and the cooperative movement.

Collapse of Tobacco Market Sparks Bingham's Actions

It was the drop in the price of tobacco during 1920–31 that brought Bingham into the cooperative picture. The collapse of the tobacco market had a paralyzing effect on the economy of Kentucky which Bingham as a public-spirited citizen could not overlook. The declining prices revived fears of night-riding and a return of the dark days of 1906–1908. Bingham concluded that night-riding would come unless some action was taken immediately to prevent conditions from becoming worse. He flew to New York City to confer with Bernard Baruch who in turn advised him to seek the aid of Aaron Sapiro, one of the foremost cooperative organizers of his day.

Following his return to Louisville Bingham called a meeting of the leading burley tobacco growers in Louisville where Sapiro presented a comprehensive plan of cooperative marketing. The Sapiro proposal was accepted and a committee of five headed by Bingham, and including James C. Stone, Ralph Barker, W. E. Simms, and John Collins, was selected to perfect a plan of organization. A thorough program was mapped out embracing the entire tobacco territory. Meanwhile Sapiro drew up a contract which required the signing member to turn over all the tobacco he raised over a five-year period to the Burley Tobacco Association. This contract became effective with the 1921 crop. An intricate system likewise was devised whereby the warehouse owners relinquished their property to the association.

The membership campaign began in earnest on June 4 and by November that year the required 75 percent of the burley growers had signed five-year contracts. Once the member delivered his crop to the warehouse, the tobacco was graded and the grower received a substantial part of the market price—the money for the purpose being secured by loans against the crop. Further payments were made during the year as the crop was sold, and final payment when all the tobacco was sold.

Securing financing was more difficult than obtaining the needed warehouses. The banks of Louisville and Cincinnati helped matters along by lending the Burley Tobacco Association $1,300,000 and Bingham advanced another $1,000,000 of his personal credit. This amounted to about half of what the association needed to make payments on the early deliveries. When rumors spread that the big tobacco companies would refrain from dealing with the association as a mean of breaking its hold on the tobacco crop, a meeting was called of all the bankers in the tobacco country. James Stone, who later became a member of the Federal Farm Board, made clear the dilemma the tobacco country found itself in and the banks lent the association $5,300,000 on its note. It came to be known as the Tobacco Growers Liberty Loan.

Bingham Co-op Act Becomes Model for States

The influence of Bingham on the burley growers was unmistakable. He became the leader of the association from the very beginning. He used his newspapers to convey the message of cooperation to every part of the burley country. In 1922 he helped draft a cooperative marketing bill that was converted into Kentucky law in six days without a dissenting vote as "The Bingham Co-operative Marketing Act." The Bingham Act has since served as a model for similar enabling legislation in most of the states. His prominence in the burley crisis may be attributed to his sense of public service and dedication to the general community of which he was a part; for he, himself, had never been a tobacco grower. In this campaign he had the active support of James Stone, Aaron Sapiro, and Ralph Barker.

In June, 1924, the Burley Tobacco Association commissioned Bingham and three others to sail for Europe to ferret out the prospects of selling its tobacco abroad. In England he conferred with representatives of the British Wholesale Cooperative Society, and in Austria, Italy, Czechoslovakia, and France with representatives of the government monopolies in tobacco. Bingham and his associates worked out possible trade agreements in these countries, and paved the way for establishing a sales office for the association in Brussels, Belgium. This office disposed of 12 million pounds of burley tobacco between 1925 and 1928.

Bingham's interests were many and varied and in the cooperative field he never again assumed the prominent role he held during the burley crisis. He served as a director of several companies and as a member of the board of trustees of Centre and Berea colleges. He supported Franklin D. Roosevelt in the presidential campaign of 1932, and shortly after the election he was named as United States Ambassador to the Court of St. James, a post he held until his death in 1937.

His influence on cooperative marketing was positive and unmistakable.

John D. Black

by Joseph G. Knapp

I WELL REMEMBER MY FIRST MEETING with Dr. John D. Black in the summer of 1925 at the University of Minnesota. I was then a graduate student at Stanford University making a study of cooperative wheat pool marketing for my doctoral dissertation.

The thing that impressed me was his zest and his interest in agricultural developments and personalities. I felt no age barrier. He talked to me on everything under the sun as if we had long known each other. I don't remember much that he told me concerning the subject of my inquiry but I do recall that he wanted me to see a man by the name of M. W. Thatcher in downtown Minneapolis who had "some rather unusual ideas on grain marketing."

From then on we were good friends and I had many opportunities to talk things over with him, and to hear him express his views in meetings of the American Farm Economic Association, the American Institute of Cooperation or like occasions.

One of my vivid memories was a 2-day seminar on agricultural cooperation, held by Black, with the assistance of John K. Galbraith, in the spring of 1939 at the Littauer Center in Cambridge. To meet with his students and staff Black had invited as resource persons E. A. Stokdyk, then Deputy Governor of the Farm Credit Administration; T. G. Stitts, Chief of the Cooperative Research and Service Division of the Farm Credit Administration; Quentin Reynolds, General Manager of the Eastern States Farmers' Exchange; and myself. It was something like a Senate Hearing. Those of us brought in were given a full opportunity to express ourselves, and then we were subjected to a barrage of questions and in the discussion all joined in the crossfire. Every assertion was carefully examined for truth or error. I came away from the seminar with a healthy respect for how things were done by Dr. Black at Harvard. Although he was favorably disposed toward cooperation he was not a blind enthusiast. It had to be logical in every respect—economic and social—to satisfy him.

My last opportunity to spend a little time with Black came in the late fall of 1959, not long before his fatal illness. He, along with Dr. Charles E. Kellogg, of the U.S.D.A.'s Soil Conservation Service, and I were in Knoxville, Tenn., as consultants to review the program of the Agricultural Division of the T.V.A. All of us had long served as consultants and friends of this program, and we were there to examine all of the ongoing activities of this Division. I recall the keen interest shown by Dr. Black in everything discussed and his satisfaction in the accomplishments and progress being made.

Of particular pleasure to me was the fact that we were quartered at the same small hotel where we were able to have several chats on items of mutual interest—and I found no let-up in his curiosity with regard to current developments relating to cooperatives. It gave him satisfaction that these organizations were coming more and more to meet the promise he had envisaged for them.

Black was a big man physically. He gave an impression of power, but of friendly power. I think most young people who came into contact with him as students or in professional relationships looked upon him as a big brother rather than as a father-figure. In his work and contacts with farmers, cooperative leaders and members he was not an austere professor—but a man interested in their problems and welfare. John Kenneth Galbraith catches the man very well in his pen portrait which introduces the volume of Black's *Selected Writings*, prepared with loving care by his former students and colleagues. Galbraith explains Black primarily as being a teacher—in the fullest meaning of this word. "Black's greatest qualification as a teacher was his confidence in the improvability of the human mind."

Back of his deep desire to improve the quality of people was a unique foundation of rigorous intellectual training. Born in a log house in Cambridge, Wis., on June 6, 1883, the fourth of 10 children, he grew up in a family that prized education. In fact, Black started his career as a teacher, and got his first two years of college at Oshkosh Normal School (1903–1905). After two years of high school teaching he went to the University of Wisconsin to train himself as a teacher of English. After graduating in 1909 with a bachelor's degree and a Phi Beta Kappa Key, he continued another year at Madison to obtain his M.A.

However, his graduate studies had led his interest into the social sciences, and his next few years as a teacher at Western Reserve University and at the Michigan College of Mines emphasized the opportunities in sociology and economics. At that period he came under the influence of E. A. Ross, an eminent sociologist, and B. H.

Hibbard, an iconoclastic economist. In 1915 he settled down in Madison to get his doctorate in Agricultural Economics. As Galbraith has noted, "The University of Wisconsin must have been an exciting place at that time. It was in that heyday of LaFollette liberation, when it listed on its faculty such names as John R. Commons, Richard T. Ely, W. A. Scott, E. A. Ross, H. C. Taylor and B. H. Hibbard."

After getting his Ph.D., Black took a position in 1918 as Assistant Professor and Acting Head of the work in Agricultural Economics at the University of Minnesota. His academic progress was startling. Within six months he was Associate Professor, and in another two years he was named Professor.

First Contribution in Co-op Field Is Wisconsin Study

This was a time when agricultural economics was just emerging as a profession and in the next seven years Black made his department one of the leading centers in this field. His interests were varied, as attested by his writings, but here we are especially concerned with his contributions in agricultural cooperation. His first publication in this field was a study of *Farmers Cooperation in Wisconsin*, with Frank Robotka, published in 1919. His interest later led him to write with H. Bruce Price a publication of seminal importance, *Cooperative Central Marketing Organization*, well-known as University of Minnesota Agricultural Experiment Station Bulletin 211.

This bulletin, issued in 1924, attracted national attention as the first careful analysis of large-scale cooperative marketing organizations. It was one of the first studies to examine the advantages of economic integration for cooperative organizations. It also recognized the importance of market structure. Black and Price did not approve of building cooperatives by appealing to class hatred. Rather, they said, "The cooperative marketing program should be presented to the growers on the basis that will inure to the common good as well as to themselves." Black and Price were interested in injecting economic analysis into studies of cooperatives and this bulletin gave them an opportunity to do so. Black was very proud of this study and he told the writer in 1946 that he would like to see it followed up with a later study that would use newer techniques—especially the concept of imperfect competition and perhaps some "Keynesian economics."

In the next few years Black participated in the annual sessions of the American Institute of Cooperation, and wrote several articles on cooperative subjects. At the first Institute, held in 1925, he gave a paper on "The Economic Possibilities of Cooperation." Although he felt that "the economic possibilities of cooperative marketing were enormous" he held that enthusiasm must be held in check so as not to "foredoom it to failure" through overselling. He was also concerned that recognition be given to local associations as the fundamental bases of cooperative organization and he warned against letting them wither away. He also saw significant opportunities in cooperation applied to purchasing, insurance, and credit.

Believed Co-op Research to Be of Utmost Value

In January, 1927, Black published an article in the *Cooperative Marketing Journal* on "The Cooperatives' Research Department." This was an appeal for research as a basis for cooperative decision making. Two years later he presented his views on "What Cooperation Can Do for Agriculture" in the same journal. In this article he said, "Progress in modern society must include an increasing amount of modification or curbing of individual action. . . . Private and cooperative businesses have a great deal in common; but they have a great deal that is not in common. . . . No research of any higher order of public service can be named than that which relates to the problems of existing cooperatives."

Black's highly important book, *Agricultural Reform in the United States,* came out in 1929. In it he favored a program of "assisted laissez faire" under which government would help farmers meet their own problems through the formation of cooperative associations. There is a chapter in this book devoted to "Cooperation."

During 1931 and 1932 Black served as part-time Economist for the Federal Farm Board. Working with Mordicai Ezekiel he helped develop the "principle of adjustment" which became part of the Agricultural Adjustment Act of 1933.

In 1929, Black undertook for the Social Science Council the editorship of the Scope and Method series of studies of research in the various sub-fields of agricultural economics and rural sociology. Before the series was completed it totaled one basic report and 21 individual reports on particular research fields. It was a herculean task and Black saw it through with unflagging interest. Of particular interest to students of cooperative enterprise is Bulletin No. 15 in this series, *Research in Agricultural Cooperation.* In this bulletin Black contributed a comprehensive introductory essay on "Cooperation as a Field of Research," and project plans for six areas of study.

Although Black continued his general interest in the progress of agricultural cooperation, his attention was increasingly diverted into other areas. However, in his Triple A study for the Brookings Institution, *The Dairy Industry in the United States* (1935) and in the general Brookings study, *Three Years of the Agricultural Adjustment Administration* (1937) by E. G. Nourse, Joseph S. Davis, and John D. Black, he did not ignore the role of cooperatives in agriculture. In a supplement to the latter volume, Black said, "The time seems to be approaching when government can resume a more vigorous program of developing agricultural cooperatives."

Black made his last significant contribution to cooperative theory in 1947 in his influential article, "Guideposts in the Development of a Marketing Program." (*Journal of Farm Economics,* August, 1947). In this article Black argued that efforts should be concentrated on "Better Integration of Marketing." He held that

> The simplest way to accomplish this integration is to set up large farmer cooperatives that handle the products all the way from the farm to the consumer; or, alternatively, large consumer cooperatives that do the same thing from the consumer end; or middleman cooperatives that operate along the same lines but from somewhere in the middle. These will put the whole marketing process under one management which is thus in a position to integrate all the steps in it and make all of them efficient.

Black was, however, opposed to marketing monopolies. He thought that in a fully integrated marketing system there would be room for "proprietary effort," provided that it was as efficient as cooperative enterprise.

Black did not think that a fully integrated marketing system would be impossible to achieve—and in his later years he was pleased to see cooperatives moving toward this general goal.

Eugene R. Bowen

by Hayes Beall

E. R. BOWEN, General Secretary of The Cooperative League of the U.S.A., 1934–1946, possesses many remarkable qualities. The two of greatest significance have been his ability to enlist men of great capacity in the work of The Cooperative League, and his success in making the concept of consumers cooperation broad and inclusive. While no man can be separated from the times in which he labors, these two factors had a special relevance to the deep depression days of 1934 when Bowen began his work with the League at the age of 53.

Twenty-five years of work in general industry preceded Bowen's executive leadership in the cooperative movement. After graduating from Cornell College, following a farm boyhood, he occupied a variety of executive positions in a pioneer farm machinery manufacturing firm—advertising manager, sales manager, and vice-president. He had amply demonstrated a drive to accomplishment and a fondness for planning for the years ahead. His Quaker religious and ethical outlook was such that he was greatly troubled by the price of wheat, for example, in relation to the cost of a tractor. Seeing the consequences of four major depressions had a profound effect upon his economic and social views.

Sees Something in Which to Make a Social Contribution

His disenchantment with profit industry finally led him to resign and to devote a year to the study of the causes of bust and boom in the hope that he might find something that made a greater social contribution and, in the process, brought more satisfaction. His search through various libraries led him from his Peoria, Ill., home to the University of Chicago library. In the course of his personal studies there, he had an opportunity to confer with Paul H. Douglas, who was then in the midst of his 25 years as a professor of economics prior to his long service as United States Senator from Illinois.

Professor Douglas who was then actively helping to establish the

Hyde Park Cooperative Society in his own community, had a pre-
scription for E. R. Bowen: Get into the cooperative movement. More
specifically, he advised getting in touch with Dr. James P. Warbasse,
president (1916 to 1940) and leading figure in The Cooperative League
of the U.S.A.

Like many people undertaking new assignments, Bowen, as he
later acknowledged, accepted Dr. Warbasse's offer of the general secretaryship without any substantial knowledge of the League's operational
problems or budgetary situation.

After appraising the new situation as he saw it from the League's
national headquarters (then in New York and since 1939 in Chicago),
Bowen wrote his highly successful tract for the times, *America's
Answer: Consumers Cooperation.*

Convinced that farm supply cooperatives, insurance, health, housing,
credit, electric, and other cooperatives were in essence *consumer cooperatives,* he began to travel to the headquarters of various state,
regional, and other cooperatives. Survival of the League depended
upon expansion.

His encounter with E. G. Cort, a founder and then manager of
Midland Cooperative Wholesale (now Midland Cooperatives, Inc.)
in Minneapolis, came at a crucial time. Cort advised him that Midland
would contribute $100 monthly to The League. This, plus other modest
income, meant a solvent organization—one that no longer need depend
on Dr. Warbasse to cover deficits from family funds.

A lifelong friendship with Murray D. Lincoln, then manager of the
Farm Bureau Cooperative Association and of several affiliated insurance companies in Columbus, Ohio, began in a most unlikely way.
Their first encounter is well described in Mr. Lincoln's autobiographical
Vice President in Charge of Revolution, pages 108–110. Lincoln's doubt
about affiliation with The League was transformed into the affirmation,
"We ought to be a part of your organization." Ohio's membership
began in 1934. Lincoln became president of the League in 1940 and
served in this capacity until 1964. Lincoln and Bowen maintained an
effective partnership that served well when there was resistance to
their drive to make the League an inclusive organization.

Against a background of 18 million unemployed and all that this
signaled with respect to the condition of the economy in the mid-
thirties, the nation's opinion makers may have been more receptive
to cooperatives than perhaps at any other time. However, it was not
by accident that many of them began to participate in, write, and speak
about cooperatives. They were systematically recruited by Bowen

and the League's small staff and friends. The then Federal Council of Churches' Dr. James Myers, Industrial Relations Secretary, and Dr. Benson Y. Landis, Research Director and editor of the *American Church Yearbook,* were most effective in reaching churchmen who were seeking forms of economic organization that could measure up to the economic ethics they felt must be fundamental to a just society. James Myers' *Cooperatives and Labor* and Benson Y. Landis' *Cooperative Economy* challenged many readers and brought a substantial number into cooperative membership and employment. Bertram Fowler's *Cooperative Challenge* was another among many popular interpretations of cooperatives.

President Franklin D. Roosevelt sent an inquiry commission headed by Jacob Baker to study cooperatives in Europe. Secretary of Agriculture (and later Vice President) Henry A. Wallace called cooperatives "The dominant economic idea of the future" and his pamphlet incorporating this into the title had a wide circulation. The Bureau of Labor Statistics in the U. S. Department of Labor, already engaged in a basic problem of consumer cooperative service and research, continued the services so long identified with Florence E. Parker.

The news media, while not always friendly, gave more attention to cooperatives than ever before. The *New York Times* gave extensive coverage to the work in which Bowen was engaged. The *Saturday Evening Post* and other mass circulation magazines published frequent feature articles about cooperatives. Foreign Policy Association, Public Affairs Pamphlets, the *Christian Century* magazine, *Catholic Rural Life* magazine and many others publicized and interpreted cooperatives.

The use of radio was expanded into a national network program. One series was "Here Is Tomorrow." It dramatized cooperative progress and it did much to improve public understanding and stimulate the formation of hundreds—possibly thousands—of cooperative buying clubs and food stores.

Believed in Education on Co-ops as Greatest Need

Education in the history, principles, and practices of cooperation was regarded by Bowen as the cornerstone of the new society he was intent upon helping to build. Study and discussion circles had played so prominent a part in the Swedish and Nova Scotian developments with which he was familiar that he reached out for ways to use these tools here. After discussions with Dr. Benson Y. Landis, he concluded that if several U. S. leaders saw the neighborhood ("kitchen")

meetings in Nova Scotia that the idea might take hold. Wisely, Murray
D. Lincoln, the restless cooperative builder and statesman whose
goals grew apace with his great achievements, was recruited to go
on one of the early study tours of Nova Scotia. Carl Hutchinson,
who accompanied him, moved from a cooperative position in
Indiana to take a leading role in the launching of what Ohio cooperators call the Advisory Council Program. With more than 1600
now functioning and well over a quarter-century of accumulated
experience, they have become one of the most effective informal
adult educational forces in the nation.

The 1935–6 lecture tour of the great Japanese Christian cooperative
leader Dr. Toyohiko Kagawa exerted a profound influence. Bowen
was informed by Dr. Helen Topping of Dr. Kagawa's desire to preach
the message of cooperation wherever possible during this tour. Starting with some major addresses to cooperative leaders in Indianapolis
in late December, 1935, Kagawa reached vast numbers of people. His
definition of cooperatives as "love applied to industry;" and his Colgate-
Rochester Divinity School lectures published under the title, *Brotherhood Economics* brought many people into membership and leadership
in cooperatives. A substantial number of today's cooperative leaders
credit Kagawa with relating their social and ethical concerns to cooperatives in a lasting and meaningful way. Kagawa properly was at the
front and center of the stage; Bowen was arranging engagements and
also promoting Kagawa's writings as well as publications about him.

The methodical and carefully organized plans that Bowen had
formulated in his first career in the power machinery business established a pattern for his cooperative work. He was convinced that cooperatives could meet a very wide range of people's needs for goods
and services. His ultimate goal was and is a cooperative economy.
Accordingly, he had a pattern in which there were places for cooperatives in food, farm supply, housing, health, savings, recreation, and all
other major fields of human endeavor. He drew up an organizational
chart and gained The Cooperative League's official approval of it.
Each type was an entity within the cooperative movement. The
Cooperative League he regarded as the catalyst. The two League staff
members on whom he depended most were Wallace J. Campbell and
C. J. McLanahan. For many years he edited the magazine, *Consumers
Cooperation.*

Many Writings Since Retirement Advance Co-op Principles

With retirement from the general secretaryship of The Cooperative
League at the end of 1946, a new chapter in E. R. Bowen's cooperative

career began to unfold. Proud of Jerry Voorhis, his distinguished successor in early 1947, Bowen scrupulously avoided any further involvement in administration or policy determination. With twenty years of retirement devoted to reading, research, and writing—and still responding to the challenge of new tasks—he remains a stalwart champion of broad-gauged consumers cooperation.

His writings since 1946 are ample evidence of his vitality and his determination to continue serving the cause of cooperation. Concerned with the causes and consequences of the depressions—1907, 1912, 1920 and 1929—through which he had lived, he wrote the pamphlet *Depressions and How You Should Prepare to Meet Them.* *The Cooperative Road to Abundance* was published in 1953 by Henry Schuman, Inc., New York. It advocates cooperation in contrast to competition and compulsion. The companion volume, *The Cooperative Organization of Consumers,* was published by The Cooperative League in 1957. It discusses the relation of consumer cooperatives to producer and public organizations. *The Coming Cooperative Economy* is scheduled for publication in late 1966. Other publications appearing in limited quantities include *A Cooperative Economic Constitution* (1963); *History of The Cooperative League, 1934 to 1946* (1961). The bulletin *Economic Trends* has treated subjects of current concern to cooperators, usually four to six issues appearing annually.

A compilation of Bowen's major writings has been assembled in one large binding and placed in the libraries of the major members of The Cooperative League, the International Cooperative Alliance in London, Kooperativa Forbundet in Stockholm, Library of Congress, and the U. S. Department of Agriculture in Washington.

Always averse to autobiographical writing, Bowen used these characteristic words when honored at the 1958 Congress of the Cooperative League in Minneapolis on the occasion of his first 25 years in the cooperative movement:

> As I see it, when a democratic organization like this throws the spotlight on a member for a few moments, it's not a matter of anyone's personal accomplishments that are really of concern. What the group really desires to do is to use some period in the life of one of its numbers as an occasion for reviewing their own past progress and foreseeing their possible future.

Respect for E. R. Bowen's views, as reflected in the words just quoted, should be evident in the context of these pages.

Mr. Bowen makes his home in a cooperative housing development in Glenview, Ill.

Charles J. Brand

by Joseph G. Knapp

CHARLES J. BRAND will live in American agricultural history as the first Chief of the Bureau of Markets and the man who first directed the cooperative marketing work of the U. S. Department of Agriculture. However, this was but one episode in his productive career. Throughout his life he gave encouragement to cooperative enterprises in agriculture in the broad sense of this term.

Charles Brand was born on a farm in Minnesota in 1879 and he gave his whole life to agriculture. As a boy and young man he lived and worked on his father's farms in Minnesota and South Dakota, taught in a country school and attended the University of Minnesota. Upon graduation in 1902 he got a job as Assistant Curator of Botany at the Field Museum of Natural History in Chicago. In December, 1903, he came to work in Washington as an assistant plant physiologist in the Bureau of Plant Industry of the U. S. Department of Agriculture. His progress was rapid and he was soon in charge of Clover and Alfalfa Investigations, and then Paper Plant Investigations. During 1912 and 1913 he was physiologist in charge of Cotton Handling and Marketing Investigations. This was one of the first scientific studies of marketing to be made by the U. S. Department of Agriculture, and this work convinced him that the marketing problems of farmers required their cooperative organization.

While Brand was experimenting with cooperative procedures in cotton marketing, forces were bringing the farmers' marketing problem to national attention. This interest caused James Wilson, then Secretary of Agriculture, to have a report prepared for Congress on "Systems of Marketing Farm Products and Demand for Such Products at Trade Centers." This was an epoch-making report in that it considered the functions of a possible "Division of Markets" in the Department of Agriculture.

Legislation was proposed at about this time to establish a marketing program in some form but agreement could not be reached on a practicable procedure. Under these circumstances, the House Committee on Agriculture proposed that a small appropriation be provided to permit the Department to expand its marketing work until Congress could determine the "feasibility and desirability of establishing at some future time the division of markets as requested." In the appropriation bill for 1914 the sum of $50,000 was provided the U. S. Department of Agriculture "to enable the Secretary of Agriculture to acquire and diffuse among the people of the United States useful information on subjects connected with the marketing and distribution of farm products."

Becomes Pioneer in U.S.D.A. Office of Markets Activity

On May 16, 1913, David Houston, then Secretary of Agriculture, followed up by creating the Office of Markets, with Charles J. Brand as its Chief. The appointment was not surprising in view of the ability Brand had demonstrated in getting a cotton marketing program underway.

The first annual report of the Chief of the Office of Markets indicated that tangible results had come from the work with cooperative cotton associations, and that other valuable information had been assembled. Congress officially recognized the Office in the agricultural appropriation act for the fiscal year 1915 by appropriating to it $200,000 for specific use in marketing work. The following year the Rural Organization Service which had been inaugurated the preceding year with funds from the General Education Board was joined to the Office of Markets and $484,050 was appropriated for the work of the Office of Markets and Rural Organization. From then on, growth was rapid, for all marketing investigations and regulatory activities were brought into its orbit, and in March, 1917, when the Office of Markets and Rural Organization took the name Bureau of Markets, the appropriation for the fiscal year ending June 30, 1918 reached $1,718,575. Thus, within five years after the beginning of its work, the Bureau of Markets had become one of the largest bureaus in the Department.

When Brand resigned in 1919 to become Vice President and General Manager of the American Fruit Growers, Inc., he could look with great pride on his accomplishments in getting marketing work established in the Department. Secretary Houston wrote him as follows:

> You have been in charge of the organizational work of the Department since its beginning in 1913. . . . When you assumed your duties you were faced with a pioneer task. There were then no marketing agencies, either in the Federal or State Services, solely designed to assist the Nation in the marketing and distribution of farm products. . . . You were confronted with the duty not

only of marking out in a definite way the paths of endeavor but also of discovering and, in a measure, training the men for the work.

Brand's Work Set Pattern for Later FCS Activities

It was under Brand that the first research, service, and education work of the Department was done with cooperatives and this largely set the pattern for the work that is now done by the Farmer Cooperative Service.

While Brand was in charge of the Department's marketing work under Secretary Houston he was a leader in getting passed much constructive agricultural legislation, such as the Cotton Futures Act, the U. S. Warehouse Act, and the Food Production Acts. He also prepared the foundation draft of the Food Control Act, administered by Herbert Hoover.

In 1923, Brand returned to Washington as consulting specialist in marketing to Secretary Henry Cantwell Wallace who was at this time greatly interested in farm relief legislation. Brand worked with George N. Peek and General Hugh S. Johnson in drafting the first McNary-Haugan Bill which was passed by Congress only to be vetoed by President Coolidge.

In 1925, he was named Executive Secretary and Treasurer of the National Fertilizer Association, and he held this post until he retired in 1945. In 1933, he was granted a leave of absence to serve as co-administrator of the Agricultural Adjustment Administration while this agency was becoming established.

It is not possible in this brief essay to capture the essence of the man who was in the forefront of national agricultural programs for some 40 years. His energies and interests led him to many parts of the world and his contributions in speeches and articles were voluminous. One of his interests was agricultural history, and while I was gathering information on the history of cooperative enterprise in the United States in the mid-forties he gave me an abundant amount of his time and much encouragement.

Mr. Brand was an impressive man—courteous, clean-cut, well groomed, and alert to everything going on about him.

Although he was not a cooperative propagandist, he was an economic and agricultural realist who helped achieve recognition for cooperatives as an important segment of our free enterprise economy.

His final testament was a little book, *What Economic System for America?*, that he wrote in 1945 to help guide the nation after World

War II. In this book his answer was "the American private enterprise system" and in it he devoted a section to "economic cooperation" in which he said, "Perhaps the best definition of a cooperative enterprise is that it is one which belongs to the persons who create and conduct it and who use its services . . . Cooperative enterprise is really private enterprise conducted by interested and participating groups."

John Brandt

by John W. Dysart

FOR OVER 30 YEARS the name of John Brandt was synonymous with that of Land O'Lakes Creameries, Inc., and the dairy industry.

Born in 1886 at Forest City, Minn., Brandt was reared on a farm near Litchfield. He acquired his first contact with cooperatives when as a young man in 1908 he joined the movement with other farmers around Litchfield to establish one of the first livestock shipping associations in the United States. A few years later he was elected president of the Litchfield Cooperative Creamery.

When Professor T. L. Haecker, the father of the cooperative movement in Minnesota, retired in 1918, he passed his mantle to A. J. McGuire, his protege. It was Extension Dairy Specialist McGuire, and A. D. Wilson, Sr., Head of the Extension Division, who set out to organize county cooperative creamery associations. They were assisted in this by county agents in the various counties.

Tom Stitts, Meeker County Agent, who later became Director of the Dairy Branch, Production and Marketing Division, U.S.D.A., called the meeting on November 23, 1920 which resulted in the formation of the Meeker Creamery Association. They elected one of the youngest men present, John Brandt, 34, as their president.

Brandt, along with Tom Stitts, collected figures which showed that if creameries pooled their shipments in carload lots, they could save 50 cents per hundredweight shipping cost. These figures were tirelessly presented to creamery after creamery by Brandt and Stitts. The Meeker County Association started shipping carload lots in April. The Association was successful, so before long creameries from adjoining counties wished to join. This resulted in the formation of Minnesota Cooperative Creameries Association, Unit No. 1, with John Brandt, President.

Members were happy, but not Brandt and Stitts, for each creamery was still selling its own butter and prices even to the same buyer varied greatly. They urged the creameries to pay 5¢ more per pound for sweet cream than for sour cream, as sweet cream butter was selling at a premium. (Here was born the idea of paying a premium for sweet cream, which was to later become the basis for Land O'Lakes' premium price for sweet cream butter meeting the association's standard of quality.)

Nels J. Holmberg, Commissioner of Agriculture, and his Director of Markets, Hugh J. Hughes, called a statewide meeting March 28, 1921, in the old state capitol building to attempt to organize a statewide cooperative marketing organization. The second meeting was held April 23. Here John Brandt made the statement that charted his course for over 30 years. He said, "We have in the past as cooperative creameries been centering our efforts in production lines. We have put forth our best efforts to produce product and completely forgotten the marketing end of the game. I think the time is fast approaching when it is going to be necessary to organize a statewide association to market our products." He urged that all "must have a determination to win," that they be "wholeheartedly" behind it and that the "personal touch" must be used.

Brandt served on the committee that drew up the Articles of Incorporation and Bylaws for the Minnesota Cooperative Creameries Association. He was chosen as member of the first board of directors, serving as secretary.

Brandt's Leadership Ability Solved Difficult Situations

Solicitors started out to obtain 300 signatures. "You'd better get down here, John, and tell these people what your outfit did in Meeker County, or there won't be any Minnesota Cooperative Creamery Association," was the telephone call by J. S. Jones, State Farm Bureau Secretary, that caused Brandt to drop his farm work and join the solicitors traveling up and down the state. Brandt acted as "clean-up" man where any difficult situation developed.

One such situation developed at the Glencoe Cooperative Creamery, which was considered the largest sweet cream creamery in the state at that time, when they received a telegram from an Eastern firm stating, "If you wish to do business with us, do not sign the pooling agreement with the association, as we will not accept your butter through it." John Brandt and Herman Meyer, Sales Manager, met with the Glencoe farmers shortly after this telegram was received. The farmers wanted to sign, but needed a steady outlet. To complicate matters a full carload of butter was on hand ready for shipment. After a long discussion with Brandt and Meyer, the creamery members exhibited both courage and faith by voting unanimously to cast their lot with the new association.

By the time of the first annual meeting on March, 1922, the required number of members had been signed. The association was in business. A. J. McGuire was General Manager.

At the association's second annual meeting on March 7, 1923, it re-elected all board members and chose its hard working secretary, John Brandt, as President, which position he held until his death, March 4, 1953.

The cooperative chose the name, Land O'Lakes, for its sweet cream butter in 1924. By 1926, the butter was far better known than the association marketing it, so the association became Land O'Lakes Creameries, Inc.

Upon the death of A. J. McGuire on October 26, 1933, Brandt was named General Manager of Land O'Lakes, in addition to his duties as President.

Sold 40 Million Pounds of Butter on One Trip

In the early days of the association the board learned to call on John Brandt if some problem arose. It was he who fought the centralizers to a standstill in the early years of the association. It was Brandt who was called on to go East, when the new association was being flooded with more butter than it could market, to find a market. He not only found a market for the association's new Sweet Cream Butter, but inaugurated the method of selling directly to the large retail outlets, thus by-passing the brokers and returning more to the farmer. It was on this same trip that he sold 40 million pounds of butter, a mark probably never equaled.

Brandt made frequent trips to Washington to appear before Congressional committees regarding legislation affecting dairy farmers.

When World War II broke out and the government called for dry milk plants to produce food for the war effort, Brandt pledged Land O'Lakes' support and supervised the construction of 22 plants. Thus Land O'Lakes became one of the largest manufacturers of dry milk powder in the U.S.

Brandt was much sought after as a speaker for cooperative and business association meetings. He was equally at home speaking to several thousand farmers gathered at a picnic; speaking at a bankers association meeting, or speaking to an assembly of Congressmen and Senators. The latter came in large numbers each year to a dinner promoted by the National Milk Producers Federation to hear him speak.

Brandt only went through the eighth grade. However, because of his magnetic personality, his rare gift of humor, and his wisdom acquired through wide experience, he became a dominant figure in the entire dairy industry. He applied untiring energy to the enlargement and betterment of this industry. That drive made of him a man of great and rare insight, rare force, fine tact, and a lover of the common man.

His 30 years of unselfish service to Land O'Lakes was rich in results. His unusual vision and diligence carried him from a modest beginning to a great record of achievement. His record is not only stamped upon the history of Land O'Lakes, but upon the activities of National Milk Producers' Federation, which he served as President for 12 years, and upon other dairy organizations to which he contributed his unsparing vigor.

Land O'Lakes will forever serve as a living monument to his work.

Marvin J. Briggs

by J. Kenneth Ward

M ARVIN J. BRIGGS was born June 2, 1892, on a Miami County, Ind., farm owned by his father and procured in the 1860s by his grandfather. His ancesters were principally English with enough Irish and German traits added to be valuable to his cooperative career.

Graduating from grade school at 12 and high school at 16, he completed his pre-law course at Indiana University at age 18. Experience on the IU debating team, which debated with most other universities in Indiana, qualified him for membership in the fraternity of oratory.

He taught rural grade schools one year, grades four, five, six in an urban school for one-half year, and urban high school for one year, and attended the university each summer.

When Marvin was 22, the judge of the county circuit court, a relative, asked him to keep his law office open during the judge's three-week vacation in the west. Experience with a woman persistently seeking a divorce and with a 35-page abstract gave this budding lawyer such an uninteresting impression of the legal profession that he told his father he believed his opportunities lay in some other field.

Immediately his father proposed a partnership with Marvin and his only brother, Robert Hurd, then 21. This partnership, known as A. M. Briggs and Sons, continued for more than 30 years, at which time his father divided all the farm between Marvin and his brother. During this 30-year period their original 400 acres was increased to 520 acres and their partnership worked efficiently, economically, and prosperously.

"May we note," Marvin says, "that this farm pattern exceeds stock market investments in dividends and capital gains. Our profits on the farms based on market value and the increment in farm value exceeds the comparable investment in industrial stock."

Today, brother Robert operates the entire 520 acres with the assistance of his son.

Oratorical Ability Gave Him Start in Farm Field

Upon joining the farm partnership, Marvin bought and studied some of Purdue's books on agriculture. Chosen to speak on a farm program in his home town on "The Boy and the Farm," his oratorical ability made such an impression on a member of the Purdue Extension Service staff that he was called upon to speak at farmers' institutes all over Indiana during the winter months of the next five years. These years, including World War I when Marvin was exempt from military service, were critical years for agriculture. The Indiana Farm Bureau was organized and began its job of building membership. Marvin joined the staff, "only in winter," and part of the time directed and managed a team of five to eight trained men making speeches and soliciting members, township by township, over a county. It was in this work that he became acquainted with Harvey Hull in La Porte County where Marvin and his team had attained 100 percent Farm Bureau membership in five townships.

After about five winters of this exhausting but constructive work, he and Mrs. Briggs, the former Sylvia True, a Pulaski County farm girl, "retired to the farm for good." This retirement to the farm was destined to be short-lived for, through Harvey Hull, Marvin was again to be called back into cooperative service.

Having managed the purchasing department of the Indiana Farm Bureau for about a year, Harvey Hull had succeeded in removing the operating deficit and instituted the Indiana Farm Bureau Co-operative Association, Inc., as an independent capital stock farmer cooperative. In December, Hull stopped at the Briggs farm and asked Marvin to join his staff. Marvin declined but an insistent Harvey Hull visited the farm a second time and in February, 1927, Marvin Briggs entered the employ of the cooperative as general field organizer. His first job was covering the whole state, dissolving the state-owned distribution centers and incorporating the county Farm Bureau Cooperative Associations. He estimates that he "signed first the Articles of Incorporation for 40 percent of the county associations simply because many farmers were skeptical of the endeavor." The county Farm Bureaus assisted materially in this program by calling meetings and encouraging farmer support. The county associations were then and are today separate from the Farm Bureaus and are capital stock cooperative corporations based on both common and preferred stock.

Helps Farmers Solve Financial Problems

In the early 1930s, Indiana farmers were almost destitute. Helping county cooperatives solve their financial problems took much more of his time and surely was a big factor in qualifying Marvin for promotion in a few years to assistant general manager, and later to the added office of treasurer of the Indiana Farm Bureau Co-operative Association, Inc.

In most counties the solution to their financial problems involved calling farmers together and inducing them to sign limited liability bonds deposited with local commercial banks as security for operating loans. In many counties, the state built bulk petroleum plants with the county repaying the state for this investment by increasing the billing by $.01 a gallon on all petroleum products. The greatest contribution, however, to building the capital structure of both county and state associations came from retention of earnings. As confidence was established in both state and county organizations, preferred stock was freely accepted by individual farmers. Today—1966—the system maintains more than $20 million of this stock and now debentures are acceptable.

In those early days Marvin worked fertilizer sales over the entire state. In this work he was accompanied by a professional salesman and owner of the plant with which the state organization had a contract for manufacturing the corporation's tonnage on a percentage basis plus a share in the profits. This continued until about 1938 when the cooperative constructed its own large, modern fertilizer plant in Indianapolis—a move which resulted in reducing fertilizer prices to all Indiana farmers by an estimated $6 a ton.

By 1938 the Indiana Farm Bureau Co-operative Association, Inc. had departmentalized its operations with a manager in charge of each department. Field work for all services was done by five fieldmen under Marvin's direction. The fieldmen concentrated on the welfare of county organizations, their management, personnel, finances, expansion plans, purchases of grain elevators, and such things.

By the time Marvin was made General Manager in 1946, the Indiana Farm Bureau Cooperative Association, Inc. had constructed, purchased or instituted three fertilizer plants, a refinery with approximately 1,000 oil wells, a wholly-owned petroleum pipe line with three distribution and storage centers, a seed cleaning plant, a separate grain cooperative with about six million bushels of storage, a feed plant—with Illinois and Wisconsin as minor owners for a short time, a farm implement department including distribution from Cockshutt of Canada, a miscellaneous department handling such items as hardware, insecticides and lawn mowers, and an oil blending plant—with Ohio and Michigan participation and now owned by United Cooperatives.

Sales Under Briggs Jump from $26 to $143 Million

When elected General Manager on April 19, 1946, the Indiana Farm Bureau Cooperative Association, Inc. annual sales were $26 million with earnings of $1.8 million. Eight years later when Marvin retired from this position, sales had increased to $143,556,000 and earnings to about $5 million. In the same period, net worth had increased from approximately $6 million to almost $45 million.

When the Rural Electrification Administration was instituted by Congress, the Indiana Farm Bureau and Indiana Farm Bureau Cooperative Associations, Inc. wrote a law which was passed by the state legislature providing for protection and incorporation of local cooperatives—Rural Electric Membership Cooperatives. The Indiana Statewide Rural Electric Cooperative was incorporated and staffed with engineers, a lawyer, and organizers to help farmers develop their county REMCs. The Indiana Farm Bureau Cooperative Association, Inc. wholly financed the state REMC and assisted the county units. Together Harvey Hull, as general manager, and Marvin Briggs, as assistant general manager, signed checks in the amount of $92,000 authorized by their board, expecting repayment from the REA. After a time, Washington refused to make money allotments to locals in Indiana to construct lines and finance development.

This impasse resulted in Marvin Briggs' being named General Manager of the Indiana statewide REMC. He immediately engaged a capable electrical engineer who managed the electrical distribution operation so capably that Marvin was able to obtain Washington REA approval along with the necessary appropriations for the construction and energizing of lines. When the $92,000 advanced by the Indiana Farm Bureau Cooperative Association, Inc. was repaid without interest, Marvin resigned as general manager and was succeeded by his assistant.

An organization as young, aggressive and fast-growing as the Indiana Farm Bureau Cooperative Association, Inc. was destined to meet with problems as well as successes. Three small lumber mills in Arkansas owned by IFBCA rendered good service to Indiana farmers during the war, but lost money later when lumber was readily available. These were sold, as was a coal mine jointly owned by Indiana and Ohio.

Entrance into the manufacture of farm implements had to be abandoned with the loss of a few million dollars sustained by the state and local organizations. The Indiana plant was sold and, as a member of the executive committee, Marvin recommended that almost $1 million recovered from this sale be applied on bank loans and the entire operation dissolved. Voted down by other members of the executive committee, the money was invested in adding to a plant in Ohio which finally was bought by Cockshutt of Canada at a loss and in the end resulted in appalling losses to all stockholder cooperatives.

After three or four state grain marketing cooperatives failed, the Indiana Grain Cooperative was organized. The Indiana Farm Bureau Cooperative Association, Inc. financed the grain co-op to a great extent and Marvin Briggs, as secretary of the grain organization, carefully scrutinized finances and operations of both the state organization and local elevators.

In 1950, the grain cooperative was merged into the Indiana Farm Bureau Cooperative Association, Inc., a move resulting in more capable management and elimination of speculation. Today, IFBCA owns and operates more than 12 million bushels of grain storage. In 1954, the IFBCA constructed its fourth fertilizer plant in Northeastern Indiana dedicated as the Briggs plant. Along with it was constructed a livestock marketing yard. In 1963, IFBCA joined Illinois, Indiana, Ohio cooperatives in building a $15 million nitrogen plant at Terre Haute.

Becomes Director of Farm Credit of Louisville

In 1936, Marvin Briggs was elected by the Indiana, Ohio, Kentucky, and Tennessee cooperatives doing business with the Louisville Bank for Cooperatives as a member of the board of directors of the Farm Credit Administration of Louisville (now Farm Credit Banks of Louisville). He served in this capacity for 17 years. After the Federal Land Banks had paid off the last of their government capital in 1947, he became interested in making the cooperative Farm Credit System completely owned by the farmers and cooperatives they served.

By this time Marvin Briggs was President of the National Council of Farmer Cooperatives and the active support and cooperation of the American Farm Bureau Federation and National Grange were solicited in furthering this project. A committee of two from each of the three national organizations was appointed to accomplish this purpose with Marvin being one of the committeemen from the NCFC. This committee was largely responsible for drafting the legislation enacted into law as the Farm Credit Act of 1953. This Act provided for the setting up of the Federal Farm Credit Board and for organizing the Farm Credit Administration under its direction to: (1) translate Farm Credit into a farmer-owned and controlled institution; (2) fully repay all of the government capital. Appointed by President Dwight D. Eisenhower, Marvin Briggs served as a member of the Federal Farm

Credit Board representing the Louisville Farm Credit District from December, 1953 until April, 1964. He served as chairman of the board for two years.

This Federal Farm Credit Board recommended modification of the law to provide for the orderly retirement of the government capital in the Banks for Cooperatives, the merger of the Production Credit Corporations into the Federal Intermediate Credit Banks with provision for their ultimate retirement of government capital, and many other adjustments necessary for the System to meet the challenge of modern farm financing. In the 12 years since the Federal Farm Credit Board was established, the cooperative Farm Credit System has increased its volume of loans outstanding to farmers and their cooperatives from $2 billion to $8 billion.

Having grappled hand-to-hand with the problems of inadequately financed cooperatives during the depression years, Marvin Briggs says with great enthusiasm, "I strongly regard the cooperative Farm Credit System as a most important asset of American farmers."

Clark Lewis Brody

by Orion Ulrey

CLARK L. BRODY was a diplomat and spokesman for farmers in state and national legislation four decades. Clark was born on a farm in St. Joseph County, Mich., on February 1, 1879, and during his active and constructive life of 82 years he helped bring about a legion of changes and developments of significance to farmers, rural life, cooperatives, education, and the total society.

After attending the local rural school, Clark went on to the Three Rivers Business College for eight months. He then worked without pay for several months at the Three Rivers National Bank where he discovered he desired another occupation. He enrolled in agriculture at Michigan Agricultural College in 1900 and graduated in 1904.

Clark returned to the home farm enthusiastic about the scientific possibilities of farming and in 1906 he was married to Margaret York, a teacher in Three Rivers. They set about to raise a family of six and to develop a dairy business and a herd of registered Holsteins. They did so well in farming that Clark was invited by the Agricultural College in 1912 to lecture on dairy subjects in nearby farmer schools. That venture in public affairs, which lasted three winters, broadened to include other farming subjects.

Becomes First President of New Farm Bureau

In 1914, Clark initiated a program to rid St. Joseph County of hog cholera through a well-organized immunization program conducted by the recently created County Farm Bureau of which he was the first president. The dairy farmers believed that the fat tests were too low, so they organized the Constantine Cooperative Creamery during the winter of 1914–15. Clark's Brother, Clarence, was its manager for many years.

In April, 1915, Clark accepted the position of Agricultural Agent in

St. Clair County. He was in a difficult spot because of the dissension over the dismissal of the previous agent. His aid in helping the beet growers to organize in 1918 brought criticism from the Michigan Sugar Company and a request for an explanation from President Snyder of the College, but his activities were approved. He helped organize the St. Clair County Farm Bureau in 1917, and assisted in creating the Michigan Farm Bureau (MFB) in August, 1919.

His services as Agricultural Agent in St. Clair County covered the World War I period of heavy demands upon agriculture. During this time he learned how to get along with people. He developed the art of compromise from bringing groups into agreement, and learned the methods of politics by winning support for the Agricultural Extension Service and its program.

During the 1915–20 period, local cooperatives and Farm Bureaus were being organized very rapidly in Michigan. The plans of the leaders were ambitious and the promises plentiful, as the writer well recalls. The farm leadership was inexperienced and many outside salesmen were used in promotion. The county agricultural agents actively helped in organizing both the Farm Bureaus and the cooperatives.

The first Executive Secretary of MFB, Charles A. Bingham, believed in the control of supply and the use of market power for determining price. His group also wanted to operate the county extension services through the County Farm Bureaus, and also to take over the established milk, potato, sugar beet, livestock, and other marketing cooperatives. The price decline, beginning in 1920, almost wrecked many of the newly-organized cooperatives.

In October, 1920, Hale Tennant of Michigan Agricultural College, who had assisted in organizing many cooperatives, was appointed MFB adviser, and a field advisory committee of six was created to consider future policies. This committee included three county agents and one was Clark Brody. Control of the MFB was changed to a more conservative board at the February, 1921, annual meeting and Mr. Bingham was swept out of office. Those who believed in decentralized control of the Farm Bureau and of the cooperatives were now in power.

Becomes Manager of Michigan Farm Bureau; Faces Crisis

The directors appealed to Michigan Agricultural College (MAC) to suggest a new Secretary-Manager, and the name of Clark L. Brody was proposed. Both the Farm Bureau and the MAC wanted someone who was tactful and friendly to the College, and Brody filled the bill.

Mr. Brody started work as Secretary-Manager of the Michigan Farm Bureau on March 1, 1921. He faced a host of tough problems: The personnel was short of experience; prices had declined and the inventory losses were large; the wool pool was in trouble also from falling prices; none of the cooperative departments was self-supporting; debts were high because of high promotion expenses and inefficient management; records had been poorly kept; the Farm Bureau membership had declined from 96,000 to 20,000 through nonpayment of dues; income was inadequate to carry on the program; and the organization was torn by factionalism and conflict even among board members. A man had to have a tremendous belief in the necessity and possibilities of farmer organizations and cooperatives to accept such a challenge.

Clark traveled the state and met with county groups to determine attitudes and to rally support for the program. He promised the county Farm Bureaus prompt action to restore the state organization to solvency and programs and personnel to maintain both good service and business efficiency. A compromise system of control was adopted for the Farm Bureau: A board of directors partly from the membership and partly from the commodity cooperatives. Clark assured the cooperatives that the Farm Bureau would not attempt to take them over or establish competing services, but would provide seed, feed, fertilizer, and legislative services to assist them. He also assured the College that the Farm Bureau would support the Agricultural Extension Service rather than compete with it.

Internal strife continued in the Farm Bureau until the February, 1926, annual convention when the opposition was thoroughly overcome. Many disagreed with Brody on issues and programs during the years, but he constantly maintained the confidence and support of a large majority of both members and boards of directors.

Steady Expansion Doubles Volume During 20's

Under Brody's direction the variety of products handled by the purchasing and seed departments of the Farm Bureau steadily expanded and volume of business almost doubled during the 20's. These departments were combined as Farm Bureau Services, Inc. (FBS) in 1929, with the common stock owned by MFB. Michigan joined with the Farm Bureaus of Indiana, Ohio, and West Virginia in 1930 to establish the Farm Bureau Milling Company to mix their own feeds, the first such joint venture. Stock in the FBS was sold to 20 local cooperatives in 1931, and a joint plan of selecting directors introduced —five from MFB and four from the member cooperatives.

Many of the local cooperatives were slow to start handling Farm Bureau products, and many areas were not served by cooperatives. In 1928, Brody was instrumental in having the MFB initiate a system of contracting with private dealers to handle supplies at points where local cooperatives were not available, and also started a system of retail stores beginning at three locations.

The late 20's and the early 30's was a difficult period for the Farm Bureau. Falling farm prices resulted in a decline in volume of business and inventory losses for the cooperative activities. Some services were discontinued, and the staff and salaries were cut. The calling of bank loans and the bank moratorium of 1933 tested the strength of the organization. Brody presented the facts to the bankers and convinced them that they must permit the Farm Bureau to carry on business operations or take heavy losses on their loans.

In 1935, John F. Yaeger, a former teacher of agriculture and newspaper man from Lapeer, joined the MFB as Organization Director. Mr. Yaeger played a leading role in shaping the pattern of organization and type of services during the following 25 years. Brody had a deep belief in a decentralized and democratic structure for the Farm Bureau and cooperatives, but he had been very busy during the previous 14 years holding the organization together—reducing internal frictions, keeping heads above water during the depression, and laying the foundation for a state structure and staff. He realized that a more solid structure would be built on the MFB system by utilizing the ideas and energies of the farmer members. Mr. Yaeger had great enthusiasm for the cooperative system as well as faith in the contribution of farm people if given pertinent roles in a farmer organization.

Brody and Yaeger together brought significant changes in the structure, services, and scope of operations of MFB and cooperatives during the 1935–52 period.

The changes which placed more responsibilities upon the local groups provided not only a sound democratic understructure but also paid off in terms of numbers of members in MFB and volume of sales of the affiliated and independent cooperatives. The local groups began to question some of the activities and arrangements of MFB, and made their ideas known at the annual meetings. They decided to change the plan of election of directors in 1944 from a joint plan of election at large and selection by commodity groups to 10 directors from districts, three at large, one by Associated Women, and one by the Junior Farm Bureau. The new plan was put into effect in 1946.

Brody's Abilities Nationally Recognized

During the war period Brody spent much time in Washington on the affairs of the regional and national cooperatives. He was Chairman of the National Farm Transportation Committee, created in 1942 to advise governmental agencies. He served as President of United Cooperatives and as Vice President of National Farm Machinery Cooperative in 1943. He was Chairman of the National Association of Cooperatives, organized in 1944 to counter the attacks on cooperatives by the National Tax Equality Association. During this time, Brody was placing more responsibility upon various staff members for the expanding activities of MFB and affiliated cooperatives. The trend was clearly recognized when John F. Yaeger was appointed Assistant Executive Secretary in 1948.

The MFB had been a member of the American Institute of Cooperation since the late 20's. Both Brody and Yaeger served on its board of directors.

Brody was relieved of administrative responsibilities on August 1, 1952, after 31 years of such service, at the age of 73, and was appointed Executive Vice President in charge of public affairs and national legislation programs.

After 1952, Brody devoted his major attention to three projects: national farm policies and legislation, services to Michigan State University, and the preparation of his memoirs, *In the Service of the Farmer: My Life in the Farm Bureau.* In 1953, he was appointed by President Eisenhower as a member of the Federal Farm Credit Board for a one-year term.

Brody retired from the Michigan Farm Bureau on February 1, 1959, when eighty years of age, and after 38 years of service. He reported in his autobiography:

> My supreme satisfaction has been working for the economic better-
> ment and freedom of the farmer. Had I my eighty years to live
> through again, I would choose to spend them at the Michigan
> Farm Bureau with the very people with whom I worked and
> remembrance of whom I cherish so.

Brody was associated with Michigan State University for 60 years as student, teacher of farmer classes, Extension agent, and member of the board of control. He was first appointed to the State Board of Agriculture in 1921 and was elected for six terms, serving for a total of 38 years. For 16 years, from 1932–38 and 1948–57, he served as its Chairman.

Services Recognized by Michigan State University

The University recognized his services in several ways. Mr. Brody was presented with a Distinguished Service to Agriculture Award at Farmer's Week in 1954. The Brody Group of five dormitories was named after him in 1955. The center building for food services, meeting rooms, and offices is known as Brody Hall. His friends and associates in the Farm Bureau and cooperatives created the Brody Scholarship Fund at MSU in 1957. The earnings are used to pay tuition for male students in agriculture selected by the Dean. The University also awarded him an Honorary Doctor of Agriculture Degree in June, 1960.

Brody's busy life left him but limited time to be with his family of six children. Their mother, a musician, encouraged the children to study music, and the members of the family orchestra were always pleased when their father would join them with his mouth organ.

What Manner of Man Was This?

What type of person was he? What were his objectives? What characteristics made him effective and successful? How did he treat others? What were his significant accomplishments? These questions were asked of his close associates. An attempt is made below to summarize their statements and opinions.

Mr. Brody was kind, considerate, friendly, and the soul of honor. He impressed all who associated with him with his sincerity and integrity. The farmers trusted him. When he realized he had not made the best decision he readily admitted it—which deepened trust in him.

Although he was quiet, soft-spoken, mild-mannered, and kindly in discussion, he was firm and when aroused was vigorous in expressing his position and opinions. He was not an orator, but he became an effective speaker and drew crowds to listen to his reasoned presentations. His talks and writing were based on his opinion of what the facts were. He sought to determine the truth as a basis for decision and action.

Brody had control of himself and of his ideas. Perhaps this was a primary reason why he became gifted in getting along with people, and in finding an effective compromise when there were differences of opinion. One of his associates reported that he was able to bring together conflicting interests and weld them into a common purpose on issues others would have considered hopeless. He was a good listener and tried to understand the views of others, especially those who disagreed with him.

He liked and believed in people, and held that if they had the facts they would make sound decisions. Consequently, he pushed programs to provide information and encourage discussions among the members of the Farm Bureaus and the cooperatives.

Brody was very industrious. He hated to waste time. He seemed to always be considering a host of ideas and plans for the future. His briefcase was filled almost every evening when he left for home. Yet he was always willing to discuss personal problems with associates and employees.

He was deeply religious and applied his religion in his daily life. An inner force impelled him to try to assist others. He was a strict prohibitionist, but his ideas of right and wrong were flexible. He once said to his secretary, "You will find in working with human beings that all is not black and white—that there are shades of gray."

During the years Clark Brody matured as an administrator. In the early years he was a man of detail, concerned with all operations. Later he learned to delegate responsibilities. At first he insisted that the other employees agree with him. Later he became more tolerant of the decisions and operations of others.

Some of his observers in Michigan considered Brody very conservative in economic and political affairs. However, he was concerned primarily with the program of the Farm Bureau and cooperatives and with specific legislation which might be of benefit or harmful to farm families. In the area of human relations he was a real liberal. He liked and treated people with kindness. He believed in their potentials. Consequently he devoted his energies to creating a favorable environment for them. To him, farm organizations and cooperatives were a means for developing farm citizens.

Brody enjoyed tough jobs and challenges and he faced them with poise. His secretary of 35 years reports "Mr. Brody's personal objectives can be summed up in one word—service."

This is a tribute he would have cherished for, truly, Clark L. Brody gave freely of himself to serve his fellowman.

D. W. Brooks

by M. C. Gay

"WHEN THE TEMPERATURE SOARED to 98 degrees in the shade and there wasn't a breeze blowing, those were always the days when my Father decided we should go to the corn field and pull fodder.

"Those were also the days when farmers in the Southeast followed pretty much the practices of their ancestors and frowned if a young man announced he would like to study agriculture at a University.

"But after one quarter at the University of Georgia I felt I learned enough about agriculture to make my entire education worthwhile. I learned in pulling fodder, you lose more corn than you gain fodder."

This is one of D. W. Brooks' favorite stories in illustrating how Dixie has developed from an area of low-income farmers to one of highly trained, skilled agricultural specialists.

A native of Royston, Ga., David Williams (D. W.) Brooks was born on September 11, 1901. His family background brought him into firsthand contact with far-ranging problems confronting farmers in the production and marketing of cotton. His Father together with other members of the family operated a number of cotton farms as well as five stores in Northeast Georgia.

Brooks' formal education included high school at Royston. This being Ty Cobb country, some of it struck D. W.'s fancy as he was Captain of his baseball team in both his junior and senior years. He went on to the University of Georgia and received his B. S. and M. S. degrees in Agriculture and taught in the Agronomy Division at the University for three years.

Motivated from Beginning by Desire to Raise Farm Income

D. W.'s outlook was greatly influenced by the agricultural depression. He observed, for instance, that the combination of such factors as 10 bushels of corn per acre, poor fertilizer, poor seed, poor management, and poor marketing contributed to a cycle of poverty that weighed heavily on the agriculture of his home community. He also observed that the low per capita income that characterized cotton farming in the Southeast suggested the need for major emphasis for better production practices and marketing. Moreover, he noted that those farmers who developed their own marketing systems were better able to improve their economic position than those who did not concern themselves with marketing.

Only a man with D. W.'s deep knowledge and concern for agriculture in the South would have been willing to devote his entire life working to improve the economic condition of farmers. The desire seemed to cling to him like ivy to a post, and in explaining the successful cooperative he heads today, he never fails to say the real reason for its organization was to raise the per capita income of farmers.

Brooks thus organized Cotton Producers Association (CPA) in the early 1930's. It was a struggle in every respect, particularly financially, and today, D. W. Brooks as General Manager simply says, "it took a lot of blood, sweat, and tears."

Dixie Boundaries Expanded to World-wide

Starting with $2,100 and only as a small cotton marketing association, in 1966 CPA and its Gold Kist divisions are now world-wide. It's Dixie boundaries were dropped when Brooks started circling the globe selling and getting more money for farm products produced by CPA members.

CPA now represents some 150,000 farmers and is almost as diversified as agriculture itself. CPA manufactures and processes feed, seed, fertilizer, pesticides, animal health products, and other farm supply items and distributes them through Farmers Mutual Exchanges located in Georgia, Florida, Alabama, and Tennessee. CPA and its Gold Kist divisions are engaged in the marketing of cotton, grain, pecans, poultry, peanuts, and livestock. Plants and facilities for marketing are located from Florida to Arizona, with marketing being world-wide.

Many of the CPA/Gold Kist operations have been so successful that they have served as examples for other businesses. For example, the completely integrated poultry operations—from feed mills to breeder flocks, hatcheries, broiler growers, to poultry processing plants, and marketing—enabled CPA/Gold Kist to make money for its members when many, many poultry businesses were literally going broke.

Also, such operations as these have dotted eroded North Georgia and Alabama hillsides with brick homes and put modern appliances in these homes. It is a striking example of what cooperatives can do for rural America. In explaining these improvements, D. W. likes to tell when he visited in farm homes back in the 30's, someone commented that the homes were in such terrible condition that a farmer could sit inside and be a geologist-by-day and an astronomer-by-night.

Growth Swift; 1966 Business $250 Million

Growth for CPA has been so swift and volume has moved up so rapidly that figures today are out-of-date before they are printed. In 1966, however, the Association did approximately a quarter of a billion dollars worth of business and net worth was around $45 million.

D. W. is in great demand as a speaker all over the United States. He actually started public speaking in the days when microphones were not always available, and today his style of delivery holds an audience to the point that there are few open days or nights on his appointment calendar.

Brooks is a man of action and has always been generous with words of advice. For example, after returning from a visit to Russia and some other Communist countries in the early 1950's he coined the term "stomach Communism." Agricultural public relations was improved greatly by the many speeches he made to urban groups on the importance of food in world peace. He was among the first to emphasize agriculture's place in reducing world tensions.

In addition to cooperative efforts, D. W.'s advice has been sought on a non-partisan basis by three Presidents of the United States. He was a member of President Truman's Board on Mobilization Policy. He was on both President Eisenhower's and President Johnson's National Agricultural Advisory Commissions. He also was a delegate to the American Assembly to work on proposed changes in the United Nations' charter.

He served two terms as President of the National Council of Farmer Cooperatives and is on the Board of Governors of the Hall of Fame at Kansas City.

Religion has always been a very vital part of his life. He is past Chairman of the Official Board of St. Marks Methodist Church, and was a delegate to the Methodist General Conference in Pittsburgh in 1964.

D. W. Brooks has been in the forefront in providing agricultural leadership to his state and nation. Through his accomplishment in strengthening cooperative organizations, farmers and other people in the rural South have developed programs of self-help that have done much to enable them to adjust to changing economic and social conditions. He has helped them demonstrate that cooperatives are a vital self-help force for rural people in building stronger communities.

It's a story that has changed history!

Alexander Edmond Cance

by Adrian H. Lindsay

A LEXANDER E. CANCE was born on a farm near Ettrick, Wis., in 1874. Like many other farm youths of this period his resources were scant and the opportunities for higher education remote. After graduation from Gale Academy in Galesville at 17 he taught physics, mathematics, and science to provide funds for his years in Macalester College in St. Paul. He was graduated from Macalester in 1896.

Here we get the first inkling of his interest in social and economic problems and human welfare. His B.A. thesis was entitled "Social Progress and Populist Discontent." During the next 10 years he held administrative and teaching positions in colleges in Missouri, North Carolina, and Pennsylvania. His teaching included Greek and English Literature. Then he switched to a major interest in economics. A fellowship for the next two years enabled him to complete the requirements for his Ph.D. from the University of Wisconsin in 1908.

With this background, Dr. Cance came to the Massachusetts Agricultural College as instructor in Agricultural Economics. At this time, L. H. Bailey was compiling his Cyclopedias, and K. L. Butterfield was active in the Country Life Commission. These two leaders were making a survey of farmers' social and economic associations to determine the purpose of these organizations and the degree of success which was experienced by them. Dr. Cance was asked to tabulate and analyze the results of the survey.

Teaches First College Course in Agricultural Cooperation

Stimulated by the results of this survey and seeing the need of more general knowledge of the basic principles of success of cooperative endeavor he began teaching a course in "Cooperation in Agriculture" in 1910.

This was the first course to be offered to college students in the United States. The course description read, "This course contemplates a somewhat comprehensive view of the history, principles, and social relations of agricultural organizations for profit." Later, such a course was given in every Land-Grant college.

Although cooperative associations had developed in Europe, their progress was slow in America. Authorities on the subject were few. In 1910–11 Dr. Cance made a survey of all of the cooperative associations that could be conveniently reached. In 1912 he visited the British Isles, France, Germany, and Denmark to study successful associations and to meet with their leaders. In 1913 he returned to Europe with President Theodore Roosevelt's committee of seven to study cooperative organization and credit. He helped to tabulate and edit the findings of this venture. The results were published as Senate Document 214 of the Sixty-third Congress. The next year Cance published a bulletin, *The Farmers Cooperative Exchange*. New laws were needed before cooperative associations could be properly organized, and Dr. Cance was instrumental in writing and promoting the enactment of such laws in Massachusetts and Vermont.

Purnell Act Result of His Recognizing Need for Research

In his work of organizing a department of agricultural economics, teaching these subjects and in serving farmer and consumer groups, Dr. Cance saw the need for research and information in the marketing activities of farmers. He took the responsibility of learning about the research being done in this field by the various agricultural experiment stations in the United States. The results of his investigation were presented to The Land-Grant College Association and through a committee of this group the findings were presented to Congress. The result was The Purnell Act which provided funds for research in marketing. In Dr. True's *History of Agricultural Experimentation in the U.S.A.* we find the statement, "Dr. Cance is given full credit for initiating the interest and action which eventually led to the enactment of the law. The passage of this Act greatly stimulated research in marketing and marketing methods. The progress which we have made in cooperative organization and credit can be accredited to research done under this Act."

After World War I, Dr. Cance was off to Europe again. He became head of the Department of Economics at the American University at Beaune, France. In addition to teaching he set up farm clubs and aided in the organization of the World Agricultural Society. For his contribution to world recovery and good will the French Ministry awarded him the Chevalier of Agriculture. While on this tour of duty he also met

May Riis, an American violinist entertaining American troops, who afterward became his wife.

Shortly after returning to the United States he was asked to be a delegate to the 1920 Hoover Conference on the Economic Crisis. He was made a member of the committee which was asked to write the agricultural report. In 1922 he spent some time in the U. S. Bureau of Agricultural Economics as Supervisor of Market Research. While there he gave a graduate series of lectures on marketing and cooperation.

To extend the field of cooperative education in 1927 he helped Dr. I. G. Davis of Connecticut inaugurate The New England Institute of Cooperation. The purpose was to inform and educate members, directors, and managers of New England cooperative associations. This organization supplemented the educational work of the American Institute of Cooperation.

Best Known as Great Teacher

To many, Dr. Cance is best known as a teacher. He was a hard taskmaster. Even in the face of unpopularity he maintained high work standards and heavy loads for his students. The test of a great teacher is what his students think of him after graduation. It may be truthfully said that no teacher at the University possessed a more loyal or grateful alumni group than did Dr. Cance. In his response to a tribute accorded him at the American Institute at Amherst in 1948 he said that he could name offhand 35 of his students who had held or were holding positions of importance in cooperatives of this country. Many more occupied positions in the management of other marketing and credit organizations. The mailing list which he maintained of his students at the time of his retirement contained over 500 names. He was a great teacher.

Being a pioneer is not an easy task. Again in his tribute response Dr. Cance said, "I had many ups and downs in my cooperative work here. Many of them have been pleasant, but twice in my career I almost lost my position because of the attitude which I took on farmer cooperatives." This new form of business enterprise was not enthusiastically received by the vested interests.

Cooperatives of today owe a great debt to Dr. Cance and his colleagues who persisted that a set of cooperative laws might be developed, that management and organizational principles might be well known, and that the general public might better understand the philosophy of the cooperative movement.

Arthur U. Chaney

by Gordon Cameron

A WINNING PERSONALITY, an organizer whose confidence in the project at hand was so great as to carry the doubters and luke-warmers along to victory, and a cooperative fundamentalist—that was Arthur U. Chaney (1874–1941) who, at the turn of the century, rallied cranberry growers scattered across half a continent and with them built a marketing cooperative.

The story goes back to 1902, and to Iowa, when Mr. Chaney bought out a half interest of a partner, and formed the A. U. Chaney Company to do a wholesale grocery business as well as to handle fresh produce. The Company handled cranberries for Wisconsin growers which were then typically sold ungraded for cash. Growers liked his style and in 1905, organized the Wisconsin Cranberry Sales Company and turned the marketing of the entire crop over to the Chaney Company.

This venture attracted the attention of growers in Massachusetts and New Jersey, and some of them asked Chaney to sell their crops in 1906. That year, as a sales tool, the A. U. Chaney Company issued the first booklet on the varieties, grades, and brands of cranberries.

The idea of growers working together caught fire. Mr. Chaney talked with the Wisconsin Cranberry Sales Company, the Cape Cod Cranberry Sales Company, and the Martin L. Haines Estate in New Jersey. They authorized him to work out an orderly plan to encourage the consumption of cranberries and the raising of more cranberries to meet the new demand.

"Mr. Chaney Will Show Us How . . ."

Excerpts from the minutes of a January 29, 1907 meeting of the organizing groups read: "One of the greatest difficulties we have met in the past has been the lack of any known sales agent who

seemed available and competent to handle a plan of such magnitude."
Later in the same meeting, "Success is assured if we will join for that
end and in the right spirit and keep our enthusiasm and determination
to succeed. Let us do this and Mr. Chaney will show us how to do
the rest." The National Fruit Exchange thus came into being with
Chaney as General Manager. He closed out his business in Iowa
and moved to New York City and devoted the rest of his life to the
cranberry business.

Pooling was a cardinal principle of the cooperative from the very
beginning. Chaney felt it was essential in order to equalize and distribute the necessary risks. Within the pool, grade differentials were
set up. Because there were no established grades that had acceptance
within the market, Chaney set out to describe and fix grades.

In 1910, the first complete catalogue of varieties, grades, color and
brands was published. Under competent inspection, the packing under
brand names was so rigidly enforced that cranberries could be correctly quoted and sold by brand without the necessity of the pur-
chaser's examining the fruit. The cooperative employed its own
inspectors at the grading stations to insure compliance. Furthermore,
whenever there was a complaint by a buyer with respect to quality,
the cooperative dispatched an inspector not only to determine the
settlement but to decide if the cooperative or the grower had failed
to perform according to the contract.

In the fledgling days of the cooperative, the country went through
the money panic of 1907. The Exchange had a number of orders for
berries which the buyers wanted cancelled because they knew they
could not pay for the purchases. After consulting with the growers to
whom he explained that they could either ship cranberries on credit
or eat them themselves, Mr. Chaney obtained their permission to
ship berries—giving the purchasers the privilege of paying at their own
convenience. He told the growers that they would probably lose
30 percent of the crop but that would be better than losing it all.
The total loss proved to be only $120, and the organization not only
helped many dealers over a difficult spot but made friends that stood
them in good stead for many years. Chaney felt the confidence of
dealers and consumers was precious beyond price, and insisted all
steps be taken to build that confidence.

Pioneered in Developing Pricing Formulae

Chaney was a pioneer in the philosophy of a market-oriented
cooperative. He said, "I do not think you can take into consideration

in pricing the cost of producing a commodity. When the fruit is produced, it has to be sold whether it cost two cents or 20 cents per pound. What you have to take into consideration is what people will pay for it."

He gave a good deal of attention to forecasting "what people will pay for it." He constantly ran market surveys and over the years developed a set of economic indicators which included such diverse items as the Federal Reserve indices, the price of grain (to measure prosperity) in farming communities, the price of sugar (much of the cranberry crop was purchased for home canning), how many fruit jars and fruit jar rings had been sold during the summer, the foreign-born mix of the population (Southern European stock did not eat cranberries, Northern Europeans did).

To these indicators he added his feel of the market, the advice given him by dealers and then he set a practical "opening price" at the beginning of the short selling season. This opening price was the highest price that would move the crop. He did not like to set the price so high that it had to be lowered later in the season as his experience had taught him that a decline from the opening price was difficult to check.

When talking about setting the price, Mr. Chaney put it this way in a talk before the American Institute of Cooperation in 1925:

> Stability of market after the price has been started for the season, is, I think, the great factor in gaining the confidence and continued good will of dealers toward any commodity, and particularly toward cranberries. Such market stability is very largely dependent upon the control and regulation of distribution. It is, therefore, the policy of our exchange, as far as it is within our power, so to regulate the distribution of cranberries as to coordinate the current supply with the consuming demand and yet distribute the whole crop while it is in prime condition.

He was not content with just measuring the demand, he had confidence he could stimulate it by advertising. When 25¢ a barrel was the accepted set-off for advertising, it was said of him that if he owned all of the cranberries himself, he would spend a dollar a barrel. He thought it was easier to get people who ate some cranberries to eat more berries than it was to start new customers who had not acquired the taste, and so he concentrated his advertising in the areas of high consumption. Once, when asked by the advertising company what he wished to accomplish, Mr. Chaney replied, "To get people to eat more cranberries." Out of this statement came the brand name EATMOR. It became famous and later became the name of the company itself. (In 1911, National Cranberry Exchange became the American Cranberry Exchange which, in turn, became known as Eatmor Cranberry Growers, Inc. It was dissolved in 1957.)

It is interesting that the dominant cranberry cooperative today— Ocean Spray—also changed its name to the brand it had popularized.

Karl D. Loos, who knew Mr. Chaney for a number of years in connection with the work of the National Council of Farmer Cooperatives and later with the Exchange, has characterized Mr. Chaney "as a fundamentalist in cooperative principles, with great emphasis on grower control and absolute equality of treatment among all growers. He was a forceful leader, a good organizer and an astute merchandiser."

"The Truth" Keystone of His Philosophy

At the 1925 American Institute of Cooperation conference, Chaney was asked, "What do you do to maintain the morale among your members and keep them interested in the organization?" He replied:

> We tell them the truth all the time; that is the first thing. We keep our records open so we can always prove the truth. If anybody wants to know where his fruit went or what happened to it, he can always see the records in the office. We aim to keep inspectors at destination as well as at shipping points. If the growers' fruit is in bad shape out in British Columbia or in Southern California or in Texas, and it is rejected, or the buyer says it is no good and he wants an allowance, we send a man there regardless of the distance, if the inspection at shipping point would indicate that that fruit should be all right. We may have made an adjustment or we may have resold it, but a man goes there just the same, and he is the representative of the grower. We make a thorough and complete report and that report goes to a committee of the growers. When it comes time to close a pool, for example, and there are 12 lots in the pool that have been in trouble or on which an allowance has been made, this committee comes in and the full facts are given them, without disclosing whose fruit it is. They vote whether or not the loss is the fault of the grower. If the loss is the fault of the grower by neglect, willful or otherwise, it is chargeable to him. If it is due to causes beyond the control of the grower, the pool stands the loss. The grower feels he is getting a square deal on that basis.

Asher Hobson summarized Mr. Chaney's contribution this way: "Before Chaney took over the marketing of cranberries, it was a distressing affair. Chaney put the Association on the map."

Miss Sue Pitman, who worked with Mr. Chaney for many years, characterized him this way: "He had a warm personality, was kindness personified, was very optimistic and always tried to cheer people up and have them look on the bright side of things. He was brilliant, honest, and the kind of person one had confidence in at first sight."

E. Clyde McGrew, a nephew who was associated with Mr. Chaney in the cranberry business and who furnished much of the background material for this paper, characterized him as one of the outstanding leaders of his time in the development and promotion of cooperation. He further said Chaney was always on the alert for the benefit of growers and shippers of farm products.

Besides the tremendous job Chaney did in getting and keeping the widespread cranberry growers together, in holding their confidence so that over half of the berries were marketed through the cooperative, he was a top notch organizer in other fields. Even before his cranberry days, he formed the Western Fruit Jobbers Association consisting of jobbers in Iowa, Nebraska, Wisconsin, Minnesota, and Colorado. Later he was instrumental in forming the American Fruit and Vegetable Shippers Association and eventually in the consolidation of several produce associations into the present United Fresh Fruit and Vegetable Association.

Chaney was active in the legislative proceedings leading to the enactment of the Perishable Agriculture Commodities Act, and in recognition of his efforts, his organization was given Certificate #1 issued under that Act. During this period, he came into contact with Herbert Hoover. Mr. Hoover was so impressed with Chaney's forcefulness and skill that in a letter to Chaney, he commented that he was the most outstanding man in the group that espoused the Act.

In summary, Chaney was a pioneer marketer, an organizer who brought to the cooperative field a skill and imagination that permitted him to adjust successfully to changing conditions, and a cooperative fundamentalist whose own character was based on first principles and on complete integrity.

Chris Lauriths Christensen

by Kelsey B. Gardner

CHRIS LAURITHS CHRISTENSEN was born at Minden, Nebr., December 29, 1894. His early life and experiences in this midwestern farming area led him directly to the study of agriculture. In 1916, he was graduated from the School of Agriculture at the University of Nebraska. World War I delayed further study. After service in the U. S. Army he returned to the University and received his degree of Bachelor of Science in Agriculture in 1920.

Graduate study followed Chris Christensen's degree from the University of Nebraska. In 1921–22 he was a Fellow of the American-Scandinavian Foundation with studies at the University of Copenhagen and at the Royal Agricultural College of Denmark.

Mr. Christensen's deep interest in cooperatives as a means of improving farmers' economic position led to work in Europe during 1922–23 as a special investigator on cooperatives for the U. S. Department of Agriculture. From this work came much information of use to cooperatives in the United States. A significant result was a Department of Agriculture bulletin *Agricultural Cooperation in Denmark* (1924).

Denmark was then known throughout the world for its extensive use of democratic cooperative principles. This study of the successful use by Danish farmers of the cooperative form of business organization was particularly timely in the United States because of the depressed condition of agriculture which had followed closely on the end of World War I. Cooperation had had substantial growth in the earlier years of the 1900's, but problems besetting cooperatives because of agriculture's difficulties made the study of cooperation in Denmark significant. On the basis of his studies Mr. Christensen emphasized the fundamental hook-up between production and marketing which he properly judged to be essential to commercial agriculture in the United States.

Mr. Christensen joined other students of Danish agriculture and cooperation in agreeing that "Denmark's agricultural progress and the cooperative movement owe their rapid growth to the people's High Schools," referred to as the Folk High Schools. These schools, begun in the middle 1800's, to quote him again, "furnished to Denmark's agriculture and the new cooperative associations, open-minded, active leaders who dared to change and try new methods; leaders who urged the people to rely upon their own capacity and strength."

Recognized and Emphasized Need for Research, Education

This recognition and emphasis in the United States on the need for research and education as bases for sound business growth and operation were the keystone of Mr. Christensen's contributions to efforts to assist agricultural cooperation in this country.

Following his sojourn in Europe he undertook during 1923–24 further graduate studies in economics and business administration at Harvard University. His analytical studies of Denmark's cooperatives and his graduate work at Harvard were important preparations for the new work he was to undertake with the U. S. Department of Agriculture in June, 1924. At that time, he was placed in charge of Agricultural Cooperation in the Bureau of Agricultural Economics. Under Mr. Christensen's direction studies of management, costs, and the factors bringing about efficient operation in cooperation were undertaken. Service and educational work in sound business principles with farmer cooperatives increased.

The need for the establishment on a more permanent basis of efforts by the Department to assist farmer cooperatives resulted in the setting up in 1926 under a new federal statute of the Division of Cooperative Marketing in the Bureau of Agricultural Economics. Because of the leadership shown by Mr. Christensen in the predecessor organization he was named chief of the new division. Despite its restrictive form of name the division was authorized to include "processing, warehousing, manufacturing, storage, the cooperative purchasing of farm supplies, credit, financing, insurance, and other cooperative activities."

It was expected that the research, service and educational work of the new division would be directed toward helping farmers build and operate sound cooperative business organizations. Policy and purpose were regarded as sound procedure at a time when numerous areas of the U. S. agricultural economy had been subjected to drives to organize farmers into cooperatives based on "iron-clad contracts" and price control of a commodity through control of the dominant part of its supply.

In this atmosphere which had its heyday in the early 1920's the efforts toward sound cooperative organization and operation were highly important. Such an approach represented in essence the earlier policies of the Department of Agriculture in its efforts to assist farmers with their problems in cooperation.

His responsibilities in the new division afforded Mr. Christensen an opportunity to build on this foundation and to expand work along both old and new lines. He met the challenge by assembling a highly capable and talented young staff whose members brought to their responsibilities competency and, what was also of utmost importance, belief in cooperatives as a necessary mechanism of farmers.

Able Administration of Division Commended

Under Mr. Christensen's direction the work in the areas of intensive studies of individual cooperatives and research in membership relations was expanded, as well as in still other significant aspects of cooperation. The program of the Division of Cooperative Marketing under his guidance was in full conformity with the hopes of the cooperative leaders who counseled with Department officials prior to the passage of the Cooperative Marketing Act of 1926. They had looked at the proposed division as "a means to give information, counsel and guidance to farmers on cooperative marketing . . . in harmony with [the Department of Agriculture's] traditional policy of service without domination." These leaders believed that such a division under wise administration would serve cooperative associations and the public welfare and that it would "render to cooperatives the kind of aid most needed by them without in any way impairing their own initiative and responsibility." Mr. Christensen's able administration of the new division resulted in the firm establishment of these goals. The impact of their sound conception has continued over the intervening 40 years through the stresses and strains of the Federal Farm Board and other subsequent changes and reorganizations which have confronted the work with cooperatives.

During the period when Mr. Christensen was Chief of the Division of Cooperative Marketing he made numerous contributions to the literature of cooperation in the United States. Two should be recognized. In November, 1926, his *Business Set-up of a Cooperative Marketing Association* was released as a USDA circular (No. 403). In April, 1929, a second publication, *Pooling as Practiced by Cooperative Marketing Associations*, appeared (USDA Misc. Pub. No. 14). This thoughtful statement of the objectives of all phases of pooling of cooperative services and activities has had a continuing application over the years when some cooperatives have made significant departures from the pooling principle, particularly in the pooling of sales returns.

Mr. Christensen's leadership and guidance were reflected in the thinking and activities of the staff. As a leader he strongly and successfully defended what he believed to be proper functions of the division. One instance had to do with the preparation of reports to individual associations on a restricted or confidential basis. Authorized under the Cooperative Marketing Act of 1926, the right of the division to carry on this aspect of its activity was successfully upheld and established by him. Another problem related to its right to make economic studies of particular concern to cooperatives. Other divisions in the Bureau of Agricultural Economics at times regarded these studies as belonging in their areas of responsibility. Mr. Christensen was able to effect working relationships with these other agencies which recognized the interests of cooperatives and of the Division of Cooperative Marketing in properly working in economic areas also.

In 1928, growers, cooperatives, and private shippers of citrus fruit worked toward the establishment of the Florida Citrus Growers Clearing House Association. Mr. Christensen summed up the basic philosophy in such a venture by stating that ". . . but clearing-house arrangements between commercial distributors and producer cooperative associations where the program goes beyond the exchange of trade information, unless absolutely in the control of producers, are fundamentally opposed to the whole theory and purpose of cooperative marketing by original producers." This Florida venture was short-lived. Anyone who may wish to explore the clearing-house idea would be well advised to go over Mr. Christensen's position as expressed in *American Cooperation—1928* (Pp. 339–353).

Named First Secretary of Federal Farm Board

In 1929, the Federal Farm Board was set up as an agency to assist farmers with serious problems arising out of the previous depressed position of agriculture which were greatly intensified by the economic depression that began in 1929. A primary objective of the Agricultural Marketing Act of 1929, under which the Board was established, was the encouragement and development of farmer-owned and farmer-controlled cooperative associations for the effective marketing of agricultural commodities.

It was to be fully expected that Mr. Christensen, with his administrative experience with cooperatives, would be directly brought into such a development. Accordingly, he was named Secretary to the Board in July, 1929, where he served until March, 1931. It was an also to-be-expected result that the Division of Cooperative Marketing, which he had so ably built and administered, would become an important part of the Board's staff. This transfer followed shortly on October 1, 1929. In the environment of the Board, Mr. Christensen found a congenial atmosphere for reception of his underlying concepts of sound organization and practices as essential features of successful cooperative operation forming the basis for loans by the Board to cooperatives.

In 1931, Mr. Christensen was appointed Dean of the College of Agriculture and Director of the Agricultural Experiment Station and the Extension Service at the University of Wisconsin. He served in this position until 1943 when he resigned to enter business. Since then he has had a distinguished business career—for 18 years he served as one of the principal executives of a major building materials manufacturing company and as a member of the board of directors of several major business corporations.

In 1934, the annual meeting of the American Institute of Cooperation was held at the University of Wisconsin. In his address of welcome, as Dean of the host university, Mr. Christensen made several observations of significance to farmers and their cooperatives. He first cited the necessity for seeing that the efforts of cooperatives "must result in a more economic and satisfactory distribution system, operating to the advantage of both producers and consumers." He also called for a "fuller appreciation of the meaning of cooperation in our country," both by members and cooperative officials and leaders. Had this admonition been fully understood and effectively carried through by those interested in farmer cooperatives, these organizations could well have over the next few years built better understanding of the economic nature of cooperatives and their objectives both within and outside the organizations. The resulting improvement in public relations would have constituted a significant bulwark against the onslaughts of the opposition to cooperatives that began in 1943 over their federal income tax status.

A second important point was included in Mr. Christensen's remarks. He emphasized the necessity for farmers to "become their own statesmen and not only organize and carry on effective organization but also meet, for the benefit of agriculture and for society as a whole, those larger economic and social issues which affect farm income."

The State of Wisconsin and its university have always been leaders in the development of farmer cooperatives. Research in cooperation has marked the programs of the university. This was an environment that afforded Mr. Christensen an additional opportunity to further his objectives in research, service, and education as essentials for the development of farmer cooperatives.

Leader in Other Activities, Including Youth Work

This profile would not be complete if it did not contain mention of some other responsibilities Mr. Christensen assumed in the fields of agriculture, education, and work with youth. Among these were: Member of the board of trustees of the Farm Foundation and chairman of its executive committee; member of the National Committee on Public Education; member of the sponsoring committee for the World Congress on Education for Democracy; service on the National Committee for the Mid-century White House Children and Youth Conference; trustee of the Rural Youth Foundation; director and President of the National Commission on Boys and Girls, 4-H Club Work; and President of the Country Life Association.

In addition to bulletins on agricultural cooperation, Mr. Christensen was co-author in 1936 of *Cooperative Principles and Practices* (Special Circular, Extension Service, University of Wisconsin). In 1939, *The Significance of the Folk School Type of Education* was released.

Mr. Christensen has retired from active managerial business responsibilities but still serves as a director on the board of several corporations, including the International Harvester Company; Armour and Company; Goff Oil Co., and the Brookside State Bank of Tulsa. He is also presently serving his sixth year as President of the National 4-H Club Service Committee. He is now a resident of Tulsa, Okla., and spends much time on his farm near Grove, Okla.

The soundness of Mr. Christensen's points of views regarding farmer cooperatives, their needs and potentials, has been demonstrated over the years. His impact is found in the work of the men who had the benefit of his direction and guidance, and in the policies of those organizations, both public and private, now working to help farmers build and operate more effective cooperative business organizations.

William Walter Cole

by C. E. Bowles

WILLIAM WALTER COLE earned for himself the title: "Father of the Cooperative Gins." This may account in part for the more intimate title, "Daddy Cole," used by those who knew him well. After reviewing his long and productive life, one quality stands out above all others: His single-purpose search for a pattern by which farmers could own and retain control of their own businesses.

Mr. Cole's background lay in cotton. He was born on a cotton farm near Savannah, Tenn., February 7, 1859. His early memories were of growing cotton under the trying conditions of reconstruction days. He picked cotton and hauled it to the gin. As a 12-year-old boy, he drove one of two teams of horses used to power a one-stand gin.

Early in his life, he was impressed with the necessity and importance of ginning in the preparation of cotton for marketing. He asked probing questions. Why did farmers have nothing to say about the charges made for ginning? Was the quality of the service received at the gin all it should be?

The Move to Texas

The Cole family moved to Texas in 1887, settling on a blackland farm near Greenville, the county seat of Hunt County. At Greenville, he came under the influence of the Farmers' Alliance, a very militant organization. The Alliance had a broad and comprehensive program intended to correct the many ills that beset the farmers of that day. Much was said in the Alliance meetings about "monopolistic trusts and greedy corporations, especially the railroads."

The Alliance was advocating a program of farmer ownership of gins, warehouses, elevators, etc. There are records of no less than 20 gins set up in Texas by groups of Alliance farmers between 1886 and 1892. One of these was a two-stand gin built by Mr. Cole and his neighbors near Greenville. He described it as a "co-partnership," but added that some of the partners failed to meet their promised contributions of capital. The effort failed and Mr. Cole learned a costly lesson in some things not to do.

Regarding this disappointment, he wrote: "Notwithstanding this failure, the experience gained seemed full of possibilities for a plan that would protect and make it possible for a farming community to own its own gins." In 1907, Mr. Cole made his second try to bring this about. He led a group of Farmers Union members in setting up a gin at Chillicothe, Tex., near his home farm at Medicine Mound. It was set up as a "joint stock" enterprise, limiting its membership to farmers belonging to the Farmers Union.

It was an up-to-date four-stand gin, a matter of much pride for the farmers. This time, each stockholder was required to put up the money or to pledge a note acceptable to the local bank. The gin was a success from the beginning and in three years, it was fully paid for with earnings from the gin. However, its very success led to its downfall. Designing men had quietly bought up 51 percent of the stock, called a stockholders' meeting and voted to sell the gin to an oil mill. This marked failure No. 2, enough to thoroughly discourage a less determined soul.

Farmers' Society Act Passed

Almost simultaneously, the Texas Legislature passed a cooperative enabling law known as the Farmers Society Act. It authorized a special type of farmers' corporation without capital stock. It could do business with members only. The Act was drafted by Walton Peteet, at that time marketing specialist for the Texas A & M Extension Service. He, too, deserves a place among the cooperative immortals. Although the law contained imperfections, it represented a breakthrough in cooperative thinking.

Encouraged by the new law, Mr. Cole again called his neighbors together for a third try setting up a cooperative gin that could remain cooperative. The Farmers Cooperative Society of Chillicothe was and is an outstanding success. Having found at last a workable pattern, Mr. Cole became an evangelist for farmers' society gins. He traveled far and wide at his own expense, teaching farmers how they could get better ginning at lower cost.

There are records of 133 of these society gins, most of which developed into highly successful businesses. As this is being written, they make up a large block of the Texas cooperative gins. All of them found it desirable to reorganize under the Texas Cooperative Marketing Act (1921) to gain certain advantages. A number of them retain "Society" in their corporate names.

Mr. Cole often compared a cooperative society to a community church. "Everyone using it owned it, yet no one could take it away from the farmers," he said. There was no allocation of equities earned in a society gin. This led to criticism from the Bureau of Internal Revenue.

Some of the societies found themselves assessed back taxes and penalties, a matter which disturbed Mr. Cole no little. The Chillicothe Farmers Cooperative Society paid an income tax, then successfully sued for a refund after establishing the equities owned by each patron. Many societies, forced to reconstruct old records, were impressed with the necessity of preserving patronage records.

Importance of Cooperative Gins

Cooperative gins in Texas now number 350. They are important in themselves as rallying points where farmers can do much more than gin cotton. They are also the "building blocks" for some highly successful regional cooperatives, oil mills, compresses, marketing associations, and cotton improvement groups. The phenomenal growth of these large cooperatives could hardly have happened without the sound foundation of the local cooperative gins.

Mr. Cole was offered attractive deals to represent gin machinery manufacturers or to endorse certain equipment. At no time would he accept a position with a salary attached—yet he worked for farmers as if he were on full pay.

At different times in his life he was active in the Farmers Alliance, the Farmers Union, and the Farm Bureau. He did not lose sight of the star on which he charted his course—businesses soundly owned and democratically controlled by farmers with the profits returned to them on a patronage basis.

Mr. Cole was one of the speakers enlisted by the Texas Farm Bureau in a gigantic membership drive in 1922. John Orr, then president of TFB, directed the campaign. He reported that 96 meetings of farmers were held in as many county seats of cotton growing counties within a two-week period.

At the Fork of the Road

During the 1920's, the leadership in Texas was uncertain which course cooperatives should take. There was still a carryover of wishful thinking that giant cooperatives could be set up so that the benefits would filter down to the farmers. In 1927, the TFB set up a subsidiary corporation, the Texas Cotton Growers' Holding Company. It was capitalized by $200,000 from TFB's reserve fund. The purpose of the company was largely to control cotton for the marketing part of TFB's activities.

Strong promotion was thrown behind establishing gins to be owned jointly by the local farmers and the holding company. Within a three-year period, 38 gins were built with the holding company investing usually 49 percent of the cost, and the local farmers subscribing 51 percent. The contract provided for distributing net margins 60 percent to the farmers ginning the cotton and 40 percent to retire the holding company's investment.

Management came from the Dallas office and the local farmers had very limited autonomy in the affairs of the gins. There was difficulty in attracting and holding patronage and farmers showed little feeling of local ownership. Most of these "Farm Bureau" gins were eventually sold to cooperative groups of local farmers, after which they developed into successful associations.

Mr. Cole did not subscribe to the "top-down" philosophy of farmer ownership. He chose the slower and more difficult course of starting near the soil. He did not overlook the need for regional federations of the gins to perform such needed services as marketing cotton, crushing cottonseed, purchasing insurance and supplies, etc. But he did not waver in his firm belief that ownership and control of the entire system should rest with the men who grew the cotton.

Belated Recognition

Recognition is often slow in coming to men who dedicate their lives to causes without thought of self promotion. Mr. Cole was 78 when the Texas Agricultural Workers Association honored him at a meeting in Houston, January 14, 1938. He was presented with a silver plaque "for distinguished service to Texas agriculture in the development of cooperative ginning."

This salute came largely as a result of efforts by Dr. W. E. Paulson, marketing specialist for the Texas Experiment Station. Dr. Paulson also earned a place among the "cooperative immortals" by his basic research into the development of farmer-owned, farmer-controlled co-operative gins.

A number of other groups recognized and honored Mr. Cole for his deep concern for the economic independence of farmers and his courage to espouse a cause which farmers were often slow to accept and which was extremely unpopular with many businessmen.

It would be impossible to bring to an end an account of Mr. Cole's useful career without at least a mention of his most ardent disciple, G. A. Vestal, of Quanah. Mr. Vestal was a man of considerable wealth. He came under Mr. Cole's teaching and from that time on, devoted much of his time to carrying these teachings to groups of farmers. He often drove Mr. Cole to meetings after it was unsafe for the old man to drive alone.

Many other men, including the writer, feel a deep personal debt to "Daddy Cole." His singleness of purpose gave all who knew him a clearer perspective of the power that lies in cooperation. This brings out another important trait in his character, his ability to inspire others to greater dedication in service to farmers.

He died April 6, 1952, at the ripe age of 93 and his remains are buried at Medicine Mound, Tex.

Charles Clements Commander

by John T. Lesley

ACCEPTING AS QUITE VALID Webster's statement that "a pioneer is one who goes before into that which is unknown or untried, to prepare the way for others," then the late Charles Clements Commander, who was General Manager of the Florida Citrus Exchange, Tampa, Fla., for more than a quarter of a century, was in every sense a pioneer; indeed a truly great Cooperative Pioneer.

Mr. Commander was a "self-made" man, having entered the business world at the very early age of 13. In the year 1903 he began his career in the State's most famous industry—citrus—and in 1909 he became connected with the Florence Citrus Growers Association, Florence Villa, Fla., one of the earliest agricultural cooperative marketing associations in Florida, where he worked in every department of packinghouse operation from grader, packer, and foreman on up to the position of manager.

In 1923, Mr. Commander was made Manager of the Polk County Citrus Sub-Exchange, a member of the Florida Citrus Exchange, and his work in this position so established his executive and administrative ability, as well as his knowledge of citrus marketing and merchandising, that he was appointed General Manager of the Exchange in 1925. He served the Exchange as General Manager until his retirement in 1951 under the Exchange's retirement plan, during which time he successfully guided that organization through many economic and political storms to its present position in the industry. No greater tribute to, or recognition of, his outstanding ability could have been paid Mr. Commander than that evidenced by the action of the board of directors of the Exchange in retaining him as Advisory Counsel to the Exchange.

The Exchange, together with its member sub-exchanges and local associations of growers, was organized in 1909 as the Florida citrus industry's first and largest cooperative marketing system and while its destiny was from the very beginning in the hands of many of the most eminent men in the industry, it seemed as though fore-designed that the increased and ever-increasing problems of the Exchange were to peak in the 1920's under Mr. Commander's administration.

Never one to procrastinate or equivocate, he struck early in a broad effort and on a broad front to create orderly marketing through cooperative effort. Deploring the then-current philosophy on the part of too many in the industry that the way to sell citrus fruit was through price-cutting, he proposed early in 1926 and constantly thereafter that quality and maturity standards be improved; that there be standardization of grades and improvements in packing-house procedures and packaging; that shippers be held to stricter accountability in their dealings with growers and that the industry impose upon itself a per-box assessment for the purpose of financing appropriate publicity and consumer-advertising of Florida citrus fruit. The Exchange itself was already expending considerable sums each year advertising its famous and internationally known trademark "Seald-Sweet."

It was quite apparent that Mr. Commander's concepts and broad program for the betterment of the Florida citrus industry were some 10 years ahead of the thinking of those outside the Florida Citrus Exchange. Voluntary agreement with his proposals was woefully lacking at the time they were first made and for too many years thereafter.

Wins Support for Florida Citrus Legislation

Since it was foreign to his very nature to give up any worthwhile fight simply because he had lost the first round, he continued his efforts and arguments throughout the industry in such way and manner as he deemed most effective and finally achieved sufficient support for the enactment in 1935 of the first broad, comprehensive citrus legislative program that embraced substantially all the features of his original proposals.

Specifically, the Legislature of the State of Florida at its 1935 Session enacted into law these principal measures:

1. A bill creating the Florida Citrus Commission as a state agency of government to administer all State citrus laws and rules and regulations promulgated thereunder, the members of such Commission to be appointed by the Governor.
2. A bill establishing maturity standards that are the highest in world for citrus fruit.

3. Three separate bills levying varying per-box excise taxes on oranges, grapefruit, and tangerines, for publicity and consumer-advertising purposes.
4. A bill requiring all citrus fruit dealers to be licensed and to post adequate bonds for the protection of producers.

Other legislative measures affecting the Florida citrus industry have been enacted into law since 1935 and those expressly mentioned above have been amended and expanded from time to time, all of which have been brought forward by a very comprehensive codification into what is now known as the "Florida Citrus Code." Under this Code, the Florida Citrus Commission is given broad power with respect to standardization of grades, the handling of publicity, sales promotion, and commodity advertising, licensing and bonding of dealers, regulating the operations of fresh fruit packing-houses and processing plants, providing for adequate inspection of citrus fruit and processed products thereof under the Florida Commissioner of Agriculture, and in general, to protect the reputation of the Florida citrus industry and the members thereof, as well as the consuming public.

Soon after enactment in 1933 of the Federal Agricultural Marketing Agreement Act, Mr. Commander started a campaign to obtain a Federal Marketing Agreement and Order regulating the handling of all fresh Florida citrus in interstate commerce. First efforts to regulate by volume limitations failed for lack of industry support. Preferring a substantial part of the loaf to no bread at all, he succeeded in obtaining industry-wide agreement on a Federal Marketing Order regulating the handling of Florida oranges, grapefruit, and tangerines by grades and sizes which, though amended from time to time, has remained in continuous force and effect ever since its original issuance in the middle 1930's.

While it is not intended to even suggest that "C.C." Commander, as he was well-known throughout the nation in fruit and vegetable circles, single-handedly accomplished all the foregoing, it is intended to assert that during the nearly 50 years that he was actively identified with the Florida citrus industry, he provided that quality of leadership which is so essential in persuading other members of an industry that the things he advocated were absolute needs and not mere personal desires in the growth, progress, and proper development of the industry.

Morris Llewellyn Cooke

by Joe Jenness

ALTHOUGH SOME 930 RURAL ELECTRIC cooperatives follow a nonprofit, cooperative-type organization, originally it was never planned nor conceived that the rural electrification of the United States would be predominantly cooperative.

Harlow S. Person, early REA economic consultant and friend of the first REA Administrator, Morris Llewellyn Cooke, has written: "Promotion of rural electrification through loans to local groups of farm people, organized as nonprofit corporations under state laws, was more easily conceived than executed."

In scores of situations throughout the country zealous promoters of cooperative organizations found themselves castigated as "radicals" and even "communists." Too many farmers were fearful that a membership application meant their farms were pledged as collateral to the federal government and in case of failure of the cooperative they would lose their farm. In addition, times were hard, the depression was still felt in farming communities, and the release of a $5 bill for membership was a major family decision.

Down through three decades of rural electrification growth and expansion, involving some $5 billion of investment, there still persists a large block of disbelievers or disclaimers of any commitment to the cooperative methods of organization. There are many, many electric systems whose officers and managers refer to themselves as an "association" or "member corporation" and avoid the term "cooperative" like the plague. Once when making an annual meeting speech, the writer used "cooperative" in referring to an organization. After the meeting was over, the president approached and declared that if ever that word "cooperative" was used again referring to their system, the writer would never be invited back!

Despite such individual attitudes the predominance of cooperative organizations in rural electrification in the United States is a triumph of a reluctant, last-ditch salvation of a fundamental economic program conceived originally as an emergency work relief effort. President Franklin Delano Roosevelt once envisioned REA as lasting not more than a year. Partially for this reason he decided not to set it up as a part of the Federal Power Commission but as an independent agency of the federal government. Later with the 1939 reorganization, REA moved into the Department of Agriculture.

Becomes First REA Administrator

Morris Llewellyn Cooke was the fortunate choice of President Roosevelt as the first Administrator of the Rural Electrification Administration. Born on May 11, 1872, in Carlisle, Pa., he was appointed REA Administrator on his 63rd birthday, May 11, 1935. He had graduated from Lehigh University in 1895 in Mechanical Engineering after gaining experience as a reporter on Philadelphia, Denver, and New York newspapers.

Early in his professional career he had come under the influence of Frederick W. Taylor, the father of scientific management, and from then on he was a dedicated management engineer. His record of public service was outstanding, and he had become deeply interested in rural electrification in the 20's as Director of Governor Gifford Pinchot's Pennsylvania Giant Power Survey. According to Arthur M. Schlesinger, Jr., in his book, *The Politics of Upheaval,* this survey "laid great emphasis on the need for public support of rural electrification." In 1933, President Roosevelt asked Cooke, who had worked with him as Trustee for the New York Power Authority, 1928-1933, to make a survey of the Mississippi Valley for the Public Works Administration. Under his chairmanship the Mississippi Valley Committee recommended federal leadership for "the great task of rural electrification."

Cooke did not come to his position as Administrator of the REA as a cooperative advocate, although he had favored the idea of making use of consumers "mutual electric companies" in 1934. Rather, the logic of the cooperative approach gradually came to him as he sought a way to achieve a workable plan of rural electrification for the country. As Schlesinger said in the book quoted, "More and more, there seemed only one means of cracking the problem—the establishment of non-profit cooperatives by the farmers themselves."

Electric cooperatives had been tried as far back as 1914 at Granite Falls, Minn. Known as the Stony Run system, arrangements were made with the City of Granite Falls to supply power from its municipally owned plant. By December, 1914, the current was turned on to 26 farms with a cost to each consumer member of $203.55 in cash, seven days of labor one man, two days of labor with man and team, and 21 free meals to men working on the line. Some 46 electric cooperatives in 13 states were set up before the advent of REA in 1935. The largest had 63 miles of line and 350 members.

These limited cooperative efforts, sometimes called "snake lines" since they meandered through the countryside, lacked the planning and application of the area coverage concept, which was a technique to push costs down and reduce investment per member. Furthermore, a small cooperative did not have the kind of engineering, legal, and financial resources or staff necessary to successful operation. The inherent limitations of the early cooperative efforts, of which only about half succeeded in staying in business, did not suggest a sure-fire, instant approach to rural electrification on a national scale.

As the first Administrator of REA Cooke faced problems, technical, sizeable, and variable, in trying to electrify the countryside and to provide immediate work relief. A logical approach called for expansion from existing power systems rather than the slower creation of entirely new and additional power systems.

However, Cooke did feel and came to know the influence of dedicated and experienced cooperative leaders, such as Dr. Joseph G. Knapp, Administrator of Farmer Cooperative Service, and Murray Lincoln, of the Ohio Farm Bureau. As Cooke tried and failed to find no other way out of his dilemma, the seeds of cooperation planted by Dr. Knapp and others found fertile soil, much as a tree growing out of a rocky crevice, and their suggestions flowered into one of the greatest social and economic programs ever conceived for rural America.

Cooke Urged to Use the Cooperative Method

Dr. Knapp recalls visiting Cooke at 2000 Massachusetts Ave., N.W., Washington, D. C., during that fateful summer of 1935 when the future of REA hung in the balance. This first functioning office of the fledgling agency was housed in a large red brick home once the residence of George Westinghouse, Jr., famous inventor and manufacturer of electrical equipment. Dr. Knapp urged the cooperative approach as one that farmers would readily understand and one which would aid in the involvement of the rural people doing something to help themselves. This, in turn, would reduce the need for so large a central federal government staff to oversee the planning, engineering and construction.

Dr. Knapp's idea of getting the consumer beneficiaries involved in solving their problem of electric service must have appealed strongly to Cooke. On the occasion of his appointment to the New York State Power Authority in 1931, the *New York Times* quoted Cooke as having written, in connection with the issue of public ownership of electric utilities, "It will be easier for us to improve things if we avoid becoming involved in any widespread move to own electrical facilities now estimated to be worth $11 billion. There is a danger also in extending the public payroll to include too large a number of patriots." Cooke's early encouragement of the Ohio and Indiana Farm Bureaus and the Wisconsin Rural Electrification Coordination Agency to plan, engineer, and supervise construction reflected his personal philosophy of keeping government control to a minimum.

Dr. Person has written that a very influential reason why cooperatives were not pushed was that at an early conference with leaders of the cooperative movement, chiefly marketing associations, some of the spokesmen not only advised Cooke but plead with him not to employ the cooperative form of enterprise for promotion of rural electrification. Serious doubts were expressed that rural electrification with government loans was a proper cooperative function. Later this attitude was to diminish.

Absorbed in the ideology of cooperation and somewhat removed from its practical aspects, James Warbasse, as head of the Cooperative League of the U.S.A. at that time, was one of the theorists who felt that any variation from the orthodox concept was bound to be harmful. He felt strongly that the state and the cooperative movement had interests so opposed as to make any harmonious relationship impossible. One existed for the commonwealth, the other for private individuals banded together, he felt.

"Should the cooperative movement," Warbasse warned, "combine with the political state, the natural outcome would be the state would take over cooperation under its control. This would be a calamity to an independent self-help enterprise."

Today, the League is a staunch supporter of cooperative rural electrification and for years has fought side by side with other friends of the program to keep it alive and adequately financed.

Through their national organization, the National Rural Electric Cooperative Association, the electric cooperatives are working now to persuade Congress to authorize a Federal Bank for Electric Cooperatives which will seek supplementary capital from the private investment market and which eventually will become owned and controlled by the cooperatives. The trend is away from government involvement and towards eventual complete ownership and control by the cooperatives.

Early Conference With Utility Executives Fails

On May 20, 1935, nine days after the White House released the Executive Order setting up REA, a conference of 16 utility executives, representing 75 percent of all utility properties in the country, met in Washington with Mr. Cooke to develop a rural electrification program. It was hoped that, notwithstanding their opposition to the creation of REA, the utility companies would be moved by a sense of duty in meeting a national emergency, and for some this lofty motivation would be sweetened by an interest rate of 3 percent and generous loan terms.

Two months later the utilities reported back with an offer which depended on the government allowing them not to lower farm rates or to simplify rate schedules. Cooke tried to show the utility committee that if they lowered their rates and did certain things the venture would mean money in their pockets. But the utility executives would not accept Cooke's proposals.

Before the end of May, 1935, a conference at the Lafayette Hotel, Washington, D. C., of municipal system managers and REA officials discussed the problems which REA faced for speedy rural electrification. Speakers made clear that in many states laws did not permit municipal utilities to operate outside their corporate limits.

In 1935, the Missouri Supreme Court ruled that municipals could not carry their lines beyond the corporate limits of their city. The court further held that the farmer could come to the boundary of a city and tap power from a municipal plant. Out of this conference came emphasis to establish organizations which could build and operate lines and secure their power supply from a municipal source.

While virtually the entire electric utility business of the country had been represented in these two conferences, what had appeared to be the quickest and most logical way to launch rural electrification on a grand scale floundered.

Farm Organizations Also Call for Co-op Way

In addition to efforts of cooperative leaders to get Cooke interested in cooperatives, there had been resolutions voiced by farm organizations, such as the Grange, American Farm Bureau Federation, National Farmers' Union, and state and local units of these groups calling for cooperative organization.

Murray Lincoln, famous Ohio Farm Bureau leader and now in retirement, gave a first-hand report of his experiences with Administrator Cooke in his autobiographical book, *Vice President in Charge of Revolution,* from which the following quotation is taken.

> ". . . sometime in 1935 I saw that one of the first New Deal alphabet agencies was the REA. I went down to Washington to meet Mr. Morris L. Cooke, the Administrator.
> "'. . . what do you know about the utility business?' Mr. Cooke asked.
> "'Not a thing,' I admitted cheerfully. 'I was trained in dairying and animal husbandry.'
> "Mr. Cooke suppressed a smile and said indulgently, as one might explain something to a child, 'Well, now, we expect about 90 percent of the rural electrification to be done by the presently existing private utilities and about 10 percent by public owned utilities and cooperatives. As you know, it is a highly technical job and I doubt whether you or your people are equipped to handle it.'
> "'I'll turn those figures around on you if you'll let us try it,' I said.
> "Mr. Cooke's demeanor changed. 'Young man, you're crazy.'
> "'Okay,' I replied. 'But just give us the opportunity.'
> "Mr. Cooke struggled a little and then sighed. 'Well, I suppose I must because the law states that I must. But I'll be frank. I I don't have much hope for you.'
> "We set up 30 cooperatives throughout Ohio so quickly that no other state caught up with us. Of the first five and a half million dollars the REA loaned to co-ops, some five million went into Ohio. We got the program well under way in seven months, although every step of it was a fight."

Lincoln proved that the use of cooperatives was not slower than the other approaches and that local involvement is superior to absentee or monopoly operations in getting a job done—even giving the established businesses a head start of being in business and functioning!

Following the two Washington meetings with power company officials and municipal representatives, Cooke called an exploratory conference of rural organizations and cooperative leaders on June 6, 1935 at the Lafayette Hotel, Washington, D. C. During the meeting Joseph C. Swidler, former Chairman of the Federal Power Commission and then serving on the TVA legal staff, recounted the earlier experiences of TVA in connection with the formation and operations of the Alcorn County Electric Power Association.

"The conference was most encouraging," Cooke has written, "and thus finally the plan for executing the program through cooperatives was devised and it has proved increasingly successful."

During June and July, 1935, Cooke found it necessary to seek the expert cooperative experience of Boyd Fisher, of Ohio, to direct cooperative activity at REA. Fisher's presence and the expected rejection of loans by private utilities caused some uneasiness to Mr. Nicholson, chief counsel for REA, and Mr. Herring, consulting engineer. These men and others in REA were convinced, even for some time after Cooke's resignation as REA Administrator, that the co-ops could not do the job. These men were charged with covertly carrying on a campaign to discredit the use of co-ops and causing a schism in the REA staff ranks.

This discontent continued until February, 1937, when John Carmody, the new Administrator succeeding Mr. Cooke, brought peace and unity to the REA ranks. Then the program began to move along the present organizational type channels with more success.

By the end of 1961 the organizational pattern of rural electrification systems totalled 992 active REA borrowers. There has been no significant change since. The active borrowers are classified as follows:

	Number	Percentage
Electric Cooperatives	930	93.8%
Public Power Districts	44	4.4%
Other Public Bodies	14	1.4%
Private Power Companies	4	.4%

Jerry Voorhis, Executive Director of The Cooperative League of the U.S.A., has written:

> The story of rural electricity since 1935 is thus one of the best illustrations of the benefits to an entire nation that can flow from consumption-oriented or consumer-directed production and distribution.
> No one farmer could make an electric system out of his need for electricity," Voorhis declares. "But a group of farmers—once their need was cooperatively organized—could do so. No one farmer could hope to monetize the credit of his single good name, but groups of farmers could do this. The bringing of electricity to rural America is thus another demonstration of the basic fact of life that what one of us cannot do alone a number of us cooperating together can frequently accomplish."

Morris Llewellyn Cooke knew electrical engineering and he knew scientific management and the problems of executive decision making. But when he found all other approaches to large-scale rural electrification were blocked, he became a "cooperator" by necessity!

On this cooperative foundation today moves the electric power for some 20 million Americans in 46 states and spread over 54 percent of the land area of the continental United States.

22 Foreign Countries Developing Rural Electrification

The American-born concept of an electric cooperative is now being expanded worldwide as part of the foreign aid program. Developing countries in South America, Africa, India and even Vietnam, while the fighting goes on, are discovering the cooperative way to get rural electrification. Surveys and construction have started in 22 countries.

Who knows? Perhaps cooperatives will some day prove more effective against communism than guns and bombs!

Cooke's contribution to cooperatives in the REA program was to serve as mid-wife for them. Others were to build on the opportunity that he opened up for other cooperators throughout the country to get the job done.

When he died in 1960 at the age of 87, many paid homage to his memory for his many national contributions. A few of them are here quoted to bring out the measure and quality of the man.

Gordon R. Clapp, formerly Chairman of the TVA, said, "All citizens owe him a great debt for his contribution to the nation's strength and conscience and for his personal administration of the wisdom of the thesis that men and their views early and forcefully expressed do make a difference in the outcome of public debate and decision."

Hugh H. Bennett, the first Administrator of the Soil Conservation Service, said: "I want to say that Morris Cooke made the greatest alltime contribution to the nation's program of optimum use of and protection of its basic national resources."

Leland Olds, former Chairman of the Federal Power Commission, said, "We may well look to the Pennsylvania Giant Power Survey of 1925, directed by Morris Cooke, under the governorship of the great conservationist, Gifford Pinchot, for many of the sprouts that grew to full stature in New Deal power and resources policy. There we find his concept of the wedding of democracy and science, management engineering applied to the Government's necessary planning functions."

It is significant that Cooke's greatest monument—the rural electrification program—could not have been erected without the spirit and practical use of cooperative principles.

E. G. Cort

by Glenn W. Thompson

E. G. CORT WAS A MAN OF ACTION. He was a man of ideas. Able, capable and dynamic, he was willing to adjust to the demands of the times.

Cooperative institutions of the Upper Midwest still bear the marks of Cort's influence and philosophy. History will have to weigh the eventual results of the dedication and convictions of one of the daring pioneer Cooperators.

Mr. Cort was born in 1885 in St. Lawrence, S. D. He graduated from Iowa State University at Ames, Iowa, in 1911. He taught school for three years. He farmed for eight years in Swift County, Minn. The Depression following World War I terminated his farm operations and launched him on his efforts to help farmers and others to help themselves through education, self-help, and mutual aid.

Mr. Cort became County Agricultural Extension Agent in Freeborn County, Minn., in 1923. In this position he became considerably aware that southern Minnesota and Iowa farmers were accepting the idea of *cooperation* and making it work, in an effort to reduce the cost of production supplies by forming local cooperative oil associations.

Tractors had replaced horses as forms of power in agriculture. Gasoline and tractor fuel had replaced corn, oats, and hay as the primary "feed" resource for the new forms of power on Upper Midwest farms. Grease and lubricants were even more extensively used—ahead of, as well as behind, the draw-bar.

Mr. Cort, as County Agent, quickly recognized these new practices and became consciously aware of his responsibilities to Freeborn County. He encouraged the farmers and townspeople to try out the idea of a Cooperative Oil Company, which had already proven successful in other southern Minnesota, Iowa, and Wisconsin communities.

By 1925 he had convinced his associates that the idea would work. One of his associates was the late Frank H. Osborne, a businessman turned farmer. Records do not show the intimate efforts between Cort and Osborne in the Mid-20's. It can be concluded, however, that these two men complemented each other. Cort was the dynamo and Osborne was the balance wheel. Cort was the idea man and Osborne was the steadying hand to prevent the throttle from being pushed too far ahead.

Freeborn County Co-op Oil Company was a forerunner to the Minnesota Co-op Oil Company. Several other co-op oil associations provided the base for the regional organization which was to grow, develop, and flourish. Many factors contributed to the circumstances which E. G. Cort recognized, and he used his influence as a leader to forge a program of cooperative development in the Upper Midwest.

There was discontent on the land in the early 20's. It was engendered by the rapid fall in farm income following World War I. The decision of the Federal Reserve Bank directors to shrink agricultural credit was to have some far-reaching effects. During the five years immediately following, farmers were unable to exchange farm-made dollars for city-made goods at city-made prices.

Inflated wartime dollars for wheat, corn, hogs, and butter, had enabled farmers to buy motor cars and tractors in 1917 and 1918. Deflated post-war dollars turned them to cooperation as a technique for buying gasoline, lube-oil, and grease.

Successful Cooperative Principles Applied to Oil

A group of farmers in Lyon County, Minn., applied the same basic principles that they had found successful in cooperative creameries, cooperative elevators, shipping associations and the early co-op stores. In 1921, the Cottonwood Co-op Oil Company went into the gas and oil business. Just a month or so after the Cottonwood Co-op was organized the farmers in and around Casco, New London, Van Dyne, and Manawa, Wis., were distributing petroleum products on a non-profit cooperative basis. The idea proved itself when Marshall, Jackson, Owatonna, Redwood Falls, Dawson, and Albert Lea in Minnesota soon followed suit.

By 1926, co-op bulk plants and filling stations were being put up all over the area. More than 20 co-op oil associations were organized that one year in Minnesota, Iowa and Wisconsin. Similar organizing campaigns were under way in Indiana, Kansas, Illinois, and other states. It all started in Minnesota and Wisconsin.

Here was an idea. Its time had come. Mr. Cort recognized the opportunity to employ the concept of collective buying for and between the several local cooperative oil companies. As he said on several occasions, if the idea of cooperative effort was good on a local basis, it would be good on a regional, or federated basis.

Directors of local cooperative oil boards and members of organizing committees attended a series of meetings throughout southern Minnesota in 1924, 1925, and 1926. Of course, there were many instances of neighbors getting together and driving 30 miles to visit a co-op set-up in another town to see how things were getting along. These unrecorded preliminaries to organizing were all a part of the cross-fertilization of ideas that produced a good crop of cooperatives and helped to make Minnesota the most cooperative state in the union.

The earliest minutes and records indicate that operations, prices, records, insurance, legislation, assistance, and advice to neighboring groups trying to start a co-op prompted delegates to attend meetings during these formative years. Caution and concern seemed to guide their actions. Unreasonably high margins of profit charged by the trade, which the co-op oil companies followed, almost guaranteed success from the beginning.

After several meetings in which the need for a central organization was discussed and debated, a committee was named in 1925 to draw up a proposed set of articles and bylaws. Several months later, incorporators were named to file the legal papers with the Secretary of State. Caution still prevailed. It was agreed that at least 10 associations should have the proposal ratified by their local boards before the filing should take place.

Minnesota Co-op Oil Company Organized

On September 8, 1926, the official incorporation of the Minnesota Co-op Oil Company [1] took place. It was expressed that the pooling of purchases for the local co-op oil associations "would give better prices and quality than obtained under the prevailing system, and that profit (sic) or resale margin would create a fund that could be used to promote and protect the local cooperative oil associations."

Without question, Mr. Cort stamped his influence on all those who served the organization he helped found and then manage. His architectural design developed from his own experience as student, teacher, farmer, County Agent, and cooperative founder, required a certain dedication and self-sacrifice. This he expected from his board of directors and the employees. Without being trite, it can be stated that Mr. Cort gave his "full measure of devotion" to an idea. This idea grew. It developed economically and organizationally.

---

[1] Later to become Midland Cooperatives, Inc.

Mr. Cort had noted the singular success of the cooperative creamery development throughout Minnesota, Wisconsin, and Iowa. He was impressed with the achievements of Land O'Lakes Creameries. He was an admirer of their first manager, A. J. McGuire. Similarly, the late W. G. Boyle of Mora, Minn., active in Land O'Lakes' development, contributed to Cort's appreciation of cooperative potential. When Mr. Cort saw an idea working successfully, he had little reservation about its efficiency. He rationalized the whole process by saying: "If you can carry cooperation in a milk can, you can carry cooperation in a gasoline can." "If farmers could ship butter by the carload, sell it and make savings in transportation and in the market; farmers could also buy gasoline by the tank car and make savings on several tank car loads."

From 1927 to 1944, the time of Cort's death, Midland grew from a broker organization, whose manager sat at a rented desk in a rented office, with a volume of $270,000 and net savings of $3,473 (enough to pay the manager's salary) to a volume of almost $11 million, net worth of $2.75 million, and savings of $750,000. By the time Cort had seen his idea, his convictions, grow from dream to reality, the country recovered from the Depression following World War I to the "prosperity" engendered by World War II.

In the decade and a half of Mr. Cort's influence on cooperative development, a number of significant things happened:

1. Cooperative education and influence moved significantly ahead. The Cooperative League of the U.S.A. became truly a national influence with E. G. Cort's support.
2. National Cooperatives, Inc., with Cort's backing was organized and has grown into an important buying and manufacturing institution serving cooperative regionals throughout the northern hemisphere. It is now located in Albert Lea, Minn., where E. G. Cort was County Agent from 1923 to 1927.
3. Midland Cooperatives, Inc., has grown from an "idea" without much resource, to an institution with assets of over $44 million, a net worth of more than $22 million, and volume of goods and services to members of about $100 million annually.

It can be said that E. G. Cort was a man of vision and dedication. Cooperation is an idea of people helping themselves without profit to middleman. Cort's life was a testimony of that simple idea. The institutions to which he and others contributed, are evidence of the validity of their conviction.

Howard A. Cowden

by Gilbert C. Fite

THE CAREER OF HOWARD A. COWDEN represents an amazing record in the history of cooperative leadership in the United States. His main contribution was in the organization and development of the Consumers Cooperative Association in Kansas City which, by the time Cowden retired as president in 1961, had become one of the largest cooperative farm supply firms in America.[1] But his influence has gone far beyond the company that he founded. Cowden has been a driving force in the farmer cooperative movement of the entire nation for some 40 years, and for the past 30 years he has been prominent in international cooperative affairs as well. Although imbued with a deep sense of idealism, this has always been tempered with a down-to-earth pragmatism. He has combined the desire to serve with practical qualities of leadership.

Cowden was born at Pleasant Hope, in southwest Missouri, in 1893. He grew to young manhood on a farm where he experienced first-hand many of the problems and frustrations common to farm life in that period. Like most rural boys, he did not get much formal education. He attended grade and high school at Pleasant Hope, and spent two short winter terms in 1910–11 and 1911–12 at the University of Missouri's College of Agriculture at Columbia. He then took the examination for a teaching certificate in 1914, and that autumn began teaching the intermediate grades at Pleasant Hope. He taught school until 1918 when he joined the Student Army Training Corps at Missouri State Normal School in Springfield.

Finds Life's Work After Chance Beginning

At the end of the first semester of the 1918–19 school year, Cowden quit college and began looking for a job. He did not want to return

---

[1] On September 1, 1966, after this sketch was prepared, the C.C.A. changed its name to Farmland Industries, Inc.

to teaching, and he had no intention of farming. Yet, he was vitally interested in the problems of agriculture. The cooperative movement was one avenue open to an energetic young man who disliked farming, but who had a deep desire to help farmers. However, it was by chance that Cowden got started in the field of agricultural cooperation and as soon as he began working with farmer cooperatives Cowden knew that he had found his place of work and service.

On March 10, 1919, he became secretary of the Polk County Farmers Association at Bolivar, Mo. The objective of this and other county associations in Missouri was to buy twine and other commodities in bulk and sell them to farmers at lower prices. It was believed that if farmers handled merchandise through their own cooperative associations they would lower the costs of production. The farmer cooperative movement in Missouri at that time rested mainly on the Farm Clubs which had been organized by William Hirth into the Missouri Farmers Association in January, 1917.

Cowden's effective work in Polk County, as well as his organization of Farm Clubs earlier, brought him to the attention of Mr. Hirth, who was also editor of *The Missouri Farmer*. Hirth found Cowden "a very bright and strong man," and predicted that "he will make one of the strongest secretaries in the state." Cowden's talent for organization, combined with sound business sense, marked him for a more important position. Early in 1920 he was named fieldman for the Missouri Farmers Association, and on January 1, 1922, he became MFA's first full-time, paid secretary. He moved to Columbia and spent the next several years organizing the farmer cooperative movement in Missouri.

Cowden was a tall, rugged, Lincolnesque looking man possessed of tremendous energy and ambition. He was self-confident and forceful, but in a firm, quiet way. Although Cowden was a warm, friendly person, he had a certain dignity and reserve which discouraged easy familiarity except among a few of his closest friends. People who had known him for years usually called him "Mister Cowden."

While Cowden did not want to make his own living on the farm, he held strong agrarian biases. He believed that agriculture was the nation's most important industry, and that farmers were the foundation upon which American greatness rested. To him the rich agricultural Midwest was both the economic and spiritual heartland of the nation. His work with cooperatives was justified to a considerable extent by his reasoning that anything which helped farmers would automatically be of value to the entire country. When it came to the purported values of farming, he held strong Jeffersonian views.

Develops Basic Philosophy of Co-op Usefulness, Value

By 1920, when Cowden went to work for MFA, he had developed a basic philosophy of agricultural cooperation which he has maintained to this day. First of all, he saw the cooperative way of doing business as a means of breaking an economic system which he believed had exploited and robbed farmers. If farmers were to improve their position in the economy, he argued, they must, through cooperative effort, increase their bargaining power in the market place.

Once cooperatives were formed, he emphasized the importance of farmer loyalty to their own buying and selling organizations. While he admitted that immediate benefits might be small, he had faith that member loyalty would ultimately pay off in lower costs of operation and better returns from sales. Consequently, Cowden stressed education in, and commitment to, cooperative principles. But he knew that regardless of how deeply farmers believed in cooperative idealism, this was not enough. He insisted that cooperatives must always be operated on sound business principles.

During the middle of the 1920's, Cowden worked hard to build the MFA and the farmer cooperative movement in Missouri. He was especially interested in developing cooperative bulk stations to supply petroleum products to farmers. The business operations of these cooperatives were simple. The cooperative bought the petroleum supplies from a major company at wholesale and passed the savings on to patrons in the form of patronage refunds.

Cowden's success in MFA affairs was partly responsible for his leaving that organization in 1927. For several years he and Hirth had experienced differences over organization techniques and business practices. The main trouble, however, was that the MFA did not have room for two such strong men as Hirth and Cowden. The struggle for power finally left Hirth in control.

After Cowden resigned as Secretary of the MFA, he formed the Cowden Oil Company in January, 1928. During the next few months he did a small wholesale petroleum business. But this firm never flourished and besides he had little interest in operating a private company. His interests were in the farmer cooperative movement and during late 1928 and early 1929 he gave careful consideration to setting up a regional wholesale cooperative to handle petroleum products. With the help of a few friends, he established the Union Oil Company (Cooperative) at Kansas City in February, 1929. Once established, the Union Oil Company began making contracts with local farmer cooperatives to supply them with a definite quantity of petroleum products.

The local associations each bought a small amount of stock in the wholesale which gave them a share in the management and earnings of the Union Oil Company. The wholesale then was owned by the member cooperatives and became a kind of cooperative federation. Savings made by the Union Oil Company were reinvested in the wholesale or refunded to the participating cooperative in accord with the decision of the board of directors.

Cowden's ambitious thinking at that time was presented at a meeting of the American Institute of Cooperation, held at Louisiana State University in Baton Rouge in the summer of 1929. In a talk on "Cooperative Oil Stations" Cowden said: "The members of the Union Oil Company are gradually developing a national chain of cooperative oil companies, the ultimate aim of which is to operate from coast to coast. In doing so they invite all organized groups of farmers to participate with them."

Despite the fact that the Union Oil Company started doing business just before the Great Depression, it made steady progress. In 1929 the wholesale sold only $309,891 worth of merchandise to 22 member cooperatives. By 1932 this figure had increased to $1,339,710, and three years later the company provided $2,994,510 worth of commodities to 258 cooperatives. Part of this remarkable record was due to Cowden's hard work and his success in selling the cooperative idea to farmers. Secondly, the Union Oil Company actually benefited from the depression because hard-pressed farmers were desperately looking for any means to cut costs and maintain their income.

Cowden also was careful to avoid the jealousies among farm organizations by keeping the Union Oil Company from being identified with any one of them. Moreover, he capitalized on the antimonopoly and big business sentiment so pronounced after 1929. But more than this, he held out the prospect of farmers owning their own company which would be able to supply all of their petroleum needs, as well as other commodities used in farm production. From the outset he talked about a national cooperative brand which would be sold by cooperative outlets throughout the nation. Cowden never thought in small terms. "Make no small plans," has always been his motto.

Was First to Consider Oil as a Farm Product

Cowden's greatest contribution to the cooperative movement was his idea of a completely integrated petroleum wholesale cooperative which would own, process, and distribute oil from the well to the consumer. He believed that farmers should own oil wells, manufacturing facilities, and distribution systems. He was probably the first cooperative leader to consider oil as a farm product. The highly integrated Consumers Cooperative Association stands as a monument to this vision.

The initial step in building an integrated cooperative oil business occurred when the Union Oil Company began compounding its own lubricating oils in July, 1929. Now the wholesale could supply local associations with cooperatively-produced brands. But Cowden was not satisfied with this development. He wanted to produce other commodities. Late in 1935 the wholesale, now called the Consumers Cooperative Association, began to manufacture grease, and early the next year CCA commenced to produce paint. While Cowden moved CCA into more and more manufacturing, the wholesale also handled an increasing list of commodities on a commission basis. These included lumber, groceries, and farm machinery all of which played an important part in the cost of farming.

During the early years of CCA's expansion, Cowden worked literally day and night. He wrote publicity, gave speeches, contacted local cooperatives in search of additional orders, and managed the growing business affairs of the wholesale. At the same time he made every effort to broaden cooperative influence throughout the nation. He was one of the founders of National Cooperatives which was organized late in 1932. In September, 1934, he attended the International Cooperative Alliance Congress in London. Cowden carried samples of CCA oil with him and within six months after his return home, CCA shipped its first oil to cooperatives in Estonia, France, and Scotland. This opened up in a small way an international trade in cooperatively-produced oil.

Outlines Plan for International Petroleum Co-op

At the ICA Paris Congress, in 1937, Cowden outlined a plan for an international cooperative petroleum association, saying:

> I am sure in my own mind that we are sincere; that we can and will work together; that the obstacles to our cooperation will grow less and less difficult as we work at the common task; that out of this meeting there shall come a new chapter in the history of international cooperation.

However, at that time nothing came of Cowden's proposal because of the clouds of war then overhanging the world.

Following World War II, Cowden again made his proposal to the Congress of the ICA and, as a result, the International Cooperative Petroleum Association was set up in 1947. The ICPA now has a membership of 38 national and regional cooperatives in 24 countries, and patronage refunds have been paid each year since its organization. Although pleased with its steady growth, Cowden looks forward to a greater future for the ICPA. In the summer of 1965 he said:

[The ICPA] has not reached the point in its development that we envisaged in Paris in 1937, but it has made substantial progress, is growing, and is of real service to thousands of people in many countries. It is needed more now than ever before.

In keeping with his idea of establishing a completely cooperative oil business, Cowden kept working to obtain a refinery. In 1938 he announced that CCA would construct a refinery which was soon located at Phillipsburg, Kans. After overcoming the serious problem of raising enough capital, the wholesale completed the plant and began refining operations in January, 1940. Construction of the Phillipsburg refinery against rather heavy odds was one of Cowden's greatest triumphs during his long career as a cooperative leader. While this was the first cooperatively-owned refinery in the United States, it was mainly important because it provided large earnings which financed expansion in other fields of endeavor.

During the 1940's, despite the war, CCA greatly expanded its manufacturing activities. The company bought other refineries, purchased two lumber mills, and began mixing commercial feeds. It also enlarged the grocery and farm machinery businesses. By 1950, CCA was furnishing patrons $62,428,460 worth of merchandise, of which about five-sixths was produced in the wholesale's own factories.

CCA next directed its efforts to building a nitrogen plant which was completed in 1954 at a cost of about $16 million. This was the largest capital outlay on a single project ever made by a farmer cooperative up to that time. Later in the decade, CCA enlarged its feed business so that when Cowden retired as president in 1961 the majority of CCA's business was in oil, fertilizer, and feeds. These were all highly successful activities.

However, not all of his schemes succeeded. Much to his distress, CCA had to discontinue the grocery, lumber, and farm machinery businesses which failed to earn savings or to be of much service to farmers. Nonetheless, in the 32 years under his management, the company expanded its annual business from $309,891 to $193,675,712. No other cooperative leader in America could point to such a gain in business volume.

Distinct Contribution Made in Fostering Co-op Education

Cooperative education is another area in which Cowden has made a distinct contribution. He spent a great deal of time and energy to further a better understanding of general cooperative principles and to train workers to manage and direct cooperative business enterprises. One of his early dreams was to establish a cooperative college. He never achieved this goal, but the CCA School of Cooperation in North Kansas City, which today serves as a training center for all kinds of cooperative activities, is a monument to his interest in this field.

After Cowden reached mandatory retirement in 1961 he became a consultant on cooperative activities for Nationwide Insurance Companies. He continues to serve as president of the International Petroleum Cooperative Association, and maintains his interest in the Agricultural Hall of Fame which he first proposed in 1957, and which was later built about 11 miles west of Kansas City, Kans. He also is a member of the board of directors of the Cooperative League of the USA, a member of the Central Committee of the International Cooperative Alliance, London, England, a member of the Board of Trustees of the International Cooperative Training Center, Madison, Wis., and Chairman of the Board of the International Cooperative Development Association, Washington, D. C.

Dominant Leader in ICDA

Two of Cowden's present interests are worthy of special mention: His work with the International Cooperative Development Association of which he has been the dominant leader; and his work with the International Cooperative Alliance as a member of its five-member Commission on Cooperative Principles.

The ICDA grew out of a resolution passed at the 1962 Biennial Congress of the Cooperative League of the USA. Its first objective is to provide a manpower bank of skills and talents in the cooperative field, from which the Agency for International Development (AID) and its contractors can draw for programs in developing countries. On January 15, 1965, ICDA was set up by a group of major American cooperatives, with an office in Washington, D. C. This organization encourages a strong people-to-people approach as a means of providing an impetus to developing economies and better living standards.

The Commission on Cooperative Principles, comprised of five members of whom Cowden was one, was set up at the 1963 Congress of the International Cooperative Alliance. The purpose was to develop and present cooperative principles in line with modern conditions throughout the world. Cowden has devoted his great energies and constructive talents to get the cooperation of all American cooperative leaders on this constructive task, and the report of the Commission is awaited with great interest by cooperators in all parts of the world.

Despite his many achievements, Cowden's most basic and significant contribution to the cooperative movement has been his concept of, and success in, applying the principles of business integration and efficiency to cooperative enterprise. He did not do this alone, but he provided the vision, leadership, courage, and even the daring needed to demonstrate that cooperatives could build great and successful businesses based on the principle of service.

Inspirational Educator

32

Verna Elsinger

by Beryle Stanton

How vividly do I remember the first time I saw her. It was at a
big meeting in Louisville where were gathered hundreds, yes, a
thousand stalwart men of the soil, growers of tobacco, demanding
a price for their crop. I had gone down with the marketing director
of the American Farm Bureau Federation, whose publicity man
I was. The meeting seemed to be getting rough . . .
Just when it seemed that we were bound to have a free-for-all I
noticed a pleasantly beautiful young girl wending her way back
and forth from group to group. Men who were mad would listen
to her reason. Leaders with set minds would let her bear and bring
a message of good will. These were pioneer days in cooperative
marketing—at least in these parts. Stubborn men who stripped
tobacco for nothing could be forgiven for paying no heed to the
niceties of cooperation. And here was a girl leading them to a real
understanding of each other. It was her life.

THIS WAS THE WAY Samuel R. Guard, Editor of *Breeders' Ga-
zette*, wrote of his first introduction to Verna Elsinger as he recalled it at the time of her death. He was telling of her work with
the Burley Tobacco Growers Cooperative Association, Louisville, as
Director of Community Organization—a position that involved what
we today would call member relations work with 108,000 members.

His comments appeared along with a number of others selected from
the hundreds received from national leaders, co-workers, and friends.
These appeared in a 17-page *In Memoriam* section of the *Ohio Farm
Bureau News* at the time of her death in 1933 at the age of 42.

Miss Elsinger was then Director of Organization for the Ohio Farm
Bureau and editor of its magazine. Murray Lincoln, retired President
of Nationwide Insurance, Columbus, Ohio, worked closely with Miss
Elsinger when he was Executive Secretary of the Ohio Farm Bureau.
In his book, *Vice President in Charge of Revolution,* he recalled how
Lee Palmer, President of the Bureau in 1928, had recommended that
she be hired as its educational director after he had heard her analyze

150

the reasons for the failure of the burley tobacco association. She gave as the major reason a lack of direct educational contact with the farmer and his family.

Mr. Lincoln wrote that although they didn't recognize the importance of the program headed by Verna Elsinger until much later, it was one of the two most significant changes in the Farm Bureau in the late 20's. The program she headed led them eventually to the establishment of the advisory councils, the backbone of the member support of cooperatives and improvements in Ohio agricultural environment and was widely copied in other areas.

Pioneered in Many Member Relations Activities

But much of what Verna Elsinger thought and said and did in her short life has been copied. She was a pioneer in member relations and educational work in farmer cooperatives. With her brilliant and analytical mind and her great spirit for humanity, she found many of the keys for helping people to help themselves through cooperatives.

The early issues of *American Cooperation,* the annual proceedings of the American Institute of Cooperation, present her thinking. At the 1929 Institute she gave a series of five lectures that are as sound today as then. And her lectures proved real forums on membership relations, where cooperative leaders from all across the nation listened and took part in the discussions.

She said in the first lecture of the series that in member relations work cooperatives have had to blaze a trail, been forced to work out their own methods, accumulate their own body of facts, and institute their own plans for experiment, research, and analysis.

She contrasted what had to be done in cooperative education with the fact that other aspects of the business operations of cooperatives could be patterned after what other businesses did.

She had also early come to the conclusion, she said, that a slower and more gradual process of education was more desirable and more permanent than an emotional appeal to crowd psychology.

Miss Elsinger herself did much original thinking in this field. She had had by that time her own baptism in cooperative failure. Instead of mourning over a lost cause to which she had devoted her time and energy unstintingly, she pinpointed the reasons for the failure and moved to forestall similar failures in other areas.

She had come to the burley tobacco association in April, 1923, after the board created a department of social services. This association— formed in 1921 to help tobacco growers do something about a price that had dropped from 30 cents to less than 13 cents a pound—had many prominent people behind it.

Robert W. Bingham—lawyer, judge, newspaper owner, and a man of great social conscience—had consulted with Bernard M. Baruch, then head of the War Industries Board, on the growers' problems. Aaron Sapiro—legal advisor to many western cooperatives who was then just emerging on the national scene as an advocate of cooperative marketing—had met with 50 prominent Kentuckians on the problem and worked with the group later on the marketing plan.

Miss Elsinger had become acquainted with Mr. Sapiro at the University of Cincinnati. In his contribution to the *In Memoriam* pages in the *Ohio Farm Bureau News,* Mr. Sapiro spoke of the soft charm of her voice, her stately dignity, her great spirit, and her marvelous directing touch.

He wrote also:

> Verna Elsinger taught men to organize . . . She advised on every type of problem—from taxes up to marketing . . . Verna Elsinger showed that there is no distinction between men and women when character, planning ability, courage, patient intelligence, and prophetic foresight are involved. There is no man living in America who saw more clearly the needs of the farmer, or who fought more bravely and persistently to bring a square deal to the farmer.

It was in Kentucky from 1923 until 1928 with the tobacco pooling experiment that she began to lay out long-lasting patterns for educational work with farm families.

Abe D. Waldauer, attorney for the association, wrote in April of 1966: "She did a magnificent job in awakening the spirit of cooperation with the farmers. Some of her pageants were works of art." At the time of her death, he had written, "It is given to few women to mold and shape movements, to impress a dynamic personality upon a large element of people. But such was the high privilege of Verna Elsinger."

Educational Activities Centered in Community Organizations

Her work in Kentucky involved a first few months of exploration, then a decision to focus the educational activities on community organizations. She provided material for meetings, worked with committees on programs, and developed local leadership talents. She set up special cooperative committees to maintain ties between community organizations and the burley association or any other cooperatives locally represented.

She stimulated discussions and informal debates to increase understanding of cooperatives; she helped stage dramatic, musical, and athletic events on a county basis with local cooperatives participating. It wasn't unusual for as many as 400 people to take part in pageants that depicted points of interest in history and development of agriculture.

It was out of this experience that she began to talk about cooperatives as "economic democracies," to point to the necessity for the involvement of the whole family as youth and women must be made to feel a part of a cooperative that is basically a matter of family interest, to stress the need for good understanding, and to point to the necessity of the "we" idea among members.

In her talks and lectures at the American Institute of Cooperation, she also outlined methods to use—all of them still in wide use by cooperatives today: printed materials, house organs or member publications as they are now more generally called, personal contacts, meetings, plant tours, and the like.

She stressed five requisites that make for good cooperative members —to have at their command current facts regarding the association, to gain an understanding of its broad relationships, to show a sense of responsibility for its success, to recognize their personal relationships with other members, and to achieve a vision of its purpose.

In one of her talks she referred to the outstanding work Vera McCrea was doing for the Dairymen's League Cooperative Association in New York to encourage the women of the member families to take an interest in cooperatives. She spoke of the reasons for this—woman's important share in the farming operation, her position as buyer and handler of much of the family budget, her influence over the views of the family, and her long-time perspective on what she sees as good for the human race.

Noted for Practical Approach with Vision, Imagination

Verna Elsinger was a practical person, as well as one with vision. She wrote, "We are not born to be good citizens any more than we are born to be good cooperators. We must learn how to participate in cooperative government; so must we learn how to participate in economic cooperation which is the economic counterpart of political cooperation."

She often spoke to the point on reasons for the failure of the tobacco association in Kentucky. She cited an opposition group that thought information to members unnecessary and unwise, meetings a potential source of trouble, and who took the laissez faire approach that difficulties would adjust themselves. But she stated that membership support must grow out of the hearts and minds of members, out of a deep-seated appreciation of the merits of cooperative action.

She did much more than her part to build this appreciation of the cooperative potential. In addition to her work in Kentucky and Ohio, she spoke often—and most effectively—at state and national gatherings of agricultural groups. These included the American Institute of Cooperation, American Farm Bureau, American Country Life Association, and National Council of Cooperative Marketing Association.

An article in the *Ohio Farm Bureau News* said, "She succeeded in her own gentle way in inspiring farm organization leaders everywhere with her own practicable philosophy of cooperation and Farm Bureau membership."

Verna Elsinger was a pioneer in another sense, that of showing what women of ability could do. She was one of the few women in a position of authority in cooperatives in her time, and one who showed that she could direct the work of as many as 11 men on her staff in Ohio.

Becomes Editor of Ohio Farm Bureau News

As Director of Organization for the State Farm Bureau organization she succeeded in keeping a well knit and loyal membership even in the worst of the depression. She had been also director of the *Ohio Farm Bureau News* and accepted its editorship, after much persuasion, just a month before she became ill with leukemia, and she died very shortly after her illness was diagnosed.

On reading back of all her accomplishments, both as a person and as an agricultural leader, I find it hard to distinguish between the two. Perhaps that's the way it should be in the cooperative context. For cooperatives have deep within them many of the same traits of good character—that is, they do if they are successful as cooperatives—as those that make for excellence in a person.

The words used to describe her in the *In Memoriam* pages illustrate this wide ranging recognition of her high stature as a person—words such as: a sane intelligence, extraordinary judgment, a gentle and sincere manner, a winsome and unusual personality, an indominatable spirit, a friendly persuasiveness, a great charm and versatility, a counselor and a friend who always had time for others' problems, a quick wit and sense of humor, a dynamic personality who radiated energy, a living presence who stimulated all. One writer described her office as a sanctuary where the great and near great could come for encouragement and for direction.

The hundreds of expressions of sympathy at the time of her death attested to both her character and her work. One came from Judge Bingham, then Ambassador to Great Britain, who stated that she shed light, with sympathy, with understanding, and with power.

Another came from Edward A. O'Neal, then President, American Farm Bureau Federation, who spoke of how she devoted her life to the economic and social betterment of rural people and the upbuilding of rural life and institutions.

Harry L. Hopkins, then Chairman of the Emergency Relief Administration for New York State, "Her integrity of purpose, her generosity, and her great capacity for leadership made her an outstanding person in the development of the cooperative movement in this country."

Perhaps a poem written at the time of her death by an Ohio woman, Mabel C. Satterthwaite, sums up what she meant to those who first heard of her work to improve cooperatives and agriculture. It said, in part:

Verna Elsinger meant life—
Energy and purpose, and a hopeful pressing forward,
A clear, keeneyed seeing of wonderful visions,
A warm, cordial hand clasp that was friendship,
A mellow voice, uttering eager, persuasive words
That carried you with them . . .

Verna Elsinger was indeed one of the best of the cooperative pioneers.

Ralph Henry Elsworth

by Anne L. Gessner

THE COMPREHENSIVE FEDERAL STATISTICS on agricultural cooperatives in the United States are largely a monument to the unflagging efforts of Ralph Henry Elsworth. Without his persistence and courageous determination to maintain the basic facts we would not have a continuing record of agricultural cooperative development for the first 40 years of this century.

Ralph Henry Elsworth was born in Whitehall, Mich., October 1, 1872. He received his B.A. degree in 1902, and his M.A. in 1904 from the University of Michigan.

During his college career he was successful in having a number of articles published. These included "How the University of Michigan Is Advertised," *Printers' Ink*, May 31, 1899; "Advertising and the Old Professor," *Fame*, July, 1903; and "The Salvation of the Country Weekly," *Newspaperdom*, April, 1903. After completing his academic work at the University of Michigan, he gave his full time for five years to newspaper work in Michigan.

In 1909 he became Chief Clerk of the Western Michigan Development Bureau, Traverse City, Mich. After two years in this position, he became Assistant Secretary of the Bureau and was responsible for arranging spraying demonstrations, bank exhibits of agricultural products, and lantern slide lectures. He handled two campaigns directed toward the improvement of the Michigan apple pack and assisted in filming a moving picture of the Michigan cherry industry.

During this period, he was instrumental in the organization of the Grand Traverse Fruit and Product Exchange at Traverse City. From March, 1915, to March, 1916, he was manager of this organization. He then accepted an appointment with the Federal Bureau of Markets. As Assistant to the Director of Markets in Michigan, he made extensive studies of the handling and marketing of agricultural products. After a few months in this position, he became the Field Agent in Marketing in Michigan for the Federal Bureau of Markets and the Michigan Agricultural College. In this capacity, he assisted in devising and installing accounting systems and in auditing the books of cooperative shipping associations.

Active in Early Development of Extension Service

Mr. Elsworth went to Washington in January, 1918, where, as Assistant, State Cooperation in Marketing, Federal Bureau of Markets, he was responsible for a study of the extension work in marketing and rural organization being conducted by the Bureau of Markets and the States Relations Service. He analyzed methods of procedure for extension work, studied problems of field agents in marketing in the field, and investigated and reported on the progress of extension work in order to coordinate the work being done by the Federal Bureau of Markets with that of the States Relations Service in the conduct of state cooperation in marketing work. He supervised the work of some 20 fieldmen in 33 states in the North and West. In this position, he did much toward the development and improvement of Extension Service.

In 1920, Acting in Charge, State Cooperation in Marketing, Federal Bureau of Markets, he was responsible for the project dealing with the collection and compilation of statistical and historical data relating to cooperative marketing. This work involved the supervision of a group of workers in Washington and in the field engaged in sending out numerous questionnaires and checking data collected.

The Federal Bureau of Markets consolidated with the Bureau of Crop Estimates in July, 1921, and became the Bureau of Markets and Crop Estimates. A Division of Cooperative Relations was established within the Bureau and research in cooperative problems became the main objective of the staff. Mr. Elsworth undertook at this time a nationwide survey of farmer cooperatives.

A year later the Bureau of Agricultural Economics came into being as a result of the consolidation of the Bureau of Markets and Crop Estimates and the Office of Farm Management and Farm Economics. A Division of Agricultural Cooperation was set up in the Bureau and work with cooperatives was expanded.

First Statistics on Cooperatives Published in 1923

Within the Division of Agricultural Cooperation, Mr. Elsworth was in charge of the project on statistics of cooperation. This Division collected annually for the first time figures on the number, memberships, and volumes of business of marketing and purchasing cooperatives. In January, 1923, the Division began the publication semi-monthly of a mimeographed circular with the title *Agricultural Cooperation.* Statistics on cooperatives collected under Mr. Elsworth's supervision were released in this publication and were of interest and value to agricultural editors, extension men, and other agricultural workers who depended on the Division of Agricultural Cooperation as their main source of information on agricultural cooperation in the United States.

With the passage of the Cooperative Marketing Act of 1926, the name of the Division was changed to the Division of Cooperative Marketing and the work was separated into distinct units. Mr. Elsworth was placed in charge of statistics and history. In this capacity, Mr. Elsworth was the author of a number of U.S.D.A. bulletins, circulars and other reports on agricultural cooperation. Many of these publications provided detailed statistics on farmers' marketing and purchasing cooperatives, usually on a nationwide basis. Particularly important among these publications was U.S.D.A. Bulletin 1302, *Development and Present Status of Farmers' Cooperative Business Organizations,* published in December, 1924, containing statistical material for the years 1921 through 1924. This was followed by U.S.D.A. Technical Bulletin 40, *Agricultural Cooperative Associations, Marketing and Purchasing, 1925,* published in 1928, which summarized and analyzed information obtained from more than 10,800 cooperative associations. Numerous other similar studies followed over the years. In 1943, Mr. Elsworth jointly authored *Farmers Cooperative Associations* with W. W. Cochrane (Farm Credit Administration Miscellaneous Circular No. 65, June 1943). This important publication dealt with reasons for discontinuance of almost 11,000 farmers' marketing and purchasing associations during the 1863–1939 period.

Mr. Elsworth saw the widespread need for improved statistics on a nationwide basis revealing the number of farmers' marketing, purchasing and related service associations, their number of memberships, and their dollar volume of business as indicators of these association's growth and importance in the agricultural economy. While the initiating moves for accumulation of such statistics were made before Mr. Elsworth's work began in this field, it was through his untiring and devoted efforts over many years that these statistics increasingly attained significance among cooperators, legislators, students, and others interested in the scope and character of farmer cooperatives.

In October 1929, the Division of Cooperative Marketing was transferred to the Federal Farm Board. Mr. Elsworth compiled *Statistics of Farmers' Selling and Buying Associations—United States, 1863–1931*, which was published in 1932 as Federal Farm Board Bulletin 9.

Collects Most Comprehensive Store of Co-op Information

With the organization of the Farm Credit Administration in May, 1933, the staff of the Division of Cooperative Marketing was attached to the newly organized Cooperative Bank Division and later became the Cooperative Research and Service Division. Within this Division, the History and Statistics Branch continued to assemble yearly information on farmer cooperatives under the direction of Mr. Elsworth. During this period, Mr. Elsworth accumulated a vast store of valuable data and information about cooperatives in the United States. It was the only comprehensive source of such information on a nationwide basis.

During the war years, to avoid possible damage in Washington, a large portion of the material Mr. Elsworth had assembled on cooperatives was microfilmed. The source information Mr. Elsworth was collecting each year on the operations of cooperatives was regarded as so important that arrangements were made for the continuation of the annual surveys even under wartime conditions.

In October, 1942, although Mr. Elsworth had reached the retirement age of 70, his reappointment for another year was approved in order that he might complete two studies on agricultural cooperation which only he could do. He retired a year later after a quarter of a century's service almost entirely in agricultural cooperation. Following his retirement, he continued to write articles and to work on publications in the cooperative field. He died in Regina, Saskatchewan, July 27, 1947, while on a vacation trip.

The vast store of historical information on farmer cooperatives assembled under the supervision of Mr. Elsworth and the many publications he authored continue to be used by students and research workers in agricultural cooperation.

Henry Ernest Erdman

by Joseph G. Knapp

O NE OF HIS MANY WELL-KNOWN STUDENTS—Dr. George
L. Mehren, formerly Head of the Giannini Foundation at the
University of California and now Assistant Secretary of the United
States Department of Agriculture—maintains that "Dr. Erdman has
influenced the development of agricultural cooperatives as much as
any other man in the nation through his research, his teaching, and
his counsel to agricultural marketing organizations." This was written
in a profile, "Henry E. Erdman—A Pioneer in Marketing," published
in the *Journal of Marketing*, April, 1960.

Henry Ernest Erdman was born on a South Dakota farm in Douglas
County on November 6, 1884. He attended a one-room school and
finished the eight grades in 1902. On account of the illness of his father
he then stayed home and ran the farm during the following winter.
Here he got his first experience with a cooperative of sorts—a horse-
breeding enterprise.

Just before his father became ill he had bought two fine black
3-year-old Percheron mares. While he was confined to the house a
promotor induced him to join with twenty-odd other farmers to buy
an imported French Percheron stallion. Some fine colts were produced
but management problems led to trouble in the "cooperative" in a
year or two so the stallion was sold. Perhaps it was well that this
cooperative "blew up" for it helped make Henry a cooperative realist.

After another year of farming Henry was able to take a year's
business course at Humboldt College in Iowa. He returned to the
farm where he remained until January, 1907, when he enrolled in
the preparatory course at South Dakota State College where he
obtained his B.S. degree in 1912 at the age of 28—several years older
than the average graduate. But he soon made up for the time lost
in his sporadic educational career.

During college years he spent summer vacations on the farm, excepting the summer of 1911 when he worked as buttermaker in a creamery. With this experience he obtained a job upon graduation as a research assistant in the Dairy Department of the college, with responsibility for running the college creamery. However, within a few months, he was appointed Deputy State Dairy Inspector. In this position he soon realized that the opportunities were limited and the duties not to his liking, so he resigned in August, 1914, to take graduate work at the University of Wisconsin in the new field of Farm Management. He was fortunate in obtaining a teaching and research assistantship the following year in the Department of Agricultural Economics under Professors Henry C. Taylor and Benjamin H. Hibbard, two men destined to become eminent in his field. Out of this work grew his interest in marketing and his first professional contribution, a bulletin written with B. H. Hibbard on the *Marketing of Wisconsin Milk* (Wisconsin Agr. Exp. State Bulletin 285, 1917).

"Marketing of Whole Milk" Was Ph.D. Study

In August, 1917, he went to Ohio State University as assistant professor of Rural Economics. There his work included teaching of courses in marketing and cooperation, a survey of the farmers' elevator movement, a survey of miscellaneous farmers organizations, talking at farmers' meetings—mostly about farmers elevator and livestock shipping associations, and (on weekends and evenings), completing his doctoral thesis. He obtained the Ph.D. Degree at Wisconsin in 1920. His thesis was published as his first book, *The Marketing of Whole Milk,* which long served as a model in agricultural marketing analysis.

In August, 1921, at the urgent request of Dr. Henry C. Taylor, he took leave from Ohio State to serve as Head of the Cost of Marketing Division of the Bureau of Markets at Washington, D. C. One year later, in June, 1922, he joined the staff of the University of California as Associate Professor of Rural Institutions where he was to give special attention to the field of agricultural cooperation. In 1925, he was made head of the new Division of Agricultural Economics. That year his recommended new curriculum for Agricultural Economics was adopted.

Here let us pause to realize that Henry Erdman was then 38 years of age and well trained for a distinguished future in agricultural economics. He came on the scene at the University of California when the work in agricultural economics was unsettled and in the process of reformulation. He found California a wonderful laboratory to explore his various interests in marketing and, particularly, the trade channels for California produce; and within a few years he was serving as head of a new department of agricultural economics.

Developed Idea of Commodity Studies

While with the Bureau in early 1922 Henry had become interested in the Agricultural Outlook approach Dr. Henry C. Taylor and others were developing as a basis for adjusting farm production to market needs. In California, Erdman soon saw that growers of numerous specialized crops for distant markets needed not only outlook data but also needed commodity studies of supply and demand in competing markets. Dr. Taylor credits him with development of the idea of commodity studies. As early as April, 1924, his "Program for the Division of Rural Institutions" had included plans for study of "price movements, relations of agriculture to the business cycle, and methods of forecasting prices." By July 1, 1925, three men had been assigned to such work.

The growing appreciation of the importance of agricultural studies was recognized in 1928 by the establishment of the Giannini Foundation of Agricultural Economics by a gift from A. P. Giannini who had risen from market gardener to banking giant. The old Division of Agricultural Economics became part of a larger, more comprehensive unit.

The Foundation was to concern itself with "the great field of Agricultural Economics" as related to such aspects as "the economic consequences" of improvements in production, overproduction arising from unusually favorable seasons, the disposition of farm products and, in fact, any questions which concern the living conditions of the individual farmer and members of his family. [Paraphrased from "Provisions of the Gift," Addresses Delivered on the Occasion of the Dedication of Giannini Hall, October 21, 1930.]

Co-op Possibilities, Limitations Analyzed

Erdman's work with cooperatives enabled him to see both their possibilities and limitations. His bulletin, *Possibilities and Limitations of Cooperative Marketing* (Cal. Exp. Station Bulletin 298, 1925), helped to give perspective at a time when more emotion than thought was being devoted to this subject. It was his contention that the full possibilities inherent in cooperative marketing were inadequately appreciated while many confused limitations with possibilities.

Henry C. and Anne Dewees Taylor in *The Story of Agricultural Economics* say with reference to this study:

Erdman's positive statements regarding the limitations of cooperatives are significant: 'Cooperative associations cannot arbitrarily
fix prices . . . Cooperative organizations cannot *eliminate the
middleman;* cooperative marketing cannot cut costs greatly.' It
took courage to make these statements in the middle 1920's. Certain agitators of that day who led farmers to believe that cooperatives could wield a large influence on prices were far more popular
with the farmers than the agricultural economist who tried to tell
them the whole truth.

In 1927, Erdman and his former student, H. R. Wellman, made
another significant contribution to cooperative literature in California
Agr. Exp. Station Bulletin 432, *Some Economic Problems Involved in
the Pooling of Fruit.* This was the first comprehensive analysis of pooling and it has long served as a guide in this important phase of
cooperative operation.

Erdman's interest in the way agricultural products were marketed
resulted in the publication of his book, *American Produce Markets,*
issued in 1928. This was the first detailed analysis of agricultural
marketing from the viewpoint of the "produce market," written to show
its evolutionary and gradual development. Dr. Edwin G. Nourse, in the
Editor's Foreword, pointed out that the method of treatment gave
"the whole book a dynamic rather than a static character."

His early work with California cooperatives paved the way for the
later more detailed cooperative studies of E. A. Stokdyk and James
Tinley, and many others. Most of the later studies of cooperatives made
at the University of California were amplifications of this pioneering
effort.

Erdman's positive thinking on the role of cooperatives in agriculture
is reflected in his report: *The California Fruit Growers Exchange: An
Example of Cooperation in the Segregation of Conflicting Interests*
(American Council of Pacific Relations, New York, 1933). This relatively unknown study was a significant analysis of the political structure
of a large farmer cooperative association.

Throughout his professional career Erdman has shown a natural taste
for history, for he has wanted to know how things came to be what
they are. This historical bent was reflected in his early studies in
Wisconsin and Ohio and in his book on *The Marketing of Whole Milk.*
In California he has been continuously interested in how California
cooperatives and California cooperative practices came into being
and developed. At one time he hoped to make or have made a whole
series of studies for various kinds of California cooperatives, but only
one was completed, *History of Cooperation in the Marketing of Cali-*

fornia Fresh Deciduous Fruits (University of California, Agricultural
Experiment Station Bulletin 557, 1933).

Cooperative Financing Long an Absorbing Interest

One of Dr. Erdman's absorbing interests has been the problems of
cooperative financing, and he has written many papers and bulletins
dealing with this subject. His latest contribution in this area is his
book (with Grace Larsen), *Revolving Finance in Agricultural Cooperatives,* published in 1965. This book provides the most complete history
available on revolving fund financing, along with a valuable analysis
of the advantages and problems inherent in this distinctively cooperative method of financing.

It is significant that one of his former students, who is now Governor
of the Farm Credit Administration, Robert B. Tootell, in a recent conversation with me, credits Dr. Erdman with being one of the first to
study in detail the financing of farmer cooperatives, and holds that
"None has made a greater contribution to this important subject."

Dr. Erdman has been a teacher throughout his life, and many well-
known persons have come under his influence in the classroom or in
personal discussions. His enthusiasm was and still is contagious, for he
gave his students some idea of the romance involved in learning and
research. Moreover, he gave them a standard of intellectual discipline
that they will never forget. It is of interest here that George Mehren
closed the essay quoted at the beginning of this sketch with these
sentences:

> His greatest contribution—possibly—is to a large number of stu-
> dents who have trained under him. Without exception, these
> students have carried respect and affection for Henry Erdman as
> man and scholar.

Although Dr. Erdman is recognized as a Pioneer in the field of
agricultural marketing, his primary interest has been the study of
agricultural and other forms of cooperative enterprise. Since his retirement some 10 years ago he has continued to work as industriously as
ever as Professor Emeritus in his chosen field, and within a few years
we may have the capstone of his career—a book on the history of agricultural cooperative enterprise in California, being written with his
colleague, Grace Larsen.

Edward A. Filene

by Tom J. Hefter

EDWARD A. FILENE, the renowned merchant from Boston, contributed significantly to the advancement of cooperative business enterprise in the United States. With advancing age, his interest in cooperative business broadened and deepened.

Filene was born in Salem, Mass., in 1860. His father was a merchant who finally centered his interests in Boston. Edward wanted to attend Harvard University but his father worked so hard establishing the Boston Store that he suffered a nervous breakdown, and so Edward was drawn into the management of the store instead. He immediately began to introduce new ideas, such as the automatic bargain basement —an innovation that made the Filene store well known as a leader in merchandising methods.

Filene's life was marked deeply by the long influence of developing his occupation as a merchant. After many successful years, he was convinced that the only way for business to better itself was to move "to the liberal position."

Indeed, the ordinary merchant assumed—and still does—that when a store or other business has made a profit, it has justified its existence. Filene denied this. To really justify its existence, he felt "the store must not merely make a profit, but must do it by expediting satisfaction of human wants."

Over 60 years ago, this kind of thinking was radical if not unheard of. Today, most American businessmen readily see the wisdom of such thinking, though they may differ to its degree.

The Boston businessman rooted most of his ideas on solving economic, social, and political problems from the standpoint of businesses as social institutions and what they could contribute to the community, the nation, and the world.

Indeed, Filene's interest in aiming his own family store toward the fuller development of a social institution eventually broke him entirely away from the family business and enabled him to turn to the development of his growing cooperative ideas.

Filene, who against his wishes was called by some as a sort of prophet, had a wide range of interests and ideas. Although he made his mark in the business world, he will live in the minds of others for his ideas, his forecast of things to come, and the wide swing of his interests, which he supported generously.

Was Far Ahead of His Time in Social, Economic Plans

While we today think nothing of discussing cooperative health clinics, credit unions, consumer cooperatives, cooperative industrial projects, chain stores, the war against poverty, and leisure-time problems, Filene discussed them publicly when such thoughts were 60 years ahead of their time and unheard of by even the most intellectual.

Among other "far out" ideas Filene attempted to bring to the attention of the world were his ideas on mass production and mass consumption. He felt strongly that for business to survive, it would have to increase volume, workers' salaries, and pass every benefit it could along to the consumer.

His reasoning for the support of the credit union idea was that through credit unions the masses of citizens would have credit readily available to them. This would enable them to purchase the numerous mass-produced items and services that were pouring out of America's ingenious production plants and business would profit as a result. He reasoned that the credit union was the necessary credit link between mass production and mass consumption.

Besides contributing nearly $1 million to the establishment of credit unions in the United States, he also founded the Edward A. Filene Good Will Fund, Inc., the Twentieth Century Fund, Inc., and the Consumer Distribution Cooperative (CDC).

The Twentieth Century Fund was established in 1919 to conduct research and educational activities on sociological and economic problems. Its major field is economics.

The Edward A. Filene Goodwill Fund was founded to "further the welfare of mankind through improvement of health conditions for workers and their dependents." The Fund also conducts research on the causes and elimination of poverty, the improvement of medical care for the masses, and the operations of consumer cooperatives.

The Goodwill Fund activities led to the creation of the Consumer Distribution Cooperative (CDC), designed as a "nationwide league of cooperative department stores."

Filene's hopes for the success of the CDC were most high, though unfortunately it later failed. The primary purpose of the CDC was to supply a chain of department stores and bring about an anticipated reduction of 10 per cent in the cost of living through "cooperative coordination."

In one of his last speeches, Filene declared that the cost of savings anticipated through the CDC operation would "open new purchase power and enrich our country." The CDC was to supply all commodities and products, including rentals and undertaking services.

"In fact, every line of business will feel the pinch of competition which our cooperative movement will be prepared to give. The cooperative idea offers a real life preserver to small merchants who must otherwise go out of business in the face of competition of larger chains and department stores," he said.

The CDC was eventually to go down in failure as had Filene's earlier attempts at the Boston store, where he encouraged the employees to take over its operation through the Filene Cooperative Association (FCA). Filene's weakness was his inability to judge people and their talents and it is said that FCA failed because the employees failed to shoulder responsibility adequately.

Filene's ideas on economics, sociology, politics and related subjects were known nationwide, for he traveled and spoke extensively. The ideas he espoused were bitterly attacked by enemies and friends as well.

Some of his friends were puzzled by what seemed to them a sudden interest in consumer cooperation after a lifetime devoted to private business. In a speech given in New York City in 1936, he elaborated on this point by explaining that he had always dealt with consumer goods and therefore had to have the consumer cooperation.

"We business men believe in publicity. We believe that what we are doing is in the public interest, which is only another way of saying that the public has an interest in our business.

"Unanimously, we business men, no matter what we have to sell, are interested in securing the cooperation of our buying public," he said in defense of the philosophical ideas he held.

It was his contention that "far from being opposed to consumer cooperation, every modern American businessman is strongly in favor of it. He not only wants his customers to cooperate with him, but he wants to cooperate with his customers. He knows he can't even continue in business if he doesn't."

Crusades for Credit Unions on Return from India

"The credit union is the one thing in my life with which I am entirely satisfied," Filene told Roy F. Bergengren, managing director of the Credit Union National Association, (CUNA), before setting sail for Europe in 1937.

Filene's interest in credit unions began in 1907 when he was in India as part of a worldwide trip. There he chanced to meet a British civil servant who had left a high position with government to devote his life to an idea—the credit union idea. The deep devotion of this man to an idea interested Filene and they traveled together on an inspection tour of credit societies, which had evolved in India. Needless to say, Filene was impressed by the idea of supplying credit on a cooperative basis.

Several years later, Filene whose interest in cooperative credit had continued to develop, hired Roy F. Bergengren and established the Credit Union Extension Bureau in Boston, Mass. Bergengren traveled nationwide to find and train credit union leadership, organize and develop credit unions, get the proper laws enacted, and to establish a national association.

Filene's generosity in supporting the Credit Union Extension Bureau kept it in existence from 1921 until the Credit Union National Association was chartered in 1934.

Though many credit union leaders knew of Filene's generous support of the credit union idea in the United States, it was not until the Credit Union National Association (CUNA) began financing itself that its leaders fully understood the magnitude of Filene's generosity in helping credit unions and leagues become established throughout the country.

Filene's business contemporaries could not understand his expenditures for credit union work or the modest way he lived but he was well satisfied with the $1 million expenditure to make credit union programs possible.

He saw in the credit union an opportunity to create a democratic economy in which the people would have cooperative control over their own wealth. Roy F. Bergengren writes in *Crusade* that "it was the potentially broad application of the credit union which most intrigued him. Here was a chance to get at the business of mass-producing a democratic economy."

More than money, Filene gave sustained devotion to an ideal, a great love for the people he was trying to serve, as well as inspiration, writing, speaking, and innumerable valuable contacts.

In *Crusade,* Bergengren writes of Filene: "Within the credit union movement, increasing steadily in millions of members, he was really loved. He will be enshrined in their affections unto many generations yet unborn. He in turn had a deep, sincere, abiding love for the credit union membership and was proud of them."

Saw Credit Unions as People's Way to Mobilize Savings

Filene's devotion to the credit union is easily understood when we evaluate his other primary interests. The credit union was to enable the people to mobilize their savings in such fashion that they could greatly increase their power of mass consumption. He hated usury because it was uneconomic. He wanted it abolished and knew that this could only be done by creating normal credit for the people. He saw the credit union as one tangible thing which worked in with his idealism.

To the critics who could not understand his support of credit unions, he said:

> I appropriate to the credit union just about what it costs a rich man to own and enjoy a steam yacht. I do not like steam yachts. I do like credit unions. Why should anyone be surprised because I spend my money the way that gives me the most pleasure and satisfaction?

While Filene was most satisfied with credit unions, he personally concentrated on other types of consumer cooperatives and their development, since he felt the credit union problems were being overcome and therefore demanded less of his personal time. Of course, he devoted many, many trips for the purpose of speaking to credit union groups but the basic organizational credit union work he left to Roy F. Bergengren and the many credit union leaders Bergengren had surfaced throughout the nation.

Filene looked upon conformity as "intellectual death." Perhaps this explains, in part, his penchant for expounding idea upon idea that was in the "far out" camp.

Well before the turn of the century Mr. Filene had already convinced himself that "the basic political problem in modern America is the problem of how the whole American people can manage to live well."

Bold Pioneer on Short Work-Week

With a firm belief that Americans would some day be living in a world abundant with leisure, Mr. Filene talked boldly about the three-hour day for wage-earners. In principle, he disapproved of the eight-hour day as being too conservative.

The Boston merchant's concern for bringing advantages within the grasp of people at all economic levels was most intense. Unheard of at the time was his early insistence on cheap transportation to Europe to bring travel abroad into the reach of middle-income people.

The lifelong bachelor was interested in the "conquest of poverty," another area of ideas in which he was well ahead of his time.

Filene, the practical man who measured all on the basis of facts, understood that in order to attack poverty, stop-gap measures were useless, and that charity or dole was an admission of defeat.

In the middle of the Great Depression, he said that things would improve when businessmen got over their traditional "age of scarcity thinking and adapt themselves to the age of plenty."

He firmly believed that general prosperity would make it more imperative to solve the problems of those who did not share in that prosperity.

His philosophy on poverty was to get to its causes and eradicate them. Usurious loan rates to the poor were continuing factors of perpetual poverty, which Filene acknowledged in his lifelong enthusiasm for the credit union idea.

He opposed individual hand-outs and mass give-away programs as firmly as he realized the futility of make-work projects in building a sound economy. "Give the workers a *buying*, not a *living* wage," he used to say.

In an era of pervasive poverty, he could anticipate the time when we would speak of "pockets" of poverty. Prosperity was still around the corner in 1937 when he died, but Filene seemed to realize that the standard of living within the United States would continue to rise with the exception of certain groups. His concern was not limited to a temporary situation of a depression. He was looking ahead. He had the vision to discern a prosperous country with increasing leisure.

"More Important to Be Informed than Sentimental"

Both businessmen and cooperative leaders can take a chapter from Edward A. Filene's concern for the facts. He was not afraid to invest in fact-finding. He was convinced that it was more important to be informed than sentimental. He was ready to experiment when his sound judgment advised it. He invested in "blue chip" ideas only—in those ideas which he believed to be sound and fruitful.

Filene's experience in merchandising made him conscious of mass consumption and in putting money in the hands of many. You might say he had an interest in seeing that people had purchasing power. Certainly, this is true. But long after Edward A. Filene had any managerial interest in the famous Filene department store of Boston, he continued to be occupied with problems of wealth and its just distribution.

A man who spent hundreds of thousands of dollars on peace prizes in Europe and a million dollars in promoting credit unions in the United States was not simply trying to guarantee a clientele for his store.

His encouragement of credit unions, cooperatives, his attack on poverty, his advocation of old age benefits and the wide scope of his other activities were part of a total effort to make America's abundance available to all.

It is difficult to tally up the totality of the contributions that Edward A. Filene made to the advancement of cooperative business enterprise in the United States. It would do little good to tally up the monetary contributions he extended to his numerous funds and special projects. At best, it can be said that the chief contribution of this diligent merchant-philosopher-philanthropist lies in the conceptual ideas he developed, expounded publicly, and supported with sound statistics.

However we as individuals regard the man Edward A. Filene and his ideas, on several main points we can agree: He foresaw many of America's trends and problems accurately, he boosted the cooperative idea a great deal, and he certainly gave credit unions in America outstanding support.

Kelsey B. Gardner

by Joseph G. Knapp

F OR OVER 40 YEARS Kelsey B. Gardner has been helping to fashion the structure and improve the business performance of agricultural cooperatives in the United States and throughout the world. His work as a public servant in the United States Department of Agriculture has brought great respect to the cooperative form of business enterprise.

Kelsey was born at Leonardsville, Kans. on July 6, 1892. Although he was not farm reared he early came to know farm life and problems through visits to the farms of his grandfather and uncles.

As a boy he learned much about the retail grocery business through working in his father's store in North Topeka, and this gave him an interest in business operations that has persisted throughout his life. As a boy he was active in church and Sunday school and interested in sports—especially basketball.

After a year at Washburn College in Topeka he became restless and decided to become a photographer. Following a year at the Illinois College of Photography in Southern Illinois, he was on the photographic staff of the University of Illinois during 1914-16. While this work was of absorbing interest, Kelsey had come to realize that a college education was essential to his ambitions. So he returned to Washburn to resume his college work.

With the outbreak of World War I, Kelsey joined the Washburn College Ambulance Company which was soon called into service at Camp Pike, Ark. Shortly thereafter he was sent to Langley Field, Va., for training in aerial photography. After service as an instructor in the U. S. Army Aerial Photographic School at Kodak Park, Rochester, N. Y., he was commissioned as a 2nd Lieutenant in the U. S. Army Air Service. In late September he became commanding officer of a photographic section and was sent to England just as the war was coming to a close.

Kelsey then resumed his work at Washburn College where he graduated in June, 1920. By this time his ambitions were settled. He had become attracted by the program of the Harvard University Graduate School of Business Administration, which was rapidly gaining national renown as a center for professional business training.

Kelsey found the atmosphere of the Harvard Graduate School of Business Administration most congenial. He liked both his professors and his fellow students, many of whom were mature persons like William A. Schoenfeld who was already trained as an agricultural economist at the University of Wisconsin under Dr. Henry C. Taylor. When Taylor became Chief of the newly-formed Bureau of Agricultural Economics in 1922 he invited Schoenfeld to serve as Assistant Chief upon completion of his work at Harvard, and encouraged him to recruit prospective employees from the Graduate School. Among those who were attracted was Kelsey B. Gardner who, after entering government service, was assigned to the Cost of Marketing Division under A. V. Swarthout. One of his first jobs was to prepare a comparative study of margins on bread for the 1923 report on the wheat situation by Secretary of Agriculture Henry C. Wallace.

First B.A.E. Assignment Led to Studies of Co-ops

Kelsey's first assignment led him directly to cooperatives—a form of business he had never heard of until he got acquainted at Harvard with Schoenfeld who was carrying on a part-time study of an onion-growers' cooperative for the Massachusetts State Department of Agriculture. Soon after he came to the B.A.E. he was sent to the Pacific Coast to study costs and operations of fruit packing cooperatives. This introduced him to the practical problems of these associations at a time when there were intense counter-currents within the cooperatives on how the job of marketing should be done.

When the Cooperative Marketing Division was set up in 1926 under Chris L. Christensen, Kelsey decided to cast his lot with it and he joined the Division to make business analyses of cooperatives. One of his first jobs was to study the joint use of a sales organization by two cooperatives—the California Fruit Growers Exchange (now Sunkist Growers, Inc.) which marketed citrus products; and the California Fruit Exchange, which marketed deciduous crops. The U.S.D.A. circular issued in 1927 giving the results of this study was Kelsey's first publication dealing with agricultural cooperatives.

His next study was *A Business Analysis of the Producers' Live Stock*

Commission Association of the National Stock Yards, Inc., issued as a U.S.D.A. circular in 1929.

When the Cooperative Marketing Division was transferred to the Federal Farm Board, in 1929, Kelsey was made Economist in Charge of the Fruit and Vegetable Section. In this capacity he was responsible for supervising and directing the organization of fruit and vegetable cooperatives, and for developing loan analyses and making recommendations to the Board on specific loan applications.

With the termination of the Federal Farm Board in 1933, the work under the Cooperative Marketing Act of 1926 for cooperatives was taken over by the Cooperative Division of the Farm Credit Administration. Kelsey then served in the Fruit and Vegetable Section directing and conducting studies and advisory service for fruit and vegetable marketing associations. During this period he made a very comprehensive study of *Terminal Fruit Auctions as Marketing Agencies for Farmers' Cooperatives,* which was issued in bulletin form.

Becomes Head of New Section on Business Organizations

In 1939 a Business Administration Section was set up in the Cooperative Research and Service Division to focus attention on business organizational and operational problems common to all cooperatives. Kelsey was made head of this new section which became the Business Administration Branch when the Farmer Cooperative Service became an independent agency in the U. S. Department of Agriculture in 1953.

This position recognized Kelsey's fine training and exceptional abilities in business analysis, and it enabled him to extend his competence to the whole range of business problems associated with all types of agricultural cooperatives. During the war period he served on the Planning Committee which was set up to help the Acting Chief direct the activities of the Division. In the period of readjustment following the war he helped re-establish the program of the Division to meet the challenging problems of postwar adjustment.

During this period, the American Institute of Cooperation, in cooperation with the American Institute of Accountants, held some 75 clinics throughout the United States to help cooperative managements adjust to problems of member and public relations and meet the adverse publicity being generated by the National Tax Equality Association with regard to federal income tax status. The clinics were based on dignified, thoughtful, authoritative presentations of problems and their possible solutions. They performed a valuable function in subjecting cooperative problems to a process of rational analysis which has had a lasting influence on cooperative operations.

Kelsey B. Gardner served as one of the three panel leaders on business procedures, along with Dr. Raymond W. Miller, President of the American Institute of Cooperation, who dealt with public relations problems, and Walter L. Bradley, who represented the American Institute of Accountants on accounting and income tax problems. Altogether, these clinics reached 10,000 cooperative leaders in every part of the nation—including directors, managers, accountants, legal counsels, and other key employees, along with representatives of the Banks for Cooperatives, the federal and state Extension Services and college and vocational teachers.

Problems relating to cooperative income taxation had grown in importance as federal income taxes were increased during World War II. At the request of the National Council of Farmer Cooperatives in 1943, Kelsey prepared a brief report on the federal income tax status of cooperatives. This report was given wide circulation and contributed to a better understanding by cooperatives and others of their responsibilities and status under the Internal Revenue Code.

Makes Outstanding Contribution to Facts About Tax Status

Following this report Kelsey worked closely with representatives of the Treasury Department on the development of the first information forms for farmer cooperatives. This liaison aided in the development in 1947 of a report of the Treasury Department on the status of farmer cooperatives under the federal income tax statutes. This report was accepted widely as an accurate and fair statement, and it helped meet a barrage of confusing and misleading statements made by those who were opposed to cooperatives.

In 1954, the Farmer Cooperative Service undertook a comprehensive study of the financial status and procedures of cooperatives under Kelsey's direction. This furnished information that helped meet the unfounded assertions that cooperatives were escaping enormous amounts of income tax payments. Facts provided by this study and presented to the Congress helped cooperatives obtain in 1962 a revision of the income tax laws based on fact rather than on fancy.

Ever since the F.A.O. was formed in the middle 40's, Farmer Cooperative Service has helped on international programs designed to improve the economies of the developing nations. This work came largely under Kelsey's direction and leadership and he gave it unflagging interest. In the past 15 years it is estimated that the Farmer

Cooperative Service has helped some 3,000 foreign visitors from almost 100 countries obtain information on American cooperative forms of organization and practices. This has been a strong force for international good will, and many countries have been assisted through these contacts in strengthening their home economies on a democratic basis.

Participates in Six International Conferences

In connection with these programs Gardner has participated as United States representative at six international conferences. The first was a technical meeting on cooperatives held for the Caribbean area in 1951 at Trinidad under the sponsorship of the Caribbean Commission and the Food and Agriculture Organization. This was followed by a second and similar conference in British Guiana, in 1956, at Georgetown. In 1957, he served as adviser on cooperatives to the U. S. Delegation at the West Indian Conference held at Willemstad, Curacao, N.A. In 1958, he served as United States observer at the Technical Meeting on Cooperatives at Port Moresby, Territory of Papua and New Guinea, sponsored by the South Pacific Commission. He also participated as U. S. observer at a second technical conference on cooperatives, held at Noumea, New Calendonia in 1961, under sponsorship of the South Pacific Commission. He took part as a member of the U. S. Delegation to the Joint Conferences on Agriculture held at Mexico City in 1960 by the Organization of American States and the Food and Agriculture Organization.

Through these various conferences Kelsey has gained international recognition for his wealth of information on cooperative business organizations and procedures, and for his sympathetic understanding of cooperative problems in developing countries.

Becomes Director of FCS Management Services

When the Farmer Cooperative Service was established in 1953, its work was placed under three major divisions and one of these was the Management Services Division. It supervises the work of four branches: Business Administration, Transportation, Membership Relations, and History and Statistics. Kelsey B. Gardner was made Director of this Division and he continued in this position until his retirement in 1962 at age 70. While Director of this Division, Kelsey served informally as deputy to the Administrator, so during this period he had both general and specific responsibilities.

As Director of the Division, Kelsey was in position to fully employ his great abilities, fine training, and very practical experience. His high standards made him, in effect, the quality control officer of the Farmer Cooperative Service. The initials "K.B.G." on a manuscript indicated that it was ready for publication.

As Division Director, Kelsey worked to bring his branches to a high state of professional efficiency. The work of the History and Statistics Branch was greatly strengthened. The membership educational program of the Membership Relations Branch was broadened and deepened. The work in the Transportation Branch was amplified through greater emphasis on research, and the Business Administration Branch undertook highly effective studies in the areas of finance, taxation, and management. While Kelsey maintained an active interest in improving the work of all of these branches, he always realized that the Farmer Cooperative Service was the sum of all of its divisions and branches, and he gave his help wherever it could be of use throughout the Service.

Kelsey Gardner was deeply interested in the training of personnel to carry on the professional traditions of the Service. When he retired he had the satisfaction of having many of his younger colleagues pay tribute to him for his guidance, assistance, and inspiration.

Since his retirement Kelsey has come back into harness on two occasions. In 1963 and 1964 he participated with Dr. E. G. Nourse, as an economic consultant, in two plywood association cases in Oregon and Washington. This task called for a great amount of research which helped establish the fact that the associations were cooperative in character. Kelsey feels that the favorable decision of the federal courts on these precedent-setting cooperative tax cases was a high-water mark in his career.

His most recent cooperative work came in the spring of 1965 when he served for several weeks at the International Cooperative Training Center at the University of Wisconsin as instructor on financial management and cooperative structure.

Kelsey received many honors during his long government career. In 1948, the American Institute of Cooperation presented him with its Distinguished Service Award. In 1955, he received a Merit Citation from the National Civil Service League; and in 1958, he received the Distinguished Service Award from the Washburn University Alumni Association for "Distinguished Service in Community, State and Nation."

Few people have had a richer life or have contributed so much to the advancement of cooperation—both as an ideal and as a form of business.

William Mountjoy Garrard

by Charles R. Sayre

WILLIAM MOUNTJOY GARRARD IV was born in Lawrenceville, Ill., August 25, 1881. The posthumous son of a newspaper editor, he was reared in Greenwood, Miss., where his mother, Zilpha Barrett Garrard, made her home with a brother. In 1908, he was married to Mabelle Mosely Smith. They had six children. He received a B.S. degree from Mississippi State College.

Early successes of his own cotton merchandising and export business attracted the originating directors of Staple Cotton Cooperative Association to Will Garrard. They beat a path to his door and urged him to take over as General Manager six short months after the first organizational meeting.

A winsome personality, courage, perseverance, depth of character, and unusual trading abilities were the tools this builder-pioneer brought to cooperative marketing in the Mississippi Delta.

From his basic blend of ideas emanated the rules of the new road that would help to carve an effective and lasting approach out of the shapeless flow of farmers' cotton to the spinner. "Selling cotton to the spinner depends upon something definite and direct; it depends upon uniform delivery of a standardized product." In 1921, Staple Cotton Association set up the first set of standard types for staples (length in cotton language). This served as a beckoner to all interested in repeatable quality in cotton as a raw material. It is a main reason why Staplcotn has made the market for cotton in the Mississippi Delta for more than 44 years—selling more than 50 percent of the crop. It was a main reason why Greenwood, Miss., headquarters of Staplcotn, could boast of the largest inland market for long staple cotton.

The Association was set up principally to sell and ship the cotton to the mill trade direct. Large volume was essential. This would enable the cooperative to out-ship the private firm with large stock from which to select shipments with dependable uniformity. Maintenance of uniform quality is difficult in cotton where each five hundred pound bale goes as a unit from the gin to the mill. Cotton cannot easily be blended, as with grain.

At the beginning, the originating group were unquestionable top leaders in the area. Their personal underwriting—10 of them at $1000 each—attracted other key members in neighboring communities. Garrard's personal magnetism was a major factor in membership build-up. This is described by a long-time member-director:

> Any association member who came to ask advice cherishes the memory of a smile which bespoke of the joy of living—a sparkle of eye that indicated uprightness, honesty of purpose, confidence, and a lack of fear both physical and mental, a directness of nature, and a warmth of personality which endeared him to all.

Brought Dynamic Principles to Cotton Marketing

Other main tenets of Garrard's early approaches in cooperative cotton marketing were:

> "Orderliness and patience is a key to cooperative selling."
> "Hold the title to the cotton until we get the money."
> "Don't let good customers get off your books."
> "Share accurate information with your customers."
> "If a problem is too technical to tell the Board, it's too technical to tackle."
> "There is nothing so secret we will not tell a member."

Statements reflecting Mr. Garrard's attitudes include these:

> In starting a cooperative organization, many of us think all we have to do is to get together and say we have a lot of cotton and the people will break their necks to buy it. It is not so. A cooperative business must be built up just like any other business. It must be built upon sound, economic lines. Just having a lot of cotton from the membership is not going to get you a lot of customers. Customers come over a period of years and only after you have rendered a definite, concrete service.

> I do not know how far it goes in other lines of business, but you do not have a Chinaman's chance to sell staple cotton unless you know your customer. Knowing your customer is a matter of fundamental importance. Associations that have not sold any quantity of cotton to the mill trade will do well to work hard along this line, for it will bring greater results than any other one thing.

You have got to keep in contact with your customer. The slightest change in kind and character of the goods he produces will make necessary a change in the raw product, and unless you keep in touch with your customer you are going to lose business. You are going to lose, because after all it is the man on the spot that takes advantage of the slight change. Suppose there are a dozen bids on any thing, and they are about the same. The fellow that offers the slightest advantage gets the order.

We have a selling agency or an agent of some kind or other in each market. Such breadth of outlet not only gives a place where every variety can be sold, but where the highest price is being paid from day to day. It is up to you to sell every known variety of cotton for more money than anybody else can. That is all your members expect, and it is up to you to assure them you do it.

Breadth of outlet is a point that many people have overlooked. If you are to get a maximum price you have to get broader outlets. If you get all you should like to have, you have to keep awake. You can't get too many legitimate outlets for your cotton.

At times it is necessary, proper, logical, and advisable to take a slightly lower price from a dependable customer than the actual market price, in order to retain his business. I think in the long run you make money. There are times when we take business from some customers who are good buyers, at one-quarter to one-half cent less than we have sold cotton, but they always give us an opportunity at their orders, and they are big customers.

During the first three years of operations—1921, 1922, and 1923— the Association offered only a pooling program for marketing the members' cotton. This method of marketing provided that all classes of like grade and staple be pooled, offered, and sold together, with participating members in the pool sharing ratably in the pool proceeds. There were two options, however:

Option 1 provided that the members would receive no advance at the time of delivery but would receive settlement as the cotton was liquidated from the Pool.

Option 2 provided that the members would receive an advance of approximately 60 percent of the estimated market value as soon as the cotton could be classed, this advance to be withheld from settlements as the cotton was liquidated from the Pool. Progress payments were made monthly as the cotton was sold, and any unsold cotton at the end of the season had to be carried over and sold from separate pools the following season.

Since there was usually some unsold cotton in both Option 1 and Option 2 of each Pool at the end of the season, the sale of this cotton along with the current-crop Pool cottons meant that sales were being made from four or more pools during the season.

Garrard Finds Ways to Meet Crisis

The insurge of the boll weevil forced Delta farmers out of the slow-maturing, long staple varieties of cotton as the 1920's advanced. This crisis tested the metal of a prodigious market-maker. Markets had to be found for the shorter, intermediate staple lengths. Numerous buyer accounts were lost as the Delta could no longer supply desired staple lengths. But men like Garrard find ways to keep in step and often ahead of change and survive. He shifted from a straight pooling operation and added a factor option. This provided for individual members' cotton to be shown on a crop-lot basis and offered separately, with offered prices to be reviewed with the grower before sale. Obviously, the premium cottons from farms remaining in the production of long staples were costing the grower more to produce and had to be fitted to the market outlets to which they were best suited. Discounts on the intermediate and short staple crops were sizeable and could not be combined with full equitableness into a uniform pooling arrangement.

The factor option resulted in some growers asking for bids at times when market conditions were particularly unsatisfactory. This was met by setting up a merchandising account under which the Association would buy in cotton from the factor accounts in order to provide more rapid liquidation. Purchases of such cotton were hedged in the New York futures market and merchandised throughout the season. This market-stabilizing approach was rather widely used until the early 1940's, when the futures market quotations became inverted and did not reflect carrying charges.

For a period prior to, during, and for a time after World War II problems were somewhat less hectic for the management in administering the business affairs of Staple Cotton Cooperative Association.

In spite of inexperienced personnel and manpower shortages due to the military demand, together with ceilings, rationing, and other war programs, there were many accomplishments. To enumerate a few—the Association was able under the direction of T. R. Wells and J. E. Coleman to carry on one of the most efficient classing services, functioning as a branch of the Greenwood Classing Office, United States Department of Agriculture. It generally was considered the best in the trade.

Entry into farm chemicals distribution in 1938 reflected membership for added services—again stemming from the problems of wartime shortages.

A prompt and efficient service for sales, sales settlements, pledging and withdrawing cotton from loan programs, as well as sales under government purchase programs, was maintained throughout the period.

Garrard's Influence Strong in Meeting More Problems

The major shift from hand to machine harvest began in the latter part of the 1940's. Again, it was Garrard's influence and leadership that cushioned the effects of generally lowering grades of cotton from the entire area which Staplcotn served. The trade had to be convinced, the mills had to be convinced that added trash content, additional ginning requirements could be met successfully.

The farm price debacle of 1920-21 hit Mississippi cotton growers a hard lick. The team of O. F. Bledsoe, the Association's president, and Garrard stepped forward with a request for a $5 million loan from the War Finance Corporation. It is impossible to assess the psychological effect of these successful negotiations. A young organization— home folks all—had come into existence. Its performance, its management, and general leadership inspired the confidence for such a loan to cotton growers at a time of high crisis. Here, was an early demonstration that the affairs of the Staple Cotton Cooperative Association affected the whole of the Delta economy—not just the pocketbooks of its members. This concept represents another Garrard imprint.

The factoring system of credit extension, crop tie-up, and market control of the farmer was the predominate structure in cotton. Growers were "tar-babied" to the supplier of 8 to 10 percent credit and could exercise little choice as to where and how they did business. Additionally, small amounts of capital and limited surpluses in Delta banks—$7,327,000, June 30, 1923—were major obstacles to cooperative marketing.

Establishes Credit Machinery

Management's answer for Staplcotn's members was to establish the Staple Cotton Discount Corporation. This was an outreach for a sound credit future for members of a precocious farmer-owned firm. The freedom from credit restraints in production, coupled with well-infomed bargaining strength in the market, became indelible markers for stable progress by Association members. When 15 Delta banks closed during the late months of 1930, Stapldiscount obtained a loan of $1 million from the Federal Farm Board. The Farm Board loan was used to augment the capital of Stapldiscount sufficiently to provide a base for production credit through the Federal Intermediate Credit Bank.

It is generally recognized that the success of the credit-arm of Staplcotn helped to stimulate and to provide guidelines for the development of the production credit associations and for its evolvement into a nation-wide farmer-owned pattern of finance organizations.

The story of Will Garrard, as an achiever, increases even my own great admiration for my predecessor. You must know more about him as a person.

He was a giant of a man who stood five feet four. He was handsome, dapper, self-assured—and surprisingly grateful for the least attention paid him, the smallest compliment given him. He was impatient with lack of appreciation wherever it occurred. "There's something you can say no matter what it is that's been done for you," he said once in exasperation. "If a man gives you nothing but a dead cat, at least you can say it is indeed the deadest cat imaginable."

It was not unusual for a little blond boy—too shy to go inside, too troubled to go away—to rap on his father's office window. Whereupon, the chief executive of what was to become a multi-million dollar cooperative would leave his desk to go out, sit on the curb, and talk over a small boy's problems.

He seemed never to have the least difficulty in coming to a decision or forming an opinion. His thinking was mercurial and concise. Characteristically, his counsel was brief, but oft-repeated proverbs and slogans: Get your story straight. Put first things first. Don't guy the clown. (Don't try to beat a man at his own game.) Comparisons are odious. Modesty is one of the attributes of greatness. Don't alibi.

He played golf and tennis; liked almost any card game; was an excellent shot, preferring to hunt quail and duck. Traveling was a hobby and he brought home many beautiful things from both hemispheres. Since a work of art makes a brief statement, he had a natural affinity with art. Most of literature he found tiresome, except for a few verses that said succinctly what they intended to say and were done. The theatre he found tedious—except for musicals and comedies intended solely to entertain.

On the other hand, he was never known to turn a deaf ear to the real problems of real people. Mr. Garrard's counsel was sought by an inestimable number of men, women, and children. Never was his tone condescending, nor was there a hint of self-aggrandizement in his manner. He was never evasive, ambiguous, or contradictory in his dealing with others. His word was his bond—and the law at his home.

He was a Baptist, a Democrat, and a leader in a host of civic activities.

The forming of Staplcotn was providential for this canny, energetic man. Will Garrard was Emersonian in his belief that but a few essentials are important: "These and the wish to serve—to add somewhat to the well-being of men." Asked why he closed his successful "Garrard and Company" to cast his lot with this new experiment in marketing, he replied with characteristic directness, "That was a business, this is a service."

He Proved It in Alabama

E. P. Garrett

by Joseph G. Knapp

E. P. GARRETT WAS BORN on March 16, 1898 in Limestone County, Ala., six miles north of Decatur, on the ancestral farm which had been owned by his family since 1818. The old plantation house where he was born and where he still lives dates back to 1859, and it witnessed the difficult days of the War Between the States. Though this home was new during the war, only minor damages were incurred as a result of the war.

Garrett's family has always taken an active interest in the affairs and responsibilities of the state and of the community. He is proud of the fact that his great, great Grandfather was Governor of the state from 1819 to 1821. The concept of public service and responsibility was born in him.

He got his preparatory school education in Athens, at Green University, 1911 to 1914, and his college education in agriculture at Alabama Polytechnic Institute at Auburn where he graduated with a B. S. degree in 1919. He served seven months in the army during World War I and was discharged as a second lieutenant.

As a young farmer he became interested in cooperatives through his inability to secure credit through the local banks for operating his farm. He was one of the incorporators of the Huntsville Production Credit Association in 1934, and he served on its board of directors for 15 years.

His first experience with the Federal Land Bank was a loan in 1921, a necessity which was brought about by the drop in the price of cotton in 1920 from 40-cents a pound to five-cents a pound. Of course, this drastic drop could not occur with today's Farm Credit program.

This experience with the cooperative Federal Land Bank and Production Credit systems naturally led him to an interest in the possibilities of farm supply and processing cooperatives.

In 1937, he became a member of a cooperative cotton gin and also served on the board of directors of the Local Soil Conservation Association. He became a member of the Farm Bureau in the early 1920's, and began working with the Extension Service and experiment station personnel from the day he left the Land-Grant college.[1]

Builds Fertilizer Co-op from Small Beginning in 1936

All of these activities and interests led to his active leadership of a group which in 1936 set up a fertilizer cooperative service in Decatur under the name, Tennessee Valley Fertilizer Cooperative. When the organization began operations he agreed to serve as Manager and he has continued to serve in this capacity to the present—although this cooperative has extended its services to other portions of the state and has taken the name, Alabama Farmers Cooperative, Inc. From a small beginning this organization has grown until it now does a business volume of $11 million, and serves some 30,000 through local member associations.

The Tennessee Valley Fertilizer Cooperative began operations in 1936 with a small dry mix fertilizer plant, but gradually it has extended its services throughout the state and broadened its line of services and facilities to include feed, seed, and miscellaneous farm supplies.

Mr. Garrett gives great credit to Sam D. Sanders for giving him the "shot in the arm" that he needed to start building cooperatives. The occasion was a Stockholders Meeting of the New Orleans Bank for Cooperatives, held at Birmingham in 1935, and Mr. Sanders as Cooperative Bank Commissioner of the Farm Credit Administration was giving down-to-earth speeches throughout the country at that time, based upon his own experience as a cooperative manager. He preached with homely example and good humor that "it could be done by well-organized and managed farmer cooperatives." Many, like Peter Garrett, took to heart the sage counsel of Sam D. Sanders.

I came to know Mr. Garrett just about this time and I was privileged to give a couple of talks to his stockholders in the late 30's. This gave me an opportunity to see how Peter Garrett was demonstrating, with the cooperation of his neighbors, that it could be done in northern Alabama as well as in Washington State, or California, or any other state.

The significance of Peter Garrett's experience was that it was a new type of cooperative venture—cooperative dry mixing of fertilizer.

---

[1] All of this led to his family being selected as the "Master Farmer Family" in 1940.

The association confined its operations to doing a good job in this one field before it spread its line of activities. It is significant that the F.C.A. used the experience of his cooperative to prepare a little government bulletin on cooperative dry-mix fertilizer plants to show their practicality.

Garrett's Leadership Abilities Sought by Many

As the business success of the Tennessee Valley Cooperatives, Inc., grew, Peter Garrett found himself increasingly involved in working in a leadership capacity for more general cooperative development with the agencies of the Farm Credit System and with the Tennessee Valley Authority. During the past 30 years he has been an active participant and leader in eight cooperatives which ranged in size from a local cooperative gin to the Presidency of Associated Cooperatives, which at one time operated a fertilizer manufacturing and distribution service in 21 states.

Associated Cooperatives was formed in cooperation with the T.V.A. during World War II to provide a source of ammonia nitrate and high analysis phosphate to help increase agricultural productions. Mr. Garrett was from the beginning an active leader in the organization which did much to expand cooperative fertilizer operations throughout the nation.

Peter Garrett's cooperative philosophy can be tersely expressed. He has believed that farmers must operate beyond the line fences of their farms if they are to get "their place in the sun," and that therefore "they must join together with other farmers and organizations and groups of farmers to obtain the necessary 'know-how' and facilities to get the job done."

He believes that the farmer cooperatives of the future must be larger and more basic in their services and facilities. This means that "they must become more willing to work together and that competition between cooperatives must stop."

Mr. Garrett can look back on his career with great satisfaction. He has held many important positions and received many honors for his great contributions to the agriculture of his state and nation. In 1958, he was named Man of the Year of Alabama Agriculture by the *Progressive Farmer* magazine. When agricultural cooperatives—or progressive agriculture—comes into conversation in Alabama the name of Peter Garrett soon comes to the front.

Milton Cleveland Gay

by J. W. Fanning

M. C. GAY WAS BORN NOVEMBER 10, 1884 on a farm near Waleska, Ga. He was educated in the country schools of Cherokee County and graduated from Tate High School. He worked his way through North Georgia College at Dahlonega, Ga., by farming and teaching in the country schools of Cherokee and Pickens County. In 1912, he received his B.S.A. degree from the University of Georgia. While attending the university he completed most of the requirements for a Masters degree, and he did graduate work at the University of Pennsylvania. For four years Mr. Gay was principal of the Ninth District A & M School, Clarksville, Ga. He also served as principal of Winterville High School, Winterville, Ga., for two years. He married Fannie Mae Cagle from Pickens County, Ga., in 1908 and they have two children, Dr. Otis F. Gay, Huntsville, Ala., and Mrs. Martha Bara, Lynbrook, Long Island, N. Y.

For 10 years Mr. Gay served as Marketing Specialist for the Agricultural Extension Service of the College of Agriculture University of Georgia. During this time he held the first Georgia cooperative carlot hog sale at Cairo, in 1916, and the first poultry sale at Griffin, in 1919. Also Mr. Gay edited for the Department of Markets the *Southern Ruralist* which was later combined with the *Progressive Farmer*. Four years he served as regional representative of a nation-wide cooperative sales agency for fruits and vegetables.

For 18 Years Helped Organize Co-ops

When the Division of Cooperative Marketing was transferred from the U.S.D.A. to the Federal Farm Board in 1930 Mr. Gay served as Marketing Specialist. For 18 years he counseled with farmer groups throughout the United States in planning new cooperatives, and advising established associations regarding their operating practices and problems. He assisted in organizing Maine Potato Growers, Inc., which is the largest potato cooperative in the world. One season he personally supervised the marketing of 9,938 cars of Maine potatoes. Much of the basic data used in planning and operating farmers' produce markets resulted from a comprehensive, nation-wide study and analysis made under Mr. Gay's supervision.

During World War II the Food Administration turned over to him the task of directing the storage and conservation of sweet potatoes with the cooperation of all state and federal agencies. While he was in Washington he was a member of the American Marketing Association and many other professional organizations. For years he was head of the Fruit and Vegetable Section of the Division now known as Farmer Cooperative Service. He is also the author of several agricultural publications. In 1949 he retired from his work in Washington only to become more active in his native state. Probably today there is no man alive who has contributed more to the cooperative way of life than Mr. M. C. Gay.

Second Co-op Career Follows Retirement

Many other outstanding accomplishments could be cited about Mr. Gay's work during his years as a national leader in the field of agricultural cooperation in the U.S.D.A., but the folks in Georgia know him best for the things he has done in Clarke County, and his own state, during the 15 years since his retirement. He was the moving spirit among farmers in a dozen Northeast Georgia counties in promoting and constructing a modern grain elevator in Athens. Today he is President of the Georgia Grain Growers Association, Inc., a position he has held since 1951. This association under Mr. Gay's leadership has acquired more than 600 members.

During his several years as President of the Clarke County Farm Bureau he assisted in 4-H and FFA programs and initiated the creation of a city-county planning commission. Today, this commission handles the future planning for all business, industrial, and residential areas of Athens and Clarke County. Mr. Gay also has devoted much time working with foreign students who attend the university in the field of agricultural cooperation.

Mr. Gay served as a member of the Clarke County Board of Education for years. During this tenure he served as chairman of numerous committees and through his guidance sprang one of the best school systems in Georgia. He helped build new and modern elementary, junior high, and high schools for Clarke County boys and girls. He is a member of the Athens Kiwanis Club. For several years he taught the Forum Bible Class at the First Baptist Church where he is an active member and deacon.

A familiar role for Mr. Gay today is main speaker for important co-op meetings. For three years he served as Secretary-Treasurer of the Alumni Association of the College of Agriculture University of Georgia. As outstanding as Mr. Gay's accomplishments have been in his professional and civic life he has probably done more for his fellowman in his daily living and personal contacts than in any other way. His enthusiasm is contagious. His zest for life at its best and look to the future with faith and optimism have inspired a great many people to a better life. He is indeed a master in the field of leadership and inspiration.

His many and varied public and civic activities have not prevented his doing an outstanding job on his 458-acre farm near Athens. Fifty to 60 acres of cotton a year have consistently produced more than a bale per acre. He is a member of the Georgia 100-Bushel Corn Club and 1000-Bushel Corn Club. "Gayland," his home located on Highway 78 is one of the show places in this area.

One of Mr. Gay's most important contributions to his own state has come in the last 10 years. During this time he has served as Secretary of the Georgia Council of Farmer Cooperatives, and he is still serving in this capacity. He was instrumental in organizing this association in 1937. He gave to it a renewed and driving forward spirit in 1956 when he became its Executive Secretary. Under his guidance this group has grown in membership from 33, in 1956, to over a hundred in 1966. The Council reaches 100,000 farm families through affiliated member cooperatives. Much of his time is spent advising with directors and managers of cooperatives, attending conferences, and planning projects.

People in Georgia recognize him as an outstanding cooperative leader. Mr. Gay has been able by virtue of his experience to bring to Georgia the most outstanding cooperative leaders in the United States for workshops and conferences. Mr. Gay and Georgia cooperatives grew up together, and for many years to come this state will reap the beneficial fruits of his efforts. Through his dedicated work a broader vision and more favorable climate for cooperatives have emerged, not only in Georgia but throughout this nation.

Harold Hedges

by Joseph G. Knapp

H AROLD HEDGES was one of the finest cooperators I have
known. He was a naturally good person and to him agricultural
cooperation was a creed to be lived and expounded. He brought great
respect for the philosophy and principles of cooperation, for his character as a man reflected his inner convictions that agricultural cooperation was essential to the welfare of farmers in all nations and to
the creation of a better world.

When cut off in his prime by a heart attack at the age of 57, he
had put his mark on agricultural cooperation as one of its great leaders,
and his influence has continued through the thousands of persons who
had come within his orbit.

In a way, all of his life Harold Hedges was associated with agricultural cooperation. His father was the manager of a cooperative
elevator. He respected him and his profession.

Harold was born in Falls City, Nebr., on May 12, 1896. After graduation from the Indianola, Nebr., high school he worked for two years
as Assistant Manager of the Red Willow Equity Exchange where he
gained experience in the practical meaning of cooperative business
through handling, buying, and selling grain, livestock and farm supplies, and keeping the accounting records. He enrolled in the College
of Agriculture at the University of Nebraska in September, 1916, but
World War I forced him to interrupt his academic studies, and from
December, 1917, to November, 1918, he served as a private in the
Air Service in Nebraska and California. He then resumed work at the
University of Nebraska where he received his B.Sc. degree in 1921.

Following graduation, he married Marjorie Phillips, his home-town
sweetheart who had been the church organist while Harold sang in
the choir. They then spent a year in Brookings, S. D., while Harold
was doing survey work in farm management and marketing for the
South Dakota Department of Agriculture. He next returned to the

University of Nebraska to obtain his Master's degree, while working as an assistant instructor to help defray expenses. It is of interest that he taught the college course in accounting for cooperative associations as part of his duties. During this period I first came to know Harold as a somewhat older classmate in the course in advanced economics given by James E. Le Rossignol. I remember him as a quiet, friendly and able student—a man with a twinkle in his eye who knew where he was going. A son, Harold Clayton, was born in 1922. His other son, Richard Henry, was born in 1926.

It is significant that his Master's thesis was a study of cooperative livestock marketing associations, which was later issued as a university bulletin. After he got his Master's degree, Harold served for a year as instructor in agricultural marketing at Kansas State University. Then he returned to the University of Nebraska as Assistant Professor of Rural Economics, and within a few years he was promoted to the rank of Associate Professor. His output of publications began to grow. Among them were two University of Nebraska Experiment Station Bulletins, *Protein as a Wheat Prime Factor* (1927) and *Types of Farming in Nebraska* (1930).

After several years with the University of Nebraska, Harold was granted a sabbatical year to work for his doctor's degree at the University of Minnesota. Although he completed all of the required course work with the high average of 90, and the language requirements in French and German in 1931-32, responsibilities piled up so fast that he was not able afterwards to find time to prepare the thesis that would have given him the doctor's degree.

Becomes Officer of New Omaha Bank for Cooperatives

The main force that interfered with the completion of the work for the doctor's degree was an opportunity in January, 1934, to serve as Vice-President and Secretary of the newly-formed Omaha Bank for Cooperatives, and this job absorbed all of his energies for the next two years. Harold was in charge of loan analysis and appraisal work, and he was responsible for field work and servicing of loans. This position gave him a wonderful laboratory in which to apply his training and experience in working with farmer cooperatives on practical problems.

Although Harold enjoyed this work, he was attracted by an opportunity to work in a broader framework. In 1936, the Cooperative Research and Service Division of the Farm Credit Administration, Washington, D. C., was looking for a man to give direction to its research, advisory service, and educational work for grain cooperatives, and with his training and experience Harold was considered the ideal man.

His performance met the highest expectations, as evidenced by official "Excellent" efficiency ratings and a fine output of helpful bulletins and other writings by himself and his staff. In the summer of 1938, at the invitation of the Province of Manitoba, he took leave to make a study of the relations of Manitoba cooperatives to government agencies, and to advise on how Manitoba cooperatives might be strengthened.

A glimpse of Harold is given us at this time in a vignette in the *Farmers' Elevator Guide* for June, 1941:

> He is a strong believer in the future of cooperative grain marketing, particularly if the associations keep their business ideas up-to-date, adhere firmly to cooperative principles, and work more closely with each other.

In the early months of 1941 the country was confronted with a serious grain storage problem arising out of the needs for war defense and from February to September Harold spent most of his time working on this problem with J. E. Wells, Deputy Governor of the Farm Credit Administration.

With the problems associated with the coming of World War II, the national farm organizations and cooperative associations set up an organization, which became well known during the war, "The National Committee for Farm Production Supplies," to represent the needs and interests of farmers in dealing with government control agencies. Harold was asked to serve as its Washington representative, and the Farm Credit Administration granted him leave for one year to get this program organized and into operation. This position gave Harold a fine opportunity to render an important national service, while extending his contacts with the general farm organizations and the principal agricultural cooperatives.

Becomes Acting Chief, then Chief of CRSD

But the heavy duties and Harold's keen sense of responsibility took their toll—and in the summer of 1942 he suffered a severe attack of coronary thrombosis. When he was able to return to the Cooperative Research and Service Division of the Farm Credit Administration, he was asked to serve in a new, and more important capacity—as Acting Chief of the Cooperative Research and Service Division. Dr. Tom G. Stitts, the Chief of this Division, was then on leave to direct the dairy program of the U.S.D.A.

From November, 1942, to November, 1945, Harold served as Acting Chief. Dr. Stitts had set up a Planning Committee to work with the Acting Chief on research and other problems before he went on leave, and I served as Chairman of this committee, along with Kelsey B. Gardner, Andrew W. McKay, C. G. Randell, and Paul Quintus. I was afforded an exceptional opportunity to appreciate Harold's fine capabilities and character.

When the war was over Dr. Stitts decided not to return to his position as Chief of the Cooperative Research and Service Division, and Harold was able to take the Acting from his title.

It was at this time that the American Institute of Cooperation was being reorganized to operate on a year-round basis, and there was much interest in broadening its scope. A committee was established on Research and Education, under the Chairmanship of Ezra Taft Benson, with Harold Hedges as Vice-Chairman, but as the former found it impossible to serve, the responsibility of developing the work of the committee fell on Harold. Under his chairmanship it became a regular feature of the annual Institute summer session to have a program devoted to research and educational matters, and this program has grown and expanded in various directions to the present day.

Gained Recognition for Marketing Research for Co-ops

One of Harold's significant achievements during the late 40's was in gaining recognition for the fact that the Cooperative Research and Service Division should be recognized under the expanded appropriations for marketing research made possible by the Research and Marketing Act of 1946. He argued persuasively that the CR&S Division had a staff competent to make significant contributions toward marketing, and that the benefits of the new program should be shared by cooperative organizations in that cooperative members had a natural stake in agricultural market reform.

In 1948, I was privileged to come into a much more intimate professional relationship with Harold. At the time the post of Associate Chief was vacant, and Harold proposed that I take it, saying "I want you as my partner." That was our relationship for the next five years until he left us.

Until then I had not fully appreciated the burdens associated with the task of being chief executive of an agency of government, especially of an organization comprised largely of professional workers. The problems were compounded in that the CR&S Division was different from the other fiscal divisions of the Farm Credit Administration and, moreover, it was the only part of the Farm Credit Administration (then a part of the U.S.D.A.) which was directly supported by appropriations from the Congress. This meant that the budget for the CR&S Division was presented by the Governor of the Farm Credit Administration, whose main concerns were the lending operations under his supervision. It was thus difficult to obtain through the legislative process adequate funds to maintain and develop our research, service, and educational program for cooperatives.

This situation placed a great strain on Harold and he did a magnificent job of trying to maintain the morale of staff while struggling to obtain sufficient support to maintain its services. The problem became very acute during the Korean War when the pinch for economy called for across-the-board cuts in appropriations. It was during this period that the House Appropriations Committee recommended that the budget of $580,000 be reduced $300,000 for the following year. Fortunately, support for the program in the Senate succeeded in reducing the cut by $100,000 and the separate appropriation for marketing research was not so drastically cut.

No one—not on the inside—could realize the strain that this placed on the Chief. Members of staff had to be discharged, and work badly needed had to be stopped or curtailed. One of the important decisions then made by Harold was not to discontinue a major part of the program, but to continue all activities with lesser intensity.

The slash in the budget made a deep impact on Harold. He could not understand how a program so important to agriculture could be so treated. I cannot but feel that his struggle to keep the Cooperative Research and Service Division in existence hastened his second, and fatal, heart attack. He gave all to the organization under his command.

It is sad to think that if he had lived only a few more months, administrative changes resulting from the Farm Credit Act of 1953 which converted the Cooperative Research and Service Division into the Farmer Cooperative Service of the U.S. Department of Agriculture would have permitted him to see the work that he loved so much have a greater opportunity for expansion.

It will be clear from the above that Harold's administrative responsibilities limited his opportunities to do creative writing. However, his written work showed the hand of a master craftsman and he was highly effective in orally presenting his views.

Major Contributions Made on Applying Co-op Principles

One of his major contributions was a statement prepared on how the Cooperative Research and Service Division worked in cooperation with Land-Grant colleges and Extension Service. In another valuable document he traced the growth of agricultural cooperation as a major policy of government.

At the American Institute of Cooperation meetings in 1951 he gave the keynote paper for a series of presentations on "Matching Cooperative Principles with Present-Day Practices." In this talk he said, "Only by effective application of [sound cooperative principles] can cooperatives serve their purposes both as business and as patron-motivated organizations." Harold was moderate in all things—but his moderation was tempered by a bull-dog tenacity to maintain fairness in all of his actions.

At the Extension Workshop held in connection with the 1952 meetings of the Institute of Cooperation he presented an outline for the study of "Cooperatives as Part of the Capitalistic Economy." He was concerned with people understanding the economic and social nature of cooperatives—for he knew that only through broad understanding of those within, as well as of those outside, could cooperatives function to maximum efficiency. It is significant that on the day of his death he completed an article, "How Cooperatives Work," for the 1954 Yearbook of the Department of Agriculture. In this article he said, "The cooperative is simply a tool fitted to the need for group action."

Study Led to U.S.D.A. Policy Statement on Co-ops

In 1951, Secretary Brannan decided to give greater attention to cooperatives in the work of the Department. A task force, under Harold's chairmanship, was directed to examine the program of the Department and offer recommendations. An outgrowth of this inquiry was the policy statement, issued by the Secretary in June, 1952. This statement, largely drafted by Harold, said among other things that the Department would "Encourage the sound development and effective utilization of cooperatives by farm people in the production and marketing of their products, and to obtain goods and services not available or not as efficiently provided otherwise."

Although this policy statement was not reaffirmed during the Eisenhower administration, it served as the model for Secretary Freeman's well-known Secretary's Memorandum No. 1540, issued on July 9, 1963, which directed all U.S.D.A. agencies to give due recognition to agricultural cooperatives in their programs.

Harold Hedges was a modest and generous man. He was concerned with what he could do for others. He lived his ideals and they became facts. He was a man of character and charm, and the influence of his work with farmer cooperatives will be felt as long as agriculture and the nation are free.

Following his death, his friends contributed some $3,000 for a Harold Hedges loan fund for students in agricultural economics at his alma mater, the University of Nebraska. Harold would have liked that —the encouragement of young men in his home state to equip themselves to be of greater service to agriculture and to the nation.

Fred E. Herndon

by C. H. Becker

FRED E. HERNDON of McDonough County, Ill., served as President of Illinois Farm Supply Company for 28 years from 1931 until his retirement in 1959. In my opinion he holds a place of high honor in any history of agricultural cooperatives. The span of years from 1915 when Fred Herndon started farming, up until the present, has never known a time when agriculture and agriculture-related cooperatives were not a part of his life and his prime concern. It is certain that these same concerns will continue to be just as important to him so long as he lives.

His business associates always called him "Mr. Herndon," and it was done out of respect, not because of any demand. He is an easy man to meet and get to know. In fact, it would be difficult to be near him and not get to know him well.

To tell the story of Fred E. Herndon is to tell the story of the period of greatest growth of farmer cooperatives in general and Illinois Farm Supply Company in particular.

Fred Herndon knew toil as a corn-hog farmer when jobs on the farm called for long hours and strong backs. He is still a corn-hog farmer today; but he uses modern tools, some of which he designed and built himself. He is still quite active and robust at age 79.

From the time Mr. Herndon started farming in 1915 he has kept farm account records in cooperation with the University of Illinois. He was a member of the University's Advisory Committee for the Department of Agricultural Economics for a number of years.

In 1918, he helped to organize the McDonough County Farm Bureau and he served on its board of directors for 12 years, 10 of these as its President. He was most prominent in the work and leadership which brought into being the two Farm Bureau-related cooperatives . . . McDonough Service Company and McDonough Grain and Milling Company.

Fred Herndon became chairman of the Bushnell Livestock Exchange in 1939, and a director of the Bushnell Producers Commission

Company. He has continued over the years to serve agriculture at the local level as well as at the state level. He also is a man who serves his community in other areas of interest. He has been a school director, active in PTA, in the Chamber of Commerce, and in his church.

Mr. Herndon's attributes as a leader have not been confined to his home state of Illinois. He has served a number of regional cooperatives as a director and an officer. He was a member of the board of directors of Central Farmers Fertilizer Company, a regional which he helped to organize.

He was one of the founders of the American Farm Research Association and served for many years on its board of directors. He was also on the board of United Cooperatives for more than 15 years, and served in the post of vice president for a number of years.

Fred Herndon has been a director on the boards of many other out-of-state cooperatives as well, such as Cooperative Plant Foods, Inc., Farm Bureau Milling Company, and Premier Refining Company.

He was called to Wisconsin in 1936 to serve a year as Executive Secretary of the Wisconsin Farm Bureau Federation, to provide his counsel and assistance through a period of reorganization.

To serve so many organizations requires an intimate knowledge of each as well as a broad general knowledge of business methods and operations. Fred Herndon had this kind of background.

Guided Growth of Illinois Farm Supply 28 Years

The years of Mr. Herndon's presidency of Illinois Farm Supply Company, from 1931 until his retirement in 1959, represent a major portion of the history of the organization. Sales of Farm Supply were $2 million in the year 1931, and had increased to more than $76,700,000 in 1959.

These years encompassed the struggles of a company in its infancy during the depression years, the war years of inadequate supplies, the aftermath of war when important decisions had to be made affecting company expansion into manufacturing and refining . . . these years were never without problems and challenge. Yet Illinois Farm Supply Company experienced continuous growth. Each year saw greater success than the year before. Certainly his leadership had a great deal to do with the success of Farm Supply and its local county member companies. His support of management's right to manage and his leadership qualities were prime factors in the organization's growth and stability.

Coincident with Mr. Herndon's first year as president, Soyoil paint was introduced to Illinois farmers. Here was a product used on the farm, one of the principal ingredients of which originated on the farm. Three years later, in 1934, the distribution of private brands of commercial fertilizers was begun.

In the next few years river transportation of fuels was undertaken and the Shawneetown and Kingston Mines Terminals came into being, with company-owned towboats and barges soon following.

The next big move into greater control over supply sources came in 1946 when the Benton Feed Mill was purchased, and this was followed by construction of the Mendota Feed Mill and the East St. Louis Fertilizer Plant in 1949.

In 1955, came the addition of the Tuscola Fertilizer Plant; and in 1957, the Springfield Feed Mill. Many new services to the farmers of Illinois were added between the years of 1931 and 1959, and Fred E. Herndon left his mark on them all.

Tremendous Interest in Farmers His Guiding Principle

A man of firm conviction, vision, courage, humor, and sound judgment, he gave the organization vigorous and wise leadership in all phases of its activities. Those who have worked with him closely, observe that his first thought has always centered on bettering the lot of his fellow farmers. It is perhaps this tremendous interest in farmers, by one who has always lived close to the soil, that is the chief factor in his successful leadership.

On matters of policy, directors' responsibilities, and organizational matters, his vast experience and knowledge have given him a perspective that many cooperatives have found of great help in improving their own operations. He has helped cooperative organizations in 20 states as a counselor and guide.

In November, 1956, cooperative leaders from all over the country gathered to honor Fred E. Herndon on the occasion of the 25th anniversary of his presidency of Illinois Farm Supply Company. A total of some 1,200 people attended the special banquet and program which were held in conjunction with Farm Supply's annual meeting.

Evidence of the high regard in which Mr. Herndon was held was evidenced in three separate news stories in 1959. Long a favorite with young people and a popular speaker at FFA and 4-H Club meetings, he was among 18 men chosen to receive the State Farmer degree with its accompanying Gold Key.

In the same year, the National Council of Farmer Cooperatives announced his appointment as vice-chairman of the Agricultural Finance and Credit Committee of the NCFC. Then, also, Mr. Herndon was elected to the Board of Governors of the Agricultural Hall of Fame.

On the occasion of Mr. Herndon's retirement from the presidency and board of directors of Farm Supply at the 1959 Annual Meeting, announcement was made of the establishment of the Fred E. Herndon Fund. A debenture bond in the amount of $15,000 was presented by Farm Supply to the University of Illinois, the proceeds each year to be used for either fellowships or scholarships in the field of agricultural business.

The awarding of honors to Fred Herndon has not come to a close even with his retirement from active relationships with cooperatives. In 1960 he was one of six men to be presented with an Award of Merit for outstanding contribution to agriculture by Gamma Sigma Delta, the honor society of agriculture at the University of Illinois.

Much in demand as a speaker, he has addressed agricultural meetings in every county in Illinois and in more than half of the states in the country. The voice of Fred Herndon is still being heard across the land wherever leaders get together to discuss the idea of cooperation.

His service to agriculture generally, and to farmer cooperatives in particular, has indeed been distinguished. Mr. Herndon has helped to write cooperative history in this nation . . . certainly he is an elder statesman par excellence in his field.

Self-help
Philosopher

42

L. S. Herron

by Gordon H. Busboom

"IF I WERE GOING TO DO A LITTLE PREACHING to older cooperators, it would be from the Apostle Paul's admonition to the Galatians, 'Be not weary in well doing.' And to the young people I would say: You are inheriting a great system of cooperatives already built. You can show your appreciation and your good economic judgment by carrying it to new heights, for cooperatives are the way to attain economic equity and justice with the preservation of freedom!" These were closing remarks of L. S. Herron in a final publication which he edited for many years for an association of Nebraska cooperatives.

L. S. Herron spent nearly 40 years promoting the cooperative movement as an editor and a speaker until his death in 1958 at the age of 74. He was born on a farm in Antelope County, Nebr., in 1884, and was a graduate of the University of Nebraska. He was active during his student days in studying the problems of agriculture, primarily cooperative marketing. In the early 1900's Herron attended and spoke at numerous meetings that were held as part of what we now historically call the "Farmers' Elevator Movement." In 1903–1904 and up until about 1914–15, many farmers' elevators were organized within the state of Nebraska. Herron was very active in this movement and was an observer of it. During this period he engaged in some teaching and journalistic work. From 1914–1917 he worked on the staff of *The Nebraska Farmer* publication, a state-wide farm magazine.

L. S. Herron was editor of the *Nebraska Union Farmer*, the official publication of the Farmers Union of Nebraska, from 1917 until 1945. He then helped organize and edited the *Nebraska Cooperator*, a publication of Associated Cooperatives, Inc., an organization of local and regional Farmers Union cooperatives within the state. He held the position of editor until his retirement in 1956 when he explained . . . "Doctors say my heart is tired."

Vigorously Supported Co-ops Through Magazines

During his editorship, Mr. Herron vigorously supported cooperatives as a voluntary and direct cure of many economic ills. He encouraged and helped build many of the Farmers Union cooperatives and helped get the cooperative enabling law through the state legislature. In 1918, he was elected to the board of the Cooperative League of the U.S.A. and continued as a director until 1933. As a speaker, Herron was frequently called upon to express his views on economic cooperation before audiences in Nebraska as well as throughout the nation. His editorials from both the *Nebraska Union Farmer* and the *Nebraska Cooperator* were picked up and widely reprinted in other cooperative publications. In the final issue of the *Nebraska Cooperator*, October, 1956, he wasted no time in "singing a swan song" but rather devoted his great memory and talents to a searching review of Nebraska cooperatives, where they came from, what they were doing and how they fulfilled their rightful place as an economic regulator and pacesetter. His concluding remarks were those quoted in the introduction to this sketch of his life.

On the day of his death, a committee of cooperative editors named him to receive the first Klinefelter Memorial Award for his distinguished service to cooperatives in the field of journalism. The award, created in memory of the late H. E. Klinefelter, former editor of the *Missouri Farmer* would have been presented at the annual meeting of the Cooperative Editors Association the next month. This award continues to be presented annually to an outstanding cooperative journalist by the Cooperative Editors Association. As an editor, Mr. Herron was widely recognized for his penetrating insight and thought-provoking editorials.

That he was a cooperative philosopher is reflected by passages from some of his editorials in the *Nebraska Cooperator:*

> Successful cooperation must be voluntary and spontaneous. It must spring from inner convictions and spirit. Inner convictions and spirit can be cultivated and developed only by education and persuasion.

> * * *

> Cooperation, as exemplified in cooperative enterprises, is an economic doctrine. It is recognized in economics as one of the associate means in which people join together to do things for themselves rather than look to the government to do things for them.

> * * *

It is the truth that the cooperative idea is the most powerful force to combat communism. By the cooperative idea we mean the idea of the people voluntarily, through their own cooperatives, establishing economic equity and justice in a free system.

* * *

Genuine competition is the effective remedy against price-fixing collusion in any line. Cooperatives furnish genuine competition because they are owned by their patrons and patrons have no incentive to practice collusion to 'gyp' themselves.

* * *

Now and again here in Nebraska we hear the lament that we do not have the fighting spirit among our members that was present in the early days of the movement. People cannot always live on a plane of intense excitement. What our movement needs at this stage, is just quiet determination not based on anger but on a well-thought-out program of cooperative expansion and extension.

The above quotes help define Herron's whole philosophy and approach to cooperatives . . . one which is based on the belief that a person should mind his own business. To do this well, people must work together by means of cooperatives. It is a simple philosophy— one that promotes neighborliness and good will to an economic theory. Some day a printed volume of his best editorials could help guide cooperative leaders throughout the land.

Without doubt, Mr. Herron's very practical thinking was based upon his early experiences with Nebraska Farmers Union cooperatives. From the period 1917 through 1919, things were going extremely well economically but from 1920 to 1922 there was a very steady decline. Many of the cooperatives then were on the brink of bankruptcy and this stimulated his interest in helping them. He worked vigorously to overcome all obstacles so as to get them back on a solid basis. When he retired in 1956 he could be proud of the strong economic position cooperatives had attained for the benefit of Nebraska farmers.

The thoughts, the philosophy, and the writings of L. S. Herron provide some genuine guidelines for all cooperative leaders in the present days of turbulent, changing agricultural economy.

Benjamin H. Hibbard

by Marvin A. Schaars

IT HAS BEEN SAID THAT "the pen is mightier than the sword." If this is true, then this cryptic statement can be applied to Professor Hibbard (1870–1955). As a teacher, writer, speaker and counsellor he wielded much influence on the thinking about cooperatives when agitators and enthusiasts needed the guidance and steadying influence of a brilliant educator. His classroom teachings, his writings, researches, and public addresses, especially during the decade of 1910 to 1920, came at a time when rural interest in cooperatives was high in the Midwest and proper direction of the movement most important. His training as a professional agricultural economist and his outstanding competence as an agricultural historian prepared him well for his role of writer and teacher on cooperatives.

Professor Hibbard's father, a one-time school teacher in Massachusetts who moved to an Iowa farm in the 1870's, died when B. H. was a 14-year-old boy. The young lad then took over the running of the farm, supported his mother, sisters, and an aunt, taught country school for several winters and at the age of 25 left home in March, 1895, to attend the College of Agriculture at Ames, which he completed with a brilliant record in 1898. He then enrolled as a graduate student at the University of Wisconsin in 1899, obtained his Ph.D. degree in 1902, returned to Ames as an instructor of economics in 1902, where he stayed until January, 1913, when he was called to the University of Wisconsin to join Professor H. C. Taylor in the Department of Agricultural Economics as a specialist in cooperation, agricultural marketing, and farmer movements. He stayed at Wisconsin throughout his academic career, was chairman of the department, after Dr. Taylor left, from 1919 to 1931, and retired in 1940 after many fruitful years of devoted public service.

Hibbard was much interested in ideas other men had and whether these agreed with his own thinking. How sound are the proposals from the standpoint of a critical economic examination? What does history tell us as to the soundness of the suggestions? These and many more penetrating questions were the kind Professor Hibbard would pose when any new proposal was brought forth. This is the way he approached suggestions that farmers should organize cooperatives for this or that purpose. He was not one to get on the "bandwagon" just because some groups "ballyhooed" a project—rather, he preferred to do his own thinking and arrive at his own conclusions. Of course, this cautious attitude antagonized some enthusiasts and gave the impression that the professor was temporizing and unsympathetic to the proponent's cause. When Dr. Hibbard once told a small group of dairymen pondering what is a fair price of milk, that "a fair price is 10 percent more than you can get" some, I am told, didn't appreciate his incisive humor and thought he belittled their serious discussion.

Pioneered in Teaching Course in Cooperatives

Hibbard was among the first university educators to teach a course in cooperatives.[1] While he was a professor on the faculty at Iowa State College, Ames (1902 to 1913) he taught agricultural economics and gave special attention to the organization of farmers for the purpose of marketing farm products. As early as 1907, Dr. Hibbard presented an outline of what he considered to be the scope and content of the relatively new field of agricultural economics before a roundtable of the American Economic Association meeting at Madison, Wis. He devoted much space to the subjects of cooperative processing, cooperative buying, cooperative marketing, and to agricultural marketing on a commodity basis. B. H.'s (as he was affectionately referred

---

[1] Note: Dr. John Lee Coulter of the University of Minnesota 1908-10 and later President of North Dakota Agricultural College might have preceded Dr. B. H. Hibbard as a teacher of the subject. As a result of Coulter's writings as early as 1909 in the *American Economic Association Quarterly,* the *Yale Review,* the *Outlook* and the *World's Work* and two years later his book *Cooperation Among Farmers,* he was in fact, better known in cooperative circles than Hibbard. When the University of Wisconsin in 1913 was looking for a professor specializing in agricultural cooperation and marketing, Dr. H. C. Taylor recommended and obtained B. H. Hibbard, whereas the State Board of Public Affairs and Charles McCarthy urged the appointment of Dr. Coulter.

to by his associates among themselves) interest in all types of co-operation—stores, insurance, credit, farming, breed associations, manufacturing, buying, and selling—as an integral and important part of the over-all field of research and teaching in agricultural economics was undoubtedly inspired by his acute awareness of the need to improve farm prices and reduce marketing costs and margins. Being a theoretician did not, however, make him less a pragmatist. Economics to be meaningful was more than a stimulating mental exercise for him.

An examination of the comprehensive lecture notes of a graduate student who was enrolled in Mr. Hibbard's course on "Cooperation and Marketing" in the first semester he taught at the University of Wisconsin (February-June, 1913) reveals what topics he considered important and what limited reference readings were available and assigned. Almost three-fifths of the course was devoted to a study of the general farm organizations—the Grange, Farmers Alliance, Agricultural Wheel, Brothers of Freedom, American Society of Equity, and the Farmers Union. Incidentally, this reveals at an early date what promised to be Hibbard's life-long interest, namely agricultural history, and may also show the impact that Frederick Jackson Turner, great historian of the American frontier, had on his student at the turn of the century. There was no Farm Bureau Federation nor National Farmers Organization (NFO) at that time, or we can be assured, these would have been also included in his lectures. About two-fifths of the time was given over to a discussion of "Business Cooperation" as he called it. This consisted of lectures on Cooperative Credit (German, French, U.S.), Cooperative Insurance, Cooperative Production—on farms, in food processing plants and by livestock and crop breeding associations, and Cooperative Marketing and Distribution of specific commodities here and abroad.

The third and last part of the course was devoted to the general topic, "What Is Cooperation?" Here, Hibbard settled for a relatively simple, but in my judgment a totally inadequate definition of business cooperation ("working together for the mutual benefit and improvement of the group"). He then explained the Rochdale Plan of co-operative organization, showed what state cooperative laws were in force (no Clayton Amendment, no Capper-Volstead Act and other federal legislation of later years had been enacted), raised the issue of how to treat nonmembers, and ended by pointing out some difficulties cooperatives face as business institutions. That was it—back in 1913, more than 50 years ago.

He Inspired, Aided Graduate Students to Achieve Fame

Hibbard's forte as an excellent teacher was principally with graduate students whom he attracted to his classrooms in large numbers. He could inspire these to no end, but I'm afraid that the poor sophomore who took his Agricultural Economics course found little inspiration in his relatively monotone lectures. At least, I must plead guilty to this charge. Many of his graduate students worked as part-time research assistants on projects in the field of agricultural cooperation and marketing, wrote their Master's and Ph.D. dissertations in these respective fields and, in turn, became teachers and researchers in this same area of study. And what a fine group of students they were—many achieving professional acclaim and national recognition.

To name just a few of his illustrious students, famed for their work in cooperatives: Henry Erdman (California), John D. Black (Minnesota and Harvard), Frank Robotka (Iowa), Theodore Macklin (Wisconsin and California), L. G. Foster (Ohio and Banks for Cooperatives at Louisville, Ky., and Columbia, S. C.), Asher Hobson (Wisconsin), E. A. Stokdyk (California), Newel Comish (Oregon), Omer W. Herrmann (Washington, D. C.), Martin A. Abrahamsen (West Virginia, North Carolina and Washington, D. C.), G. Burton Wood (Oregon). To be sure, others could be listed, but this is a sampling. Like the shadows of the spreading chestnut tree, those of Professor Hibbard extended to many campuses in this country and abroad through the top ranking Ph.D.'s and Master's he sent forth and through his own writings.

Hibbard was no apologist for cooperatives. He saw them as business institutions—not some form of life or way of living, not as an Owenite or Fourierite. He believed they could be positively beneficial to farmers. It must be remembered that he was a product of the soil. He had a farm of his own near Madison, Wis., raised Brown Swiss cattle and sold the milk through a milk-bargaining association. He experienced farm depressions in Iowa and knew what hardships were like when farm prices dropped pitifully low. He had faith, however, that the solution to farm problems rested with farmers, rather than with a beneficent government. At the same time, he was clearly aware of the fact that, to quote him, "The farmer was easily misled by the superficial views concerning the possibilities of cooperation." His idealism was not lacking in realism.

Many bulletins, circulars, book reviews and articles about cooperatives were written by Mr. Hibbard either alone or with some graduate student before the 1920's. During the two preceding decades hundreds of local associations were started in the United States, some regional federated and centralized associations also appeared, state laws in the pattern of the Wisconsin Cooperative Law of 1911 were being enacted and, in general, a great deal of agitation for cooperatives was in the air.

In Wisconsin, there was the additional ferment created by the dynamism of the Wisconsin division of the American Society of Equity and of the Right Relationship League, by the active interest in promoting cooperation among farmers of the State Board of Public Affairs (largely instigated by Charles McCarthy), by Senator Henry Krumrey's organizing efforts to set up the Wisconsin Cheese Producers Federation, and by the echoings and reechoings of the National Conference on Marketing and Farm Credits held in Chicago 1913–14–15–16, also largely engineered by the inimitable Charles McCarthy of the Wisconsin Legislative Reference Library. It was in these tumultuous times, that Hibbard appeared on the scene in Wisconsin and did his writing, teaching, and counseling.

Hibbard Selected to Make Basic Farm Marketing Studies

Pressure for more work and more active participation on the part of the University in the fields of agricultural marketing and farmer cooperation came in 1912 from the State Board of Public Affairs of which the Governor was the chairman. Hibbard was hired and immediately marketing studies were undertaken to show what happened to cheese, milk, and butter from the time the milk left the farm until the finished product reached the consumer. What services, charges and prices were involved and what happened to the consumer's dollar were things farmers wanted to know. Hibbard and his associates found out and wrote Wisconsin bulletins on the subjects.

These studies provided the foundations for his judgments as to whether cooperatives might be helpful in solving marketing problems for specific commodities and how much might be expected from efficient operations. As a result, some promotors became impatient with Hibbard when he did not acquiesce in their price control schemes, but in the end, I believe it fair to say, Hibbard's ideas prevailed and he was respected for his sound judgments.

Although Dr. Hibbard was no Robert Owen, a Dr. William King, or a George Holyoake, nevertheless, his writings carried much weight and bore the imprint of a sympathetic but at the same time a discernful analyst. He was not superficial—more inclined to create understanding than to agitate for a cause or to urge hasty action. His roundtable discussion on "Agricultural Economics" at the 20th Annual Meeting of the American Economics Association in 1907, mentioned above, helped to establish him as a leader of the professional economists interested in cooperatives.

To this day historians of the farmer cooperative movement cite the beginning of the cooperative grain elevator movement with the first elevator started at Madison, Wis., in 1857, a fact brought to light by Hibbard in his 1902 doctoral dissertation on "The History of Agriculture in Dane County, Wisconsin" (page 141). In 1909, his article on "Cooperation in the Grain Elevator Business" appeared in Bailey's *Cyclopedia of American Agriculture* and, in 1913, another article on the same subject plus one on "Farm Organizations" appeared in *Iowa State College Bulletin No. 12*. In that same year he wrote reviews for the *American Economic Review* of Henry W. Wolff's *Cooperation in Agriculture* and of James Ford's *Cooperation in New England— Urban and Rural*. His light as a writer and student of farmer cooperation, and of other agricultural economics topics as well, was beginning to shine more brightly at this early date as this recognition of his talents by the editors of the American Economic Association reveals.

Was Conservative in His Philosophy About Cooperatives

It was, however, in June, 1914, that Hibbard's first full length bulletin on *Agricultural Cooperation* appeared (Wis. Agr. Expt. Sta. Bul. 238—32 pp.). This bulletin is a combination of philosophy, suggestions, and a manual for organization. Unlike Aaron Sapiro who later had a specific plan of organization to recommend, Hibbard's suggestions by comparison were quite orthodox and in line with the more or less accepted doctrines of the day with one major exception as we shall see.

He saw cooperation in agriculture as "organized working together of farmers for the transaction of business;" that "in true cooperation there are no profits, but rather savings," a point not clearly understood to this day by many of its detractors; and that organizations should preferably be local in character and restricted to relatively simple operations ("The business which they are to direct should therefore be simple like the manufacture and sale of butter, the sale of grain or the purchase of feeds. The management of intricate manufacturing establishments or complex transportation companies should not be undertaken"). His conservatism is reflected in his warning that cooperatives should not engage in speculative operations or at least keep them at a minimum ("Some speculations are sure to be disastrous. If an association speculates and loses there will be severe criticism and in most cases trouble").

Had Strong Views Modifying One-Man-One-Vote Principle

Hibbard, of course, believed that "a cooperative company which is not democratic is not in a real sense cooperative, although it may be such in form." However, it is most interesting to note that he did not willy-nilly believe that the only way to vote was on a one-man-one-vote basis, but rather that voting on a patronage basis in cases where there are large and small producer members is reasonable and just and not undemocratic. Here's what he wrote in that bulletin back in 1914 when practically all writers took it for an accepted fact that the one-man-one-vote was immutable cooperative doctrine:

> Under most circumstances the plan (one-man-one-vote) is to be commended—. Under some circumstances the "one-man-one-vote" may prove to be too rigid a safeguard. Where the interests of the members are nearly identical, or equal, there would seem to be no good reason why each man should not have an equal voice in control of policies. But where the members have widely varying interests at stake, it is often hard to get those whose interests are greatest to agree to the "one-man-one-vote" plan. It may happen that one member has ten acres of strawberries and relies on strawberry sales almost exclusively, for his income. Another man may have a tenth of an acre and get a trifling part of his income from the sale of such fruit. It is not likely that the big grower will take kindly to the proposition giving the small grower the same voice as himself in the marketing policies. And it hardly seems reasonable that the two should be put on an equal basis with respect to authority in control . . . One very satisfactory way of bringing the large and the small producer together on a basis fair to both is to permit voting in proportion to business furnished . . . (Underlining is mine). This plan gives each member an influence corresponding to the interests he has at stake, and while a single small producer might seem to be swallowed up by his larger neighbors a group of them would be able to compel recognition.

This must have sounded like heresy to the self-designated cooperative purists at that time, just as it does even to this day, but it clearly shows that Hibbard wrote as he believed even if this went counter to the current of thought of his day.

This bulletin was widely distributed and in January, 1917, a revised and expanded edition appeared. Earlier, in January, 1915,

Hibbard with his student Frank Robotka (later a Professor of Agricultural Economics at Iowa State University, Ames, and an eminent theoretician, writer, and teacher in the field of cooperatives) published *Farm Credit in Wisconsin* (Wis. Agr. Expt. Sta. Bul. 247) in which they discussed land mortgage associations that were started pursuant to a Wisconsin law of 1913 and also in which they recommended passage of a law providing for farmers' credit unions. With Asher Hobson (also later a well-known specialist in cooperatives and agricultural marketing) Hibbard published another bulletin *Cooperation in Wisconsin* (Wis. Agr. Expt. Sta. Bul. 282—May 1917) which gave the history and extent of farmer cooperatives in Wisconsin.

Authored 155 Writings

Many other bulletins, articles, book reviews and full-length books were written by B. H. Hibbard, either alone or in collaboration with a graduate assistant, on cooperatives, agricultural marketing, public land policy, farmer movements, production and prices—in fact, almost every topic which came to the attention of agricultural economists during the first 50 years of this century is included in the 155 writings bearing his authorship. And with what clarity he could write and express himself!

Little thus far has been said of the unpublished, yet in many ways just as effective, public service, which Hibbard contributed through his counseling with cooperative leaders, with his informal conferences with general farm organization men, and with his voluminous correspondence, numerous public addresses, and personal contacts with rural people. As chairman of the Department of Agricultural Economics for so many years (1919–1931) innumerable inquiries and requests for information and advice came to him personally. After about the first 15 years when his staff became larger, others could share in these responsibilities to the public and lighten his load.

Professor Hibbard—renowned scholar, profound historian, brilliant essayist, perceptive thinker—lived and wrote at a crucial time in American cooperative history. He made his high mark principally as a combination teacher and philosopher. As he wrote of himself, "My connections with farming have always been too close to permit any other than a sympathetic view of farm problems, yet at the same time the mistakes made by farmers in their efforts to correct unfortunate situations are often such as to demand criticism." And though he could be sharply critical, even to the point of being caustic, his intentions were kindly indeed.

"Equality for Agriculture"

Bill Hirth

by Jack Hackethorn

WILLIAM A. (BILL) HIRTH was a champion of "equality for agriculture," and for a quarter of a century he built and headed the influential Missouri Farmers' Association.

The colorful Hirth preferred, however, to be called a producer of purebred Percheron horses, Jersey cattle, Poland China hogs, and Shropshire sheep.

He studied law and was admitted to the bar, but instead of practicing, he purchased the *Columbia Statesman* and developed it into one of the leading weeklies in Missouri. In 1908 he started publishing *The Missouri Farmer* through which he launched the Missouri Farmers Association.

Hirth was not one to be frightened by his opponents or discouraged by defeat. As chairman of the Corn Belt Committee he battled for the McNary-Haugen Bill and when the Tom Pendergast machine was at its peak of power, Hirth ran against the machine's handpicked candidate for the Democratic nomination for Governor of Missouri.

Hirth was born at Tarrytown, N. Y., on March 23, 1875. His parents were German immigrants. After coming to this country his father worked as a teamster for an iron foundry in New York City for several years. The family moved to Pike County, Mo., and purchased a farm on Lead Creek. Later they purchased a larger farm near Rush Hill, in Audrain County. When Hirth was 17 years old he started selling books and building and loan stock and made enough money to pay his way through three years of college. In 1900, he married Miss Lillian Vincent, daughter of a former Kansas Congressman, and they moved to Columbia. He died on March 24, 1940, and is buried in the Rock Hill Cemetery near Rush Hill, Mo.

As Youth Became Interested in Farmer Cooperatives

In an article entitled "The Romance of the Missouri Farmers' Association" written by Hirth in 1934 he said:

> As a 16-year-old farm boy in Audrain County, Mo., I joined the Farmers Alliance which led to the People's Party movement back in the 90's, and I took an active part in its affairs until I left for school.
>
> It was while closely associated with the grizzled old Alliance leaders of Central Missouri that I gradually formed the ideas which later became the foundation of the MFA. The Alliance was almost wholly political. I did not believe that such an organization could be permanent—that while it is imperative that farmers shall battle for their economic rights in an organized way through the dominant political parties, in the final analysis "production cost and a reasonable profit for the fruits of the farmer's sweat and toil" depends upon farmers owning and controlling the agencies which market their grain, livestock, poultry, and dairy products, and which supply feed, flour, fertilizer, binder twine, etc. Such a marketing machine would not only make their political demands infinitely more effective, but the resulting profits would cause farmers to "stick," thus guarding against the efforts finally winding up in the farm organization graveyard in which so many of the farm movements of the past are nothing more than dim memories.

The largely social organizations, such as the National Grange, didn't appeal to Hirth. He wrote: "for while a more interesting rural life is of tremendous importance, there is no reason why this cannot go hand in hand with constructive achievement."

It was back in 1911 when Hirth began to definitely crystallize his plans for the MFA. "Realizing that I couldn't hope to get anywhere without a mouthpiece of some kind, I launched *The Missouri Farmer* about this time," he explained. "Single-handed and without funds I started to work and for several years I not only hammered away at the kind of an organization I had in mind through *The Missouri Farmer*, but I delivered hundreds of public addresses whenever a handful of farmers would listen."

His "Farm Club" Movement Takes Fire!

In the winter of 1914, Aaron Bachtel and the Heisel boys organized the first Farm Club in the little Newcomer schoolhouse in Chariton county. This was the opportunity for which Hirth had been waiting. "As soon as Mr. Bachtel wrote me I sent him the Farm Club bylaws which I had prepared . . . then I urged him and his neighbors to organize Clubs in adjoining school districts as quickly as possible,

promising to supply good flour, bran, and shorts at the wholesale price
when the membership was large enough to order a minimum carload," Hirth wrote.

In less than two weeks this order was made up. This first car saved
the participating farmers approximately $400 as against the prevailing
retail prices—and "this set the woods on fire." Before spring they
had more than 300 members in the Brunswick district.

Hirth declared:

> Retail profit margins were outrageously high at that time, and
> citing the big savings which these Chariton county farmers were
> realizing to other farmers, the movement began to spread like a
> prairie fire into different parts of the state. Soon the school-
> houses were lit up in every direction, and the Fords rattled far
> into the night. Meanwhile, I often made three and four speeches
> per day. To demonstrate to farmers that they couldn't afford
> to stay out, I made a contract for binder twine which during
> the following harvest saved the average farmer his annual dues
> of $1.50 (including *The Missouri Farmer*) several times over,
> leaving his savings on flour and feed clear. Before I knew it we
> had better than 10,000 members, and the organization of new
> Farm Clubs went on with ever increasing speed.

Hirth continued:

> I recall that the first maximum carload of flour and feed which
> I ordered for Peter Wansing in Maries county saved over $1,100,
> and in varying degrees these savings were made in literally
> scores of communities . . . Once a Farm Club was organized in
> a new trade district, I urged its leaders to "carry the message to
> Garcia" in the adjoining districts so they would be able to make
> up carload orders of bran, shorts and flour, and it worked just as
> I thought it would.
>
> On every meeting night the schoolhouses were crowded as
> farmers made up their orders for the next shipment. Out of
> these schoolhouse Farm Clubs were developed the most militant
> farm leadership that was ever marshalled behind a farm or-
> ganization. As time has passed, this leadership has become in-
> creasingly aggressive and able, until today, it is without an equal
> in the United States. Everywhere farmers flocked to the MFA
> because it paid them to do so. This confirmed my early convic-
> tion that farmers would "stick" whenever they were offered an
> organization that was worth sticking to, for as the old saying
> goes, "money talks."

300 Elevators, Exchanges Organized, Financed

As the Farm Clubs expanded, and as farmers began to complain of
unloading commodities from the car door, the next step was to begin
financing elevators and exchanges. Again the Fords rattled far into

the night and the MFA was building a real foundation. In approximately three years' time Elevators and Exchanges were financed in nearly 300 towns.

Once the Elevators and Exchanges were going concerns, the next momentous step was to begin buying eggs, poultry, and cream. "I knew that we could force a big advance in the price of eggs and poultry to the farmer, but in order to not be at the mercy of the big handlers of produce, I also knew that we had to ship by the car," Hirth wrote. He suggested the financing of "central plants" and the directors approved. In a little while, the "chicken fight" was on and the feathers flew. "At first the big produce dealers laughed at us, but when in many communities we forced up the price of eggs 5¢ per dozen, and poultry in proportion, and as carloads of these commodities began to roll to the Eastern markets, their laughter turned to dismay," Hirth later wrote.

The Producers Creamery Company and the FMA Milling Company, both at Springfield, were soon going concerns and the Farmers Livestock Commission Company was in operation at the National Stock Yards. The MFA Oil Company was launched in 1929.

As a young man, still active in the Farmers Alliance, Hirth campaigned for William Jennings Bryan in 1896. Through later years he corresponded with Congressmen, Senators, Cabinet members, newspaper publishers, bankers, businessmen and others of influence.

His roll-top desk was described by an associate, H. E. Klinefelter, "as organized confusion." It was always cluttered, but Hirth always knew where to reach into a stack of papers to find the exact information for which he was looking. Letters, papers, and magazines would be piled high on his desk and Hirth would clear a space about six inches square for doing his writing in long hand. He refused to use a typewriter and he always used a pocket knife to sharpen his pencils.

Becomes Active in Politics to Build Farm Prosperity

Hundreds of MFA livestock associations, exchanges, and elevators dotted the agricultural landscape of Missouri when the first McNary-Haugen bill was introduced in 1924. The savings realized by the farmers through the MFA were substantial, but to Hirth these alone were hardly adequate to compensate for the inequity caused by the tariff structure.

"He (Hirth) was in the mainstream of Populist tradition," explained Richard O. Davies in the October, 1964, issue of *Agricultural History*. Davis continued:

Like the man he supported for the Presidency, William Jennings Bryan, Hirth believed that national prosperity rested directly upon a healthy agricultural economy. To prevent grass from growing in the city streets, the farmer had to be restored to prosperity first. The major purpose of his Missouri Farmers' Association was to enable the family farm to prosper . . . . Hirth, therefore, fully recognized the importance of governmental aid for the farmer. If the family farm were to endure, such aid—preferably in the form of McNary-Haugen—was mandatory.

The tariff suppressed competition and by artificial devices, maintained prices of goods and service for business and labor, but this did not help farmers. There was little likelihood of scaling down industrial tariffs so Hirth sought a way to make the tariff effective for agricultural products. The McNary-Haugen bills he thought, would do this.

He was convinced that if the "exportable surplus" was segregated from the domestic market, the farmer would enjoy the prosperity that was rightfully his.

After the defeat of the first McNary-Haugen bill, Hirth in 1925 was made chairman of the Corn Belt Committee, a group organized to solidify farm support behind the bill.

With Hirth's help and solid farm backing, the Congress twice passed the McNary-Haugen bill only to have it vetoed by Coolidge. Shortly after Hoover was inaugurated, Hirth wrote fellow Missourian, Arthur Hyde, the Secretary of Agriculture, "I confess that I have a feeling of hopelessness, and this is because I shall always believe the President was the chief inspiration of the Coolidge vetoes."

Hirth also wrote Hyde: "You know, of course, that my interest in agriculture is so deep that it transcends friendship and everything else, and this because, in my opinion, unless the new administration meets the situation squarely and courageously, the day of disaster is not far off and unless I am very much mistaken that disaster will apply not merely to agriculture itself, but to our whole industrial fabric."

Hirth called Hoover's farm program a "shrieking farce" and was a caustic critic of the Federal Farm Board, its members and its policies.

He considered Hoover's defeat in 1932 to be "a national necessity." Senator James A. Reed was Missouri's favorite son candidate for the nomination but Hirth endorsed Roosevelt immediately after he visited Albany in February, 1932. Endorsement of Roosevelt by progressive political leaders whom Hirth admired—George Norris,

Robert M. LaFollette, Jr., and Gifford Pinchot—reinforced Hirth's enthusiasm. Hirth worked hard for Roosevelt. He editorialized in *The Missouri Farmer,* gave five radio speeches at Farley's request to counter Hoover's last-ditch attempt to win Midwestern farm votes, and corresponded with farm leaders in every section of the country.

Hirth was an uncompromising McNary-Haugenite and felt deep disappointment when Roosevelt appointed Henry Wallace Secretary of Agriculture. The Iowa publisher was looked upon as "an outsider, an interloper by the leaders of McNary-Haugenism," according to Gilbert Fite in his book *George N. Peek and the Fight for Farm Parity.*

Wallace and most other farm leaders now supported Domestic Allotment but Hirth remained loyal to McNary-Haugenism.

MFA Influence in Missouri Built by Hirth

Hirth was having considerable legislative success in Missouri during this period. The influence of the MFA was demonstrated when the General Assembly in 1931 after a bitter fight, passed the state income tax law. Most of the income tax revenue was set aside for rural schools for the purpose of providing a minimum of an eight-months school term and to assure a high school education regardless of where a boy or girl might live.

In the fall of 1932 the MFA created the Committee on Taxation and Governmental Reform to make a study of state and county government. The record of this study committee was impressive. Among the achievements were: adoption of a constitutional amendment to limit the number of employees of the General Assembly to 150 whereas previous sessions had employed between 800 and 900; adoption of a constitutional amendment requiring a budget to guide the Legislature in making appropriations and giving the Governor an item veto of appropriation bills; passage of a law requiring that all excess fees be turned into the State Treasury and made available for the state school fund; passage of a law reducing cost of collecting back taxes, and providing for a two-year redemption period for farmers and town and city home owners; a law giving the governor the right to have any state agency audited; a law creating a state purchasing agent; a law requiring that the last census be used as the basis of population for salaries of county officials; a law reducing the salary of county collectors; a law consolidating offices of county treasurer and collector in counties having less than 40,000 population; a law consolidating the office of circuit clerk and recorder in counties of less than 20,000 population; a law requiring counties to budget their expenditures; a law reducing the election judges from six to four in precincts polling less than 300 votes; a law abolishing the State Board of Agriculture, State Fair Board, Bureau of Dairying, Plant Board, Apiary Board, Forestry Department, Egg Inspection Department, and Pure Food and Drug Department and the duties of these boards and commissions were consolidated under the newly created Commissioner of Agriculture.

In announcing as a candidate for the Democratic nomination for Governor in 1936 against political boss Tom Pendergast's hand-picked candidate, Lloyd Stark, Hirth confided to friends: "Of course I don't expect to win, because the machine is too strong, but what I do hope to do is to open the eyes of thousands of our voters to the fact that our state government has fallen into the hands of the biggest gang of crooks that ever went unhung. I never look at our beautiful state capitol that I don't imagine I can see a flock of buzzards circling around over it."

After Stark became Governor, and broke with the Pendergast machine, Hirth promptly went to his side.

In Hirth's opinion, agriculture largely built the nation during its formative period and has always been its basic industry. He often said, "Nothing is so essential to the wholesome prosperity of our country as to assure the millions on the farms of fair purchasing power— that is, to assure a price for the products of their toil based on their costs of production, as so largely determined by industry and labor."

The reason that Hirth had an advantage over the average farm leader in a public discussion was because as a young man he began taking a hand in the rough and tumble of politics. He loved a fight and was not awed by the great and near great in public life.

Shortly before his death he told a friend,

> I have done the work of three average men in my time and no doubt this will shorten my life by at least 10 or a dozen years. If I had 10 more fighting years ahead of me, I believe I could so strengthen the MFA as a business machine for the farmer that it would soon be duplicated in every state in the Union. For years the great trouble with farm organizations has been the lack of sound leaders. They mean well enough, but lack experience. They don't know how to build sound cooperative agencies. And the same is true of such leaders in a political way. Instead of building up a powerful group of voters who can reward or punish at the ballot box, they content themselves with passing high-sounding resolutions, etc.

Asher Hobson

by Milo K. Swanton

ASHER HOBSON, agricultural economist, professor, friend and counselor to cooperatives, both in and outside of Wisconsin, gave decades of constructive service to agricultural well-being in America. As a long-time advocate and designer of self-help procedures, he contributed much to strengthening the farm family system of American agriculture.

Born in Quenemo, Kan., in 1889, and raised in the midwest environment of rapidly developing agriculture, Asher naturally acquired an early and deep interest in the economics of farming, the self-help efforts of farmers, and in rural life generally.

At the University of Kansas in Lawrence he majored in economics, receiving his B.A. degree in 1913. He then came to the University of Wisconsin for graduate work in marketing. After receiving his Master's degree he accepted a position on Wisconsin's agricultural economics staff as Research Assistant.

Becomes First Washington Director of Farm Markets

Few young men have ever gained from such fine experiences and broad contacts as came to Asher Hobson in the next intervening years. In 1916, he went to the Pacific Coast as Assistant Professor of Agricultural Economics at Washington State. A year later he became the first Director of Farm Markets for the State of Washington. In this position young Hobson put to work his basic philosophy of intelligent self-help by cooperative marketing. Much in the fashion of a political campaigner, he stumped the state of Washington in behalf of organizing dairymen then selling milk to condensaries. He put much emphasis on the mechanics of sound business-like cooperative structures.

Not alone with dairymen, but also with apple growers and potato farmers, Marketing Director Hobson advocated group action in marketing. He laid the early groundwork for cooperative dairy marketing in the Seattle area and for cooperative marketing of fruits and potatoes in the Pacific Northwest.

Attracted by the driving energy and sound marketing concepts of this young man, the U.S. Department of Agriculture invited him to Washington, D. C., in 1919, to take over the position of Assistant Chief, Office of Farm Management. However, within a year the academic field invited his service and he accepted an associate professorship in agricultural economics at Columbia University in New York City.

Next came seven years of most valuable experience in foreign service as American Delegate to the International Institute of Agriculture in Rome, Italy. There he gained significant insight concerning international trade relationships, centered on the common denominator of food and agriculture. He conducted a thorough study of cooperatives in Switzerland where he traveled extensively. He spent one entire summer walking through agricultural districts while making a detailed analysis of the operation and organizational structure of the Swiss Farmers Union (L'Union Suisse des Paysans), a most remarkable farmer's cooperative.

Hobson's findings as reported in *Agricultural Survey of Europe-Switzerland,* (U.S.D.A. Technical Bulletin #101) presented a clear picture of European, and especially of Swiss, agriculture and rural people in the late 1920's. He revealed how struggling energetic people were employing group action to grapple with the then current cost-price squeeze problem. Whether in the form of bee associations, bull clubs or agricultural cooperative bakeries, whether dairy, wine making or credit services, Hobson's published survey revealed the growth and operation of America's cooperative counterparts in Europe.

Back to this country in 1929, Asher Hobson became consulting economist with the Federal Farm Board and in 1930 was asked to take over as Chief of the Division of Foreign Agricultural Service, U.S.D.A. In that capacity, no administrator has ever stood more staunchly in support of foreign markets building. During that period of economic chaos when in desperation the trend moved toward economic isolationism by means of foreign trade restrictions, Hobson spoke and wrote forcefully against barriers to international trade.

In the July, 1934, *Journal of Farm Economics* when discussing "International Aspects of the Agricultural Adjustment Act" he said: "Protection is contagious. It is both a disease and a vaccine against the effects of the disease. If national isolation was a cure for the depression, the world should now be on the high road to perfect economic health."

Prior to this time, Asher Hobson completed further graduate study and in 1931 received his Ph.D. degree from the University of Geneva, Switzerland. Following this, he accepted an invitation to return to the University of Wisconsin as Chairman of the Department of Agricultural Economics, which position he held for 17 years.

Wisconsin Agriculture Profits from His Exceptional Background

With this exceptional background of education and experience, Dr. Hobson came to the agricultural cooperatively minded state of Wisconsin. Because of the dairy marketing field surveys he had previously made when a graduate student and staff instructor, he was immediately at home among dairy farmers and with the marketing problems they faced. It was here in Wisconsin 16 years before, that the team of Hibbard and Hobson had made the significant surveys of "Markets and Prices of Wisconsin Cheese" and "The Marketing of Wisconsin Butter." In fact, Hobson's return to Wisconsin in 1931 brought him back to the scenes of his earlier cooperative pioneering. In 1917, jointly with Professor B. H. Hibbard, he had surveyed, researched and written Bulletin 282, *Cooperation in Wisconsin,* a very comprehensive report on farmer cooperatives and farmer movements in the state. This treatise presented information and guide lines that basically influenced future cooperative developments in Wisconsin.

Likewise, contacts and observations during those earlier years with Wisconsin's cranberry industry had provided Asher with knowledge that contributed significantly to his outstanding cooperative cranberry study published by the U. S. Department of Agriculture as Bulletin No. 1109,—*Sales Methods and Policies of a Growers National Marketing Agency.*

This publication became a national pacemaker in the field of cooperative business generally. Producers' group action in coping with seasonal market gluts, self-help by central sales backed by grading and standards of quality, more adequate financing and better cooperative business methods as presented in that Hobson report made it, and for decades it remained, a master treatise on cooperative endeavor.

As Chairman of the Department of Agricultural Economics at the University of Wisconsin, Dr. Hobson put great emphasis on cooperative marketing. He brought increased cooperative interest both within the department and among the farm leaders of the state. He was never too busy to take time to advise farmers. In spite of heavy administrative duties, he continued in the role of lecturer and teacher. Because he looked upon the Short Course boys as being closest to actual farming performance in the future, he always considered it a great privilege to personally give them a course in agricultural cooperation.

Advocated Cooperatives as "Tool" for Farm People

When meeting in the classroom with students at graduate or undergraduate levels, Professor Hobson gave more than historical and statistical information about cooperatives. He stressed the role they had played and could continue to play in strengthening the social and economic position of farm people. He emphasized always that farmer cooperatives were not an end-point in themselves, but were a tool—a means to gain improved status for farm people and others patronizing cooperatives.

It has always been Dr. Hobson's conviction that preservation of individual farm operation (the family-type farm) is in the national interest. He held that preservation of family farm operation depends in large measure upon increased bargaining power among farmers. Such bargaining power must be backed by good quality products, orderly and intelligently fed into markets. He stressed rational collective bargaining. He endorsed farmer-owned and controlled processing cooperatives and purchasing associations, when and where needed, to satisfy demands for products and services, to broaden market opportunities, to obtain production supplies not currently available, and at prices commensurate with actual costs based on efficiency. He emphasized in the classroom and at the conference table that always the existence of a cooperative—its birth and its continuance—must be founded on need.

Asher stood for, advocated and promoted cooperative action based on factual information. He insisted that just as an individual's judgment is no better than his information, so also cooperative procedure must be based on full knowledge of such factors as: supply-demand relationships, degree and nature of competition, and a high level of co-op member understanding.

Dr. Hobson held firmly to the belief that just as ownership of private property begets interest and a feeling of individual responsibility, so also cooperative membership and outright investment in cooperative capital begets deeper interest in, and greater responsibility

for, the marketing, servicing and purchasing events that take place
beyond production at the farm.

Hobson Widely Sought for His Realism, Practical Guidance

As a trained economist and as an experienced business practitioner
with a background of national and international contacts, Dr. Hobson
met farm economic problems with a deep sense of realism. His
services were requested extensively throughout Wisconsin and beyond. General farm organizations and cooperatives looked to him
constantly for guidance.

Because he expressed himself frankly and understandably he was
always in demand as a speaker at annual cooperative meetings. Frequently he was called on to meet with boards of directors and to
consult with co-op managers.

Repeatedly upon the urging of farm and cooperative leaders, Asher
"made the circuit" of Co-op Marketing Conferences and Cooperative
Short Courses scheduled by the Wisconsin Council of Agriculture
Cooperative. His constructive messages on Sound Cooperative Financing, Better Membership Understanding, and Board of Directors-Man-
agement Relations were in constant demand.

Hobson's sound economic statesmanship was a stabilizing influence
during the adverse conditions of the depression years. His constructive cooperative guidance shone clearly during the vicious death-
dealing 1933 milk strike in Wisconsin when widespread emotionalism
and hatred challenged economic bravery and tended to drive com-
mon-sense underground. During this time the College of Agriculture's
economic leaders, with Dr. Hobson at the helm, held to a firm,
realistic, but oft-times unpopular position of dependable influence.
With diplomacy and with firmness, Asher Hobson and his staff met
criticism, defended the work of existing tried-and-true dairy marketing cooperatives and advised on courses of action helpful to future
cooperative marketing procedures.

Shows Statesmanship in Strong Advocacy of Co-ops

Dr. Hobson's statesmanship in meeting cooperative issues was further shown in his analysis of reasons for passage of the Capper-Volstead
Act which so often has been under attack in some business circles.
Repeatedly he stressed that this Act is not a blanket exemption. It
safeguards farmer cooperatives from certain anti-trust provisions only,
and merely confers upon farmer co-ops the same rights that other

businesses have under corporation law—the right to organize in large groups for the conduct of legitimate business. At the same time he often reiterated before cooperatives as well as among noncooperative groups that while Capper-Volstead assures cooperatives the right to organize, it does not grant them the right to corner markets, fix prices, nor to enter into agreements to restrict supplies.

In his addresses throughout the United States, often before foes as well as among friends of farmer cooperatives, Asher left no doubt about cooperatives being an integral and valuable part of America's capitalistic economy. Often he forcefully stated:

> Contrary to those who picture cooperatives as socialistic institutions, let me assure you that cooperatives operate within the framework of our free competitive system and are an integral part of our capitalistic economy. The cooperative owns property and works to safeguard both property and personal rights.

There has never been a stronger supporter of self-help through cooperation than Dr. Hobson. There has never been a more devoted advocate of democratic group action by means of cooperative enterprise as contrasted with extensive dependence on government programs. When stressing his philosophy on this, he points to experiences abroad saying:

> Having lived five years in Rome under "master planner" Mussolini, I speak with feeling on the dangers to cooperatives when dominated by a controlled economy. You name a country that has abolished private capital or that exercises rigid controls over capital and I will name that country as one that has no cooperatives, or at least none that would qualify under the term as we use it.

During his 22-year period of outstanding service as a member of the Agricultural Economics Department at the University of Wisconsin (17 years as chairman), Dr. Hobson authored numerous economic papers, cooperative bulletins, and circulars. His 125-page publication, *Cooperation—Principles and Practices*, published in 1952, met a great educational need for information about the origin, growth, and service methods of cooperatives. Practices, possibilities, and limitations, as well as organizational structure and functional operations, are well presented in this cooperative text.

Abilities Widely Recognized by Organizations

Asher Hobson's abilities were widely recognized and they extended over a long period of time. He was an American member of the

Council of International Conference of Agricultural Economists. He was chairman of the American Section. He played an active role in the American Farm Economic Association. Almost singlehandedly, as Secretary-Treasurer, he placed that group on a sound financial footing. He served as its President in 1947. In 1957 the American Farm Economic Association's highest award, that of FELLOW, was bestowed upon Dr. Hobson.

In 1944 he was elected to the board of trustees of the American Institute of Cooperation. He served with distinction as Chairman of the Board from April, 1949, to the time of his retirement in August, 1953. In the words of J. Kenneth Stern, President of the Institute: "Asher Hobson contributed broad understanding on how the efforts of Land-Grant College people and cooperative leaders and educators could be coordinated so as to be more effective and objective in their efforts." In 1962, the American Institute of Cooperation awarded Honorary Recognition to Asher Hobson, "For outstanding leadership during this organization's most critical years of growth and development."

Now retired from academic assignments and although no longer an active participant in cooperative work, Asher Hobson, nevertheless, still continues to be an interested and deeply concerned partisan in present-day cooperative policies and programs.

Among beloved books in their extensive library at their beautiful country home nestled among the hills near Blue Mounds, west of Madison, Dr. and Mrs. Hobson are thoroughly enjoying the quiet and enduring values of rural living. Here also their devotion to rural history and their interest in the cultural heritage of the Vikings is manifest in their development of *Little Norway*, visited each season by many thousands of tourists.

Meanwhile, the cooperatives of this country, and especially the vast number of farm families they serve, are deeply indebted to Asher Hobson—trained economist and experienced public servant. His devotion to rural life objectives, coupled with his broad knowledge of the socio-economic tugs and pulls at the crossroads, make him a most constructive and understanding ally of rural people in America. As researcher, educator, advisor, and above all, as *cooperative statesman*, this man has done so much to clarify the image of farmer cooperatives, to improve the quality of their services, and to strengthen their structure throughout America.

Charles W. Holman

by Joseph G. Knapp

THERE ARE MANY WHO REMEMBER Charles W. Holman as
the premier agricultural lobbyist of the years from 1915 to 1955,
but there are few who know of his outstanding cooperative statesmanship that gained recognition for agricultural cooperation as a
major force in American agriculture. This essay will emphasize his
constructive contributions to the progress of agricultural cooperation.

Holman was born in Winona, Miss., on October 3, 1886, but he
spent his boyhood on a ranch near Sherman, Tex., where grain and
cotton were taking over pasture lands. Most of his early schooling
came from the library, and he did most of his reading as a boy, on
horseback. In 1898, his family moved to Sherman where he attended
a private school and then two years of high school. He worked his
way through Austin College, a school which had high requirements in
Latin and Greek. As a reporter during the summer at Lake Charles,
La., he came to know well Seaman A. Knapp, who was then developing his views on the demonstration approach to agricultural
education. Holman's first published article, written when he was 16,
dealt with child labor in a cotton mill.

In 1908 he joined the staff of *Farm and Ranch,* which was then
edited by Colonel Frank P. Holland, who gave him complete freedom
as a feature article writer. During this period he became deeply
interested in the Social Center Movement which was then sponsoring a library unit plan for country schools. He also wrote some 30
articles on the farm tenancy problem and became interested in cooperative marketing. In 1912, Colonel Holland sent him as a roving
reporter to study emerging cooperative developments in Oklahoma,
Colorado, Utah, California, and Oregon.

Holman's Outstanding Organizational Work Began in 1913

Soon after this trip, Colonel Holland called a conference on marketing at the Dallas Fair, and this gave him the idea of the first National Conference on Marketing and Farm Credits which he called jointly with a group of agricultural magazine editors in 1913. He made Holman the organizing secretary. After this conference dissension arose among the sponsors, so Holman arranged to have the conference continued with $5.00 personal contributions and by the sale of the Proceedings. He accepted a job with President Van Hise as Press Secretary for the University of Wisconsin, and took all of the conference records with him to the University. The fourth and last National Conference, held in Chicago, was attended by some 2,000 persons. Entry into World War I forced discontinuance of the conferences.

An examination of the Proceedings of these four conferences show their importance in gaining support for the Federal Farm Loan Act of 1916 and in encouraging an interest in cooperative marketing. It is also of interest that the National Milk Producers Federation got its start in February, 1917, from these meetings. These conferences and the well-edited Proceedings were a monument to Holman's organizational and journalistic abilities.

While at the University of Wisconsin, Holman worked closely with Charles McCarthy, the Head of the Legislative Library, who was a great admirer of Irish achievements in agricultural cooperation under the outstanding leadership of Sir Horace Plunkett. One of the outgrowths of the National Conference on Marketing and Farm Credits was the formation of the National Agricultural Organization Society, based on the general ideas of the Irish Agricultural Organization Society, and Plunkett helped secure a grant for it of $40,000 from the Carnegie Corporation. In order to get this program started, it was decided that Holman and Charles Lyman should go to Ireland to study the procedures and methods of the I.A.O.S., and Holman in 1915 spent six months in this way. The influence that it had on him is reflected in his excellent paper, "Sir Horace Plunkett's Influence on Agricultural Cooperation in the United States," presented at the American Institute of Cooperation sessions in 1937.

Early Writings Advocated U. S. Farmer Cooperatives

After Holman returned from Ireland he served as Secretary of the N.A.O.S. until it was forced to discontinue in 1917 because of the war.

The N.A.O.S. issued a number of attractively printed pamphlets—two of them prepared under his authorship. In one Holman dealt effectively with the problem of spurious cooperative packing plants; in the other, entitled, *First Aid to Farming Business*, he described how the N.A.O.S. could help farmers organize cooperatives.

With the stimulation of the National Conferences on Marketing and Farm Credits, Holman helped set up in Washington, D. C., an organization which endeavored to bring together all general farm organizations in a conference body known as the National Board of Farm Organizations, and he served as its first Secretary.

With the outbreak of World War I, Holman came to Washington to work with Herbert Hoover and in this position he helped form sentiment for a separate Food Administration. Following the war, as a member of Hoover's staff, he spent some time in the Far East and this gave him an opportunity to study Siberian cooperatives.

Returning to Washington, Holman was soon installed as Secretary to the rapidly-growing National Milk Producers Federation which soon became one of the strongest political organizations representing farmers. Many problems following the war called for attention, especially legislation to protect and assure opportunities for cooperatives. Holman worked closely with John D. Miller, Senator Capper, and other agricultural and political leaders to secure the enactment of the Capper-Volstead Act of 1922.

Sparks Plan to Organize American Institute of Cooperation

In 1923 at the World's Dairy Congress, Holman proposed that consideration be given to revising the Agricultural and Credit Conferences. However, it was agreed that the name should be changed to Institute of International Cooperation. At the next meeting of the National Milk Producers Federation, Richard Pattee proposed that the Federation undertake the formation of this Institute with the cooperation of other farm organizations. Holman then undertook to build support and enlisted the interest of Secretary of Agriculture Henry C. Wallace and Henry C. Taylor, Chief of the Bureau of Agricultural Economics. The organization plans were perfected in the offices of Dr. Taylor and those present included Dr. Edwin G. Nourse, then Chief of the Agricultural Division of the Institute of Economics; Lyman S. Hulbert, Attorney of the U.S.D.A.; Richard Pattee; and Charles W. Holman. The work of drafting the organization papers was done largely by "Judge" Hulbert.

To finance the Institute as a University a committee, comprised of Taylor, Nourse, and Holman, went to New York and persuaded Beardsly Ruml of the Rockefeller Foundation to provide funds to help finance the Institute which, under the persuasion of Ruml, adopted the name, American Institute of Cooperation.

Plans were made for the first Annual Session of the American Institute of Cooperation to be held at the University of Pennsylvania in the summer of 1925, and the job of program building was turned over to Dr. Nourse who devoted several months to this object. From the beginning it was assumed as a natural fact that Holman would be in general charge as Secretary, and he continued in that capacity while serving as Secretary of the National Milk Producers Federation until the end of World War II when the Institute was reorganized with a full-time President, Raymond W. Miller, in charge.

At about the time that the A.I.C. was being established the cooperative organizations of the country, largely led by the National Milk Producers Federation, undertook to get the research and educational work of the Department of Agriculture with cooperatives set up on a permanent basis. After much intensive effort the Cooperative Marketing Act of 1926 was enacted. Holman served as one of the key persons in getting this Act passed, as attested by its legislative history. In the Hearings on the Bill he said, "We consider that the bill is a very important forward step in a long-range or long-time policy of assistance to agriculture . . . We think that the bill is non-controversial and noncontentious."

Helped Organize National Council of Farmer Cooperatives

Holman was in favor of all measures to create greater unity and power among the cooperatives and national farm organizations. He was one of the organizers of the National Council of Farmers' Cooperative Marketing Associations in 1924, and in 1928 he was a prime mover in setting up the National Council of Farmer Cooperatives, which was formed in 1929. At the 1928 American Institute of Cooperation meetings held in Berkeley, Calif., he called for "national unity for cooperatives." He said, "Today's session of the Institute will deal with the question of better coordination of agricultural cooperatives for the solution of their common national problems." He urged the need of consolidating the strength of existing cooperative organizations, citing the experience of the National Milk Producers Federation to show what could be accomplished by working together.

During the Federal Farm Board and early New Deal days, Holman devoted his primary attention to the many problems of the National Milk Producers Federation, which had become one of the most powerful commodity organizations in agriculture. However, he never neglected the affairs of the American Institute of Cooperation. Up until 1942, when war forced discontinuance of such meetings until 1946, an annual session of the Institute was held with the cooperation of a Land-Grant or general university.

The writer was privileged to work closely with Holman during this period; in indexing the Annual Proceedings for 1927; in writing publicity for the 1928 sessions; in serving as local representative for the 1933 session held at North Carolina State, Raleigh, N. C., and as editor of the Proceedings for that year; in helping develop annual programs while on the staff of the Cooperative Research and Service Division of the Farm Credit Administration from 1934 to 1942.

I recall how Holman, in the spring of 1940, persuaded me to go to Lansing, Mich., to meet with the program committee for that year's Institute. The Michigan representatives were determined that the program should be built around the regional interests of the state. They saw no need to have prominent speakers from California or other leading cooperative states. When these views were vigorously pressed, Holman said, "The Institute of Cooperation is the *American* Institute of Cooperation. It is not a sectional organization and cannot so function."

Militant, Practical, But Idealistic, Too

While Holman was an intensely practical man, he recognized that agricultural cooperation must appeal to the heart as well as the head. The social-minded side of Holman is perhaps best illustrated by his talk on "The Contribution of Horace Plunkett to American Agricultural Cooperation." Anyone who knew him intimately realized that Holman was a man deeply interested in culture, literature, and the finer things of life. The other side reflected the man who had to fight every inch of the way for his ideals and ambitions. As a result, many saw in Holman the crafty, political organizer who knew how to create and use power, without realizing that his impelling drive was to improve the lot of agricultural producers and rural communities.

In his last Institute of Cooperation address, given at Oklahoma State University in 1950, Holman looked back over his career and referred to the 1920's—when all of his great energies were being devoted to pushing cooperatives ahead—as the Golden Age of Agricultural Cooperation. He said:

> Then we were young. Then we were fighting the battle of a young movement. Then we thought the ideal of more importance than the penny profit. . . .
> The great farmer cooperatives are those whose members are practical individualists and who so recognize themselves. These farmers see cooperatives as a mechanism of which they are a part, and through which they have the best chance of success under the private enterprise system. The cooperatives whose members have lost that idealism will disappear.

His last publication was a booklet of 89 pages entitled, *The Cooperative Way Wins in America,* issued by the Metropolitan Cooperative Milk Producers Bargaining Agency, Inc., in February, 1957. In this he could say with pride, "I have spent 43 years of my life in active contact with the general farm organizations and the agricultural cooperatives. I have worked with them all, helped organize and served three great cooperative groups." This pamphlet is remarkably modest in tone, in view of what he accomplished in making the cooperative way win. Probably no one justifiably could take greater pride for his contributions to agricultural cooperation in America.

In this essay I have not portrayed the man, who was about five feet seven, and a dynamic and persuasive speaker with a slight Southern accent. He was jaunty in appearance, and he loved to be attractively dressed. He had the charm and courtliness of the old South but he was "a militant effective fighter for cooperatives." When Charles Holman was about—you knew it.

He is now living in Washington, D.C.

Robin Hood

by Joseph G. Knapp

FIRST AND FOREMOST, Robin Hood was a publicist. Writing and editing were in his blood—and his greatest contributions to cooperative progress came through his writings or through the publications that he edited. But he was more than an able cooperative publicist. He was a person of keen intellect who equipped himself by searching study and travel to play a major role in cooperative advancement during the late 1920's and the 30's when new cooperative institutions were being formed. As first secretary and spokesman of the National Council of Farmer Cooperatives he helped it gain recognition in agricultural and political circles.

Robin was born in Chicago, Ill., on March 8, 1898, and he was reared in the city and on a farm. As a boy of nine he got out a neighborhood handset newspaper and took a lively interest in photography. After attending McKinley High School in Chicago he majored in Journalism at the University of Wisconsin where he was graduated with a B.S. degree in 1919. This followed a short period at Ft. Sheridan during 1918 as 2nd Lieutenant Training Officer in the U. S. Army.

Following his university training he worked on the Ojibwa (Wisconsin) Land Development project and was then editor of the *County News,* published in Bay City, Tex., from 1920–23, and the *Beacon,* published in Palaciors, Tex., from 1920–26. During this time he was swept up in the wave of interest in agricultural cooperatives engendered by Aaron Sapiro, and he helped develop publicity material for the commodity cooperative campaigns among farmers in the South.

In this work he became closely associated with Walton Peteet, who was director of cooperative marketing for the American Farm Bureau Federation in 1923. When Peteet became Secretary of the National Council of Cooperative Marketing Associations, set up in 1924 by a group of Sapiro-minded commodity marketing cooperatives, he induced Robin Hood to join this organization as director of information.

While Robin was serving in this capacity in 1925–26 he was able to take advantage of courses and lectures given at the Brookings Graduate School in Washington, D. C. He also visited Ireland, England, and the Scandinavian countries to broaden his knowledge of agricultural cooperatives.

Edits Influential "Cooperative Marketing Journal"

In 1926 Peteet and Hood launched the influential *Cooperative Marketing Journal*. In the fall of 1926, Peteet was stricken by illness following the collapse of the Sapiro-dominated Council, so the *Journal* was continued as an independent venture by Robin, although the name of Peteet was carried on the masthead of the *Journal* until his death in 1930.

During the years from 1927 to 1929 Robin also was in charge of publications for the Tennessee Cotton Growers, Memphis. Early in this period he married a charming girl, Ruth Vivian Frohlich, and conducted a Cooperative Marketing School for vocational agricultural teachers at Colorado State University.

When the National Cooperative Council was established in Washington, D. C., in 1929, Robin Hood was made Temporary Secretary, and the *Cooperative Marketing Journal* became its semi-official publication. However, in January, 1935, it took the name, *Cooperative Journal*.

It should be said here that the National Cooperative Council, established in 1929, was not a continuation of the National Council of Cooperative Marketing Associations which had completely disintegrated in 1926. The National Council, as set up in 1929, represented a clean break from Sapiro's cooperative philosophy, and it included all types of agricultural cooperative associations. In early 1940 it became the present National Council of Farmer Cooperatives.

Served Eight Years as Council Secretary

At the July, 1930, meeting of the National Cooperative Council, held in Columbus, Ohio, Robin was made Secretary-Treasurer, and he held this position until he resigned in December, 1938.

The National Council was born in 1929, soon after the Federal Farm Board was established and there was then great need for a national organization to represent the common interests of agricultural cooperatives. This was a time of rapid advancement, and the *Cooperative Marketing Journal*, issued monthly, did an excellent job in keeping cooperatives and government officials well informed on matters of current interest to agricultural cooperatives.

Under Robin Hood's editorship the Journal reflected the best thinking available on cooperative problems. Its authors included public officials and men of academic standing, as well as managers and leaders in various forms of cooperative enterprise. Hood's forte was an ability to bring ideas into focus.

One problem that gave concern to the National Council during the Farm Board period was the absorption of the U.S.D.A.'s Cooperative Marketing Division by the Federal Farm Board so that it ceased to have the independent status provided for by the Cooperative Marketing Act of 1926. When the Farm Board gave way to the Farm Credit Administration in 1933, Robin Hood, as the representative of the Council, successfully worked with other agricultural organizations to get the research and service work for cooperatives re-established.

With the coming of the New Deal other problems needed attention. Many of the NRA industry codes at first refused to recognize the distinctive characteristics of cooperatives, and especially their practice of distributing savings in the form of patronage refunds. Robin vigorously represented the Council in helping correct this situation.

In the early days of the New Deal great interest also developed in consumer cooperation, and some of the consumer cooperative theorists of that day were very critical of the "slow-moving, conservative" agricultural cooperatives. Many of the enthusiasts saw in consumer cooperation a panacea that would meet all economic and social problems. One prominent consumer cooperative leader maintained that "in every country the socialist movement is close to the consumers cooperative movement because of the similarity of ultimate aims . . . In the cooperative movement the ultimate tendency is toward the creation of a social structure capable of supplanting both profit-making industry and the compulsory state." Robin Hood, as Secretary of the National Cooperative Council and as Editor of the *Cooperative Journal*, effectively questioned the realism of such statements.

In January, 1936, the publication of Marquis Childs' book, *Sweden —the Middle Way*, aroused great interest in European cooperatives as an answer to American economic and social problems. This book

stimulated President Roosevelt to set up a commission to study and
report on Cooperative Enterprise in Europe. As originally set up,
the Commission was to be comprised of three members, but in view
of the fact that the only government funds available for the inquiry
were in the U.S.D.A. it was deemed appropriate to add three members to represent the viewpoint of agriculture. In this way Robin
Hood along with Clifford Gregory, Editor of the *Prairie Farmer*
became members of the inquiry.

The Commission spent two and a half months during the summer
of 1936 surveying "mainly consumer cooperative enterprise" in the
British Isles and Northern European countries.

Conservative Views About Consumer Cooperatives Assailed

The report of the Commission was published as a comprehensive
government document in early 1937, and its findings were more
realistic and conservative than had been anticipated—possibly due to
the presence on the Commission of Robin Hood and Clifford Gregory
who reflected the experience and thinking of American agricultural
cooperative leaders. The report recognized the important role that
cooperatives could play as part of the American private enterprise
system but it stopped short of outright propaganda in their behalf.
In the report each member of the Commission also presented his or
her independent views. The following excerpts represent some of the
views expressed by Robin Hood:

> It therefore appears that present American conditions are not
> particularly conducive to the rapid and widespread development
> of consumer cooperatives.
>
> ——
>
> Finally, consumer cooperation is not a highway to Utopia. It
> developed in Europe because it served an economic need. It will
> develop in the United States to the extent that it can serve an
> economic need.
>
> ——
>
> Any group of people who believe they can purchase their re-
> quirements more advantageously through cooperatives . . .
> should be fairly afforded an opportunity to make the effort. But
> European cooperative leaders themselves uniformly advise us
> against government subsidies and high-pressure government pro-
> motion.

Robin Hood's views were bitterly assailed by certain of the consumer cooperative leaders of the time but he stood his ground in the
Cooperative Journal and on public platforms. In this way he helped

crystallize thinking toward a more constructive view of what co-operatives could properly be expected to contribute to the nation's economy.

Strongly Advocated Research, Education

Robin Hood believed in the power of research and education and, as Secretary of the National Council, he worked to get the research and educational work of the Farm Credit Administration more firmly established. At its annual convention in January, 1938, the Council made its position clear. Its resolutions stated:

> The National Cooperative Council believes that the government's policy in regard to agricultural cooperatives is as important as any policy relating to agriculture. . . . The Council further believes that commendation is due to the Farm Credit Administration for its efforts and accomplishments in furthering cooperative marketing development. It questions, however, the advisability of placing the administration of the Cooperative Marketing Act of 1926 in too close association with the Banks for Cooperatives, in the fear that the intention of a strong research and extension program may be subordinated to the loaning functions of the Banks . . .

Robin Hood kept these views before the officials of the Farm Credit Administration and, as a result, the Cooperative Research and Service Division was established in early 1939 within the Farm Credit Administration.

Shortly after Robin Hood resigned as Secretary-Treasurer of the National Cooperative Council in late 1938, an expression of appreciation was adopted at the Council's Eleventh Annual Assembly of Delegates. It is here given in part:

> WHEREAS, Mr. Robin Hood, who has continuously served as secretary-treasurer of the National Cooperative Council since its formation, has recently tendered his resignation, and

> WHEREAS, the standing and influence of the Council during those years has been especially constructive and outstanding, and has placed the organization in a position of major importance in national affairs, and . . .

> WHEREAS, the increased interest and concert of effort have been in substantial part due to the leadership of the secretary of the Council and to the confidence which the members have in his wisdom, honesty, and sincerity of purpose, and

> WHEREAS, Mr. Hood has given unstintingly of his time and energy to develop bonds of friendship, a will to work together, and unity of purpose and effort among cooperatives and co-

operative leaders, and striving toward that end, he was, in a substantial measure, responsible for the organization and the early development of the Cooperative Council,

NOW, THEREFORE, BE IT RESOLVED that the delegates of this annual meeting unanimously express their appreciation and thanks for his devotion and enthusiastic cooperation and express the gratitude and indebtedness to a sincere and effective worker, a true cooperator, a gentleman, and a friend."

Following his resignation from the Council, Robin was very active in the Coast Guard. He had long been interested in boats and one of his great pleasures was a small yacht for week-end cruising. With the approach of World War II he organized the Defense Flotilla on the East Coast, and later was on transport duty to Africa and to the South Seas and Manila. From 1941 to 1943 as Lt. Commander he was in charge of the Narsarssuak base in Greenland.

After the war he went back to newspaper work—his first love—and from 1946–1954 published the *Muskogee (Oklahoma) County News,* which won many awards. He then taught and studied Journalism at Oklahoma A. & M., and was granted the M.A. degree there in 1955. In 1956–57 he was head of the Journalism and Graphic Arts Department of the University of Houston. He also taught Journalism at the University of Nevada in 1959–60.

Only a few oldtimers—such as myself—can recall Robin Hood in his heyday as Secretary of the National Cooperative Council. One of them is Stanley Andrews who gives me this remembrance in a recent letter:

Hood in those days was rather heavy for his height but that did not keep down a sort of restless energy which kept him always needling farmers and his friends toward what we then called the "Cooperative Way." While he did not organize any cooperatives nor manage any and was not of the whoop and holler type, his great persistence and steady push on those with whom he came in contact did much to solidify and make for a really successful beginning of a combined educational effort.

To me, Robin Hood was a good and generous friend from 1927— when I began submitting articles to the *Cooperative Marketing Journal*—until his death from a heart attack in Arizona in 1962. His patient inquiring mind and warm human spirit helped open the road for sound cooperative advancement in the United States.

Arthur Howland

by Orion Ulrey

THE NAME OF ARTHUR HOWLAND is revered in Michigan for the 30 years of constructive service that he devoted to the farmer cooperatives of that state.

Art was born in 1892 and grew up on a farm near Breckenridge, about 60 miles directly north of East Lansing where Michigan State University is located. He served with the U. S. Army during World War I, and afterwards was a herdsman on a dairy farm near Alma.

He worked as a research assistant on dairy and farm management studies in Michigan before he resigned in 1921 to enter Michigan State as a student in agriculture. He was an excellent student, as attested by his membership in Alpha Zeta, an honorary fraternity. He assisted in organizing the MAC Dairy Club in 1924 and was its first president.

After his graduation in 1925 he worked for one year at the McIntyre Dairy Company in Saginaw and six months for the Arctic Dairy Company in Detroit. On January 1, 1927, he was appointed as an extension worker in the Department of Economics of Michigan State College, to assist primarily "in the accounting and business practices of cooperatives." He retired on June 30, 1957, 30 years and six months later, without a single leave of absence from his work except once on full pay following serious surgery in 1946.

Most of Howland's work was with people and his written contributions were few. In 1955 he prepared *A Directory of Farmer Cooperatives in Michigan* and, jointly with Orion Ulrey in 1956, *The Cooperatives and Nonprofit Dairy Associations in Michigan*. For many years, however, he presented papers and participated in discussions at the meetings of the American Institute of Cooperation and in workshops for marketing and cooperative specialists.

Howland was project leader of the Marketing Section of the Department of Agricultural Economics for several years beginning in

1949. He was active as a director for several years and was president of the Michigan State Association of Extension Specialists for one term. He was a member of Epsilon Sigma Phi, national honorary extension fraternity. He served for a time as an adviser of a cooperative house for men students at Michigan State. In fact, the Howland House, organized in 1945, was named for him.

Arthur Howland joined the Extension Service soon after the programs for the constructive building of the farmer cooperatives were initiated by Michigan State, by the new federations of cooperatives and by the Michigan Farm Bureau. His services during the three decades might be classified as follows: (1) accounting, records, and financial statements; (2) organization and legal structure, especially in relation to the corporation laws, the federal corporation income tax, and the requirements for loans by the Banks for Cooperatives; and (3) economic analysis and recommendations for the cooperative businesses.

Active in Developing Co-op Legal Structure

During the early years he devoted considerable time to the establishment of adequate accounting systems for several score societies. He collaborated with attorneys and other legal counsel in the preparation of standard articles and bylaws for various types of cooperatives. These were widely adopted by the societies of the state. Art, along with attorneys and other cooperative specialists, assisted in the preparation and filing of articles for a legion of cooperatives; and worked with the boards in evolving bylaws which fitted the statutory laws and the activities of the individual cooperatives.

Art collaborated with both the Corporation Division and the Securities Division of the Michigan Corporation and Securities Commission in an advisory and consultant capacity on statutory and regulatory requirements applicable to farmer cooperatives. He also assisted many cooperatives to obtain financial aid from the St. Paul Bank for Cooperatives, and served as an adviser to the cooperative banks on the economic potential and management of borrowing cooperatives.

Many of the early cooperatives were formed as farmer-owned stock companies. The stock of some of these became concentrated in the hands of a few, and they became profit corporations. Many groups wished to retain their cooperative status. Early members were deceased. The new patrons did not become stockholders. The assets, of course, belonged to the stockholders although frequently created largely from nonmember business. Art took the lead in reorganizing many cooperatives to permit current patrons to become the owners of the associations.

Art introduced and promoted the automatic membership system and the rotating plan of financing among the farmer cooperatives of the state in order to guarantee the continuous cooperative nature of the business and to obtain finance from the owner-users. Where the plans were properly followed, the results have been very favorable. Under the plan, the owners have consisted only of active patrons.

Insisted on Proper Legal Procedures

In the early years, many of the cooperatives did not employ proper legal procedures for the annual and special meetings of members and for the meetings of the boards of directors. Art made sure that every meeting he attended was legal, and thus assisted in establishing legal procedures among the farmer cooperatives. He drove thousands of miles each year to attend membership meetings and especially to confer with boards and management. He knew the problems of a host of cooperatives, and was constantly encouraging the leaders to make the proper adjustments and corrections. His advice to local boards was always sincere and dealt with pertinent issues. In the analysis which preceded his recommendations, he was careful to check in great detail the records and operations of the cooperatives.

Art assisted in the consolidation and reorganization of a large number of cooperatives. One of his jobs in which he took considerable pride, and justifiably so, was the organization of the farmers who sold milk to the McDonald Dairy Company of Flint to purchase the facilities of that company. Beginning in 1942, deduction from the monthly milk checks were used to pay for the facilities. The former owners became the initial managers of the McDonald Cooperative Dairy Company. The volume and facilities of the cooperative have expanded several times since the company was purchased by the dairy farmers.

The cooperative leaders of Michigan have placed a high value on the services of Howland and the other cooperative specialists. The following are typical of the comments about Art:

"He saved the cooperatives a lot of headaches."
"He checked every detail."
"He was always conscientious—dedicated and sincere in his work."
"He insisted that the cooperative jobs be done right."
"He was always on the job—always ready to provide service."

"He was as much, if not more, concerned about the problems of the cooperatives as any employee."

"We had great confidence in him."

"He provided us with tools and ideas."

Art was interested not only in the role of cooperatives in serving Michigan farmers but also in the possible services of cooperatives to urban consumer groups and to the strengthening of economic democracy. His office files contained records of almost 200 cooperatives of many types, which he serviced during his three decades as a staff member at Michigan State. He was an educator in the finest tradition of the Extension Service—and cooperation found in him one of its most sturdy advocates.

Lyman S. Hulbert

by John C. Bagwell

I REMEMBER THE DAY I walked into "Judge" Hulbert's office for the first time. It was 1933. I was reporting for a new job and he was to be my boss and my friend for years to come. But the day stands out in my memory for other reasons.

Lyman S. Hulbert, affectionately and respectfully known as "Judge" to his friends and associates, was a well-known name. I knew it because Judge Hulbert was even then a recognized authority on the law of cooperative associations—the business organizations of farmers that helped farmers through the depression of the 1930s.

As a young lawyer reporting for my first assignment on the legal staff of the Farm Credit Administration, I was a bit apprehensive about this first meeting. Any fears I had, however, proved groundless. Judge Hulbert greeted me warmly and we had a long visit. In no time at all, we talked as if we were old friends.

This quality—this ability to make people feel at ease under difficult circumstances as he had done with me—is, I believe, one of the qualities that made Lyman Hulbert so perfectly suited to work with and for farmer cooperatives.

In putting this biography together, it is difficult for me to be objective in describing the singularly outstanding career of this man. He was my first supervisor and I have been privileged to know him and to learn from him all of these years. After he retired from government service in December, 1950, he opened an office specializing in the practice of cooperative corporation law. Today, as much as ever, it is a welcome treat to visit with the Judge. He frequently stops by to discuss current cooperative legal matters when he can get away from his active law practice. His wisdom and counsel have contributed to the solution of many difficult problems.

Authored "Legal Phases of Cooperative Associations"

Among Judge Hulbert's countless achievements in the field of cooperative law one stands out—his authorship and the subsequent revisions of *Legal Phases of Cooperative Associations*. But more about this later.

Lyman Hulbert is the oldest of four brothers. He and his one older sister were born at Manchester, Mich. His brothers were born on a farm near Manchester, where the family moved after he was born. Distance, horse and buggy transportation, and farm work complicated and delayed his formal high school education. When his father died, it was decided to sell the farm and move to Ann Arbor, Mich., where he and his brothers would have an opportunity for a university education. While just a young man, Lyman assumed the responsibilities of head of the family. He thus became not only provider, but head of the household for a whole family while other young men his age followed less demanding pursuits. To help earn his way through college he sold aluminum ware and books door-to-door several summers.

In June, 1914, when most young men his age had already finished school, Lyman graduated from the University of Michigan Law School and was admitted to the Michigan bar. Devotion to his family and the desire to insure an opportunity for the education and well-being of his younger brothers and sister were uppermost in his mind at this period.

With an eye to the future, he decided to take a federal law exam offered in July, 1914. Nearly 700 applicants took the three-day test. When results were announced, Lyman had placed eleventh but there was no immediate prospect of a job. Opportunities for a young lawyer in Michigan were limited, so he moved to Atlanta, Ga., and engaged in the general practice of law.

Some three years later when he had almost forgotten about the federal law exam, Chester Morrill, an attorney in the Solicitor's Office of the United States Department of Agriculture, came to his office in Atlanta with an offer of a job in Washington, D. C., at $1,600 a year. He accepted on the spot.

On December 1, 1917, Judge Hulbert entered government service as a member of the Solicitor's Office of the Department. It was the beginning of a long and colorful career for this man who would become a foremost authority on the law of farmer cooperatives.

His first office was located in a red brick house which had been converted into offices and was situated on Independence Avenue between 12th and 14th Streets where Agriculture's South Building stands today. There were 21 or 22 lawyers on the Solicitor's staff at the time and the Judge was assigned to work involving the country's agricultural problems incident to World War I. Within six months his salary was raised to $1,800 a year.

In 1923, Judge Hulbert married Virginia Southgate. They have one daughter and two grandchildren.

Analyzed Capper-Volstead Act Aid to Co-ops

Judge Hulbert remained on the Solicitor's staff until he was asked to take charge of the legal work for cooperatives in a new agency of the Department—the Bureau of Agricultural Economics. Centered in this agency would be research, advisory, and educational services for farmer cooperatives. It was also at about this same time that the Judge prepared a statement concerning the meaning and scope of the Capper-Volstead Act. This 1922 law, frequently called the bill of rights for farmer cooperatives, supplemented the Clayton Amendment to the antitrust laws by specifically permitting farmers to act together in associations without danger of prosecution under the antitrust statutes. Copies of the Judge's statement were sent to thousands of cooperative associations all over the country in response to requests for information about this new legislation.

One of the main areas of cooperative work in BAE dealt with legal phases of cooperation. Publication of Department Bulletin No. 1106, *Legal Phases of Cooperative Associations,* took place in October, 1922. This event deserves special mention. It was entirely the work of Judge Hulbert and it was a basic contribution. It marked the origin of a publication which today is the "desk or handbook" of cooperative officials and advisors all over the world.

The Judge's Bulletin provided the first extensive discussion of legal problems in the organization and operation of cooperatives. It has been revised and extended several times (three by the Judge himself)—the last time in 1958 as *Legal Phases of Farmer Cooperatives, FCS Bulletin 10.* It has played a significant part in the development of the statute law and judicial precedents affecting the legal status of farmer cooperatives everywhere. Few publications have received such wide and favorable reception and use by those responsible for providing legal advice to farmer cooperatives.

Other works were to follow, including many basic legal opinions, articles for various cooperative publications, and the summary of cases and decisions affecting cooperatives. Space does not permit a listing of all of them. Of the many legal opinions he has written, the Judge recalls with pride the part he played in one. "It was," he says, "a matter of great importance. We concluded after much study and research that, under the law, a corporation may be a farmer."

He conducted and participated in numerous clinics, institutes, and seminars throughout the country where cooperative officials, directors, and attorneys could get first-hand information and help. His vast experience and legal knowledge, combined with his patience and understanding, kept him in constant demand. He would think nothing of working hours and days, if necessary, in solving a complex problem for lawyers or others who came to consult him.

Helped to Draft Basic Farm Legislation

He had a major role in drafting much of the farm legislation of the day. Following the stock market crash of 1929, he worked on a bill which became the Agricultural Marketing Act establishing the Federal Farm Board. The Cooperative Marketing Act of 1926, the legislation which is the basic law under which the Farmer Cooperative Service operates today, was largely the work of Judge Hulbert. Amendments to the Commodity Exchange Act are also examples of legislation which the Judge helped write.

One of his major assignments was to help set up the Federal Farm Board. He was on the legal staff of the original Farm Credit Administration, the agency which succeeded the Federal Farm Board.

During World War II, when many government agencies were transferred out of war-time Washington, Judge Hulbert remained as liaison attorney for the Farm Credit Administration which had been moved to Kansas City, Mo. As Assistant General Counsel of FCA he was in charge of all legal work for the 13 Banks for Cooperatives. This title, according to the Judge, was the highest position he held during his 33 years with the government. But title or position do not measure the man.

Private Legal Practice Aids Co-ops, A.I.C.

Retirement from government service in 1950 only served to intensify his activity in behalf of cooperatives. As a part of his private practice, he is associated as Legal Consultant with the American Institute of Cooperation, the national educational and research organization of farmer cooperatives. For many years Judge Hulbert's work with the American Institute has included appearances as guest lecturer at some 20 or more different law schools throughout the country. The Judge has talked to hundreds of law students on the subject of cooperatives and the law. His lectures covered the nature, character, objectives, and tax status of farmer cooperatives.

Helim Hulbert, the Judge's younger brother, a retired career employee of the Department of Agriculture, recently told me:

> The Judge has always been my inspiration. All my life I have tried to follow in his footsteps. He has provided the spark—the driving force behind much of my own activity. It is the Judge, you know, who gets us on the tennis court these days.

It is a well-known fact that the Judge can be found on a tennis court almost every weekend throughout the year. His friends say that the Judge is at home in any court—whether it be law or tennis.

Judge Hulbert's way with a legal draft is memorable. He never made a correction merely to change a word here or to add a bit of punctuation there. But if he could improve the thought and clarify it—if he could point up the subject by "cutting away the underbrush"—he did it. His method, I recall from first-hand knowledge, consisted of adding his thoughts and ideas on the page, across and through the page at every angle, and if necessary, around the margins until, finally, the draft resembled a "sunburst." No more apt metaphor could be used, because the Judge's comments, corrections and additions always threw light on murky legal problems, and warmed you with their clarity and wit.

Millions of members of cooperatives all over the country have benefited from his sharp legal mind, his gentle humor, his boundless capacity for labor in their behalf, and his total grasp of the law.

In 1948, the Judge received the Department of Agriculture's Superior Service Award. The University of Wisconsin honored him in 1947 with a testimonial from its College of Agriculture for his service to cooperatives and for his contribution to the law of cooperatives. He was named a "Pioneer in Agricultural Marketing" by the American Marketing Association, in 1963.

Of the scores of anecdotes about Judge Hulbert, one is my favorite. When I was a member of his staff in the early days of the Farm Credit Administration, he once laughingly told me when I came in carrying a single volume of the U. S. Supreme Court Reports, "Beware of the lawyer with one book." The Judge obviously felt that a lawyer who comes in with a stack of law books under each arm is giving away the fact that he is not well prepared or that he is not sure of his case. "But," the Judge warned me, "the lawyer with one book is a formidable foe. He is prepared. He is sure of his facts. He has done his research well and has found the precedent that will prove his point and win the case." If memory serves me well, the Judge never had more than one lawbook with him at any given time.

I. H. Hull

by Herbert C. Fledderjohn

ISAAC HARVEY HULL—Harvey to his friends—farmer, surveyor, active Methodist layman, cooperative leader—especially *cooperative leader*. My first close-up look at I. H. Hull, General Manager of the Indiana Farm Bureau Cooperative Association, came in the early spring of 1932. As a recently hired bookkeeper I had seen him in the halls or on the elevator a few times and had heard his booming voice when he spoke at a meeting, but never had I had the chance to see him in action close up. The occasion was a meeting that we had of the office force.

There was a widely-circulated rumor that a change was to be made in the management of the office, and when Mr. Hull asked that the group gather around their desks, we assumed that he was to announce who our new office manager would be. When he called the meeting to order, he explained briefly about the necessity for selecting a new manager, commented on the importance of an accurate, up-to-date, well-run office, and then said, "Since all of you are going to have to work together under the supervision of the new office manager, I think it would be appropriate that you elect him rather than for me to appoint him."

I was dumbfounded. Fresh out of college, I had been studying all about personnel management, testing, selection, organization charts, and all of the paraphernalia of business management. You just didn't ask employees to elect their supervisor. *But we did!* It was completely unbusinesslike, unscientific—a dangerous deviation from the traditional dictatorial power of "the boss." The only thing that could be said for it was that it worked. Since we had made the decision, we had to work twice as hard as normal in order to prove that our judgment was right. And, of course, we had made the right choice. William Kenneth Miller, who was the one selected, later became Treasurer and Assistant General Manager of the organization.

This story is told because it typifies the kind of man that Harvey Hull was, and is. His leadership was based on an unbounded faith in the capacity of ordinary human beings to do things for themselves, given the basic facts that they needed, and an organization technique that would make it possible for them to work together effectively. And on this theory, he built the Indiana Farm Bureau Cooperative Association into one of the leading agricultural cooperatives in the United States.

Harvey was born (1884) and grew up on an Illinois farm, and it was one of those typical midwestern farms where the whole family had to work from daylight to dark in order to produce enough to keep the mortgage paid and body and soul together. As a matter of fact, farm work had to come before education, and it was necessary for Harvey to miss several years of school. However, like another great resident of the state of Illinois, Abraham Lincoln, Harvey had learned about the value of education, and he managed to finish high school long after he was of the age for it, and went on to Northwestern University to get his B.S. degree in 1909 as a surveyor.

As Farmer, Hull Saw Need for Group Action

A few years later, he was to be found farming in LaPorte County, Ind., where he learned first-hand the problems of a farmer. Low prices for what he sold—high prices for what he bought—the uncertainties of the weather—the risks of pests—and the realities of an "every man for himself" business world. This combination of circumstances, which faced all Indiana farmers after World War I, would inevitably lead to some kind of group action, if for no other reason than that it was necessary for their survival. Out of it came the Indiana Farm Bureau, and Harvey Hull enlisted in the struggle. Almost immediately he was named as president of the LaPorte County unit and soon was elected to the state board of directors representing the First District.

Among the early programs of the Indiana Farm Bureau was an effort to help farmers with their operating costs. This took many forms. On some occasions, reports of profiteering in the sale of farm supplies were published in the official organ, the *Hoosier Farmer*. On other occasions, agents helped farmers to pool their orders for fertilizer, coal, or feed, so that they could get the advantage of bulk buying. They even tried a "buyers' strike" to force down the price of fertilizer. Finally, under a subsidiary corporation, the Indiana Farm Bureau organized a group of farm supply stores over Indiana from which farmers would be able to purchase their supplies at substantial savings.

Something went wrong with the plan, and in 1926 the Farm Bureau Board named a committee consisting of Harvey Hull, James Mason, and Lewis Taylor to study the operation and come in with a recommendation for improvement before this operation destroyed the parent organization. By some miracle they discovered the Rochdale Weavers and their method of cooperative operation, and recommended to the Farm Bureau that this serve as a pattern for the organization of Indiana farmers into an effective cooperative. The Farm Bureau Board was more than willing to be relieved of this direct responsibility, so they asked Harvey to take on the task of directing the reorganization of their buying service into a federated cooperative, and to serve as its General Manager.

Hull's Faith in Farmers Working Together Built I.F.B.C.A.

It was a wonderful assignment. The organization had no capital, and in fact, had debts of $12,000 with no resources to pay them. There were no local cooperatives and the general attitude among farmers was one of discouragement and disillusionment. A wonderful opportunity for a young man with formal training in Civil Engineering and no business experience. But *Harvey Hull made it work.*

Emerson observed that "an organization is the lengthened shadow of a man." And the Indiana Farm Bureau Cooperative Association is the lengthened shadow of I. H. Hull. Of course, he didn't do it all himself. He gathered around him a group who had caught the vision of what farmers could do working together, and as a group, they built the cooperatives in Indiana, organization by organization, service by service, dollar by dollar. Harvey's insistent faith that people could do anything that they wanted to do if they worked together governed the whole operating policy of the organization. The people who were selected were those who had demonstrated a commitment to the idea through their voluntary activities—not any specialized skills. As a matter of fact, there was not more than one college graduate in the whole group. But Harvey's enthusiasm and confidence was infectious, and not knowing that they couldn't compete with the likes of Standard Oil and Ralston Purina and Swift, they went out and did it.

The way was not always easy. At the depth of the depression cash became short in the co-op and Mr. Hull asked that each employee take two weeks vacation without pay. True to his sympathies for the "little people," any married employee who was making less than $25 per week didn't have to take a vacation. There was hardly a murmur in the whole employee group, and most of them took the two weeks without pay in stride, although few of them actually took the vacation. Such was the morale of the organization.

From $1 to 50 Million in Net Worth

It was no wonder that starting with a $12,000 deficit they were able within a few years to achieve a net worth in the wholesale cooperative of $1 million. In the annual meeting where General Manager Hull announced to the delegates the achievement of this milestone, he pointed out in all seriousness that the first million dollars was the hardest, and that future millions would come easier.

This seemed to be a great joke to the delegates, because few of them felt that they could grow much larger. However, now the organization has a net worth in excess of $50 million, and counts its volume in the hundreds of millions. Such is the power of a man of conviction who has the capacity to stir others to accept his vision and act on it.

The business of organizing cooperatives is habit-forming. It was as early as 1929 that Mr. Hull saw the necessity for expanding the base of operations in certain kinds of activities if they were to be successful. On this basis, he invited the Ohio Farm Bureau Cooperative Association and the Michigan Farm Bureau Services to join with Indiana Farm Bureau Cooperative in the ownership and operation of an oil-compounding plant to be located in Indianapolis.

All three of these cooperative states had made a beginning in the petroleum business and all were finding that it was difficult to purchase consistently high-quality motor oils at reasonable prices. The three state cooperatives did join in and launched what was to be a very successful interregional cooperative—so successful in fact, that in 1936 other state and regional cooperatives in the United States requested permission to join, and the organization became United Cooperatives, now a very successful coast-to-coast federation of regional farm supply purchasing cooperatives.

"National Cooperatives" Follows "United Cooperatives"

With the Farm Bureau Oil Company well launched, Mr. Hull joined with Howard Cowden, the General Manager of Consumers Cooperative Association in Kansas City, to convene a meeting of petroleum cooperatives over the country which might be interested in jointly contracting for liquid fuel supplies. Again other cooperatives saw the wisdom of this, and National Cooperatives was launched. It has since evolved into a nationwide manufacturing and purchasing organization, servicing regional cooperative wholesales.

By happy chance, in 1934 the Board of Directors of the Indiana Farm Bureau Cooperative Association insisted that their General Manager take some respite from the driving pace which he maintained, and join the first Cooperative League tour of Europe. U. S. cooperatives had made a beginning, but they were for the most part small and struggling. For Mr. Hull to see the grand scale of operation of the cooperatives in England, Denmark, Sweden, and Finland, was to apply a forced draft to the spark of cooperative conviction that had grown out of his experience in Indiana.

Early in the tour a trip to the Toad Lane store of the Rochdale Pioneers was scheduled, which had then become a museum for the cooperative movement in England. Harvey stood in obvious awe of what the simple weavers had accomplished from their humble beginnings in that little store. And here was proof positive of his basic philosophy that ordinary people can do anything if they get the facts and are willing to work together.

Harvey walked from the Toad Lane store down the street to one of the modern emporiums of the Rochdale Society of Equitable Pioneers and saw by contrast what these people had really accomplished. So struck by the store was he that he made a purchase. When the tour had left the United States, the temperatures in the Midwest were hovering near 100°, so that Harvey had taken only light clothing and no hat. The coolness of the English summer was beginning to bother his bald head, so he emerged from the Rochdale store wearing the most wonderful English bowler that anyone had ever seen. Through the rest of the tour it was a sort of badge as he proudly announced that it came from the Rochdale Cooperative.

Was First to Work for Rural Electric Co-ops

Later in the tour, the Danish farms were visited and Harvey was impressed by the way in which cooperatives provided electrical service in these rural Danish areas. In fact, it wasn't long after he got back to Indiana that he again got into the business of organizing cooperatives. He asked the staff of the Indiana Farm Bureau Cooperative Association to prepare a bill to be introduced in the state legislature which would authorize the organization of rural electric cooperatives. Actually the Indiana statute was passed two months before the national Rural Electrification Act became law, and the first rural electric cooperative in the United States was in Boone County, Ind.

Some who knew more about the electrical utility business, who understood the difficulty of serving the sparsely populated rural areas, and the amount of revenue necessary to support a mile of line, were sure that these rural electric cooperatives would fail, and in the process embarrass the whole cooperative movement. But Harvey never wavered. True to his conviction that the people can do anything if they want to and are willing to stick together, he arranged for funds to be advanced to the rural electric cooperatives from the Indiana Farm Bureau Cooperative, and pushed aggressively for their extension. Of course, time has proved that he was right.

Advocated First Rural Credit Unions

Harvey Hull has made it a consistent part of his cooperative strategy that it is important for people to organize and control their financial resources. Out of this conviction came a drive in the 30's to organize the first rural credit unions in the United States. Several of these have now become multi-million dollar organizations and the idea has spread to many other areas. On the basis of the record, it can be said that Harvey Hull was always in the business of starting something. Those of us who are the beneficiaries of his foresight can be glad he did.

It would be a mistake to leave the impression that everything which Harvey touched was successful. There were some notable failures too, but Harvey always insisted that these were failures of the people, and not of the plan. If the people would stick together and learn the facts, there was nothing they couldn't do. One of his great disappointments was in the failure of the cooperatives in the farm machinery business. Years of earnest toil and hundreds of meetings that resulted ultimately in the organization of National Farm Machinery Cooperative, proved to be of no avail. The cooperatives lacked the internal discipline and the sophisticated know-how to succeed in this complicated field of operation.

Consistent with his basic philosophy, Harvey never criticized an employee if he was *trying*—failures or mistakes could be overlooked if you were making an honest effort. The one unforgivable sin was to not try your best. A central theme ran through all the communications between Harvey Hull and his executive staff, office and plant workers, directors, and local cooperative management employees. This theme was that we were to make careful plans, keeping fully in mind our objective, and then to work aggressively toward the realization of these plans.

He liked to tell the story of his courting days when he set out to win the hand of a young neighbor girl. Harvey tells that in order to impress her, he bought the most spirited team that he could afford and hitched it to a new buggy and went courting. He reported with great seriousness that he made no progress at all, and finally discovered that he was so busy driving the spirited horses that he had no time for courting. "I lost sight of my objective," he was fond of saying. Then he would tell how he traded this team for a more gentle one that could be handled with one hand, and it wasn't long before Minnie had decided to become Mrs. Hull.

In retrospect, one wonders about the modern techniques in cooperative development. Harvey Hull came to manage a bankrupt organization. He knew nothing about the sophisticated management techniques of budgets, and manning tables, and financial ratios. He had never heard of a job description or a market research study. But a combination of firm belief in the cooperative principle, a faith in men, and ordinary business judgment created highly successful cooperative business institutions.

Maybe you can't do it this way any more. Maybe the modern situation calls for electronic data processing and sophisticated feasibility studies and high-powered promotion based on an understanding of motivation research. But we can say, "Thank God for the Harvey Hulls." They inspired us to do things that we didn't know we could do. They put handles on our aspirations and convinced us that we can stand tall if we are willing to work together. They gave us back our human dignity by making the opportunity for us to count for something in a group that was working for total social progress. They gave meaning to the humble day-to-day job without which man becomes nothing more than a machine. Yes, thank God for the Harvey Hulls.

A. L. Jerdan

by J. Franklin Nix

"He paweth in the valley, and rejoiceth in his strength: he goeth on to meet the armed men. He mocketh at fear, and is not affrighted; neither turneth he back from the sword" (Job 39:21–22).

JOB COULD HAVE EASILY BEEN WRITING about Alabama's greatest contribution to Tennessee, the old war horse, A. L. Jerdan. Mr. Jerdan, or Al as he is known to his friends, came to Tennessee in 1920 as a livestock specialist; and in 1921 he became Extension Marketing Specialist. This was about the time the Agricultural Extension Service was getting started and many years before marketing and cooperative purchasing was an accepted practice in this state.

Al then held B.S. degrees from Alabama Polytechnic Institute (now Auburn University) and the University of Missouri, and the M.S. degree from the University of Illinois.

Prior to his coming to Tennessee, he had served two years as Extension Livestock Specialist in North Carolina and had ably served in World War I as the commanding officer of Company B, 52nd Infantry, in the American Expeditionary Forces in France and Germany. (Incidentally to this day, Mr. Al can tell you the names and hometowns of many of the officers and enlisted men with whom he served.) Following cessation of hostilities in 1918, he spent a year as instructor in animal nutrition in the College of Agriculture, A.E.F. University, Beaune, France.

In these early years, many of the better Tennessee farmers were not moved to action by Al's early efforts and many business men condemned his soul to the everlasting fires of eternal damnation. And since the program of cooperative marketing, which he promoted, was not at that time politically expedient for his superiors and some of his contemporaries in the service, he received little help and daily opposition. However, this fellow, Al, is a determined character. Having survived the impact of being born in rural Alabama, the First World War, and the influence and contempt of some of his friends and co-workers, he started out slowly yet deliberately to build farmer-owned, farmer-controlled, organizations in Tennessee.

Succeeded in Organizing Co-op in Spite of Opposition

This was not an easy task for he was encountered on all sides and at all levels by adverse circumstances. Many people, even some farmers, honestly believed that it was wrong and downright sinful for farmers to organize and many, many other people, because of vested interests or political expediency, fought him and his farmer projects every step of the way.

To those who have admired and worked with him, Al was and is, without any doubts or reservations, the spirit, power, and enlightment of all successful cooperative efforts in Tennessee, be it in the fields of fruits, tobacco, peanuts, poultry, cattle, calves, lambs, wool, farm supplies, cotton, grains, or a county fair. The Tennessee Farmers Cooperative is perhaps the best example of the work and determination and philosophy of this man Jerdan. He has and still is guiding it every step of the way. To most Tennesseans at the present time, he is our "Mr. Co-op," and his cooperative tracks grow larger each year. His friends love and cherish him and he has out-lived most of his enemies. As for the latter, they either writhed in ignorance or were enemies of all cooperative activities of farm people.

His efforts were not confined to this one field of endeavor. He had many other interests and talents. His charts of the grain markets are still worth studying. He assisted in obtaining the charter for the Tennessee 4-H Club Foundation. In fact, he drafted the charter and the bylaws for the organization and assisted with the proper organizational structure and procedure just as he had for hundreds of other cooperative groups. His was one of the most articulate voices of Tennessee as related to farmer-owned, farmer-controlled organizations, proper organizational structure, and adherence to the legal aspects of director and delegate action. It was his voice that made the plea for educated and informed directors and delegates and it was his voice that sounded the warnings of proper and legal roles to be performed by those who make policy and those who perform the role of management.

The dozens of co-op failures in Tennessee's earlier years were the result of ignoring Al's words of wisdom and precise instructions. As an Extension worker, he had to help incorporate any cooperative group who requested his services; but not one can stand or testify that Al didn't warn with a roar and a prophecy that unless they adhered to basic cooperate principles and sound financing, their birthday would go down in history as a miscarriage rather than a happy memory.

Fought for Sound Financing, High Principles

He has very definite ideas as related to economics and again his ideas run counter to some modern trends. Perhaps the understatement of this thesis follows: He believes in adequate financing and is opposed to deficit spending or the unbalanced budget. A look at Tennessee Farmers Cooperative's balance sheet today strongly reflects Al's financial philosophy.

You can find Al Jerdan's deeply embedded beliefs in his own stout assertion that "there is just one kind of constructive help, and that is *self*-help." His approach is that self-help can take one of three forms: do the job alone, with the strength of your family, or banded into a group driven by the same desire or need. One of his operating principles is that we should spur on the slower horses instead of tying hobbles on the fastest horse.

And therein lies Al Jerdan's belief in cooperatives. When the job is too big to be budged by the individual, the cooperative—through pooling strength and resources and competent management—can render the self-help the individual needs and deserves for betterment.

Those who have known and worked with Mr. Al recognize him as a man who doesn't flinch when the going gets rough. Rather than duck a problem or surrender his convictions, he lives by a quotation from Huxley: "God give me strength to face a fact, though it slay me."

Mr. Al sees a continuing need for every person to have a sane spiritual belief. He holds personal freedom to be one of our priceless possessions. He looks on better schools and education, homes and churches, as our right as well as our need—and believes that if we don't develop them, we're "flat failures."

Perhaps, when he faced the long haul of helping to form and develop cooperatives, he drew strength from such experiences as acquiring an education when "they said it couldn't be done." At the age for high school, he lacked the training and schooling to pass an entrance examination, but he convinced the authorities to give him a three months' trial anyhow, and he led his class. Then, when he applied for entrance to Auburn he was again told he didn't qualify. Once more he sold those in authority on letting him stand or fall on his own accomplishments in the classroom. This three-months' period of grace gave him the opportunity he needed, and at the end of the year he was awarded a certificate of honor and a distinction ribbon for special achievement.

He was always the best dressed man and with few exceptions the most popular man at the party. He played the fiddle much better than some radio and TV artists and was known far and wide as a good dancer—when dancing was an art rather than a twist, a shake, and a shudder. Probably he was able to withstand the impact of the problems of the day because he could enjoy the company of close friends.

Perhaps his wisest decision, and the one that resulted in his greatest accomplishment, was the decision to give up the role of Tennessee's most eligible bachelor. No doubt that his era of greatest happiness started on December 30, 1941, when he was married to Miss Ivye Peek of Hermitage, Tenn.

One of his friends described Al like this:

Nature threw away the mold after Al was cut. There just isn't anymore like him. He is the ruggedest of rugged individuals, a rock of independence, a self-reliant thinker, a man who believes working out one's own earthly salvation is the only way, who lives by the precept that one should create and capitalize upon his own opportunities rather than have "security at the price of liberty."

That is Al Jerdan. He would give you the shirt and galluses off his back . . . . but he would resist to the death your taking them without "the consent of the governed."

An over-all evaluation of Al and his services, his characteristics, his nobility, and his genuine Americanism could best be summed up by saying "what this country needs is more Al Jerdans."

Oscar B. Jesness

by E. Fred Koller

DR. JESNESS WAS A PIONEER on several frontiers of activity. His long and outstanding career has included service in research, government service, teaching and—in later years—as an agricultural policy leader and agribusiness statesman. In true pioneer manner he dared to explore new fields of endeavor and to try new approaches.

Dr. Jesness was a member of a pioneer midwestern family. His parents homesteaded in western Minnesota (Stevens County). He was born February 4, 1889, the last in a family of eight children. As a youth he experienced the challenge of pioneer life, but also some of the frustrations, long hours and hard work. Throughout his career Jesness was a prodigious worker and one who did not worry about the hours when there was a job to be done.

About the time of Jesness' birth and youth the pioneer farmers of Minnesota were turning to cooperation in a great ground swell of organizational activity and development. There were innumerable agricultural problems to be solved. In the 1870's and 80's there was a surge of farmer elevator openings in Minnesota followed in the 1890's by an even larger wave of cooperative creamery formations. Jesness grew up with this great wave of cooperative activity. This background and experience served him well as he turned to the intensive study of cooperation after his graduation from college.

Jesness attended the University of Minnesota from 1908–1912 where he was a student in the Department of Agriculture. Courses in the curriculum at that time devoted little or no attention to cooperation. Among the teachers at the university who played a large part in awakening Jesness' interest in agricultural economics was his faculty adviser, Andrew Boss. Professor Boss founded the work in farm management at Minnesota and was a great inspiration to Jesness.

At Minnesota Jesness met A. D. Wilson, then Superintendent of Farmers Institutes, who also helped shape his program. A. D. Wilson

displayed considerable interest in cooperatives as indicated by one
of the early Minnesota Farm Institute annuals being devoted to cooperation. In his undergraduate work Jesness took a course in the
principles of economics from Dr. John Lee Coulter, who about this
time wrote his book on *Cooperation Among Farmers.*

Pioneer in Cooperative Research at Minnesota

After one year of high school teaching (1912–13) Jesness returned
to Minnesota for a year of graduate study. At this time L. D. H.
Weld, who became widely known as the author of *The Marketing
of Farm Products* (the first textbook in the field), was appointed Chief
of the newly created Division of Agricultural Economics at Minnesota. He taught a graduate seminar in marketing in which Jesness
registered and it started him on his research career. The seminar
members were required to write reports on various phases of marketing. It turned out that these papers were considered good enough to
publish in *Studies in the Social Sciences, No. 4* issued by the university in 1915. The section prepared by Jesness was on the "Cooperative Marketing of Potatoes" and was his first published research report.

Contact with Weld during that year led to his finding some university funds and encouraged Charles J. Brand, Chief of the Office of
Markets, U.S.D.A., to provide some additional funds for Jesness' full-
time appointment as "Assistant in Marketing" with the rank of instructor. Jesness was assigned to participate in a study of butter marketing in cooperation with the Office of Markets (1914–15). This study
involved interviewing many creamery officials to obtain data. As the
majority of the creameries in Minnesota were cooperative, this provided Jesness with the opportunity to study the organization and
operation of cooperatives in detail. This experience proved to be
invaluable when Jesness moved to Washington a year later to specialize in cooperative studies.

In 1913, the Minnesota legislature directed the university to gather
information on cooperatives and this job was assigned to the Division
of Agricultural Economics. Weld prepared a questionnaire which was
mailed to all of the known cooperatives in the state. Jesness worked
with Weld on the study and had rather close contact with the progress
of the survey. The resulting report—Minnesota Bulletin 146, *Statistics of Cooperation Among Farmers in Minnesota,* 1914—was the
first State Experiment Station report of this type anywhere in the
country.

Pioneer in Cooperative Research in U.S.D.A.

In 1915, Jesness became a full-time U.S.D.A. employee and was transferred to Washington. He was assigned to the section of the Office of Markets and Rural Organization dealing with cooperatives under the leadership of Charles E. Bassett. One of his major assignments was to take an active part in a national mail survey of farmer cooperatives, similar to that completed earlier at Minnesota. Jesness worked under the immediate direction of W. H. Kerr. In addition to analyzing the mail survey materials, Jesness studied the history and development of the earlier general farm organizations such as the National Grange. He also assembled copies of the cooperative laws of the states which had enacted such statutes.

One product of this research was U.S.D.A. Bulletin No. 547, *Cooperative Purchasing and Marketing Organizations Among Farmers in the United States* (O. B. Jesness and W. H. Kerr), 1917. This was the first publication dealing comprehensively with farmer cooperatives on a national basis. It truly blazed a pioneer trail along which many others were to follow. It was the forerunner of a series of statistical and research reports which have been issued from time to time during the intervening half century by Farmer Cooperative Service (U.S.D.A.) and others.

The Clayton Amendment to the antitrust laws had been enacted in 1914 so this was a period of rising interest in the nonstock, nonprofit form of organization for which Section 6 of that amendment appeared to grant some exemption from antitrust action. As most states lacked available laws for the incorporation of nonstock organizations, the Office of Markets decided to prepare a suggested bill to serve as a guide to the states. Jesness took an active part in its formulation. The bill was published as "Service and Regulatory Announcements, No. 20" of the Office of Markets. Here, again, was a study which blazed a trail for developing cooperatives. About this time another U.S.D.A. bulletin—No. 541 *Cooperative Organization By-Laws*, 1918, by C. E. Bassett and O. B. Jesness discussed Section 6 of the Clayton Amendment in some detail and presented the first comprehensive suggested set of bylaws for nonstock, nonprofit cooperatives.

The crowning achievement of Jesness' Washington years was the publication of U.S.D.A. Farmers Bulletin 1144, *Cooperative Marketing*, 1920, by O. B. Jesness. This bulletin was a tremendous success. It had one of the largest circulations of any U.S.D.A. publication of that period (about 200,000 copies). Indicative of its merit is the fact that it was translated into Russian by private interests in the early 1920's with the thought that Russia would adopt democratic ideas and that this bulletin would be useful to them.

Bulletin 1144 was written in a manner which typified the "Jesness style" over a lifetime of writing. The style was simple and direct—no wasted words. Jesness became well-known to his students for his rough treatment of any manuscript with excess wordage. The publication presented practical pointers to the developing cooperatives of the period—when to organize, essentials for success, the place of contracts, pooling, financing, and many others. A unique feature of the bulletin was the use of a number of boxed-in statements in large type which emphasized basic points. One of these which read, in part, "Necessity is a good foundation for a cooperative organization" illustrates one of the author's points of emphasis.

During his period of service in Washington, Jesness shared in the preparation and authorship of several other Department cooperative publications, including farmers' elevators, cooperative milk plants, and livestock shipping associations.

Upon the resignation of C. E. Bassett, Jesness was placed in charge of the work in cooperation in the Office of Markets. He occupied this post until resigning in 1920 to head up the work in marketing at the University of Kentucky.

Dr. Joseph G. Knapp, Administrator of Farmer Cooperative Service, summarizes Jesness' contribution in his Washington years as follows: "He was one of our real pioneers in government service work with cooperatives. He helped set the mold."

Pioneer in Cooperative Research in the Mid-South

The Kentucky years were most productive ones for the young cooperative researcher. In rapid succession he authored or shared in authoring several Kentucky bulletins including the following: *Cooperative Livestock Shipping Associations*, 1921; *The Marketing of Kentucky Strawberries*, 1922; *Cooperative Marketing*, 1922; *Plans for Cooperative Marketing*, 1922; *Cooperative Marketing and Price Control*, 1926; and *The Cooperative Marketing of Tobacco*, 1928.

He arrived on the Kentucky scene when there was widespread concern over the price prospects for the 1920 tobacco crop. When the auction sales of burley tobacco opened in December, 1920, the bids showed that the concern was well founded. The talk in 1920 centered on the need to stage another tobacco "cut-out" to cut supplies, such as occurred in 1908 and which resulted in widespread "night-riding" and other rough tactics to enforce conformance.

Aaron Sapiro, a California attorney, had come into the limelight about that time and advocated commodity cooperatives with strong supply control through binding contracts with a large proportion of the growers of that commodity. He was invited to present his plan to tobacco leaders in Kentucky. This was followed up with a whirlwind signup campaign in the summer of 1921, which placed about 55,000 burley tobacco growers under six-year binding contracts with the association.

Jesness' background in cooperative research and service and his position at the university provided him with a front-row seat from which to follow these developments. Previous acquaintance with Mr. Sapiro and meetings with him on many occasions in Kentucky helped develop considerable mutual understanding and respect. Jesness early took note of the danger of overexpectation created by the enthusiasm of Sapiro and his followers in the ability of the association to dictate prices. He saw the need for a vigorous campaign of membership education in problems and possibilities. This took real courage under the circumstances.

Henry C. and Anne Dewees Taylor, in their monumental work, *The Story of Agricultural Economics* took special note of the service performed by Jesness in his capacity as critic. Thus, they included an extended quotation from Ken. Bulletin 271, *Cooperative Marketing and Price Control.* This quotation was followed by the statement (p. 683) that,

> Jesness' analysis of price control has been presented rather fully for several reasons. It is a clean-cut statement. It was made at a time (1926) when few agricultural economists found themselves in a position to publish in an experiment station bulletin a statement so far out of line with the propaganda of the professional organizers of centralized selling agencies organized under the laws providing for farmers' cooperative associations. Jesness had the courage to say what he thought."

The Taylors also commented that "Jesness could speak boldly on the limitations of cooperatives in the field of price control because he was known to be an advocate of the cooperative principle and its practice. . . ."

Pioneer in Cooperative Education

Another pioneering activity of this agricultural economist was the development of one of the early college courses in cooperation soon after his arrival at the University of Kentucky. The structure and content of this course was the basis for his book *The Cooperative Marketing of Farm Products* (Lippincott 1923), a pioneer text in this field. His philosophy with regard to cooperatives is illustrated by the observation in the introduction to this book (p. 6) that "Marketing is a business and carrying on marketing through a cooperative organization does not remove it from the sphere of business. It is as a business that this type of cooperative endeavor is to be considered in this volume." This made clear that he does not view cooperation as a "religion" or "cause" or an end in itself but rather as the means of serving an end.

In 1928 he returned to the University of Minnesota as head of the Department of Agricultural Economics. He took over the course in Cooperative Organization which was one of the offerings. He also conducted a graduate seminar in cooperative marketing. Administrative and public service demands limited the time he could devote to research relating to cooperatives, but he was able to share in the authorship of various Minnesota bulletins on this subject.

Over the years Dr. Jesness' interest in cooperatives continued. He addressed numerous state and national meetings and conferences on various phases of cooperation. He could enrich these occasions with a wealth of experience and philosophy. For instance, in the FCS and A.I.C. sponsored Research Conference on Agricultural Cooperation held at Kansas State College in 1957 he pointed to the "coming of age" of cooperation in this country as follows:

> Fortunately, with the passage of time and learning from experience much of the emotionalism has cooled down. This is not to deny the value of enthusiasm and loyal support of cooperatives. However, no lasting gain will come from unbridled enthusiasm which creates goals impossible of attainment. Experience shows that disillusionment in the wake of over-promise is hard for a cooperative to live with.

Believes in Widespread Contacts

Jesness holds strongly to the view that persons in academic posts, particularly in agricultural business fields, need to keep in the closest possible contact with the outside world and to avoid cloistering themselves in ivory towers. The demand for his services has made it relatively easy for him to develop and retain these contacts. From the mid 40's until 1965, he served as a member of the Advisory Council of the Agricultural Committee of the American Bankers Association.

From 1955 through 1960 he was a member of the National Agricultural Advisory Commission by presidential appointment. He has been a member of some advisory committees of the U.S.D.A. Also, he has served as an adviser to some CED committees. He has been a member of the National Agricultural Credit Committee for the past 20 years.

Jesness served as a director of the Midland National Bank (Minneapolis) for about 10 years until his appointment to the Board of Directors of the Federal Reserve Bank of Minneapolis. He served successively as Deputy Chairman and Chairman of that board.

He continues to hold directorships in the Minneapolis Grain Exchange, the Green Giant Company and the Green Giant Foundation of which he is President. He is a member of the board of trustees of the Farm House Foundation and is Chairman of the board of Experience, Incorporated. He played an active role in developing the Minneapolis Farm Forum and was a director and vice president of the Minneapolis Chamber of Commerce for a term.

Jesness is highly respected in his profession. From 1933–35 he served as editor of the *Journal of Farm Economics*. In 1937 he was elected President of the American Farm Economic Association. In 1958 he was accorded the top honor of Fellow in the Association.

Dr. Jesness is best known for his stimulating writing and for his sparkling commentary in meetings of top economists, business leaders or farmers. Jesness loves to talk. At the height of his career he presented an address or two each week. They were always well organized, analytical, to the point, and no holds barred.

Reference has been made to Jesness' readiness to speak out on controversial issues. He was always more concerned with being right than with popularity. This should not be interpreted to mean that he was argumentative for the sake of argument. Instead, it was a case of unwillingness to compromise his professional standing in an endeavor to please. His frankness, however, led those persons who initially found themselves opposed to his views to value his opinions and advice, knowing that they were frank and reflected his best judgment.

In long years of service Dr. Jesness has contributed significantly to agriculture, to agriculturally related business, and to higher education as an ardent scholar, diligent researcher, and counsellor. His ideas have left an indelible mark on agricultural economics, cooperative development, and farm policy.

"Spark Plug" for Livestock Cooperatives

53

Forrest G. Ketner

by George H. Thomson

MOST SUCCESSFUL FARMER COOPERATIVES have had a "spark plug" whose ideas and actions became woven into the very fabric of the organization.

In Ohio, where cooperative livestock marketing and Producers Livestock Association are virtually synonymous, seek out Forrest G. Ketner and you will have found the source of many of the ideas and actions which created one of the nation's most progressive farmer-owned livestock marketing organizations.

History records that Welsh pioneers living near Granville in the central part of Ohio, took the first cooperative livestock marketing step in 1820. They drove their hogs overland to Lake Erie, slaughtered them, packed the pork in barrels, and shipped it to Montreal where it was sold to buyers from England. It was 100 years later that Mr. Ketner came on the marketing scene, but he definitely left his mark on Ohio history in the next 40 years.

Born on a farm near Lancaster, January 23, 1888, he graduated from Otterbein College, Westerville, Ohio, in 1910; (Otterbein gave him an L. L. D. degree in 1958) served as a lecturer and instructor in Ohio's Farmer Institutes from 1913 to 1918, and for the next two years was the first county agricultural agent in Delaware County.

Becomes First Director of Marketing

His induction into the specific area of livestock marketing came in May, 1920, when the Ohio Farm Bureau Federation appointed him its first Director of Marketing. At that time 22 cooperative elevators and 17 local shipping associations were handling livestock. The first shipping association had been formed in 1916 at New Concord, later to become renowned as the home town of Astronaut John Glenn.

The new director recommended that marketing associations be organized on a county-wide rather than a local basis. Following this plan, Morgan County became the first county association, dating its service from June 21, 1920. Four counties were organized in 1920, 46 in 1921, 12 in 1922, and 1 in 1925.

Formation of the National Live Stock Producers Association as recommended by the Farmers' Live Stock Marketing Committee of Fifteen, provided new impetus for organizational work in the eastern Corn Belt. Producers commission firms were established at Buffalo, N. Y., in 1922; Cleveland, Ohio, and Pittsburgh, Pa., in 1923; and Cincinnati, Ohio, in 1925. F. G. Ketner was one of the organizers, secretary-treasurer, and director of each of these firms. He served as director of the National Live Stock Producers Association from 1923 to 1936, and was its secretary-treasurer from 1925 to 1936.

These were days of long hours, night meetings by the dozen, extensive travel, and constant problems in convincing thousands of stockmen that they should work together in a new harness—owning and operating their own commission firms. Mr. Ketner was untiring in his efforts, and effective through the use of logic, cajolery, diplomacy, psychology, and any other "weapon" at his command.

One major problem encountered early was a boycott of the new firms by local buyers. The solution was to establish an order buying company in 1923 which secured orders for slaughter livestock from distant packers. The Eastern States Company broke the boycott, and as the Eastern Order Buying Company to this day remains an important subsidiary of Producers.

At the depth of the depression, when credit was much needed but difficult to obtain, Producers Live Stock Credit Association was organized in 1932. Since that time, this wholly-owned subsidiary of Producers has loaned more than $57 million to stockmen.

At Helm of Producers for 25 Years

The big break-through in cooperative efforts came in 1934 with the consolidation of the farmer-owned agencies at Cleveland, Pittsburgh, and Columbus, the order buying and credit subsidiaries, into one organization—The Producers Livestock Association. Mr. Ketner became the Secretary-Treasurer and General Manager, posts he held until his retirement at the close of 1959. During his 25 years at the helm, Producers grew from three markets with total assets of $318,000, to 35 markets with assets approximating $6.5 million, (now over $8 million).

Under Mr. Ketner's management, Producers maintained services at the terminal markets, but was first in the nation to establish a network of farmer-owned near-home markets served by centralized sales services. It was instrumental in securing passage of the Ohio Livestock Sanitary, Weighing and Bonding Law, and legislation to control the movement of cattle with Bang's disease.

Producers brought integrity to livestock marketing; it banished fear on the part of consignors that they might not get paid for their livestock. The association has sold more than $3 billion worth of livestock without the loss of a penny due member-patrons. The cooperatives brought a new dimension to marketing, sponsoring research and instigating and supporting numerous programs to improve livestock production as well as marketing. Producers related the sale of lambs on merit to production of quality lambs as early as 1932. The association was a major factor in Ohio's pioneer position in development of meat hogs, the first efforts to develop such hogs having been made prior to World War II. Regular sale of hogs on merit was begun in 1951. The Extension Service, Ohio State University, cooperated in all such programs.

The advantages of working with other organizations were always apparent to "F. G.," as Mr. Ketner was known to many of his associates and friends. Producers Pork Improvement Association and Eastern Order Buyers, Inc., the hog sales arm of Producers, are both joint subsidiaries of Producers at Columbus and Producers Marketing Association, Indianapolis, Ind. He long advocated consolidation of Producers at Columbus and Cincinnati into one organization. This was accomplished July 1, 1962.

"F. G." had a good nose for ferreting out projects that proved to be successful even though many others gave them slim chances for success. He led Producers into an association with P and C. Food Markets, founded in 1945 in New York State. Producers made a small investment in P and C and for several years sold livestock to the packer which provided the markets with most of their meat. As P and C grew to 55 supermarkets plus a warehouse service to many independent stores, Producers' ownership grew into 80,000 shares of stock with a market value of nearly $1 million.

Never the type of individual to confine his activities to a single project or a single industry, Mr. Ketner served as president of the Ohio Council of Farmer Cooperatives from 1943 to 1949; was a director and member of the Executive Committee of the National Council of Farmer Cooperatives; director of P and C Food Stores; trustee for 14 years of Ohio State University and the Ohio State University Research Foundation, and member the Board of Control of the Ohio Agricultural Experiment Station. He served as a member of the Executive Committee and as president of the Association of Governing Boards of State Universities and Allied Institutions.

In his long association with the National Live Stock and Meat Board, he promoted research, instruction and public relations on behalf of livestock and meat throughout the United States. He is a life member of the Board.

He has been an officer of a savings association, a bank; is a member of the Farm Bureau, the Grange, the Chamber of Commerce, the Bexley Methodist Church, and numerous civic, fraternal and livestock groups. His 1,200-acre "Ketner Farms" south of Columbus, are devoted to livestock and grain.

Forrest Ketner's 40 years of service to farmers bear the imprints of a man who knows and loves the land, the livestock and its people. He stands tall among the tall timber of cooperative leaders.

Promoter and   54
Organizer

Henry Krumery

by Theodore Saloutos

HENRY KRUMERY, a farmer-politican and cheese cooperative organizer, was born on a farm on February 3, 1852, near Plymouth, Sheboygan County, Wis., in the heart of what was to become one of the biggest cheese-producing areas in the state.

Krumery operated a farm and was a livestock dealer, but he found time to become active in the political life of his community. Educated in the public and private German schools of Plymouth, he held the offices of supervisor, town treasurer, and chairman of the town board; and for 14 years he was director of the school board of his district which took in the town of Plymouth. A friend and supporter of Robert M. LaFollette, a Progressive Republican Governor and United States Senator, he served in the Wisconsin State Assembly from 1901–1902, and in the State Senate from 1909–1912. He was chairman of the Republican State Central Committee in 1910 and a delegate to the Republican national convention on three occasions. He was a member of the historic Wisconsin legislative session of 1911 which enacted much social legislation that brought national recognition to the state.

Spearheaded Fight of Cheese Producers

Krumery is better known for his work in organizing and heading the cheese producers during the early years than his accomplishments in state politics. For years the farmers complained about their haphazard methods of marketing their products, but made few efforts to improve conditions. The sudden decline of the price of cheese during the summer of 1912 had a jarring effect on the producers of Sheboygan County who felt that the time had come for them to take a more effective course of action. Krumery headed the fight. In a series of articles and speeches, he voiced the grievances of the farmers and urged them to undertake the marketing of the cheese themselves. As a result of his efforts more farmers came to understand that because the storage facilities were under the control of private groups they suffered from low prices during the summer months when production was at its peak, and failed to benefit from the prevailing higher prices of the winter months. The idea was to establish their own storage facilities, feed the market gradually, and stabilize prices during the year.

Although Krumery spearheaded the initial campaign, and assumed command of the early organization effort, he had the support of other groups and individuals. A general program of education was launched by the Wisconsin Society of Equity of which Krumery had become a member. When conditions were favorable, a mass meeting was called which was attended by representatives of the Wisconsin College of Agriculture, the Wisconsin State Board of Public Affairs, and the Wisconsin Society of Equity.

A committee on organization presented a plan to the farmers which they accepted. During the summer of 1913 some 43 cheese factories were organized and incorporated under the cooperative law of Wisconsin. These companies then formed the Sheboygan County Cheese Producers Federation, which was incorporated under the same law. The company was ready for business with the opening of the selling season in 1914, and, after a slow start, began receiving orders from all parts of the country.

Became First President of State Federation

The Wisconsin Cheese Producers Federation was an outgrowth of the movement that began in Sheboygan County. The Wisconsin College of Agriculture and the Wisconsin Department of Markets frequently came to the assistance of the Federation by placing at its disposal some of the best knowledge and experience available in helping a real constructive organization. Krumery became the first president. When Krumery died in early 1922, the Wisconsin Cheese Producers Federation had at least 140 cheese factories as members.

The contributions of Krumery to the cooperative marketing of cheese were genuine. His accomplishments were promotional and organizational, instead of those of a business manager. A contemporary who was close to the scene and a student of the cooperative cheese marketing movement in Wisconsin wrote in 1925, ". . . there is another story, one that probably will never be written, which centers around the work of Henry Krumery, who unselfishly gave his time and health to the cause of cooperation; who had to bear the brunt of the preliminary organization work; who had been slandered, vilified and threatened at every step by the enemies of the cooperative movement and sometimes even by those who were to be ultimately benefited by his activities."

John Lawler

by Alyce Lowrie Jewett

UNDER HIS GUIDANCE, Poultry Producers of Central California grew from an unknown, uncertain infant cooperative to the largest egg marketing cooperative in the world, unsurpassed in fiscal solidarity. As its general manager, constantly mindful of its fiscal operations, he was more responsible than any other man for that growth and financial stature. It could have been truly said of him, "He made his money minding his own business." Since the business was a cooperative, it was the members' money. And he never forgot that.

When young John Lawler graduated from a small rural high school in Jack London's fabled "Valley of the Moon" in Sonoma County, Calif., where he was born on August 5, 1887 and spent his boyhood, he went to work for a bank in nearby Petaluma, then the hub of the foremost egg-producing area in the United States. He applied himself diligently to learning banking principles and practices—so successfully that he was appointed cashier of both the Sonoma County National and the Petaluma Savings Banks when he was 21 years old, establishing an age record for that position. He enjoyed his associations with Sonoma County farmers because of his youthful years on a farm in that area.

His father had bred and raised trotting horses, so it was appropriate that trotters were John Lawler's sole hobby. He drove trotting horses on the track often and skillfully while he was still a schoolboy. From the time he was 18 years old and throughout his life, John Lawler had two absorbing interests—farming and fiscal security; in 1920, he added a third—farmer cooperatives.

It was John Lawler's habit to walk from his residence to the bank, early each morning. On a morning in 1920, he was briskly on his way when a friend, John J. Bergstedt, offered him a ride to the bank in his Model T Ford. Mr. Bergstedt was president of a fledgling cooperative association, organized four years earlier for the purpose of marketing the vast quantities of eggs laid by the productive White Leghorn hens that dotted the rolling hills of southern Sonoma County. He asked John Lawler how he would like to work for the organization. Its manager at the beginning was J. H. Barber. He was not a young man and he conscientiously tried to handle every detail of the operation, so he needed an assistant who could tactfully and dependably carry some of the managerial load. The young banker listened thoughtfully; he told Mr. Bergstedt that he was interested in his proposal and that he might convey that reaction to his board of directors. The board interviewed John Lawler, was favorably impressed and offered him the position of assistant manager in the cooperative.

The choice between the "cloistered halls" of the banking fraternity and the uncharted course of an egg marketing cooperative was not easy to make. Banks were respected by the community and provided essential services. John Lawler held positions of responsibility and was reasonably certain of future advancement. Farmer cooperatives were fairly new in California. Two previous egg marketing cooperatives had failed, causing heavy losses to producers. Eggs were a perishable commodity for which consumer demand was largely centered along the Atlantic coast, 3,000 miles east of Petaluma. Would egg producers consider membership in and marketing through a cooperative somehow detrimental to the independence that they cherished?

Work with Cooperative Selected as Challenge

John Lawler was intrigued by the challenge offered in the cooperative position. He possessed initiative, determination, ingenuity, and courage and he was stimulated by challenge. He talked to George P. McNear, president of the Petaluma Savings Bank; Mr. McNear was not happy at the prospect of losing his capable young cashier. When he sought to dissuade him from making the move, John Lawler replied that the cooperative organization was young and it appealed to his own youth. With unusual perception, John Lawler foresaw that he might, through the cooperative egg marketing endeavor, accomplish economic betterment for egg producers in that area, increase per capita egg consumption by improving and standardizing the market quality of eggs, and demonstrate progressive egg marketing techniques which could be adopted by other areas of concentrated egg production in the United States.

When he accepted the assistant managership of the small egg marketing cooperative in 1920, he brought to it a sound and thorough knowledge of financial requirements and relationships in business. He consistently and rigidly adhered to conservative banking principles in cooperative finance. His exceptional acumen and leadership talent were promptly appreciated by the board of directors and he succeeded Mr. Barber as manager in 1921. A heart attack necessitated his retirement in 1954. During his 33 years as general manager, he had witnessed phenomenal growth of Poultry Producers of Central California—growth in its dollar volume of business, its membership, its functions and services, and its esteem in the business community. For two decades, he had been surrounded by a large and competent staff, but he personally supervised the cooperative's fiscal operations.

In the mid-twenties, a Feed Department and a Poultry Department were added. The former manufactured and distributed a variety of poultry feeds and subsequently some dairy and livestock concentrates, which attracted farmers other than egg producers to membership. John Lawler strongly favored the signing of an egg marketing agreement by ALL members which stated that all eggs which they produced or might produce in future, other than those for home use or hatching purposes, would be marketed through the cooperative, so long as they remained members of it. He also preferred that the various supplies carried and distributed by the Feed Department be *farm* supplies. The Poultry Department chiefly marketed cull hens and the broilers raised from male chicks, usually fresh-killed (not frozen).

In his personal life, John Lawler was gracious and abstemious. He enjoyed hosting small dinners. He neither smoked nor drank but he served a variety of beverages to his guests. He and his first wife had two sons, John and Glenn, but Mrs. Lawler passed away while they were quite small. In 1921 he married a gifted pianist, Edna Shores. They were the parents of one daughter, Elizabeth. He developed an appreciation of music in response to his wife's talent and musical interests. He was a staunch Republican and a man of consistently conservative business and personal attitudes.

During his lifetime, John Lawler purchased and sold numerous farm properties. His earnings therefrom augmented his salary income which was never large. He was opposed to high salaries for cooperative employees and asked that his own compensation be decreased during the depression years. At the time of his death, he owned five rather extensive ranches in California. On one, he and Mrs. Lawler rehabilitated a century-old house and he built a half-mile track for trotters. Despite his continued enthusiasm for harness-racing, he limited his betting to placement of $2.00 on his own horse. When the 19th century stern-wheeler, T. C. Walker, was retired from river service, he purchased it, brought it to his delta island ranch and converted it to a duck club.

Cited for Service to California Agriculture

John Lawler had a profound interest in and respect for education and research. He maintained close contact with the Poultry Department and Agricultural Economics faculty of the University of California. The professor who once headed the Poultry Department on the Davis campus was subsequently PPCC editor and afterwards a director of that cooperative. In the 1940s, Mr. Lawler was appointed to serve on a committee which recommended subjects and procedure in higher agricultural education for California. With the creation of the Grand National Livestock Exposition at the Cow Palace, San Francisco, the Governor (Earl Warren) appointed John Lawler a director. In 1952, he received one of three citations ever awarded by the University of California to men who nobly served agriculture in the state.

As general manager of Poultry Producers of Central California, John Lawler consulted his board of directors on every phase of the cooperative's policy and on many operational aspects of the business. This resulted in prolonged board meetings (held monthly) but it kept the organization aligned with members' needs and preferences because every director was a member and reflected members' attitudes. In cases of deadlock or unduly prolonged board discussion, Mr. Lawler tactfully suggested "tabling" the matter until the next meeting. He never took one director into his confidence or discussed an issue with one or two members of the board (of 11 members). Perhaps his own knowledge of money and banking caused him to favor lengthy and detailed financial statements and comprehensive monthly auditor's reports, although it is doubtful whether many directors were able to fully digest this material. He did not hold frequent staff meetings; he paid almost daily visits to the various departments in his general office, thereby keeping himself informed of their respective activities and problems and providing for them a source of counsel and wisdom.

His keen and searching mind was always aware of every phase of the organization's operations. He infallibly encouraged creditable undertakings and discouraged injudicious endeavors. He inspired his department heads; under his leadership, they achieved maximum performance. He effectuated cooperation between administrative staff members with ease. He had a matchless capacity for friendship and was warmly regarded by all of his 250 employees and by members. No one—employees, friends, business associates—was familiar with him; he had the respect and affection of all his associates.

Occasionally, discussions grew heated at membership meetings. When tensions mounted and voices rose, John Lawler would often go to the front of the room, seat himself causually on the corner of table or desk, fold his hands and ask smilingly, "Now, have we considered this question from all angles? Let us weigh the pros and cons of all approaches. . . ." Oil was poured on the troubled waters and the mood of the meeting swiftly changed.

Strong Advocate for Co-op Fiscal Soundness

He won the respect and esteem of the business community with the fiscal soundness of the cooperative business which he managed. He worked with attorneys Aaron and Milton Sapiro in adapting the newly-developed revolving finance idea to the needs of the association. Under his guidance the plan became a model for other cooperatives. The revolving fund cycles were kept short, ranging from two to four years in length. The Egg, Feed, and Poultry Capital Funds were kept separate. Interest (usually five percent) was paid on revolving fund certificates. When used as loan collateral, those certificates were "good as gold." The leading banks in central and northern California would lend up to 90 percent of face value on such certificates at the same rate of interest that the cooperative was paying on them. Members' purchases of feed and supplies were limited to cash and loans were not made to members for any purpose. Members received returns for their eggs, which were marketed promptly, within a fortnight, minus one cent per dozen withheld for the Egg Capital Fund, about six cents per dozen retained to cover costs of packing and marketing, and a small deferred payment (usually not exceeding two cents per dozen) which they received at the end of the year.

At a time when few women were employed by farmer cooperatives, John Lawler respected women's capabilities. For the last five years of his managership, he had three women on his administrative staff: an editor, administrative assistant, and executive secretary (who was also secretary to the board of directors). When he hired the administrative assistant, he told her that she was the first in that position in Poultry Producers and gave her permission to plan the course and scope of her work. He depended on her to assist with public relations, member relations, and employee education. At one time, he asked her to serve as manager of the poultry department and to organize and conduct a live poultry auction—the first in western United States. He said to her on the day that she was hired: "Whatever you do, remember that I am always behind you—giving you support and encouragement. Hitherto, you have been a lone woman in a man's field. Now you are no longer standing alone."

He had little respect for public relations, as such. Rather, he believed that a well-managed, efficiently operated, financially "respectable" business would win the esteem of the public and attract friends to its door. To John Lawler, honest and creditable business relations automatically led to good public relations.

It is doubtful whether anyone respected him more than his secretary. She admired him for his meticulous attention to detail, for his exceptional skill in dictation, his remarkably discerning mind. He was very considerate of her during her mother's long and final illness and habitually included her in social gatherings at his home.

Six Principles Strongly Advocated

John Lawler will be long remembered for his steadfast advocacy of several principles and procedures which were basic to the stature and success of Poultry Producers of Central California between 1920 and 1954: (1) a strong, enforceable and enforced marketing agreement as a condition of membership; (2) emphasis on quality of eggs—its standardization and maintenance in production and marketing and its use as a basis of payment to producers; (3) marketing of branded and protectively packaged eggs; (4) restriction of members' purchases of feed and supplies to cash transactions; (5) relative brevity of revolving fund cycles; (6) no loans by the Association to members.

John Lawler was widely acclaimed as a cooperative leader. He served as an officer of the Agricultural Council of California (that state's cooperative council) and of the National Council of Farmer Cooperatives. At their meetings, he listened attentively to addresses and discussions, reached swift and firm conclusions and could be depended upon for frank, sage, and succinct comments when they were solicited. Frequently, when action had been long and heatedly debated, John Lawler could summarize the advantages and disadvantages effectively so that a decisive vote or passage of a resolution was hastened and facilitated. Cooperative managers and directors from California, Oregon, Washington, and Utah frequently telephoned him for advice in regard to the handling of controversial matters. He had amazing ability to clarify and classify, thereby enabling the inquirer to decide.

This master of money management and minder of his own business was a confirmed champion of marketing cooperatives and a powerful advocate of standardized commodity quality. He was a pathfinder and a pillar of strength in farmer cooperative endeavor.

Murray Danforth Lincoln

by Davis Douthit

IT WAS ANOTHER MEETING OF FARMERS in the mid-'thirties. In Ohio.

They wanted electricity like the people in the towns and cities had.

So they were listening carefully to a lanky, intense man with a New England accent. He was talking about electricity, and he was blurting it out and putting it on the line. The way he always did.

"It's up to you," he challenged the farmers, "whether you get power for profit or power for use. Are you going to do it yourselves, the cooperative way, or are you going to sit back and wait for someone else to do it?"

He paid attention to any possible skeptics or faint of heart in the crowd.

"Not too long ago," he reminded them, "They were telling us we couldn't run our own fertilizer, or feed, or livestock, or insurance businesses. I sure get a kick out of poking our financial statements under their noses. We've proved we *can* run our own business."

He paused to let that sink in. Then the clincher:

"To me there's only one answer. If we don't do it ourselves, we're going to wait and wait for electricity, and then pay and pay and pay."

The farmers liked the blunt way this tall, bald Yankee got down to cases. And they agreed with what he said. So did others at similar meetings throughout the state. Result: farmers all over Ohio got electrical power the co-op way.

It wasn't the first time Murray Danforth Lincoln had pushed and prodded and pleaded with farmers to work together to tackle their problems, and it wouldn't be the last time. "There's no problem can't be solved if people want to get together and solve it," he said again and again. "We can make anything we want out of what we've got."

Becomes First County Agent in New England

Back in 1914, fresh out of Massachusetts Agricultural College, Lincoln had gone to work in Connecticut's New London County as New England's first county agent. His job description: find out what the farmers want and help them get it.

He's been working away at this job ever since, except that it wasn't too long before he discovered he needed to change one word in the description: find out what *people* want and help them get it.

"I've come to the belief right or wrong," he told the American Institute of Cooperation in 1936, "that as farmers by ourselves, there's not much hope of our securing our rightful share of the nation's income. But I do believe that if we can find the proper basis of relationship with consumers, together we can dominate the whole field of economic production and distribution."

The farm "problem," he decided, was also the city problem; indeed it was the human problem—how to learn to work together and live together, with your neighbors, next door and around the world, helpfully and cooperatively.

It's a problem, Lincoln found, that seems so simple to solve but isn't. Many people just plain don't want to be helped, like the Connecticut farmer who told the young county agent, "Heck, boy, I don't farm as well as I know how already." Many people don't want to cooperate; they'd rather go it alone. Especially if the other fellow lives and works in the city and they don't; especially if the other fellow talks a different language or has a different color of skin.

Lincoln always bounced back from such "blue funk" thinking.

"I've been spending as much spare time as I can out on the farm," he wrote a friend, "and while working rather hard physically it's given me lots of time for thinking. I could not help thinking that irrespective of what the Russians or Americans do, the wheat is growing, and the oats and grass will soon be coming up, and in our particular case, little calves are popping up all over the barn. I quit reading the newspapers and listening to the radio and by Sunday night was convinced the world wasn't such a bad place after all."

He started off helping Connecticut farmers get what they wanted by showing them how to home-mix fertilizer and save $17 a ton (and deprive the local fertilizer company of some business). He began to set up a cow-testing association and a cooperative milk-distributing plant.

An order from the U. S. Department of Agriculture, which paid a third of his salary, to "lay off those economic things" stopped him only temporarily. He moved over to Brockton, Mass., organized pig clubs and a milk plant co-op, and then got his "call" to Ohio.

Promotes Cooperation as Key to Farmer's Salvation

He became Executive Secretary of the newly formed Ohio Farm Bureau Federation in March, 1920, and almost at once began convincing the state's farmers that cooperation was the key to their salvation.

Without question, the farmer cooperative movement in Ohio was and is the lengthened shadow of Murray D. Lincoln. He created a storm of rural excitement, hope, and action which resulted in a raft of purchasing and marketing cooperatives of all kinds, as well as the cooperatively-oriented Nationwide (originally Farm Bureau) Insurance Companies.

But he couldn't confine himself to helping one group of people in one state. He itched for a national and an international field to operate in. He tried to talk the American Farm Bureau Federation into getting into "those economic things."

"The vision I've always had," he said back in 1932, "is a great group of farmers joined together in one common enterprise. What limits progress today is the inability of farm organizations and farmers to get together in sufficient numbers to be felt legislatively and economically."

By this time the Lincoln-led insurance company was six years old, and insurance was much on his mind.

"We all need insurance," he wrote. "If all our insurance were together in one big company, a sum of money five times greater than the total amount of income to the American Farm Bureau could be legitimately taken from insurance margins to promote this program of education that the farmer needs to convince him of the efficacy and opportunities of cooperative endeavor."

But things didn't work out that way. So Lincoln took another tack. ("When I find one road blocked, I pull and haul and twist and try to go down another avenue.") He discovered that the leadership of The Cooperative League, a national federation of consumer and purchasing cooperatives, thought the same way he did about the need to get rural and urban people to work together. And he cajoled and argued and browbeat and persuaded until finally, in 1934, he was able to talk his Farm Bureau Co-op board of directors into joining the League.

In 1938, Lincoln asked his board to decide on one of four directions for the Ohio Farm Bureau insurance company to go: (1) develop as a farm company just in Ohio; or (2) as a general company in Ohio; or (3) as a company covering several states but serving only, or principally, farmers and rural folks; or (4) as a general company appealing to all classes of people and attempting to serve the insurance needs of the growing cooperative movement.

Becomes Forceful, Energetic International Leader

The board, egged on by Lincoln, went for Number Four, and the country boy from New England was off and running again.

He became President of the Cooperative League in 1941.

The next 20 years or so saw Lincoln in full stride—and he could take long ones both physically and mentally. He became one of the world's better known cooperative leaders. He served on the central committee of the International Cooperative Alliance. He was President of the Fund for International Cooperative Development. He was a founder and served for many years as President of CARE, the international cooperative relief organization.

He became president or board chairman of a dozen other business and social enterprises, in addition to heading the Nationwide insurance companies. President Roosevelt named him to represent agriculture at the UN Conference on Food and Agriculture in 1943. President Truman named him to his Commission on Higher Education. President Kennedy appointed him task force chairman of the Food for Peace program. He was a permanent consultant to the United Nations Economic and Social Council. And the list of his works in behalf of people goes on and on.

The cooperatively-oriented Nationwide organization became, under his leadership, one of the largest (assets now total about $750 million) and most influential multiple-line insurance outfits in the nation. The *Christian Science Monitor* described it awhile back as "one of the United States' most interesting companies."

But Lincoln sees insurance primarily as a means to the larger end of amassing the wherewithal to help people provide themselves with other necessities of life, including the need to have an economic, as well as a political, voice in what happens to their money and their lives.

"We're in insurance," he said once, "and insurance brings together people and money, two mighty important assets. But insurance is just one means to prove that people are better off if they work together and do things for themselves, instead of letting things be done for them—and to them."

As Norman Cousins, editor of the *Saturday Review,* observed to a meeting of Nationwide agents, "Murray Lincoln is a man concerned with insurance of civilization itself, because no other insurance can mean anything without that kind of insurance."

This was why Lincoln was forever impatient for the organizations he led to "build every kind of people's institution we could think of," to get bigger—"so we can bury our mistakes, because we're bound to make some"—to get into many different kinds of business, like oil, banking, communications, food. He launched a valiant effort—so far unsuccessful—to figure out some way for cooperatives to take over one of the great national food store chains.

Preached Cooperation With Zeal, Passion

No missionary ever preached with more zeal and passionate conviction than Murray Lincoln preached the gospel of cooperation.

"I believe," he said, "that cooperatives, properly directed, can help save the world from the self-destruction toward which it seems to be headed. If anybody knows a better way to help people, it's time to trot it out, for the world is in trouble, and if I knew anything better to do than what I'm doing, I'd do it."

This belief in cooperatives didn't stop him from "scolding" his cooperative colleagues. He denounced "small thinking" and selfish provincialism. He kept goading and berating and driving other co-op managers and leaders to become more aggressive, to show more initiative and ingenuity.

"We need something to wake these guys up to co-op possibilities," he kept saying. "They don't seem to understand that when you start out to meet a big human need, if you do even a half-way decent job, you'll succeed."

Lincoln owns up to some pretty bad spells of discouragement now and then. Well, perhaps not so much discouragement as dissatisfaction with the rate of progress. He once told members of his staff, half-apologetically, "It's not that I don't appreciate what you've been doing; it's just that I've been pondering whether we could find a better way."

"I've been saying for a long time that people have within their own hands the tools to fashion their own destiny," he reminisced once, "but I have to admit to dark moments when I wondered whether people really *want* to use those tools.

"I've worried because we haven't moved faster and because of what has seemed to me to be a lack of independent thought and action in advancing the cooperative idea. Nevertheless, we've won more than we've lost; we've demonstrated that people *can* work together to help themselves.

"In fact, we've come a long way in the past 50 years. But not nearly far enough. And when I think over what we've done in relation to what I believe we can do, I say we've just begun to scratch the surface of our potential for human service. The time for cooperative pioneering is not in the past. It is right now."

It has taken the creeping ravages of Parkinson's disease to slow Lincoln down. Over the past two years he's had to relinquish his many presidencies and many of his other posts. He is, however, still a member of the board of directors of the Nationwide insurance companies and regularly makes the trip from his farm home near Columbus to attend the monthly meetings. He requires help in getting around and it is difficult for him to talk, but at the age of 74 he continues to be as concerned and as alert as ever to what goes on in the world.[1]

---

[1] Mr. Lincoln died on November 7, 1966, while this book was in production.

Andrew George Lohman

by Orion Ulrey

ANDREW LOHMAN, builder of a successful community cooperative which in turn has been largely responsible for the efficient
poultry farms in the area around Hamilton, Mich.: poultryman and
farmer; community leader in educational and religious activities; and
a devoted worker in developing the poultry industry of the region
and nation, was born on a farm two miles west of Hamilton, Allegan
County, in western Michigan, July 19, 1896. In early 1966 he was
vigorously serving as secretary-manager of the Hamilton Farm Bureau
Cooperative (HFBC) which he first joined as bookkeeper in September,
1921.

Andy Lohman attended the local primary school, and spent a total
of 10 months during three winters in the Holland Business College.
He assisted his father on a general farm and was married before
serving in the U. S. Army for a few months during World War I.
The course in bookkeeping at the College and the training in
mechanics while in the Army were of material use in later activities
with the cooperative. Mr. Lohman was self-educated through managing a cooperative, reading journals and college publications, obtaining information from friends in the markets, contacts with college
research and extension staff for four decades, and through travels
primarily to obtain information and ideas.

The HFBC was established in 1920 to buy supplies and market farm
products. The first manager was a local farmer without business experience. Records were inadequately kept. The post-war depression
resulted in inventory losses. The cooperative was considered a failure
in 1921 as the assets were found to be a minus $3,000.

A few members, including John Lohman, the father of Andy and a
board member, however, were convinced that the cooperative could
survive. In September, 1921, Andy was requested to set up a book-

keeping system and he soon was installed as the bookkeeper and manager at a salary of $50 a month.

The majority of farmers in the area are of Dutch descent, and are active members of the Reformed or the Christian Reformed Churches. They are industrious, frugal, and sharp in their economic decisions. Their loyalty to the cooperative is closely related to price gains and quality of service. All of the board members have been Dutch farmers. Some visitors have concluded that the national origin and religious affiliations of the farmer members have been significant factors responsible for the success of the cooperative. The writer questions such a conclusion. These two churches frequently have had their differences and the cooperative has been a primary factor in bringing harmony among them. The writer also believes that the training and code of ethics obtained by the secretary-manager from his church may have been a very important factor in the success of the co-operative.

"Andy Lohman Is the Cooperative"

During the life of the cooperative, Hamilton has been a small village of around 500 to 700 persons, with a few stores and service shops, and a dog food plant in recent years. The cooperative employed around 100 persons in 1965. The association has been the main business of the area. Through the years, one has heard such statements as "The cooperative is Hamilton and Andy Lohman is the cooperative." Those who have analyzed the conditions seem to agree that "the cooperative has been largely the shadow of the man," and that the story of the Hamilton Farm Bureau Cooperative and of Andy Lohman are closely interrelated.

Under Andy's leadership the HFBC has grown to an annual volume of over $6 million as of 1965. It provides 75 percent of the farm marketing and farm supply business in its trade area. It has achieved a high degree of economic integration—discontinuing services no longer required as agricultural conditions have changed and adding new ones to meet changing farm requirements. Major attention has been given to the poultry enterprise of members. In this connection Andy and the cooperative have given major attention to improving the quality of eggs through feeding, sanitation, and care on the farm; through handling and grading in the plant; and through an incentive price program which has paid poultrymen to produce superior eggs, starting July 1, 1958.

HFBC has become a member of most state-wide cooperative associations and of the Michigan Association of Farmer Cooperatives. Andy, too, has been and is a most active community and cooperative citizen with participation in the following state and national organizations:

State Organizations

    Member—Advisory Committee of Michigan Department of Agriculture
    Member—Committee to assist in formulation of Michigan Egg Laws
    President—Michigan Allied Poultry Industries, Inc.
    Director—Michigan Egg Grading Association
    President—Michigan Farm Defense Board, World War II
    Member—Michigan Farm-Labor Public Relations Council
    President—Michigan Feed Manufacturers Association
    Director—Michigan Feed Manufacturers and Dealers Association
    President—Michigan Poultry Improvement Association
    President—Michigan Poultry Industry Defense Committee, World War II
    Director—Michigan Record of Performance Association
    Member—Selective Service Appeal Board, World War II

National Organizations

    Member—American Farm Bureau Federation Poultry Committee
    Director—Chicago Mercantile Exchange
    Director—Institute of American Poultry Industries
    Member—National Committee on grades and standards for eggs and poultry
    Vice President—National Poultry Industry Defense Committee, World War II
    Director—Poultry and Egg National Board, representing American Farm Bureau Federation
    Member—National Shell Egg Advisory Committee, World War II

Develops Close Relations with Michigan State University

By the late 20's, Mr. Lohman realized that an efficient and successful poultry industry in the area of Hamilton would have to be built on the application of research in production and in processing the eggs and poultry. Consequently, he utilized the services of many departments of Michigan State University. Arthur Morley, county agricultural agent in Allegan County, beginning in 1929, played a leading role in opening up the services of Michigan State for the cooperative.

The personnel of the Poultry Science Department suggested formulas for poultry feeds for the cooperative. They aided the quality egg program by examination and grading of eggs. They assisted in setting up the processing line when the cooperative began to process hens and broilers in 1933. Andy encouraged staff members of the University to utilize the facilities of the plant and farms of members for various studies. He conducted trips through the entire operation for numerous classes in marketing and poultry science. He cooperated in collecting data used for college publications, and assisted on various projects at Michigan State. Andy also adopted the policy of not dealing with commercial feed ingredient companies until their materials and ideas were presented and approved by members of the Poultry Science Department.

Andy Lohman has given major attention to breeding, feeding, and handling to improve the quality and to lower the cost of production of eggs. He has used many resources of Michigan State to accomplish these objectives. After the retirement of J. M. Moore, poultry extension specialist at Michigan State, he was hired by Andy, for three days a week for a period of 18 months during 1958–59, to work on production and processing problems.

Andy has also made extensive use of the services of Arthur Howland, a cooperative specialist of the Department of Agricultural Economics. Through the assistance of Howland, the bylaws were changed in 1935 so that the organization became a true cooperative: patronage refunds to all patrons, and shares issued automatically to all farmer patrons. In 1944, the bylaws were changed to use revolving certificates of indebtedness for financing. The objectives of such changes were to improve the cooperative plan and the system of financing, and also to qualify as an exempt cooperative under the Federal Corporation Income Tax laws. The balance sheet of December 31, 1965 showed that 94 percent of the assets were being financed by shareholders; and three-fifths by rotating certificates of indebtedness.

Andy has also used the Soil Science Department faculty for formulas for the mixing of fertilizers; the Dairy Department personnel for feeds for dairy cows; and the Animal Husbandry Department members for hog feeds. The agricultural agents of Allegan County and the special extension agents of the district have worked closely with him in servicing the cooperative and the farmers of the area.

Thus Lohman was one of the most extensive users and boosters of the University from the late 20's to the mid-60's.

Many Groups and M.S.U. Commend His Efforts

The efforts, services, and accomplishments of Andy Lohman have been recognized by many groups. During the World War II period the State Board of Education presented him with a recognition statement for the training of war veterans; and Selective Service gave him a medal for service on the Selective Service Appeal Board.

In 1955, Michigan State University presented him with a Centennial Award "in recognition of distinguished services which have contributed to the benefit of mankind." Again, at Farmers Week in 1959, Michigan State presented him with a Distinguished Service to Agriculture Award.

In 1960, the Commission on Agriculture of the State of Michigan presented him with a plaque for "his contributions to agriculture, farm cooperatives and the poultry industry."

The Poultry and Egg National Board, in 1961, presented him with the famous Blue Rooster Award "for outstanding leadership of the poultry industry."

The Michigan Farm Bureau gave him the Distinguished Service Award in 1963 "for his nationwide influence in the integration of production and marketing of eggs and poultry—and for his outstanding services to the farm people of Michigan."

The U. S. Agency for International Development, through the Farmer Cooperative Service of the U.S.D.A., presented a certificate to the cooperative for its generous assistance to foreign guests.

However, the finest recognition of Andy perhaps are the commendatory statements generally made by members of the poultry industry, by staff members of Michigan State, and by the rural people of Allegan County and Michigan.

The following characteristics of Andy Lohman as manager have been significant in the success of HFBC:

1. Concern about the welfare of farm people.
2. Industry and attention to details.
3. Integrity in all relationships.
4. Desire to be a leader in new ideas, operations and services.
5. An investigational mind which resulted in the extensive use of research.
6. Ability to analyze the factors affecting the operations and future of the business and to make sound decisions on needed adjustments and changes.

How and why did Andy Lohman develop a successful cooperative? What were his objectives? What type of man has he been? These and other questions were asked of a number of persons who have worked with him for years. Their opinions are summarized below.

Lohman is mild-mannered and soft-spoken in discussion. He is very humble but sure of himself in areas of his experience. He has been very appreciative of assistance and friendships. He has been frank and honest but not necessarily tactful. One always knows where he stands on issues involving poultry, cooperatives, and the community. His concern and integrity undoubtedly have been important reasons for the confidence placed in him by his boards, patrons, and other citizens of the community and state. His teetotaler position and his refusal to accept spirits as gifts undoubtedly strengthened him in the Dutch community where Calvinism has had such a strong foothold. Mr. Lohman has practiced his religion both on Sunday and every day during the week.

Andy has not seemed to take himself seriously. He has had a clever sense of humor as indicated by frequent salty remarks.

What Motivates a Man Like Lohman?

What have been his objectives? Certainly they haven't been financial. He has been underpaid considering his responsibilities and accomplishments. He has refused salary increases proposed for him by the board. He has refused compensation to pay for any of his few vacation trips. Lohman has thoroughly enjoyed his experiences and the challenges faced. He has enjoyed being a pioneer—in experimenting with new ideas for the community. His remarks, "I have had a lot of fun," and "I have gotten a big kick out of life," may explain part of his motivation.

Lohman has a keen memory and his mind holds a lot of useful, practical information. He has read extensively in poultry and financial journals; in publications where he could obtain ideas of value for the cooperative and poultry industry. He has regularly read *American Business, U. S. News and World Report,* and the *Wall Street Journal.* He has had a deep appreciation of the values of informative records, and has constantly examined the financial statements. He has been sharp in business affairs; has practically never missed the trends in egg prices, and has been over 80 percent accurate in estimating the price trends for the ingredients used in mixed feeds and mixed fertilizers. He has done the designing and engineering for all of the two-score buildings of the cooperative except for the push-button elevator completed in 1964.

The operations and success of the services of the cooperative have been by far his primary concern. He has lived within a block of the cooperative, and has arrived at his office by 6:00 or 6:30 a.m., approximately an hour before the other employees. His wife is reported to have said, "If fires should break out simultaneously at home and at the cooperative, Andy would go to save the cooperative."

Mr. Lohman seems to be always planning—always thinking ahead. As one walks with him around the facilities, one hears him constantly using such terms as "revamp," "change," "add," "remodel," and "take this out."

The direction of his thinking is reflected also by such expressions as "modernize," "volume per man," "lifters for men," "speed up operations," "bulk mixing and bulk delivery," "lower the costs," "push-button operations," "special services for farmers," and "only four or five farm supply cooperatives are needed in Michigan."

His attitude toward business operations and management are reflected in such statements as: "One must be ahead of the crowd," "you have got to beat your competitors or they will beat you," and "one must always be figuring." Such views certainly tend to develop the imagination and to stimulate innovation.

Through the years, Lohman has obtained so much satisfaction from his daily experiences with the cooperatives and the poultry industry that he has not wished to make special vacation trips. He has taken a lot of pride in his markmanship with his 22 rifle on sparrows, starlings, and crows. For many years he has written a weekly column for the *Allegan County Echo*.

One of the finest tributes paid to Andy Lohman was a remark of a friend, "Andy has done for his community what others have done for themselves."

The writer has frequently wondered: Why haven't there been more Andy Lohmans for the cooperatives of Michigan? Perhaps one also should add: Where will we find the Andy Lohmans for the cooperatives in the dynamic, mechanized, and computerized society of tomorrow? Will another Andy Lohman show up for the Hamilton Farm Bureau Cooperative, or will another efficient system of management and operations be evolved for the cooperative?

Innovator, Activist,
and Humanitarian

Charles McCarthy

by Marvin A. Schaars

CHARLES McCARTHY OF WISCONSIN may be unknown to most readers of this brief biographical sketch but he was not so to every legislator, governor, university administrator, farm leader, and public official in the state in the two decades from 1901 to 1921. These were the fiery days of Robert M. LaFollette, Sr. These were the decades when much progressive social legislation was passed in the state. This was the time when farmer cooperatives appeared everywhere in the state. These were the Charles McCarthy years.

The facts of his life are: He was born in Brockton, Mass., June 29, 1873 of immigrant Irish parents who moved to this country following the Irish potato famine of the 1850's. After attending the local public elementary and high schools, he went to Brown University as a special student from 1892 to 1896. Here he distinguished himself much more so as an All-American football player than as a scholarly student. He became deeply interested in the struggle of American democracy, in the plight of immigrants, and of poor people generally. He concentrated especially upon history which he found not only fascinating but enlightening as well.

He served as football coach for two seasons at the University of Georgia. The burning desire to study more about social and economic problems and ways to do something constructively about them caused him to come to the University of Wisconsin, in 1898, to study under Frederick Jackson Turner, the renowned historian of the American frontier; Richard T. Ely, eminent liberal economist; William T. Scott, economist well-known in his day; and others at the university. McCarthy must have been a joy to his history, economic, and political science professors with his insatiable desire to read and to concentrate upon it, his ability to express himself clearly, and with his constant alertness to problems that needed solving. His Ph.D. thesis on the

Anti-Masonic Party was awarded the Justin-Winsor Prize by the American Historical Association in 1902.

Sees Opportunity for Public Service in Legislative Drafting

Upon receiving his Ph.D. degree in 1901 at the age of 28, he accepted a position as "document clerk" or "document cataloger" for the Wisconsin Free Library Commission. The low salary ($83.33 a month) might easily have discouraged a lesser man from accepting the position, but Dr. McCarthy evidently envisioned the greater opportunities for public service which the position offered. He became the originator and the official director of the Wisconsin Legislative Reference Library. This was, and is to this day, a unique institution, the first of its kind, which provided a marvelous opportunity for the exuberant and militant McCarthy to serve as a catalyst in the drafting and passing of significant social legislation. This began at a time when the elder LaFollette was governor. He, as is well known, championed liberal, progressive legislation which McCarthy approved so heartily.

The library was dubbed by some as McCarthy's "bill factory." He conceived it as serving two major purposes: first, to assemble accurate, timely, and comprehensive information upon the subjects which legislators intended to embody into legislative bills; and secondly, to actually draft the bills upon request. McCarthy was the architect and soul of this service institution. It was the forerunner of a number of others like it in other states. Its critics, particularly certain legislators and one governor of a lesser social bent, saw it as generating new legislation and not merely as polishing off the bills that legislators brought to it in rather crude form.

This bureau, this bill-perfecting office, this catalyst and adjunct to progressive legislation is in many respects a lasting memorial to Dr. McCarthy. It is mentioned early in this sketch because this institution provided the springboard for McCarthy to get involved deeply in the states' cooperative movement and in other agricultural activities outside the legislative sphere. It was a vantage point from which he could observe and participate in the trend of events at the state level as they were taking place.

Although Dr. McCarthy was city-born and city-raised, he had great sympathy for farmers. He was convinced that the existing marketing system did not work *for* the farmer but *against* him. How else could the wide margin between what the farmer received for his products and what the consumer paid be explained? Certainly, it was not simply in the cost of providing marketing services, but rather in the very poor bargaining position in which the farmer found himself and in the lack of standardization of products marketed, so McCarthy thought. These needed correction if the avaricious middlemen were to be controlled.

Decides to Help Correct Situation by Promoting Co-ops

And how was this to be corrected? Through cooperation—that was McCarthy's answer! That's how the Irish did it in their creamery movement; that's how the Danes did it with their dairy, egg, and meat packing plants; that's how the Germans cut the usurious rates of money lenders in their Raiffeisen credit societies. Proof galore to Dr. McCarthy—if only the farmers could be told these things and guidance provided for the establishment of cooperatives!

McCarthy did not choose to sit idly by and do nothing. Economics which he studied so intently as a graduate student was far more than some mental gymnastics for him or an expose of solutions to problems that don't exist. It had to become "the living word," the basis for action, the yeast for better times, much as it did for Bishop Grundtvig in his Danish Folk Schools. Low farm prices and low incomes constituted a challenge—not simply sterile statistical figures. They needed to be corrected and he was going to do something about them. He was determined to take up the cudgel in the farmers' behalf.

During the two decades of McCarthy's activities in the state, the American Society of Equity was very active as a general farm organization. It started many Equity exchanges (supply co-ops) and livestock shipping associations. It organized a cooperative to buy and operate the first cooperative meat packing plant in the United States at La Crosse, Wis. (1914). It was successful in getting the legislature to provide for the manufacture of binder twine at the state prison circa 1912; it supported the passage of the Wisconsin cooperative law of 1911. It urged the University of Wisconsin to change its passive policy toward cooperatives to one of more direct assistance.

McCarthy worked hand-in-glove with the officers of the state organization and with many Equity members elected to the state legislature. He was their confidante, their counselor, their inspiration and source of new ideas. He chided them when he disapproved of their actions and warned them of pursuing ill-conceived projects, such as the purchase of the run-down, bankrupt meat packing plant at La Crosse. The Equity found a champion of its zeal to organize in McCarthy, and McCarthy had a state-wide group through which he could advance his ideas for improved marketing and social change. The two complemented each other nicely.

Actively Promotes Cheese Marketing Cooperative

McCarthy was an important cog in the establishment of the Wisconsin Cheese Producers Federation, for many years Wisconsin's largest cooperative. At that time (1911 to 1914) there were several thousand cheese factories in the state and the prices payable to farmers for their milk depended upon the prices for cheese established on the cheese boards. The price of cheddar cheese in the summer of 1911 was 11 cents to 13 cents a pound on the boards and netted the farmers less than $1 per cwt. for milk. This same cheese left the dealers' warehouses in winter at prices as high as 18¢ to 22¢ a pound. And in May, 1912, when the current demand for cheese was still high, prices again slid from 15¢ to 12¢ a pound on the dealer controlled board ostensibly for the purpose of enabling the dealers to fill the storage warehouses for winter sale at higher prices. Senator Henry Krumrey, a dairy farmer near Plymouth, Wis., in the heart of the cheese producing country, believed the dealer margins completely unjustified, became determined to give battle to the "cheese trust" and to set up a cooperative cheese selling organization. Krumrey sought McCarthy's support and received it in full measure.

McCarthy, who loved a fight where justice and equity were involved, was active throughout the campaign to set up the federation. When discouragement faced Krumrey, Dr. McCarthy knew just how to give him the adrenilin shot of encouragement with a well-timed letter. When Prof. H. C. Taylor of the university suggested in 1912 that all cheese in the Plymouth area, rather than a mere fraction of it as was the custom, be sold on the cheese board on a competitive-bid basis, Krumrey and McCarthy considered this much too simple a solution to the farmers' marketing problem. They wanted a cooperative sales agency run by the farmers to sell the cheese and not, as Taylor proposed, a continuation of the dealer-dominated boards. Their plan prevailed, and later Taylor and Prof. B. H. Hibbard, who arrived in Wisconsin as a specialist in cooperatives and agricultural marketing early in 1913, helped the two men formulate the plans for the sales organization.

McCarthy's interest in cooperatives was genuine. He was a close personal friend of Sir Horace Plunkett and thought highly of his views on cooperatives. He knew of the successful struggle of the Irish dairymen to revise their creamery system on a cooperative basis.

When Plunkett was in this country, he worked closely with McCarthy on schemes to educate farmers about cooperatives and to assist in organizing them. This was the purpose of the informal organization, the American Agricultural Organization Committee, of which Sir Horace Plunkett was a member with McCarthy. McCarthy assisted the Country Life Commission in some of its investigations of agricultural marketing, and later made several trips to Europe to study cooperation in Germany, Denmark, Belgium, England, and Ireland.

His thorough knowledge of American history, his understanding of economics, his intimate contacts with farm leaders and farmers' problems, and his investigations of cooperation in foreign lands eminently qualified McCarthy to play a conspicuous role in rural organizations. He did this principally by suggesting the original ideas to farm leaders, oftentimes by proposing full-fledged plans of organization, by appointing committees and commissions since he was a great believer in the democratic process and group action, and by continuous writing of sharp letters, notes, reports, and explanatory memoranda to key individuals. Only one book, *The Wisconsin Idea* (1912) was written by McCarthy. In this he expounded his broad social philosophy. It was, therefore, not in published books and bulletins written by himself that McCarthy carved his niche in the history of cooperation. It was rather in his genius to get others to investigate and to write, to organize committees for collective action, to call meetings of responsible persons—in short, to get things done. He worked adroitly through others and his influence, was, therefore, tenfold.

Drafts Wisconsin Cooperative Law of 1911

Both the American Society of Equity and the Right Relationship League claimed credit for getting the Wisconsin legislature to enact the Cooperative Law of 1911. However, William Kirsch who was close to the scene and an admirer of Dr. McCarthy writes, "At a conference between Senator Krumrey, Dr. McCarthy, and Professor H. C. Taylor, it was decided to introduce a bill in the legislature. This bill, drafted by Dr. McCarthy with the assistance of Miles Riley (an attorney working for McCarthy in the Legislative Reference Library) of Madison was enacted into law at the legislative session of 1911." Unquestionably, McCarthy's continual contacts with the Equity men in and out of the legislature and his direct supervision over bill drafting in the Reference Library suggest that McCarthy also shared in getting this law enacted.

McCarthy was largely instrumental in getting another law passed in 1919 which required the State Department of Agriculture to provide auditing service for cooperatives large and small, (still being provided to this day) and to assist them in installing uniform accounting systems. This service quickly found favor among the farmers and helped many associations to adopt businesslike methods of operations. McCarthy got the idea of this service during his visit to Ireland and made the Wisconsin farmers beneficiaries of it.

In the spring of 1913 the legislature of Wisconsin passed an Act authorizing the incorporation of credit associations for loaning money to farmers on long-term mortgage credit. Although this cooperative credit law differed from the proposal McCarthy made in 1912 to finance farmers, cooperative organizations, and other state development projects by banks using state funds, it, undoubtedly, met with McCarthy's approval for he constantly agitated for better agricultural credit and knew of the European experience in this field.

To help cooperatives in the preparation of their legal papers— articles of incorporation, bylaws, constitutions, membership agreements, marketing contracts, capitalization, number and value of shares —McCarthy utilized the services of Attorney Miles Riley, his assistant in the Legislative Reference Library. As McCarthy's "legal-man-Friday," Riley aided many cooperatives in the state on matters about which the farmers knew little and thus smoothed the way in organizational details at little or no expense to those helped. This was an invaluable service initiated by McCarthy and one so vital to the new organizations being started throughout the state.

Used State Board of Public Affairs to Advance His Ideas

One state agency which was in many respects the dream-child of Dr. McCarthy and which he, as its de facto director, used effectively to advance his ideas pertaining to farmer cooperatives, agricultural marketing and credit, and other social legislation was the State Board of Public Affairs. It came into existence in 1911 and immediately McCarthy drafted an extensive plan of operation for the board. "The State Board of Public Affairs as a legislative brain trust and state-planning board combined was exactly the free wide-ranging investigative and research agency he needed to supplement the more confined and limited activities of the Legislative Reference Library, and give effect to the 'ideas' of his fertile and ever active mind." (Fitzpatrick in *McCarthy of Wisconsin*, p. 146).

Numerous investigations were started at once. Pressure was also brought to bear on the university to make marketing studies of specific agricultural commodities, to do more work in the field of cooperatives and in agricultural credit, and to teach cooperation in the short course. Professor H. C. Taylor who insisted that the university's function was to investigate and not to agitate on organizing marketing institutions brought B. H. Hibbard to Wisconsin as a marketing and cooperative specialist partly in response to McCarthy's and the Society of Equity's prodding of the university.

At least a dozen different publications were issued by the board and a number of laws resulted from its work. The report on cooperation and marketing consisted of four parts: agricultural cooperation, cooperative credit, municipal markets, and distributive or store cooperation. A marketing bill to create a bureau of markets in the state department of agriculture was introduced in 1912 and after several sessions of the legislature was ultimately passed. McCarthy saw the great need for this and other types of legislation and repeatedly urged their adoption. Writing to the governor, who was the chairman of the State Board of Public Affairs committee, in 1912, McCarthy gave an indication of the wide range of activities for agriculture he had in mind, when he wrote:

"If it is the wish of your committee, I shall draft bills (1) for a cooperative credit plan along the lines which I have laid down; (2) for the teaching of cooperation and marketing in the rural schools; (3) for the establishment of a paper or report of some kind along the lines which I have suggested (which would tell monthly or perhaps quarterly exactly what the cooperative agricultural warehouses had, their prices, etc.), and also for the establishment of cooperation in the short course at the University; and (4) the establishment of cooperative credit. It may be that some of these can be taken up with the Regents of the University without legislation. I believe it wise, however, to have legislation set forth in definite shape, so that if the Regents do not take it up or that those in charge of the rural school work do not take it up, the plan can be put through by your Board." (quoted by Fitzpatrick in *McCarthy of Wisconsin*, p. 152)

McCarthy was also the guiding influence in the national Conferences on Marketing and Farm Credits held in Chicago in 1913-14-15-16. A review of the speeches at the conferences and the working committees that were appointed indicate the great interest shown in cooperatives, in marketing practices and efficiencies, and in problems of distribution. At the conference held in 1915, a National Agricultural Organization Society (N.A.O.S.), modeled after the structure of the

Irish Agricultural Organization Society, was created. McCarthy was named to the committee to draft its provisional constitution and by-laws. N.A.O.S. had a broad program to encourage the organization of cooperatives, to improve marketing, to encourage educational institutions to be active in helping farmers solve the problems of finance and marketing, and in general, provide assistance to farmers largely through associated action. N.A.O.S. established headquarters in Madison under McCarthy's general direction and with Charles Holman, a protegé of McCarthy's, in direct charge.

Described as Leading Contributor to Co-op Development

McCarthy's contributions to the development and expansion of cooperatives in Wisconsin during the 20 years, 1901 to 1921, were greater than those of any other single individual in my opinion. He was the idea-man—others carried them out. He was the innovator, the planner, and the pragmatist. He prodded others. He planted the germ—others nurtured it. He was a humanitarian with a vision—he inspired others to action. He was a dynamic leader, imaginative, liked controversy, and was interested in so many things—sports, travel, politics, history, economics, mankind. He was a non-conformist, brilliant, adamant, often impatient with persons of lesser talents or those slow to act. He thrived on involvement. He was in the thick of the fight—not on the side-lines. He made enemies.

He was gregarious, talkative, and almost mesmeric in his personal magnetism. He saw the social and economic problems of his day with a clarity held by few. In all of these, his concern for the welfare of the farmer was deeply rooted. He tried to instill in his protegés the need to get the spirit of cooperation as exemplified in his Irish friends, Sir Horace Plunkett, George Wm. "A.E." Russell, Father Finlay, and R. A. Anderson of Ireland. This spirit of cooperation was likened by him to the powerful force of public opinion within nations. This spirit had to be caught if cooperation was to manifest itself among the farmers. His untimely death at the age of 48 silenced the peoples' statesman, but many of the ideas he advocated have taken root and proclaim his dedicated service.

James G. K. McClure

by Claud L. Scroggs

"THE GOOD LORD MUST OF SENT HIM TO US, 'cause we needed him so bad." This statement made by a mountain farmer of western North Carolina in the early 20's sums up much of the reverence, respect, and humble appreciation for a man who devoted the final 35 years of his life to the economic and spiritual welfare of rural families in the mountains of the Tarheel state.

James G. K. McClure was, in fact, a crusader, an innovator, a one-man pioneer blazing the trail of economic development of an under-developed area. And especially important in his kit of tools were the self-help features of cooperative activities. To him, cooperation was not an economic institution alone; rather it was an activator that could propel a whole set of social and economic endeavors in the direction of improved living standards, better roads, improved schools, and last but not least, stronger churches and social institutions.

Having come to Western North Carolina in 1916 for his health, McClure's background and experience provided him with the qualifications which guided him naturally into the niche for which he seemed destined. Son of a Presbyterian minister who later became president of McCormick Theological Seminary in Chicago, McClure also became a Presbyterian minister following his education at Yale Univeristy, McCormick Theological Seminary, and at New College in Edinburgh, Scotland, with terms at the University of Tubingen, Jena, and Berlin in Germany. Before going to college, he spent a year on a ranch in Texas, where he became an expert bronco buster and earned extra money by breaking "broncs" for $2.00 per head. While in Texas he became familiar with Hereford cattle, which he later helped introduce into Western North Carolina.

Being the kind of man who involved himself in community organizations, he became an active member of a local Farmers Union and was greatly engrossed with the possibilities of cooperative buying and

301

selling. Recognizing that the Farmers Union was a dying cause in the area and had very little local support, McClure provided the leadership for starting a new organization which would "provide a marketing system that would stimulate production and make for less waste of money and effort in distribution."

Originally known as the Fairview Farmers Federation and serving only the community in which McClure resided, the pattern was being set. Because of the period of depressed farm prices following World War I and the fact that the average net income of mountain farmers was around $86.00, farmers were allowed to buy stock with building material at market price or labor at the following rates: (1) Muscle men, $3.00 per day; (2) man and team, $5.00 per day. Much of the stock purchased by the first members was paid for by a few days work on the warehouse or in laying track for the railroad siding. A considerable portion of the labor required in building the first warehouse consisted of such volunteer labor. Favorable civic support and considerable newspaper publicity about this first effort resulted in requests from many other communities for help in providing their own marketing and farm supply businesses.

Soon after this humble beginning, the name was changed to Farmers Federation—a federation of effort but organized structurally as a centralized cooperative. At the time of McClure's death in 1956, the cooperative had 24 warehouses and eight freezer-locker plants serving 15 mountain counties in western North Carolina. He had seen the marketing and farm supply business of this association reach almost $7 million annually. Dollarwise, this is far from the entire story. For several other cooperative operations—independent of the Federation but spawned by it and by McClure's leadership—had business volumes that would increase this annual figure to as much as $12-$15 million during this great innovator's lifetime.

Co-op's Objectives Both Economic and Social

Because of McClure's spiritual outlook and strong feeling about social conditions, the Farmers Federation was unique among contemporary cooperatives of those early years because emphasis was given not only to economic objectives but to social objectives as well. McClure lumped these into a four-fold purpose: (1) To find or create markets for things that can be produced on the farms of western North Carolina; (2) To secure for the individual farmers the advantages of wholesale buying; (3) To develop new sources of wealth for farm people; and (4) To strengthen and develop spiritual resources of the territory the cooperative serves.

Under McClure's guidance, the Federation took the pioneer approach in achieving many of these goals. In many ways these efforts could be termed a Point IV program at home or an early-day regional development—a determined attempt to harness undeveloped human and soil resources in an area hampered by the size of small mountain farms. Marketable surpluses above home needs were usually in small volume and lacking in uniformity. Thus, from the beginning, the Federation considered marketing as its *big* job. In the early years it was outstandingly successful in operating sweetpotato curing and storage houses. This let members hold their potatoes over and sell in the spring, when they brought almost double the price farmers usually received in the fall.

In 1928, the cooperative built a cannery in Henderson County to stimulate production of green vegetables. It sold yellow and red tomato juice, okra, tomatoes, and snapbeans under its own labels— Carolina Sunshine and Carolina Mountains. From this facility developed a large vegetable producing area which each summer ships many tons of fresh vegetables to cities in Florida and other markets. Following the practice of reaching for the market with the highest prices, the cannery was abandoned when fresh vegetable prices exceeded those that could be paid by the processing plant.

In the beginning, the Federation also helped members market mountain shrubs, locust fence posts, chestnut rails, and large volumes of pulp wood and acid wood. It discontinued this particular job when other markets opened up. As a result of these activities in timber marketing, McClure's contacts became so widespread that he served for several years as president of the American Forestry Association. In addition, he was also president of the North Carolina Forestry Association.

Over the years, and through trial and error, McClure pushed the organization into simple marketing functions that helped promote varied products that would provide mountaineer farmers with added income. Included among these were such unusual items as beeswax, potted flowers, herbs, and quartz crystals. During World War II, the Federation operated two plants which manufactured pipe bowls from the knobby roots of mountain laurel, replacing imported brier.

Develops Long-Range Program To Build Poultry Industry

Outstanding among its efforts to fill the first objective of finding or creating markets was the Federation's energetic, long-range program to develop a poultry industry—broilers, supply flocks to furnish hatching eggs, turkeys, and commercial egg flocks. Beginning in 1921 the organization handled about $2,500 worth of poultry the first year; volume increased to $50,000 by 1925. Unique in this early effort were the live poultry cars operated over the railroads in the western counties of North Carolina, with regular weekly stops at each strategic point. Cash was paid at the car door, a policy which McClure insisted on as necessary for installing a reliable market that would automatically increase poultry production. By 1929 these live poultry railroad cars had reached a volume of almost a half million dollars annually.

This early poultry effort was continued throughout McClure's lifetime and by the end of his career this department had grown close to the $3 million mark annually.

Bulwark of successful poultry activity was the hatchery department which by the mid-fifties was turning out about two million certified baby chicks per year. The Federation maintained rigid standards and not a single case of Pullorum was traced to the hatchery over several years of operation.

While McClure was still at the helm of the cooperative, it had continued to promote the broiler industry because it fitted so well into the scheme of managing small farms. This great crusader was known to be very proud of the fact that the organization was marketing approximately 40,000 broilers a week, and he could call the names of members who were "growing off" about a quarter of a million of chicks in any one period.

In searching for income sources, McClure was a great force in persuading mountain farmers to increase their production of burley tobacco because of the high value of crop per acre. Because of his interests, McClure served as head of the Chamber of Commerce committee to build a burley warehouse at Asheville. As a result of his efforts, the auction tobacco market was opened in 1930. In his lifetime he saw this market grow until local warehouses were paying farmers of the region more than $5 million annually for their burley leaf. The Federation served an important role in this market, operating three sales floors and administering the support program of the Commodity Credit Corporation.

Another example of McClure's efforts to open new markets to small farmers was the establishment of a department to promote production of gladiolus bulbs. In this venture, like many others he envisioned, major emphasis was given to the potential income to farmer producers.

Whereas McClure was ofttimes heard to advocate marketing activities in order "to collar the dollar," he was constantly stressing the fact that farmers must work together in cooperative purchasing because producers are "forced to sell at wholesale and buy at retail." Moreover, he was constantly reminding farmers that cottonseed meal was selling at $4.10 per bag when the Federation came into existence in 1920, and the price was immediately reduced to $2.50.

McClure, Starting Small, Builds Co-op Services

From the meager beginnings that amounted to only a few thousand dollars per year, McClure was, during his lifetime, able to see farmer members of the Federation buy hundreds of carloads of fertilizer, feed, seed, farm implements, and numerous other farm and home supply needs through the 24 warehouses operated by the centralized association. He saw this farm supply volume reach something over $3 million per year, or almost one-half the dollar volume of cooperative business. Feed accounted for almost one-third of the supply volume and was constantly growing with increased poultry and dairy production in the mountain counties.

In maximizing the services that could be rendered to members as the organization grew, McClure insisted on small grinding and feed mixing mills at the local warehouses. This permitted farmers to bring in their own grain and have it mixed with other ingredients which the warehouses kept on hand to make well-rounded dairy and poultry feeds. At some local warehouses, these services included a grist mill, a corn sheller, and a feed mixer. The Federation was one of the early cooperatives that provided farmer-members with freezer locker services, and at the last annual meeting over which McClure presided he reported that the eight locker plants processed over a million pounds of beef and pork and many thousands of pounds of vegetables during the year.

As another facet of marketing operations, country-cured hams became a growing business in connection with locker plants. These hams gained a reputation because of their fine quality, and many local residents as well as the horde of tourists in the mountain area made up the growing market.

Since low-income farmers were inadequately provided with transportation facilities, McClure recognized early in the cooperative's activities that transportation services had to be provided by the organization. So, trucks operated by the cooperative played an important part in all these many marketing and farm supply services provided to members on 28 different truck routes. The average truck route was about 50 miles roundtrip, delivering farm supplies and picking up broilers, eggs from hatchery supply and commercial flocks, and other farm produce to be marketed by the association. These trucks operated mostly on mountain dirt roads and thus required top-notch repair and maintenance. The cooperative had its own garage for such work, also using the mechanics for tractor and equipment repair at the Asheville headquarters. It had a second tractor and equipment repair department at the Hendersonville warehouse.

McClure's interest in improving transportation and farm-to-market roads was instrumental in his appointment in 1949 as chairman for Western North Carolina to carry the referendum for a state bond issue of $200 million for improved rural roads and schools. This referendum was successful largely because of the big majority rolled up for it under McClure's leadership in the western tier of counties.

McClure Finds Other Ways to Help Farmers Increase Income

The complete story on Crusader McClure cannot be limited to the Farmers Federation and its efforts in the marketing and farm supply field. Through hard work and faith, he and those he led made remarkable achievements with other enterprises, fostered and promoted by the cooperative until the new activities were able to pay their own way. Important among these "god children" was the Treasure Chest Cooperative Mutual, composed of skilled native craftsmen in the mountains of Western North Carolina. This organization was set up to market hand-hooked rugs and similar items. The rugs are folk art, handed down within families from generation to generation. By carefully controlling design, quality, color, and workmanship, Treasure Chest products soon found a unique place in American rug merchandising. McClure lived to see this association become the largest shipper of hand-hooked rugs in the country, thus making good use of surplus family labor available on many small mountain farms. Some families actually made their entire living from hooked-rug production. Children have been sent to college on money earned from rug making.

The Treasure Chest Mutual is just one example of the institutions created to help farmers increase their income. This and other efforts led, in 1946, to formation of the non-profit organization known as "The

Development Foundation of Western North Carolina, Inc." This organization was founded to develop the resources and economic life of the area by research, demonstration, education, and other methods. This foundation was so organized as to include such home industry associations as the Treasure Chest Mutual, the Handicraft Mutual, Biltmore Spinning Company, Appalachian Textile Company, and Swannanoa Textile Company; the Farmers Loan Corporation, a credit organization; the *Farmers Federation News*, a house organ for the entire family of cooperatives; and certain other cooperative enterprises.

Believing firmly that more high-producing milk cows would add to the income of the mountain farmers, McClure provided tremendous leadership in promoting the dairy industry. Although incorporated as an independent dairy cooperative, Skyline Cooperative Dairies, Asheville, was a member of the Federation-sired family of cooperatives. To market the milk, the dairy cooperative was set up to provide both wholesale and retail milk routes in five of the mountain counties.

McClure also helped establish an artificial breeding program to improve the quality of dairy herds. At his instigation and invitation, the American Breeders Service leased buildings and facilities the Federation put up and provided semen to local breeding cooperatives throughout the Southeast. In one of McClure's articles in the *Farmers Federation News* in 1952, he proudly reported that more than 105,000 cows were bred from this stud that year.

From its very inception, the Farmers Federation under McClure's guidance worked closely with the State Extension Service to increase yields per acre and production per animal. The association sponsored corn luncheons for all corn growers in the area growing 100 bushels or more per acre. It also worked with 4-H Club members in pullet chains. The boys and girls grew out these pullets, selling 12 at a special poultry show and sale in the fall and keeping the rest at home as a laying flock. The money from the sale of pullets was kept by County Agents to carry on the chain the following year.

McClure was a great believer in combining economic activities and social events. The annual picnics of the Federation year-after-year became important social events and happy affairs for cooperative members. Singing of hymns and ballads handed down by God-fearing generations always played an important part in the proceedings. The Federation had its own string bands and choral groups which added to the festivities. It was at such events that McClure showed his exceptional talents. A man of great speaking ability, a keen sense of humor, and outstandingly successful as a toastmaster, he had the talent to meet the demands of his audiences whether a gathering of relatively uneducated farmers or a most sophisticated civic group.

Religious Dept. in Co-op Unique Development

McClure's intense feeling about spiritual values resulted in the establishment within the Farmers Federation of a religious department. This made the association unique among cooperatives in the whole country and, of course, this was the step needed in accomplishing the fourth purpose for which the organization was founded—to strengthen and develop the spiritual resources of the mountain territory. It was within this department that the activities of "The Lord's Acre" evolved. In actual practice, members of a rural congregation are asked to dedicate to their church a portion of a farm crop or of livestock which will be sold and the proceeds given to the church. Begun in 1930, since that time the movement has been instrumental in giving financial stability to many churches in the mountain area of North Carolina, and its influence has spread to congregations of many denominations throughout the United States and in many foreign countries.

An ordained minister, Rev. Dumont Clarke, a brother-in-law of McClure, was persuaded to take over this department. Until his death in 1963, Clarke promoted the Lord's Acre movement and other activities of the religious department in the territory served by the Federation. From the inception of the idea, the Federation offered to help market any product dedicated to a Lord's Acre project. Close associates of McClure say that he was never happier than when speaking at Lord's Acre movement meetings in small, rural churches, his remarks ofttimes being disturbed by the bleating of a lamb tethered in the church yard or the raucous crow of a rooster or two that may have been brought as offerings.

A further indication of McClure's broad interest in the general welfare of the mountain people was his influence in fostering a non-profit health insurance program among farmers of the mountain area. In fact, McClure was one of the staunchest supporters of a state-wide movement begun in 1946 by the Governor to improve health conditions in the rural areas.

Even though new hospitals had been constructed and additional practicing physicians were induced to serve in the rural area, McClure realized that the largest problem facing the better health program was some kind of health insurance at group rates for farm families. Most health organizations claimed the loss in time, labor, and expense was too great to canvass the many rural families who would be eligible.

As in so many other pace-setting activities for the benefit of farm folks in Federation territory, President McClure conceived the idea for a health insurance program which he worked out with Doctor George Bond of the Valley Clinic and Hospital at Bat Cave, N.C. By means of this program, the Hospital Care Association made Blue Cross benefits available to farm families at group rates for the first time. The financial assistance for this plan was given by the Commonwealth Fund of New York City which made a grant to underwrite the high initial cost and preliminary educational expenses of the program. The Division of Health Affairs of the University of North Carolina helped to plan the program.

This type of activity is so illustrative of McClure's ability to reach out for resources and services that could be brought into effective play in uplifting the mountain people he loved so well. In earlier Federation days he successfully solicited funds from well-to-do friends and interested firms and established what was called an Educational and Development Fund for carrying on some of the activities envisioned and to provide some of the needed capital. Since McClure himself was donating his time in these early years, he felt free to ask for the help of others who could afford to donate to such a worthy cause.

McClure was widely recognized for his innovations and dare-do ventures—many of which were carried out on an economic "shoestring." Berea College awarded him the honorary degree of Doctor of Science in 1929. His Alma Mater, Yale University, gave him an honorary M.A. degree in 1939; and the same honor was given him by Harvard in 1941. The University of North Carolina awarded him an honorary LL.D. in 1942. In addition, he served in many other civic, state, and national positions with distinction. But, probably no title would have made him happier than the one assured him in the annals of Western North Carolina history—"cooperative crusader."

James A. McConnell

by *Joseph G. Knapp*

W HEN ED BABCOCK gave up the management of the Cooperative Grange League Federation Exchange (the G.L.F.)[1] in 1937,
at the age of 47, Jim McConnell was the ideal man to succeed him.
Babcock was a great innovator and he had built the G.L.F. into an
impressive cooperative organization. What was now required was a
great administrator, one who could build on the foundation given him.
Let us see how well trained McConnell was for this task.

Jim was born on a farm near Mansfield, Pa., in 1891. As a boy he
was bashful, shy, retiring, and given to dreaming. He had a sharp
conscience when he felt that he had done something wrong.

He loved to read general adventure stories and his dream hero
always carried a six-shooter. Like other boys of his time he was a
fan of "Golden Days" and "The Youth's Companion," and an avid
devotee of Horatio Alger stories. Later he turned to historical novels
and never lost his taste for them. He had no ambition to be President,
but for a time he aspired to be a teacher because this seemed to be
attainable, for in those days teaching in a country school was open
to farm kids who could learn to read, write, and figure.

As a boy on the farm he did his share of the chores and work, and
attended country school until he was 17. Then in the fall of 1909,
with the encouragement of his mother, he went to Mansfield Normal
School for two main reasons: (1) It was only six miles from home;
and (2) it took very little cash, being a State school.

After a year at Mansfield Normal he was able to get a teaching
job in a nearby country school at $40 per month under a "provisional"
teacher's certificate. He held this job for three years and got his
salary up to $50 a month. With the death of his dad during this

[1] In recent years, the G.L.F., and Eastern States Farmers' Exchange, and Pennsylvania Farm Bureau Cooperative Association have merged to form Agway, Inc.

period, Jim ran the home farm with his mother while also teaching in the country school.

However, Jim's older brother, Carl, who later became a prominent Methodist minister in Elmira, N.Y., persuaded him that there wasn't much opportunity in teaching country school and running a small farm. At Carl's urging Jim decided to enter Cornell if possible. When he went to Ithaca in the fall of 1916 to try his luck he found that it would be necessary to work a year so as to establish New York State residence in order to avoid having to pay out-of-state residence tuition. Fortunately, his brother knew the foreman on Professor G. W. Warren's farm near Ithaca, and this was a fine break as Dr. Warren was the leading Farm Management teacher in the United States. Work on Warren's farm gave Jim his first experience with large-scale farming, and under an expert. In those days dairy cattle, large flocks of hens, and fruit were all part of the farming operation.

With his residence status settled, Jim was able to enter Cornell in the fall of 1917.

His college career was interrupted briefly by a short time in the Navy in 1918 after he had made two unsuccessful attempts to get into the Service. He first applied for admission to the first Officers Training Camp. Eventually he was notified that he "lacked executive ability." Later he applied for pilot training in the Air Service but was rejected because of his eyes.

The year on Professor Warren's farm was a great help when Jim got into Cornell University for his associates on the farm and off were largely college students and instructors. This gave him a "great seasoning" and taught him a lot of good farm practices being put to use. Jim has always held that he had a five-year college course—one year at Warren's farm and four years of formal education.

When Jim entered Cornell as a Freshman he was 25 years of age and had little money. He had to earn whatever he needed for tuition, etc., and he had little time for outside activities. His recreation was centered around music and country dancing and playing his banjo. During his Freshman year he continued to work for Professor Warren as a hired man, and later Professor Warren would refer to him as "the best hired man who ever went through Cornell." Jim says that he never knew how to take this remark—whether as a "compliment or an insult."

One of his jobs for Professor Warren was running a milk route to Forest Home Inn near the Campus. In this way he became acquainted with Lois Zimmerman, who was working her way through college and living at Forest Home Inn. This friendship carried through from work days to college and eventually they became engaged. They were married in June, 1920. Lois recognized in Jim potentials that he didn't quite see in himself, and from the time of their marriage until her death in 1963 they were a team that contributed to the growth and fulfillment of each other.

Attracted by the competence of his professors at Cornell—especially George F. Warren, Elmer Seth Savage, Frank Pearson, H. E. Babcock, and Dean Albert Russell Mann, and stimulated by the hovering presence at Cornell of Liberty Hyde Bailey of whom Jim says: "I sat at his feet, a long way off;" and happily married to a wife who was ambitious for him, Jim decided to continue at Cornell for a Master's Degree after his graduation in June, 1921, with a B.Sc. Degree in Agriculture. His main source of support was an Instructorship in Animal Husbandry which paid $60 per month.

Joins Babcock in Helping To Build G.L.F.

If fate had not intervened he might have continued until he had a Ph.D. and become a Professor of Animal Husbandry. But in the spring of 1922 Jim came under the challenging influence of H. E. ("Ed") Babcock who was teaching an unorthodox course in Cooperative Marketing—a subject of great interest in New York State because of the efforts being made by the G.L.F. to establish itself. When Babcock took over the management of the G.L.F. on July 1, 1922, he drew several of his students, including Jim, to help him make a go of this floundering organization.

Jim admits that at this time he had not yet become a "real convert to the farmer cooperative way of life." He says, "I was really following a man."

His decision to join with Babcock was influenced by two other factors—an allergy test showed that his bad attacks of asthma were caused by being around cattle and his doctor advised him to "get out of the cow barn." Secondly, as a married man with a family on the way he found that the couldn't live on the $60 a month received as a graduate student instructor. (His daughter, Jean, was born on November 7, 1922. His son, Joe, came on March 30, 1924, and his second daughter, Carroll, on December 8, 1930.)

So when Ed Babcock became General Manager of the G.L.F., Jim informed him that he was available for a job. Ed put him to work, but Jim found that this didn't cause him to give up his planned profession— for as he expresses it, "I have spent the remainder of my life 'teaching.' "

Babcock's immediate need was to get the G.L.F. rooted, and he needed fieldmen who could speak the farmer's language and "get the business." McConnell and the other fieldmen soon found that the best way to get the business was through the utilization of local dealers, and gradually on this pragmatic base the unique G.L.F. system of Agent-Buyers was developed.

One of the serious problems of the new organization was to produce a feed of good quality. In 1923, Babcock needed someone in whom he had complete confidence to take charge of quality control at the Buffalo Mill—someone who knew what farmers needed and wanted. Jim was the ideal man for this job and he did it so well that in 1924 he was made mill superintendent.

In the early days of the G.L.F. it operated on a partnership basis with the American Milling Company, and drew much of its mixed feed from the A.M.C. feed mill located at Peoria, Ill. In 1925, Ed Babcock decided that the G.L.F. needed a representative on the spot so Jim was sent to Peoria. This position gave him a new perspective and an inside knowledge of the management of a big business. He came to have great respect for the management ability and broadmindedness of H. G. Atwood, President of the American Milling Company, and they developed a working relationship that proved helpful in solving problems that arose within the partnership.

In 1927, Jim returned to Buffalo as manager of the G.L.F.'s feed division and in 1928, when Babcock was forced by illness to take a few months of needed rest, Jim served for him as Acting Manager.

In 1929, Jim was placed in charge of all G.L.F. wholesale operations, and from 1933 to 1936 he served as Assistant General Manager. During this period he spent a year as Executive Vice-President of the Commercial Molasses Company, an organization in which G.L.F. had a vital interest because of the large molasses purchases needed for its feed mixing operations. This experience in New York City further widened Jim's knowledge of industrial management and marketing methods.

McConnell Was Logical Choice to Follow Babcock

When Babcock gave up the post of General Manager in October, 1936, Jim's appointment was both logical and natural. Ed Babcock said at this time, "Jim has worked up from the ranks. You will find that he is idealistic but also practical and level-headed. He has courage and, above everything else, he is fair. I know the G.L.F. will go forward under his leadership."

During the next 16 years Jim built upon the solid foundations that Babcock had developed with his close assistance. In fact, the two men had complemented each other for Jim, since 1922, had been Babcock's right arm in making programs work. Jim's wife, Lois, once said to me, "Ed lays the eggs and Jim hatches them."

Although great decisions were made by the G.L.F. while Jim was General Manager, the essential farmer-controlled character of the organization remained unchanged. During his administration the wholesale business volume of the G.L.F. grew from $35 to $184 million, and the total assets of the G.L.F. system grew from $9 to $55 million.

During the years of Jim McConnell's stewardship the G.L.F. accomplished many things.

- It simplified its highly complex structure.
- It began a program of returning savings in the form of patronage refunds.
- It developed across-the-board marketing services.
- It greatly broadened its line of supplies and services.
- It inaugurated an integrated petroleum service program.
- It made great contributions to the war effort.
- It greatly amplified its research activities.
- It developed the member-ownership plan that eventually led G.L.F. to give up voluntarily its Federal income tax exemption.
- It carried forward employee and membership education so that the morale of G.L.F. was outstanding among cooperative organizations.

These accomplishments came from a continuous ferment for improvement which was encouraged and directed by Jim McConnell. He had the gift of being able to work with all associates on a personal, friendly basis, but he was not a complacent, easy-going manager. He expected and got the best possible performance. Probably no cooperative organization ever achieved and maintained for so long a time a higher morale than G.L.F. under Jim McConnell.

Employees, Members Made to Feel They Were Partners

This was not all due to Jim, but it was he who gave all employees and members of the organization the feeling that they were partners in a common enterprise. The name Jim McConnell became loved and respected by all related to the G.L.F.

Jim continuously strove to keep the G.L.F. essentially democratic. In his annual report for 1943, he said:

The only objective of the member ownership campaign is to have a large body of stockholders, with sufficient investment on the part of each one so that they feel a sense of ownership and responsibility.

He was very much disturbed by the general public's misunderstanding of cooperatives and he believed that the member ownership program would demonstrate that farmers were supporting G.L.F. not only with their purchasing but with their funds.

In his 1947 annual report he said:

> If I were to pick out one central theme which has run continuously through top policy, it would be: *"Let's not build a G.L.F. which is so strongly centralized that its effectiveness depends on the decisions and actions of a few men at the top."*

I have many letters from Jim which indicate his continuous searching interest to improve the G.L.F. In one letter he dealt with a criticism that I had made of one phase of G.L.F. operations which had upset certain members of his staff. He remarked, "I take it from this that the talk was well worth-while."

In another letter to me in June, 1945, he said, "A cooperative without a research program and an educational program among its employees is much like a ship without a compass or a rudder. The research is the compass."

The executive leadership of Jim McConnell made the Cooperative Grange League Federation Exchange a living organism—a demonstration of what farmers could do cooperatively under effective administration. When he retired as General Manager in 1952, after 30 years of continuous service to the G.L.F., to become Administrator of the Agricultural Stabilization Administration and, later, Assistant Secretary of Agriculture, he left a strong organization which was in position to reach new heights.

Jim is now back where he started from, living on the farm near Mansfield, Pa., where he grew up as a boy. In 1963 he married Betty Beach, a pianist and water color artist, and a longtime friend of himself and Lois, and he continues his keen interests in agricultural and national affairs, and in his grandchildren.

In a recent letter to me he said:

> When it is all over—I'd like to be remembered for the job of putting a great business organization, which is successfully operating, into a democratic framework, using all the devices available to the business world, and still keeping the essential controls in the hands of farmers.

Arthur J. McGuire

by Gordon W. Sprague

AMONG THE LEADERS in the development of the Cooperative Dairy Industry in Minnesota was A. J. McGuire. As a young man in the University Extension Service he traveled up and down the state over the dirt roads on a bicycle, gathering information on cream and butter prices. These facts showed the dairymen how an increase in income could come to them if they would organize cooperatives for the improvement of marketing and quality programs.

Arthur James McGuire was born in Swift County, Minn., on July 27, 1874. He was "a green, awkward, unsophisticated country boy" when he first showed up at University Farm. As he was also poor, he had to earn money to get through the university. He then came under the inspiring influence of Professor T. L. Haecker, "the father of the cooperative movement in Minnesota." Professor Haecker asked him this question when he sought a job, "Can you milk cows?" Young McGuire replied "That is just what I *can* do!" Needless to say, he got the job of milking cows, and he gradually was promoted to greater responsibilities until he was finally making butter and cheese in the college dairy plant.

McGuire graduated in 1904, and was made superintendent of the university's branch station at Grand Rapids. During his 10 years in this position he made a great contribution to the improvement of dairy production throughout the state and in land clearing work.

McGuire then went back to University Farm and served until 1921 as Extension Specialist. It was in 1921 that he began his great task of forming the cooperatives of Minnesota into a great marketing federation.

Becomes First Land O'Lakes General Manager

He became the first General Manager of the Minnesota Cooperative Creameries Association. He was at first hired by the Organizing

Committee to serve as Organizational Manager and to direct the work of building a membership. In order to accept this appointment it was necessary for McGuire to obtain a leave of absence from the Extension Division of the University of Minnesota. He continued as Manager of the Minnesota Cooperative Creameries Association until it was renamed Land O'Lakes Creameries, Inc., in 1926. He then became the first General Manager of the new organization.

To those who have had the experience of organizing a new cooperative and getting members to contribute, the task which confronted McGuire will be easily understood. There was general agreement that action to improve the dairymen's participation in the butter market was needed but money was scarce. His sincerity and honesty, however, were unquestioned and these facts stood him in good stead. Slowly the organization began to gain membership and with membership, prestige.

As evidence of success began to crown his efforts the activities of competition increased. Some creamery operators also opposed the activities of the new organization because it infringed on their freedom of action. But the organization grew, and with it the earnings of Minnesota dairymen.

It is easy to over-simplify the statement about any one of the persons active at the inception of the Minnesota Cooperative Creameries Association. Nothing about it was simple. It was new and had to earn its way at every step. It is also easy to over-simplify the explanation of the reason for growth. The contribution of A. J. McGuire was tremendous, but he was not alone; there were many others at the College of Agriculture and in the state government to help.

Outstanding among the leaders was a farmer named John Brandt, whose name came to be almost synonymous with that of Land O'Lakes Creameries. But it is doubtful that Brandt and McGuire together could have accomplished the development of a successful cooperative. The obvious sincerity of McGuire, the work of many others, and the fact that they trusted each other were the essential ingredients. It was on these bases that A. J. McGuire left his name indelibly engraved on the history of cooperative accomplishment in Minnesota and on the memories of the persons with whom he labored to reach his goal.

Many pages could be written about the life and activities of Arthur J. McGuire. Perhaps the following words from a resolution passed following his death, October 26, 1933, by the Minnesota House of Representatives, catches his unique influence:

"His contribution to the dairy industry of Minnesota can never be measured. He was a true cooperator. Cooperation, to him, was more than a better way of doing business. It was a living principle which he labored to extend to all of the relations of human life."

Andrew W. McKay

by Martin A. Abrahamsen

ANDREW W. McKAY is a distinguished pioneer in cooperative research and educational work. Like other early pioneers in this field his recognition of the possibilities of cooperatives grew out of his early employment experiences. These experiences gave him an opportunity to observe first-hand the economic implications of agricultural production, and the contributions of cooperatives in helping farmers achieve for themselves the benefits of organizing and operating their own businesses.

McKay was born in River John, Nova Scotia, Canada, in 1883. He attended the Ithaca, N. Y., High School and after 2½ years earned credits necessary for admission to the College of Agriculture of Cornell University in 1904. There he received a Bachelor of Science Degree in January, 1908. In view of his later literary output it is not surprising that he won the Laura A. Messenger Prize for an essay on human progress that year. During the following spring and summer terms he took graduate work in pomology and plant physiology.

In the fall of 1908 McKay joined the Bureau of Plant Industry, U. S. Department of Agriculture. In this position he gained valuable knowledge about fruit production. His assignment covered problems of fruit storage and transportation—functions that have come to be recognized as among the more important areas of marketing. One of his early publications, issued in 1918, was *Loading and Transporting Western Cantaloupes*. Thus began a career of public service that was to cover 40 years and include contributions in the field of agricultural cooperation that marked him as a nationally recognized cooperative pioneer and leader.

From 1914 to 1916 and again from 1919 to 1921, McKay supplemented his governmental employment with first-hand industry experience. During the first period he was employed by H. C. Shreader Company, Jacksonville, Fla., to direct and supervise picking, grading, and packing of citrus fruit. During the latter period, he served as Vice President of the Southern States Produce Distributors, Valdosta, Ga. He then rejoined the U. S. Department of Agriculture in 1921 as an employee of the Bureau of Markets and Crop Estimates.

McKay rose rapidly in the ranks of this and its successor agencies. One of the early reports of the Bureau of Markets and Crop Estimates stated that he studied the cooperative marketing of Vermont Maple Products. Even at that time close cooperation prevailed between Land-Grant-Colleges and U.S.D.A. agencies responsible for work with cooperatives. For example, the Vermont Experiment Station published findings of his study.

Takes Charge of U.S.D.A. Work on Economics of Cooperation

McKay was actively engaged in cooperative work throughout the time when it was centered in the Bureau of Agricultural Economics from 1922 to 1929.

As the Division of Agricultural Cooperation got underway in the Bureau, three work areas were identified: economics, statistics, and legal phases of cooperation. He was placed in charge of work on the economics of cooperation. Such other contemporary pioneers as R. H. Ellsworth and L. S. Hulbert, respectively, were assigned to work with statistics and legal phases of cooperation.

Drawing on his background and experience in fruit and vegetable work, McKay naturally did much of his pioneering work with fruit and vegetable cooperatives. He was the senior author with W. MacKenzie Stevens of U. S. Department of Agriculture Bulletin No. 1237, *Organization and Development of Citrus-Fruit Marketing Agency,* issued in 1924.

This publication was developed in response to numerous requests for information on the operation of California Fruit Growers Exchange, Los Angeles, the cooperative now known as Sunkist Growers. It provided valuable information on basic cooperative organization and operating principles, useful not only to members and employees of the Exchange but also to other types of cooperatives and to cooperative students as well.

In addition to providing fundamental information on operating practices, the report identified the following practices as fundamentals of the Exchange system: (1) Operation for mutual benefit; (2) limitation of membership; (3) informing and consulting with members; (4) conservative practices; (5) cooperation with other agencies; (6) member withdrawal privilege; and (7) membership loyalty.

The usefulness of this study is indicated by the fact that it was updated in 1937 as FCA Circular C-121 with McKay again as the senior author. Since then, thousands of copies of this report have been distributed by Farmer Cooperative Service, U.S.D.A., and its predecessor agencies to both cooperative leaders in the United States and abroad.

It has served virtually as a textbook on the basic organization features and operating practices of a national cooperative recognized as being in the forefront in organization features and operating practices. It was revised in 1950 and again in 1960 when it was published as FCS Circular 27, *Sunkist Growers, Inc.—A California Adventure in Agricultural Cooperation.*

As McKay's interest broadened to problems of cooperative management, he co-authored with W. J. Kuhrt, Department of Agriculture Bulletin 1414, *Management Problems of Cooperative Associations Marketing Fruits and Vegetables,* which was issued in 1926.

This bulletin was prepared in response to problems growing out of the very substantial growth of these associations during the prior decade. It, for instance, pointed to a 170 percent increase in volume between 1915 and 1924 as well as the existence of nearly 1,000 cooperatives providing marketing service for fruit and vegetable producers.

Using a pragmatic approach of going to cooperative managers and other officials to identify problems, the authors found that the following were among the most frequently mentioned as problems concerning officials:

1. The volume of business handled by the association often was not sufficient to stabilize the market.
2. Too many varieties were produced, including many varieties difficult to sell or of poor keeping quality.
3. Poor packing, careless handling, inadequate storage facilities, a lack of grade standards, and other difficulties were encountered incidental to the preparation of the products for market.
4. The association was unable to control the delivery of the product or to specify the time of delivery.
5. Sales service was inefficient. Small markets were not supplied regularly and directly, while the large markets were often oversupplied. Too many shipments are moved unsold or consigned to commission merchants or auctions.
6. Retailing methods and margins restricted the consumption of fruits and vegetables.
7. Car shortages, delays in transit, and other difficulties incident to transportation were frequently encountered.

The study then went on to develop suggestions for management as to how to deal with these basic problems.

With the passage of the Cooperative Marketing Act in 1926 work with cooperatives in the Department expanded. The Division of Agricultural Cooperation was designated the Division of Cooperative Marketing and a number of specific work units were set up. Because of his wide experience with fruit cooperatives McKay was placed in charge of the unit responsible for work in this area.

Co-Author of Pioneering Book on Co-op Marketing

While an employee of the Cooperative Division, McKay in collaboration with Charles H. Lane authored one of the pioneering books in Agricultural Cooperation, *Practical Cooperative Marketing*. It was published in 1928.

The book had an introduction by W. M. Jardine, Secretary of Agriculture. The Secretary called attention to the need for farmers to organize and direct their own marketing agencies and the necessity to emphasize the importance of education in cooperative marketing. Referring to this book, the Secretary stated:

> In this volume, the authors have undertaken to present an unbiased description of the policies and practices of successful cooperative marketing associations. As a textbook of cooperative marketing, it should be useful in so far as it enables farmers and agricultural high school students to study the organization and operation of associations in their communities, in the light of the experiences of successful organizations. It will be useful also, if it can give farm people, particularly the boys and girls on the farm, a broader outlook on their production and marketing problems and an increased pride in their occupation.

The book included a scholarly description of the basic features of cooperatives. It gave attention to basic cooperative characteristics, services cooperatives could perform, essentials for successful organization, problems of membership, management and financing, and price policies and pooling.

This was followed by a description of various types of marketing cooperatives—those handling dairy products, poultry and eggs, potatoes, fruits and vegetables, livestock, cotton, grain, wool, purchasing, and supplies.

The authors showed a keen insight into problems of cooperatives when they listed as essentials to successful operation the following points:

1. Does the association meet an economic need?
2. Is the association soundly organized?
3. Is the association guided and supported by its members?
4. Has the association improved handling practices?
5. Does the association handle an adequate volume of business?
6. Has the association efficient management and financial stability?
7. Is the association making the community a better place in which to live?

A separate chapter covered each of these questions. In them McKay and Lane demonstrated a depth of understanding of many problems that continue to concern cooperative management today. They developed basic and fundamental suggestions as guideposts for the successful operation of cooperatives.

Becomes Chief, Division of Cooperative Marketing

With the transfer of cooperative work by Executive Order to the Federal Farm Board for a period that extended from 1929 to 1933, Chris L. Christensen became Secretary of the Board and McKay was elevated to the position of Chief of the Board's Division of Cooperative Marketing. In this position he directed the work of the Board in its program of assistance to various commodity groups as well as the wide range of educational activities carried on by the Board.

In the early part of World War II, McKay took leave from the Department of Agriculture to accept a War Service Appointment. This involved directing the Fruit and Vegetable Program of the War Food Commission. His interests took on international dimensions in 1944 when he accepted an assignment with the Ministry of Finance of the Government of Iran. His responsibilities included advising and directing officials of the government in management and operation of public lands, including farming projects and collecting and selling crops from these lands. In the latter capacity he drew on his wide cooperative experience and helped to introduce cooperative methods of business operation in that country.

Upon the completion of this assignment McKay again returned to the Cooperative Research and Service Division of the Farm Credit Administration. His positions there included that of head of the Fruit and Vegetable Section and later head of the Member Education Section. Because of his varied background in cooperative work, he was appointed Assistant to Chief of the Cooperative Research and Service Division in 1950 and served in that capacity until his retirement on November 30, 1953.

During this latter period, in addition to his administrative responsibilities, he found time to issue a number of basic publications in the field of agricultural cooperation. These included publications relating both to new developments in fruit and vegetables and to membership education.

In his research and educational work, McKay achieved an enviable reputation for his integrity, his ability to focus attention on the basic issues without being diverted by less important considerations, and for his ability to express himself clearly both as a speaker and as a writer. As one observer stated, "he characterizes the outstanding admirable qualities which have been dominant in the official leadership of the cooperatives. . . ."

Prepares History of U.S.D.A. Work with Cooperatives

Because McKay was so much a part of the pioneering developments in agricultural cooperation, he was re-employed by Farmer Cooperative Service following his retirement to prepare a history of work in the U. S. Department of Agriculture with cooperatives.

This report covered the period 1913 to 1953, and was updated and issued in 1962 as FCS Circular 31, *Helping Farmers Build Cooperatives —The Evolution of Farmer Cooperative Service* to commemorate the centennial observance of the founding of the U. S. Department of Agriculture.

In speaking of his contributions to this work, Joseph G. Knapp, Administrator, Farmer Cooperative Service, said:

> Mr. McKay took part in many of the events here described. His interest in cooperative organizations started in 1908 . . .
> From then on, with minor interruptions, he was active in helping farmers organize and operate their cooperatives until his retirement in 1953. No one can speak of the record of this work of the Department with farmer cooperatives with more intimate knowledge, perceptiveness, and authority.

Andy or Mac as he is affectionately known to his associates, however, did not end his work with cooperatives with the completion of this publication. In 1956 he taught a graduate course in advanced agricultural cooperation at the University of Maryland where he was able to bring his vast knowledge of cooperative activity to students interested in exploring this field.

His knowledge of cooperatives also was called upon by American National Foods, Inc., when that organization employed him on a part-time basis to serve as a consultant on policies of organization and operation. He also prepared a special report on its operations and contributed substantially to its monthly house organ.

Throughout his cooperative career, McKay combined in the most admirable way humility with a high degree of performance and outstanding achievement with high esteem and admiration. McKay possessed unique ability in training and coaching young employees. He never was known to speak ill of any person; rather he had words of encouragement for aspiring cooperators, be they students, teachers, federal employees, or cooperative directors and employees.

As a pioneer in cooperative work, Andy's warm, friendly, and understanding human qualities did much to mark the path and lighten the load for those who followed.

Charles Leonard McNeil

by Ewell P. Roy

LOW COTTON PRICES and the relatively high cost of farm supplies after World War I accentuated poverty in the Southern United States. Disappointed with the defeat of the McNary-Haugen Bill and not yet pacified by the Federal Farm Board, cotton farmers in the Gulf South sought relief through cooperative efforts. Sapiro's ideas had helped stir the imagination of farm leaders in the Deep South in the direction of cooperation. Everywhere farmers and others looked to cooperatives as a means for survival.

What were these specific economic conditions in the 1920's and 30's which plagued the farmers of Mississippi, Arkansas, Louisiana, and Alabama? First, their extreme poverty as an aftermath of the Civil War and World War I. Second, many small farmers both white and colored located in the upland cotton areas of all four states. Third, the extensiveness of tenancy and sharecropping. Fourth, the low literacy among the farmers and farm people. Fifth, the low standards of living in rural areas, poor health, housing, electrification, and transportation. Sixth, high cost of credit if it could be obtained at all. Seventh, lack of rural industries to accommodate surplus labor. Eighth, extreme dependence upon a one-crop economy (cotton). Ninth, lack of marketing systems for commodities other than cotton. Tenth, widespread lack of leadership and managerial talents to further agricultural cooperative progress.

As a means of alleviating some of these difficulties, farmers in all four states turned to their state Farm Bureaus for assistance recognizing that in numbers there must be strength. As we look back now, we see that the Mississippi Farm Bureau mustered better its political and economic resources than did Farm Bureaus in the other states and molded them into a cooperative effort of considerable magnitude, enlightment, and preseverance. The *economic* and *cooperative* aspect of Mississippi Farm Bureau's attack on farm problems was largely in the person of *Charles Leonard McNeil.*

McNeil had been born in Tupelo, Miss., on September 9, 1888. After attending elementary school in Tupelo and graduating from high school in Nettleton, Miss., he first taught school in Lee County and then attended Mississippi A. & M. College (now, Mississippi State University) for two years.

After leaving Mississippi A. & M., for the next five years he was high school superintendent in Monroe and Lee Counties. From 1915 to 1917 he re-entered Mississippi A. & M. and was, first, instructor and, later, assistant professor of mathematics. During the time he was on the faculty of A. & M. College, he completed all college work and was awarded a B.S. Degree in Agriculture in 1917. He also attended the University of Tennessee for two summer terms, taking postgraduate work.

Named "County Agent of the Century"

From 1917 to 1919, he worked with the Mississippi Agricultural Extension Service as County Agent in Tate County and spent 1920 as district agent in 4-H Club work at the A. & M. College. During the year 1921 he entered private business in Senatobia, Miss., but after a brief spell he rejoined the Extension Service as County Agent in Madison County which position he held from 1921 to the latter part of 1929 when he became general manager of Mississippi Farm Bureau Federation. In 1964, some 35 years after leaving Madison County, McNeil was still so well remembered and revered that he was named *County Agent of the Century* by the people of that county.

The Charlie McNeil who had become general manager of a statewide farmers' organization at age 41 was idealistic, visionary but extremely practical, and cautious. He was acutely concerned with the economic problems of Mississippi farmers and their lack of political and economic organization. His point-of-view was broad for his day—having taught school, worked with rural youth, operated a business, and worked with farmers. McNeil was ready in 1929-1930 to launch the second period of his career entirely in the field of farmer organization, particularly in farm supplies and commodity marketing.

Cooperative purchasing of farm supplies in Mississippi had started about 1920, when several county agricultural agents (including McNeil) began purchasing fertilizer cooperatively for groups of farmers in their respective counties. In 1923, these purchasing activities were taken over by the Mississippi Farm Bureau Federation, which set up a statewide cooperative wholesale purchasing service to serve its local county units. Beginning in early 1930 the different purchasing units, both county and state, were incorporated as cooperative associations under the Mississippi Agricultural Association Law as amended in 1930.

Becomes Manager of New State Association

The new state association was called the Mississippi Farm Bureau Federation (A.A.L.) with Charlie McNeil as general manager. Fellow county agents and agricultural workers in Mississippi insisted upon McNeil being called to manage the new co-op organization. The scope of service of the new associations, which originally included only the purchase of fertilizer, was enlarged to include the purchase of seed, feed, and miscellaneous farm supplies, and the marketing of farm products, especially cotton. It should be noted here that at the time McNeil assumed managership of Mississippi Farm Bureau it was, for all practical purposes, bankrupt. He borrowed $5,000 from a close relative and in turn lent these funds to the association. Therefore, his managerial tenure actually began under very trying conditions.

In January, 1935, the charters of the Mississippi Farm Bureau Federation (A.A.L.) and its member county cooperatives were amended so as to separate these organizations from the state and county farm bureau units. The name of the state purchasing association then became Mississippi Federated Cooperatives (A.A.L.), and each county unit used the name of its county with the addition "Cooperative (A.A.L.)." McNeil remained as general manager of M.F.C., while the Mississippi Farm Bureau Federation continued along more farm policy and legislative lines.

At the time of M.F.C.'s formation in 1935, McNeil had a nucelus of 36 affiliated county co-ops. M.F.C. had $15,380 of common stock, no preferred stock and $27,785 in surplus and reserves for a total equity capitalization of $43,165. Furthermore, M.F.C.'s base of operations lay primarily in East Central and Northeast Mississippi, which constituted the poorer areas of Mississippi. The M.F.C. staff consisted of McNeil, six office employees and one traveling auditor. With the fiscal year ending June 30, 1936, M.F.C. had wholesale farm supply sales of $570,000, of which fertilizer accounted for $284,000; seed, $221,000; feed, $29,000; and other supplies, $34,000. It also was marketing limited quantities of potatoes and cane syrup.

From this austere beginning, McNeil set out to build M.F.C. in an aggressive but methodical manner characteristic of his personality.

His leadership was not of the emotional type but rather of one who contemplates building an organization block-by-block, not erecting more roadblocks than are already present. He was always looking to future accomplishments, not past glories.

Sees Need for Co-op to Move into Manufacturing

McNeil realized early that wholesaling farm supplies was not going to be enough. The co-op would have to move further into economic integration, that is, it would have to enter those markets with margins fat enough that M.F.C. could melt-down for the farmers' benefit. This kind of philosophy stimulated McNeil and others in Mississippi to consider entry into fertilizer manufacturing. Mixed fertilizer plants at Canton and Laurel were begun variously as early as 1939 which served not only farmers' fertilizer needs but also became a competitive yard-stick for the fertilizer industry in the Gulf South. In 1948, McNeil was also instrumental in putting the strength of M.F.C. into Mississippi Chemical Corporation at Yazoo City, Miss., which proved an extremely wise move into the field of nitrogen fertilizer manufacturing for all concerned. McNeil was sincere in his beliefs that cooperatives should cooperate in order to get more basic in supplies. For example, by 1953, M.F.C. had invested over $304,000 in other co-ops.

In seeds, M.F.C. followed a procurement program relying as much as possible on local seed growers and out-of-state cooperatives. Further, a central seed processing plant at Canton was established in 1950 to more adequately serve the seed needs of farmers. McNeil also believed that farmers' total supply needs should be procured coopera-tively and he steadily and steadfastly expanded M.F.C.'s activities into bags, heavy hardware, inoculants, insecticides, petroleum products, tires, batteries and accessories, farm equipment, hardware, fencing, and steel products, among others.

In late 1952, McNeil and the M.F.C. board realized that Mississippi's agricultural economy had become quite diversified with increasing emphasis on a livestock and poultry economy. Since M.F.C. was lack-ing in experience with feed compounding, it first turned to M.F.A. Milling Co-op in Springfield, Mo., for a feed distributorship. Almost overnight gross margins on feed in Mississippi fell from between $.05 to $1.00 per hundred-weight. This entrance into feed distribution was a most significant step because, later, it would become the heart of a forward-looking integrated poultry and egg program, discussed somewhat later.

At the same time that the feed distribution program was instituted

(1952) M.F.C. made another alliance, this one with M.F.A. Oil Company to distribute petroleum products mostly in North Mississippi.

It would be erroneous to believe that McNeil and M.F.C. were interested only in farm supplies. Marketing had always been of concern to McNeil. For example, in 1939, M.F.C. had begun a cotton marketing and loan service to its members which continued until about 1964 when cotton marketing efforts were coordinated and combined with Staple Cotton Co-op in a more formal relationship. These earlier cotton marketing efforts were the first in a series of later efforts to improve the marketing of seeds, grains, livestock, pecans, vegetables, and broilers and eggs.

McNeil Demonstrates Soundness of Total Integration

M.F.C.'s broiler and egg ventures deserve special note. These efforts started about 1955, near the end of McNeil's active management of M.F.C. It is apparent that McNeil was tormented about this decision to enter the poultry and egg field. He knew full well the risks and tribulations connected with poultry and egg marketing. Personally, McNeil might have preferred to steer M.F.C. into other ventures, particularly the agricultural chemical business for which he had taken a special liking (after Mississippi Chemical's fantastic success).

However, he did not back off from the poultry and egg venture. The issues of *contract farming* and *vertical integration* were at their peak about 1955 and there was much talk about how small farmers were going to be swallowed up by large companies. This issue intrigued him as it did his two principal assistants, E. G. Spivey and Earl Beall. McNeil and the M.F.C. organization committed themselves to an integrated poultry and egg program by having risks, profits, and losses rest upon the growers' shoulders as part of a cooperatively integrated program and to make this program successful plans were laid to integrate feed milling, chick hatching, supplies processing, and marketing into one totally integrated whole. M.F.C. demonstrated, once again, the soundness of a totally integrated program and justified McNeil's original co-op philosophy to do whatever job needed to improve the growers' economic status, be it fertilizer, cotton or poultry.

McNeil retired as general manager March 1, 1958, but continued as management consultant to M.F.C. up to the time of his death. As he left M.F.C., McNeil could recount a growth in M.F.C.'s county affiliates from 36 to 55; net worth from $43,165 in 1936 to $7 million in

1958, and a growth in dollar volume of business from $570,000 in 1936 to $26 million in 1958. He left behind a team of personnel highly skilled and devoted to his cooperative philosophy serving over 75,000 farmers. McNeil was a good judge of men and, much to his credit, his appointees and associates worked hard for him and put out their best efforts always. This team spirit continues in the present-day M.F.C. organization.

McNeil's tenure as M.F.C. manager spanned almost 30 years. He had given all his efforts and energy to one sole objective—to improve the economic lot and bargaining strength of farmers. He was a kind and generous person with high Christian principles which were never compromised.

Active in Many Co-op, Agricultural Organizations

But, McNeil was more than a co-op manager. For a number of years he served as a member of the board of directors of Mississippi Farm Bureau Federation and for several years was vice-president of that organization. He devoted many years of his life in helping develop and promote state and national legislation beneficial to agriculture which included a successful attempt at the American Farm Bureau Federation Convention in Baltimore in 1938 to gain backing for cotton price supports of 85 percent of parity. Also, he aggressively sponsored and promoted all agencies having to do with improvement of agricultural conditions in Mississippi and the Gulf South. For this accomplishment, the *Progressive Farmer* magazine named him as Mississippi's *Man of the Year* in 1955.

During all this period, since 10 years of age, McNeil actively farmed. He operated a farm in Pontotoc County, Miss., which his grandfather bought from the government soon after the Indians were moved to Indian Territory.

McNeil served as president of the Mississippi Seedsmen's Association and the Mississippi Council of Farmer Cooperatives; was a member of the board of directors and the executive committee of the National Council of Farmer Cooperatives; producer delegate to the National Cotton Council; member of the board of directors of Associated Cooperatives, Inc.; member of the board and executive committee and first vice-president of Mississippi Chemical Corporation and of the Coastal Chemical Corporation; and, honorary member of the board of directors of the Mississippi Farm Bureau Federation. His membership in fraternal and civic organizations included that of a Shriner, Mason, Knight Templar, and member of the Rotary Club,

Chamber of Commerce, and First Presbyterian Church of Jackson, Miss. He died on November 30, 1964 survived by his wife and one daughter.

The organization which McNeil so devotedly endowed, Mississippi Federated Cooperatives, continues to flourish. It is now active in both Mississippi and Louisiana serving 70 affiliated co-ops, endeavoring to strengthen all past programs and initiating new ones. M.F.C. now works even closer with other farmer cooperatives, has capable technical and managerial talent and is aggressively pursuing a supply and marketing program for all farmers in its trade area. Its most recent activities indicate a wholesale farm supply business of $30 million and a marketing volume of $45 million, with a net worth of $12 million.

The poverty-stricken South which had so stirred McNeil in the 1920's is no more. In the wake of this poverty, one can find productive fields and prosperous farm families. The countryside has been balanced with resource conservation, cooperation, and contentment. McNeil had constructed the main roadbed of agricultural cooperation in the Gulf South. Because of him, his able successors and followers had an easier road on which to travel toward an improved cooperative destination.

Manly G. Mann

by Joseph G. Knapp

AS a boy, Manly Mann's dream was to be a conductor on the Atlantic and North Carolina Railroad which runs from Goldsboro to Morehead City, and he never lost his love of trains. As a man he had an elaborate system of miniature railroad yards in the attic of his home and it gave him great pleasure to escape from the cares of the day to spend a little time as a railroad man. Lucky were the children who were invited up to see Mr. Mann's trains, for his joy in watching them run equalled theirs. Many a time I have been riding with him when he would stop his automobile so that he could see a train go by.

His love of trains, which never left him, was indicative of the bull-dog attachment that he gave to all things that he loved, and as his vision widened, the desire to improve the lot of rural people in his native state became his driving ambition. But, to go back to rail-roading for a moment, he did not realize his dream of becoming a conductor on the Atlantic and North Carolina but he did become its President. By the time this goal was realized the position was largely honorary—but he did preside over four board meetings a year. One thing that he achieved as President of the railroad was to persuade the Southern Railway to lease this small line. It took the Southern $3 million to bring the road bed up to Southern's standards but it proved to be a profitable operation. Two years after Mr. Mann's death in 1958, the A & N C paid a dividend on its stock—the first paid since the Civil War, and it has continued to pay generous cash and extra dividends since that time.

Manly Glenwood Mann was born on June 6, 1889 in Newport, a village near the coast in Eastern North Carolina. His father was a general merchant who found it hard to get ahead with economically depressed farmers as customers. While Manly never lived on a farm, he lived close to farm conditions. He early found that his future depended on his own efforts.

Young Manly was able to complete seven grades in school, but there was no high school in the county at that time. He started his business career by clerking in his father's store but he soon gave that up to sell shoes on a house-to-house basis in his county. After a year or so he found that he could make more money working in a local logging camp and soon he was a foreman.

Like many of his generation, Manly's ambitions were nourished by the "rags to riches" stories of Horatio Alger, and the "rugged individualism" "preachments" of Elbert Hubbard, who never ceased to be his favorite author.

With savings from selling shoes and logging, Manly was able to go to Raleigh for further education at King's Business College. Upon graduation in 1906 he was able to get a job in the freight auditor's office of the Atlantic Coast Line at Wilmington, N. C.

While working for the railroad Mann met and married Cora Eagles of Tarboro, in 1912, and this gave him contacts and interests in that city that led to an offer as assistant cashier in the First National Bank of Tarboro in 1914. Although the salary was less than he was getting as a freight auditor he saw wider horizons in banking and accepted the offer. Mann was now 25 and at last in a position where he could find an outlet for his capabilities.

His Analytical Ability Helps Bank

He was not long in the bank when he realized that it was not progressing as it should. He began a systematic study of the bank's transactions after work at night and his explorations revealed that the bank was losing money on many of its checking accounts. He conceived the idea of levying a bank service charge on checking accounts which failed to maintain minimum balances or drew more than a certain number of checks per month, and he persuaded the bank's directors to adopt this as a policy. Many neighboring bankers were aghast and the action even attracted the adverse criticism of the president of the American Bankers Association.

The First National Bank of Tarboro operated in a cash crop economy of cotton and peanuts that was rapidly eroding the soil. Mann saw that a more diversified agriculture was essential to the success of the bank. He began to advocate cover crops but farmers were loath to accept change. But this did not daunt Mann. He purchased seed on the recommendation of the Extension Service and stored it in the bank under prescribed conditions. Then when a prospective borrower sought a loan it was not granted until he procured seed for a cover crop. This brought results and within a few years no county had more acreage in cover crops.

Mann was also aware that a balanced agriculture required livestock and there was then little livestock production in Eastern North Carolina. He began to make trips to the Midwest to arrange for shipments of sheep and cattle to the bank, which resold them to the farmers of the area, with loans where necessary. When shipments arrived they would be met by Mann, as Vice President of the bank, and, with the help of a herdsman, he would lead them down Main Street to the Bank where individual sales were made near its premises.

These innovations in farming, brought about by the aggressive young banker, soon paid off in better farm income in the area with resulting improvement in the balance sheets of the bank. Although neighboring bankers referred to him as "mad and radical" his achievements soon attracted statewide attention. In 1923, he was invited to address the Farm and Home Week Convention at North Carolina State College on the subject, "The Banker's Place in the Agricultural Program." In his talk he stressed the need for more and better livestock and the expansion of extension and vocational educational work.

During his years at Tarboro, Mann realized his weakness as a speaker. He met this problem by buying a set of books on public speaking and by training himself. He got practice and self-confidence by "preaching" at Negro churches near Tarboro.

Sees Opportunity in Co-op; Leaves Banking

In 1926 Mann was forced to make a decision. As a result of his success at Tarboro he was offered a more lucrative position as Vice-President in the much stronger Commercial National Bank of Raleigh. He had agreed to take the new post when U. B. Blalock, the general manager of the North Carolina Cotton Growers Association, offered him a position as Director of Field Service. Although the beginning salary was even less than he was earning at Tarboro, Mann saw an opportunity to widen his influence and do something that he was uniquely qualified to do.

In 1926, the wave of enthusiasm for large scale farmer cooperatives formed in the early 20's in North Carolina and other states under the magnetic influence of Aaron Sapiro had subsided and it was becoming realized that such organizations could succeed only with membership education and public understanding. In Manly G. Mann the cotton association found the man who could give leadership to this task, a person with a warm and engaging personality who believed that education was essential for progress, and one who saw in the cooperative form of organization a practical method of bringing "better business" to the farm. His services as Director of Field Service led to his appointment in 1929 as Assistant General Manager and in 1934 he became its General Manager.

However, Mann's first assignment was to improve the relationship of the association with the bankers of the state. At that time many would not even honor a draft on the association. With his banker's experience and acquaintance with bankers as a former officer in the North Carolina Bankers Association, Mann was soon able to improve the association's image to the extent that drafts were honored and necessary lines of credit established.

With the banking problem overcome, Mann could direct his talents toward the building of a stronger association as Director of Field Service. He knew that the success of the association depended upon the support of its members and that the association had to have trained men in the field who could represent it in business relationships. He realized above all that the future of cooperatives depended upon the education of the youths who would later become their members.

In 1927, Mann's life was saddened by the death of his wife, which left him with the responsibilities of raising his 11-year-old son. In January, 1930, he married Norma Sanders of Tarboro who helped him again make a home.

Inaugurates Unique Youth Essay Contest

In his second year with the cotton association he inaugurated an essay contest in the high schools of the state to get boys and girls to give more attention to the agricultural problems of their communities. This program was continued as long as Mann was active in the association, and he gave it his boundless enthusiasm and drive. Each year up to the time of World War II he would address the entire student body of over 100 rural high schools, and the number of essays written one year reached 16,000. This contest was not a perfunctory matter, for it was organized on a local, district, and state basis, and the contestants were judged not only on the quality of their essays but on their oral presentation at local, district and state contests. It was an honor to be a winner and, moreover, educational scholarships and cash prizes were given to the winners. Nothing gave Mann more joy than these essay contests for they stimulated many boys and girls to strive for excellence and helped a number get college educations. He felt that these contests were reaching the farmers of tomorrow. During Mann's lifetime some 150,000 students participated in these contests—which were unique among cooperatives in the United States.

Mann's interest in helping farmers obtain supplies for production purposes was afforded greater scope in his new position. Under his guidance the association introduced a commodity cotton improvement program with seeds best adapted for the area. This led in 1928 to the formation of a subsidiary company—the Cotton Growers Supply Cooperative—which furnished seeds and fertilizers for members. This organization served as a forerunner of the F.C.X. and was dissolved in 1934.

My close friendship with Mr. Mann began soon after I joined the staff of North Carolina State College of Agriculture as Associate Professor of Marketing and Agricultural Cooperation in 1929 and for the five years that I was with the college we were in close rapport on agricultural problems in the state. This was the time of the great depression and the "Live at Home" campaign of Governor O. Max Gardner, and the plight of the farmer called for innovations in agricultural organization.

Many of us thought that only through cooperation by farmers themselves could prosperity be brought to North Carolina agriculture. For years it had been impossible to get farmers to pull together as a group. The high expectations which had been dashed to the ground by the failure in the mid-twenties of the grandiosely conceived Tri-State Tobacco Cooperative had left as a legacy a sense of frustration and disillusionment that impaired confidence in any new cooperative ventures. But with the acute problems brought by the depression, interest in cooperative remedies had begun to rise again.

F.C.X. Formed with Mann as Manager

It was at this time that the foundations were laid for a great common cooperative effort in cooperative purchasing that resulted in the formation of the Farmers Cooperative Exchange—the F.C.X.—in 1934, with Mann as Manager. I have told how the F.C.X. came into being in *Farmers in Business*, and there is no need to retell it. However, here it is important to say that it is doubtful if anyone else could have nursed this embryonic organization into the great cooperative institution that it became under his managership. Mann was the one person who could fuse discordant elements into a common front and give them the blend of leadership and confidence that the times demanded. He had the gift of enthusiasm and faith, and he imparted it to his associates. He also knew that people make cooperatives and he had the fervor and industry of a great evangelist as he went up and down the roads to the farmers and rural communities of North Carolina preaching the gospel that farmers must work together if they were to achieve prosperity for themselves and their families.

But Mann also had the attributes of a master politician. He understood the fallibility of human nature and the importance of attracting the good will and support of the newspapers, the bankers, and the industrial and religious leaders if the F.C.X. were to succeed in its mission.

By a master stroke he enlisted the undivided support of the agricultural agencies of the state even before the F.C.X. was officially born. He was at that time being pushed to accept the managership of the new organization being formed. He realized that he could not be successful in this position without assurance of complete support from those in charge of all agricultural agencies in the state. He achieved his end by arranging a luncheon at the Sir Walter Hotel, with the following present: Dr. Frank P. Graham, President of the Greater University of North Carolina; I. O. Schaub, State Director of the Extension Service; T. E. Brown, State Director of Vocational Education; U. B. Blalock, General Manager of the North Carolina Cotton Growers Cooperative Association; R. B. Etheridge, Chief of the State Division of Markets; and E. S. Vanatta, Master of the State Grange.

After a pleasant luncheon in which all present expressed their cordial goodwill toward the organization about to be formed, Mann in effect said, "I know that all of you are behind this great effort and that you will be willing to sign the little document that I have here." He then took from his pocket a brief typewritten statement that had been prepared with the assistance of his close friend, L. C. Salter of the Division of Markets. It was headed "A Covenant," and it contained these words, "In order that there may be no misunderstanding and that all may know our position in regard to the cooperative movement, we the undersigned . . pledge our full support and cooperation and that of our respective organizations in the development and in the program of the North Carolina Farmers Association." At this time the name, Farmers Cooperative Exchange, had not yet been selected for the proposed organization.

Mann then handed this document to one of those present who

read it and passed it to another. Then Dr. Graham said, "Let me have it." He then took out his pen and signed it and handed it to Dean Schaub who then signed, and the others followed.

This was a significant act, for it gave Mann the assurance of support upon which a great organization could be built.

Mann realized that nothing is more important in selling an idea or a product than confidence in its merits and he strove to build confidence in the success of the organization even before it was born.

Soon after Mann assumed the management of the F.C.X. he was made General Manager of the cotton association, and he served as General Manager of both organizations until his death in 1958.

Daring Experiment on Cotton Marketing Worked

As General Manager of the cotton association, Mann introduced the repurchase pool method of marketing cotton, an innovation in cotton cooperative marketing. This was a daring experiment which depended upon the ability of the association to market the grower's cotton more efficiently than competitors, but it worked and it has continued in operation to this day, although it is less used under the government loan program.

Although Mann never lost his interest in the welfare of the cotton cooperative, his energies were unceasingly absorbed by the problems of the F.C.X. which flourished under his guidance. In time the F.C.X. widened its services in farm production supplies and expanded to undertake the marketing of other farm products—except cotton. It also overflowed into South Carolina with the result that it now serves farmers in both of the Carolinas. When Mann died in 1958 it was doing a volume of business of over $50 million and serving almost 200,000 farmers.

One of Mann's great strengths was his belief that the cooperative form of business was essential to farm prosperity. He effectively carried the gospel to the farmers and business leaders of the Carolinas, and to the educational and governmental organizations with whom he worked closely. His interest in education came from his own efforts to self-educate himself. If he had lived only a few more months he would have had the great satisfaction of receiving an honorary L.H.D. degree voted by the Trustees of North Carolina State College.

His agricultural and cooperative leadership brought him wide recognition. In 1951, the North Carolina State Grange conferred on him its Distinguished Service Award, and in 1956 the *Progressive Farmer* named him North Carolina "Man of the Year in Agriculture" with this statement, "Marketing efficiency is agriculture's Number 1 need. Few men have brought greater benefit to farmers through pioneering in this field than M. G. Mann."

In a tribute to the memory of M. G. Mann shortly after his death, Dr. Frank P. Graham, former President of the Greater University of North Carolina, said, "It was an honor and a joy to work under the leadership of M. G. Mann for the mutual cooperation of the farm families as a basic point of that brotherhood called North Carolina." Mann would have liked this sentence coming from Dr. Frank Graham —and especially the reference to joy—for all his life he did his best to bring joy to others.

One of those who worked with Mann in the early days of the F.C.X., Roy H. Park, Editor of the *Cooperative Digest*, treasures a portrait of M. G. Mann on the wall of his office. The quality in Mann that most impressed him was his great "empathy—his capacity to feel the sorrows and joys of others. Many lives have been enriched, including my own, by the thoughtfulness of M. G. Mann."

Bert W. Kenyon, now with the Farmer Cooperative Service, also was privileged to work intimately for many years with M. G. Mann. To him the three qualities that consistently stood out in Mann's character were compassion, empathy, and loyalty.

These are qualities essential to the leadership of great enterprises and they have been building blocks in the progress of cooperation in the Carolinas.

Hutzel Metzger

by Lloyd L. Ullyot

HUTZEL METZGER was born December 12, 1894, on a farm at
Athens, Tenn. Upon graduation from high school at Grandview,
Tenn., he taught for three years in a public school before attending
college. At the end of his sophomore year at Michigan State Agricultural College, he enlisted in the armed services. The last two years
were spent in the Army Air Corps as a pilot during World War I
where he held the rank of First Lieutenant. During the years from
1919 to 1923 he attended North Dakota Agricultural College, receiving
a B.S. degree in 1920 and an M.S. degree in 1923. During part of
the three years at North Dakota, he held the position of Assistant
Agricultural Economist and then Associate Agricultural Economist and
Farm Management Demonstrator.

After obtaining the M.S. degree, he went to the University of
Minnesota as a Research Assistant, and enrolled in further graduate
studies. He received a Ph.D. degree in Agricultural Economics from
the University of Minnesota in 1925. He then joined the staff of the
Division of Cooperative Marketing of the United States Department
of Agriculture as an Agricultural Economist in the field of cooperatives handling dairy products, where he made significant studies. In
1929, this Division was transferred to the Federal Farm Board
created under the Agricultural Marketing Act of 1929. Dr. Metzger
was made Assistant Chief of the Division. One of his outstanding
publications of this period was *Cooperative Marketing of Fluid Milk,*
(U.S. Department of Agriculture Technical Bulletin 179, published in
1930).

In 1932, he became Regional Representative of the Federal Farm
Board for the Western States, and held this position until he became
first president of the St. Paul Bank for Cooperatives.

Guided St. Paul Bank for Cooperatives for 18 Years

"Doc," as he was affectionately called, was eminently qualified by background, education, and experience to be the first president of the St. Paul Bank for Cooperatives and to guide that organization's operation from its beginning in October, 1933, until his untimely death in December, 1951.

The task that confronted Doc in locating suitable office space and equipment, in procuring and training personnel, in setting up operating procedures and policies, and in acquainting the boards of directors and managers of farmer cooperatives and the general public with the services and objectives of the Bank was a tremendous one. How well he accomplished the job is evidenced by the fact that, during the 18-year period, loans in excess of $425 million were made to 1,085 farmer cooperatives in the states of North Dakota, Minnesota, Wisconsin, and Michigan, and the net loss on this loan volume was only $40,000.

It is not for the excellent record of loan volume and the loss record that Doc should best be remembered, but rather for his brilliant mind, sound judgment, sense of justice, and sincere desire to find solutions to the problems of people.

A borrower or a prospective borrower of the Bank, an employee, or anybody, could always go to Doc and get a sympathetic hearing and sound counsel and advice. He sincerely believed that the Bank's most important function was that of counseling with boards of directors and managers of farmer cooperatives. Doc set high standards of performance in everything he did, and was a tireless worker. He expected and demanded the same from those with whom he was associated. However, he was a keen judge of people, and recognized their strengths and weaknesses. Perhaps his greatest contribution was the development of people to carry out the objectives of the Bank he so ably guided for 18 years.

Encouraged Employees to Improve Knowledge About Co-ops

Even though Doc had a Ph.D. degree in Agricultural Economics, he kept up-to-date by taking night school courses at the University of Minnesota. He encouraged all of the employees to do so, too, and particularly to take those courses that would not only help them directly as employees of the Bank, but those which would broaden their interests. On a number of occasions he said:

> "Cooperatives should encourage and assist their younger men in improving themselves in order to develop employees who take a

real interest in the success of their organization. Cooperatives should take advantage of the opportunities presented through cooperative management courses and schools sponsored by our state colleges, the cooperative wholesales, or other cooperatives. Payment of a part or all of the expenses of a promising second man or other employee, while in attendance at short courses, may be money wisely invested."

Doc wrote a number of articles and speeches on agricultural and cooperative topics. The following excerpts give their flavor:

"I think the co-ops are doing their job well—some think, too well. To me, there is little justification for setting up a cooperative if someone else is doing the job just as well as the co-op can do it. The development of our cooperative system to where it is today is evidence that the co-ops are doing a better and more economical job. Serving an economic need, rendering a service both to their members and the public, giving their members and patrons a greater share by influencing prices and by returning savings, and preserving democratic free enterprise—all these amply justify a place under the sun for cooperatives."

"Probably no factor which our institution must consider in the financing of farmers' cooperatives is of greater importance than that of management. I am thinking of management in its broader sense—the responsibility which lies directly on the board of directors and the manager. On these men falls the responsibility for failure or success of our cooperative business enterprises."

His counsel and advice were valued highly by those in Farm Credit and in agricultural circles, and he made a major contribution to the development and success of farmer cooperatives as established business enterprises in our economy.

John D. Miller

by Bruce V. Snow

EFFECTIVE LEADERSHIP TAKES MANY FORMS. For some it is the center of the stage, the eloquent speech, and the magnetic personality. For others, equally effective, it is conference tables, the hours spent in patient research and thought and the continuous, year to year, effort to consolidate progress and move on to the next plateau.

Ranking high in the latter category was John D. Miller, long-time General Counsel and First Vice President of the Dairymen's League Cooperative Association, New York City. At his death in November, 1946, at the age of 90, Judge Miller had been an active leader in the dairy industry for almost half a century.

Three great farmer organizations stand as a monument to John D. Miller's leadership and ability. Foremost in building the Dairymen's League, he vitalized it with his dynamic energy and then went on to greater achievement. He was a Director of the League from 1916 to 1935, First Vice President from 1918 to 1939, and was General Counsel from 1917 to his death.

He became president of the National Cooperative Milk Producers Federation in 1922 when that organization was young and weak. Under his vital leadership, the Federation became a recognized and powerful spokesman for the organized dairy farmers of the nation.

Later, in 1933, he was called to the still bigger task of heading the National Cooperative Council (now the National Council of Farmer Cooperatives) when that organization was still little known. During the nine years of his presidency, the Council achieved nationwide status as the leading spokesman for and champion of farmer cooperatives.

Recognized Hardships of Dairy Farmers; Helps Organize Co-op

Judge Miller's interest in cooperative marketing for farmers began almost with his admittance to the Pennsylvania Bar as a country lawyer back in 1892. Then, he was the owner of a dairy farm near the little village of Thompson, Pa. He recognized at once the economic handicaps against which dairy farmers were struggling. He watched their struggle go on locally until in 1900 he took a hand in helping to organize a small cooperative in his community. He soon discovered that not only did farmers need cooperative marketing, but before they could have it, there was need of new laws to make such cooperative marketing workable and legal.

His increasing interest in cooperative law and in cooperatives led him to membership in the Dairymen's League. When he came home one night and announced to his son, Allan, that he had been asked if he would serve as a director of the Dairymen's League, Allan replied, "Well, Dad, you have been wanting to take it a little easier, this is something you can do to occupy your mind." His son's words could be classified as the "understatement of the year" because Judge Miller was "occupied" at full tilt for the next 30 years. The farmer cooperative era was just beginning and fate had selected him to lead farmers in their greatest economic advance.

In addition to his great work as a builder and leader of cooperative organizations, Judge Miller was the recipient of many other important honors because of his achievements in the field of cooperative marketing. In 1928 he was appointed by President Calvin Coolidge as one of the delegates from the United States to attend the World's Dairy Congress in England. He was a director of the Central Bank for Cooperatives and a trustee of the American Institute of Cooperation. In few men existed such a combination of lawyer, farmer, business executive ,organizer, leader and author of legislation.

Greatest Service in Field of Co-op Legislation

But it is in the field of cooperative legislation, local, state and national, that Judge Miller rendered perhaps his greatest service to American cooperatives and American farmers. When cooperatives began to engage in interstate business along about 1919, Judge Miller forsaw the necessities of obtaining clarifying amendments to the federal anti-trust laws. He was instructed by the directors of the Dairymen's League to prepare such a bill and present it to the National Cooperative Milk Producers Federation. This was done and Judge Miller was made chairman of the Federation's committee to present it to Congress.

Was Real Author of Capper-Volstead Act

The legislative fight that followed became historic. Entrenched interests saw in it the rise of powerful farmer cooperatives and the end of dealer domination of markets. The Milk Producers Federation and Judge Miller became a target for an intensive campaign of villification which more than ever put cooperatives and their leaders not only in the spotlight but "on the spot." The legislation became law in the form of the Capper-Volstead Act, now known far and wide across the land as the "Bill of Rights" for farmer cooperatives. Judge Miller as a representative of the organized dairy farmers of the nation, was the real author and sponsor of this great law.

"He, more than anyone else, is entitled to the credit for the drafting of the Capper-Volstead cooperative marketing law," wrote Senator Capper in 1940. Judge Miller's conspicuous work in connection with this epoch-making legislation not only brought him national prestige in the field of cooperative legislation, but also carried him to a new pinnacle of cooperative leadership and fame.

In the words of the late Albert S. Goss, Master of the National Grange:

> No man in America did more to establish farmer cooperatives on a sound basis than John D. Miller. The rights presently assured to farmers and their organizations under the Capper-Volstead Act will always stand as a monument to this man who envisioned what few could see and made a sound foundation when others ridiculed.

Raymond W. Miller

by A. Ladru Jensen

R AYMOND W. MILLER'S STRONG BELIEF in agricultural cooperation is the natural result of a birthright inherited from his
late father, David Wiley Miller, a pioneer fruit and nut grower in the
San Joaquin Valley of California.

The elder Miller had been raised on a farm in New England, but
grew discouraged as a young man with rolling rocks and harvesting
stones each spring, they being the only "regular crop." Leaving
Massachusetts, he traveled to California by way of the Isthmus of
Panama and then up the Pacific Coast by sailing vessel. He herded
sheep, drove teams, and ultimately saved enough money to acquire a
piece of land in Linden, which was to become one of the first farm
areas in central California devoted to orchards. Ray Miller's mother
also came from a farm background, having been born in Iowa, and
raised in rural Nebraska. He, therefore, as a boy came to love and
respect the land.

Ray was born in San Jose on January 21, 1895, but his family moved
to Linden when he was about 10 years old. As there was no high
school in Linden, young Ray went a hundred miles away to San Jose
to the Methodist academy of the University of the Pacific, and later
graduated from the San Jose Normal School, now known as San
Jose State College. As a young man of 21 Ray demonstrated his
innate, personable, intellectual and executive qualities by becoming
principal of the elementary school at Colfax, Calif. He enlisted in
the Veterinary Corps during World War I, and reached the rank of
sergeant.

Years earlier, as an eight-year old lad, he had met a little girl,
Florence Burk, who was riding on the back of an immense tortoise
which her uncle, Rollo Beck, the eminent naturalist and ornothologist,
had brought back with him from the Galapagos Islands off the coast
of Peru. They met again, much later, at San Jose Normal, where they

were co-editors of the college yearbook and members of the same graduating class. After Ray was discharged from military service, they were married and settled down to farming a piece of property Miller had purchased adjoining the family home farm in Linden and since then their life together has been a love story that cannot be told here. During the years Ray has consistently farmed this land, developing it into a walnut grove. His brother, David W. Miller, now handles its operation with his own groves, and the farm is still home to Ray and Florence.

Walnuts were a new crop in Linden when the young Millers took up farming after World War I. Ray was one of the organizers of the first walnut growers association of the San Joaquin Valley—the old San Joaquin Valley Walnut Growers Association. It is interesting to note that the former California Walnut Growers Association, now Diamond Walnut Growers, presently has state headquarters only 15 miles from the Miller farm, in the city of Stockton, Calif. Ray became a director of the local association and later Vice President of the central association. Walnuts from his groves have been delivered to the Diamond Walnut Growers for a period of almost half a century.

As a result of his work with the association and because of the experience he gained there, Miller was requested to help organize other farm groups. He became President of the San Joaquin County Farm Bureau Federation and during his administration it gained the honor of being the largest county Farm Bureau in the United States.

Becomes World-Known "Trouble-Shooter"

In 1935, the Agricultural Council of California was asked to advise and counsel some of the larger food distributors—chain stores then just beginning to gain in size—as to how they might best serve agriculture and the consuming public at the same time. Ray was invited to assume the job of finding what might be done. He developed an organization, Agricultural Trade Relations, Inc., now World Trade Relations, Inc. Miller has always held the attitude that a job should be studied, problems changed into projects, and the client started on the road to following through himself. From this beginning Ray has become a world-wide trouble shooter for companies, governments, churches, educational institutions and other groups, and the philosophy gained from dealing with his fellow walnut growers in the cooperatives in Linden has stayed with him all these years. It is, primarily: get the facts, explore and explain them, endeavor to hold people to the truth, let the chips fall—and the results will be good.

In the early 40's, the cooperatives of the United States were under vicious attack by various groups which held that farmer cooperatives represented a subversive and tax-evading phase of American life. In response to this propaganda the National Council of Farmer Cooperatives, in 1943, asked Ray to make a basic study of the public relations problems facing agricultural cooperatives in the United States. During the following year he and his associates interviewed thousands of people in almost every nook and corner of the United States and came up with some basic recommendations.

Chief among them was that the American Institute of Cooperation, which had been forced to discontinue its sessions during the war, be revitalized, reorganized, and encouraged to expand its activities so as to better perform a public relations and educational function for farmer cooperatives. The board of directors of the National Council of Farmer Cooperatives unanimously adopted Miller's proposals and steps were then taken to provide a sizable budget to enable the Institute to perform a broader year around service under his direction. For a period of three years Ray served the A.I.C. as its President.

Provides Leadership for Making A.I.C. Valuable Co-op Educational Research Force

Under his leadership, the Institute took on added stature by greatly expanding its encouragement of research and educational work for cooperatives. One of the most important projects started by the Institute during this period was a series of seminars and clinics for executives of cooperatives and others who came together to study business, public relations, and tax and accounting problems. The idea for this program came from Dr. Ellis A. Stokdyk, President of the Berkeley Bank for Cooperatives, and was given leadership by Ray Miller; Kelsey Gardner of the Cooperative Research and Service Division of the Farm Credit Administration; and Walter Bradley, well-known auditor for cooperatives, who represented the American Society of Accountants.

In the years 1945–47 some hundred clinics of this type were held in all areas of the United States and they did much to enhance the public image of agricultural cooperation in the United States in the postwar period.

While President of the American Institute of Cooperation, Ray placed great emphasis on the importance of establishing solid legal principles for cooperative development. As a Member of the Bar he had learned that every lasting social-economic movement must have a solid legal foundation in the society in which it struggles for growth. He appointed A. Ladru Jensen, Professor of Law at the University of Utah—and a student and disciple of Frank Evans, the eminent attorney for the American Farm Bureau Federation and the Federal Farm Board, and the author with E. A. Stokdyk of *The Law of Cooperative Marketing*—as part-time Director of Legal Education of the Institute; and together Miller and Jensen induced Sidney E. Teiser, Chairman of the American Bar Association Committee on Corporations and Mercantile Law, to establish a Division of Cooperative Law within the Section in 1946.

For the next four years articles on cooperative law and taxation were presented at the annual meetings of the Corporation Section of the A.B.A., and from 1948 to 1949 were published in the Legal magazine of the Section.

Dr. Miller and Dr. Jensen wrote or planned, secured and edited most of the articles in a legal symposium in "Law and Contemporary Problems," the *Law Journal of Duke University*, Vol. 13, Summer 1948. By thorough legal briefing and personal conferences they quieted the attacks against cooperatives.

The results of these efforts to secure legal understanding and support for cooperatives can be realized by these facts. Only about 80 lawyers were known to be practicing cooperative law in 1945. By 1950 the Institute's legal mailing list of cooperative lawyers had grown to about 420.

In 1950 the Institute published *Cooperative Corporate Association Law and Accounting*, by Dr. Jensen and others. Within about three years the entire edition of 2000 copies was sold.

When Miller resigned his official position with the Institute in 1948 he was made a member of the Board of Trustees and he has held this position ever since. Ray is eloquent when he talks about the grand work being done by his successor, J. Kenneth Stern, and he takes great satisfaction in the substantial progress made by the Institute under Stern's direction.

Becomes Faculty Member of Harvard Business School

Just prior to withdrawing as head of the Institute, Ray had been selected by the Harvard Graduate School of Business Administration to conduct seminars with its graduate students, to meet with its alumni around the world, and to hold conferences with its faculty concerning the whole new world in transition from an exploitive capitalism to a service capitalism. As a member of the faculty of the Harvard Business School, a position he held for 16 years, he worked with hundreds of young men to help them understand the philosophy of cooperative service capitalism.

Within a few months after he went to Harvard, Ray was requested by Norris E. Dodd, Director General of the Food and Agriculture Organization of the United Nations, to become his international troubleshooter in the 55 countries that were then members of the FAO. The President and the Dean of Harvard encouraged Miller to do this, so for the next six years he served as consultant to FAO's Director General and adjusted his seminars at Harvard to fit in with his trips around the world. During this period, he drafted the program of the FAO in regard to cooperatives.

Miller traveled some 300,000 miles for the FAO through most of the trouble spots of its member countries, always on the alert for ways to help cooperatives. With Dr. Horace Belshaw of New Zealand he arranged for a most important conference held in Lucknow, India, in October, 1949. Delegates present represented Japan and areas from the Pacific and Indian oceans as far west as Iran. Out of this meeting crystallized Ray's idea that cooperatives were the natural answer to the threat of Communism.

Later, in 1954, Miller made a report to the Indian Planning Commission, then presided over by Mr. Nehru, on the place of cooperatives in India and this document was translated into the many languages of India. In this report Ray said, "The flame of cooperation eternally flares through the night of despair, and enough sparks from it ignite the combustible materials to prove that there is nothing wrong with the philosophy of cooperation, but only with its application."

Prolific Writer on Co-op Subjects

Ray Miller has written a number of books on various phases of international and domestic affairs, as well as many articles. Running through all of them is his very firm, strong belief that non-profit cooperatives are the greatest economic tool the free world has to defeat Communism. In 1959 his book, *Can Capitalism Compete?*, was published, and in 1964 followed his semi-autobiographical book, *A Conservative Looks at Cooperatives*. He is now working on a new book to be called *Most of the World's Problems Are Rural*.

Ray is a member of the Advisory Committee on Cooperatives of the Agency for International Development of the U. S. Department of State, and carries on a wide correspondence with cooperative leaders around the world. As a part of his continuing activity with the American Bar Association, he is a member of ABA's Standing Committee on Education About Communism in Contrast with Liberty Under the Law. The Committee recently published *The New Czars vs. The Rule of Law*, which included Ray Miller's "Communism—Capitalism—Cooperation," a reprint from *American Cooperation, 1961*. This essay emphasizes Miller's theme that cooperatives are the antithesis of Communism.

Ray's influence in support of agricultural cooperatives will live long after he is gone. It is a permeating influence that infiltrates its way into the consciousness of many people who are innoculated without knowing it. His other great contribution rests in his writings on the philosophy, the ethical merit and demonstration of the practicality of incorporated cooperatives.

A Great Friend
of Farm People

Horace A. Moses

by Kenneth Hinshaw

H ORACE AUGUSTUS MOSES should be long remembered by
farm people of the Northeast. He was a farmer's son who
excelled in a great array of business undertakings, prospered, and so
sought to serve his fellowmen that he left to this world many helpful
enterprises, some of them particularly useful to the rural people
for whom he had great love and respect.

As a lad, Horace Moses saved his earnings and set off to get a
business education at Troy Conference Academy in Poultney, Vt.
He got his first steady job at 19, the year he finished his academy
training. This was an office job in a small factory that made fine
papers. In seven years, he undertook and mastered various jobs
in the factory and became mill superintendent.

Then at the age of 30 he organized a paper company of his own,
built a mill and bought control of still another mill. He went to
Europe and studied paper-making skills. A trip to the Scottish
Highlands so impressed him that he named his new paper company
Strathmore in tribute to the beauty of the heather-covered hills of
the Strathmore barony in Scotland. And then he made it his life work
to make *Strathmore* papers excel in quality and beauty.

Exhibits Foresight, Initiative in Improving Farms, Homes

His new paper company was only two years old when farmers
found him leading their efforts to organize a program to promote
better methods and higher standards for the farms and homes of
his community. In 1912, he founded and became the first president
of a farm and homemaker association known as the Hampden County
Improvement League. Some idea of the foresight and initiative in
this program may be appreciated by the fact that here was a full-
fledged agricultural extension service program set up to serve a
county . . . and it was started and was functioning remarkably

well *two years before extension service as such was launched by an Act of Congress in 1914.*

Through a series of "bureaus" the Hampden County Improvement League, you might say, mothered first the Eastern States Exposition (1915–1916), the Eastern States Farmers' Exchange (1918), and the Eastern States League (1919). The latter was a community betterment project intended to give greater range to the type of program successfully demonstrated by the Hampden county organization.

It was jointly sponsored by agricultural and industrial leaders—a tie-in which reflected the Moses philosophy that courageous improvement of the community called for united study, planning, and effort on the part of both town and country citizens.

The Eastern States League mothered Junior Achievement, a program of boys' and girls' clubs which taught youngsters the principles of American business through youth groups organized as miniature corporations to produce and market craftwork.

If you throw into the story here a long, long list of projects ranging from a remarkable research of the historical significance of his home town of Ticonderoga, N. Y., the building and endowment of libraries, hospitals, churches, YMCA's, an international leader training school for 4-H, on through to banks, factories, and real estate developments, you have just a rough idea of the dynamic energy Horace Moses gave to activities that interested him.

Just why Horace Moses bothered with a non-profit cooperative enterprise, the Eastern States Farmers' Exchange, and what he did for it is a long story in itself. Probably at the root of his interest in this farmers' association was his opinion that the erosion of the country home in eastern communities was disastrous not only to farmers but also to industry in the cities and towns. He grew up at a time when the new land of the Western States produced drastic competition for the worn out soils of the Northeast. He foresaw that if eastern farming could not survive, abandoned farms would mean impoverished communities, an unfavorable tax burden on town properties, a dependence of workers on foodstuffs hauled a long way to market, a drying up of the flow of country youth to the factories and businesses of the cities. His idea of a model community was a busy industrial center surrounded by prosperous, well-run farms.

His attempt to help agriculture through the Hampden county program was of an educational nature. It set up the means to demonstrate and preach good farming. But he could see some things preaching wouldn't cure. For instance, the farmer was, according to industry's comparisons, a blindfolded buyer and a clumsy salesman. He bought supplies at retail (knowing none too well what it was he bought) and sold his produce wholesale—just the reverse of other kinds of businesses.

Moses' Vision Leads to Organization of Eastern States Co-op

So out of his search for something solid to help the farmer operate more successfully, there was set up within the Hampden county league a "bureau" devoted to purchasing and marketing. A young chap who had effectively built up a vegetable marketing business in Philadelphia was employed to head this project. Through his contributions to the league, Horace Moses paid most of the expenses. The new bureau's head was a leader in the Rotary Club and was sent to a convention in Copenhagen, Denmark. This was fortunate for it exposed him to the remarkable achievements of the Danes in cooperative associations.

So he brought back some ideas about how the purchasing of farm supplies and the marketing of eastern eggs and milk might follow the Danish pattern. This appealed to Moses and he instigated a mass meeting of farm leaders at the city hall in Springfield. It was here that the Eastern States Farmers' Exchange was born late in 1917. It began business and was incorporated in January, 1918.

The Hampden "bureau," now having outgrown its county origin, was transferred to a borrowed desk in the downtown office of the Eastern States Exposition—Horace Moses being godfather of the league, the exposition, and the new "exchange."

The cooperative had no money, so it was decided to solicit farmers to have them buy stock to finance it. This they did reluctantly, and when a lot of compaigning produced only $19,000 in subscriptions, Moses concluded some better and faster way should be found. He rounded up about 50 of his friends and persuaded them to sign their personal notes for sums ranging from $500 to $5000 to give to the cooperative as a basis for credit. The Chicopee bank, of which Moses was a director, accepted these notes as collateral for a loan of half their face value. It was this loan that gave the Eastern States cooperative the cash to get started.

The new cooperative found that the first service which interested eastern farmers was the purchase of carlots of grain for dairy cows. The first patronage came through county exchanges—purchasing associations—of which there were many at that time. Originally, Eastern States was conceived as a wholesale agency owned and controlled through a federation of these exchanges. The purchasing service grew so fast that it completely overshadowed a trial effort in marketing, an undertaking that was dormant for 40 years although it was provided for in the Eastern States bylaws and charter.

By 1925, the Eastern States feed business had grown to the point where it either became the major agent of a feed manufacturer or cut loose and provided its own mill service. While it had grown credit resources of its own and had long since released the credit loaned by its founding friends, it still had no such money as would be needed to buy a mill as big as was needed. There was such a mill on the market—and its price was $300,000.

Helps Eastern States Finance Feed Mill

Horace Moses persuaded one of his wealthy friends, Edward W. Hazen, to join him in financing the mill's purchase. Each put up $100,000 and Moses took a mortgage for an additional $100,000 . . . and Eastern States got its mill. Without a feed business to go with it, that mill was just a pile of steel and concrete. The money put up by the cooperative's two friends—Moses and Hazen—might pay them five percent, but the risk was very real. What Horace Moses staked his $200,000 on was his faith in cooperating farmers.

Much to the credit of the pioneer Eastern States members, the mortgage and preferred stock of the mill was all paid off and retired by 1932. Horace Moses through his able supervision, hard work, and financial risk in Eastern States, made it possible for thousands of farmers in the Northeast to create and own cooperatively what had thus become a multi-million dollar property. Often he told friends that of all his business ventures he took greatest satisfaction in seeing Eastern States thrive, grow—almost to a $100 million a year—and become so useful to so many rural people.

Horace Moses looked more like a history professor from an Ivy League college than like the combination of dynamic tycoon and part-time farmer that in fact he was. He was of medium stature, with a bit of the sags and bulges the indoorsman acquires. For years he wore a mustache and small vandyke beard—the whiskers of which could crackle and snap like charged wires, according to one of his associates who often saw this human dynamo respond to emergencies in the complex of businesses which he controlled. Although Moses led, inspired, and counselled many groups, he was no great shakes as a speaker. Certainly not a spellbinding evangelist for any of the uplifting community movements to which he was dedicated. His speeches, conversations, and letters were brief, blunt, somewhat crisp . . . and his voice had an almost crochety quality although much of what it had to say was of kindly benefit to a great many people.

Horace Moses Also a Master Farmer

It annoyed some of the more bucolic agrarians that a multi-million-aire corporation president should hold a place on the board of directors of the Eastern States Farmers' Exchange for almost 30 years. One by one, farmer directors had replaced the businessmen and industrialists that Moses had enlisted as the cooperative's note signers and who had been compensated by more or less honorary directorships. The fact was, however, that Horace Moses himself was in the master farmer class. On the farm which was his country place—Woronoake Heights—he put together one of the country's finest Ayrshire herds, and for years cattle of his breeding ranked among the breed's best in both milk production and show winnings. Also, he developed one of the best apple orchards in Massachusetts . . . an enterprise complete with grading equipment, refrigerated storages, and gift box packing facilities—years before these became common in eastern fruit farming.

In 1924, Horace Moses contributed a trophy cup—the Moses Leadership Trophy—as an award to the highest scoring leader among the country's 4-H Club members. He paid the expenses of each year's winner to the National 4-H Club Congress in Chicago. The third winner (1926) of this trophy was a lad from the state of Washington who said he wanted to be a journalist. Moses learned that before long the young magazine published for Eastern States members would be needing an editorial assistant. That was why he sent for the young fellow out there in Washington, said he just wanted to look him over . . . and two years later when the young journalist was finishing college, Moses urged the general manager of Eastern States to offer him a job. That's how Eastern States got its editor for the members' magazine, the *Eastern States Cooperator*, that once had a circulation of 140,000 farm homes . . . and for years ranked as one of the best periodicals published by a farmer cooperative.

And that's the story of Horace A. Moses—the story of how to be helpful in countless ways.

There's no better way to close this story than exactly the way it closed. On April 21, Mr. Moses was 85. His room at the Springfield Hospital was filled with baskets of flowers from his hosts of friends. When Mrs. Moses came to see him next day he had a message for her . . . please see that these flowers are taken to the children's wards so the youngsters can enjoy them. And while the flowers were being received by little tots with troubles, the great and good man died. He was sharing something good down to the very last moments of his life.

W. I. Myers

by W. Gifford Hoag

THE COOPERATIVE FARM CREDIT SYSTEM, as we know it
today, started in 1917, with the Federal Land Banks and National
Farm Loan Associations (later to become Federal Land Bank Associations). These organizations were organized to provide a nationwide
source of farm mortgage loans. Congress added to the System by
establishing the Federal Intermediate Credit Banks in 1923. These
banks were established as wholesalers of operating credit. They dis-
counted loans for commercial banks, agricultural credit corporations,
and livestock loan companies.

When W. I. (Bill) Myers came to Washington immediately after
the election of Franklin D. Roosevelt as President in the Fall of
1932, the System had 15 years of experience. It had made a good
beginning. Many of the farm leaders who fought for its establishment
had had a great deal of faith in the cooperative idea. They insisted
that the Federal Land Bank System be set up on that basis, even
though private investors were given the opportunity to establish a
parallel system of joint stock land banks. The previous 15 years had
been a period of trial and error. The depression had greatly reduced
the effectiveness of the Federal Land Bank System, along with all
other types of financial institutions. President-elect Roosevelt sent
Henry Morgenthau, Jr. to Washington to work with the farm organizations to draw up emergency legislation. Morgenthau took Myers
with him. Morgenthau and Myers soon decided to concentrate on
developing emergency financing plans that would relieve the financial
stress of farmers all across the country.

At that time, thousands of farmers were losing their farms by
foreclosure and many hundreds of thousands more were facing the
threat of foreclosure in the very near future. Commercial banks were
failing. Insurance companies were pressed for funds by policyholders'
requests for loans and they could not collect even interest on many

of their farm loans. Their solvency was threatened. Sources of credit
for farmers had dried up. Myers tackled the job with quiet enthusiasm and determination, not only to relieve farmers' present financial ills, but to round out the Federal Land Bank—Federal Intermediate Credit Bank System to make it a complete source of credit
for farmers and their cooperatives. He was determined to build a
permanent, dependable source of credit for farmers—credit that was
tailored to suit their needs, rather than the desires or needs of
lenders.

Myers Recognized as Designer of Farm Credit System

While many farm leaders have had a hand in shaping the Cooperative Farm Credit System in its modern dress, W. I. Myers is generally recognized as the chief architect who conceived and drew the
basic plans for the expansion of the System. Morgenthau and Myers
presented their plans, which had been approved by the farm organizations, to Governor Roosevelt in Albany in December, 1932.
Roosevelt approved the plans and they became the Administration's
farm credit program and withstood the challenge of a proposal for a
government-owned corporation drawn up by Senator McAdoo who
had been Roosevelt's opponent for the presidential nomination.
Morgenthau was made chairman of the Federal Farm Board when
Roosevelt assumed the Presidency on March 4. Twenty days later the
President by executive order effective after 60 days unless disapproved
by Congress, consolidated all existing agricultural credit programs in
the new Farm Credit Administration. The Emergency Farm Mortgage
Act was passed almost immediately. The Farm Credit Act of 1933
rounding out the Cooperative Farm Credit System became law on
June 16, 1933.

From the background of a boyhood on a farm in southern New
York state, where he was born in 1891, and as a student and teacher
of farm management, farm finance, and cooperatives at Cornell University, where he received his B.S. degree in 1914 and his Ph.D. in
1918, Myers knew that the constant availability of credit on terms
suited to farmers' needs was a basic necessity for farmers throughout
the country. He realized the Federal Intermediate Credit Banks
had not been able to establish a nationwide system of retail outlets.
Thus, his legislative proposal provided for local production credit
associations—to be capitalized and supervised by 12 district production credit corporations, owned by the government.

Myers had seen the failures of many of the attempts of Aaron

Sapiro and the Federal Farm Board to build national cooperatives from the top down. He used what could be salvaged from the Federal Farm Board's revolving fund to capitalize a system of district Banks for Cooperatives to help build and finance farmer cooperatives from the ground up. In addition, he provided for a Central Bank for Cooperatives to finance large, established regional and national cooperatives.

Believed Farmers Should Eventually Own System

Myers was a thorough believer in the idea that, while farmers needed government help, particularly in the depression days, to put renewed life and strength in the land banks and to start the new parts of the System, farmers should participate in running the System and should eventually assume complete ownership of the System.

He saw to it that provisions for working toward these goals were put in the original legislation for starting the Production Credit Associations and the Banks for Cooperatives.

Myers would be the first one to say that these ideas were not new. He knew the strength and weaknesses of the Federal Land Banks and the National Farm Loan Associations. He tried to build on their strengths and find ways to eliminate their weaknesses. He also used their experience in designing and building the Production Credit Associations and Banks for Cooperatives.

He wanted eventually to have a strong, farmer-owned and controlled system of credit that could stand on its own feet. But his plans included emergency measures for rescuing farmers who faced foreclosure by using government money to strengthen the Federal Land Banks and to provide these Banks with access to government money to make the more risky, second mortgage loans on behalf of the Federal Farm Mortgage Corporation. He was willing to do this, even though his ultimate aim was to see the System obtain all of its lending funds from investors through the sale of securities. He was also willing to see farmers temporarily receive subsidized interest rates.

It is of interest that Myers addressed the 1936 Annual Meeting of the American Farm Bureau Federation and asked it not to request Congress to continue the subsidized interest rate on Land Bank loans. He based his plea on the premise that the Farm Credit System was a cooperative organization that should stand on its own feet as quickly as possible.

The Federal Land Banks administered the Land Bank Commissioner loans so well on behalf of the Federal Farm Mortgage Corporation that they not only helped save hundreds of thousands of farmers from losing their farms by foreclosure, but the government received dividends of $150 million on its $200 million investment in the Corporation, along with the return of its investment.

Becomes FCA Governor in Nov., 1933

Early in 1933, Bill Myers became Deputy Governor of the newly-created Farm Credit Administration, designed to supervise the Co-operative Farm Credit System, under the Farm Credit Administration's first Governor, Henry Morgenthau, Jr. On November 17, 1933, when Morgenthau became Secretary of the Treasury, Myers succeeded him as Governor. Myers immediately set about the task of organizing the new parts of the Farm Credit System and putting the old ones in high gear.

All leaders in the cooperative movement have had some outstanding strength. Bill Myers, however, came to his position with an unusual number of strengths and an unusually small number of weaknesses. His quiet confidence, his vision, his organizational ability, his constant humility, coupled with his determination and ability to work with others, and get them to work with him, soon earned the respect and admiration of a large proportion of the people with whom he worked. His vision, confidence and pride in the Farm Credit System didn't stop with the people with whom he worked. It spread out across the country to people in the district banks and local associations who heard him speak, or merely heard about him from their friends.

Myers Kept Vision of Ultimate Goal; Worked Toward It

Myers had the ability to visualize and translate into definite plans, broad goals, and objectives. Even when current problems and circumstances made it necessary to make compromises, he never gave up the vision of the ultimate goals for which he was sure farmers would want to reach.

Although many of the founders of the Federal Land Banks and the local National Farm Loan Associations (now Federal Land Bank Associations) had believed in the idea that the System should be controlled and operated by farmers, many of the administrators who were chosen to carry out the idea in the 1920s had not made very great efforts to develop that concept. Myers, however, set about trying to make it work, not only in the Federal Land Banks, but in the newly-organized Production Credit Associations and Banks for Cooperatives.

Myers, together with F. F. Hill, who became his Deputy when he assumed the role of Governor; Albert S. Goss, Land Bank Commissioner; Francis W. Peck, Cooperative Bank Commissioner; S. M. Garwood, Production Credit Commissioner; and Garwood's Deputy, C. R. (Cap) Arnold, set up standards for the type of people they wanted as officers of the district Land Banks, Production Credit Corporations and Banks for Cooperatives.

They felt that the officers of these organizations should include men well grounded in credit, as well as men who knew agriculture of their territory and who had had successful experience in dealing with farmers.

To a large degree, they were successful in finding men who had qualifications they had specified. Myers and Hill also set about the job of training not only the leaders but the followers, in the Farm Credit Administration and the organizations it supervised. Visions Myers had of the future structure and role of the Cooperative Farm Credit System he imparted to people all across the country. Some leaders of men are able to impart their vision enthusiastically and with zeal and emotional appeal. Myers had the enthusiasm—but he substituted logic and well-laid-out plans, carefully explained, for the emotion and zeal of many other leaders. As a result, he earned and kept the respect and support of his co-workers throughout the country, as well as that of the leaders of the national farm organizations.

In fact, when the System was later attacked by people who wanted to substitute government ownership and control for the objective of complete farmer-ownership and control, people within the System—not only its officers, but also boards of directors and farmer-members of the local associations—rose to protect the System from a change in goals. They were backed by most of the national farm leaders.

Myers' Ability to Deal with Congressman Pays Off

One of Myers' strengths was his ability to deal with Members of Congress. He understood their problems, and their need to satisfy their constituents. However, he was not willing to sacrifice the ideal of building a strong organization to the pressures to appoint to top positions men whose chief qualifications were their political activity. He was able to impart his vision to Members of Congress and, by building an efficient organization, gained their respect and support. At the time, it was said that when he picked a man, he never asked his politics, but turned over his name to W. Forbes Morgan, a former investment banker, who was one of his Deputies and Treasurer of the Democratic Party, and asked Morgan to explain to the interested Members of Congress why the man was needed.

As a result, members of both Parties quickly realized that here was a man who was sympathetic to their problems but one who would not play partisan politics. At a time when most of the new or- ganizations in government were highly affected by political overtones, Myers kept the Farm Credit Administration's vision focused on the job of serving farmers by helping them help themselves. One result has been that over the years Farm Credit-trained men have risen to important positions throughout government as well as in private life. But, as one of them said recently, "We never lose our respect for and loyalty to Farm Credit."

Farm Credit System Perfected on Myers' Foundation

Over the years, there have been many, many refinements made in the organization and operation of the Cooperative Farm Credit Sys- tem. Many leaders have come along in recent years—such as R. B. Tootell, currently Governor of the Farm Credit Administration, and the members of the part-time, policy-making Federal Farm Credit Board. They have changed and perfected the details of the System, which is now largely owned by 900,000 farmer-members and their cooperatives and loans $7 billion a year, to meet the changing nature of agriculture. But today's leaders have built on the solid foundation that Bill Myers helped design and build so carefully and so well.

They have kept his vision expanding and moving forward. He would be among the first to agree with most of the changes that have been made, and has urged more, because his objective has always been to give farmers the best possible service—not merely to build institutions. For example, from the beginning, he strove for close coordination of Federal Land Bank Associations and Production Credit Associations so they could best serve farmers' total credit needs.

Myers' dream of a completely farmer-owned Farm Credit System is rapidly coming true. The Federal Land Banks repaid the last of their government capital in 1947. All but three of the 474 Production Credit Associations have repaid all their government-owned stock. Two of the 13 Banks for Cooperatives repaid the last of their govern- ment capital in 1965. The others plan to do the same soon.

In 1938, Myers returned to Cornell University, first as Head of the Department of Agricultural Economics. Later he became Dean of the University's College of Agriculture (1943–59). In those years, Myers was called on time and time again to fill a wide variety of important part-time committee and commission assignments. He turned down the offer of the Presidency of one of the largest state universities.

Becomes Chairman of Reorganized A.I.C.

Right after World War II, Myers was chosen by farmer cooperative leaders to serve as Chairman of the Board of Trustees of the American Institute of Cooperation, when that organization was trying to get back into operation after a wartime eclipse. Together with its full-time President, Raymond W. Miller, he guided the organization in developing a broad and significant full-time educational program to replace its pre-war summer program.

He was called on by President Truman, at World War II's close, to serve on two important committees. They were the Famine Emergency Committee (1946) and the Committee on Foreign Aid (1947). The latter committee, under the chairmanship of Averill Harriman, then Secretary of Commerce, made recommendations that led to the Marshall Plan to rehabilitate Europe.

President Eisenhower appointed Myers the first Chairman of the President's National Agricultural Advisory Council and he served in that capacity until 1959.

His broad interests in education have resulted in Myers serving for many years as a Trustee of the Rockefeller Foundation, the General Education Board, the Carnegie Institution of Washington, the Eisenhower Exchange Fellowships, the Agricultural Development Council, Elmira College, and Vassar College. Stretching from his active career into his retirement, he has traveled as a consultant to such far-off places as the Philippines and India for organizations such as Cornell University and the Ford Foundation.

In the international field, Myers for five years served on the International Development Advisory Board of the International Cooperation Administration.

Myers Active in Business, Finance, and Co-ops

In the field of finance and business, Myers has been sought after to hold a string of directorships that would do credit to a Wall Street tycoon. But mixed in the list of big businesses were several farmer cooperatives. For 12 years, he served on the Board of Directors and was Deputy Chairman of the Federal Reserve Bank of New York. Other directorships which he still holds are Avco Corporation, Continental Can Company, Grand Union Company, SCM Corporation (Smith-Corona-Marchant), New York State Electric and Gas Corporation, Marine Midland Corporation, American Agriculturalist, Inc. (a farm paper), P. & C. Food Markets, Inc. (organized and largely owned by farmer cooperatives), the Mutual Life Insurance Company of New York, and the Marine Midland Trust Company of Southern New York.

Apparently Myers' business judgment over the years has proved just as sound for large businesses as it was in the early 1920s when he was a frequent advisor to a young and struggling farmer-owned organization that was to become the Nation's largest farm supply cooperative—now Agway—then the Cooperative Grange League Federation Exchange.

Myers' work on behalf of farmers has not gone unnoticed by his fellow workers in agriculture. He served as President of the American Farm Economic Association in 1934 after having been its Secretary-Treasurer for three years. He is now one of a small group of Fellows of that organization. He was made an Honorary American Farmer by the Future Farmers of America, and received Agricultural Service Awards from the American Farm Bureau Federation and the American Association of Agricultural Editors.

Farmer cooperatives can be proud of claiming such a well-rounded man as Bill Myers as one of their own pioneers!

Edwin Griswold Nourse

by Orion Ulrey

D R. NOURSE WAS THE TEACHER of a course, Principles of
Cooperation, in which the writer was a student, at the second
annual session of the American Institute of Cooperation (A.I.C.) held
at the Agricultural College of the University of Minnesota in 1926—
40 short years ago. The teacher impressed his students as being very
fair in his analysis of the fundamentals and possibilities of cooperative business to serve American farmers. Dr. Nourse was one of
the founders of A.I.C. at a Cleveland meeting in 1924, and served as
program chairman, as a trustee, and a member of the executive committee during 1925–29.

The nearby Alpha Zeta House provided rooms and meals for Dr.
Nourse, Dr. Jesness, Dr. Ezekiel, Richard Pattee, and several students
of the Institute. The discussions about cooperatives and the rural
economy at meals and during the evenings, left deep impressions on
the students who were searching for ideas on "improved systems."
In fact, the experiences at the Institute, along with significant articles
by Dr. Nourse, may have been major reasons for the writer's deep
interest in cooperatives during the following four decades.

As anyone who associated with Dr. Nourse for a period of time, the
writer became very fond of the man, his sincerity, his depth, his wide
interests, and his personal concern about others. Occasionally during
the 30's, the writer was brash enough to call, without previous arrangements, on Dr. Nourse at the Brookings Institution in Washington.
He always made one feel that he was pleased to be visited although
he was a very busy person.

Edwin G. Nourse was born in Lockport, N.Y., on May 20, 1883, but
was reared on a small farm in northern Illinois. He attended the
Lewis Institute in Chicago in 1901–02, and received an A.B. degree
at Cornell University in 1906. He was an instructor at the Wharton
School of Finance and Commerce, 1909–10, and professor and head

of the Department of Economics and Sociology at the University of South Dakota, 1910–12. He completed his Ph.D. at the University of Chicago in 1915, was professor and head of the Department of Economics at the University of Arkansas, 1915–18, and was professor of economics and chief of the Agricultural Economics Section at Iowa State College, 1918–23. His experience in studying the economic problems of farmers in these three Midwest states during an inflation and deflation period apparently aroused his interest in the possibilities of cooperatives to serve farmers.

Becomes First Chairman of Council of Economic Advisers

Dr. Nourse was in charge of agricultural studies for the Institute of Economics from 1923 to 1927. When the Brookings Institution was established in 1927 he became Director of the Institute of Economics in the Brookings Institution, and from 1942 to 1946 he was Vice President of the Brookings Institution. He was appointed by President Harry Truman as the first Chairman of the Council of Economic Advisers in the Executive Office, under the Employment Act of 1946. There he assisted in pioneering a new function in government, since he was uniquely able to focus his fruitful experiences in economic analysis on governmental policy and the national economy.

He was a fellow of the Guggenheim Memorial Foundation, 1950–52, which provided for a continuation of his research, writing, and lecturing, especially on subjects dealing with governmental and national economic policy. He served for a number of years as vice chairman of the Joint Council on Economic Education, and is continuing his research and writings, in early 1966, in the offices of the Brookings Institution.

Dr. Nourse was an active developer of the American Farm Economic Association, and was its president in 1924, editor of its Journal for two years, 1925–1926, and chairman of its committee for awards of graduate fellowships in Agricultural Economics and Rural Sociology, 1928–30. He was voted as one of the initial group of 10 fellows of the American Farm Economics Association in 1957. The statement of recognition said in part:

> As one of the senior statesmen among agricultural economists, Dr. Nourse has for many years inspired others in agricultural economics. He has incessantly pioneered the arduous pathway that agricultural economists have traveled during the past four decades. He has helped to establish the young and growing discipline on a firm foundation of objective analysis, intellectual integrity and

dedication to the preservation and strengthening of a progressive agricultural economy in a dynamic and expanding America.

Dr. Nourse has been requested to serve on many other significant committees and organizations. He was appointed an American delegate to the International Institute of Agriculture in Rome in 1924 and 1936; was a member of the League of Nations Committee on Nutrition, 1935–37; was president of the American Economic Association in 1942; and chairman of the Social Science Research Council, 1942–45. He has received many other awards, including: Honorary LLD at the Illinois Institute of Technology in 1950, Honorary Doctor of Science at Iowa State University in 1958, and the Rosenberger Medal at the University of Chicago in 1959.

Dr. Nourse has been a member of the Alpha Zeta, Phi Kappa Phi and Phi Gamma Mu fraternities; of the Chevy Chase and Cosmos Clubs; of the American Philosophical Society, of the American Academy of Arts and Sciences, and of the Unitarian Church.

Dr. Nourse's writings have covered a wide range of topics dealing especially with agricultural economics, cooperatives, the price system, and the total economy. He has published 12 books: *Agricultural Economics* (editor) 1916; the *Chicago Produce Market* (Ph.D. thesis), 1918; *American Agriculture and the European Market*, 1924; *The Legal Status of Agricultural Cooperation*, 1927; *The Cooperative Marketing of Livestock* (with Joseph G. Knapp), 1931; *Marketing Agreements under the Agricultural Adjustment Administration*, 1935; *America's Capacity to Produce*, 1936; *Three Years of the Agricultural Adjustment Administration* (with Joseph S. Davis and John D. Black), 1937; *Price Policies and Economic Progress*, 1938; *Price Making in a Democracy*, 1944; *The 1950's Come First*, 1951; and *Economics in the Public Service: Administrative Aspects of the Employment Act*, 1953.

His articles on similar topics have appeared primarily in the Journal of Farm Economics, the American Economic Review, and in *American Cooperation*: the proceedings of the American Institute of Cooperation.

Makes Significant Contributions to Better Understanding of Co-ops

Farmer cooperatives were being developed very rapidly during much of the period when Dr. Nourse served at three Land-Grant institutions in the Midwest. Farmers were actively attempting to improve the marketing of their products. Special laws for cooperatives were being discussed and introduced in the states. The legal meaning, economic significance, and organizational structure of cooperatives were being debated. Opinions varied widely on these issues. A few agricultural economists were giving attention to this "new" type of business. It was logical, consequently, that Dr. Nourse with his experiences in three farm states, his concern for farm people, and his inquiring and analytical mind should give considerable attention to farmer cooperatives, especially during the 20's and 30's.

Dr. Nourse, in a letter of March 15, 1966, states that his major objective was "to get the theory of cooperation as a distinctive (important, but neglected) phase of business organization in perspective in the economic literature and among the leaders of cooperative enterprises. Later, I tried to build on this foundation a structure of description and analysis covering the application of this general theory and legal recognition in various commodity areas."

Two papers, published in 1922, were very significant in presenting his views and concerns about farmer cooperatives; and also in laying the foundations for future papers and books.

In the paper "Outlook for Cooperative Marketing" in the April, 1922, issue of the *Journal of Farm Economics,* Dr. Nourse stated his belief "that the cooperative is a form of business organization which is slowly evolving . . . is designed to play a role as brilliant as the old-line corporation and the trust . . . and the largest field of usefulness appears to be in farm marketing."

He pointed out the danger of killing cooperatives by kindness and by over-promotion, since they were a popular solution for the agricultural depression of that period. He distinguished two major goals—business efficiency of the organization and central market control. He was fearful of attempts to use cooperatives to manipulate or control supply and fix farm prices on a cost plus basis. He pointed out many improvements that should be made: on business operations and management, in solving internal problems, in coordinating activities among cooperatives, in organizing and educating members, in developing strong federations, in developing overhead service organizations, in improving leadership and in selecting and training management and other employees—before attention could be given, with safety, to the market control possibilities.

The article expressed optimism about the future of farmer cooperatives because of the recent state laws; understanding by only a few lawyers; the attention given by agricultural colleges in research, teaching, and extension activities; and the opportunities available for well-trained young men in cooperative business. Dr. Nourse emphasized the need for practical and penetrating investigation to improve these many aspects of the cooperative. He cautioned his readers to consider the slow growth processes necessary to build sound business and membership organization for maximizing the potential of the cooperative.

The second paper, "The Economic Philosophy of Cooperation," appeared in the December, 1922, issue of *American Economic Review*. Dr. Nourse observed that the cooperative leaders were short on theory and in understanding of principles; that cooperative legislation, organization, operations and member contracts should be based on sound theory; and that the Rochdale principles should be examined and interpreted in terms of current conditions and problems.

He examined the case for farmer marketing cooperatives, consumer purchasing cooperatives, and labor-production associations; and came to the conclusion there might be a place for each from the standpoint of marketing efficiency. He favored cooperation within each of these groups, and collective bargaining among the groups. He expressed the belief that labor might obtain greater gains through collective bargaining than through ownership and profit sharing. He pointed out that if the cooperative scheme were pushed to its logical conclusion a new system of making prices would evolve: comprehensive collective bargaining. Dr. Nourse recognized that extreme application of cooperation might produce some form of socialism, but concluded that American citizens would not voluntarily develop into such a "cooperative commonwealth" as was being discussed abroad because of the regimentation involved.

Consequently, he gave attention in a later paper to the role of voluntary farmer cooperatives in the American brand of free enterprise, capitalism, and "mixed" economy. This paper discussed principles of cooperation in terms of American conditions and problems: actually an application of the principles evolved at Rochdale and elsewhere. As was common in his articles, he challenged the economists to research all of the economic and human aspects of cooperatives. He expressed optimism about the cooperative as an instrument for economic efficiency and ethical distribution of the economic shares, but he questioned the monopolistic and central control objective of some cooperatives.

Has Major Role in Building A.I.C. Program Policies

After such provocative early articles, it was logical that Dr. Nourse would be requested to play a major role in the creation and the policies of the American Institute of Cooperation during the formative 1924–29 period. As program chairman of this educational institution for five years, he, along with others, was concerned with finding out more about the business cooperative, its application to American economic life, with developing the various aspects so it could compete and make real contributions in the economy, and about how it could effectively serve the thousands of small and independent farmers. Consequently, the A.I.C. has served as an institution to bring together the leaders especially from farmer cooperatives and the agricultural colleges to present and exchange ideas, and to mobilize action in the areas of research, education, and training.

In the 1926 annual meeting in St. Louis of the American Farm Economic Association in his paper, "The Outlook for Agriculture," Dr. Nourse listed cooperation as one of five significant forces which would affect agriculture over the long period. He stated, "cooperation —a plant of slow growth—offers in the long run, quite probably, the most important single opportunity for improving the economic organization of agriculture."

Dr. Nourse, in fact, is one of the few well-known economists of any type, who over a period of time, has recognized and been concerned about the potential of cooperatives. One wonders if this scarce breed is disappearing!

The most important single contribution of Dr. Nourse to the understanding of cooperatives may have been the book, the *Legal Status of American Cooperation*, published in 1927. The objectives were to examine: the economic philosophy and motives; the manner of expressing the economic purposes in the specialized statutes; the relation of the laws and practices to the general body of corporation law; the attitudes of the courts in interpreting both general and special statutes; and the effects of the cooperative laws on competition, business stabilization, and restraint of trade.

The book traces the history of cooperative legislation in America up to the mid-20's, describes the Rochdale influence, analyzes the objectives of the nonstock Acts, the origin of the uniform cooperative Acts, and the effects of commodity marketing programs upon legislation. The legal aspects of problems presented and analyzed include: the cooperative pools, membership contracts and enforcement, restraint of trade; and the courts' attitudes and findings on cases involving the areas of conflict.

Dr. Nourse realized that efficient cooperatives must have a sound economic and legal base. Consequently, the book, the first thorough analysis of the legal statutes and problems of American cooperatives, was prepared. He was critical of some trends found in the legislation for cooperatives, such as: providing special privileges for agriculture, or class legislation. He contended that all groups should have comparable opportunities to utilize cooperative business. He again stated many of the economic reasons for farmers to use cooperatives. He believed that there was no reason to fear the large cooperatives because of the checks of competition and the courts. He discussed the problems of equity of treatment of members and nonmembers, and decided that there was no final remedy at law. Information and education were necessary to build the foundations for contracts and laws.

Dr. Nourse gave special attention to the conflicts in the cases presented to the courts, and seemed to agree with the rule of reason which apparently was frequently applied. He concluded that there was no perfect or final formula for regulating a dynamic and evolving society.

Basic Theory, Principles Applied to Co-op Livestock Marketing

The next book, the *Cooperative Marketing of Livestock*, in collaboration with Joseph G. Knapp, was published in 1931. In this book, the authors attempted to apply the general theory and principles evolved in previous studies, to the cooperative marketing of livestock. The book is divided into three parts: the evolution, organization and problems of the shipping association; the development and services of the commission and terminal companies, the national producers' movements, and the effects of and relations to direct buying; and an analysis of the current development such as: the effects on costs and services, the effects on market price, and the program for a national livestock marketing system launched by the Federal Farm Board.

The authors concluded that much economic and legal progress had been made in less than two decades in the cooperative marketing of livestock: first by the shipping associations which were largely destroyed by improved roads, trucks and direct marketing; and later by commission and terminal companies and their affiliated services. They seemed to give approval of the attempt, underway in 1931, to create a national livestock marketing system. They pointed out, however, that a sound national system should rest on organizations of farmer associations at several levels and be thoroughly coordinated. They were skeptical of promotion by governmental agencies. They stated that if the national movement failed, a primary reason would be inadequacy in the leadership. They were critical of much of the Farm Board livestock program: as being based too much on political expediency rather than cooperative doctrine and economic fundamentals; as being overpromoted or at too rapid a pace; as being intolerant of other types of cooperative efforts among livestock producers; and as lacking proper organization of producers. They emphasized the need for research and education as a basis for the possible future evolutionary development of a national livestock system.

The writer, who lived through much of the period analyzed in detail by the authors, was impressed as he again reviewed the book; by the clarity, logic, and scope of the study. He wonders why such studies are not repeated every decade or so, if the agricultural economists are really concerned about the farm segment of the economy!

Fundamental Questions Posed on Marketing Agreements, Collective Bargaining

The third book of Dr. Nourse which dealt largely with cooperatives, *Marketing Agreements under the Agricultural Adjustment Administration*, was published in 1936. This book was the fifth of six studies of the Brookings Institution on the AAA. The book traces the origin of the marketing agreements, licensing and orders by the federal government; the procedures and policies of the agreements; the use by the various commodities; the administrative processes and issues; the problems of enforcement and legality; the price objectives and strategy; and an evaluation of the results.

The experiment with federal marketing agreements grew out of the Agricultural Marketing Act of 1929, and the program of the Federal Farm Board. Later, a marketing agreement provision was added to the Domestic Allotment Act of 1934. The agreement was dependent upon action by a cooperative group of producers. After hearings, the dealers and processors could be licensed so they would be placed under the provisions of the agreements. Later, marketing orders were used instead of licenses to bring the middlemen and the nonmembers under the market plan. The general objectives were to raise and stabilize farm prices, and to obtain a higher degree of price equity among farmers and middlemen. Marketing agreements were used primarily for the perishables, and especially for milk, where price wars and disturbances had traditionally caused very unstable conditions.

Dr. Nourse noted that the scope of economic operations was not legally clear. The agreements permitted the producers to move from collective bargaining with dealers to practically collective control of the market. The minority, nonmembers and dealers who did not buy from the cooperative, were required to participate in the market price and control plan. The agreements permitted several devices for supply control: removal of inferior grades and distribution of shipments by time and areas; and the use of a two-price or multi-price system.

The author raised the question of how far the government could assist producers, under the marketing agreements, within the limits of sound economics. He had several fears about the possible use of marketing agreements: the greater dependence upon the government rather than upon the cooperatives; the inadequate use of economic analysis for determining prices; the possibility that economics might not give the best answer even if used; and the over-stimulation of production if prices were unduly enhanced. However, he doubted whether it would be economically desirable to go back to the tug-of-war marketing procedures. He favored the continuation of the experiment, but suggested the need for regular study of all aspects, especially to find a desirable system of checks and balances.

Dr. Nourse's presidential address at the December, 1942, meeting of the American Economic Association was on a pertinent topic, "Collective Bargaining and the Common Interest." He traced the economic trends: the growth in size of the business corporation, the transition from individual to collective bargaining for labor and agriculture, and the unfolding role of the government in assisting in the goals and operations of collective bargaining. He expressed the belief that collective bargaining, as used, was moving towards more government. Since individualism in the market is inadequate, he concluded that the economist must work with, analyze, and assist the new forces.

He ably presented the case for a system of group price making: for multilateral bargaining for a major part of the economy, as best in the long run. He expressed the belief that such a system would provide the best opportunity for economic self-expression and for technical efficiency. His listing of the shortcomings of the government included the following: that the government decisions wouldn't result in achieving the common good; that unwise compromises would result from group pressures and political trades; that the result might be a dictatorship by a group; that administration and operations might be based on dead data from the past; and that rewards and responsibility would not be directly related. He drew examples from experiences with the Agricultural Adjustment Administration to prove some of his beliefs about the operations of governmental agencies.

Dr. Nourse raised questions on problems created by the group power and bargaining system: How best to organize for voluntary group action, how to find the best data and apply the best economic answers to the complex problems and the place of the individual in the total scheme.

He pointed out the need for well-trained and motivated economists and political scientists to serve with the private organizations and with the governmental agencies. He emphasized the necessity to use statesmanship and science, instead of guerilla war and group power politics, in the modern society—partly to escape the expansion of government. He expressed the belief that the economist must gain more proficiency to serve effectively in the large administrative groups; and that they must be prepared to deliver knowledge to the groups during the years ahead. He again reminded the economists that they must continue to operate to win respect for the scientific approach.

This paper rounded out his philosophy on the role of cooperative economic action in the modern society.

The paper, "From Dogma to Science in Cooperative Thinking," presented at the 1946 meeting of the American Institute of Cooperation, reviewed progress made in understanding cooperatives during the previous decades. He stated we had learned the values of limiting the return on capital, of distributing returns to patrons, the possibilities of the revolving plan of financing, the necessity for considering the rest of the economy, the importance of constant research and information, that cooperation was based on voluntary and not compulsory action, and that there were many ways of applying the cooperative principles.

He concluded we had learned that the large-scale marketing organization with the binding contract, as promoted by Sapiro and the Farm Board, was not the best answer. An unsolved problem was: what combination of cooperation or self-government and governmental assistance would be best for a variety of conditions? He proposed additional attention to two types of research: the meaning of an "equitable" association, and social research along with economic investigation. He cautioned against being dogmatic about a specific application of a cooperative principle in such a dynamic society. He stated that the principles had an ethical as well as an economic basis.

In his talk, Dr. Nourse emphasized as forcefully as in any previous statement that the cooperative movement was an antimonopoly crusade, and a crusade for both political and economic democracy.

He recommended that the A.I.C. continue its program of investigation and discussion to find out more about the cooperative institutions, as proposed by Richard Pattee, one of the founders, in the early meetings.

Continues Contributions to Understanding of Co-ops

In his talk, "Changes Necessary to Meet Tomorrow's Problems," at the 1952 sessions of the A.I.C. at Michigan State, he repeated some of his observations of 1946 and added a few. He continued to oppose reliance on government to solve the farm problems, and the movements of the cooperatives towards restrictions and monopoly. The cooperatives grew as a protest against restrictions and restraints, and consequently shouldn't follow such practices.

He gave attention to the place of cooperatives in the growing dynamic urban society, in the mixed economy, and in strengthening the free enterprise system. He stated that one of the problems was to find out how to combine science, productive machinery, the price-income system, and proper economic behavior—in order to further expand the economy of abundance. He was not optimistic that organized management and labor would have the best answers. He asked the question: Do cooperatives offer the machinery and the system to assist? He pointed out that the emphasis on opportunity, freedom, and individualism in our society must be balanced by social consciousness, integrity, information available for all, and the constant search for truth.

In the paper presented before the 1962 Meeting of the American Farm Economic Association, "Lessons for Farm Economists from Recent Anti-Trust Decisions: or—Desirable Public Policy," Dr. Nourse reviewed a few of the court decisions since the mid-30's. He pointed out that the Supreme Court had moved quite a way in accepting group action and supply control of farmer cooperatives, but that cooperatives do not have immunity from the anti-monopoly rules applied to profit business corporations. The two lessons were: cooperatives had been given a wide latitude in administration of supply, because of such factors as the small size of business units and the available substitutes; and cooperatives could use modern business organization and techniques to obtain higher income, but not including conspiracy and collusion. The courts had concluded that the marketing agreements were not deemed to be, just because of their nature, unlawful as in violation of any antitrust laws.

Dr. Nourse stated that legislation and action to assist farmers, under the general welfare philosophy, must also protect consumers against undue price enhancement from any concentration of market power. The theory for any action must rest on the equal opportunity principle of the political system, and the rationale of efficiency in use of resources developed by the economists. He raised the question: If consumer groups were to attack the agricultural price-support system as beneficial to a few and contended that the supply could be produced at a lower cost, what would be the view of the Court!

He concluded that the Supreme Court had considered the rule of reason and public interest criteria in its decisions; and that it was assuming the responsibility of acting as a conscience of the nation in such areas of conflict of economic interests. He challenged the economists to obtain the information, to make the analysis, and to be economic statesmen; and thus serve to assist the courts to make wise decisions, and to assist the farmer cooperatives to make proper judgments in the pricing and supply control operations.

Dr. Nourse returned to the two aspects of cooperation which he discussed in a paper in the *Journal of Farm Economics* 40 years earlier. He concluded that the public and the courts had accepted the goal of economic efficiency, but that the position of the goal of market power of cooperatives was less clear.

The writer, after reviewing three books and seven articles by Dr. Nourse dealing with cooperatives, arrived at a few conclusions: Dr. Nourse was concerned with protecting the rights and developing the potentials of the individual. He had faith in the actions of man if the best use were made of science, research, and analysis; if man's actions were supported by consideration of ethics and responsibilities; and if his institutions were operating in a system with adequate checks and balances. Economic cooperation was one of the means of furthering the rights of the individual to more adequately share but also meant an extension of his responsibilities.

He had a deep belief in the potential of the cooperative to serve the American farmer. He wished to foster it through his services as an economist and as a statesman. He realized its limitations without the assistance of research, education, training, and experience. He came to the conclusion that the cooperative also could function in a society of big business, big labor organization, and big government: if it had the tools, perhaps including some government assistance.

Dr. Nourse was fearful of extreme cooperation, since he realized that extensive discipline and regulations were involved. He was also fearful of the large and powerful state: the pressures, slowness of operations, limited incentives, and frequently not the best decisions. He recognized the need for an extension of the government in the complex urban society; that it be assisted by science and research; but never quite trusted its operations as he did the private segments of the economy. He seems to subscribe to the theory of need for countervailing forces in the modern society of group bargaining giants. He was always a supporter of the system of free enterprise.

What were his major accomplishments in his contributions to cooperatives? He stated in his letter of March 15, 1966:

> I like to think that I did something toward raising agricultural cooperation from the level of amateur fumbling towards a professional level of organizational theory and managerial practice. I tried to keep cooperative leadership oriented towards economic efficiency and social service rather than towards market power as a coercive weapon. I feel that the American Institute of Cooperation, with the strong emphasis on education of members and especially the rising generation, its emphasis on the principles and social ideal of the cooperative movement, is something of a star in my crown.

The writer agrees.

Florence C. Parker

by Erma Angevine

A STATISTICIAN WITH A SENSE OF HUMOR; a cooperator with a sense of proportion; a historian with a sense of words. Florence E. Parker is at 75 one of the most vital, witty, and stimulating persons. She retired in 1952, 10 years ahead of schedule, to write a book. She went to San Diego to relax in the sunshine and live a life of quiet ease.

Miss Parker isn't the type for quiet ease. She set about at once to help organize a cooperative memorial association and at the same time to help coordinate a federation of California memorial societies. She's still at it.

Let's go back a bit.

Florence E. Parker was born in Minneapolis August 19, 1891. She was graduated from the University of Minnesota, where she majored in English, and joined the working force at a time when opportunities for women were extremely limited.

Miss Parker's first job was to proofread a 1250-page compilation of labor laws for the United States Bureau of Labor Statistics in Washington, D. C. Rather than let this document overwhelm her, she characteristically amused herself and her fellow workers by reading to them ridiculous statements that she unearthed: "Sponges shall not be shipped from any port less than six inches in diameter," a Florida law read. "Miners shall not be lowered into nor hoisted out of any mine with gunpowder," was the law in Colorado.

Miss Parker says her sense of humor won her a place on the editorial staff of the department "in spite of my being a woman." Having worked her way through college, she sympathized with labor. These liberal, pro-labor feelings led her into field studies on union activities—pension plans, welfare measures for disabled and aged members, and a 300-page volume on care of the aged in the United States.

Finds "Life-Long Absorption" in Co-op Development

Cooperatives entered her life in 1920 when she accepted an assignment to look into self-help projects and found a "life-long absorption."

She wrote, and the Bureau of Labor Statistics published reports on consumer, self-help, worker, student, and housing cooperatives. She wrote about taxation of cooperatives and turned out the annual reports on statistics of operation and developments among cooperatives.

Second in command of the editorial division and assistant editor of the Bureau's *Monthly Labor Review,* Miss Parker interested herself in the ups and downs of co-ops throughout the U. S. She was a charter member and organizer of the Department of Labor Credit Union; president and director of Rochdale Cooperative in the nation's capital; and a director of the Cooperative League of the USA.

In 1946, Miss Parker became the Bureau's full-time Specialist on Cooperatives. Of her new job, she said, "It's like going to heaven without having to die!"

The Bureau sent her to co-op meetings here and abroad. She attended all biennial congresses of the Cooperative League from 1920 to 1956. She sat on the back row at Eastern Cooperative League (now called Eastern Cooperatives) meetings and was usually introduced as "Miss Parker, the aunt of the cooperative movement."

She knew more about what was going on than many co-op leaders—and she could both praise and scold those responsible. She understood the co-op's operating statement and could take it apart digit by digit.

In addition to many pamphlets and articles about U. S. cooperatives, she wrote two books based on her observations at International Cooperative Alliance Congresses in Czechoslovakia in 1948 and Denmark in 1951: *Cooperatives in Postwar Europe* and *International Aspects of the Cooperative Movement.* Joining with Helen Cowan she also wrote *Cooperative Associations in Europe and Their Possibilities for Postwar Reconstruction.*

Writes Monumental History of Consumer Co-ops

One reason she elected to retire early was to concentrate on a special project she'd been planning for years. She wanted to write a history of consumer cooperatives in this country. Miss Parker already had much of the research on file. She knew of obscure cooperatives that others had never heard about. She knew managers, directors, and members. Her reputation for research gave her access to personal files of cooperative leaders.

For the first five months after she retired, she visited cooperatives and co-op people all over the country. For the following 18 months she wrote. Her first draft was monumental—1,800 single-spaced legal size pages. She revised her manuscript three times and then looked for a publisher.

The First 125 Years: a History of Distributive and Service Cooperation in the United States, 1829–1954, was published by the Cooperative League in 1956.

In her book Miss Parker centers her attention on consumer and service cooperatives. Her meticulous research, however, led her to examine all kinds of cooperatives. Her book is the definitive volume on the history of consumer cooperation in the U. S. She notes the early beginnings with the New England Association of Farmers, Mechanics, and other Workingmen in 1831, the farm co-ops of the Grange after the Civil War, and the 45 electric power cooperatives that predated the Rural Electrification Administration. Her book is not just a history. It is an evaluation of cooperatives past, present and future.

In the dedication of *The First 125 Years,* Miss Parker writes:

> Still fairly young when I first began to read cooperative literature, attend meetings, and absorb the cooperative philosophy, I then envisioned cooperatives as instruments entirely of brotherhood and sweetness and light. This illusion was rudely shattered at the very first Cooperative Congress I attended—that of 1920. For that meeting was marked by a knock-down and drag-out oral battle between the Cooperative League's representatives (notably its president) and those of regional organizations of the Midwest and Far West whose practices deviated from accepted Rochdale methods. At that Congress I learned that even cooperators were not exempt from the American passion for bigness and speed and that some of them would resort to questionable tactics to obtain "results."
>
> This was the first of a long series of revelations showing that the cooperative movement is above all one of people—people of all sorts and descriptions: Some who joined only because of what they could get out of it in dollars and cents. Some who did not by any means disdain the possible economic advantages, but also caught a gleam of something shining beyond. And some who envisioned the store or other enterprise merely as a valuable means to the larger end of a broader, fuller life open to an ever-growing circle of people, with services provided for use and not profit. For this ultimate aim, thousands have worked and sacrificed with single-minded devotion and a few have even laid down their lives.
>
> This is not to say that anywhere near all the effort has been on a selfless, lofty plane. The cooperative movement has by no means been free of personal ambition, of bitter antipathies, of petty bickering and politicking, or of many honest differences of opinion as to ways and means. All of these have been present, and many

a cooperative has been torn and even wrecked, primarily because two men or two factions could not get along with each other and neither would yield.

Since the cooperative movement is one of personalities, it is peculiarly subject to all of the human characteristics. Its successes are the result of the higher qualities of leadership, high ideals, perseverance, and courage. Its failures have been the result of human frailties, of inexperience and short vision.

By and large, I venture to say, few if any economic movements have elicited more devoted, disinterested service than the cooperative movement. Over the years certain cooperators stand out like beacon lights.

One of those beacon lights now and always will be Florence E. Parker.

Richard Pattee

by Kenneth Hinshaw

"THE NEW ENGLAND MILK PRODUCERS' ASSOCIATION *will never get anywhere by being a namby-pamby-kid-glove-grandmotherly organization*" was the "Personal Word" written by Richard Pattee in the cold December of 1917.

Pattee was a man born to fight for a cause, and the cause he found and for which he fought courageously and competently was to overcome the dairy farmers' milk price problems.

Born on a farm in Alexandria, N. H., in 1872, he grew up partaking of the two kinds of education a New England youth could readily acquire in the late 80's—first, the on-the-job training in the austerity of rural economics, and then some of the scholarly knowledge that distinguished the region's numerous academies, institutes, colleges, and universities. Pattee went from his home state's New Hampton Institute to special courses at Dartmouth College and the University of Minnesota. For a few years, he worked for newspapers, taking assignments that provided opportunity for him to travel throughout the United States.

As Grange Lecturer, Finds Co-op as "Cause" Needing Leadership

In 1898, he returned to New Hampshire where he became prominent in Grange work. He advanced through the organization's offices to become State Lecturer in 1904. It was then that he found the "cause" that needed leadership—the dairy farmers' need for an organized effort to improve their incomes.

Consequently, during the years he was a Grange Lecturer, Pattee's became the voice that urged New England's milk producers to form a strong cooperative to attain fair prices for dairy products.

Early in 1913, the Boston Cooperative Milk Producers' Company was dissolved following a series of legal snarls, and this created a crisis which set the stage for bolder leadership to forge a bigger and stronger organization. The leadership was ready, and Richard Pattee was employed in August, 1913, to direct the affairs of the newly organized New England Milk Producers' Association.

For three years, Pattee devoted most of his time to organization work. The NEMPA grew to a membership of more than 2,000 dairy farmers and managed to pay all its bills and keep a bank balance of almost $100.

In October, 1916, a new crisis developed. A quarrel flared between Boston milk dealers and NEMPA and this led to a milk strike. The strike caused dairy farmers to recognize the inter-dependence of New England markets, and this resulted in re-organization of NEMPA to extend its services to dairy farmers shipping milk not only to Boston but also to other southern New England markets. In January, 1917, Pattee was elected secretary and executive officer of the re-organized NEMPA. Now the association was gaining members at the rate of a thousand a month.

In the fall of 1917, a series of events thrust the NEMPA's pricing policies into public controversy. In August, the association had worked out a program of new and simpler pricing procedures with its milk distributors. A price of seven cents a quart delivered in Boston was agreed upon. This was a substantial advance over the price agreed to in April. The advance, of course, was passed on to consumers and this drew considerable newspaper comment and criticism.

While this publicity was running its course, the Boston Chamber of Commerce issued a report on a cost study which it had begun months before at the suggestion of NEMPA. It showed the farm cost of a quart of New England milk to be six cents, with eight cents the appropriate price for a quart delivered at Boston. Accordingly, NEMPA announced it would raise its price to eight cents in October.

This was during World War I, and the immediate consequence of NEMPA's announcement was a request from the Massachusetts Food Administration to suspend the price advance. One thing led to another until Herbert Hoover, top man in the nation's wartime administration of foods and prices, gave it his personal attention and advised New Englanders to form a Federal Milk Commission for the region's milk markets. The commission was formed—and it negotiated a price reduction of half a cent a quart.

Ill with pneumonia, and ordered to bed by his doctor, Richard Pattee reluctantly accepted the situation. He said: "I was seriously embarrassed by the agreement to accept even temporarily a reduction that I had been urging producers to fight against."

Continues Fight for Satisfactory Milk Price

And fight he did—for 10 years as a leader in the New England dairyman's battle to make cooperative effort yield a satisfactory price for milk. To keep NEMPA members informed about their organization and its problems and accomplishments, Pattee developed a monthly publication, *New England Dairymen,* for which he wrote a message that bore the title "My Personal Word."

Here are examples of his courageous cooperative spirit—

1918—

I know there is tremendous work ahead to put dairying, as a business, on its feet in New England. If we cannot put dairying on a paying basis, we owe it to the wife and kiddies to quit and go into something else that will pay. But it's worth while to try and the only way is: Organize! Organize! Organize!

1920—

It all sums up in realizing that the farmers themselves must have an organization to protect their business, big enough and broad enough and with competent men enough to really study every branch of the business and act intelligently for the whole industry in every question affecting its welfare.

1923—

The present scope and method of (NEMPA) operations were never intended to be permanent. They were but steps, a flight of steps perhaps, that led up to a higher level but not to the summit of organized possibilities. We have in fact come up from the dark cellar in which New England dairy farming was drearily dying 10 years ago to about ground level. Another rise is due.

1926—

I want to live among, and be of those who, not content, are willing to fight for improvement. And somehow, the uncertainties of the farmer's life, the chances he must take, the risks he must run, make him the sort of man who has the courage to fight against every element that would check or hinder or destroy his progress.

The last of Richard Pattee's "My Personal Word" was written for the August, 1927, issue of *New England Dairyman*— and in November the small, white-haired man who made a strong cooperative force out of 20,000 individual dairy farmers was gone.

But he left his footprints on the sands of cooperative effort.

Served A.I.C. as First Chairman

In addition to being an organizer and manager of NEMPA, Richard Pattee was a leader in establishing the National Milk Producers Federation and the American Institute of Cooperation, which he served as its first Chairman. His deep interest in the need for the Institute and his appreciation of what it could do for the benefit of agriculture and the whole economy is reflected in many comments throughout the Proceedings of the first Annual Institute. In the opening address he said: "The purpose of the American Institute of Cooperation is to collect and make available accurate information concerning the history and practical application of the principle of cooperation as a business practice, its relation to personal prosperity and to the public welfare."

In a tribute to Mr. Pattee's contributions to the Institute, Dr. Edwin G. Nourse said at the 1932 sessions held at the University of New Hampshire, "Mr. Pattee sensed the distinctive character of the cooperative movement as a protest against the abuse of capitalism which has been growing up in this country. He was reaching forward in his own mind and was helping the rest of us study the essential character of cooperation."

Dr. Nourse has given me this further statement for use in this article:

> While Richard Pattee was clearly a militant leader in the cooperative movement, his leadership was not one of "muscle" merely, but of mind and heart. Though he was a partisan for the hardpressed New England dairy farmer, he saw the problem in terms of economic "justice," not raw power. He was intrigued with cooperative association as a means of protecting the small independent farmer in a day of growing urbanization and the consolidation of distributor corporations. But his chief concern as one of the major architects of the American Institute of Cooperation was to have scholars and practitioners probe deeply into the distinctive nature and possibilities of cooperation as an economic institution and the requirements for its success in general and in the long run, not merely as an emergency device.

A full statement on the "Cooperative Philosophy of Richard Pattee," by Charles W. Holman, then Secretary of the American Institute of Cooperation, and Secretary of the National Milk Producers Federation, was published in the *Cooperative Marketing Journal* of September-October, 1932, when the Richard Pattee Fellowship was established by various New England agricultural organizations "to help qualify young men for intelligent leadership in marketing farm products."

In his statement Mr. Holman said:

Unfortunately, Pattee was cut off from life just at the time when he was becoming a real national figure in the cooperative world. What impact he might have made upon the larger matrix of public consciousness is a matter of speculation, but I am inclined to believe that had he lived a few years longer . . . he would have created a body of literature which would have stamped him as one of the most constructive builders of rural civilization of his day.

Francis W. Peck

by Oren R. Shelley

FRANCIS W. PECK was recognized early as an outstanding agricultural educator and he has devoted his life to the improvement of farm conditions.

Born in St. Paul, Minn., on May 20, 1885, and farm reared, he graduated from the College of Agriculture, University of Minnesota, in 1912. He served on the staff of the college as assistant professor of farm management from 1912 to 1915. He was granted the Master's degree in 1917, and served as associate professor, 1918–1919. He then was a farm economist in the Office of Farm Management, U. S. Department of Agriculture, from 1919 to 1921, when he was appointed Director of Agricultural Extension of the University of Minnesota. He continued in this capacity until 1933. During these years of professional development he prepared a number of bulletins and reports on farm costs of production and on farm organization and management. He became a member of Sigma Xi, Honorary Scientific Fraternity, and served as Secretary of the American Farm Economic Association.

Selected as First Cooperative Bank Commissioner

In 1933, Mr. Peck came to the attention of Henry Morgenthau, Jr., who was then chairman of the Federal Farm Board. When President Roosevelt, in consolidating the various agricultural credit agencies into the Farm Credit Administration, designated Mr. Morgenthau as the Governor of the new Farm Credit Administration, on April 11, 1933, Mr. Morgenthau announced he had selected Mr. Peck as one of his assistants who would have the responsibility of direct supervision over the functions of the Federal Farm Board having to do with assisting farmer cooperative marketing enterprises. On July 6, 1933, President Roosevelt announced that he had named Francis W. Peck, Cooperative Bank Commissioner in the new Farm Credit Administration.

Mr. Morgenthau was appointed Secretary of the Treasury and President Roosevelt then appointed W. I. Myers as the Governor of the Farm Credit Administration. As Cooperative Bank Commissioner, Mr. Peck was one of four commissioners appointed by the President. The other commissioners supervised the work of the Federal Land Banks, the Production Credit Associations, and the Federal Intermediate Credit Banks, respectively. Mr. Peck, along with Mr. Myers, had the responsibility of organizing the new Banks for Cooperatives and seeing to it that these Banks were staffed with top men to head them. Twelve regional Banks for Cooperatives were formed, plus the Central Bank for Cooperatives. Mr. Peck, as Cooperative Bank Commissioner, also served as President of the newly established Central Bank. As Commissioner, however, under the direction of the Governor, Mr. Peck supervised the 12 regional Banks for Cooperatives.

Mr. Peck, on many occasions, has recalled some of the problems confronting him in getting the kind of personnel needed to head the new regional Banks for Cooperatives. Many pressures were put on him politically and otherwise to select favorite persons of certain groups or individuals, but he stood fast and selected men who he felt had the integrity and professional competence and ability to head the new regional Banks. History evidences the keen insight of Mr. Peck in being able to search out and help select the most capable men to head each of the regional Banks for Cooperatives.

Every one of the Banks from the very beginning provided credit services and leadership in cooperative business endeavors that had not been equalled up to that time or since. Each of the Banks has been successful and has grown to a point where all now provide the major amount of borrowed funds used by farmer cooperatives in the United States. Even though there were many attempts to modify the function of the Banks, Mr. Peck stood firm in his conviction that if these Banks were to succeed and provide farmer cooperatives with proper guidance and credit, they would have to be operated on a sound business basis. He was dedicated to carry out the expressed declaration of Congress in enacting the Farm Credit Act of 1933.

Primary Purpose: To Help Borrowers Out of Debt

In a paper Mr. Peck gave in July, 1933, at the meeting of the American Institute of Cooperation held at the State College of Agriculture and Engineering, Raleigh, N. C., he outlined the objectives of the Farm Credit Administration as related to cooperation. Following are some excerpts of the comments he made which are illustrative of his thinking and conviction:

> One of the first objectives of any credit agency should be the attempt to get borrowers out of debt rather than into debt. That is, the primary purpose of any financing operation is constructively to assist the individual or agency in creating a profit from the business operation involved, and through the excess of receipts over expenses develop such current conditions as to be unembarrassed by its borrowed capital. Credit should be effective as well as safe. . . .
>
> Another fundamental objective involves the desire of the Farm Credit Administration to help others to help themselves. In financing, this means assuming only a share of the financial burden. Locally-subscribed capital should be added to borrowed capital to complete the financing of any cooperative . . . .

Mr. Peck pointed out that it was ". . . .the desire to be sympathetic, fair, helpful, sincere in its grower or member interest; patient in its insistence upon sound business methods; reasonable in its consideration of the needs of cooperatives, but firm and insistent upon sound business financing in the belief that it can best serve the permanent development of agriculture with these points of view."

Mr. Peck carried out his responsibilities as the first Cooperative Bank Commissioner forcefully as well as with enthusiasm so as to assure farmers that the Banks for Cooperatives would provide a permanent and assured source of credit for cooperatives operating on a sound business basis. By 1936, Mr. Peck felt that he had accomplished most of the objectives in establishing the Banks for Cooperatives System and returned in January, 1936, to resume his position as Director of Agricultural Extension at the University of Minnesota.

As Land Bank President Helps Farmers Retain Farms

In early 1938, Mr. Peck was asked to come back into the Cooperative Farm Credit System. On February 1, 1938, he started as President of the Federal Land Bank of St. Paul to take over the helm from retiring President, Mr. Roy A. Nelson. Mr. Peck brought to the Bank a sympathetic understanding of the credit problems confronting farmers as they were working out of the great depression. This was a difficult period as thousands of farmers lost their farms through foreclosure and hardships created by a series of drought years, particularly in North Dakota. He was confronted with the dilemma of helping farmers to save their farms and at the same time maintain the soundness of the Bank's operations. Here again he demonstrated his resourcefulness as an outstanding leader in agricultural credit as evidenced by the thousands of loans that were made to help farmers retain their farms and solvency and at the same time permit the Bank to grow and prosper.

In the July 29, 1945, issue of the *St. Paul Pioneer Press,* Dick Wilcox summarized the conditions that existed during Mr. Peck's tenure as President:

> A few years past no one could see any sun peeping through the clouds. Most of the North Dakota land on which the Bank had mortgages had little of value to apply on the principal. Farmers had to be urged to stay on the land. The drought had hit the whole Northwest and especially the Northern Great Plains, but what did the most damage was the low prices. Wheat was selling at not much more than it was worth to haul it to town.
>
> But in the three last years heavy crops and much better prices have enabled most of the farmers to pull out with a considerable amount of money in the bank.
>
> Thus much of the credit for the improved condition must go to the weather and prices, but the policies adopted by the Bank under Mr. Peck's leadership did have much to do with the excellent position the Bank was in to take advantage of the improved situation, with an outcome favorable both to the farmer and to the Bank."

On October 1, 1945, Mr. Peck retired as President and was succeeded by Col. M. D. Avery.

Although Mr. Peck retired as President of the Federal Land Bank of St. Paul, agricultural leaders did not allow him to become inactive. Furthermore, he thrived on challenges to help people. He was appointed Director of the Farm Foundation with headquarters in Chicago. Mr. Peck was well prepared for the position since he was considered one of the nation's outstanding experts on farm management and was deeply interested and sympathetic toward improving the social and economic position of farmers. Mr. Peck headed the Farm Foundation during the period from 1945 to 1953.

Then, in 1953, Secretary of Agriculture Ezra Taft Benson named him as the thirteenth member of the newly created Federal Farm Credit Board that was established under the Farm Credit Act of 1953. Mr. Peck brought to the board his knowledge of the Cooperative Farm Credit System having had the background as an administrator at the Washington level and as the operating head of the Federal Land Bank of St. Paul. He was extremely helpful to the board in giving of his knowledge and relating the tremendous experience that he had in the agricultural field and in farm problems. He represented the Secretary of Agriculture until the end of 1960 when he finally retired.

Mr. Francis W. Peck over the years earned the respect and admiration of all those who came to know him and he stands high among the great agricultural leaders of his time. American agriculture is indeed deeply indebted to him for his leadership and the contributions he made. The Banks for Cooperatives, particularly, and the Cooperative Farm Credit System as a whole in large measure are the fine institutions they are today because of the part Mr. Peck played in helping to shape and guide their destinies.

Mr. and Mrs. Peck currently live at 444 Otis Avenue, St. Paul, Minn., enjoying retirement.[1]

---

[1] While this book was in production, Mr. Peck died on August 18, 1966.

Edmond Adrian Perregaux

by *Willis H. Hayes*

F OR OVER 40 YEARS E. A. Perregaux has helped farmers, citizens, and students further their knowledge of cooperatives.

Perregaux was one of Ed Babcock's students in his famous 1922 Cooperative Marketing Class at Cornell University, and for a time he served on the GLF field force. His doctoral dissertation on the costs and efficiency of feed stores, completed in 1926, provided evidence that feed distribution costs were too high and this evidence enabled the GLF to demonstrate the value of its services.

Perre was born on January 25, 1895, in Mount Bethel, N. J., a son of Swiss parents who came to this country to operate a dairy farm. He moved to Rhode Island with his family at an early age and was reared in that state.

After Army service in World War I, he enrolled in Cornell University. Upon obtaining his Ph.D. degree in 1926 he joined the faculty of the University of Connecticut in 1927 as a professor of agricultural economics and he served in that post until he retired from the university in 1955.

Teaches About Co-ops; Helps Farmers Organize Them

As an instructor he taught undergraduate courses in cooperation and dairy marketing, and as an extensionist he helped farmers in Connecticut organize many successful cooperatives. He became head of the Department of Agricultural Economics in 1941 and was then responsible for the selection of personnel that made research, teaching, and extension a significant aspect of the University of Connecticut's agricultural curriculum. He was not "only" a teacher, nor "only" an administrator.

He found time to serve on the executive committee and was, at one time, president of the New England Institute of Cooperation, which was established in 1927. He also helped organize and was chairman of the Business Management Conference for Poultry Cooperatives, a concern that ultimately became part and parcel of the Northeastern Poultry Producers Council (NEPPCO).

He was instrumental, too, in the founding of a farm credit school at the University of Connecticut, and organized Connecticut's prominent Conference Board of Farm Organizations.

Becomes A.I.C. Land-Grant College Consultant

During a sabbatical absence in the early 1950's Perre also spent a year as a consultant for the American Institute of Cooperation, visiting 33 of the nation's Land-Grant Colleges to discuss and review teaching techniques with other instructors in the field of agricultural cooperation.

He was asked to join the Marshall Plan staff after World War II and went to Europe to assist in the U.S.-sponsored recovery program. So highly regarded were his efforts that he was awarded the "Officer de Merite Agricole" decoration by the French government, a tribute accorded "in recognition of his contribution to French agriculture."

Perre assumed the post of director with Connecticut Milk for Health in 1958. During his five-year tenure he helped encourage the establishment of an annual budget for promoting the use of dairy products in Connecticut. This program gained the support of over 90 percent of the dairymen in the area—a clear indication of the significance of the efforts of its chief protagonist.

Perre has received many tributes, awards, and recognitions. In 1962, he was cited by Alpha chapter of Epsilon Sigma Phi, national extension fraternity, for "outstanding service" as an extensionist in Connecticut. The state's Grange lauded him in 1964 for "outstanding contributions" in the field of agricultural economics, and the Washington chapter of the American Marketing Association acknowledged him in 1963 as a "pioneer" in agricultural marketing. In 1963 he received a plaque from Gamma Sigma Delta, national honorary agricultural fraternity, bearing this inscription, "In grateful recognition of Mr. Perregaux's faithful and devoted service, fruitful ideas and untiring enthusiasm, we wish to thank him for his years of effort in bettering the Connecticut dairy farmer's position in the market place."

Mr. Perregaux's retirement has taken him from agricultural cooperation's active roles, but while he is "resting and relaxing," he can still be counted on to champion that segment of agriculture he has so long served.

Henry C. Peterson

by Merle E. Betts

R ANCHER, BANKER, COOPERATIVE LEADER—these are a
few of the successful careers which have been pursued by
Henry C. Peterson, of Chappell, Nebr.

Henry was born on February 15, 1882, in Iowa during a stopover
while the family was moving by covered wagon from Racine, Wis.,
to the ranch area of Nebraska. Their first home in western Nebraska
was the wagon box with the cloth cover still on it. Later the dwelling
was expanded by digging a cave adjacent to the wagon box and
covering it with boards and soil.

Henry's father, Peter S. Peterson, and his mother, Lena (Hanson)
Peterson, were both born in Denmark and came to the United States
in their youth. Peter Peterson's first job in America was in Chicago
cleaning up debris after the Chicago fire. It was in 1887 that the
family settled in Nebraska.

Henry's early years were spent in western Nebraska where he
learned to ride and rope cattle—both of which he continues to do
at the age of 84. He lived under conditions that have characterized
development of the Old West as one of the pioneer epochs of our
great country. His education was pursued in a little sod schoolhouse
for three months of each year until he reached the age of 17. At
the same time, through practical experience, he was getting "vocational
training" to become a rancher.

One of the memorable events of Henry's boyhood was a family
vacation trip nearly 75 years ago when his parents and the children
returned to Racine, Wis. by covered wagon. The trip required 30
days but greater speed was generated on the return journey which
took only 26 days.

In 1902, he married a girl who lived on a neighboring ranch
and became a full-fledged rancher shortly thereafter when the man
for whom he had been working as a cowpuncher decided to move

to California. The couple lived in a sod house in the early years of their married life. In 1903 the Petersons homesteaded in Garden County. Later the land was sold to one of Henry's brothers.

Rheumatism had bothered him on the ranch and the family thought it would help to get away from the damp climate of the river bottom where the ranch headquarters was located. He moved to Oshkosh, Nebr., in 1909 where he ran for county treasurer of Deuel County and was elected. This meant moving to Chappell, the county seat. He served as county treasurer for five years and started the Chappell State Bank in 1912. He became the executive officer and controlling stockholder. He soon built a reputation as a banker who had a deep interest in people and deserves much credit for the development of the region as an important wheat- and cattle-producing area.

One of the characteristics of Henry Peterson was his ability to come back in the face of adversity. The bank failed in 1931 and later paid out 91 cents on the dollar to depositors. In view of the difficult times prevailing in those depression years of the 30's this was a monumental achievement. Considering the depreciated value of the collateral, many recognized in retrospect that the bank should never have been closed.

Saw Need for Farmer Co-ops to Market Wheat

Although a strong individualist, he could see the need for farmers working together in cooperatives to market wheat in the Western Plains. During the late 1920's and early 1930's, his interest in farmer cooperatives was heightened by service on the board of directors of the Farmers National Grain Company of Chicago, which had been set up by the Federal Farm Board.

He helped organize the Westcentral Cooperative Grain Company and served as its president from 1938 to 1949. Despite early difficulties, Westcentral went on under his leadership to become one of the great regional grain cooperatives in the Midwest, serving thousands of farmers across Nebraska, northwest Kansas, and southwest Iowa. A plaque was presented to Henry in 1949 by the board of directors of Westcentral citing him for wisdom, skill, perseverance and leadership as President of the organization.

In early 1933, when the Banks for Cooperatives were being organized, Henry Peterson was called by the Governor of the Farm Credit Administration to become the first treasurer and vice president of the Omaha Bank for Cooperatives. He moved his family to Omaha and served for three years, until the Bank was well under way.

John E. Eidam, the Bank's first attorney, who currently serves as President, has this to say about Henry Peterson's service to the new Bank:

> H. C. Peterson's good business sense, along with his deep understanding of cooperatives and farm people, was a primary factor in the development of a strong Bank for Cooperatives in Omaha. His ability to concentrate on a problem, gather all the facts, and arrive at a sound decision, made him one of the outstanding treasurers in the Cooperative Bank System.

Henry's love for the open plains was great, and in 1936 he returned to Deuel County and again went into the cattle ranching business. Full of energy and enthusiasm, he wasn't satisfied to settle down to ranching as a single occupation. Shortly after moving to Chappell, he bought an interest in the Chappell and Oshkosh Livestock Commission firms and operated them in partnership for several years.

Transmits Interest in Co-ops to Three Sons

His interest in cooperatives was transmitted to his sons Chester, Walter, and Wayne. All of them have been active members of cooperatives. His second son, Walter W. Peterson, served as manager of the Farmer's Elevator Company at Chappell for 32 years and has been secretary of Westcentral since 1949. He was elected by cooperatives to serve on the Farm Credit Board of Omaha and is also a member of the board of directors of the Central Bank for Cooperatives in Washington, D.C.

Henry still maintains a strong interest in cooperatives although he has not been active in recent years. He is a living tribute to the rugged spirit of the Old West.

One of the windows to Henry Peterson's character is the poetry he has written. Most of the poems are sagas of the plains, picturesquely portraying the spirit of the Old West. Here are some examples:

> There wasn't a fence in the country we knew,
> The West and its people were honest and new.
> The range stretched away to the sky for a lid,
> I am old, but I am glad, that I lived when I did.

Later he wrote. . . .

> When my old soul hunts range and rest
> Beyond the last divide,
> Just plant me in some stretch out west

That's sunny, lone and wide.
Let cattle rub my tombstone down
And coyotes mourn their kin,
Let hawses paw and stomp the mound,
But don't you fence me in.

Henry C. Peterson was tall in the saddle, and tall in the eyes of the countless farm and ranch people who knew him as an early leader in the development of agriculture and farmer cooperatives in the United States.

Crusader for
Happier Rural Living

Clarence Poe

by Manly G. Mann, Jr.

NO OTHER TITLE WOULD BE AS APPROPRIATE for Dr. Clarence Poe as "Crusader" for improved agriculture and happier rural living in the South.

During his 67 years as editor of the South's largest and most influential farm journal, *The Progressive Farmer,* he gave his full support to every movement that held promise of relieving the problems of an impoverished agriculture that had plagued the South since the Civil War.

Clarence Poe was born on a farm in Chatham County, N. C. on January 10, 1881, the son of William B. and Susan (Dismukes) Poe, whom he once described as "plain, hardworking farmer-folk."

Young Poe quickly acquired a love of the land and a compassion for all who till the soil that was to remain with him all his life.

While his own parents were able to maintain a comfortable standard of living at the time, Poe was concerned with the fact that so many farmers were so poor. He felt that the land should be able to provide a higher standard of living.

Poe's education incorporated many sources. At that time, public education in his area was limited to a four-month school term each year. Many rural children didn't even take advantage of that limited amount of schooling, because compulsory attendance was held by many to be "a damnable meddling with control by parents."

His public education was supplemented by study in a private subscription school, but perhaps even more important was his love for reading all the magazines and books he could get his hands on. He was especially fond of agricultural publications.

Recognized Plight of Southern Farmer as Pre-Teenager

While Poe was still a pre-teenager, he already formed ideas within his own mind of why farmers in the South were so poor. First, and foremost, was lack of education. Next, perhaps, was a blind devotion to one-crop farming—cotton. Cotton, at most, was only a five-month business. The remainer of the year the land was not only idle but usually barren and exposed to all the ravages of erosion. A ruinous credit system based on the time-merchant plan, with hidden interest rates running as high as 60 percent per annum, certainly took its toll. The fact that so many farmers were tenants rather than land-owners contributed heavily to the poverty of southern farmers.

But Poe, at the time, also sensed a need for organization among farmers, not only for the purpose of standing up for their rights and their welfare wherever their voices needed to be heard, but also for buying supplies and selling produce.

The severe farm depression that struck while he was still in his early teens left no farmers untouched, including his father.

Out of that depression came the Farmers' Alliance movement. As Poe later said, "I was too young to join the Alliance, but I felt a hearty boyish enthusiasm." And a hearty enthusiasm it was, because he attended every Alliance meeting within a reasonable distance of his home, and he read every word of each issue of the Alliance paper, *The Progressive Farmer*, that was published in Raleigh.

There can be no doubt that his enthusiasm for the Farmers' Alliance was the forerunner of his lifetime support of and devotion for farmer cooperatives and other farm organizations.

When Poe was only 16 he wrote an article supporting improved public education and submitted it to the editor of *The Progressive Farmer*. He ended his letter accompanying the article with these words, "I, too, should like to become an editor someday."

The Progressive Farmer not only published his letter, but the editor requested that he come to Raleigh for an interview. As a result of that interview, he became assistant editor and moved to Raleigh.

Two years later the editor resigned, and at the early age of 18 Poe became editor of *The Progressive Farmer*.

Just prior to his promotion, he had made plans to enter Wake Forest College, which was then located 16 miles from Raleigh.

Among those who influenced his decision to remain in journalism was Josiah W. Bailey, who was then editor of *The Baptist Biblical Recorder*, and who was later to serve his state in the U. S. Senate.

Becomes Editor of "The Progressive Farmer"

When Poe became editor of *The Progressive Farmer*, it was a weekly farm paper with a circulation of 5,000. Today it is the South's largest farm journal (a monthly magazine) with a circulation of nearly one and one-half million copies. It carries more advertising than any other farm journal in America, and it is published in five separate regional editions, completely covering the South.

A few years after he became editor, Poe was able to purchase the publication from its owners. He sold some of the stock to four of his associates and friends, and incorporated the business.

After he purchased the paper he had the following words incorporated into the bylaws:

> . . . The paper should not be only a farm journal, but a farmer's journal—interested in rural mail delivery as well as in cotton growing, in good rural schools, and good country roads as well as in fertilizers and soils. In short, it will be devoted to everything that makes for the uplift or betterment of farm life.

He also announced at the time that *The Progressive Farmer* would be a crusading journal. And a crusading journal, indeed, it was to become under his leadership.

Throughout his long and brilliant career Clarence Poe demonstrated an almost uncanny ability to discern the things that were wrong with southern agriculture, come up with the correct solution, and then write and speak incessantly until action was taken.

Among his many crusades were improved rural education and compulsory school attendance, better rural roads and rural health, a better balance between crop farming and livestock farming for the South, experiment stations and cooperative demonstrations, the county agent system, 4-H and FFA Clubs, more favorable freight rates for the South, better pastures, business-like farm credit for southern farmers, to mention just a few.

In his efforts to make farming in the South a more profitable business, Poe never lost sight of his goal of also making rural living a happier life. In 1906, he employed a home department editor for *The Progressive Farmer*, the first to be employed by any agricultural journal in America. Throughout his career he continued in his efforts to persuade farmers and farm wives to beautify their homes and grounds.

Poe's enthusiasm for farmer cooperatives was ignited during a trip to Europe prior to World War I. He was amazed to find how much cooperatives had helped the farmers of Denmark, France, Ireland, and England.

Sees in Co-ops Antidote for Unfair Practices

He returned home convinced that cooperatives could do as much for the farmers of this country. He was particularly fond of repeating the following quotation from Sir Horace Plunkett: "The greatest result of agricultural cooperation in Ireland is not the profits we have made, but the fact that we have made businessmen out of farmers."

Soon after Poe returned home from Europe he wrote a book, *How Farmers Cooperate and Double Profits*, which has been used as a textbook in cooperative marketing in colleges.

Notwithstanding efforts to diversify, the rural South remained after World War I pretty much a land of cotton. Dr. Poe had long deplored such marketing practices as the "hog round" system under which the buyers paid to farmers only the average price for cotton, although the cotton might be of premium grade and staple length. He also disliked the lack of competition among buyers. Buyers would "take turns" in bidding on a farmer's cotton, on the basis of "I'll bid in the next wagonload, and you can have the one following." The farmer was completely at the mercy of such a system because he didn't know the true worth of his cotton, and often he didn't even know the current market price in his local town, much less the prices quoted on the exchanges.

Poe saw in cooperative marketing a chance to do something for the cotton farmer, and in the tenacious manner that had become his custom he embarked on a writing and speaking campaign that played a major role in the establishment of cotton marketing associations throughout the South in the early 1920's. In his own state he was a charter member of the N. C. Cotton Growers Cooperative Association, and a member of the organization committee that led to its incorporation in 1922.

Poe also gave his full support to Tri-State (N. C., S. C., Va.) Tobacco Cooperative Association which was established at about the same time.

While the Cotton Association, under the recently changed name of Carolinas Cotton Growers Association, is still in successful operation today, the Tri-State Tobacco Association failed within a few years of its establishment. Its inability to make a go of it was due to many factors, the most important being that farmers expected too much from it, and were so disappointed in it when it couldn't provide instant miracles that they deserted it in droves, although they had signed iron-clad contracts.

The failure of Tri-State, and the hundreds of lawsuits against farmers for breaking their contracts, caused, as one could well imagine, the word "co-op" to become a dirty word among many farmers in the area. The cotton cooperative was often referred to as being a "sister cooperative" to Tri-State, although there was no legal connection. So one can well imagine what effect the failure of Tri-State, and the resulting bitterness of farmers, had on this association. The N. C. Cotton Association barely managed to pull through that critical period and to live to the day when the word "co-op" would once again become a decent word that could be used at the family dinner table. And this association might very well not have pulled through if it had not been for the work of one man—Clarence Poe. While he admitted that Tri-State had made certain mistakes, he constantly fought on his editorial page and in meetings for the principle of cooperative marketing and the N. C. Cotton Association in particular. He kept assuring and reassuring his readers and his listeners that the Cotton Association had managed to avoid the mistakes of Tri-State, and that they would have everything to gain and nothing to lose by supporting their cooperative.

Keeps Up Fight to Prove Virtues of Cooperation

In scanning the back issues of *The Progressive Farmer* during those critical times it is almost impossible to find a single weekly issue that did not have at least one editorial or article expounding the virtues of agricultural cooperatives. With the tenacity of a bull dog he stayed in the ring and fought the fight on the side of cooperatives. There can be no doubt that he lost some advertisers and some subscribers during the time, but he was dedicated to a larger cause.

Dr. Poe's service to his state and his nation was not limited to strictly agricultural matters. Among his other areas of service were the following: Chairman of the executive committee of the board of trustees of N. C. State College (now North Carolina State University), 1916–31; member of executive committee of board of trustees of University of North Carolina, 1931–55; member State Board of Agriculture, 1913–31; member Federal Board for Vocational Education, 1936–45; member of National Commission on Hospital Care, 1944–46; member Committee on Health Needs of Nation, 1951–52; member International Development Advisory Board (Rockefeller Commission), 1951–53; president N. C. Conference for Social Service, 1913–15; member State Literature and Historical Commission, 1914–15, and director of N. C. Art Society, 1926–60.

Although Poe did not attend college he often repeated Thomas Carlyle's famous saying: "The true university is a collection of books." Through the use of his own library, as well as college and public libraries, he continued his education throughout his life.

In recognition of his work and his devotion to scholarship he received the following honorary degrees: Litt. D., Wake Forest College, 1914; LL. D., University of North Carolina, 1928; LL. D., Washington College (Md.), 1929; and Sc. D., Clemson College, 1937.

Among the books of which he was the author are the following: *Cotton: Cultivation, Marketing and Manufacture* (with C. W. Burkett); *A Southerner in Europe; Where Half the World Is Waking Up; How Farmers Cooperate and Double Profits; True Tales of the South at War: How Soldiers Fought and Families Lived; Carolina's Courageous Crusaders*, and *My First 80 Years*.

The most appropriate tribute to the life and work of Clarence Poe was his selection as the first member to be admitted to the North Carolina Agricultural Hall of Fame, which was established recently.

G. Harold Powell

by F. R. Wilcox

G. HAROLD POWELL was a scientist with great administrative ability who understood the principles of cooperative marketing. With these talents he guided Sunkist Growers, Inc., then known as California Fruit Growers Exchange, as general manager for almost 10 years during the period from September, 1912, to the time of his death in February, 1922. During this period, which embraced World War I, production of citrus in California increased 50 percent. The Sunkist organization also grew during this period to the point that the organization marketed 76 percent of the total production.

In spite of the heavy work load of his own organization during that period, Mr. Powell found time and energy to work closely with other cooperative organizations and to represent the food industry at the national level.

Mr. Powell was born in Ghent, N. Y., in 1872, and was farm reared. After completing his public school work in that state, he was graduated from Cornell University in 1895 with a B.S. degree and the following year received an M.S. in Agriculture from the same institution. He became known as a horticulturist and devoted the first five years of his post school work to development of the horticultural industry at Delaware Agricultural College.

From 1901 through 1910 he was associated with the U. S. Department of Agriculture. He was constantly given increased responsibilities and finally was Assistant Chief of the Bureau of Plant Industry.

Protective Work Commended; Becomes Sunkist Manager

Because of his outstanding work he was induced to become Secretary-Manager of the Citrus Protective League of California in 1911. Under his direction, but largely due to his personal efforts, the damaging effects to citrus of blue mold fungus was eradicated by improved handling practices. The following year, in recognition of his capabilities and natural aptitude, he was named general manager of the Sunkist organization, with headquarters in Los Angeles, Calif.

In 1913, Powell wrote his well-known treatise on "Cooperation in Agriculture," largely as an outgrowth of his early experience in managing the California Fruit Growers Exchange. This pioneering book, according to one cooperative authority, "did much to set the course for the modern development of cooperative enterprise in agriculture."

During his management of Sunkist there was great progress made in the handling, storage, and shipping of citrus fruit. Consequently, producers, trade, and consumers became aware of the changes and there was established a confidence in the quality of this product, which has lasted until the present time. Losses of fruit through decay and through other means were greatly reduced, to the great benefit of producers and consumers. Mr. Powell understood how to attack such problems, beginning at the orchard and carrying through to the retail store. He was untiring in his efforts to improve quality.

Excerpts from his associates indicate not only his understanding of physical problems relating to the handling of commodities, but also his understanding of people. One of these associates stated that Mr. Powell "had a way of showing us his confidence that inspired us to make an effort to deserve it."

The reputation and work of Mr. Powell, even during this busy period, was not confined to California and Arizona because his services were sought at the national level. During World War I, the U. S. Food Administrator, Honorable Herbert Hoover, called on Mr. Powell to take charge of the distribution of a large part of food during the war period. Mr. Hoover commented on his work as follows:

> The importance of his services cannot be measured because it is impossible to reconstruct the problems and difficulties in the setting of those difficult times in which he served."

This is only one of his services performed on a national basis by Mr. Powell that typifies his leadership. In addition he served the State of California and the Southern California area by actively participating in the Chamber of Commerce, the University of California, the All Year Club and many others. History records that in all of these activities he was a leader and his judgment had the respect of all of those with whom he worked.

Powell's Practical Business Approach Praised

In 1932, at the annual meeting of the American Institute of Cooperation, held at the University of New Hampshire, Charles W. Holman, Secretary of the Institute, paid tribute to Powell as one who had

made an "impress upon the character of our agricultural institutions."
He said, "The thoughts and practices of G. Harold Powell gave a
practical turn and business standards to the cooperative movement."
At this same meeting Dr. Edwin G. Nourse said:

> Mr. Powell did an enormous service to the cooperative move-
> ment, by expressing in persuasive, businesslike terms the distinc-
> tive character and the distinctive ideals of cooperation as a
> different form of business. He was a businessman and he expressed
> that in a way that businessmen understood.

Mr. Powell left many valuable documents for those who have in
later years become interested in the fruit industry and in cooperative
marketing. One of these, *The Fundamental Principles of Cooperation
in Agriculture*, prepared as a circular for the University of California
in 1914 and revised in 1920, has long stood as "a classic statement of
cooperative fundamentals." His bulletins covering the growing, transportation, and storage of fruit are still read by students and persons
who are actively engaged in this industry.

Agricultural cooperation is indebted to this man for the contribution
which he made and those who had the privilege of knowing him had
their lives enriched because he was in the true sense a great man.

H. B. Price

by Wendell C. Binkley

G ENTLEMAN—SCHOLAR—RESEARCHER—TEACHER—AD-
MINISTRATOR. These terms take on special significance when
linked with the name of Dr. H. B. Price for the thousands who know
him as a friend, professional colleague or teacher.

Dr. Price's effective leadership in cooperative research and teaching
during the most active period of cooperative development in the
United States, when reviewed, helps any student of cooperatives
better understand the tremendous developments which have occurred
in the United States in a relatively short period of time, and also provides insights into the intellectual leadership which has been instrumental in helping shape these developments.

Hugh Bruce Price was born in 1888 at Tulare in the Dakota Territory, in the homeland of the Sioux Indians—of Big Foot, Kicking
Bear, and Sitting Bull, one year before South Dakota became a state.
Famous "Custer's Last Stand" occurred only 12 years earlier, and the
last warfare between the Indians and whites occurred two years after
Price was born, as did also the passage of the Sherman Act which
was to hold real significance in the development of the legal status
of farmer cooperatives.

Graduating from the University of Wisconsin in 1914, Price received his M.A. from the University of Minnesota in 1916, and his
Ph.D. from Yale University in 1921. In addition to publishing one
book on marketing farm products which represented a comprehensive
study of the marketing organizations and functions for all major agri-
cultural commodities sold on the Minneapolis and St. Paul markets,
Price has authored hundreds of scholarly articles appearing in the
*Journal of Farm Economics, American Economic Review, Annals of
American Academy of Political and Social Science, Proceedings of the
International Conference of Agricultural Economists,* bulletins of the
Social Science Research Council, and publications of the American
Institute of Cooperation.

Within the field of his continuing primary interest of research, Dr. Price has personally authored, or co-authored, 10 or more bulletins published by the University of Minnesota. The importance, timeliness, and quality of these, plus the evidence of their influence on the nature and progress of cooperative developments, especially in grain marketing and dairy products marketing during the most dynamic period in such developments, and literally at the heart of such developments in Minnesota from 1921 to 1929, warrant additional comments later.

Interest in Tobacco Co-ops Began in 1929

Coming to the University of Kentucky in 1929, Price became head of the department then called Markets and Rural Finance. It was here that his interest in tobacco cooperatives developed and intensified, but not to the exclusion of broad research interests in marketing, including other cooperative marketing. In addition to his administrative and teaching responsibilities in his new position, Price immediately became actively involved in research out of which came numerous research bulletins covering a wide range of interest to farmers, to agriculture, and to cooperatives. These, of which he was either author or coauthor, included studies of agricultural credit, farm real estate taxes, the organization and management of the Louisville Fruit and Vegetable Market, the organization and management of the largest cooperative milk producers association in Kentucky, the tobacco auction markets of Kentucky, farmers' cooperative fire insurance companies in Kentucky, and an over-all survey of the total scope of formal cooperative business efforts by Kentucky farmers.

Evidence of Price's deep commitment to sound research in an admittedly challenging field of exploration is to be found in the no less than seven articles on research methods in agricultural economics which he prepared for publication in the bulletins of the Social Science Research Council in the relatively short period of six years from 1928 through 1933. These ranged from "Analysis of Financial Aspects of Local Grain Elevator Organization and Operation," to "Effect of Motor Trucking upon Methods of Transportation" "Improvement of Quality and Standardization of Products by Cooperatives," "Cooperative Aspects of Local Selling Units," and even included an early exploration of the possibilities and limitations of "Using Commercial Audits as Sources of Data" for research purposes in studying cooperative business organizations.

Makes Valuable Contributions to First A.I.C. Institutes

During the early years of the American Institute of Cooperation, beginning in 1925, when the annual summer "Institutes" were of four weeks duration, Dr. Price was both a teacher and student, as were others whose names are well-known for having provided the real intellectual and organizational leadership for cooperatives during a critically important time in the total development.

For example, in 1926, at the second summer meeting of the American Institute of Cooperation, Price drew on his research studies of local farmers' elevators in Minnesota to present two of the important papers on cooperative grain marketing. One dealt with the "Business Setup of Farmers' Elevators," and not only provided research-based information, but also offered suggestions for improvements. The other, dealing with "Management Problems of Local Farmers' Elevators" did likewise, including the offering of specific suggestions for improvement of management—which might well be read by students of cooperative management today, and for others than managers of cooperative elevators.

Again, in 1927, at the third annual summer institute of the American Institute of Cooperation, Price presented and discussed a paper on "Group Management for Farmers' Elevators." Here he drew on his continuing concern with, and study of, how to gradually integrate the business functions of local cooperatives. In his scholarly and forthright manner he presented the discussion as an "inquiry into the nature of the services that such an overhead organization may give local elevators . . . because it seems to be the next step in the logical development of local cooperative grain marketing."

Here also, Dr. Price clearly stated his personal philosophy with regard to the sound development of cooperatives in these words: "For history teaches us that evolution is the most certain and the least costly road to economic progress." He clearly and correctly identified, in advance, the "next step in the farmer cooperative elevator movement . . .," based on the stated hypothesis that "grain producers have faith in their farmers' elevators after 50 years of experience," and also promised disappointment to those who were looking for large further immediate gains by adoption of the recommendations. Interestingly, Price's recommendations here were also in part the result of his studies of similar developments in the cooperative marketing of dairy products, and specifically of some of his studies of similar functions performed by Land O'Lakes for its local cooperatives in the early stages of that development.

It seems significant that in 1927, while he was engaged with other scholars of national repute in studying and trying to anticipate the next stages in the sound development of cooperative grain elevators, of dairy products marketing and of other specialized cooperatives, he also edited the one book of his life which represented a more or less "across the board" approach to examining and making recommendations for the improvement of all the marketing organizations in the St. Paul-Minneapolis market for all major agricultural commodities marketed there, regardless of whether or not or to what extent such were cooperative in nature. The book represented the work of many scholars at the University of Minnesota who had conducted a series of seminars on the topic.

Makes Scholarly Study on Future for Tobacco Co-ops

Dr. Price's remarkable ability to rapidly acquaint himself with the relevant facts regarding any marketing or cooperative development, and his continuing insistence on the importance of true historical perspective in understanding any such situation is typified in his presentation and discussion as one of the instructors at the 1934 summer institute of the American Institute of Cooperation. At this 10th summer meeting, Price, still relatively new in Kentucky, discussed "What Future for Tobacco Cooperatives?" Here he carefully identified and examined the factors influencing the uncertainty and the generally unsatisfactory system of marketing tobacco, including a penetrating analysis of the then three different approaches which tobacco farmers had attempted, in turn, to use in their efforts to deal with the problems cooperatively, beginning in 1904. His comments were direct, critically analytical, and even today this one paper is no doubt the single best scholarly presentation on the subject. In studying the paper, one gets the impression that Price was rather painfully aware of the fact that the "pattern" of cooperative tobacco marketing efforts in Kentucky offered striking contrasts to both his earlier experiences in the study of cooperatives in Minnesota, and also challenged his philosophy as to the orderly and "evolutionary" development of cooperative marketing efforts.

No brief discussion of the contributions of H. B. Price to sound cooperative developments in the United States can do more than highlight a few of his contributions, and the selection of these must inevitably reflect the judgment and perhaps the bias of the writer. Direct contributions of the sort herein mentioned briefly represent such an infinitesimally small part of Dr. Price's contributions that one must at least mention his contributions in the superior teaching of literally thousands of students, both graduate and undergraduate, in a wide variety of subjects including basic economics, agricultural policy, agricultural prices, marketing, research methods, in addition to cooperatives.

Teachings Have Far-Reaching Influence on Co-op Executives

Just to enumerate the key executives of various cooperatives all over the United States who owe their initial interest in cooperatives to having been students of Dr. Price, were this possible, would provide additional evidence of his far-ranging contributions. Important leaders in academic work, including those engaged in research and teaching on cooperatives, admitting to the influence of Dr. Price on their choice of professional careers adds to the evidence. Price himself would, however, insist that he owes much to the time, place, and the circumstances, including the forceful intellectual and organizational leaders with whom he was privileged to associate during the most dynamic period in agricultural cooperative development in the United States. To hazard mentioning any of these here would pose the problem of at what point to end the list.

At the University of Kentucky, where Dr. H. B. Price is actively engaged in tobacco marketing research, albeit at a more leisurely pace than in some of his former years, there exists a "Statement of Policy on Cooperation" which represents the official policy statement of the University of Kentucky. Price, as the formulator of this policy statement which was initially announced by Dr. Thomas Poe Cooper, in 1945, as Dean and Director of the College of Agriculture and Home Economics, captured in the policy statement part of his sustaining personal philosophy and position as an educator in institutions of higher learning having both responsibilities and opportunities to help farmers help themselves through cooperatively organized business efforts.

This policy statement, adopted at a time when increased emphasis was being placed on cooperative purchasing efforts by farmers throughout the nation, has stood the test of time—has been reaffirmed by each succeeding administrator at the University of Kentucky—and has been carefully reviewed by key administrators in many other Land-Grant Universities as they coped with the challenge of a "position" relative to cooperative work. One brief and partial quotation from this policy statement follows:

> Thus, it is the policy of the College of Agriculture and Home Economics to include cooperation as part of a comprehensive

program of research, teaching and extension. . . . The College serves farm people and others in all forms of business enterprise. In including cooperation in its plan of work, the College is mindful of the small size of the individual farm enterprise and the competitive disadvantage of the farmer in an increasingly complex economy when individually selling farm products or when purchasing supplies and services. It recognizes that the modern cooperative association, either large or small, is consistent with the traditional desires of people to solve problems through mutual self-help while using modern corporate organization and business practice.

Edward Newton Puckett

by Roy Bender

EDWARD NEWTON PUCKETT was born September 30, 1879, in Guion, Izard County, Ark. He was educated in Arkansas Schools. When he finished high school at age 16, the superintendent suggested that he take the Teachers Examination just for practice. He decided to do so and was surprised that he passed the examination and was issued a Teachers Certificate. The superintendent then gave him a job teaching school and he taught for two years. Shortly after that he was married and for several years operated a small farm in Arkansas.

In 1909, he loaded his wife and children in a wagon and moved to Ochiltree County in the Panhandle of Texas. They located on a farm near the present site of Perryton, Tex. In addition to farming he operated a freight line from the railroad point of Canadian, Tex., to various inland points in the Panhandle. He continued this type of operation until 1916 at which time he sold out and moved his family back to Arkansas and was associated with his brother in operating a general merchandise store and post office. In 1918, he made a trip back to the Texas Panhandle to see about the opportunity of relocating in that area as the wide open spaces appealed to him.

Leaders of New Co-op Select Puckett as Manager

The farmers in the vicinity of Perryton, with the assistance of C. O. Drayton, national president of the Farmers Equity Union of Greenville, Ill., had just been successful in organizing the Perryton Equity Exchange, to cooperatively market the grain of the area. E. N., as he was known by everyone who knew him, was a born cooperator. The leaders in this cooperative undertaking knew his background and they asked him to take the management of their new cooperative organization. E. N. was the type of man who always liked a challenge, hence he readily accepted the position and moved his family to Perryton.

While his new position was a real challenge, he never seemed to worry. He was a deeply religious man and had as his motto, "All things are possible with God." He commenced each day with a devotional and prayer bringing his family about him at the breakfast table for that purpose.

These were very difficult times in the Texas Panhandle, both on the farm and in the marketing of grain. In addition to his deep faith in God, E. N. had an exceptional characteristic and that was when he started out on a program he felt was right and that he had God's blessing, he would never turn back. He never did know what the word "defeat" meant. He always said, "Make God your every-day partner. Talk to Him and listen to Him and He will see you through to success on any project that is right and worthwhile."

E. N. was attracted to cooperative work because he felt, and was convinced, that it was a way to be of service to his fellowman. From early childhood he demonstrated exceptional ability in many ways but when he reached manhood it was apparent that he had outstanding ability to conduct business in a profitable way and at the same time in an honest and above-the-board manner. He soon proved himself to the grain farmers of the Perryton area and as a result these farmers rallied to the support of their new cooperative and it experienced remarkable success, both in net savings and outstanding service. E. N. was always quick to give God the credit for any success of any adventure that he was connected with.

Four Local Co-ops See Need to Merge; Puckett Becomes Manager

In addition to the Perryton Equity Exchange, during the early 20's, cooperative elevators were organized at Darrouzett, Booker, and Spearman on the Spearman Branch of the Santa Fe Railroad that runs through the Panhandle. These cooperative elevators, which were separately owned and operated at these four points, were handicapped because they had no marketing facilities in the grain centers. Hence, they had no option other than during harvest to ship the grain to the grain centers and dump it on the market because they did not have local facilities adequate to hold it for more orderly marketing.

The leaders in these respective cooperatives recognized the problem and were diligently seeking some ways to improve their marketing position. A number of meetings were held and in 1925, the stockholders of the cooperative elevators at Perryton, Spearman, Darrouzett, and Booker, approved the organization of Union Equity Exchange and incorporated it under the Warehouse and Marketing

Laws of the state of Texas. The authorized capital was $5,000. Additional meetings were held and it was decided to select Enid, Okla., as the location for their central marketing agency. Enid was selected because of its good rail connections and transit privileges.

The position as manager was offered to the local managers of these four cooperatives, with the result that E. N. was readily selected. He was so passionately imbued with the idea, and felt so keenly the necessity for establishing such an agency to help with the marketing of the grain in the Panhandle area, that he promptly accepted the position.

In June, 1926, he opened the office in Enid with $3,260 paid-in capital with which to start the business. In the beginning he operated only as a broker, marketing the grain for its member organizations in the Panhandle. In 1927, there was almost a complete crop failure in the Panhandle and in his usual resourceful manner, the Agency started buying and selling the grain of any cooperative elevator organization that desired to sell to them. Due to E. N.'s exceptional business ability and honest dealing the Agency operated quite successfully and the cooperative elevators at Follett, Tex., and also at Carmen and Meno, Okla., became stockholders during 1927 and 1928.

Early in 1929 the Farmers Cooperative Grain Dealers Association of Oklahoma decided to provide a Cooperative Grain Sales Agency through which their membership could market their grain on a voluntary basis. The directors of both the Association and Union Equity Exchange were of the opinion that there should not be two such organizations operating in the same territory on a competitive basis.

A plan was easily worked out whereby the Union Equity Exchange was to be the official grain sales agency for the Association, and the Association would continue as the cooperative service association. The offices of the two organizations were moved together in June, 1929, and in October, 1929, Union Equity Exchange was reorganized and incorporated under Oklahoma Cooperative Laws with the name Union Equity Cooperative Exchange.

Puckett Attributes Equity Success to God's Help

The development of Union Equity Cooperative Exchange, under the management and leadership of E. N. Puckett is a success story far beyond his fondest dreams and those of his associates, beginning with $3,260 paid-in capital, and with a net worth of over $12 million when he passed away. The first grain storage elevator of 100,000 bushels was built in Enid in 1930, with almost continual building until his death in 1954 to a total of 50,300,000 bushels. He lived to see the first unit of the last elevator completed. The number of stockholder organizations increased from the original four to over 100 and the volume increased comparatively.

Early in the history of Union Equity, a policy was established to start each business day with a short devotional period on company time. All office employees came together in the offices and the elevator employees at their respective elevators, for scripture reading and a prayer before going to work. One of the office employees remarked, "These morning devotionals are invaluable. We seem to get an inner urge of power and energy that stays with us throughout the day." One of the elevator employees said, "I seldom went to church before, but these morning devotionals do something to you. You feel like God is with you all day and you are doing something really important like helping Him feed the world."

Mr. Puckett often remarked that God's will has been our guiding light in the formation and development of Union Equity. He, for a long time, had been critical of the multiple cylinder type grain elevator as a wasteful method of construction. As a result he decided to do something about it. One night in a hotel room he was praying and asking God how the new elevators that were being planned to be constructed in Enid should be built. He stated that he looked down at the floor and there God had given him the answer. There was a multiple hexagon design right on the rug, the very geometrical design God and nature had made for beehives. He immediately reported his findings to the construction engineers and all Union Equity elevators constructed following that date were built on the hexagon plan at a great savings of construction costs over the cost of the conventional design. The hexagon design of construction has become extensively used throughout the nation.

Mr. Puckett, in addition to being deeply religious, was indeed a benevolent man. He was always helping those in need. He felt deeply that if everyone would read his Bible more and try to follow its teachings, most of the world's problems would be solved. He was almost a one-man Gideon Society. During one five-year period he personally paid for and gave away more than $5,000 worth of Bibles. In addition he persuaded his board of directors that it was good business practice to spread the Gospel of the Golden Rule by distributing Bibles among those with whom they did business. Bibles were given to all types of people, cynical lawyers, hard-headed railroad presidents, bank presidents, people of wealth and people in despair; always with the admonition, "It's the greatest book in the world but it's of no use to you if you don't read it."

While Mr. Puckett was a man of deep religious convictions, he recognized the demanding responsibility of good citizenship and good government. Those who had the privilege of working closely with him not only loved him but were inspired and helped by his example for good.

Truly he was a man who walked and talked with God.

The Champion of
Cooperative Livestock Marketing

Cortes Gilbert Randell

by Raymond L. Fox

FOR MORE THAN 40 YEARS the name "Gib" Randell has been linked with cooperative livestock marketing. His influence in building strong and effective livestock marketing cooperatives is reflected not only in the livestock marketing cooperatives of this country but it extends into Canada, South America, and Africa.

Cortes Gilbert Randell was born on a farm near Lawrenceburg, in Southern Indiana, in 1896, and he grew up in a community where cooperation came naturally to the people. He recently described his rural background to me in these words:

> On our farm we produced a wide variety of products. We tapped our maple trees and made maple syrup. We grew our own cane and processed our sorghum. We had our own horse power to grind grain for home and feed consumption; our own forge and blacksmith shop; our own sawmill; and a small lake where we put up ice for the whole community.
>
> We raised cattle, hogs, and sheep and slaughtered them and sold the meat at retail. We had our own large stone smoke-house. We smoked our pork products for 6 weeks using hickory and apple wood. We had the best meat and sausage in the country.
>
> A fact that is often lost sight of is that practically every major job on our farms and most projects in our rural communities 60 years ago were carried on cooperatively. It was a way of life. We had our threshing rings where we exchanged labor, our barn raisings, and our cornhusking bees.

Knowledge of, Interest in Co-ops Started When Young Boy

When Gib was nine years old the farmers of his community built their own mutual telephone system. Gib helped cut locust posts, skinned them, dug the holes, and helped put up the insulators and strung the wire. It gave him and his family a thrill to be able to telephone a neighbor or a doctor instead of getting on a horse and riding for help.

419

In 1907, when Gib was 11 years old, he helped build a cooperative creamery for the community. Plans were obtained from Purdue University and the farmers built the plant and equipped it, and then hired a buttermaker from Purdue to operate it.

With this background, it was only logical that Gib was attracted to a career of cooperative service.

Gib was always energetic. He ran a painting and decorating business while in Lawrenceburg High School, and raised potatoes in a big potato project.

He entered Purdue University in 1915 after graduation from high school. There he joined the National Guard and soon afterwards was sent to the Mexican border as a gunner. Back at Purdue he played on the Freshman football varsity team, but crippled his knee so he couldn't continue football. However, even with his bad knee he got into the Army briefly before the war closed in October, 1918.

During the summer of 1919 Gib worked with the Nebraska Sub-Experiment Station at North Platte. Here he got some county agent experience.

After graduating from Purdue in 1920 Gib got a job running a ranch in Kansas. Then, in 1921 and 1922, he served as agricultural director of schools at Marysville, Kan. Here he helped build a municipal feed and transit yard.

In June, 1923, he joined the Producers Livestock Commission Company when it opened in Oklahoma City. The problems of this organization, in endeavoring to provide service on the Oklahoma City Market, opened Gib's eyes to the nature of the opposition that confronted livestock producers in establishing their own commission firms. He soon came to realize that producers must have strong cooperatives if they were to improve their position in marketing livestock. A rigid boycott by commission agencies, dealers, and traders, who refused to purchase farmers' livestock handled by the cooperative, made it necessary to cease operations before a federal indictment could be secured against the boycotters under the P & S Act.

Experiences Convince Him of Need for Strong Co-ops

This experience convinced Gib that the livestock producers could not rely on the government to maintain open and competitive markets. The only solution seemed to be the building of a strong and adequately financed system of livestock marketing cooperatives.

Gib realized that he needed further basic training to improve his capacity to cope with this problem and in the fall of 1923 he was able to obtain a legislative scholarship at the University of Wisconsin for graduate work. By working day and night he was able to complete the work for a Master's degree in June, 1924, and immediately afterwards he accepted a position as Assistant Manager of the Producers Commission Association at Kansas City. Here he found the same forces opposing cooperatives that had forced the collapse of the Producers at Oklahoma City.

This experience intensified his feeling that the development of a strong national livestock association was necessary to combat boycotts and provide producers with the services they needed.

Gib's work and training in livestock marketing made him the logical person to head up the Livestock Section of the Division of Cooperative Marketing when it was set up in 1926, and in this new position he immediately began a survey to find out the strengths and weaknesses of livestock marketing associations. The results of this study were published in 1928 as USDA Technical Bulletin 57, *Co-operative Marketing of Livestock in the United States by Terminal Associations.* This important study provided a blueprint for the future development of a national livestock marketing association.

The opportunity to carry this program forward came with the establishment of the Federal Farm Board in 1929 which was provided with a revolving fund of $500 million to help promote effective cooperatives along with its other functions. With the transfer of the Division of Cooperative Marketing to the Federal Farm Board, Gib was soon at work for the Board developing articles and bylaws for a National Livestock Marketing Association.

After various meetings the plans for the organization were approved on May 10, 1930, and the association began business on July 14, 1930. The directors of the National immediately voted to make Gib the General Manager, but Alexander Legge, Chairman of the Farm Board, took the position that this would give the impression that Randell— or "Bully Beef," as he always called him—had built a job for himself, and so he refused to permit it. However, Gib was authorized to do everything possible to assist the new organization in a research and advisory capacity.

During the next few years the National established itself as a strong force in livestock marketing. With Gib's direct encouragement, an order-buying service, a National Feeder and Finance Corporation, along with a number of regional livestock credit cooperatives were developed. This proved invaluable in building an effective livestock marketing service on a national basis.

Gib also took a leading role in the establishment of the National Wool Marketing Corporation which was incorporated in late 1929, and its subsidiary, the National Wool Credit Company.

It is of considerable significance that, of all of the national marketing agencies organized under Farm Board auspices, only the National Livestock and Wool Associations, in modified form, have survived down to the present.

Becomes Head of FCS Livestock and Wool Branch

When the work of the Federal Farm Board with cooperatives was taken over by the Farm Credit Administration in 1933, Gib continued in charge of the Livestock and Wool Section of the Cooperative Division, and when this program of work became the Farmer Cooperative Service of the U. S. Department of Agriculture in 1953, Gib took the title, Chief of the Livestock and Wool Branch, and he continued as Chief until his retirement in July, 1962, to engage in management consultant activities.

Gib's work with livestock and wool cooperatives extended to every part of the nation, and whenever a group of livestock producers needed help on a livestock or wool marketing problem, he or members of his staff were there carrying on research or providing advisory services.

One of his outstanding jobs was to help a group of Michigan livestock producers learn how to operate a cooperative livestock packing company, which functioned for years under the name, Detroit Packing Company. This became a pilot operation for livestock processing. It was here that tests were run to determine the advantage of meat-type hogs, and this experience gave the U.S.D.A. the basic data for new grades of hogs.

There was no information available on formulas for sausage, smoked meat, etc., and these had to be learned the hard way through experimentation in the plant. Randell was never daunted by lack of knowledge or experience for he knew that he could find ways to get it. He gradually built up a fund of information that could be used on almost any problem confronting livestock producers.

All of this experience and know-how gained in helping the Detroit Packing Company to establish itself was put to work in helping farmers in the Shenandoah Valley set-up—the Shen Valley Meat Packers—at the end of World War II. After a difficult period this organization got on its feet, and has long provided a needed service.

During World War II when leather was in critical supply, Randell was requested to take charge of the national hide and leather conservation program for the government and also head up the production of shearlings to make flying suits for our aviators.

Gib has been a strong force in encouraging cooperatives to follow good management, financing, and membership practices. Many cooperatives throughout the United States are indebted to him for technical assistance, advice, and that unique personal quality—called leadership. His indomitable spirit has infected many who needed to build up their confidence in themselves.

Assists Many Foreign Countries

Even before Gib retired from government service he had become active in helping improve agricultural conditions in foreign countries. Much of this work was done on his own annual leave periods. His first foreign job was done in Colombia, in 1945, where he helped set up elevators and potato storage facilities. In 1951, he made a comprehensive study of livestock production, marketing and processing in Ethiopia. In 1953, he returned to Colombia to develop a livestock producing, financing, transportation, marketing, and processing program.

In 1957, Randell worked out a program to assist a concern in developing a large meat plant for Paraguay and Argentina. Other similar work followed in Colombia, Venezuela, Honduras, and Uruguay.

Gib has received many honors during his long and varied career. Included among these is his election to membership in Alpha Zeta, national honorary agricultural fraternity; and in Phi Delta Kappa, national honorary educational fraternity. He received an award in 1952 from the Producers Livestock Association, Columbus, Ohio, for national and international service to the livestock and meat packing industries. In 1958, he received the U.S.D.A. Superior Service Award "for major contributions in organizing and developing livestock marketing and processing cooperatives and for posing solutions to numerous problems that have resulted in outstanding benefits to livestock producers and their cooperatives."

Gib's colleagues know him as a man of joyous, indubitable courage and spirit, a humanitarian who loves his fellowman, and a fighter against injustice wherever found. He has marked cooperative livestock marketing with some of his own sterling character.

Quentin Reynolds

by Kenneth Hinshaw

IN THE BACKYARD of a Montclair, N.J., lawyer's home Quentin Reynolds had his first taste of farming. During his boyhood, the future general manager of the Eastern States Farmers' Exchange defied the residential traditions of his neighborhood by indulging in the chicken business. It was not a large indulgence, but it was enough to make the poultry dealers over in nearby New York City familiar with a certain one-hen-at-a-time buyer. A critical buyer, too, who would insist on having just that certain hen from somewhere in the whole stack of crates piled high in the market place.

One good story of those days is the one about Quentin's newly purchased Black Minorca hen. He marched into his father's law offices with the black hen in a cardboard box and he parked her, box and all, down among the law books. Just as he was leaving with his father at the close of the day's business one of the members of the firm jokingly asked to see the hen. When Quentin displayed his purchase, lo! there was an egg as well as a hen.

Quentin was the youngest of the lawyer's four sons. One of his father's legal assignments took the family to Italy for about seven years and it was in the ancient city of Florence in the year 1890 that Quentin was born. Older brothers called him "Babe," which never was very appropriate for the tall and sturdy stature he developed—but the nicknomer stuck among his associates even through his top executive days.

As befits the traditions of success in the profession of law, the Reynolds' sons were schooled in the public classes of their home town; then "prepped" at Andover and later graduated from Harvard.

There Quentin's six-foot chassis equipped with "over-drive" and a custom built body of the leanest, toughest muscles got an annual spring showing in the crew shells on the River Charles. For three years he rowed bow on the varsity, was captain and competed in all the races of the crew during his three years of eligibility.

First Job with Small New York Ad Agency

Young Reynolds found a market for his Harvard economics first in a small advertising agency in New York City. Three years later he was selling space on the advertising staff of the mellow old *Farm and Fireside.* Always an idealist, he had his first cold world disillusionment over a food account. This was after he married Sylvia Crowell, the daughter of Thomas Crowell, the book publisher, and the Reynolds' baby daughter was in the cereal food stage.

Quentin Reynolds read the advertising that filled the space he sold. Some of this copy glorified a by-product food—and the Reynolds baby got her chance to show how sincerely the copywriters served their public. She ate the stuff and thrived.

Reynolds buoyantly reported his first-hand testimonial to the food company's representative, and then it happened! Instead of beaming proudly at this show of interest in his company's goods, the man first looked shocked and then exclaimed something like: "Great Scot! You're not feeding that STUFF to *your* kid!"

Other disillusionments followed until Quentin Reynolds was just plain sick of what he began to think was a world of make-believe, sick enough to pack up kit and kaboodle and seek a more wholesome world in up-country New England—on a farm! The place was near Littleton, N. H. This was in 1920, about the time the country was side-slipping into the postwar economic air pockets—and you may remember farmers felt these jolts first and hard.

The young woman who found herself the wife of a Harvard farmer was a tall, pleasant person whose girlhood was in an environment of culture and sophistication. She was a Vassar College graduate— and how many farmers' wives that school can boast is not statistically important, but certainly few of them would have matched Sylvia Reynolds in enthusiasm for becoming the working partner of a man determined to get mud on his boots.

The couple went at farming the hardest of hard ways . . . untrained. And you can be sure, too, that fitting such a couple of North Jersey accents into a community full of Yankee twangs of two centuries nativity was just about as hard as learning to milk 10 Jerseys night and morning with hands softened by years of signing advertising contracts.

There was a little cooperative marketing venture undertaken among the farmers around Littleton to sell their products to summer hotels. To this Reynolds brought his potent stock of idealism, his cooperative friendliness, his backlog of college economics—and his own farm's market-needing products.

Joins Eastern States as Fieldman—Becomes Manager

About this time word was going round that farmers were organizing a regional purchasing association known as the Eastern States Farmers' Exchange. When some of the New Hampshire farmers held a meeting to hear about the new cooperative, Reynolds was there. The enterprise fascinated him and the next step in his agricultural life was to become an Eastern States fieldman. This was in 1923 and in another year the cooperative's management found a place to use more extensively QR's talent for expressing his organization's ideals in print. He was assigned the young cooperative's publicity work, and in 1925 brought forth the first issue of the *Eastern States Cooperator*. As Eastern States grew, so did the scope and significance of this pioneer among American cooperative journals.

When industry bid away the Eastern States general manager in early 1930, QR was made the captain of another crew—the cooperative's fast-growing managerial staff.

The whim of fate that placed QR in charge of Eastern States could be described as something hard to believe . . . but nevertheless very fortunate for all concerned. One can point to many reasons why QR seemed to be an unlikely choice for general manager of a large-scale, vigorously competitive, farmers' business. For instance—

He had the wrong background. He came from another world, a society of prosperous, well educated, sophisticated citizenry who spoke a language one just didn't hear in the up-country cow barns.

He was exactly the opposite of the hard-boiled, shrewd horse trader type of businessman who was considered most likely to be successful in this period.

Was an Idealist With Many Positive Abilities

He was long on ideals and theories and short on demonstrated ability to master personally any kind of farm enterprise. The type of farm economy that he pictured as ideal—the self-sufficient, free-of-debt homestead—was fast fading from the scene while QR clung to the theory that its revival was the answer to the nation's farm problem.

He opposed the use of credit—except under the most conservative circumstances—by individuals, businesses, and government . . . at a time when credit expansion was having its greatest impact on our economic development.

He wasn't a "joiner." The new general manager of Eastern States was to become the leader of a cooperative association that had been created and kept alive for years by aid from a long list of community spirited clubs, societies, company boards of directors, and busy executives of various enterprises who volunteered their assistance to the fledgling farmers' co-op. By contrast, QR rejected membership in service clubs; opposed the customary practice of supporting community betterment projects with contributions from company treasuries. If the businessmen who contributed their time and money to get Eastern States started had had QR's philosophy, there'd have been no Eastern States for him to manage.

He emphatically didn't like aggressiveness in business. Although he was enough of a realist to recognize that advertising and salesmanship are essential to the success of businesses, he preached that there should be more *customer buymanship* inclined toward austerity instead of affluence. In retrospect, it is rather surprising to note that even though QR's attitude was well-known to his associates, Eastern States grew for 25 years at a pace that is rarely matched by any hell-for-leather volume-seeking business. And the volume charts during most of QR's 25 years rose in spite of many years of Depression and War!

The negative elements in QR's qualifications for management of a booming cooperative, however, were far outweighed by his salient positive qualities.

Perhaps the greatest of these was his genuine sincerity in striving to live a business life that gave more than it received. The bottom had fallen out of the economy when he stepped into his Eastern States responsibilities. His first years as manager were those years "that tried men's souls" . . . a period when men's faith in one another was practically the only resource they had. The sincerity, the reliability, the dedication to helpful service that Quentin Reynolds brought into every Eastern States policy and action gave the cooperative exactly what it needed to convert the vicissitudes of the Depression into a stairway of growth and progress.

People who knew Quentin Reynolds had the greatest respect for his high principles. During the years of his leadership of Eastern States, it was this intangible but confidence-inspiring quality that became the *image* of the cooperative. And no business ever produced a better one!

Reynolds Right Man, Right Place, Right Time

In other times, in other circumstances, QR's dedication to high principles in business might not have motivated his "team" so effectively, and the cooperative's membership, too, might not have been so responsive to sterling product quality and the sternest kind of thrift. And QR's remarkable disregard for the usual business tactics and his abhorrence of hard sell promotion might have so handicapped the cooperative that it could not grow. But all of the dark possibilities that might have occurred in QR's managerial career didn't happen. He was the right man in the right place at the right time.

During the 25 years that QR managed Eastern States, the cooperative grew in volume from $10 million to a high mark of $98 million . . . and its achievements included continuous expansion during the economic stringencies of the Great Depression, a series of large scale increases in services to food producing enterprises during World War II, and the development of a highly capable research program to aid the region's agricultural progress during the adjustments necessary in the postwar years.

In spite of a reluctance to get into activities apart from his position at Eastern States, Reynolds was long recognized as one of the nation's distinguished leaders in farmer cooperative enterprises. In the National Council of Farmer Cooperatives he was an executive committeeman and President; for American Institute of Cooperation, he was a trustee; for the National Planning Association, the New England Council, and the Twentieth Century Fund, he served as director or agricultural advisor.

The story of Quentin Reynolds is unique. He didn't seem to be designed for his job, but he became eminently successful in it. He wasn't the go-getter type, but few businesses ever grew so fast under such adverse circumstances as the one he managed. He wasn't a publicity seeker, but he did indeed become one of the country's great personalities in the field of agricultural businesses and organizations.

The Gadfly
of Cooperation

Frank Robotka

by Richard Phillips

PROFESSOR FRANK ROBOTKA, the gadfly of cooperation—a title given to Frank out of respect and kindness by his good friends among the Canadian cooperative leaders and worn by him with some pride. In a nutshell, the title reflects Frank's persistent and penetrating, yes even annoying, approach to find the real problems and spur cooperative leaders to greater achievement. More than one reader will remember the shock of Frank's blunt approach the first time he received the reply to the usual "Good morning, Frank" of "What's good about it?" This typifies his approach to cooperation—from the Rochdale Principles to the operation of the local cooperative.

In spite of his characteristic approach, Professor Robotka never viewed cooperatives cynically. The welfare and progress of cooperatives have been his sole professional concern. Dating from his boyhood and undergraduate days in Wisconsin and graduate training in economics at the Universities of Minnesota and Chicago, Frank has been a staunch supporter of cooperatives. Beginning in 1920 and throughout his long career as Professor at Iowa State University, he has devoted his life to cooperation. His apparent cynicism from time to time comes from his high standards for cooperatives and his strong desire to see these standards achieved.

Robotka Felt that Co-op Commercial Success Not Enough

Frank has always believed that commercial success for cooperatives is not enough—that there also must be "economic success" and "cooperative success." In his thinking, economic success is the fulfillment by cooperatives of their true economic role, and cooperative success requires fruitful application of a true cooperative structure. None of the three types of success is automatic with achievement of the others; of the three, commercial success is the most common and cooperative success the most rare.

As a student of cooperation, Frank Robotka has been constantly in search for the answers to "Why?" Major examples of these why questions to Frank have been the following:

1. Why should cooperatives follow cooperative principles? e.g., what are the basic economic characteristics about cooperatives that make it consistent for them to follow cooperative principles?
2. Why should patronage refunds be excludable from corporate income tax to the cooperative? e.g., what are the unique economic characteristics of patronage refunds by cooperatives that provide a basis for legal interpretations?
3. Why is revolving fund financing consistent with the economic nature of cooperatives?
4. Why is constant cooperative education so important to cooperative success?
5. Why are true (perfect) cooperatives so hard to find in practice?
6. Why haven't the various disciplines which have application to cooperative problems been more successfully integrated into a common approach to these problems?

Although one may tend to think first of his theoretical contributions to cooperation, Frank was never one to be happy remaining in his Ivory Tower. Through the years his mind has been as active for pondering practical questions as for pondering those of a theoretical nature. His two-match ritual for lighting his much-used pipe applies equally well to both kinds of pondering. This pondering of practical cooperative questions has resulted in big payoff for farmer cooperatives on more than one occasion.

Robotka's "Miracle" Revives and Stabilizes Iowa Co-ops

One such occasion was Professor Robotka's hand in the creation and application of the 1935 Iowa cooperative law. Prior to the enactment of the new law, many cooperatives in the state were in serious difficulty. In the wake of the Great Depression, those organized under the old stock-company law could attract neither the membership nor the volume of business for successful operation. Some had completely lost track of many of their original stockholders, or the heirs thereto. The existing non-stock law under which they might have reorganized was unpopular and in many ways unsuited to the immediate needs, particularly in the case of the farmers' elevators. A miracle was needed which would enable the Iowa cooperatives to pull themselves up by their own economic bootstraps.

Frank conceived this miracle, and together with cooperative leaders and attorneys drafted what was to become the 1935 cooperative law. The provisions of the new law were specific and detailed, and tailored to the needs of the times. Farmers were permitted to subscribe for and earn their membership stock. All patronage refunds were to be placed in a revolving fund and retired on an "oldest first" basis. Funds were to be set aside for cooperative education. Special provisions were made to facilitate reorganization to come under the new law. Specific provisions were included for the formation of federated regional cooperatives.

With the new law on the books, the educational work began. For more than two years Frank worked closely with cooperative leaders and attorneys to help the farmer stock companies reorganize. Sample articles and bylaws were prepared. State-wide and district meetings were conducted. Literature was prepared to explain the new law and its advantages to cooperatives. Educational and planning sessions were held with local boards of directors over the entire state. In the end most of the associations had been reorganized successfully and established on a course of economic recovery. The 1935 law had proven its value. For 25 dynamic years Iowa cooperatives grew and prospered without amendment to this basic enabling law.

In many ways Frank Robotka's story is the story of Iowa cooperatives from 1920 through 1950 and beyond. In the earlier part of this period he was active in helping to form and organize local cooperatives. Then there was the period of major reorganization starting in 1935. In more recent times he was active in helping Iowa cooperatives to add major functions, to organize federated regional cooperatives, and to bring about cooperative mergers and consolidations. He played a major role in the formation of the Iowa Institute of Cooperation.

Strongly Backed Co-op Education Programs

Throughout this period Professor Robotka carried out aggressive programs of cooperative education over the state, usually in close cooperation with regional cooperatives, the Omaha Bank for Cooperatives and, in the more recent years, with the Iowa Institute of Cooperation. Clinics for cooperative directors always were favored activities for Frank, not only because of his dedicated belief in their value, but also because he thoroughly enjoyed working face-to-face with directors. Subjects of discussion for the clinics and other educational activities covered the full range of cooperative topics—distinguishing characteristics, organizational structure, methods of operation, responsibilities of directors and members, control and management, financing, accounting, legal aspects, taxation, history, economic role, public policy, and membership education. Frank was never at a loss to discuss any cooperative topic, and discuss it in depth, whether by pen, from the podium, or from the floor.

Professor Robotka's contributions to practical cooperative problems are by no means limited to those in Iowa. Over the years he has been active in regional and national activities. For many years he was one of the few members from the academic world on the Board of Trustees for the American Institute of Cooperation. The summer institute session of the A.I.C. on the Iowa State College campus in 1937 was one of the highlights of his career. Many of Frank's respected associates—leaders like Dean W. I. Myers, Charles Holman, E. G. Nourse, Ted Shultz, O. B. Jesness, J. R. Barton, B. B. Derrick, Quentin Reynolds, Wilbur Thompson, Harold Hedges, and Joe Knapp —were prominent speakers at the Ames sessions. The name Robotka appeared on that program, and is sprinkled generously through the annals of the A.I.C. Yearbook *American Cooperation* over the years. Even with the editing of side comments, Frank's head-on approach clearly shines through in most of his published papers dealing with practical cooperative problems.

In spite of his many contributions to the practice of cooperation in Iowa and the United States, Frank Robotka probably is best known as a cooperative scholar. His research work, teachings and writings are familiar to students of cooperation around the world. Through the years scholars from abroad have corresponded with him, and some have come to Ames to learn from him.

Frank's students at Iowa State soon learned that as a professor his bark was far worse than his bite. Although a challenging instructor, he always encouraged self-expression and free exchange of ideas. Most students found him easy to communicate with and get to know, both as a scholar and as a person.

On the campus and off, Frank would rather discuss cooperation than any other subject. However, he never turned down a chance for a general bull session or a friendly poker game with his students and colleagues. He enjoyed the added personality color that derived from driving the same car for more than 20 years, from his fur-collared coat and from the small burned holes in his conservative suit and tie.

Frank rarely took a vacation during his long active tenure at Iowa State University. Most of his free time was devoted to his home in Ames. His wife, Helen, was a semi-invalid for many years and Frank served as both nurse and housekeeper for her. He pursued his hobby of flower gardening with vigor, and his beds produced champion blossoms from early spring until late fall. He was an early dark room enthusiast, and many will recall his beautiful hand-done Christmas cards portraying college life.

Impact Was on Men's Minds

The full impact of a true scholar of cooperation such as Frank Robotka is difficult to measure, even to comprehend, because much of the impact comes through the influence on other men's minds. Frank's thinking and his penetrating way of putting his thoughts forward surely have helped shape the thinking of many with whom he has come in contact. Perhaps his contribution to cooperative thought would have been somewhat more widespread had he believed a little less in perfection and published more of his thoughts and draft manuscripts. Whether or not this be true, Professor Robotka certainly has helped to mold the thinking of scholars of cooperation in such fields as law, accounting, statistics, political science, sociology and history, as well as in his own field of economics. He certainly has influenced cooperative leaders and through them the development of agricultural cooperatives.

Now in his middle 70's, and handicapped by eye trouble, Frank is busy on an analysis of cooperative "principles" for those who will come later.

It has been an honor to draft Frank Robotka's sketch for inclusion in *Cooperative Pioneers*. A great deal of personal pride and satisfaction derive from having been closely associated with Frank as his graduate student and colleague, and from a deep appreciation for his thinking and approach to cooperation.

Arthur Richards Rule

by A. E. Mercker

ARTHUR RICHARDS RULE was born at Goshen, Ky., December 6, 1878, the son of the Reverend John and Mary W. Richards Rule. He was educated in the area's private schools and Academy, and married Elizabeth Becket Wright on March 21, 1903. They had five children. Mr. Rule died in 1950.

Mr. Rule started in the fresh fruit and vegetable business with the firm of Crutchfield and Wollfolk of Pittsburgh, Pa., with whom he was connected from 1898 until 1911. He learned his marketing by first-hand experience, not only as a salesman and as a solicitor in country shipping areas for various fruits and vegetables for his firm, but also in an administrative capacity. He was a most forward-looking, practical planner of operations. He spent a great deal of time in the field studying the inefficiencies and weaknesses in the marketing of produce. This led to his interest to develop and organize cooperative associations at a very early date.

He tried to keep in mind the interest, needs, and responsibilities of all concerned, and developed a close relationship with both producer and consumer in intimate harmony which inspired him further to develop cooperative marketing associations. When a grower or shipper discussed his problems with him Mr. Rule had the rare ability to place himself in the other person's place and see the problem through his eyes. He would then proceed to take remedial action from that viewpoint but adjusted to the practicalities of the situation.

Inspired Organization of Co-op Associations in Many States

His high ideals and forward planning inspired the formation of cooperative fruit and vegetable associations in every state of the Union. He spearheaded the organization of fruit and vegetable associations in the West Coast states; of fruit, vegetable, and onion growers in the Rocky Mountain states; strawberry and vegetable growers in the Middle Western states; potato growers from Florida to Maine, and in practically every northern state west to Idaho; the fruit growers, such as the peach and apple growers in Georgia, in the Ozark section of Missouri, in North Carolina, Virginia, West Virginia, Maryland, Pennsylvania, New Jersey, New York, New England, Michigan, Illinois; and west to Utah, Idaho, Oregon, Washington, and California, of grape growers in Michigan, Pennsylvania, and New York; of onion growers from New York state to Indiana, Colorado, Idaho, and Oregon; of fruit and vegetable growers in Florida; and of watermelon growers. His guidance was responsible for the formation of the South Carolina Asparagus Growers Association and the Florida Citrus Exchange.

In 1911, he formed the North American Fruit Exchange—a capital stock sales organization to centralize the selling and distributing of products of the many associations in the Northwest. He organized the General Sales Agency of America in 1915. This organization represented the many shipping area cooperative associations in the terminal markets which also sold the produce of several large independent growers, and some corporate operators who produced, or financed growers to produce fruits and vegetables. This arrangement was dissolved in 1922 and was replaced by the Federated Fruit and Vegetable Growers which sold only the produce of associations of growers or individual growers.

The fruit growers associations varied from joint stock companies composed of growers or dealers, or both, who distributed their own products or the products of others to the non-profit form of cooperative association which purchased the supplies and distributed the salable products of its members at cost. Voting power varied from a single vote for each member to a vote proportional to the amount of stock owned by each or to the acreage held by each.

At the earliest date he took upon himself the task of changing the fresh fruit and vegetable business from a consignment operation to one of selling the produce at shipping point. Although he sold f.o.b. he believed the auction method concentrated the supply and demand at one point—selling cars after arrival had its good points. Of the 30,000 to 40,000 carloads sold annually by his organization the type of sales were about 88 per cent f.o.b.; 5.4 per cent at auction; and 6.6 per cent after arrival. These included some sales made cash track, storage house sales, jobbing, and export sales. Although his major efforts were directed towards selling the produce f.o.b. point of production he held no prejudice toward any method of selling as long as the producer or association received the best possible price attainable, and the entire proceeds of the sale less the selling charge, transportation, and other charges.

In bringing about this concept he had to create confidence in the buyers, and to this end he developed standards of quality, writing grade specifications for the various levels of quality and the packaging of uniform size in the packages, and properly marking them. This increased sales and required a larger volume of the various products and their handling in central packing houses.

He believed in identity of the product and the early established individual brands for the individual associations and consolidated their output into larger groups under a master brand in order to fulfill increased business. Many of these brands gained not only a most favorable national reputation but were in great demand in other countries.

He guarded against lowering of standards by devising a system of brands well associated with the various levels of the quality premium and giving assurance as to dependability. He believed that nothing was sold until it was actually consumed with satisfaction and pleasure. The consumer, in his opinion, was not half as troublesome as the middleman, for the consumer's needs were determined by heredity and environment.

An outstanding example of this standardization was his revolution of the watermelon industry. He developed standards for watermelons, grading them more accurately for size, contour and shape, and labeling them SOWEGA. The first such labeled watermelons were those from the Southeast and this label—SOWEGA—assured the dependability of the watermelons as to maturity and quality. He prevailed on the chain stores to merchandise for the first time in their history such labeled watermelons.

OSMA His Magic Formula

OSMA was his magic word—Organize, Standardize, Merchandise, Advertise. The first requirement was *volume*. This meant that growers must organize themselves into cooperative associations. By concentration on big operations the growers could obtain efficient sales organizations and low costs of operation. The next step was to attract the buyers. This was done by standardizing the produce and giving the buyer the assurance of a continuity of a dependable supply. With such assurance the buyer could organize and establish an all-out merchandising program to attract the trade and the consumer. To further this end he organized advertising programs that appealed to the consumers, the retailers, and the distribution outlets. In all of these efforts quality was never permitted to be sacrificed. Mr. Rule's theory was that a good reputation is more easily lost than gained; a bad reputation is a whole lot harder to get rid of than a good one.

Mr. Rule contended that the producer's responsibility did not end when his product was sold and out of sight. Repeat orders depended upon the quality and appearance, and the satisfaction of the consumer. He never let his salesmen become "order-takers" but made them merchandisers and advertisers. To this end he tried to satisfy the small buyers by making up so-called "drugstore" or "manifest" carloads which contained several kinds of fruits and vegetables in different types of packages. This innovation required a new set of freight rates on the part of carriers, which broke all precedent.

Why did the organizations that he helped form, live and prosper? They lived because they served and accomplished much good. He did this by hiring professional salesmen and compensated them by paying them high salaries. These professionals located and developed new markets at home and abroad. However, to assist his salesmen and supply them with the facts on which to base their vision and judgment of values and market trends, he set up a service to gather statistical, production, price, distribution, and weather information. He persuaded the U. S. Department of Agriculture's Fruit and Vegetable Market News Service to estimate and forecast bi-weekly the estimated movement of potatoes from each major area. He stimulated the use of the Federal-State Fruit and Vegetable Service, and persuaded practically every grower association he dealt with to use it. He provided a complete service to producers, setting up a traffic and claims division, financial and accounting system, revolving funds for their use, well-grounded legal service, a department of general information, and a field organ. Many of the associations that he helped develop and to which he gave of himself and his practical knowledge are still serving the fruit and vegetable industry.

Works Vigorously for "Orderly" Marketing

He worked closely with the leading national farm organizations, and in 1921 convinced the American Farm Bureau Federation to form "The Fruit Marketing Committee of 21." This was a most revolutionary and constructive step. There were many interesting aspects—prices of agricultural commodities had dropped 44 percent from May, 1920, to June, 1921, resulting in pressure from farm groups for relief legislation. This led to formation of the Farm Bloc in Congress. In 1922, President Harding called a National Agricultural Conference which stressed the need for re-establishing a "fair exchange value for all farm products with that of non-farm commodities." "Equality for Agriculture" became a popular slogan but no legislative action was taken at the conference.

Mr. Rule drafted, and was a leading force in having the Congress pass and the President approve legislation which established the Division of Cooperative Marketing in the Bureau of Agricultural Economics in the U. S. Department of Agriculture. In 1928-29 he was one of the draftees of the first over-all farm legislation which became the Agricultural Marketing Act of 1929. This became law in June, 1929. The principal objective of this Act was the promotion of "orderly" marketing of farm products.

This was done by encouraging organization and expansion of farmer-owned cooperative marketing associations, making loans to cooperatives, and it created the Stabilization Corporation which was authorized to purchase and store cotton and grains.

During World War I, Mr. Rule was a close advisor to the late President Herbert C. Hoover who was then War Food Administrator, and was instrumental in developing rules of conduct, practices, and grade standards for the industry.

In agriculture policy matters Presidents Harding, Coolidge, and Hoover frequently consulted with him. He formulated policies to stabilize dealings with cooperative organizations and developed a permanent national policy and programs. To further these objectives he was instrumental in outlining the credit needs of the farmers and assisting in developing the Farm Loan Act of 1923.

In 1927, he was Chairman of the Organization Committee of the United Growers of America. He was selected to be a member of the General Organization Committee of the Pan American Standardization Conference by Secretary of Commerce Herbert C. Hoover, and was Chairman of the U. S. Section of the Inter-American High Commission. He was a member of the Organization Committee (1923) and the Executive Committee, National Council of Farmer Cooperative Marketing Associations; charter member and Director of the American Committee on the International Institute of Cooperation at Rome in 1923, representing 62 nations and 96 percent of the world total area, and 97 percent of the total world population. He was charter member and Trustee of the American Institute of Cooperation in 1925.

At the first annual meeting of the A.I.C. in 1925 he said:

> Cooperative marketing tends to orderly marketing. Orderly
> marketing tends to stability of prices. Stability of prices tends
> to narrower margins of profit by jobbers and retailers. This means
> lower average cost to consumers. Thus the cooperative movement
> eliminates waste and inevitably reduces the cost of living. The
> cooperative movement thus justifies the wholehearted support of
> consumers, but consumers generally are uninformed as to the
> benefits they may receive from it. The story needs to be told
> them plainly and fully by the cooperatives.

Arthur Rule was the best posted man in the marketing of fresh
fruits and vegetables. He had more ability than anyone else to teach
and train young men in practical marketing and practices. These
young men became his second line of salesmen. When many companies or local associations went on their own they would hire the
first line of men and this presented opportunities for advancement
for his second line men. Mr. Rule trained more top men and his
organizations served as a source of well-trained personnel, many of
whom became outstanding leaders in the fresh fruit and vegetable
business. M. C. Gay, now Secretary of the Georgia Council of Farmer
Cooperatives, maintains that he "learned more from him than from
all other sources combined."

The constructive imprints that the fruit and vegetable industry
inherited and adopted from Mr. Rule are lasting and of great benefit
to the industry to this day. In many respects he was a generation
ahead of his time.

Samuel D. Sanders

by Joseph Douglas Lawrence

SAMUEL D. SANDERS held no college degree other than an honorary doctor's degree from the University of Wisconsin. The award was in recognition of his outstanding contribution to cooperative organization and business methods and to the development of the Banks for Cooperatives.

Mr. Sanders' conventional education ended in the third grade in a little country school in the Ozarks of Arkansas, an educational institution somewhat less advanced than one would expect to find in the large metropolitan communities. There was some "post graduate" work however in an "academy" but it was not extensive.

Despite his brief conventional education, Mr. Sanders was a highly educated man in the important science of business operations and the art of human relations. His master's degree in these subjects came from his native honesty and great depth of common sense and solid judgment.

Mr. Sanders acquired knowledge of important matters because his good sense told him it was the profitable thing to do. From what he told his close friends, his early childhood fell short of the minimum environment usually considered necessary for the development of character. Yet Mr. Sanders was a man of high character. His good sense told him that character was proper and necessary. He said that an uncle taught him to "cuss" when he was five years old. Yet he was not in the least profane. Those who were close to him never heard him use a "cuss" word. His good sense told him that "cussing" was foolish. He was a religious man in a practical way. He was not religious because he had been preached to or because he wanted to be on the side of the good people. He was religious because his good sense told him that it would be well to recognize the Supreme Being and obey His commandments.

While Mr. Sanders was not a student of English literature as such

440

he had a broad vocabulary and a sense of phraseology that he used very effectively and convincingly. While he had a little trouble on rare occasions with verb conjugation his spoken English was good and easy on the ears.

This is a brief background outline of the man who came to Washington, D. C., from Seattle, Washington, to succeed the popular Frank W. Peck as Cooperative Bank Commissioner of the Farm Credit Administration on January 1, 1936.

When Commissioner Peck decided to return to his work in his home state of Minnesota the then-governor of the Farm Credit Administration, Dr. William I. Myers, (the father of the Farm Credit Administration) looked the country over for a practical, experienced, and successful cooperative operator to carry on the work that Commissioner Peck had begun. With the help of Land Bank Commissioner Albert Goss he picked Samuel D. Sanders, Chairman of the Board, President, and General Manager of the highly successful Washington Cooperative Egg and Poultry Association of Seattle, Wash., now the Western Farmers Association.

Provided Practical Leadership

Mr. Sanders came to Washington with a background of experience and a record of success that eminently qualified him for leadership in the development of agricultural cooperatives. At the time he took up his duties as Cooperative Bank Commissioner the cooperative movement was growing rapidly under the stimulus of available capital from the newly organized Banks for Cooperatives system.

It was indeed fortunate that this developing cooperative financing system had the quality of practical leadership that Mr. Sanders provided. The success stories of the Banks for Cooperatives and their patrons might have been greatly different if a lesser man had been Commissioner at that time.

Mr. Sanders learned how cooperatives should be organized and operated the hard way and in the best possible school, namely, the school of how-not-to-starve-to-death. He had been a wheat grower in east Washington state at a time when the small farmers had to cooperate to survive. He organized his neighbors to do necessary things together that none could do alone.

After wheat growing in the area where Mr. Sanders farmed became economically impracticable, cooperative marketing notwithstanding, he acquired a poultry farm near Puyallup, Wash. He took a short course in poultry and egg production at the University of Washington

and began business. He peddled eggs up and down the streets of
Puyallup. So did his neighboring egg producers.

It did not take him long to convince his neighbors that competing
with each other up and down the streets of Puyallup was not the way
to market eggs.

The Washington Cooperative Egg and Poultry Association was
organized with Mr. Sanders in the forefront. Under his leadership
and the dedicated efforts of his able "co-workers," as he called them,
this cooperative grew to be one of the largest and most successful in
the nation. It became one of the most important suppliers of eggs
in the eastern markets. Every sound cooperative and business principle was employed in developing this big successful cooperative
business institution. Mr. Sanders knew them all. He knew as few
other contemporaries knew what it takes to make a cooperative business successful.

Mr. Sanders was a great teacher. He lectured interestingly, convincingly, and simply. One would learn his lessons so easily and
enthusiastically from him that he, the student, was prone to accept
what he absorbed as if the ideas had been his all along.

On one occasion Mr. Sanders was talking to a group of agricultural
economists and cooperative promoters in his office. He explained how
a cooperative should be organized, how it should capitalize itself, and
how it should operate. He laid the facts out in orderly fashion for
everybody to see. One of the economists, who later became an able
manager of a successful poultry processing and marketing cooperative, listened very carefully to what Mr. Sanders said. Later during
the round-table discussion this man spoke up and gave his ideas of
how a cooperative should be organized, capitalized, and operated,
repeating what Mr. Sanders had said word for word. When he finished
he said, "Mr. Sanders, that is my philosophy. Do you agree with it?"
The operation had been so skillful and painless that the man actually
believed that what Mr. Sanders had injected into him had been his
own ideas all along.

When Mr. Sanders talked about cooperatives and his blue ribbon
flock of white leghorn layers he threw himself totally into the subject.
As he talked along he worked up a pantomime and his listeners could
see in him an image of his subject.

He liked to talk about his prize white leghorn hens. He would say
that in spite of all-out efforts for perfection there were always a few
culls that had a way of making themselves irritatingly conspicuous.
When he would show off his flock one or two of these ungraceful

birds would make its way to the front and impair the image of the whole flock. As he talked one could see in him a droopy-winged, knock-kneed, big eyed, long beaked, molty hen.

He would use his cull chicken story to illustrate how a minor but unsightly defect could mar the image of a good program or a good institution.

Supervised Extension of Credit by 13 Banks

Mr. Sanders was not a banker but he knew how to lend money to cooperatives and get it back after it had served its intended useful purpose. In addition to his position of Cooperative Bank Commissioner where he maintained general supervision over the extension of credit by the 12 regional Banks for Cooperatives he was chief executive officer of the Central Bank for Cooperatives that, at that time, made the larger loans to cooperatives directly.

While he had men on his staff who had conventional credit experience he was the leader in the development of sound constructive lending throughout the cooperative bank system. A sound credit policy at the control center was of great importance at this stage of the formative period of the Banks for Cooperatives.

Credit experience in the regional banks in the beginning was either almost non-existent or inappropriate. The presidents of the Banks, who were the chairmen of the loan committees, were mostly educators. There were four Ph.D's among them, several politicians, and others of demonstrated ability. None were bankers. The other two members of the loan committees were the secretary and the treasurer. The secretaries were largely educators, and other men active in the agricultural cooperative field. They were not bankers, either.

In selecting the first treasurers it was deemed wise to select country bankers for these positions to temper the exuberant promotional spirit of the other officers. This philosophy did not work. The experienced bankers could not absorb the shock of extending credit to farmer groups without commercial experience and gilt-edged security. They had no stomach for becoming dedicated development bankers in a new and uncertain field.

Paradoxically, the officers who knew the least about credit extension became the best credit men, with two exceptions where there had been some specialized credit experience. These newcomers into the credit field did not have anything to "unlearn." A whole new field was ahead of them. They were mostly men trained and experienced in searching out facts and developing methods and means. They understood the objective. They knew that it was not smart to lose money by making bad loans. They accepted the truism that an unsound loan is bad for both the borrower and the lender. They also knew that if the money were kept locked in the safe the objective would not be reached. So, under Mr. Sanders' practical leadership they set about in a professional way to develop sound objective lending policies and procedures.

How well they succeeded is attested by the record. One bank, over a period of 25 years had a loss record of $\frac{1}{64}$ of one percent of money loaned. The bank approached closely the goal of making all of the loans that should have been made. A city banker said to the president of this bank, "You have some loans that I would not touch with a 10-foot pole." Yet the Bank for Cooperatives had a better loss record than did his bank. This situation is typical throughout the system. There were losses, of course. Some were heavy, but the percentage loss record has been very good indeed.

The cooperative banks operate to a large extent in a marginal area. They have had to find substitutes for conventional credit-base components. Governor Myers, in the course of a briefing lecture said to the presidents of the Banks, "Find ways to make loans, not ways to not make them."

Suggests Guidelines to Tell Good from Poor Risks

Early in the development period before clear-cut guide lines had been established there was some confusion as to how to tell a good credit risk from a bad one. The Farm Credit Administration examiners were required to review and evaluate all of the loans of the Banks for Cooperatives. In the early years they had trouble classifying the loans as to good, problem, or probable loss.

One day, in exasperation, the Chief Examiner said to a staff member of the Cooperative Bank Division, "I wish you fellows would give us a yard stick so we can measure these loans." The staff member said, "Mr. Sanders has a yard stick in his mind. Let us go in and see if he can put it into words." They went into Mr. Sanders' office and the staff member asked him if he could tell them what were the necessary elements for a cooperative to have to be successful and thereby be a good credit risk. Mr. Sanders replied quickly that there should be an economic need for the cooperative, it must have satisfactory member support, it must have sufficient capital to do business, and it must have good management.

Thereupon emerged the yard stick. It was soon published in

pamphlet form; and became the core around which the credit guidelines of the cooperative bank system crystalized. In summary it is as follows:

1. Economic need
2. Member support
3. Adequate capital
4. Efficient operations—(Good management)

Simple as it appears, it took Mr. Sanders to find it and put it into words.

Mr. Sanders was an avid advocate of the retain and revolving method of capitalizing a cooperative, that is: withholding a small fraction of the value of the commodities handled to be used for capital and refunding it progressively in due time as new capital comes in due course.

He would say, "A cent a bushel of wheat won't make or break the farmer but it will make or break his cooperative." What he meant was that the farmers would not miss the cent a bushel but a cent per bushel from many bushels of many farmers would painlessly capitalize a cooperative. At the same time the farmer would be making a good investment in his own cooperative. Under the revolving process the investment would be liquidated in due time.

Mr. Sanders' strong advocacy of this method of capitalization with the results obtained was one of his great contributions to the development and growth of agricultural cooperatives.

Samuel D. Sanders was a developer and an operator. When the development was completed and operations became routine he was like a race horse without a race to run. He became bored under such circumstances and retired in 1947.

There are more, better, and bigger agricultural cooperatives in the United States today because there was a Samuel D. Sanders.

Aaron Sapiro

by Grace H. Larsen

A ARON SAPIRO earned space in college textbooks of American
history because of the nature of his work with agricultural
cooperatives. He remains one of the most controversial figures ever
to appear on the nation's agricultural scene, yet one of the most
significant. Whether appraised (as he has been) as the peerless
evangelist of cooperation or as the agricultural Napoleon of the
20th Century, he merits attention particularly because his influence
has lingered on. Ideas associated with him have continued to appear
and find acceptance in government programs and among leaders in
the agricultural industry.

Sapiro's private life was as dramatic as his public career. Born in
San Francisco in 1884, he lived in Oakland where he sold matches
and newspapers on street corners from the age of five to supplement
the income of the family, which included several children and an
alcoholic father. When he was nine, he was sent to live in a San
Francisco orphanage. One of its trustees, Rabbi Jacob Nieto, observed
young Sapiro's extraordinary intelligence and arranged, in time, for
him to attend the Hebrew Union College at Cincinnati to prepare
for the rabbinate. Sapiro abandoned this program of study but
earned an A.B. and an M.A. degree in history at the University of
Cincinnati as well as election to Phi Beta Kappa before returning to
San Francisco. In 1911, he graduated among the top in his class at
the Hastings Law College of the University of California and passed
the state bar examination. While a student, he gained experience and
earned money working in the office of the prominent attorney, Jesse W.
Lilienthal.

---

* Note: This is a condensed version of the article by Grace H. Larsen and
Henry E. Erdman, "Aaron Sapiro: Genius of Farm Co-operative Promotion," *The
Mississippi Valley Historical Review*, Vol. XLIX, No. 2 (September, 1962), pp. 242-
268.

Sapiro acquired an interest in agriculture during the course of numerous conversations with Harris Weinstock and David Lubin, half-brothers who drew fortunes from their Sacramento and San Francisco dry goods stores and won esteem for their public service. Farmers as well, they took part in efforts to cope with agricultural marketing problems from the 1880's. Although he returned for occasional visits, Lubin settled in Rome where in 1905 he established the International Institute of Agriculture, predecessor of the Food and Agriculture Organization of the United Nations.

Weinstock and Sapiro formed a close relationship. They were immediately attracted to each other upon first meeting in 1905 at the home of Weinstock's daughter in Stockton, Calif. Sapiro's theological school had sent him out to the town to conduct religious services. It was the merchant who recommended Sapiro, at the time he was studying law, to Attorney Lilienthal and, in 1911, for a state position as secretary of the newly formed Industrial Accident Board. Governor Hiram Johnson was glad to approve the appointment for he had sat in the audience at the Hastings commencement exercises in 1911 and had listened, greatly impressed, to Sapiro's valedictory address.

Starts Private Practice; Studies Co-op Legal Status

Following in Weinstock's footsteps, Sapiro began to lecture to various audiences in the state on liberal causes. In 1913, he left state service to start a private law practice in San Francisco. When Weinstock became California's first Market Director in 1915, he asked Sapiro to serve as legal counsel for this office which had headquarters in San Francisco. Sapiro had been acting as Weinstock's personal attorney and accepted the offer with enthusiasm. Since the law that authorized the appointment of a State Market Director made no provision for legal services, Weinstock paid the young and gifted lawyer from his own pocket.

To prepare for his work with the Market Director, who intended to use his position to organize as many of the state's farmers as he could into cooperative associations, Sapiro read every scrap he could find on cooperative marketing in Weinstock's large personal library as well as in the library of the University of California. Most of the literature available to him not only indicated that agricultural cooperation was still in a formative stage but pointed out the need for leadership. The writings stressed that farmer enterprises were held back by the inadequacy of legal arrangements. It was a situation made to order for a brilliant and dynamic young lawyer who, while ambitious for himself, was also an idealist wanting to engage in socially useful work.

Sapiro's involvement in organizing work began with his listening to the growers who came to the Market Director's office to tell their problems. He helped in forming into organizing committees farmers who represented various crops, and he went out to the farming regions with Weinstock and these committees to interest other producers in starting cooperative associations. As soon as the Market Director decided that enough growers were ready for organization, Sapiro drafted the legal papers.

Assisted by other lawyers in his firm, he borrowed freely from legal documents of existing cooperatives, adapting them to the special needs of each commodity group. Following the accepted lines of the ordinary business corporation, the first articles of incorporation and bylaws were simple and brief. But as the requirements of farmer cooperative corporations became apparent, provisions of their legal instruments became more explicit and elaborate. To enable the associations to control an adequate volume, Sapiro's firm worked out a contract (or marketing agreement) between the cooperative and its members. Suits were filed by the new associations against members who failed to comply with their contracts. In their defense, members fell back on claims of lack of mutuality and inapplicability of liquidated damages. To meet this situation, the lawyers rephrased the contract to obtain an enforceable arrangement. Legal preparation was made also for the different types of activities which cooperatives began to add to their services. To help the Sapiro firm in its work, its office kept a chart of laws governing cooperatives in every part of the nation and a record of the legal experiences of cooperatives operating under these laws. This information proved of great value in serving cooperative clients, especially in courtroom defense of contracts and the process of revising them.

Sapiro Develops "Iron-Clad" Contract with Growers

The contract or marketing agreement developed by this process became known as the Sapiro or "iron-clad" contract. Sapiro did not originate either the idea of such a contract or its provisions. But all the associations he helped to organize in California and elsewhere at a later date adopted it. It became identified with him because he insisted that it was essential to the success of cooperatives.

The contract obligated the grower to deliver to the association over a specified period of several years all the merchantable products of his farm. It attempted to protect the association against actual or threatened breach of contract by providing remedies and relief in the form of the injunction, decrees of specific performance, and provisions for liquidated damages, as well as payment of legal costs by violators of the contract. The association had to agree to accept its members' products exclusively, to pool the products delivered to it, market them, and return to members the proceeds after deducting costs. The contract also contained a provision for the method of financing the cooperative, a statement of the purposes of the organization, and a clause making the instrument effective only when the signup among farmers assured a designated volume of business.

Since many of the cooperative associations that were thus started with state aid became private clients of the Sapiro firm, it began to enjoy an enlarged and profitable practice. Consequently, Sapiro concentrated on cooperative work. By 1920 he and his legal associates were recognized as one of the strongest and most respected firms of younger attorneys in San Francisco. Those active in his legal office at some time during the period 1915–1920 were: Philip S. Ehrlich, John Francis Neylan, Lawrence and David Levy, Elystus L. Hayes, George J. Hatfield, and Leo J. Rabinowitz, as well as Aaron's brother-in-law, Stanley M. Arndt and Aaron's younger brother, Milton Sapiro. All later became noted attorneys in their own right.

Develops and Uses New Co-op Financial Plan

Another development in cooperative marketing that bore the imprint of Sapiro's work before he left California to gain fame and fortune by promoting cooperation among the nation's farmers and those of Canada was the nonvoting preferred stock system of financing corporate subsidiaries of cooperatives. Several bankers on boards of directors of cooperatives that Sapiro served supplied some of the ideas of the plan, the details of which were worked out by Sapiro. It was a scheme designed to enable farmers to undertake functions calling for large expenditures, for example, those requiring acquisition of packing facilities. Upon the formation of a capital stock subsidiary for the purpose of buying, building, or operating packing plants, its nonvoting preferred stock was sold to interested growers or outside investors while the parent (or member) organization held the common stock. Arrangements were made for the subsidiary to repurchase part of the preferred stock each year using, for this purpose, withholdings from the proceeds of the product sold by the cooperative. After a period of a few years, the parent organization acquired ownership of the facilities through its ownership of the common stock.

Sapiro made extensive use of this financing technique. He made it the central feature of the northwestern fruit, grain, and dairy organizations and of southern and midwestern tobacco, wheat, and cotton associations that he was instrumental in establishing. He also supplied copies of the plan to other groups scattered through the United States and Canada. According to his estimate, this procedure was used in the acquisition of more than $100 million worth of properties before the cooperatives had "as much as a cent of cash to pay for any of them." In time, the plan proved inadequate as banks became alarmed over the close relationship between the member and subsidiary companies and turned down loans using warehouse receipts as collateral. Other methods were required to meet the increasing financial needs of cooperatives.

In 1919, Sapiro began to answer with increasing frequency requests coming into his office from outside the state from desperately troubled farm groups who were eager for help in solving the problems of their industries. About the same time, his association with Weinstock ended, the result of a difference over a private legal matter. In the next few years, Sapiro independently built his national reputation by effectively proposing across the continent adoption of the "commodity method" of cooperative marketing.

Sapiro asserted in speech after speech and in published articles that California had been the laboratory where the "fundamental principles of cooperative marketing" had been developed. Success in agriculture and improvement of the farmers' lot would be virtually guaranteed if the farmers of the country would follow his simple directions for applying these principles. The plan he proposed was variously called the California plan or California idea or commodity method of cooperative marketing. He proclaimed it with such vigor and so often that by 1925 the plan was usually referred to as the Sapiro plan. He was not always consistent or accurate in presenting his message; but promoters are not noteworthy for either trait, and it was as promoter that he made a major contribution to farmer cooperation.

Success of Co-op Only If All Points of Plan Adopted

Sapiro usually implied and occasionally asserted that only by adopting all the basic points of the proposed plan would a cooperative succeed. The first point was organization with regard to the commodity involved, not the locality. He claimed that the aim of the cooperative was "to control flow of supply as to time, place, and quantity so that you have something to say about the conditions that affect price values. You cannot do it as individuals, you cannot do it as local units, but if you take the local units and you federate them from a commodity viewpoint, then you can do something to affect the price."

His plan also called for the cooperative to be strictly a business, composed only of farmers in order to prevent the development of any diversity of interests among members. A third provision consisted of enforceable contracts covering a long span of time and taking effect only after a fixed minimum signup was achieved. The designated signup varied with each organization and might be 30, 50, or even 75 percent of qualified growers, depending on the commodity and the local conditions. The cooperative must provide for pooling of growers' products to assure that "every man in the association gets the same as every other man for the same type, grade, quantity, and quality of product." Sapiro proposed formation of nonstock corporations, reasoning that capital stock was not essential for their regular operation since the basis of the marketing association was the contract with the growers who agreed to provide the products it was to sell. Capital stock subsidiaries would provide the selling agencies with funds to finance facilities.

An attractive person with extraordinary charm and powers of persuasion, Sapiro presented his theme to countless audiences. His highly emotional entreaties appeared to have mesmerized the huge crowds he drew. In his artful appeals were sentimental anecdotes about anguished farmers who recovered by forming cooperatives, stirring slogans that aroused enthusiasm for organization, and a credible plan of action to follow. Next to reform, he told farmers, there was nothing worthier than cooperatives to which they could consecrate themselves. As one commentator noted, he made the "marketing of a barrel of apples more exciting than a Tale from Boccaccio and the signing of a cooperative agreement seem as vital to social justice and progress as the Magna Charta." Apostles carried Sapiro's ideas into nearly every producing region. As part of their membership drives, they distributed pamphlets outlining the purposes and promises of Sapiro's new type of organization.

In response to his electric eloquence, farmers signed cooperative marketing agreements in droves. By 1922, he had organized or represented at least 55 associations in 19 states, including California. By the following year, when he moved his residence to Chicago, he had organized, or served as counsel, cooperative groups whose membership totaled over half a million persons. The same year he helped in establishing the vast wheat pool movement among Canadian farmers. Another tabulation noted that by 1923 he had organized 66 associations in the United States, having an estimated annual volume of $400 million. To serve his clients, he maintained, at the peak of his work, law offices in Dallas and New York, as well as in San Francisco and Chicago.

Further evidence of the extent and nature of Sapiro's influence was evident in his relationship with the American Farm Bureau Federation. He attended almost all its early meetings to foster marketing cooperatives and in 1923 was appointed legal advisor of its Department of Cooperative Marketing. The first president of the Farm Bureau, James R. Howard, considered him the country's leading authority on cooperative marketing. But controversy over him within the Federation came close to destroying it. Sapiro resigned early in 1924 when it became obvious that new officers regarded the Bureau's attention to organizing cooperatives with far less favor.

Credited with Many State Adoptions of Co-op Marketing Act

Sapiro did more than organize cooperatives. He publicized the need for a uniform cooperative marketing act before state legislatures, legislative committees, and farm groups and participated in preparing the model. More than any other person, he received credit for the adoption by most states during the years 1920–1928 of some version of the so-called standard cooperative marketing act. The existence of the standard act served as a definition of public policy and was instrumental in obtaining court acceptance of cooperative operations. In 1927, Sapiro also defended before the U. S. Supreme Court the Bingham Cooperative Marketing Act of Kentucky, which he thought was the best representative of the standard act. The Court's decision has been considered a landmark in the expression of approval of the rights of states to provide specifically for the organization of cooperative associations.

Acting on a suggestion made to him by Senator Arthur Capper, Sapiro took an active role in creating the National Council of Farmers' Cooperative Marketing Associations in 1922. He was also its mainstay. Founded to give commodity-type cooperatives a chance to express views on federal agricultural credit legislation and to provide a forum for other problems of the associations, the National Council held four national conferences attended by delegates from the country's largest associations before it became defunct in 1926.

Honored as the foremost expert on the law of cooperative marketing and leader in organizing cooperatives, Sapiro was approached for information, opinions, and advice not only by Farm Bloc Congressmen but by officers and other personnel of the U. S. Department of Agriculture. In 1923, he had support from the Secretary of Agriculture, Henry C. Wallace. This waned, however, and before long there was evidence of open opposition to him from within the Department. Wallace denied charges of some of Sapiro's supporters that any Department member had obstructed adoption of the commodity plan of cooperative marketing. He announced that Department members would continue to encourage cooperatives in every legitimate way but regarded it as a duty to point out difficulties that farmers might encounter under any contemplated plan of organization.

By 1926, many of the Sapiro associations had ceased to function and the attorney's meteoric career of promoting farmer cooperatives was at an end. When asked about the lack of success of organizations formed according to his plan, he stated that most of the dissolutions occurred after his relationship with the associations was over and often because his rules had not been followed. He commented in 1925 that he had learned through personal experience that organizing cooperatives was not easy and there was no fixed plan for them. The types of farmers and commodities involved as well as local conditions had to be studied.

Sapiro's procedures had significant defects. In a sense, he was a victim of his own legal approach. He assumed that cooperatives set up on his plan would operate smoothly if left in the hands of experts. Once he had organized a body of farmers he traveled on to answer the call for help from another group. Serious conflicts emerged when he ignored or opposed existing organizations built over the years by local efforts. He tended to underestimate the complexities of administering large-scale cooperatives and oversimplified the job of marketing regional supplies of an agricultural product. Also, he did not appreciate some aspects of membership problems. Placing too much faith in the contract as a guarantee of grower loyalty, he overestimated the adequacy of legal instruments for maintaining member enthusiasm.

Momentary acclaim returned as a result of a $1 million damage suit that Sapiro filed against Henry Ford in 1925 for statements printed in his Dearborn *Independent* in a series of articles dating from April, 1924. The articles insinuated that Sapiro was more interested in personal gain than farmers' profits and predicted financial loss if not disaster for those who joined his enterprises. Among other claims, the newspaper stated that Weinstock's employment of Sapiro began the "history of Jewish attempts to seize control of the agricultural and horticultural resources and production of America."

In 1927, in an out-of-court settlement, Sapiro obtained a retraction and an apology for these irrational statements to "the whole Jewish people; retraction of the charges against cooperative marketing, [and] retraction of the personal insinuations." Although Sapiro blamed the articles for ruining his usefulness in the farmers' cooperative movement, the evidence reveals that his effectiveness in promoting cooperatives had ended earlier. He continued to practice law until his death in Los Angeles in 1959 but the great clamor for him in the rural areas vanished in the mid-20's with his organizations.

Sapiro's ideas and activities contributed greatly to the growth of large-scale agricultural cooperatives. Through the extensive publicity that he gave to experiences of California farmers, he stimulated an unprecedented interest in producers' marketing associations. He also had a leading part in making available in the states adequate legal machinery for their development. In addition, he deserves credit for bringing these organizations closer to sources of financial backing and winning for them much sympathy from outside interests. As recently as 1960, a knowledgeable observer of cooperative development wrote that "probably no man has made more of a mark on the character of American agriculture and the agriculture of the world during the last 40 years."

John J. Scanlan

by Roy W. Lennartson

THE ILLUSTRIOUS CAREER of John J. Scanlan is quite typical of a comprehensive number of pioneer-oriented and farm-raised youth who have made outstanding contributions to the nation's agriculture and its general welfare.

Born to vigorous pioneers of Irish background, John appeared on the homestead farm in Lincoln County, Minn., in July, 1896. He was to be one of five children. Tragedy struck the family when he was but two years old—his father being killed in a runaway team accident.

John's formative years are a familiar story. Grade school—no ready access to a high school so he lived away from home to attend and did so by working for his room and board—graduated with honors—a freshman college scholarship award.

His college career began at St. Thomas in St. Paul, Minn., in 1915 —then on to the Mankato Normal School in that state where he obtained a Rural Teachers Certificate. In the war year of 1918 he joined the Student Army Training Corps only to be stricken with flu and pneumonia at Fort Snelling. Rejected for further duty he taught school until 1920 when he was offered a four-year scholarship to Notre Dame University. This he turned down and continued teaching until 1921 when he entered the University of Minnesota.

At Minnesota he combined agriculture and business administration and received his B.S. Degree in the latter subject in 1924. A Master's Degree followed in Agricultural Economics in 1925. Enmeshed in this academic pursuit was the usual pattern of farm students: Summer farm labor, nursery stock salesman, part-time research and the like as a means of financing the educational desire.

Federal Career Begins in U.S.D.A. Co-op Marketing Division

In 1926, he joined the Division of Cooperative Marketing in U.S.D.A. as a Junior Economist and began his long and outstanding federal service career.

Although John's first assignment was to make a business analysis study of the Poultry Producers of Central California, San Francisco, he was called on for work in other fields. Of considerable professional interest was the study that he made with J.M. Tinley to determine the causes for the failure of a Sapiro-inspired largescale cooperative tobacco marketing association. The report on this study, *Business Analysis of the Tobacco Growers Cooperative Association,* published in 1929 as U.S.D.A. Circular No. 100, provides an invaluable record of this experience, and offers lessons that are still of practical value.

Firmly established with a steady income, John found it possible in 1928 to marry his college sweetheart, Agnes Mary Galvin, an Iowa-born Irish lass who was then teaching home economics at the University of South Dakota. Together they have represented all that is wholesome and good as parents, citizens, and close friends to a multitude of people.

The pioneering heritage which John assimilated from his parents has been an important element in his success. Through most of his career in cooperative development and service, he has been closely associated with the poultry industry. During these years it was an industry subject to dramatic changes in production, distribution, and institutions. Essentially, it has been an industry providing wide latitude for a pioneering spirit. It was an ideal setting for a man of John's attributes.

Makes Many Contributions to Poultry Co-op Effectiveness

Unlike the major commodities which generally represented regional concentrations and formed the major income to individual farm families, poultry, egg, and turkey production was scattered far and wide. This usually constituted a supplementary income to the farm endeavor. Nevertheless, numerous attempts at cooperative effort in assembling, quality improvement, continuous supply, and merchandising efforts were attempted under a variety of arrangements. In his patient and understanding way John soon evolved a set of guiding principles for use by interested groups which were highly effective, and in the long run, prevented many impractical and futile efforts being undertaken.

On the other hand, as areas of concentration and specialization in production evolved providing appropriate environment and opportunity for cooperative efforts, John was alert and became a moving force in guiding, analyzing, educating, and servicing these associations to their ultimate benefit. An illustrious set of organizational names appear in his portfolio of studies and assistance during his span of service with the federal government—Utah Poultry Producers Association; Washington Farmers Association; Pacific Egg Producers Association; Land O'Lakes Creameries; Northwestern Egg and Poultry Cooperators; Flemington, Brockton, Vineland, Derry Egg Auction Associations, Norbest Turkey Growers Association; and so on and on.

Intermingled with such specific efforts is a wide spectrum of activities closely associated with the poultry industry. He appeared frequently on annual programs of the American Institute of Cooperation, American Farm Bureau Federation, Institute of American Poultry Industry, Northeastern Poultry Producers Council, and numerous other regional associations. His portfolio of writings cover 66 research reports, 48 magazine articles, 18 speeches, and 19 other documents. They present an excellent panorama of knowledge in his field of specialization.

Aside from his strenuous analytical efforts, John reflected an attribute which too few enjoyed throughout his career. The young men who in their formative years were fortunate to have worked for and with him came to know this attribute. He was a big man in terms of tolerance, understanding, and compassion. He reflected an environment of character and intelligence which could be and was readily absorbed by his understudies and his associates.

One of those who speaks the views of all who came to know and love John through his work was C. M. Ferguson who, prior to becoming Director of the Federal Extension Service in the 50's, had been Extension Poultryman at Ohio State University. "Fergie" wrote as follows to Joseph G. Knapp, Administrator of the Farmer Cooperative Service, on February 7, 1966:

> I have many wonderful memories of the help John gave us in Ohio when we were struggling to get some cooperatives organized and working. This was in the dark days of the thirties. John's publication on *Guides to Organizing Co-ops* became our Bible. John skillfully put into print, in a clear-cut, easily understood way, the essentials without clouding his material with a lot of supplemental material which may have been relevant but not necessary to the person in the field faced with developing sound procedures. His visits with us during those years were most helpful. His quiet, sincere manner and sound counsel always made you not only feel good but gave you the encouragement to go ahead. American agriculture owes a full measure of gratitude to John Scanlan.

U.S.D.A. Award Recognizes Superior Service

Over-all he was always a fine public servant and was recognized as such by the United States Department of Agriculture with a Superior

Service Award in 1960. The citation speaks not only for his work with the Farmer Cooperative Service but for the poultry industry as a whole: "For national leadership, initiative and sustained high level of performance in helping farmers develop and build effective poultry and egg marketing cooperatives."

Perhaps no one has enjoyed greater standing among all elements of the American poultry industry, and it is significant that he attended and presented papers for the Department of Agriculture at four World Poultry Congresses: Cleveland, Ohio, 1939; Copenhagen, 1948; Mexico City, 1958; and Sydney, Australia, 1962. He has also prepared a paper for presentation at the 1966 Congress at Kiev in Russia.

As John drew the curtain on his interesting and productive career at the age of 69, he had a few choice words which were nicely put:

> It has been my over-all purpose to encourage and help poultry and other cooperatives grow and be successful, progressive, resourceful, and pacesetters in their fields. In the drastically changing poultry field, the challenges to the cooperatives have been many, complex, and serious. They have needed and requested much help from us. My chief regret is that we have been unable to help these cooperatives to more fully meet the challenges, take advantage of new opportunities, and solve their many and varied problems. We have tried but were limited by our abilities and small staff. Another regret is that I have been unable to complete some work underway and planned because of retirement earlier than anticipated.

Vera McCrea Searles

by Helen Smith

A S DAIRY FARMERS IN THE EARLY 1900's were striving for better markets for their product, they recognized the aid and assistance of farm wives and families to their business. The faith in the Home Department movement by the directors and members during these early years made Home Department a reality.

On retirement of Vera McCrea Searles, H. H. Rathbun, then President of the Dairymen's League, said:

> . . . when you think of Vera McCrea Searles, you think of the Home Department, and when you think of the Home Department, you think of Vera McCrea Searles. She has done a lot for the League and we hope there will be opportunity for her to render more service to the League in the broader field of the cooperative movement.

In responding, Mrs. Searles said that her great satisfaction was the realization that thousands of farm women have been able through the League's Home Department, to cooperate with other farm organizations and to benefit through organization as well as to help carry forward the work of the Dairymen's League.

In 1923, Vera McCrea joined the Dairymen's League staff as a field representative of the Membership Service Department. The addition of a woman to this staff indicated the belief of these leaders in the value and assistance that women had given and could give to the organization.

Born on a farm in DeKalb in St. Lawrence County, N.Y., she attended country school, Canton High School, St. Lawrence University, and Columbia University. Miss McCrea came to the Dairymen's League with a background of Home Economics teaching and food conservation work. She had also helped organize Home Bureaus in Cortland and Tompkins Counties.

She brought with her a vast knowledge, understanding, and appreciation of the problems of farm people.

Sparks First Inclusion of Women in Co-op Program

Through her pioneer efforts in the field of women in cooperatives, through her understanding of rural problems and her belief in the ability of women and young people to enrich the program, the Dairymen's League officially organized the Home Department in 1925. No cooperative marketing association had ever before included women in its program. The objectives of the department were:

1. To help stabilize morale.
2. To inform League members as to the purpose, progress, and ultimate goals of the Association.
3. To extend womens' interest to state-wide organization work and translate it into active participation as a group representing the Dairymen's League.
4. To interest boys and girls in the work of the Association.

As she moved throughout the milkshed, her calm, stabilizing, effective guidance, her sound judgment, and exceptional organizational ability, as well as her warm and sympathetic understanding of farm people and their problems, led to activity by the farm women in local meetings as well as sub-district meetings of the organization.

It soon became evident that these women were also attending and participating in meetings of many other farm organizations. The influence of this group, as they became more active and forceful in their own organization, extended far beyond their own organization and to both state and national legislative halls.

Working with other women leaders in the fields of agriculture and nutrition, Miss McCrea helped organize the New York State Council of Rural Women. This was an organization of leaders—New York State Grange, New York State Home Bureau, Home Department of Dairymen's League Cooperative Association, and later the Council of Rural Churches. These leaders, working together, gave understanding and combined action to the programs instigated by the parent organizations in behalf of better life for rural New York Staters.

Farm Women Led into Positions of Influence

The New York State Women's Joint Legislative Forum was another study group where the leadership of Vera McCrea led the women of the Dairymen's League into positions of influence and responsibility. Membership in this non-partisan group, representing many women's organizations in the state of New York, gave the women of the Dairymen's League an opportunity to broaden womens' understanding of rural and dairy farm problems. The public of New York state certainly was influenced in sound legislation for the dairy industry through the understanding and appreciation which was developed through participation and action of this group.

While serving the Dairymen's League, she participated actively in many other organizations. Some of these were—President of New York League of Business and Professional Women, President of Business and Professional Women's Clubs of New York State, Chairman of the Educational Committee for New York State Home Bureau Federation, President of the Conference Board of New York State Women's Educational Organization, advisory member of the Farm Committee on National Safety Council, member of New York State Home and Farm Safety Committee.

In 1936, a trip abroad to England, France, Denmark, Sweden, Norway, and Germany, with the study of cooperatives as the objective, gave the Dairymen's League and its members a much broader picture of cooperatives and an appreciation of their own cooperative.

Miss McCrea was editor of the Home Page of the *Dairymen's League News*, which grew to include pages devoted to the "Ko-op Kiddie Korner," Nutrition, Young Cooperators, and Membership News.

Youth Recognition Leads to Organizing "Young Cooperators"

There was a steady growth in the Home Department in recognition of the youth in the organization. These programs included information and understanding, as well as leadership. The Young Cooperators were officially recognized in 1940 as a part of the Home Department, and became a Service in their own right in 1946 when Home Department became a part of Membership Service—Home Service.

Miss McCrea organized and was director of the Health Education Department in 1928. This program was discontinued in 1938 when the State Milk Education Program was developed. Through this program, the nutritional value and importance of milk in the diet was reinforced in the minds of children and adults across the milkshed.

She retired from the Dairymen's League in April, 1946, to what better place than a farm—Nutmeg Farm in Bridgewater, Conn., where she and her husband entered into the areas of poultry and general farming. Here she maintained her interest in cooperatives and rural organizations, as they were members of the Connecticut Egg Producers' Cooperative, as well as Farm and Home Bureau, and Grange. The 150-year old colonial farm home was completely restored and furnished with antiques of the period by the Searles. Here she died February 25, 1963.

The Home Department Creed, written by Vera McCrea as she set the foundation stones of Home Department, reflected her convictions and ideas with regard to women in cooperative work. . . . .

> To maintain the highest ideals for the Dairymen's League Cooperative Association; to develop a love for and a loyalty to the organization and thus assure a permanent and stable foundation. To think actively and intelligently about the League. To work for the highest type of leadership and for the highest quality products, and constantly to broaden and to extend the League's influence and its membership.

It is easy to see the far-sightedness of this woman in this Creed as penned in the early 1920's. It still reflects the need for, value of, and guidance necessary as the women's program continues to support and reinforce the membership program of the Dairymen's League Cooperative Association. This implies a well-informed, well-educated group of cooperative members being helped at every angle by the group who do this so well—the women behind the men.

At the time of her appointment, her introduction in the *League News* recognized the potential of this woman, which showed as she pioneered in the development of programs for women in cooperatives. . .

> Miss McCrea is on the staff of the organization department to serve League women. No better woman could have been secured for the job. She knows practical farm conditions, and she has a big vision of what the successful marketing of milk and other farm products will mean for the farm homes and the farm women and children. When all the League women get that vision too, economic success is in sight.

Her 22 years with the Dairymen's League laid a firm foundation on which this program has continued helping the women of the organization understand, appreciate, and interpret their organization to friends, members, and neighbors throughout the Northeast.

Ralph Snyder

by Harold Hamil

AS A FARM BOY IN EASTERN KANSAS, Ralph Snyder heard
about cooperatives from his father. And most of what he heard
was in troubled tones. The father lived close to the problems of a
struggling little Grange-sponsored cooperative store in the nearby
county seat of Oskaloosa. He talked about these problems at home
and gave young Ralph every reason to associate cooperatives with
things unpleasant and irritating. Yet Ralph Snyder grew up to become
one of the most ardent supporters that farmer cooperatives ever had.

What the boy heard from his father was not critical of the basic
structure or the primary objectives of the cooperative. Most of the
complaints, Ralph recalled in later years, had to do with the fact that
too many farmer members had their hands in the prune barrel, so
to speak. Too many wanted more from the co-op than they gave in
return. And too many didn't pay their bills. Finally, there was the
fact that in the Oskaloosa cooperative, as in many other early cooperatives, the farmers who owned the store were inclined to pick their
managers from among neighbors who hadn't done well at farming.

While Ralph Snyder stayed hitched to cooperatives up to the time
of his death in 1962 at the age of 90, he was never one to stick with
the crowd or with a given way of doing things just for the sake of
avoiding conflict or controversy. A banker for many years, he cham-
pioned causes that were unpopular with other bankers. While a
member of the Kansas Legislature, he broke with his party on occasion,
defied the governor when he felt the latter was out of line, and con-
founded a lot of people once when he, a conventional banker, supported a cooperative banking bill. (The bill got through the Lower
House, with Snyder's leadership, but was killed in the Senate.) And
the railroad and utility lobbyists, it was said, never could quite understand this banker-farmer who chose to reach his own conclusions
as to how to vote on certain issues.

During his first term on the board of the American Farm Bureau
Federation, he picked up some "bad boy" characteristics, as he once

put it, and failed of re-election. He did get back on the board a few years later for a second term. With the coming of the New Deal this lifelong Republican became an ardent supporter of the farm programs of a Democratic administration, and the head of a branch of one of the new federally-sponsored agencies.

Consistent in Advocacy of Cooperatives

It is a bit of a paradox perhaps that this man who was quick to disagree with fellow workers in many situations was a consistent and energetic advocate of cooperation. His role of dissenter must be analyzed in the light of situations or conditions that provoked dissent.

The great consistency of the man was in his determination to bring farmers together so that their interests and welfare could be better served. Along with many other farm leaders, he had the capacity to diagnose motives. He was quick to detect those situations in which farmers might be used to serve the interests of everyone except the farmer.

During a long and active lifetime it was Ralph Snyder's privilege to talk with presidents and to sit in the councils of important national farm policy-making. Yet there were few things in his record to which he pointed with greater pride than to his role in the founding of the Kansas Committee of Farm Organizations. This committee, probably unique, still exists. It is made up of representatives of all the major farm organizations, cooperatives, and farm commodity groups. It is active only during legislative sessions, but it has provided for Kansas agriculture a quiet, but effective, organization to lobby in behalf of those measures on which the various segments of agriculture can agree.

Ralph Snyder was 77 years of age when he retired from the Presidency of the Wichita Bank for Cooperatives. For the next 13 years he retained an amazingly keen interest in what was going on in Kansas agriculture. He attended the annual meetings of various farm organizations and cooperatives and wrote letters to those involved in the affairs of those organizations.

In the history of American agriculture his achievements probably will not loom up as big as those of Senator Arthur Capper, and he certainly did not create as much of a national sensation as did "Sockless Jerry" Simpson. Ralph Snyder, nevertheless, wrote his name in large letters in the history of Kansas agriculture and in the history of farmer cooperatives.

Ralph Snyder's boyhood was typical of that of all boys born on the frontier of western movement following the Civil War. His father, Edwin Snyder, had served in the Union Army. He and his bride started west from Ohio shortly after their marriage in 1866. They settled on a homestead relinquishment in Jefferson County, Kan., and it was on this farm that Ralph was born in 1871.

When Ralph was 14, he was confident that his country school education had sufficiently prepared him to enter the new State College of Agriculture and Applied Sciences at Manhattan. While his formal preparation was short of what the college expected, he took a special examination and was accepted. In 1890, at 19 years of age, he was one of the 26 who were graduated from what is now Kansas State University.

After two years of teaching a country school, he and Miss Nellie M. Finney, whom he later referred to as having been one of his "advanced pupils," were married. They settled on a farm a mile east of Oskaloosa, where their three children were born.

In 1908, the Jefferson County Bank in Oskaloosa was placed in the hands of the State Banking Commission. Someone convinced Ralph Snyder that he should reorganize the bank and preserve it for the community. He carried out this assignment and then became the bank's President.

During World War I, Snyder responded to an appeal from the extension department of Kansas State College to serve as emergency county agent. His job was to work in two counties and help farmers increase production to meet the war-time demand for food.

In 1918, a friend put Ralph's name on the Republican ballot as State Representative. He was unopposed in the primary and general elections and thus began the first of two periods in the Kansas legislature. His second round as a lawmaker came some 30 years later— after retirement from the Wichita bank presidency.

Helped in Adoption of State Co-op Marketing Act

It was during the 1919 legislative session that he introduced a cooperative banking bill, and it was during his second term, in 1921, that he took issue with Governor Henry J. Allen and opposed a move to change the manner of selecting the state board of agriculture. During the same session Snyder was at the forefront of the legislative campaign that brought about the Kansas Cooperative Marketing Act, which contributed materially to the development of cooperatives in Kansas.

While serving in the legislature, Snyder found time to participate in the bringing of county farm bureaus into a statewide organization. When the organization finally took shape, in 1919, he found himself in the office of President of the Kansas Farm Bureau. He was re-elected without opposition at 14 successive annual meetings. His tenure might have gone on, had he not resigned in 1934 to become President of the Wichita Bank for Cooperatives. Snyder liked to reminisce about his years as Kansas Farm Bureau President. He was especially proud of the two insurance companies that got their start under his leadership.

There was no question about Snyder's position as a top man in Kansas agriculture through the 1920's and early '30's. Along with other farm organization leaders, he saw the need for some special attention to agriculture on the part of the federal government. He was in on the formation of the Corn Belt Committee and participated in the development of the McNary-Haugen approach to federal farm legislation. This took him on frequent trips to the nation's capital.

Referring to the McNary-Haugen bill in some reminiscent writing in later years, Snyder summed up some of the political temper of the time with the following:

> We pushed the bill through Congress twice and President Coolidge vetoed it each time. All the Kansas congressional delegation supported it except Poly Tincher (Jasper Napoleon Tincher) of the 7th district. He said it was "economically unsound." We didn't know what that expression meant and could not seem to find out. Poly stayed home thereafter.

Ultimately Snyder and his contemporaries found themselves in a more friendly atmosphere. With the election of Franklin D. Roosevelt, a committee of 36 met in Washington for a new try at getting a comprehensive farm bill through Congress. One of four Kansans in the final group of 15, Snyder was selected as Chairman to present the program to the President. Many years later he recalled the circumstances:

> As far as I know, President Roosevelt had never seen the bill and certainly had nothing to do with framing its policies. We knew, however, that we would get a sympathetic hearing. Its three objectives were: 1. To adjust production to effective demand; 2. To develop a rural credit policy that would be a dependable source of credit to farmers and organized farmer business; 3. To provide a more flexible medium of exchange. It was our plan to present it to Congress in three bills.
> We discussed the measure with the President for a good two hours. He finally said, "Well, boys, you're asking a good deal. But if you can get Congress' approval, I'll go along with you.

But why make it three bills? Let's put it all in one bill." And so we did, and then went to work again on Congress. It will be remembered that this happened in the midst of the worst of all depressions that the United States had ever known. We really did not have a hard time convincing Congress of the efficacy of this measure and in May, 1933, the Agricultural Adjustment Act became a law.

Becomes President of New Wichita Bank

Within less than a year, Snyder was called upon to accept the Presidency of the new Wichita Bank for Cooperatives, and from January, 1934, to July, 1948, he was closely identified with the progress of cooperatives throughout the bank's area of jurisdiction which included, besides Kansas, the states of Oklahoma, Colorado, and New Mexico. In this territory there were many grain elevator companies that had been in existence from as early as 1907. Some of these had already banded together into regional cooperative organizations. When Snyder left the Wichita Bank in 1948, he enjoyed looking back on the tremendous growth of these regional organizations and the part the bank had played in helping expand and strengthen these and other cooperatives.

Among cooperatives financed by the Wichita Bank were several irrigation associations, a rabbit wool-producing co-op, and an association of fox fur producers. Snyder found himself on the receiving end of some jokes about the kind of cooperatives his bank was sponsoring. Especially did this come from men identified with cooperative banks in the East. Of the variety of Wichita loans the one that invited the most derisive comment was what a fellow cooperative bank president referred to as the "distillery" loan. Actually, this loan was made for an oil refinery—the first cooperative oil refinery in the United States.

Snyder recalled in later years that practically no one in bank circles had encouraged him to lend money to Consumers Cooperative Association for the building of a refinery at Phillipsburg, Kan. As it turned out, this Phillipsburg refinery paid off rapidly and the Wichita Bank, under Snyder's supervision, participated in additional loans which enabled CCA to acquire other "distilleries" and become undisputed leader in the farmer-owned segment of the petroleum industry.

Snyder had been a close friend of Howard A. Cowden, founder of CCA, and had served briefly on the CCA board. It was quite proper that he should have a prominent place on the dedicatory program at Phillipsburg. He poured a vial of gasoline into an old horse-drawn tankwagon and said: "Let it (the gasoline) represent new ideas, new and better ideas, trickling through and permeating and modifying the old (economic) structure."

While not exactly a fire-eater on the platform, he was a popular speaker at farm meetings and attained a degree of fame for a stock of stories on which he could draw for most any occasion. In 1957, after he had passed his 85th birthday, he wrote out all of these stories he could recall and arranged for their publication in booklet form. Knowing how effective these stories had been when Ralph Snyder told them, some of his friends tried them, only to learn that the success of an anecdote depends more on the telling sometimes than on the content. There was a touch of Lincoln in the way Snyder could support his point with a humorous illustration.

Writes "We Kansas Farmers"; Emphasizes Strong Co-ops

In the early 1950's, Ralph wrote a small book on the history of farm movements and organizations in Kansas. He called it *We Kansas Farmers*. While he had not been active in the Farmers Alliance and the Peoples (Populist) Party, he was a youthful observer of the Kansas political scene during the peak period of the nineteenth century agrarian revolt. He devoted a short chapter to a summary of events and personalities of the period. He made no attempt to hide his sympathy with the fundamental objectives of those who led the uprising. No one, he wrote, could say that the Alliance and the Populists had been a total loss to Kansas.

The best parts of the little book, however, had to do with those activities of which Snyder was a part. He could write in the first person about the Corn Belt Committee and the founding years of the Farm Bureau Federation. He could draw on conversations with Herbert Hoover, and his first-person description of the farm bill discussion with Franklin D. Roosevelt was one man's recollection of a momentous date in the history of American agriculture.

Throughout his book, Ralph reflected his consistent belief in the desirability of strong farmer cooperatives. He devoted a full chapter to Consumers Cooperative Association, and in his closing chapter he wrote this paragraph:

> I am proud of having had some part in the progress the co-operatives have made in Kansas, and in the country. There has hardly been a major cooperative failure in the past 20 or 25 years. We have developed regional marketing and purchasing organizations as they have never been dreamed of before. The

total volume of cooperative business is far beyond our fondest hopes of 25 years ago. Financial returns in cash have been quite satisfactory. The cooperative philosophy is almost universally understood by those who wish to know. Benefits to nonmembers as well as to members is understood. Indirect benefit to the community as a whole has become the unexpressed result of successful operation of the cooperative enterprise. Where the farmer's cooperative was originally considered as a sort of social outcast, it is now taken and accepted as an important factor in community life. We are proud now to wear the cooperative label.

Ralph Snyder, well past three score and ten when he wrote this, emphasized the positive. That was characteristic of him in his youth, and it was characteristic of the Ralph Snyder I last visited with as he approached his 90th birthday.

Thomas G. Stitts

by Joseph G. Knapp

I LIKE TO THINK OF TOM STITTS when he was my Chief of the Cooperative Research and Service Division of the Farm Credit Administration. He was a colorful character and there was never a dull moment when Tom was Chief. He was very industrious himself and he expected all on his staff to be likewise. However, he had a high good humor and I have found few people whose laughter was so infectious. He could enjoy a joke on himself as well as on the other fellow.

In the summer of 1940 I was planning to spend a month at my summer cabin in Colorado and I knew that Tom was planning to attend some meetings in the Northwest. I suggested that he spend a few days with us loafing in the mountains.

Tom replied with a huff, "Don't you know that I never loaf. I've got more important things to do."

Seeing how the ground lay, I took a different tack, and said, "I had hoped to get you out there to help me saw up a big pine tree for firewood." On the alert, Tom said, "Do you really have a tree? How big is it? I love to saw wood."

I had the tree—an enormous tree that had been about 300 years old—and Tom came and spent two days with us. He got me up before breakfast to saw off a few rounds and we kept busy sawing wood until he had to leave.

He had a wonderful time, and I got my tree cut up for firewood.

This may seem a queer introduction to this sketch of a pioneer cooperator, but I think it reflects the man, industrious, purposeful and cooperative—for he liked to help his neighbors.

Thomas G. Stitts was born on March 25, 1891, at Burlington, N. Y. He was reared on a farm and lived there until he entered the School of Agriculture of Cornell University in 1911.

While in college during the summer months he worked in a cheese factory which he operated during the summer of 1913. During the following summer he was herdsman for a herd of 100 pure-bred Holstein producing fluid milk. During the summer of 1915 he worked for the Cortland County Seed Potato Growers' Association inspecting potatoes and assisting in producer work such as in spraying and fertilization problems.

After graduation in June, 1915, he taught agriculture for two years at the New Berlin High School, New Berlin, N. Y. During this period he worked part time and summers for the Dairymen's League; first in planning and organizational work, and later in helping prepare the plant for handling milk.

He then entered the Army in 1917 as a private. After serving three months as a cook and three months as a staff sergeant he was sent to the Officers Training Corps. He then taught water and rail transportation in officers training for the Quartermasters Corps Service for four months. He then organized a Company (Motor Transportation Corps) and went to France as Company Commander. In France he was responsible for a Transport Center of 70 trucks and 100 men. In this work he traveled throughout France, Belgium, Germany, and Italy.

After being demobilized from the Army in 1919 he was elected County Agricultural Agent in Meeker County, Minn.

It was in this job at Litchfield, Minn., during the next five years that Tom Stitts got deeply involved in cooperative marketing. He helped in the organization and management of a cooperative egg association; he assisted 10 cooperative creameries in the organization of egg departments, and developed a county plan for egg marketing. He organized three cooperative livestock shipping associations, and handled the cattle shipments for several months until a manager could be employed.

Organizational Work Forerunner of Land O'Lakes

But his major cooperative achievement in this field was the organization of the first Creamery District in Minnesota which comprised 22 cooperative creameries. This was a forerunner of the Minnesota Cooperative Creamery Association and the Land O'Lakes Creameries. It was in this work that he came to be associated with John Brandt and, together, they made a formidable organizational team. Tom also made an exhaustive study of cooperative creamery business practices, financing, organization, pricing policies, pooling methods, and other

phases of operations, which was used as a basis for extension work
with these creameries.

With the encouragement of Dr. John D. Black, Stitts decided to
take graduate work in 1924 at the University of Minnesota, where
he majored in agricultural economics and minored in business and
dairy technology. Concurrent with his last year of graduate study
he was employed by the University as Instructor in Agricultural
Economics and Extension Specialist in Marketing. While he was
working for his Ph.D., which was granted him in 1927, he helped
with local arrangements for the 1926 American Institute of Cooperation, did research work for the Land O'Lakes Creameries and Lake
Region Egg and Poultry Exchange, and served in a consulting capacity
to a number of cooperatives on problems of organization and administrative procedures for creameries and dry buttermilk plants.

In 1927, Tom came to Washington to work as Marketing Specialist
in the newly-created Division of Cooperative Marketing in the Bureau
of Agricultural Economics of the U.S.D.A. This gave him an opportunity to work with dairy marketing cooperatives throughout the
nation, and in this capacity he produced a number of important
bulletins.

When the Federal Farm Board took over the Division of Cooperative Marketing, Tom became active in the organization and developing of cooperative marketing associations from Coast to Coast.

In 1933, when the Federal Farm Board ceased operations, Tom
was transferred to the Cooperative Division of the Farm Credit Administration where he was placed in charge of dairy and poultry work.

Becomes First Chief of Co-op Research, Service Division

In 1937, the Cooperative Research and Service Division of the
Farm Credit Administration was created with Tom as Chief.

Tom continued to serve as Chief of this Division until 1946, but
during the years from 1942-46, this work was directed by an Acting
Chief, for Tom's major responsibility during these years was as
Director of the Dairy and Poultry Branch of the U.S. D.A., and the War
Food Administration. In this work he had direct responsibility for
all federal food orders issued by the War Food Administration relating
to dairy and poultry produce, purchase programs for dairy and poultry
products for the Lend Lease Administration, and many other similar
wartime responsibilities. In this work his knowledge of cooperative
leaders and organizations was of the greatest importance, in view of
their importance in the total agricultural marketing structure.

In 1946, Tom left the government to serve as Director of Public Policy and member of the Senior Board of Executives of H. P. Hood & Sons, Inc., Charlestown, Mass., and he served in this capacity until his retirement in 1957. Since retirement Tom has spent a good share of his time in Clearwater, Fla., which is his present address.

This record of Tom's life may show the progress of his professional career but it does not fully indicate the great influence that he had on the development of cooperative organizations during the 25 years from 1919 to 1946. As much as any other man he helped build the strong dairy cooperative organizations that now do a total annual business of over $2 billion.

Herbert L. Forest, Director of the Dairy Division of the U.S.D.A. Consumer and Marketing Service, says this with regard to his contribution:

> Tom did the first real research in the problems of cooperatives in marketing milk with the cooperation of several bright young fellows. . . . Tom's work actually dealt with the practical problems of the cooperatives. . . I think that all the people acquainted with cooperatives have more respect and confidence in his judgment than anybody before or since. He not only advised them on financial problems but on problems connected with their personnel, management, and public relations.

Architect
of Cooperation

90

E. A. Stokdyk

by Joseph G. Knapp

DR. ELLIS A. STOKDYK was born near Sheboygan, Wisc., in 1897. His father and mother were immigrants from Holland. He was reared on a small Wisconsin farm and educated at the College of Agriculture of the University of Wisconsin, with an intervening period in the Navy during World War I.

After graduation from the University in 1920 he started out on his professional career as an Assistant 4-H Club Leader. Let us pause for a minute to see this young chap at the age of 23. He was, from all accounts, keen and attractive. His college record was excellent—his personality was warm and friendly. He already had a professional interest in horticulture and he had found that he liked to work with people. Dr. Hutzel Metzger recalls him as "a good looking chap with a bag of tricks to entertain the 4-H Club kids."

He had been in this work only a few months when he accepted a job as Extension Horticulturist at Kansas State College. He jumped into this new work with elan and was soon actively working on several jobs. Almost immediately we find circulars and bulletins coming out under his name.

Stok had landed in Kansas almost simultaneously with the agricultural depression following World War I. He couldn't escape its impact. The emphasis of the times was on better marketing. What good to save potatoes or other crops from disease just to have them rot in the fields for lack of markets.

With the completion of his work for the M. A. degree in horticulture in 1924 at Kansas State, a cycle in Stok's life was completed. He then shifted from his field of plant pathology to agricultural economics. He was just the man Dr. W. E. Grimes, head of the Department of Agricultural Economics, was looking for—and in October, 1924, he became the first marketing specialist to be employed by the Kansas State College of Agriculture.

The new work brought him in close touch with Professor Roy Green who was then making significant studies of grain prices. He also traveled about the state attending farm meetings with Ralph Snyder, then President of the Kansas Farm Bureau, and a national figure in "the fight for farm equality." Snyder saw in Stok "a comer."

This was a period of intensive development in the field of agricultural economics. The field was new—the problems were challenging. Cooperation was being prescribed as a solution to all evils. However, many were turning to the state for help via such routes as the McNary-Haugen plan.

Determines to Become Authority on Ag Economics, Marketing

The way he imbedded himself in the life of the state's agriculture in the next four years was remarkable. All of this time he was studying, thinking, writing, and speaking. He was determined to make himself an authority in the field of agricultural economics and marketing.

Realizing that more education and training were required, Stok in 1928 went back to the University of Wisconsin for advanced training. He was clearly a man of coming power.

His viewpoint was already mature. He knew what he wanted and what he wanted it for—not personal wealth—but the power of knowledge—the tools for building a sounder agriculture. His intellectual appetite was voracious. The University of Wisconsin gave him the challenge of such men as Professors B. H. Hibbard and John R. Commons.

Just at this time—1929—the University of California, with the new Giannini Foundation established—was reaching out in the field of agricultural marketing. Dr. Henry Erdman, in charge of marketing, was looking for a man to help him who would be a research man, a teacher, and an extension man—a thinker and a doer. Dr. Hibbard, head of the Department of Agricultural Economics at the University of Wisconsin, had just the man, then working for his Ph.D., to recommend—Stok—and he more than filled the bill.

In the next few years Stok infused a new spirit into California agricultural cooperation. Probably at no time in its history has the University of California contributed more fruitfully to the development of sound cooperative programs, and at the center of the ferment was Dr. E. A. Stokdyk.

He was a natural. He liked the people—the people liked him. He grappled with their problems with a trained and original mind. He

offered sound programs—they were adopted. His reputation grew
as a professor with a mission—he had the practical touch. He brought
respect to education because he used it for solving problems. His
studies were among the finest marketing analyses the country has
known, and his output was large and uniformly good.

Selected as President of New Berkeley Bank

When the Farm Credit Administration was established in 1933, and
the Berkeley Bank for Cooperatives was set up, there was little doubt
as to the man for the job. The farm organizations, the cooperatives,
the University authorities saw in Stok one who could lead the new
institution and he was made President. He served in this position
until his death 12 years later, except for one year, 1938-39, when he
was on leave of absence as Deputy Governor of the Farm Credit
Administration in charge of research.

Stokdyk was a student of the cooperative form of enterprise. He
came to the field with a fresh mind and on the basis of his studies
he steadily deepened his understanding of cooperatives. He saw
that they were economic institutions of a political and social nature.
He was a pragmatist. Cooperative theory had no significance to him
unless it could be worked out in practice.

He was concerned with the way in which the cooperatives could
be used to solve problems. He knew that they had to be able to do
things at least as well as other enterprises if they were to survive.
He knew that they must be soundly organized in the light of their
own special problems if they were to perform efficiently. He also
knew that effective operation with competent management was essential. To him a weakly-formed and operated cooperative was hardly
worthy of the name.

The name of Dr. Stokdyk is closely linked to the revolving fund
method of financing. He was not its originator, but few people have
had a greater influence in developing and extending the plan. Its
possibilities intrigued him and he analyzed it from every point of
view to see how the idea could be most effectively utilized.

To Stok the revolving fund plan of financing was the ideal method
for financing a cooperative, for he believed that costs and benefits
should be harmonized in a true cooperative organization so that all
individuals would bear expense and share in benefits equitably. To
him, the revolving fund plan as a cooperative device was almost as
important as the concept of patronage refunds.

Stok was a voluminous writer and his publications were persuasive because they were simply written and well organized. He believed in short sentences and short paragraphs. He believed also in supporting his arguments with careful analysis, both logical and statistical. One could always see what Stok was driving at and his writings answered or threw light upon vital questions. There was almost no phase of cooperative economics—price theory, market or cost control, membership administration—that Stok did not consider in some of his various publications.

Stok, as a student of cooperative enterprise, early came to realize that the sound development of cooperative organizations was handicapped by their inaccessibility to sources of credit comparable to those enjoyed by large corporate organizations. He saw that one of their difficulties in obtaining financial assistance was that their methods of organization and operation were not understood by those whose experience was limited to dealing with commercial business firms that operated for profit.

Believed that Banks Should Do More than Merely Lend

To Stok a cooperative banker had to be more than a lender to cooperatives, for he believed that to be effective as a cooperative banker one had to understand the formation and workings of cooperative organizations. He believed that the power of finance should be used wisely to help in the building of efficient cooperatives.

Stok soon impressed his views on the Banks for Cooperatives. Soon after his appointment as President he presented a paper on the "Economics of Cooperative Loans" at a conference of the Bank presidents. He pointed out that:

> The ultimate test of our services to cooperative enterprise is based upon our understanding of the economics of cooperative loans. If we make unsound loans, we will be given little credit for developing procedures and policies or conforming to legal requirements. On the other hand, if we pass up sound loans because we do not comprehend the economic phases, we fail to render maximum service.

It is of interest that Stok was the principal proponent of the plan for making the cooperative banks fully cooperative. It will be recalled that the Banks for Cooperatives were established originally with government capital and that no provision was made for gradually supplanting government capital with capital furnished by the cooperatives themselves. With the passage of time, he became convinced that the Banks for Cooperatives, like the other parts of the Farm

Credit Administration, should be cooperatively financed by those served. As the protagonist of this view, Stok was named chairman of a committee within the Farm Credit Administration to consider how the cooperatives might gradually acquire the capital then held by the federal government. The Farm Credit Act of 1955, which brought about the change to cooperative ownership was a belated monument to his efforts.

Stok was an evolutionist. He believed in the gradual transformation of organizations so as to take advantage of prior achievements. He appreciated that time was required for the gestation of ideas as well as for their execution. His plan for transforming the Banks for Cooperatives from federal ownership to cooperative ownership provided for a painless transition over a long period of years, during which government capital would gradually give way to capital furnished by the cooperatives served. He was not concerned with all of the questions which might arise because he felt that one sure achievement would lead to others, while too large a program at the outset might bog down.

As an Economist He Recognized Economic-Legal Mutuality

Although Dr. Stokdyk's name has been identified with cooperative law through his co-authorship of *The Law of Cooperative Marketing*, with Frank Evans, he was not a trained lawyer in the strict sense of the word. Rather, he was an economist who saw the inter-relationship of economic and legal institutions. Trained under the influence of John R. Commons at the University of Wisconsin, he was an "institutional economist"—one who recognized legal structures as economic facts. Stok was always intrigued by the law and he was a careful student of the influence of law on our society. However, as a specialist in economics he fully appreciated his limitations as a specialist in the technical field of law.

Stok's contribution to cooperative law was thus that of a student of legal concepts and methods. Laws to him were made by people to achieve ends and law was a living force, not the sole property of lawyers. He impressed on lawyers the ideas of economic analysis while he impressed on economic analysts the importance of legal institutions. As one economist has told me, "Stok taught me the importance of cooperative law. The book by Evans and Stokdyk made me realize that cooperative law was as important to the economist as to the lawyer."

When the American Institute of Cooperation was revitalized in

1944, Stok was impressed with its educational opportunity, and he was the natural person on its Board of Trustees to serve as Chairman of the Committee on Education. The report which Stok presented as Chairman of this Committee is a document of great importance, and many of its recommendations have yet to be carried into effect.

One idea especially appealed to Stok—A correspondence course for young men and women on cooperative principles and their application. He felt that a course of this kind would train leadership so essential for cooperative vitality. Working with his friend, Dr. Erdman of the University of California, this course was brought to reality in the closing days of his life as his last great contribution to agricultural cooperation.

Stok's work in the field of public relations for cooperatives was outstanding. He believed in cooperative principles of organization and felt that they were in keeping with the system of private enterprise of the United States.

His authoritative grasp of cooperative principles and his incomparable knowledge of how cooperation worked in practice made it possible for him to win support for the cooperative method through his addresses, meetings, and conversations.

His practical wisdom, pleasant good humor, tolerance, and kindliness gave standing to the cooperatives. He was no fanatic. He recognized the problems of labor, industry, and business, and he respected the role of capable executives in making our free enterprise system work. To him, cooperatives were simply business organizations set up by farmers to serve themselves—an extension of the farming enterprise.

Made Outstanding Contribution in Public Relations Area

Stok realized that good public relations for any man or institution depends upon character, and the effective performance of important functions. He encouraged cooperatives to so operate as to merit the respect of the communities in which they lived.

It is my opinion that Stok's contribution in the area of public relations work was of unique importance. I believe that the public relations of cooperative associations would be better than they are today, if he had lived longer, for he was a master in this field where we have needed sound counsel and sound interpreters of the role of cooperatives to national well-being. As one of his friends, Fran Wilcox, has well said, "Dr. Stokdyk was the symbol of defense for cooperatives."

Stok drew people to him and gave them encouragement and inspiration. He had great prestige, due to his analytical abilities and unusual strength of personality. He was both a natural and a trained leader.

In whatever group Stok found himself he was in the forefront. He was not "too" perfect, but he had a quiet competence and an ability to put over his ideas. His training as a research man and teacher helped him in organizing his thoughts. He was gifted as a storyteller and effectively used anecdotes to illuminate his points. His rich sense of humor was kindly and fun loving. To him a good story or humorous situation was a cause for rejoicing.

Probably a clue to his character was his forthrightness. People knew where he stood. He differed with them frequently—but not harshly. Even those he opposed respected him for his polite and considerate behavior. He won by his charm as well as by his logic.

There are many men who found out from Stok what they could do. Young men, particularly, were caught by his insight, vision, and determination, and were challenged to make good.

Over the years his prestige and influence grew. His judgment and confidence affected the character of many organizations. He gave his well-considered views generously—and they were quietly absorbed.

Cooperation has had few exponents of his stature. The number is small who have had a greater effect in raising the standards, or in broadening the influence of agricultural cooperation.

It was because of my love and respect for him that I wrote *Stokdyk— Architect of Cooperation*, published by the American Institute of Cooperation in 1953.

Frank Tracy Swett

by Henry E. Erdman

THE NAME FRANK T. SWETT came onto the cooperative marketing scene in the San Francisco area in the summers of 1916 and 1917 when Frank took an active part in the formation of the California Pear Growers Association, and became its first President and only Manager. But the name was already well known on two counts: (1) his father, John Swett, had been a prominent and often controversial figure in California public school affairs at a time when teachers' jobs were often considered political spoils, and (2) Frank had already demonstrated his own ability and public spirit.

Frank was born in San Francisco on November 22, 1869. Here he grew up, attended public schools, and for two years commuted to the University of California across the bay in Berkeley. There he studied chemistry as a major, including such courses as botany, literature, and mathematics; but for him perhaps most meaningful were courses in horticulture and viticulture. But events diverted him from his studies at the end of his sophomore year.

Frank's father had acquired a 185-acre farm in 1882 near Martinez, some 25 miles as the crow flies, northeast of San Francisco. The farm had been bought "as a sort of old age home to which we could retire after schoolwork was ended." He had immediately hired a foreman and had proceeded to plant a vineyard. In 1889, he gave up his school job rather than fight a losing battle with the political machine. When the family moved out to the farm, he found conditions such that he asked Frank to leave school for a year while they got things in order. He made Frank foreman at $600 a year and board. But the aroused citizens of San Francisco nominated and then easily elected Frank's father the Superintendent of Public Schools for a four-year term. So, he went back to the city that fall leaving the family on the farm with Frank as foreman.

Upon John's return to the farm after completion of his term in

January, 1895, he established the firm of "John Swett and Son," paying Frank a "fair salary," as he put it, for keeping the books and conducting the business correspondence, "leaving me free to select the work best suited to my tastes."

In 1897, Frank was married to Myrta Wallace More, who had come to the Swett household as a "roomer" while she was teaching the nearby country school. "As a wedding present to Frank," wrote the father, "we deeded him a one-fourth undivided interest in Hill Girt farm"—the name Frank's mother had bestowed on it upon noting the ring of hills around it.

In 1910, John Swett wrote of Frank as "business manager," and added, "Besides, he owns and cultivates a new 20-acre vineyard contiguous to Hill Girt, living now in his own home with his wife and two children—Margaret and Elizabeth."

Recognized as "Practical Expert" on Fruit Stock

By 1916–17 when the movement to form a pear growers association was taking shape, Frank Swett had already won recognition among fruit growers of Central California. He had been County Horticultural Commissioner in his home county (Contra Costa) for a number of years (1905–1909, and again in 1915–1919). He had been a member and Vice-President of the California Viticultural Commission (1913–1919). He had frequently participated in affairs of the State Fruit Growers and Farmers Conventions and had presented papers at its sessions.

In one such paper in December, 1912, he castigated those who mislead the unwary to plant fruit acreage when fruit is already in surplus. He suggested the establishment at the University of "a chair of agricultural and horticultural economics." He had become recognized as a "practical expert" on grape growing and on disease resistant fruit stock and had been called on to lecture on these subjects at Farmers Institutes conducted by the University of California in that period. His farm experience was underscored by the way he handled a phylloxera infestation of the vineyard in 1898. The heavy cost of replanting with resistant stock was reduced by availability of suitable stock at the firm's own nursery.

During the time he had a business office in San Francisco, he was an active member of the Commonwealth Club of California and for some 10 years was chairman of its agricultural study section.

In 1936, he acted as Regional Supervisor of Farm Debt Adjustment in the Resettlement Administration.

Chaotic Pear Marketing Situation Leads to Co-op Development

Early in 1916, Harris Weinstock, the Director of the newly-established State Market Commission, had embarked on a program of helping groups of farmers organize on a commodity basis to solve their own marketing problems. A few prominent pear growers—among them Frank T. Swett, then a County Horticultural Commissioner as well as a pear grower—called the new Director's attention to the chaotic condition of the pear market. The Director suggested and shortly addressed a meeting of pear growers which appointed a committee of five to confer with the Director on plans for organizing. But the matter was dropped because growers showed little interest. They were in the habit of acting as individuals. Moreover, canners expecting an increase in European demand were soon offering $50 a ton as compared with $30 paid the previous season, this in spite of prospects for a bumper crop.

In the summer of 1917, when canners were talking of $35 a ton for pears, a more representative meeting of pear growers led to the appointment of a committee of 11 growers who were authorized to organize. They did so by electing Swett as Chairman and then incorporating as the California Pear Growers Association with Frank T. Swett unanimously elected as its President.

Although it was too late that season to do any selling, the organization campaign alerted producers to the facts that the Eastern market promised to be better than the cannery outlet and that the European dried fruit outlet might be good. The result was sharp increases in quantities shipped fresh and dried, sharp decreases in quantities canned, and increased prices to growers in all three outlets for the 1917 crop.

Mr. Swett was appointed as Manager on July 1, 1918, a position he was to retain until the association was dissolved in 1936.

As President and Manager of the new association, he brought to its service a wide knowledge of the problems of fruit growing and of the economic factors involved in reaching marketing decisions. His business experience of over two decades from the mid-1890's to 1916 had included much of the detail involved in raising and marketing the product of over 100 acres of fruit land planted to grapes, pears, peaches, cherries, prunes, and walnuts. In addition, in pre-Prohibition days, the partnership operated a small winery and, for a time, two nurseries.

He was always a keen observer, a good listener, and a wide reader. As Manager, he was included in numerous conferences on industry problems. Thus, he kept abreast of changing conditions in or affecting the fresh, canned, or dried fruit industries. Naturally the duties of the new position gave him added stimulus to keep fully informed and, of course, to keep his directors abreast of affairs not only in the industry but more particularly in the association.

Described as "One of Co-op's Greatest Assets"

The directors often seemed to have relied heavily on his judgment not only in reaching decisions on agreements with buyers but also on such matters as investments, insurance policies, reserve funds, and member relationships. His leadership was sufficiently reflective of his own ideas to have antagonized some members, but it may fairly be said that Swett was one of the cooperative's greatest assets.

As President, Swett also had frequent occasion to represent the association at such diverse meetings as those called by Weinstock in 1917–18 to form the California Federation of Cooperative Marketing Associations, the cooperative conference called in 1929 by the Federal Farm Board, and some conferences designed to coordinate activities of California and Northwest pear grower groups.

Once his work with the pear growers had demonstrated his ability, he was called upon by other associations. In 1920, he was asked to advise the cherry growers then forming an association. For a number of years, he served on the boards of the California Grape Exchange, the California Canning Peach Growers, the California Cherry Growers Association, the California Prune and Apricot Growers Association, and the California Growers and Shippers' Protective League. At a later date, he served as temporary Manager of the California Canning Peach Growers.

Goal of 85 Percent of Pear Crop Not Reached

Throughout the period of his management he was very much in charge of affairs. The minutes of the board of directors show him to have had very nearly a perfect record of acting as chairman, and the brief notes on discussions suggest that he was alert to the basic problems involved. But the association never succeeded in reaching the goal he had set for it. He had hoped to sign up a minimum of 85 percent of the California pear crop. He believed that with such support it would be possible to do national advertising of fresh, canned, and dried pears that would take care of the oncoming crops from vast new acreage being planted in California and the Northwest. He never lost his enthusiasm for advertising, but both he and successive boards of directors refused to "carry the umbrella for the non-members" by supporting more than some experimental advertising. When the depression hit pear growers badly in 1930, he noted that other producer groups had lost too. Citrus growers had received $23 million less than in 1929. "Did they quit advertising?" he asked. Answering his own question he said, "No, they increased their advertising budget for 1931 by $500,000!"

The depression found California pear growers with a record crop that was not to be exceeded for another eight years. Said Swett: "No depression has been permanent, and, in the course of time this one will pass."

Swett seems never to have favored having the association do its own canning. It would weaken the association's hand in bargaining and was risky. In January, 1933, he noted in his annual report that since the Association began selling in 1918 "we have seen over 40 canners fade out of the picture, some with heavy losses." But the association had been able to collect on all but one-tenth of one percent of its sales to canners. The depression seemed to breed dissension within the ranks of pear growers. Neither between the Northwest and California nor between the various sections of California did any consensus on procedures emerge from the innumerable conferences. Instead, splinter movements favoring conflicting proposals developed and finally led to cessation of activity as a bargaining association. Finally in 1936 this led to dissolution.

Mr. Swett and his directors deferred dissolution of the corporation, apparently hoping it could again become useful. From early 1933 on, Swett urged curtailment of shipments, advised against signing long-term sales contracts, showed how curtailment plans would work, etc. In 1933, the association distributed the revolving fund and sold crops for those members desiring it. In his reports, Swett repeatedly showed how the association was still helping growers. In one of his last letters he questioned whether growers had really learned that organization pays; then he quoted an old saying:

When the devil was sick, the devil a monk would be;
When the devil got well, the devil a monk was he.

Emil A. Syftestad

by T. H. Steichen

EMIL A. SYFTESTAD spent the major part of his life, nearly 45 years, building cooperatives. For 26 of these years, he served as General Manager of the Farmers Union Central Exchange, a regional farm supply cooperative headquartered in South St. Paul, Minn. Organized in 1927 as the Farmers Union Exchange, a subsidiary of the Farmers Union Terminal Association, a grain marketing cooperative, the Farmers Union Central Exchange acquired its own identity with its re-incorporation on January 15, 1931.

When E.A., as he was known to his closest associates, was appointed General Manager on April 1, 1932, the Central Exchange was surviving on loans from the Terminal Association and from its own limited line of credit. The darkest days of the depression were ahead of it.

With the patient loyalty and confidence of the farmers, E.A. guided the company to solvency and beyond. His last report to stockholders at the annual meeting of March, 1957, showed the previous year's volume at nearly $68 million. The co-op's first year had a volume of less than a million.

Advocated Co-op Ownership of Manufacturing Facilities, Raw Materials

The guiding spirit behind E.A.'s management of the Central Exchange was his determination to reduce the cost of farm supplies. He felt this could best be done cooperatively, and by the regional cooperatives owning manufacturing facilities and the sources of raw material.

During 1932, his first year as Manager, he helped to organize National Cooperatives, Albert Lea, Minn., as a supplier of automotive items and appliances to wholesale co-op members. It was under his spirited leadership that the Central Exchange made one of its wisest moves. In 1943, it purchased a refinery from the Independent Refining

Company, Laurel, Mont. Later that same year, the CE participated in the formation of the National Cooperative Refinery Association to purchase the refinery at McPherson, Kan.

Still expanding the idea of becoming a basic producer and manufacturer, the Exchange again joined with other co-ops, in 1945, to form Northwest Co-op Mills in St. Paul, a feed, seed and fertilizer manufacturing cooperative. And, in 1946, Central Farmers Fertilizer Company, Chicago, Ill., was formed with the Exchange as a member. That same year CE's first producing oil well came in. Only eight years later, in 1954, the Oil Basin pipeline was constructed to carry petroleum products from the refinery at Laurel to Glendive, Mont.

The rapid growth of the Central Exchange during its early years made increased facilities for an expanding business a necessity. By the end of 1934, it had out-grown its rented offices in St. Paul. On May 1, 1935, the Exchange moved into its own new building in South St. Paul, a building which included a warehouse, office, and CE's first manufacturing operation: a lube oil blending plant. In response to continued growth, additions were made to the main plant and home office in 1941 and 1947, doubling the capacity of the facilities. On February 22, 1957, its offices moved into a new four-story building across the street. By this time, the Exchange had built a network of eight branch warehouses in four states, as well as 20 LP Gas plants and the first of many soil service center bulk fertilizer plants.

The Central Exchange was Mr. Syftestad's whole life; it was his work and his hobby. Those who remember him best say E.A. was the company's watchman; he was on the job seven days a week and far into most of every night. He ruled with a firm but just and respected hand. His strength in building the Central Exchange helped strengthen the cooperative movement throughout the company's trade area from the Great Lakes to the Pacific Ocean. And he had gone far in accomplishing his desire to reduce farm costs through cooperative action. He won many honors for his devotion to the cooperative cause, among them the 1953 National Farmers Union Award for Meritorious Service to Agriculture.

Praised for Devotion to Cooperative Movement

In presenting this award, James G. Patton, then President of the National Farmers Union said in part:

> Owned and operated by farmers, the Farmers Union Central Exchange has never lost sight of its purpose, its goals and its

responsibilities. As a result of these policies, it has been of great economic service to farmers throughout the country . . . working from a broad base to make a better way of life for farm families everywhere.

In the forefront of this cooperative, since its beginning, has been a man who is respected, admired, and liked by all who know him, Emil Syftestad. He has devoted his life to cooperatives, and the debt that is owed him by farmers and those in the cooperative movement cannot be estimated.

Emil A. Syftestad was born in Appleton, Minn., on November 26, 1891. His family moved shortly thereafter to homestead near New Rockford, N.D. He attended schools there and was graduated valedictorian of his high school class. He also acquired a reputation as an athlete in both basketball and baseball. After graduation, he went to Seattle, Wash., to attend Wilson Business College.

Learning of a position with a cooperative in St. Paul, he moved there in 1915 to become a clerk for the Equity Cooperative Exchange, moving two years later to Big Sandy, Mont., where he was employed as a bookkeeper for the Farmers Union Elevator Company. With the coming of World War I, he volunteered for two years of medical service with the army in France. After the armistice, he returned to St. Paul and became a bookkeeper and accountant for Equity, the cooperative for which he had previously worked and which would eventually grow into the Farmers Union Terminal Association. Throughout those early troubled years for cooperatives, Emil Syftestad's responsibilities grew greater and greater—until that day in 1932 when he was named the General Manager of the Farmers Union Central Exchange. Then he had all the responsibility, but for him it was fun and a time for total devotion to his principles and goals.

On July 16, 1957, Emil was at his desk "as usual." That evening he complained of not feeling well. He was rushed to the hospital, where he was pronounced dead of a heart attack upon arrival. Surviving were his wife and two daughters and the thousands of cooperators for whom he had fought so long and so well.

Carl C. Taylor

by Joseph G. Knapp

CARL TAYLOR THINKS THAT HE INHERITED his interest in cooperatives. His father was President of a farmers' cooperative store in Harlan, Iowa, back in the 1890's.

Carl was born on a farm in Shelby County, Iowa, on December 16, 1884. He grew up during a period of agricultural ferment, with Populism still a dominant force in the Mid-West. As a child he loved to read and he found much intellectual nourishment and entertainment in the *Youth's Companion* which was almost a bible in his home.

Carl was ambitious to prove that he was a man just as soon as possible, and he didn't see the advantage of education until he was nearly grown. From the time he was nine until he was 16 he missed many terms of the country school, and after 16 he didn't attend at all for the simple reason that he had bragged that he was going to run the farm without hired men when he reached 16. His father let him do it.

He was so imbued with being a "heap big farmer" that he had no notion of going to college—but gradually he became aware of his ignorance. So when his father decided to sell the farm, Carl began prep work at Eureka College in 1904 so that he could enter Drake University in Des Moines.

He found himself at Drake University from which he graduated with a Phi Beta Kappa key and a B.A. degree in 1911. He then got a job as instructor in public speaking at the University of Texas. Here he met and married Miss Euphie Ramsey, and also obtained his Master's degree in 1914. His next job was as instructor in economics and sociology at Mt. Holyoke College in Massachusetts and, after a half-year of that, he got an assistant professorship in sociology at the University of Missouri where he could take the work for his doctor's degree. After receiving the degree in 1918 he was promoted to the rank of associate professor.

Became Vitally Interested in Rural Sociology

Taylor had become interested in rural problems through articles in *Wallace's Farmer* and the *Iowa Homestead*. He found of special interest the writings of Charles Harlan Cooley, then professor of sociology at the University of Michigan. He liked Cooley's line of analysis which recognized the importance of "the social order" in each individual's life. He was attracted also by the writings of such prominent sociologists of the time as E. A. Ross, Franklin Giddings, Kenyon Butterfield, and the broad philosophical rural writings of Liberty Hyde Bailey. When he was in college at Drake University, Theodore Roosevelt's Country Life Commission was attracting national attention to the social and economic problems of agriculture.

His special interest in the emerging field of rural sociology came from a graduate seminar at the University of Missouri, where he chose to answer the question "Are American farmers a social class?" In writing up this paper he read every agricultural journal he could lay his hands on over a period of time and in that process he became interested in what he came to call "The Farmers' Movement," the subject which became his lifetime interest.

In 1920, a real opportunity opened for him. North Carolina State College of Agriculture and Engineering was looking for a man to head up a new Department of Agricultural Economics, and Taylor was selected for this post. Although the University of Missouri offered him a full professorship to stay there he was anxious to have experience in the Old South and the position in North Carolina offered a golden opportunity for his widening ambitions.

Until that time his interest in cooperation was largely academic, although he had helped organize a faculty cooperative purchasing club while at the University of Missouri. At North Carolina State he couldn't avoid becoming actively interested, for Sapiroism in the form of large-scale commodity cooperatives was beginning to sweep the South. He was soon pulled into all the discussions that led to the formation of the ill-fated Tri-State Tobacco Association and the North Carolina Cotton Growers Cooperative which has continued to this day.

Gave Serious Study to Cooperative Marketing Methods

Taylor recognized that there was no one in the area with a basic knowledge of cooperative marketing and he began to give this field serious study. In 1922, after teaching at the summer school of the University of Texas, he went on to California where he devoted two months to finding out for himself how California cooperatives worked.

For one thing, he found that Sapiro's philosophy was more honored by cooperative leaders in other states than in California where he got his start.

Although skeptical of Sapiro's philosophy and methods he couldn't ignore the gigantic experiment in cooperative organization Sapiro initiated. The job was to make the Tri-State and the North Carolina Cotton Cooperative Associations work. At this time the outstanding agricultural leaders in North Carolina were Dr. Clarence Poe and Dr. B. W. Kilgore, Director of the North Carolina Agricultural Extension Service. These men were committed to cooperation and they called upon Carl Taylor for help. As a result he made something like 200 speeches in North Carolina, South Carolina, and Virginia in a 30-month period in 1922–1924, and he sat in on all of the councils on cooperative marketing problems.

He came to know Sapiro well and often appeared on the same program with him. At one meeting in Richmond he publicly refused to go along with Sapiro's position that if they signed up enough tobacco they could control the market and literally dictate the prices. On another occasion he sharply disagreed with Sapiro's position that the growers' iron-clad contracts to deliver their crops to the tobacco association were legally airtight. Taylor foresaw that no legal action could possibly stem a tide of contract-breaking; that so many thousands of suits would clog the courts that even legal contracts would be of no avail in the face of the resulting upheaval.

Taylor was convinced that the one thing that would enable these gigantic cooperatives to succeed was a great educational movement with field persons employed to explain cooperative marketing to growers, and he promoted this idea in his numerous speeches. To a large extent he was responsible for the inauguration of field service work in the Tri-State and cotton cooperative associations.

However, before the educational program could become effective, the Tri-State began to have serious trouble. As a result, in 1925, the Tri-State directors asked the three State Colleges to each appoint a person to make an analysis of its problems. Clarence Poe, who represented North Carolina State on this committee, asked Taylor to serve for him. Taylor sat through all of the hearings and served as rapporteur for working up the report. The report made in April, 1925, found that one of the most serious problems was due to lack of attention to membership education. However, by this time the situation had grown so bad that it could not be remedied and, after a critical study by the Federal Trade Commission, the Tri-State association was thrown into receivership from which it never recovered.

Worked Hard to Rebuild Tobacco Cooperative

With the Federal Farm Board's encouragement an attempt was made to re-establish statewide tobacco cooperatives in North Carolina. At the request of Governor O. Max Gardner, Taylor was relieved from teaching in 1930 to give talks throughout the state in behalf of the new effort. However, it was impossible to rebuild upon the still warm ashes of the old Tri-State.

In 1933, at the American Institute of Cooperation, Taylor relived the experience of the Tri-State Tobacco Cooperative and the later efforts to reorganize on a more modest scale in a talk entitled, "The Story and the Lesson of the Tri-State Tobacco Cooperative Association." This is a fine eye-witness account of this interesting social and economic experiment and it is told with dispassion.

In the early 30's, Taylor encouraged the Virginia Seed Service to extend its supply purchasing services into North Carolina and assisted it in organization within the state. When it was reorganized as the Southern States Cooperative in 1933, Taylor was asked to serve as a Director.

These experiences afforded Taylor laboratory experience to test his theories that membership education was essential to cooperative success—and in his 1933 speech referred to above he concluded:

> No cooperative marketing organization can be built on the backs of a tenant-cropper, crop-mortgage-ridden population. . . No cooperative can survive on the basis of purely contractual relations and corporation ideas of operation.

In 1931, a crisis occurred in Taylor's life. Up to then his career in North Carolina had been a brilliant success. In 1923 he had been made Dean of the Graduate School and he had been a leader in remaking the institution. He had served as Chairman of the library committee, which within a year got a new library for the college, and as Chairman of the athletic committee which took athletics out from under the control of the alumni.

No agricultural leader in North Carolina was better known or more highly respected. But his liberal views and aggressiveness were resented by the "old order," and this element considered him a dangerous free-thinking radical. He was very popular with the students for they found in him a staunch and fearless friend.

University Clique Abolishes His Position as Dean

Then out of the blue, Taylor was informed that the Board of Trustees had voted to discontinue the Graduate School and his post as its Dean in the interests of economy. This action, contrived by a clique on the Board, came as a shock, not only to Taylor but to the entire college community—and Taylor found himself an outcast from the position of importance he had held so long.

Taylor's first reaction was one of shock and bewilderment. His whole career had been that of a professional educator, and this way of life was temporarily closed to him, at least in a position of eminence such as he had enjoyed. He had always been generous to causes and people and he had practically no resources to fall back on. Although he tried to support his wife and family for a time by selling insurance his heart was not in this work. There was one helpful side. The enforced retirement from professional work gave him an opportunity to work on a book that he had long been gathering information for—on Farmers Movements.

Through the Whitney Foundation he obtained a small grant of $2,000 to enable him to work on that project. Many years later, when this book was published, Taylor said in the preface:

> The author owes long-delayed thanks to Mr. and Mrs. Elmhurst who, through the solicitation of my longtime personal and professional friend, Professor Edward C. Lindeman, made a grant of $2,000 from the Whitney Foundation which enabled me in 1932 to work intensively for about six months consolidating the ground I had covered over previous years of work.

Later in 1933, John W. Studebaker, then Superintendent of Schools in Des Moines, Iowa, called for Taylor's help on a program of adult education forums in Iowa. Taylor's popularity in this work attracted national attention, and especially that of Henry A. Wallace, who was soon to become Secretary of Agriculture under Franklin D. Roosevelt.

After Difficulty, Enters Field of Rural Sociology

This was a stop-gap job but it brought Taylor into Wallace's mind when he began to make plans with M. L. Wilson for a program of agricultural settlement to be undertaken through the Department of the Interior. In a conversation with Wallace at a rural conference in Blacksburg, Va., in late July, 1933, Wallace inquired as to his availability for work on this new program. Taylor was able to give impressive evidence that he had given much attention to the problems involved in an analysis of the Hugh McRae Colonies near Wilmington,

N.C., and in a professional paper on the subject. Wallace asked him to write to Wilson and let him know of his interest in being of help on the new program.

Taylor was then at about the end of his rope. In his letter to Wilson he said:

> I do need a job like the devil. I have sacrified about all of my life insurance and will have to sacrifice my home unless I have promise of some earning position within a month. I suppose I was foolish to allow myself to get in such a position. I did so because I have steadfastly refused to accept positions which were not of my professional line and because I have clung to the arrogant faith that my services would be sought sooner or later by some institution or agency . . . It was because I was faced with the end of the road that I have been thinking of writing you. I don't know what I would have done, but when H. A. [Wallace] opened the conversation himself and made the suggestion without my solicitation, I will confess that I was ready and eager to follow the suggestion.

Taylor was first named sociologist of the Subsistence Homesteads Division of the Department of the Interior. In 1934, he was appointed regional director of the Land Policy Section of the Agricultural Adjustment Administration, with headquarters in Raleigh. In 1935, Taylor was named director of the Division of Rural Settlement of the Resettlement Administration. In 1937, he was made Head of the Division of Farm Population and Rural Life and he continued in this post until he retired from the Department of Agriculture in 1952 to make a study for the United Nations of rural social centers in the Caribbean area and Mexico. One of his many contributions in the Division of Farm Population and Rural Life was the publication of a book on the *Rural Life Problems in the United States* (1949), prepared with the cooperation of his co-workers.

But Taylor's work reached a new high after his retirement. He had become interested in the rural life problems of foreign countries before he left government. His first major study in the international area came in 1942–43 when he spent more than a year on a special research assignment for the United States Department of State. Out of this came his book, *Rural Life in Argentina* (1948). In it, as in all of his writings, he carefully examined the place and importance of agricultural cooperatives.

In 1952 Taylor joined the staff of Stanley Andrews, Director of the Foreign Agricultural Organization in the U.S.D.A. to serve as adviser on community development in the Middle East and South Asia. In this work he tried to "get down to the common people."

After he reached the age of government retirement in January, 1955, he carried on studies as a consultant on rural development for the Ford Foundation in India and Pakistan. Out of this experience grew the comprehensive study by Taylor, Ensminger, Johnson, and Joyce, *India's Roots of Democracy*. This book is widely acknowledged as the most thorough examination of the rural problems of India. Of special interest here is the enlightening chapter on "The Prospects and Problems of Developing Cooperatives" which reflects Taylor's long experience with cooperative institutions in various parts of the world. With regard to India there is this sentence:

> There is a high probability that the necessity for, and effective organization and operation of service cooperatives will do more than any other one thing to gradually remake the social structure of Indian rural society.

At the present time Taylor, now 82, is almost as busy as ever, working on the second volume of his study of *Farmers Movements* at his home in Arlington, Va. He still enjoys his golf twice a week although he reports that his score "is no longer a little over par."

Carl C. Taylor's contributions to agricultural cooperation have been unique both in the United States and abroad, for he has brought to the field the professional disciplines and insights of the trained sociologist, along with those of the agricultural economist. As some of his friends say of him, this combination has given him "hybrid vigor."

Henry C. Taylor

by Martin A. Abrahamsen

DR. HENRY C. TAYLOR, a distinguished teacher and a pioneer university and U. S. Department of Agriculture administrator, brought a scholarly and systematic approach to the many unfolding problems of agricultural cooperatives during the first 25 years of the 20th century. Moreover, as an agricultural economist of international renown, he has continued until this day to have a lively interest in the problems and possibilities of cooperatives.

"Red" Taylor, as he was known to many of his associates, was the son of an Iowa farmer. This coupled with his early experience as a graduate student and a teacher were important forces in developing his interest in agricultural economics and in cooperatives. It was primarily as an administrator, however, that he deserves recognition for his contributions to cooperatives.

Dr. Taylor received his Ph.D. from the University of Wisconsin in 1902 after having graduated from Iowa State College at Ames in 1896. He immediately joined the staff of the Commerce Department at Wisconsin to teach Economic History and Economic Geography. In assuming this position, Professor Taylor had an understanding that he could develop his interest in agricultural economics as a sideline. He did this quite largely through his course in Economic Geography in which he spent considerable time exploring areas of production and consumption. He then integrated production patterns and consumer needs by showing the interrelationships of such market functions as processing, merchandising, and transportation. Being conscious of the marketing problems of farmers, it was natural that his intellectual curiosity would lead to an examination of cooperatives and their role in helping farmers with the complex problems of marketing.

Taylor's disciplined approach to problems of agricultural economics and cooperation no doubt also was influenced by his studies abroad. From 1899 to 1901 he studied agricultural economics at Berlin and

Halle—Wittenberg Universities in Germany and at the London School of Economics and the British Museum in England. His first course in agricultural economics was given to Farm Short Course students at Wisconsin in 1902–03—a course consisting of 14 lectures on farm management.

Confronted by Problem of Working with Co-ops

Later, as the first Chairman of the Department of Agricultural Economics, Taylor during the period 1910 to 1913 became confronted with a practical problem of determining the role of that Department in working with cooperatives. Three strong, and to some extent, contending forces existed in Wisconsin at that time. These were: The American Society of Equity; the State Board of Public Affairs, and the University of Wisconsin.

Taylor credited the State Board of Public Affairs, under the domination of Charles McCarthy, with bringing pressure on the university to initiate a program of study and teaching in agricultural cooperation and marketing. This pressure, he stated, proved most helpful in obtaining funds and necessary support for the university to initiate work in cooperative marketing.

He responded to the demand for this work by hiring, on a part-time basis, two university students, George S. Wehrwein and William A. Schoenfeld, to study cheese marketing problems—the most critical marketing problems of farmers in the state at that time. Wehrwein studied cheese marketing practices and prices within the state, and Schoenfeld examined the outside markets for Wisconsin cheese. In later years, Professor Wehrwein became known nationally and internationally as an outstanding land economist at the University of Wisconsin. Schoenfeld in addition to serving as Assistant Chief of the Bureau of Agricultural Economics, U.S.D.A., under Taylor, later became Dean of the College of Agriculture at Oregon State University, a position that he occupied for 19 years.

Henry Krumrey, a dairy farmer, state Senator, and member of the American Society of Equity, drew on the finding of the cheese marketing study to support his idea that a cheese producer's association should be organized to give farmers in the state a more effective voice in marketing their products.

Urges Federation of Cheese Producers

Taylor evidently was somewhat skeptical as to whether farmers were ready to take such a step. He pointed out to Krumrey that since most of the cheese factories in the Plymouth area of Wisconsin were owned by the cheese makers, it would do no good to organize individual farmers. Taylor, therefore, suggested that a federation of cheese producers made up of individual cooperatives that hired their own cheese maker and ran their own association should be set up. Krumrey's first reaction was that this would be a tough and expensive job.

He was challenged, however, by Taylor with the statement: "Unless you and your friends are willing to work for nothing, board yourself, and buy your own gasoline for doing this job of organizing locals, there can be no cheese producers federation."

Taylor credits Mr. Krumrey with meeting the challenge head on. He even was successful in organizing some 40 cheese factories into a federation and in raising $50,000 among the farmers to build a warehouse to store cheese for the federation. Taylor helped in drafting organization plans for the federation and also addressed a mass meeting of farmers at the Plymouth fairground.

In the meantime, in response to encouragement for the increased emphasis on cooperative work at the university, Taylor was successful in 1913 in hiring Dr. B. H. Hibbard, a former graduate of the University of Wisconsin and at that time on the staff of Iowa State College, to carry on research and teaching in agricultural cooperation and marketing. Hibbard no sooner reported on the job, however, than there arose a question as to the future role of the university in working with cooperatives.

This was threshed out in a conference in the office of President Van Hise of the University with representatives of both the American Society of Equity, and McCarthy of the Legislative Reference Library. It was agreed at that time that the university would conduct studies, present facts, and in general provide educational information as to cooperative principles and operations. It was further agreed that the Equity would assume active responsibility for promotion and instigation of cooperative activity.

In a letter to Dean H. L. Russell of the College of Agriculture, University of Wisconsin in 1913, Taylor referred to this conference as follows: "As I see it, our function is to investigate and educate and not to agitate or organize marketing institutions."

In general, this policy was continued at the university for the next five years. During this time Hibbard was actively engaged in teaching and research.

More Aggressive Co-op Promotion Program Urged

Conditions, however, were changing at the university. In a letter written to Dean Russell in 1918 Taylor stated that both he and President Van Hise felt that "the time was ripe for the College to become somewhat more aggressive in the question of dealing directly with cooperatives on the subject of cooperation."

The idea for such an approach may well have been set by President Van Hise himself, who at the first National Conference of Marketing in Farm Credits gave the keynote address under the subject "Waste in Distribution." In this talk, President Van Hise, according to Taylor, proposed what would now be called "integrated cooperation." This, in effect, was cooperation that would not only involve producers at one end and consumers on the other, but also the various agencies providing processing, transportation, wholesaling, and retailing services in moving farm products from production to consumption.

Taylor further stated in his letter to Dean Russell:

> . . . that the educational campaign on the subject of cooperation should be pushed with new vigor. For example, brief, pointed statements with regard to the advantages of cooperation should be continually pushed into the press; that the county agents should take favorable opportunities for calling the farmer's attention to the possibilities of cooperation whenever the farmers bring the matter up by discussing the marketing problems. This should be done in the form of an educational activity; that the county agent should not take the responsibility of promoting a specific organization for a specific purpose but should educate the farmers to the point where they themselves should undertake something of this kind.

Another interesting sidelight appeared in this letter as Taylor referred to a discussion of a cooperative problem that led to the somewhat unique development in Wisconsin whereby the State Department of Agriculture developed an auditing service for cooperative organizations. On this point, in his letter to Dean Russell, Taylor stated:

> Another line of activity which was suggested, I believe especially by Professor Commons, is the provision for auditing the accounts of cooperative companies, the idea being that the one in charge should really be an accounting advisor for these companies, not simply auditing but helping them to get their books and keep their books in proper form. One of the stumbling blocks of cooperation has been the lack of accounts. . . . .

It is obvious that Taylor, the teacher, scholar, administrator, and political scientist, played a very important role in the development of cooperatives in Wisconsin during this early period. Within a year he was to leave the university (1919) and it was his firm belief that the university was then in a position to carry on a more aggressive role with cooperative organizations.

He believed that this was so because the educational campaign would be taken directly to farmers, more help would be given farmers in organizing and re-organizing cooperatives, and the provision for auditing association accounts would help improve the operating performance of cooperatives.

His Influence on Co-op Development Becomes National

For the next six years Taylor's influence on cooperatives became national in scope. As Chief of the U.S.D.A. Office of Farm Management and Costs and later Chief of the Bureau of Agricultural Economics, Taylor had general responsibility for work with cooperatives.

While first, L. S. Tenny and later Chris L. Christensen were directly in charge of the Cooperative Marketing Division of the Bureau, Taylor's interest and understanding of problems of cooperatives as well as his support was in evidence on many occasions.

Many of the problems that confronted him at Wisconsin were reappearing on the national level. This was a period of enthusiasm in which the sky was promised by many cooperative enthusiasts. They held strongly to their particular views and philosophy and often more heat than light was generated in discussing the problems of the day. Taylor's guiding hand did much to help steer a straight course on cooperative problems at this time.

Taylor's observations on the cooperative views of H. C. Wallace, then Secretary of Agriculture, are interesting. He believed Secretary Wallace at first was inclined to favor the centralized type of cooperative organization. Following a conference between Secretary Wallace and Sir Horace Plunkett, it was evident that they were far apart on the question of types of cooperatives that might most effectively serve farm members. Following that conference, Taylor sent a note to Secretary Wallace that, in part, read as follows:

> It takes more personal courage for a man who possesses the power of leadership to devote himself to the use of democratic methods and the building of democratic institutions than it does to proceed by autocratic methods. The former involves the education of the masses to wise conscious action. The latter involves gaining control of the masses and directing them in accordance with the leader's plan. The former means education from the top down and control from the bottom up. The latter means control from the top down and less attention to education. . .

These two methods of approach have been made to the problem of agricultural organization. . . . Sir Horace Plunkett is the outstanding leader of the very large group of workers throughout the world who believe in taking the time to educate the people and help the people build for themselves the agricultural organization which they require to improve their living conditions. It may be pointed out that this is the method that has led to permanent success in various European countries, notably in Denmark. And it is the one method that has until recently been used in the organization of agriculture in this country.

Taylor Believed to Have Shaped Secretary Wallace's Views

It appears that Taylor believed that he had been somewhat successful in shaping Secretary Wallace's views on cooperation for he later quoted at considerable length a talk he gave in 1924 at an in-service training conference of the Bureau of Agricultural Economics. At this meeting Secretary Wallace had said:

> Everybody seems to be talking cooperative marketing. People who don't know anything about it are endorsing it one hundred percent. . . . The tendency with a great many of these people is to assume that the mere organization of a cooperative is the solution of their troubles, but of course those who have some knowledge of cooperatives know better than that. . . .
>
> It seems to me two or three things are fairly clear. A cooperative marketing association cannot be successful unless it renders a service equal in value to the service that has been rendered by the middleman whom it seeks to displace, and at a price not very much greater. . . .
>
> Now the U. S. Department of Agriculture must try to steer a clear course on these matters. I think the Department cannot set itself up to say that one particular type of cooperative marketing is the only type that can be successful; I think we cannot take that position. This is a Department of service.

Under Taylor's general direction and with his encouragement the Department made a number of basic cooperative studies. These were directed to accounting, legal phases, management aspects, and case studies that would be useful in providing basic information for other producers interested in organization and operation of cooperatives.

In 1925, Taylor along with Professor B. H. Hibbard, his earlier colleague at Wisconsin, were among the 21 founding Trustees of the American Institute of Cooperation.

Taylor together with E. G. Nourse and Charlie Holman worked for a month drawing up plans for the Institute. They then approached Beardsley Ruml of the Rockefeller Foundation and on a matching fund basis arranged for a grant to help finance its operations, an arrangement that was in force for several years.

While Taylor's direct responsibility with cooperatives ended when he left the U.S. Department of Agriculture in 1925, his interest in them has continued until the present time. In all his writings and undertakings he has demonstrated a scientific approach to the solution of problems.

He has directed attention to a wide range of subjects including, among others, the agricultural depression, protection for farmers, evaluation of the Federal Farm Board, national policies affecting agriculture, tariffs, and international aspects of agriculture. Taylor is a productive writer, as he is the author of 305 publications related to the economic problems of farmers. Outstanding among them is his monumental work, *The Story of Agricultural Economics,* (1952) prepared with the collaboration of his wife, Anne Deweese Taylor. This is a treasure house of information on state and federal studies relating to agricultural cooperation as a part of the general field of agricultural economics.

In his book, *The Outlines of Agricultural Economics,* (McMillan Company, 1925) Taylor devoted two chapters to cooperation. These chapters explain his philosophy; namely, that sound advice and effective educational programs must be based on getting the facts and that this can only be done through a realistic program of research.

Emphasizes Nine Principles for Co-op Success

In this book, he also outlined nine points he believed essential if cooperation failures were to be avoided. These were:

1. Organization must perform definite functions
2. Association should be built around a single commodity
3. An adequate amount of produce must be controlled
4. Good management is essential
5. Membership contracts should be used
6. There must be an educated membership with all facts available to members through proper accounting
7. A cooperative association must be controlled by its members
8. It must be a self-perpetuating organization
9. Financial risks should be distributed.

Through the years, Taylor's interest in cooperation has been unflagging. This is illustrated by the importance he attached to cooperatives in a recently prepared manuscript on the agriculture in Japan. In this manuscript he identified individual associations and by a case study brought into focus the important ways in which these organizations are helping farmers in that country.

He emphasized a pragmatic approach to the problems of cooperation. As an administrator he demonstrated his ability to work out realistic solutions to questions of jurisdictional responsibility. He did much to help integrate cooperation into the general field of agricultural economics and identify it as an important part of that discipline. He made significant contributions in directing research and educational programs of both state and national levels into sound channels.

Cooperators today owe a debt of gratitude to Taylor for the competent way in which he approached problems during formative years of cooperative development and for the continuing interest he has demonstrated in cooperatives as a way for improving the lot of rural people.

Charles Collins Teague

by Kelsey B. Gardner

CHARLES COLLINS TEAGUE was a distinguished national leader in agriculture and in cooperation. His more than 50-year career in agriculture covered the development of the California citrus and walnut industries and his efforts influenced both production and distribution. His interests were broad and he was unstinting in his assumption of responsibilities that he believed would help agriculture generally and cooperatives in particular at both state and national levels.

Charles Teague was born June 11, 1873 in Caribou, Maine. He came from a line of New England pioneers who were dependent on their individual efforts and resources to meet the hardships of a life in a frontier environment. When he was eight years old, his family moved to Salina, Kan., where they lived for the next 11 years. At age 16 a summer railroad construction job found him in Colorado driving a team of mules pulling a dump scraper. Compelled to leave school at 17 years of age because of family financial reverses, he first took a job as a clerk in a dry goods store for about a year. Following this he was employed to close out a bankrupt hardware store in a nearby town.

During the Salina period Charles Teague made his first real contacts with the soil on his father's and great-uncle's farms, from which developed the deep interests that were determining influences in his life.

In 1893, the Teague family moved to Santa Paula, Calif. where Charles Teague began his long identification with the California citrus and walnut industries. His beginning jobs included pruning windbreaks and picking lemons. The latter job soon led to his acting as foreman of a gang of Chinese lemon pickers. Out of these early lemon handling experiences grew recognition of the necessity for handling, picking, and grading lemons without injury so as to retain full keeping quality in the fruit. Thus began Charles Teague's lifetime in the then infant lemon industry of California.

Achieves Management Competence in Diverse Enterprises

Responsibilities came quickly. With the death of his father in the same year the family arrived in Santa Paula, Charles Teague began sole care of a small lemon grove which he and his father had planted. In 1896, he took over management with full authority of the business interests of a great-uncle, whose new interests required his presence in South America. Included in these properties was a half interest in the Limoneira Company. Beginning in 1898 Charles Teague was to manage this company for the next half century. Under his direction and ownership interests the Limoneira Ranch was to grow into a great enterprise. Other property included an interest in a water company (important for irrigation), a residential subdivision, a small oil company, and a horse and cattle ranch. The management responsibilities of these diverse enterprises were ably met.

Mr. Teague grew with the lemon industry. Management of Limoneira involved serious problems which called for solution. Washing, curing, and storing of lemons were first. Then, loss in storage from Brown Rot Fungus soon threatened the industry. Through his driving insistence, research assistance from the University of California was successful in meeting this threat. This use of research to obtain pertinent facts was a marked characteristic of Charles Teague which revealed itself under many situations. Research was carried on at Limoneira during his long administration and the results were made available to all. His interest in the results of research was carried into the California Fruit Growers Exchange, the Federal Farm Board, and wherever else his activities took him.

Mr. Teague early became convinced that citrus and walnut growers should own and control their own cooperative marketing organizations. He recognized that only through these mechanisms could growers determine the quantity and quality of fruit to be shipped and the distribution to be made to individual markets, and at the same time bring about the lowest cost of operation.

Responsibilities in many businesses including cooperative organizations came to Mr. Teague as a result of his interest in citrus and walnut production and distribution. Some of these activities that should be mentioned include: Long-time Presidencies of the Teague McKevett Company, Santa Paula, Calif.; Limoneira Company; three water companies; Fruit Growers Supply Company, Los Angeles; and the Teague McKevett Association, Santa Paula. In 1911, he was named a director of the California Fruit Growers Exchange. In 1920, he became its President, a position in which he served with distinction until his death on March 20, 1950. In 1912, he helped organize the California Walnut Growers Association, serving as its President until 1942.

Great Support Given Co-op Marketing of Citrus, Walnuts

Mr. Teague brought to his work with cooperatives the best possible background of experience in both production and distribution. Having been faced early in his career with problems of producing, handling, storing and marketing of crops that included citrus, walnuts, lima beans, and apricots, he had the first-hand knowledge essential to a full understanding of their production and distribution problems. His firm determination to aid in the development of cooperative marketing of citrus and walnuts carried with it the resolution to give all the support he could to its achievement. His life is a record of unselfish efforts and accomplishment toward this goal.

It was his considered belief that the most important fact in the growth of the California citrus industry was the California Fruit Growers Exchange. His many public and private discussions and his writings, presenting the values and accomplishments of cooperative marketing were drawn from the organizations he knew best—the Exchange, and the California Walnut Growers Association. Product quality achieved through proper methods of handling and selling including grading, standardization, packing and storing; demand stimulation through advertised brands, competent sales organizations and proration, when necessary, of available supplies among markets and to surplus operations were important elements in his presentations.

These efforts to further cooperation as an aid to meeting the problems of agriculture brought many responsibilities to Mr. Teague. Some of these included: Member of the Federal Farm Board, 1929–31; Vice-Chairman, American Institute of Cooperation, 1933–44; President, National Council of Farmer Cooperatives, 1942–43; and consultant on cooperative marketing, Graduate School of Business, Stanford University, 1935–40. For 25 years he was President of the Agricultural Council of California. In the latter organization, as well as in the National Council of Farmer Cooperatives, there was opportunity to give further attention to legislative matters of concern to agriculture as well as to farmer cooperatives.

It was at the insistence of President Herbert Hoover that Mr. Teague accepted appointment as a member of the Federal Farm Board in 1929 for one year's service which was extended an additional year to early 1931. One of the challenges presented by the Agricultural Marketing Act of 1929 under which the Board was set up appealed strongly to him. This was the Act itself and the Board's interpretation of its authority to establish grower-owned and grower-controlled cooperatives for the marketing of farm products and the purchase of supplies essential to the production and marketing of agricultural commodities as a means of meeting problems of the depression in which agriculture found itself in 1929. He was an active proponent of having the Board in 1929 take over the Division of Cooperative Marketing from the U. S. Department of Agriculture in order to employ the Division's staff and experience in furthering this objective.

Teague's Practical Approach Wins Chairman Legge's Acceptance

Mr. Teague's practical approach to problems soon led him into an early situation in conflict with Alexander Legge, Chairman of the Board. As the Board in the first two months of its life was proceeding on a basis of personally hearing representatives of many distressed cooperatives, the resulting confusion convinced Mr. Teague that the only way to meet this dilemma was to set up an examination division. This unit was to consider loan applications of associations in order to determine whether they were qualified applicants under the Act, were soundly organized, and operated or could be reorganized so as to qualify. Meeting a rebuff from Chairman Legge in this effort, he offered his resignation as he was convinced that orderly examination procedure had to be set up. Out of the successful solution of this situation based on his ideas grew a close working relationship between Mr. Teague and the Chairman. Mr. Legge had come to the Board with no experience with cooperatives but he came to believe firmly that help in cooperative development comprised the greatest assistance that could be given to agriculture.

Mr. Teague had a continuing belief in the usefulness of facts developed through competent research. His belief in and his support of research evidenced themselves in one Board session that I observed. The Division of Cooperative Marketing maintained a continuing annual record of the number of farmers' marketing and purchasing associations, their memberships, and dollar volume of business. Mr. Teague recognized and had made use of these national statistics as informative sources of the scope and trends of cooperation among farmers. He firmly and successfully opposed another Federal Farm Board member who did not clearly see the usefulness of the information and urged discontinuance of the statistics.

Those of us who worked closely with Mr. Teague during his service on the Federal Farm Board were continually impressed by his courtesy, his sense of fairness, his respect for others' opinions, his willingness to examine their positions objectively, and his complete confidence in the values and potentials of farmer cooperatives when soundly organized and operated.

A substantial portion of Alexander Legge's estate was left to the Farm Foundation. Mr. Teague was named a trustee but he referred to the experience as "not a happy one." He was well aware of Mr. Legge's belief in cooperatives. Among objectives of the Foundation was the encouragement and development of cooperative effort. Mr. Teague presented to the trustees of the Farm Foundation a proposal for a study of cooperatives with special emphasis on reasons underlying their success or failure. Failing in his effort to have this study made, he was unwilling to compromise with his convictions and shortly thereafter resigned from the Foundation's Board of Trustees.

We are indeed fortunate that Mr. Teague recorded many of his experiences, ideas and conclusions in his book, *Fifty Years a Rancher,* published privately in 1944. Numerous talks in which he clearly and forcibly presented his experiences and viewpoints are available in the series of annuals, *American Cooperation,* published by the American Institute of Cooperation.

Believed Co-op Success Based on Willingness to Work Together

Mr. Teague's principal concepts of the spirit of cooperation can be briefly summarized. He believed that the fundamental success factor in cooperation was the willingness of the principal proponents to work together for the good of all. In this connection he held that "the chief essential of cooperative management is the ability to understand people and work for them and with them effectively." Although he recognized that the personal interests of the participants were directly dependent on the success or failure of the cooperative, he believed that their chief satisfaction came from a sense of service to the grower group. He was also convinced that there is an identity of interests of both small and large producers, so that both groups are essential to a cooperative.

In his broad approach to cooperatives and their position in agriculture and the economy, Mr. Teague's concept of the distinction between a farmer cooperative and the usual business enterprise as it relates to their responsibility is worthy of quotation:

A large-scale cooperative, especially if it is dominant in its field, must exercise leadership in the industry, concern itself with the factors that establish the basic price levels, with building consumer demand with research, by-product development, legislation, and many things done for the good of the industry as a whole, the efforts and expense of which are not necessarily helpful to the competitive position of the cooperative within its own industry. (*American Cooperation*, 1936, p. 69).

After Mr. Teague had decided to aid cooperative development in any way he could, his subsequent path was unswerving. An illustration of his willingness to "talk straight" was his address to a group of California bankers. (*California Citrograph*, January 1933). This was an appeal to the bankers in their own interests as sources of grower credit to influence growers through education to support citrus and walnut cooperatives as instruments for effective control in marketing. In 1938, he gave a series of 10 radio talks, attempting to overcome the opposition of non-exchange shippers to an orange prorate program under a Federal marketing agreement. In these talks he presented forthrightly the effects on growers of the failure of the program to function. In doing so, he explained the nature, objectives, and methods of operation of the California Fruit Growers Exchange. He emphasized its relation to the citrus industry and especially its functions as a stabilizing influence in citrus distribution. The talks promptly broke the impasse.

Numerous honors came to Mr. Teague for his efforts on behalf of agriculture. In 1924, the University of California conferred an honorary degree of Doctor of Laws, with the citation: "Pioneer in the great citrus and walnut industries of California; supporter and prosecutor of agricultural research; untiring advocate of improved agricultural methods; worthy representative of the State's largest industry." In 1931, his native state of Maine, through its University, conferred a similar honor. In 1930 he was named a regent of the University of California at Berkeley, a position that he held until his death in 1950.

In 1945, Mr. Teague's fellow directors on the board of the California Fruit Growers Exchange presented a silver plaque to him in commemoration of his 25 years as President. This recognition by those who knew him well bespeaks his leadership. His widespread effective services to agriculture and to cooperatives are recognized far beyond the confines of the California citrus and walnut areas where his primary interests were based. At the 1950 annual session of the American Institute of Cooperation, Charles W. Holman, Secretary of the Institute for almost 20 years, in referring to Mr. Teague's lifetime of effort to build cooperatives spoke for all when he said, "I am sure historians will place him among the American giants of the cooperative movement."

M. W. Thatcher

by Robert Handschin

E ARLY IN 1915, M. W. "BILL" THATCHER had to choose between testifying for a young co-op under heavy attack by powerful interests, and his good job in a Minneapolis accounting firm. He
chose to help the Equity Cooperative Exchange of St. Paul, the first
co-op grain commission firm in the U.S. Thus began a long career
working for farmers.

Born at Valpariso, Ind. May 5, 1883, son of a former Granger,
Thatcher studied accounting in Chicago, and in 1906 audited grain
and milling firms at Minneapolis and Duluth, which were amassing
fortunes while grain producers struggled to live. In 1909, he moved
to nearby Osceola, Wis. to manage for five years a chain of flour and
feed mills in distress. He bought grain from George Loftus who on
August 1, 1912 became the Equity's second manager. When Thatcher
returned to his Minneapolis accounting job in the fall of 1914, Loftus
asked him to audit the Equity's books.

In 1908, farmers had set up the Equity to sell their grain on the
Minneapolis and Duluth markets but were barred from membership.
When Loftus took over, he vigorously attacked the entrenched grain
trade, which began a powerful conspiracy against the Equity. When
the North Dakota Attorney General, in April, 1915, sued to dissolve
the co-op, Loftus packed the Fargo courtroom with hundreds of
farmers, got their pledges for $41,000 if needed, and with Thatcher's
expert testimony, the suit was dismissed. Thatcher went into business
for himself, until 1918 auditing the Equity.

Equity in Receivership; Thatcher Becomes Manager

The conspiracy went on until the Equity entered voluntary receivership March 10, 1923, with Thatcher named Manager of the busted
co-op. (For details see FTC Docket 694, a 39-page Cease-and-Desist
order issued December 28, 1923, too late to help the Equity.) Poor
management, internal dissension, the severe price drop which began

in May, 1920, and losses in the U. S. Grain Growers 1921 pool, all aided the Equity's downfall. But it pioneered terminal grain marketing and in 1916 built both the first co-op terminal elevator (on St. Paul's riverfront), and the first livestock commission co-op (now Farmers Union Marketing Association).

Earlier, North Dakota Equity members had revived older demands for a state-owned terminal elevator, and voters in 1912 and 1914 twice approved 3 to 1, only to have the 1915 legislature balk, resulting in the Non-Partisan League which swept the state. Its state flour mill and terminal elevator were successful—its many reforms a New Deal years before Roosevelt's. Thatcher audited some League ventures, learned effective politics from such Senators as Wheeler, Walsh, Frazier, Ladd, Nye, Langer, Norbeck, Magnus Johnson, Shipstead, the LaFollettes, Lenroot, and other "sons of the wild jackass" as New Hampshire Senator Moses labeled the farm bloc of the 1920's. Years later, FDR's interest in this opened the White House door for Thatcher and led to a close and mutually-productive friendship.

To revive the Equity, Thatcher personally visited each of over 600 farmers who had $133,000 due from their pooled grain, driving 27,000 miles over dirt roads to do so. He got their approval and eventually every cent was repaid. To put a more solid foundation under the co-op, Thatcher turned to the National Farmers Union, which in 1925 gave him and two others (C. C. Talbott, A. W. Ricker) $500 to organize Minnesota, Wisconsin, North Dakota, and Montana. The Union could tie together co-op and legislative goals, and carry on co-op education and promotion with five percent of co-op savings. Farmers would gain power through their "bushels, hooves, and ballots." Soon scores of new oil co-ops added another department, which in 1931 became the Farmers Union Central Exchange.

Grain marketing revived in the Farmers Union Terminal Association (FUTA) which in 1926 replaced the Equity. In 1927–28, in the "battle of tin cans," thousands of farmers sent in wheat samples to get free protein tests, selling their wheat for as much as 42¢ a bushel more, thus gaining hundreds of dollars of most welcome income. Thus began protein premiums which since have ranged from a few cents to a high of $1.21 in 1947, and averaging at least $20 million extra per year.

Farmers' ballots couldn't stop Coolidge's two vetoes of the McNary-Haugen farm relief bill, but Hoover promised a new approach through co-op marketing. Thatcher worked for both, and FUTA joined the new Farmers National Grain Corporation which began October 29,

1929, just as the stock market crashed. Farmers struggled to make nation-wide marketing work. FUTA made the first farm storage loans in 1930 in Montana and North Dakota, since widely used by millions of farmers.

In a celebrated trial in 1931–32 involving FUTA's elevator "M," Governor Floyd B. Olson of Minnesota found the co-op not guilty of false grading and other charges brought by the grain trade.

Thatcher's Work in Nation's Capital Effective

In April, 1932, FNGC assigned Thatcher to Washington, D. C. He called the conferences of farm leaders in September and December, 1932, which laid the ground for future action, as farm commodities sank to a nearly "free market" for buyers. He helped prepare, testified, and lobbied for the wheat processing tax and benefit payments of the first AAA, the wheat loan and parity payments which in 1938 replaced it, and the various credit acts.

Thatcher deserves principal credit for three laws. The first was the 1935 amendment to reduce federal farm mortgage rates to 3½ percent which saved farmers $334 million, and helped lower all interest rates. Secondly, he worked three years to pass the Commodity Exchange Act of 1936, placing farm commodity markets "in a goldfish bowl" and guaranteeing farmer co-ops entrance to them. Thirdly, he saved what became the Farm Security Administration (F.S.A., now F.H.A.) from oblivion in 1936 so that it could continue loans to hundreds of thousands of hardup farm families.

By 1937 co-op grain marketing had to be turned back to the regionals but after three years of drought and depression they were without funds. Thatcher went to President Roosevelt who on December 29, 1937, inscribed on Thatcher's short memo "HW: Try to work out, FDR," "HW" being Secretary of Agriculture Henry A. Wallace. It was done. The new Banks for Cooperatives helped the regionals start again, and F. S. A. lent farmers money to buy co-op shares in locals and regionals.

On June 1, 1938, Farmers Union Grain Terminal Association (GTA) began with 121 local association members, adding in the next two years another 129 aided by FSA loans, all repaid before due.

The first year, 17 million bushels of grain was handled. In building GTA Thatcher had the able help of key men who had worked with him from Equity days.

Becomes President of New National Federation

In February, 1939, Thatcher called together nine regionals to form the National Federation of Grain Cooperatives (NFGC) which since has annually elected him its President. Its purposes have been to stop the government's Commodity Credit Corporation from competing with the co-ops, and to give them a common voice in Washington.

In 1939, Thatcher also became legislative representative for the National Farmers Union, previously having represented only some Northwest states. Thatcher urged Congress to pass a wheat income certificate bill giving family-sized operators full parity, others less.

Farm foreclosures by the Farm Credit Administration were halted and a drive further to liberalize FCA led to a giant meeting of 21,000 key Midwest farmers at St. Paul April 27, 1940, where the campaign to make Wallace Vice-President was launched. His selection made U.S. World War II policies more progressive both at home and abroad.

As GTA grew, so did opposition, which turned to vicious personal attacks on Thatcher. And once again, the legal right of a co-op to buy its own members' consigned grain was challenged. After years of dispute, the Minnesota Supreme Court backed GTA unanimously on February 14, 1947, and the Federal District Court dismissed a grain trade appeal on December 31, 1947.

In 1941, a dream held by Northwest farmers since 1891 came true with the building of a 4.5 million bushel elevator at Superior, Wis. Thatcher erected the tallest, fastest-operating elevator in the world, not to be matched for many years.

In May, 1942, GTA took over a durum wheat mill at Rush City, Minn. to become the first U.S. grain co-op to go into milling, and foreshadowing later moves into feeds and oilseed processing.

Thatcher in Key Role Fighting NTEA

On May 1, 1943 GTA bought the 57-year-old St. Anthony and Dakota Elevator Company with 135 elevators and 38 lumber yards. This shocked the private grain trade into forming with other farm co-op competitors the National Tax Equality Association. The NTEA spent millions to convince Main Street that farm co-ops were a mortal threat, tax dodgers, and unAmerican. The bitter battle over tax laws, government credits, and co-op purposes was to last many years. Thatcher played a key role in setting up state and co-op associations and national committees to answer the NTEA and to put backbone into wavering cooperators.

In January, 1943, Thatcher began "Food for Freedom" radio talks on a four-state network, proposing a postwar food-for-peace program and a farm program going far beyond pre-war. A National Agricultural Relations Act (NARA) would grant farmers the same rights organized labor enjoys under their National Labor Relations (Wagner) Act. Self-financing self-run commodity programs, using co-ops, could be voted in by the farmers concerned. Supporters of government-run programs were not willing to risk collective bargaining for farmers but it remained a Thatcher goal anyway.

When FDR died, postwar reaction set in, with the Cold War shifting power away from farmers and labor, and forcing Henry A. Wallace out of the government. Attacks on farm programs and farm co-ops sharpened in the 80th Congress. The grain trade moved to eliminate CCC storage bins, block the Wheat Agreement, take back the export trade, double-tax farm co-ops, and weaken or kill farm price supports. Aroused Midwest farmers re-elected Truman, sent Hubert H. Humphrey to the Senate and defeated the anti-co-op Ways and Means Chairman, the veteran Republican Harold Knutson of Minnesota.

Then began a delaying action of several years before price supports were substantially lowered and depopulation of U.S. farm areas became official policy, which Thatcher was to fight under the slogan "Farm Prices Are Made in Washington."

Thatcher Builds GTA to Largest Grain Co-op

By 1950 GTA had become the largest U.S. grain co-op with many services for members. Annual sales were 100 million bushels, a quarter of the area's total, with savings averaging $2 million per year. Membership had grown to 615 local or line elevators with 28 million bushels capacity owned by some 150,000 producers. Terminal elevators held another 19 million bushels, that at Superior with 11.5 million one of the world's best. Savings since 1938 were $22 million with nearly $3 million paid back in cash, the rest reinvested. This, together with $1 million not from savings, left a net worth of $20 million. From GTA alone another million dollars had been paid the Farmers Union in educational funds.

These terminal savings of a few cents a bushel did not measure the full gains to producers from price supports, better markets and lowered margins, bigger local savings and better service, plus the personal satisfaction and common pride in achievement gained through their organization.

By 1950, the National Federation of Grain Co-ops had grown from nine weak regionals to 16 thriving members, Farm Bureau as well as Farmers Union, handling nearly 400 million bushels. Since 1946 it had a Washington office with an able secretary, Roy F. Hendrickson, Iowa farmboy, newsman, and U.S.D.A. Administrator. Co-op grain farmers had come a long way from the days when they had no voice in the grain business. Thatcher, already dean of American farm leaders, in 1950 could look back on a turbulent but highly productive life in the service of American farmers and their cooperatives.

Thatcher brought business ability to his co-op career but other leadership skills he learned over the years. He knew how to concentrate on a single issue, how to make it clear to farmers and others, and how to select the best time and means for action. Above all, he fully understood the need to combine economics and politics if farmers were to protect themselves from those who often dominated both.

His personal warmth to those he served or worked with also characterized his platform speaking, at which he became a master. Friend of Presidents, Senators and Congressmen, he also could make each farmer and his wife in a large audience feel his personal concern for them, or could be thoughtful about small details in the lives of those he met. This is probably why he chose to be a cooperator and why he could lead thousands of others to do so.

The confidence he inspired in people made it possible for them to drop their fears and band together in hope for their common good.

He always told co-operators that the main goal of a co-op should be the welfare of the family on the farm, not just a good balance sheet or large patronage dividends.

Among his monuments are the co-op he twice rescued from defeat; the Farmers Union which without his help might not have survived; the Federation of Grain Co-ops, to which he gave vital leadership in its founding years; and the farm and co-op laws that were his contribution to the "legislated economy" of which he so frequently spoke to farmers.

At mid-century co-op grain farmers had both great growth and heavy competition ahead of them, while M. W. Thatcher, already at an age when most managers retire, was yet to achieve some of his greatest successes.

Victor Nelson Valgren

by French M. Hyre

VICTOR NELSON VALGREN, authority on cooperative insurance
for farmers was born in Sweden in 1876 and came to this country
at the age of six. With his parents he settled on a 160-acre homestead
farm in South Dakota.

He received his early education in the public schools of South
Dakota and later he studied at the University of Minnesota and the
University of Chicago. He received a PhD degree in economics from
the latter institution in 1914.

Choosing a career in farm mutual insurance, Dr. Valgren pioneered
in developing research and education programs in this field. He
worked unceasingly to give the farm mutuals a better understanding
of their functions, problems, and opportunities, and in later years
came to be recognized as the nation's foremost authority in this area
of rural economics and cooperation.

Dr. Valgren's interest in mutual insurance was stimulated at an
early age by the fact that he grew up on a farm where the insurance
was provided by a local farmer-owned mutual company. In explaining
this in later years he said:

> I once calculated that the savings on my father's insurance bill
> was approximately sufficient to buy a suit of clothes for one
> member of the family each year, and in that frontier community
> new suits of clothes came none too often.

While a graduate student at the University of Minnesota Dr. Valgren
completed his first research study, "Farmer Mutual Insurance Companies in Minnesota." The results of this study were published in
the *Quarterly Journal of Economics,* Harvard University, February,
1911.

At the University of Chicago Dr. Valgren continued his studies of
farmers mutual insurance companies "with a view of using the results

in a so-called doctors dissertation or thesis, and this ambition was fulfilled a number of years later."

In 1915, Dr. Valgren accepted an appointment with the United States Department of Agriculture in Washington, D. C., as Special Investigator in Agricultural Insurance. With the exception of a three-year period from 1923 to 1926 when he served as manager of the Crop and Weather Division of the Automobile Insurance Company, Hartford, Conn., he was continuously associated with the Department of Agriculture and the Farm Credit Administration until his retirement in 1946.

Becomes Authority in Mutual Farm Insurance

During his 28 years with the Department of Agriculture and the Farm Credit Administration, Dr. Valgren devoted himself almost exclusively to the betterment of farm mutual insurance and the strengthening of farmer-owned mutual insurance companies.

His first Department publication, "Farmers Mutual Fire Insurance" appeared in the *1916 Yearbook of Agriculture*. This was followed in 1917 by U.S.D.A. Bulletin No. 530, *The Organization and Management of a Farmers Mutual Fire Insurance Company*, and in 1919 by U.S.D.A. Bulletin No. 786, *Prevailing Plans and Practices Among Farmers Mutual Fire Insurance Companies*.

These early publications attracted wide attention and helped Dr. Valgren build his reputation as an authority in this field. Furthermore, these publications laid the foundation for a continuing educational program that has helped the farm mutuals to adjust, refine, and build their programs to better meet the expanding insurance needs of their members as farms in this country became larger and more highly commercialized.

At the request of the Governor of the Farm Credit Administration, Dr. Valgren was transferred to that agency in 1936 and made Head of the Insurance Section of the Cooperative Research and Service Division. His first task was to help farm mutuals standardize their policy forms in order that their insurance might be more readily accepted by the Federal Land Banks and other lending agencies.

The non-standard forms used by many of the smaller mutuals prior to that time were not being readily accepted by lending agencies. The problem was that every time one of these non-standard unfamiliar forms was submitted by a farmer to provide the insurance required by the mortgage holder someone in the lending agency had to study it carefully—and in some cases get a legal interpretation in order to determine whether the lending agency was properly protected in the event that fire damaged or destroyed the property on which the mortgage was issued.

His Work Resulted in Wide Acceptance of Standard Forms

Dr. Valgren worked with the National Association of Mutual Insurance Companies to encourage and assist the various state associations to develop standard policy forms for use by their member companies. Within a year or two these standardized forms were being widely used throughout the industry and they have been a factor in the progress and growth made by the farm mutuals.

During his seven years with the Cooperative Research and Service Division, FCA, Dr. Valgren continued his research work with farmers mutuals and issued a number of publications including the following: *Problems and Trends in Farmers Mutual Insurance Companies,* FCA Bulletin No. 23, 1938; *Using Your Farmers Mutual,* FCA Circular E15, 1939; *Summary of the Illinois Agricultural Mutual Insurance Company,* FCA Miscellaneous Report 22, 1940; and *Reinsurance Among Farmers Mutual Insurance Companies,* FCA Bulletin 45, 1941.

Dr. Valgren was a frequent and popular speaker at state and national meetings and conventions of farm mutual people. At these meetings he talked on management, organization, policy forms, loss prevention, reinsurance rating systems, record keeping, and all the things that farmer directors and officers needed to know in order to operate their companies successfully.

One thing that added to his popularity as a speaker was the fact that he could talk the farmers' language. Having grown up on a farm he was able to weave into his talks illustrations and relate personal incidents that not only added humor but also added a rural flavor that his listeners fully understood and enjoyed. For example, on one occasion he concluded his talk with the following statement:

> In conclusion let me say that I do not flatter myself that I have covered all the factors in farm mutual success. My views on farm mutuals and their accomplishments may perhaps be colored by inherent or acquired prejudice in their favor. Few if any of us, it may be conceded, are entirely free from prejudice in our views and conclusions.
>
> I recall, for example, an incident of my early youth in South Dakota. I had the privilege one sunny day in early autumn of riding with a neighbor to Sioux Falls and back. This ride of about 14 miles each way in a lumber wagon drawn by a team of work horses, naturally gave ample time for conversation and observa-

tion of the farms and fields that we passed. My neighbor, it happened, was an incurable optimist as to his own interests and was also a man of rather picturesque language. On our ride to town we passed a field on which the corn was turning white on the higher ground. My neighbor's comment was: "By golly! this must be awfully poor sandy land. Look how the corn is drying up in spots!" On our return from town by a different road we finally came alongside my neighbor's own cornfield and here, too, the corn was turning white on certain gravelly knolls. My neighbor, looking out over his field, remarked: "By golly! my corn is beginning to ripen!

During the early 1940's Dr. Valgren contributed significantly to the war effort with a nationwide campaign that stressed conservation of agricultural resources. He stressed the increased need to reduce fire losses on the farm since building materials for repair and replacement were urgently needed in the war effort. He urged the farm mutuals to step up and intensify their fire prevention campaigns through inspection of farm buildings and educational programs with members.

In 1943, Dr. Valgren transferred to the Bureau of Agricultural Economics where he continued his work with the farm mutual insurance companies until his retirement in 1946.

Dr. Valgren died in his 87th year in Sioux Falls, S. D., April 11, 1963. His body was interred in a community cemetery near where the family homesteaded 80 years earlier.

He left a heritage of more than 170 articles, bulletins, and speeches, and 1,500 farm mutual insurance companies which his lifetime effort had helped to build. He was the first person to be elected to honorary membership in the National Association of Mutual Insurance Companies.

James Peter Warbasse

by Wallace J. Campbell

THE COOPERATIVE LEAGUE was organized in the home of Dr. James Peter Warbasse on March 18, 1919. He was its founder, its first President—a post he held for 25 years, and a director for 41 years. He gave up a distinguished career in surgery to devote full time to his cooperative interests, and for a generation was the most influential single figure in guiding the Cooperative League's policy and direction. He led it through turbulent days and lived long enough to see it mature to the point where it wished to go in directions other than he himself would have chosen.

Dr. Warbasse was born in 1866, and was a graduate of the Medical College of Colombia University, did post-graduate work in medicine in Germany and Austria, served as chief surgeon of the German Hospital in Brooklyn, N. Y., for 13 years, was editor of the *New York State Journal of Medicine,* a fellow of the American College of Surgeons, and author of a three-volume masterpiece, *Surgical Treatment,* that was a standard textbook for a generation after his retirement from medicine.

Three years after Dr. Warbasse founded the Cooperative League, he gave up his first career and devoted himself to his second. He was then 53 years old, and from that time until he died at 91 his chief work was in behalf of the cooperative movement. He had become interested in cooperatives during his medical studies in Germany before World War I. Two active cooperators, Hyman Cohn and Albert Sonnichsen, asked his help in forming a cooperative federation, and the League was begun.

He led it, financed it, kept it alive and breathing, and brought to it a generosity and a viewpoint that in the end almost killed it.

Dr. Warbasse wrote with great honesty about himself as a cooperator in his book, *North Star,* which he wrote shortly before his death:

> Not all people are cooperative. I am by nature a non-cooperative person. I lack the natural gregariousness of most persons.

I was happy when alone, and my surgical experience tended to breed the autocrat in my nature. During my surgical career I made decisions and gave orders. There was no time for consultation. Put a surgeon on a committee, and make him chairman, and you will find that he prefers to do the work himself rather than be bothered by the opinion of others. My board of directors sometimes asked why I had taken action on some matter without consulting them. The fact was I was afraid the board might not agree with me, and the thing I was for was so important that I did not care to take chances. In short, I am by nature an individualist, rather than a cooperator.

Fought Against League "Take-over" by Communists

It was this candid but autocratic approach that led Dr. Warbasse through the most troublesome days for the Cooperative League. Early in the depression, the Communist Party of the U.S. decided to take over the League and make it an instrument of revolution. Dr. Warbasse resisted this with all of his force and ability. Adhering to democratic methods, he rallied cooperative leaders to his support and was successful as chairman of the meeting when Communists were expelled from membership. It is significant that the Cooperative League was one of the first organizations scheduled for "takeover" by the Communists and was one of the first to throw them out in open battle. With his leadership, it did not become a bloody battle.

But the autocracy had its limiting aspects. Both Dr. Warbasse and his wife, Agnes, who served for many years without pay as the League's education director, gave so much financial support to the League that it became looked upon as an automatic subsidy and failed to build an economic system for self-support. It was not until the League's new executive secretary, E. R. Bowen, took office in 1934 and demanded that League members pay their own way that the organization became an independent, democratic institution.

Bowen and Warbasse broke bitterly over policy matters and fought each other within the framework of the Cooperative League for seven years. Both were entirely dedicated to the cooperative philosophy and the democratic, economic movement which both sought to lead. The League was separated into two camps, one under Bowen who was determined to organize and develop a self-supporting structure, and the second under Warbasse who believed in education, rejecting a program of active organization. Warbasse, too, looked with some suspicion on the farm supply cooperatives which he felt might water down the strong consumer influence of the League.

League Structure Changed to a Federation

This fight was won by Bowen. At his insistence, the League changed from a group of individuals directing an economic movement to a federation of representatives of local, regional, and national cooperative organizations who were elected to positions on the Cooperative League Board and whose memberships contributed to League economic support to make it a viable cooperative organization.

Murray D. Lincoln, then President of what is now Nationwide Insurance, succeeded Dr. Warbasse when he retired as President in 1941. Lincoln had brought his organization into the Cooperative League only when Bowen assured him that the philosophy of cooperation stated by Dr. Warbasse in his classic book, *Cooperative Democracy*, was not the official policy of the Cooperative League. Warbasse had advocated the extension of the consumer cooperative movement to the point of ownership and operation of the major farms of the U.S. Lincoln, a staunch advocate of individual ownership of the family-size farm, and then the Manager of the Ohio Farm Bureau Cooperative Association, was appalled at this concept.

From 1941, when the internecine warfare ended, until Bowen's retirement in 1947, the Cooperative League was a substantially different organization from the one that Dr. Warbasse had led in its earlier years.

A third step in the League's evolution was taken with the election of Jerry Voorhis as Executive Director in the spring of 1947. Under the leadership of the former Congressman from California, the League again enlarged to become a federation of national federations in the cooperative field and embraced such organizations as the National Rural Electric Cooperative Association, the Credit Union National Association, the National Cooperatives, the Group Health Association of America, the National Association of Housing Cooperatives, and other cooperative organizations.

From a handful of individuals in April, 1916, the Cooperative League of the USA had grown to become a federation of consumer, service, and purchasing cooperatives with about 18 million members. The institution had grown beyond James Peter Warbasse's fondest dreams. It had also changed substantially in philosophy and character.

But for all the differences, there was one man who maintains the great distinction of being founder of the League. His biography should list many of his other contributions: he was a lecturer on medical sociology at the Long Island College of Medicine after his retirement from surgical practice; he continued to write and lecture after retiring as president of the Cooperative League in 1941 when he was 75. His books include *The Doctor and the Public, Cooperation, a Way of Peace, Problems of Cooperation, The Cooperative Way,* and *Poems of the Family Circle.*

He lived a full and active life, gave generously of it, and perhaps endured no than most parents who live to see their offspring come to independent adulthood. Heroes and founders are people of the past; the present often speaks with blunt reality.

Harris Weinstock

by Grace H. Larsen

IT HAS BEEN SAID THAT MORE farmer cooperative associations were formed between 1915 and 1921 than in any like number of years before or since. Harris Weinstock (1854–1922) attracted national attention during these years as one of the leaders in the organization of agriculture. An energetic proponent of industry-wide producers' cooperatives while serving as California's State Market Director from 1915 to 1920, he brought into being during that time no less than 16 major cooperative marketing associations. More significant than this number was the new stimulus he gave to cooperative marketing.

An awakening had been occurring in California, as one farm editor described the situation in 1913 on the eve of Weinstock's designation as the state's first Market Director. A strong public sentiment had been developing concerning the need for producers and consumers to obtain relief, the producers from depression, and the consumers from high living costs. To remove the wrongs in their industries, farmers had for years been making starts and stops in forming local marketing organizations. The number and variety of their independent associations reflected their differences in methods of attacking their problems. In almost every agricultural industry there had been years of fumbling and floundering about in efforts to cooperate, with the resultant disappointments that led to mistrust of cooperation and frustrations that brought discouragement if not apathy. The obvious need, the editor insisted, was to originate some broad cooperative plan or set of policies that would be safe and workable and that would command general support to replace the lack of coordination that characterized the business of marketing almost every commercially grown crop.

Had Unusual Ability to Create Confidence in Co-op Benefits

Weinstock appeared, as if by prophecy, to present with unflagging enthusiasm just such a program. His success was possible not alone because "cooperation was in the air," but because he had an extraordinary ability to create among farmers confidence that they would benefit from the cooperation he advocated.

Perhaps Weinstock's career accounts for his own outlook of almost unfailing optimism. He overcame the obscurity and poverty of New York City's Canal Street where his family lived after fleeing the persecution of Jews in Europe. At a very early age he left home and after some wandering about followed his half brother David Lubin to settle in 1869 in California. They accumulated a fortune merchandising dry goods in Sacramento and San Francisco, using such unusual sales methods of the day as a single price for all customers. With business success they gained prominence in the public mind.

Although the press identified Weinstock as a wealthy merchant, by other activities he acquired popularity as a public-spirited citizen—an asset of inestimable value in detracting from opposition to his cooperative marketing work. He wrote articles for newspapers and popular journals. He gave effective lectures to various types of groups on such topics as civil rights, tolerance for religious beliefs, morality in trade and government, aims of public education, and the status of women. Audiences everywhere in the state esteemed him for his exceptional character. His magnetism and dignity combined with an unimpeachable integrity set him apart. Considered "saintly" by close associates, he was styled as "one of nature's noblemen."

Weinstock was a doer as well as a talker in reform movements. He worked for political reform, civic improvement, renovation of public education, and numerous other causes. A progressive in politics, he was approached in 1910 for the gubernatorial candidacy by Lincoln-Roosevelt forces of the Republican Party. Instead, he helped to persuade a close family friend, Hiram Johnson, to accept the candidacy.

Weinstock retired from active private business in 1908, following Lubin's lead, to give most of his time to work of a public nature. Lubin left the management of Weinstock, Lubin and Co. in 1896 to begin in a few years his pioneer efforts for international cooperation with the formation of the International Institute of Agriculture in Rome. Weinstock's primary interests after leaving the store were labor and agriculture.

With a commission from a California governor to search for solutions to the problems of industrial relations, he made a personally financed trip around the world in 1908 and 1909. It added both to his store of knowledge and his public stature. In 1912, another governor commissioned him to investigate riots in San Diego involving the Industrial Workers of the World, and the following year he was appointed to the newly-organized State Industrial Accident Board. President Wilson had named him the same year to the National Commission on Industrial Relations.

Major Contributions in Marketing, Rural Credit

The areas in agriculture in which Weinstock made major contributions were marketing and, to a lesser extent, rural credit. He became aware of farmers' complaints as he talked to store customers but was confronted directly by the problems of agriculture when he and Lubin ventured into farming. In 1884, a decade after opening their Sacramento store, they acquired two sections of wheatland and a large vineyard. They began to attend and participate in the annual conventions of fruit growers which leading growers and shippers had formed in 1880 to discuss common problems.

The convention's transportation committee which Weinstock served as President obtained improvements in rates and services on eastern fruit shipments. He also helped to organize and acted as a director of the California Fruit Union, a cooperative formed in 1885 to market fresh deciduous fruit. Three years later he was active in the formation of the California Dried Fruit Union. Neither survived for long, but they were soon replaced by similar organizations in which Weinstock took a prominent part. They, too, were short-lived.

Nonetheless, Weinstock earned credit during these early years of California's agricultural development for his efforts to insure more even distribution of the ever-increasing amounts of California farm products going to out-of-state markets and for adoption of the auction sales plan for the deciduous fruit shipped. For a brief time his clearing house plan or scheme of regulated distribution found favor with organizations formed under the auspices of the fruit growers' conventions. Lubin shared in some of these endeavors until, as noted, he went his separate way. Prompted by a sense of mission, he tried to promote world peace and justice by improving world agricultural conditions. This zeal to raise the status of farmers probably influenced Weinstock to some extent.

Weinstock's agricultural work was deeply affected by his own business experience. He drew upon techniques of merchandising dry goods to urge fellow farmers to figure unit costs, to standardize their products, to expand markets by advertising, to cooperate with shippers to send their products to receptive markets, and to put money into their own associations as a means of giving them strength. With standardized products to sell and collective bargaining associations, farmers would command better credit terms and higher prices. In his first annual report as State Market Director he said, "It is, in my judgment, essential that each of our leading industries be effectively organized along marketing lines in order to regulate supplies, minimize gluts, and develop interstate and foreign markets, while filling the demands of our smaller markets at home."

Believed Deeply in and Worked Toward Collective Action

The concern he felt about bettering the lot of farmers reflected his belief that agriculture was the basic segment in the economy. He considered farm prosperity crucial to the country's well-being and believed that the national welfare depended on ownership of farms and homes by their occupants. It was his conviction, moreover, that the age of collectivism had arrived: Salvation for any economic group, business, labor, or agricultural, depended on collective action. Not doctrinaire with respect to cooperatives before he became State Market Director in 1915, he determined to use this office to form farmer cooperatives like those of the California citrus and raisin growers. Thereafter, he found in organization the solutions to all agricultural marketing problems. Probably this enthusiasm was stimulated by discussions of other cooperative leaders including those attending the third annual sessions of the National Conference on Marketing and Farm Credits in Chicago in 1915. Weinstock attended these meetings immediately after receiving his appointment as State Market Director.

He was also profoundly impressed by the organization of German farmers and the assistance given them by the German government. He obtained his information about German agriculture firsthand during his travels. His observations during a trip in 1913 led to his participation in reforming rural credit facilities in the United States and in turn to his concentrating his energy on organizing cooperatives.

In 1913, the governor of California appointed him as a state representative of the American Commission on Agricultural Credit and Cooperation which was composed of delegates from the United States and the Canadian provinces. With the United States Commission appointed by President Wilson, it toured Europe for three months to study cooperatives and rural credit programs. David Lubin initiated the scheme, and the Southern Commercial Congress sponsored it in the United States. Weinstock found the days of investigation in Germany the most valuable; in fact, he said that they were "the most educational 25 days that I have ever spent anywhere."

After the Commissions returned, they published a lengthy report which added publicity to a problem already a public issue. This document influenced the course of rural credit legislation including the Federal Farm Loan Act of 1916. Early in 1915, Weinstock was asked to serve in California on a committee to advise the government about developing a state rural credit program. In response to the committee's report, the legislature created the State Colonization and Rural Credits Commission on which Weinstock served. It concluded that the federal program for rural credit would meet most state needs, but it had held hearings which revealed extensive farmer discontent. Not surprisingly, legislators responded by supporting a measure providing for the appointment of a State Market Director.

Becomes California State Market Director

Weinstock did not share in the formulation of this law which progressives in the state adopted. He saw in it, however, a means of implementing farm marketing ideas that he had been developing from the 1880's when he first acquired a vineyard but could not find a market for his grapes. At his urging, Governor Johnson signed it and put Weinstock in charge of its administration.

The law was the first of two under which Weinstock held the office of State Market Director and was called the State Commission Market Act of 1915. It was followed by the State Market Commission Act of 1917. The slight variation in wording represented completely different interpretations of the duties of the State Market Director. When asked about the discrepancy, Weinstock remarked that the two laws were as different as a horse chestnut was from a chestnut horse.

The first law gave the Market Director no explicit power to organize producers into cooperatives but contained discretionary power to create public markets when and where he judged conditions to be suitable. Weinstock opposed state marketing of farm products. Thus, he did not judge either the time or place appropriate for starting any public market. What he did was to interpret a section of the law that obligated the Market Director to provide producers with market information as authorization to organize farmers, commodity by commodity, into strong marketing enterprises. He reasoned that the Market Director could not give farmers individually the information they needed, but he could help farmers by supplying their organization with useful market information. He started with the industry that seemed in greatest need, the dried fruit industry, and went on to help organize poultry producers, dairy farmers, rice and olive growers, and others as they asked for state aid. Through speeches, newspaper interviews, and conferences with representative growers in his office and out in farming communities, he directed his efforts toward organizing the greatest possible number of growers.

Aaron Sapiro a Protege

In most phases of his work as Market Director, Weinstock had the assistance of able young associates. These included the secretary of the State Commission Market (later, Market Commission) whose position was established by the law under which the agency functioned, and a gifted lawyer, Aaron Sapiro, for whose services the law did not provide. Weinstock used his own money to pay him for his help. A protege of Weinstock, Sapiro was often present in the early stages of the Market Director's work to talk to growers who called at the Commission Market office and frequently went along on trips into the farming regions to promote the formation of associations. He worked with growers' organizing committees in the signing up process and drafted legal papers for the new associations. Once launched, these enterprises often retained him out of their own resources for their legal needs. Consequently, he and his firm began to specialize in cooperative work. They not only built a thriving practice but in the process contributed to the development of cooperative law. In this fashion, work with the State Commission Market served as the training ground for Sapiro's later achievements in organizing cooperatives throughout the United States and Canada on what he called "the California plan."

The energetic activities of the Market Director and his staff generated numerous and often bitter protests, but they came from diverse sources—from organized consumer groups who insisted that the state establish public markets to lower the cost of living; from canners, packers, and grocer associations; and from politicians who had voted for the bill and objected to Weinstock's use of it, to name his highly vocal critics. The lack of agreement among them in contrast to the unified support from organized farmers combined with the widespread respect for Weinstock in the state enabled him in 1917 to push through the Legislature the second law. It repealed the law of 1915 but provided once again for the appointment of a State Market Director. The new law specifically directed him to organize farmers into cooperatives. Provisions for public markets were deliberately omitted.

While serving under these laws, Weinstock dispelled much mistrust of cooperatives and successfully encouraged farmers up and down the state to join forces in marketing associations. But he suffered keen disappointment in trying to obtain adequate backing for his "pet projects," a state distributing agency—the Bureau of Distribution as he called it—and his plan to unite all of the cooperatives into the California Federation of Farmers' Cooperative Marketing Associations. This ambitious plan which, he thought, would be the envy of all the farmers outside the state, was realized only on paper. Meetings were held and a federation formed. The plans for a state distribution bureau did not develop beyond the discussion stage. The old established cooperatives, not seeing enough to their interests in either scheme, remained aloof. Without their support, the projects fell by the wayside.

Few of the cooperatives formed in the Weinstock era outlasted the postwar depression; most of the survivors were forced to undergo substantial reorganization to adapt operations to changing conditions. Some had a highly uncertain existence for most of the following decade, although each had distinctive problems.

Weinstock's ambitions for organized farmers were not entirely realistic. He may have appreciated the necessity for farmers to maintain a constant alertness to the way their business was functioning, but his message to farmers stressed, rather, the advantages of organization along industry lines. Yet few leaders can match the significance of his role in cooperative history. He helped to shape the pattern of California cooperative development intermittently over a period of 35 years. Not only were the state's farmers imbued with the benefits of organization, but respect for cooperatives spread widely among nonfarmers as a result of his work.

In 1920, during a serious illness, Weinstock resigned from the position of State Market Director. His immediate successors did not receive the good press that he enjoyed. That the office never again reached the peak of influence that it attained under Weinstock was most of all a commentary on his remarkable ability, energy, and popularity.

Carl Williams

by John D. Campbell

CARL WILLIAMS WAS AMONG THE EARLY LEADERS of modern cotton cooperatives. Grange organizations attempted to market cotton in 1873—five years before he was born—but most of the first cotton cooperatives lasted only but a few years.

The Oklahoma cotton lint marketing association and other cotton cooperatives that Carl Williams helped organize in the early 1920's are active now—more than 40 years later. The Oklahoma cotton cooperative that he sponsored and of which he was one of the first directors, changed names and recently merged with the Plains Cotton Cooperative Association. In effect, this cooperative has been in continuous operation now for 45 years.

Carl Williams was born in Indiana in 1878 and was reared on a farm. When he was 19 years of age, he started work as a copy boy on a newspaper and became the managing editor in a short time.

His interest in farming led him into the editing of farm papers. He edited *Scientific Farming* in 1905–1906, then farmed in Colorado from 1906 to 1911, where he was a seed-breeder and stockman. In 1913, he became editor of *The Oklahoma Farmer-Stockman* and was its active editor for 16 years.

In the National Conference on Marketing and Farm Credits, held in Chicago in 1915, Williams gave an address on "The Tenant of the South and the Marketing of His Crop." He was then deeply aware of the farmer's plight and although he saw in cooperative organizations a ray of hope, he felt that the deepest need was education for the cotton farmer himself so that "he may see the heights above him and may be moved to climb them instead of sitting inert in the valley below and deluding himself with self-pity into an attitude which is not helpful to the community welfare."

While his abilities took him into many fields, cotton cooperatives were his major interest. He was writing editorials and articles favorable to cooperatives several years before he began to organize the Oklahoma Cotton Growers' Association.

For example, in the December 25, 1916 issue of *The Oklahoma Farmer-Stockman*, Williams wrote that cooperation was the best weapon of farmers to get higher prices.

Enthusiatic Co-op Supporter, But Realized and Wrote About Problems

Although Williams was an enthusiastic supporter of cooperatives, he recognized their problems. In an editorial in April, 1920, he wrote: "Nobody is going to acuse me of knocking if I indulge in a few cooperative dont's. I have preached cooperative marketing among farmers, in season and out for so many years, that I cannot remember when I really began it . . ." He then proceeded to caution farmers on the need for adequate volumes, adequate capital and management, and other matters. His recommendations included many given groups interested in organizing new cooperatives today.

Following the belt-wide Montgomery, Ala., meeting, April 13–16, 1920, Williams started an intensive educational campaign on cooperative marketing of cotton. He used both editorials and articles in *The Oklahoma Farmer-Stockman* and made speeches to inform farmers and lay the foundation for organizing the Cotton Marketing Association.

By June, 1920, delegates from 32 of the 50 cotton-producing counties in Oklahoma had met at Oklahoma City and adopted a plan for organizing a statewide association to handle the 1921 crop. Carl Williams was chairman of the organization committee that had charge of the campaign. The plan adopted by the Oklahoma cotton growers was patterned after the centralized associations in California rather than federated locals as proposed by the committee of the American Cotton Association at Montgomery. He was at this time an ardent admirer of Aaron Sapiro.

The campaign to organize the Oklahoma Cotton Growers' Association got underway in September, 1920, and was completed April 1, 1921. Contracts were signed by 35,000 growers, representing 400,000 bales. The goal had been 30,000 grower contracts and 300,000 bales. Carl Williams was due a large share of the credit for the success of the campaign.

He was a recognized leader of the large-scale commodity marketing associations of that period. The Oklahoma plan was followed by nearly all the other similar cotton marketing associations formed in the next

several years. He advocated the organization of a nationwide cooperative marketing organization and was a sponsor in the organization
of the American Cotton Growers Exchange in 1921, which was later
reorganized with broader activities and renamed the American Cotton
Cooperative Association.

While Carl Williams saw the potentialities of cotton cooperatives,
he was not a visionary. An editorial by him in the July 10, 1921, issue
of *The Oklahoma Farmer-Stockman* accurately anticipated some of
the opposition that would be encountered, and he recognized that
rumors of graft and exorbitant costs would be circulated in an attempt
to undermine the associations.

Accepts Pres. Hoover Appointment to Federal Farm Board

His editorials and articles gave him a reputation that extended far
beyond the borders of Oklahoma. In July, 1929, President Hoover
offered him an appointment to the Federal Farm Board on the advice
of farm organizations representing two million farmers. Although
loathe to do so he took a leave of absence as editor of *The Oklahoma
Farmer-Stockman* and accepted the offer, for he recognized that the
Federal Farm Board was pioneering in a new area and that it was
his duty to do what he could to help strengthen cooperative marketing associations.

While a member of Federal Farm Board Carl Williams was a very
active protagonist of cooperatives and he was often the board's spokesman. In a challenging address at the A.I.C. meeting at the University
of New Hampshire in the summer of 1932, he defended the policies
of the Federal Farm Board with respect to its encouragement of
nationwide cooperative marketing organizations. In a critical paper
on the Board's shortcomings, Dr. Edwin G. Nourse took issue with
him and this set off one of the most spirited debates in the annals
of the A.I.C., and one which left both men with higher respect for
the other. In his rebuttal comments Dr. Nourse said:

> I think it is a wonderful achievement when a man in official
> position connected with a Board which has occupied such a
> delicate and difficult position, takes the time and exerts the effort
> to make the contribution Mr. Williams has . . . I am going to say
> before Mr. Williams what I have said behind his back, that I think
> he is intellectually one of the most able members, if not the most
> able, the Board has ever had. Added to that are a personal
> courtesy and friendliness, and spirit of sportsmanship which makes
> his participation all we could hope for . . .

After his service with the Federal Farm Board, Carl Williams moved to Fort Pierce, Fla., where he was active in civic affairs until his death in 1953.

Although some of his views on cooperatives are still visionary, much of his thinking has been adopted. The accomplishments of cotton cooperatives in Oklahoma and Texas since his death would have greatly pleased him if he could have lived to see them.

101

Founder of
Southern States Cooperative

William Geoffrey Wysor

by W. M. Corwin

I F THERE BE TRUTH IN THE STATEMENT that the successful business organization is but the lengthening shadow of a man who is or has one time been its leader, then the growing, versatile Southern States Cooperative which operates "at the top of the South" reflects the sound foundation laid for it by its founder and General Manager for 25 years, William Geoffrey Wysor, a Virginian, born and bred of sturdy English and German stock.

It was this man, born December 1, 1892 in the little farming community of New River in Pulaski county in Virginia's rugged southwestern territory and educated in a one-room school, who went on to become President of the student body at his college, Manager of the largest farm east of the Mississippi, and Secretary to a Virginia governor. And it was he who, despite offers of top positions in private business at then "fabulous" salaries, refused to give up his crusade for farmers, remained faithful to the task of helping his fellowman by teaching him the philosophy of self-help—the idea that many men, working together, can better their economic well-being through the exercise of their own initiative and resourcefulness.

From his home community and the one-room school, young Wysor moved to Dublin Institute, a private educational institution in the area, and then to Virginia Polytechnic Institute at Blacksburg, where he was graduated "with honors" in agriculture in 1914, and acquired the popular nickname of "Bud" after a well-known beverage. During his senior year at V. P. I., he was ranking captain in the cadet corps, President of the VPI Athletic Association, and of course, President of the student body.

He entered V. P. I. after only five years of formal schooling, and earned his way through four years of college by waiting on tables, distributing the mail, working in the registrar's office and, in his senior year, teaching two freshmen classes. Notwithstanding these handicaps, he finished first in his class with a four-year average grade of 94.6 per cent.

Following graduation he served as county agricultural agent in Russell county (Va.), then took a job as General Manager of the Georgia Land and Livestock Company, a corporation which owned and operated a farm of 128,000 acres in South Georgia. Here indeed was a task which called for coordination, organization, good judgment, and dedication. And here it was, his friends and admirers expect, that young Wysor learned of the opportunities offered by "bigness"— mass purchasing of supplies, mass marketing, proper application and assignment of manpower.

To merge these things with an inborn "individualism" fostered by his farm background and with the needs of thousands of struggling Virginia farmers immediately after the first World War, was just another step down the road for this quiet, soft-spoken man with a sparkle in his eye and a keen sense of humor. Here, too, was a man who was a wise judge of manpower, a natural leader who at times was a taskmaster, but who never expected more from his subordinates than he had already done himself.

In 1918, Wysor resigned from the position in Georgia to enter the Artillery Officers Training Camp at Fort Zachary Taylor. The war ended shortly thereafter and he joined the Stuart Land and Cattle Co., of Elk Garden, Va. as Secretary-Treasurer. This operation was owned by the then governor of Virginia, Henry C. Stuart, and young Wysor also acted as the governor's Secretary in the handling of the latter's personal and business affairs.

Organizes Crop Improvement Association in 1921

After two years Wysor was back at V. P. I., this time as a member of the Agricultural Extension Service agronomy staff. And there it was that he came face to face with his "destiny." In 1921 he organized the Virginia Crop Improvement Association for the breeding, production, and distribution of certified seed under rigid rules and with a careful inspection system designed to insure superior strains, adaptation, higher yielding ability, and high quality generally. It was from this organization which has ever since been a major factor in seed improvement in Virginia, that the idea of an association like Southern States was born in W. G. Wysor's fertile mind.

By 1922, the Crop Improvement Association had more than 500 members scattered throughout Virginia, producing certified seed in considerable quantities. But though the association solicited, entreated, cajoled, and pleaded, the existing seed trade refused to handle certified seed produced by the farmers. This seed, because of higher promotion costs, would not bear the rather large profit margins normally realized by the commercial seed trade.

To Wysor it was obvious that association members, unable to sell through existing channels, must do the marketing job themselves.

At the same time, Virginia farmers faced another serious problem. In fact, it had existed for some time. Getting good stands and yields from the clover and alfalfa generally distributed by the seed trade was almost impossible.

But in 1922, the Virginia Experiment Station, after years of research, came up with the answer. The alfalfa and clover failures, it reported, was due to the use of unadapted seed—seed which lacked winter hardiness and which was susceptible to anthracnose. Some domestically produced seed and substantially all imported seed had been proved guilty of these inferiorities.

Yet, even when the Experiment Station reported these findings in a special bulletin, in the public press, and at farmers' meetings, urgently requesting seed dealers to handle clover and alfalfa of known origin, to discontinue importing seed which was unsuitable, and to supply only seed adapted to Virginia's climate and soil and high yielding under Virginia conditions, the answer was a ringing "no."

Not one commercial seed handler was willing to serve as a distribution unit for adapted seed. None were willing to afford farmers a choice by providing information as to seed origin. In Wysor's own words: "Some actually attacked the colleges for even recommending that seed be purchased on the basis of its origin."

Virginia Seed Service Succeeds CIA in 1923

Needless to say, this situation was as fuel to the fire which burned in the breast of the young Crop Improvement Association Secretary. His determination to lick this situation grew ever stronger. So it was, at his strong urging and with his guidance, that a meeting was called in Richmond in April, 1923, mostly of members of the Crop Improvement Association. Here 150 farmers organized a cooperative to handle seed on a non-profit basis in the interest of the men who planted the seed and hoped for a crop. They named it Virginia Seed Service. They elected a board of directors, including W. G. Wysor. They subscribed for capital stock. At the first board meeting Wysor was chosen General Manager, whereupon he immediately resigned as a board member, saying he did not want "to be in the position of sitting in judgment as a director over my own performance as an employed manager."

Some years later, after more experience and maturity, Wysor pursued this philosophy a bit further and wrote a letter to the board of directors in which he said:

> Since the General Manager is an employee most responsible for good operating results, he should be the easiest employee to remove. To facilitate my removal, at the discretion of the directors, I herewith submit my resignation to be accepted at the pleasure of the board.

The directors, without exception, objected, but Wysor insisted the letter go into the minutes as a part of the permanent record. It did.

The infant cooperative opened July 1, 1923 with paid-in capital of $11,000, two employes (Wysor and one other), and leased space in a Richmond warehouse. Office equipment consisted of a second-hand typewriter, a battered desk, two old chairs. Purchase of a seed cleaner took a tenth of the original capital. It is hard to conceive of any organization having a less auspicious beginning.

That the VSS lived at all was a miracle. No existing seed dealers would handle VSS seeds. Many farmers were suspicious of it. Few farmers of that day were aware of the greater yields possible through use of adapted seed of superior breeding and quality. Another deterrent was that such seed, of necessity, was more costly to produce and had to be relatively high priced.

The Virginia Seed Service survived, said Wysor, because "it applied a business principle entirely different from that motivating the commercial seed trade—operation in the interest of the users of the business rather than operation in the interest of the owners of the business . . . handling of seed on a value-in-use basis, rather than on the basis of merchandising profit.

Mr. Wysor was right. But there was another reason . . . Wysor himself.

Without his zeal, his determination and his inexhaustible energy, the VSS might well have failed. The early going—the first 10 years in fact—were plenty tough and time after time financial extinction was very close. Payrolls often could not be met, and Wysor was the first to hold back his meager salary. Along with other employees he gave personal notes to tide the organization over some rough spots, even reduced his own salary to curtail expenses. Hours of work meant nothing to him.

When dealers refused to handle Virginia co-op seed, it was Wysor who organized a "pooler" system of distribution, encouraging individual farmers to take their neighbors' orders for seeds and thus "pool" together enough volume for a carload or at least a substantial quantity for a particular locality. For getting the order, and collecting the money when the seed arrived, the pooler got a five percent commission, hardly enough to cover travel expenses. But this was the spirit of these early cooperative-minded farmers and indicative of the zeal which they caught from Wysor, their leader. As a matter of fact, quite a number of the farmers serving as seed poolers believed so strongly in what the VSS was undertaking to do that they refused to take any commissions whatever.

Now let's back up a bit, to the period Wysor was working in Russell county not long after graduation from college. One Sunday afternoon, while motoring near town he came upon a group of girls, some of whom he knew, taking a stroll. They introduced him to pretty Ruth Gaines Puckett, of Rosedale, Va., and though Wysor didn't know it then, another part of his "destiny" was sealed on the spot.

Some time elapsed, he said, "before I ever saw her again," but Wysor and Miss Puckett did begin "seeing each other on a regular basis" a little later and on September 12, 1922, at a quiet home wedding they were united in matrimony.

The Wysors became parents of two children—a son, William Geoffrey, Jr., who became a physician, and a daughter, Betty Ruth, now Mrs. S. M. Pearman. Mrs. Wysor died in 1960 of a heart attack while vacationing with her husband in Florida. Later Mr. Wysor was married again—to Mrs. Margaret Aston Barker, an old friend of earlier years.

"Open Formula" Introduced by Wysor on Feeds

In 1925, the Virginia Seed Service took the first step towards enlarging its service beyond the handling of seed. Here, once more, Wysor was able to muster a crusade for farmers which not only enlisted new recruits to the cause of cooperation, but brought livestock feed prices tumbling and pioneered another landmark within the feed industry— public specifications or "open formula"—telling the patron exactly what ingredients and how much of each was in every bag he purchased. The idea was basically the same as the VSS had pioneered on seed—giving the patrons all the facts about origin, variety, germination, and weed content.

The mixed feed industry of the middle 20's was a profitable business because (1) mixed or formula feeds were very generally, unfairly, and unreasonably priced; and (2) the quality often left much to be desired (cheap ingredients like grain screenings, rice bran, cottonseed hulls and ground-up hay, which were low in nutritional value, were popular). It was also standard practice to promote some feeds like chick starters as mysterious concoctions and apply unreasonably high prices to them.

It was simple enough to produce feeds using top quality ingredients. And it was simple, too, to offer VSS feeds at savings under other feeds because the VSS priced its feeds at actual cost, plus a small margin for safety. The savings to farmers who used them averaged about $3 per ton on dairy feeds and laying mashes, while on chick starting mashes the savings were usually at least $20 per ton ($1 per bag) under prices charged by reputable feed manufacturers who were producing good quality feeds for that day.

Such savings, however, did not result in farmers rushing to the VSS to buy their feeds. On the contrary! Many farmers literally were afraid to buy VSS starting mash because they thought it couldn't possibly be as good as others at such a low price. It was some time before VSS feed volume was more than a mere trickle. But it did grow, and once farmers learned they could buy nothing better, it grew fast—eventually to well beyond the half-million ton mark annually.

S.S. Fertilizer Program Also Becomes Pace-Setter

By 1927, the VSS, and Wysor, were ready to tackle fertilizer—another of the farmer's "big three" production supplies. Here, too, farmers at the time were paying unreasonably high prices for the actual amount af plant food they were getting. The most generally used fertilizer was of 2-8-2 analysis, which could not be made without using over 600 pounds per ton of filler, usually sand.

So it was that the VSS, though at that time it had no plants of its own and had to contract its production through other facilities, established an effective fertilizer program which soon became a pace-setter for farmers on quality, price, and service. The VSS preached the recommendations of the colleges for better, higher analyses and greater all-round use of fertilizer. In fact, in production of all supplies, Southern States has always listened to the sound, unbiased advice and recommendations of the agricultural colleges and experiment stations.

Having taken agriculture at V. P. I. and having served later on the college's agronomy staff, it was natural that Wysor should look to his alma mater and its research for guidance as to what was best for farmers.

When a feed service was inaugurated, he recommended to his board of directors an "open formula" policy, and urged that such a policy of public specifications be pursued insofar as feasible with respect to all farm supplies produced or purchased by the organization. This policy was adopted and has since been adhered to.

The essence of it is to inform the patron by tag or otherwise the origin and variety of seed and all other pertinent information. In feed and fertilizer it means telling the patrons the ingredients used and exactly the quantity in each ton. Application of the same principle to other supplies is contemplated.

With reference to recommendations from the colleges, Wysor said:

> The Land-Grant Colleges are public institutions supported with public funds. They have the best available information and are unprejudiced in using it, in the best interests of farmers. How logical it is for a farm cooperative to look to their knowledge and research for specifications and guidance.

After VSS (Southern States) services were extended to farmers in other states beyond Virginia, this policy was modified to employ the research and guidance of all the Land Grant Colleges in the operating area. This was done by organizing boards made up of appropriate representatives of each of the colleges. There is now a College Dairy Feed Conference Board, a Poultry Feed Conference Board, a Fertilizer Board, a Seed Board and a Farm Supply Board. The latter gives counsel on hundreds of supplies and commodities used by farmers.

With the seed, feed, and fertilizer in the VSS fold, Wysor could see that a complete one-stop service on all production supplies used by farmers should follow. Such a cooperative purchasing service would be convenient for patrons, would provide them with dependable quality at a saving, would reduce prices, would spread costs more thinly and thus improve operating efficiency.

The farm supply phase of VSS service grew slowly, an item at a time. The first was baler twine. Today's complete line ranges from appliances to Zorbit litter for poultry houses and embraces roofing, fencing, paint, tools, tires, automotive supplies, motor oils and greases, lawn and garden supplies, dairy, poultry, and swine raising equipment and hundreds of other items and services.

Decision Made in Early 30's to Expand to Other States

By 1930 it was obvious to Wysor and others that a large enough volume of business could not be put together within the state of Virginia to gain maximum efficiency in rendering a wholesale cooperative service to supply the local community retail agencies, the outgrowth of the old pooler system. (Some early poolers actually became local agencies, built warehouses, and handled cooperative supplies under franchise. In other areas, groups of farmers organized their own local cooperatives to provide local community retail service.)

The first crossing of the borders was into North Carolina where farmers soon began reaping some of the benefits of cooperation available to their Virginia cousins. This was highly unpleasing to the competing manufacturers of farm production supplies. They threatened to, and actually did slash prices in Virginia and spent considerable money and effort to "break" the VSS. They expanded their sales staffs, offered to set up local cooperatives for farmers, even tried to hire Wysor himself for more than double his salary with the struggling cooperative, plus a long time contract. But the organization, its General Manager, and other leaders stood firm. The "price war" was finally called off by the commercial business which started it. The VSS was left with the major problem of building more volume in the midst of a rapidly deepening economic depression.

By 1934, several cooperative groups in North Carolina, all performing similar services for farmers, were brought together in a new organization called Farmers Cooperative Exchange and the VSS gracefully withdrew from the state to avoid further duplication of services to farmers and to make possible greater savings for farmers there. The new FCX continued to use the wholesale and production facilities of the VSS as sources of supplies. Relationships between the two organizations have remained close and harmonious to this day—a splendid example of the ability of cooperatives to cooperate, thereby enabling each to serve its membership better and more efficiently.

Before the next territorial expansion—into Maryland in 1934—the VSS changed its name to Southern States Cooperative, a title more appropriate for an association with broadened services and territory.

Services were extended to Delaware also in 1934, to West Virginia in 1941, to Kentucky in 1945, and to northeastern Tennessee in 1947 (SSC later withdrew from that state under mutual agreement with the growing Tennessee Farmers Cooperative).

The Southern States territory today embraces the five states of Virginia, West Virginia, Maryland, Delaware, and Kentucky. Its membership was 220,000 by the mid 60's, its annual business volume above $125 million, its net worth exclusive of affiliates, near $36 million.

In addition to the basic services on seed, feed, fertilizer, and farm supplies, it now handles petroleum and LP gas in certain parts of its territory, operates a marketing service on eggs and grain, owns interests in a large oil refinery, a nitrogen plant, and in phosphorus and potash production facilities under construction, operates bulk feed, fertilizer spreading, nitrogen application and numerous other services. Nearly 30 modern mills, plants, warehouses, and other wholesale facilities produce, process and purchase supplies which reach farmers through 600 local cooperative service agencies making up one of the largest and most effective cooperative distribution systems in the nation.

Wysor Honored Widely on Retirement at 54

All these are fulfillments of the dreams of William Geoffrey Wysor. For 25 years he led the cooperative as General Manager—through the trying early years of development, through the fierce competition from all sides in the depression years, through the period of tremendous growth just prior to, during and just after World War II. Then he stepped down, at 54, from the general managership to a less demanding post as Management Counsel which he held for another 10 years until full retirement in 1958.

Speaking of his retirement as General Manager in 1947 (climaxed by a silver anniversary testimonial dinner which brought messages and comments from farm and business leaders all over the nation) a Virginia newspaper commented:

> Rarely have regret and applause been so mingled as in the retirement of W. G. Wysor. . . . The regret, of course, lies in losing a leader who has fought the hard fight for farmer cooperatives. . . ."
>
> The applause lies in the reasons advanced by Mr. Wysor for his leaving. He will not be 55 until December 1. His associates believe few men half his age can match his vigor. Yet Mr. Wysor expresses these convictions: "The management of such a business as this must have the stamina to take a lot of strain, pressure, and pounding. In good conscience, I also have to recognize that any reasonably successful management is always in position to overstay its time. If I allow myself to commit that offense I would be guilty of basic ingratitude for the generosity of Southern States to me and the honors it has bestowed upon me. It is my conviction that the future welfare, success, and usefulness of Southern States Cooperative will most effectively be promoted if the position in management is filled by a younger man.
>
> Every student of business and public administration will praise his forthright view. Too often, we see men cling to positions long after they should have stepped aside in fairness to their associates and themselves.

In addition to duties with Southern States, Wysor has had a distinguished business career. He was a member of the board of directors of the Federal Reserve Bank of Richmond for 18 years, during which time he served for some time as Deputy Chairman and later as Chairman of the board.

He was also for 13 years a director of the Central Bank for Cooperatives. He served as President of a number of Southern States subsidiaries and affiliates.

For many years he served on the board of directors and the executive committee of the National Council of Farmer Cooperatives. He was a Trustee of the American Institute of Cooperation, and for 15 years was on the board of the Foundation of American Agriculture. He was also a member of the executive committee of the Agricultural Conference Board of Virginia.

Wysor received in 1962 the highest honor his alma mater could bestow upon him—the VPI Citation—"for meritorious service and outstanding contributions to his profession, his nation and his alma mater." He was particularly cited for his "leadership in organizing and developing the Southern States Cooperative." The citation also expressed appreciation of his service as Chairman of the Federal Reserve Bank board and his chairmanship for 14 years of the VPI Alumni Fund Council.

What was the motivating philosophy which this man used to form and build one of the nation's largest and strongest farmer cooperatives? What were some of the principles which underlay the planning, the organization and the management of that cooperative? What were the secrets of its success . . . and that of Wysor?

Though Mr. Wysor gave voluminous credit to the late H. E. Babcock, one of the founders and early General Manager of the GLF of New York state (now a part of Agway) for ideas, assistance, and guidance in founding VSS and to other GLF workers for advice and counsel, it was Wysor's own perseverance and determination that were major factors in the later success of Southern States Cooperative.

Wysor believes firmly that the farmer as an individual is all but helpless in the market place . . . that he can exercise little control over either the price he pays or the quality of the supplies he gets . . . that when he goes as an individual to sell his farm products he must generally accept what is offered. This fundamental problem implies that farmers must join together in their own cooperative organizations to strengthen their bargaining position . . . in fact, to have any bargaining position at all.

Wysor Book Explains Co-op Principles; Praises Co-op Values

As Wysor said in his book, *The Southern States Story,* there "is no way to increase the net income of farmers other than through self-help cooperatives owned by farmers, controlled by farmers, and operated by farmers in their own interest on a cost-of-doing-business basis."

The solution, says Wysor, is for farmers to pool their resources, their buying, and their selling power. "In a free society such as we have in America," he points out, "farmer cooperatives which purchase farm supplies and market farm products are economic and social instruments which (1) promote and protect the opportunities of the individual, and (2) safeguard our cherished free enterprise system."

Wysor sees cooperatives as contributing to farmers' self-reliance and morale . . . as organizers of competition to prevent monopolies and monopolistic practices by other business . . . as the off-the-farm purchasing and marketing "arm" of the farmer in nearly every phase of fiber and food production.

He believes that cooperatives are more successful and effective in improving the farmer-members' net income when they operate "across the board" services—owning and operating the facilities which enable their farmer owners to control every step of production from raw materials to the finished supply delivered to the farm, thus gaining savings on each individual operation.

He believes strongly in farmers using their cooperatives on a voluntary basis . . . thinks cooperatives must be so effective and so efficient they will "deserve" the farmer's business, rather than having members coerced or forced, through stringent contracts and agreements, to deal with their cooperatives.

Wysor stressed "ownership" and "loyalty" through the years as he talked with farmers, urging them to consider their shares of cooperative membership stock as significant an investment as that in their own land, buildings and equipment and capable of producing an even greater return.

He was strong for the principle of "one man—one vote." And he never failed to remind Southern States members that by keeping quality of farm supplies up and costs down, their cooperative was setting a pace which other suppliers to the farm must follow . . . bringing benefits not just to cooperative members but to all farmers alike.

One of Wysor's outstanding characteristics is humility. Never has he claimed personal credit for the success and usefulness to agriculture of Southern States Cooperative. He says the cooperative "has succeeded because it was economically needed and because farmers intelligently supported it." In the dedication of his *Southern States Story*, he wrote:

> To the man on the land who has demonstrated his courage, initiative, and resourcefulness in solving his problems and bettering his economic well-being through self-help cooperation.

As one of cooperatives' "strong men" of the century, "William Geoffrey Wysor spent an entire career in the service of agriculture. He believes as strongly today in the fundamental principles of cooperation as on that April day in 1923 when he helped organize Virginia Seed Service.

"In the last analysis," he says, "the objective of farmer cooperatives is a fuller, richer, more independent and happier life for the man on the land. Cooperation has already achieved much in this direction. And I'm sure that progress, through farmer cooperation, will continue."

Part III

The Pioneers of
Cooperative Credit

102

The Federal Land Banks

by Robert B. Tootell

T HE GENESIS OF MANY PIONEERING INSTITUTIONS is traceable to the vision and leadership of a single person. Others have no clearly identifiable person who warrants the major credit for their being. In this latter category is the federal Land Bank system that began its career as a cooperative pioneer half a century ago—in 1917, and largely set a pattern for the cooperative Farm Credit system.

Land Banks, as a source of financing for farmers, are not exclusively a phenomenon of the 20th century, however. Farmers since colonial times have been plagued by capital shortage in varying degree, and have tried many schemes to ease the problem. More than 200 years ago, private land banks and public land banks or loan offices were organized in the Colonies using land mortgages as security for paper money. These banks were neither soundly conceived nor soundly managed with the result they proved to be failures. A related development was the "property" banks, state institutions organized to help meet capital needs of planters in the South before the Civil War. They issued and sold bonds backed by real estate mortgages. They were also authorized to issue bank notes and perform other functions of a commercial bank. Sparks, in his *History and Theory of Agricultural Credit in the United States* (p. 97) gives the following evaluation:

> In the development of real estate banking in the United States, the property banks may be regarded as the connecting link between the colonial land banks and the present federal loan banks. With the Federal Farm Loan Act of 1916, paper money was finally divorced from land banking, and only the loan function was retained. But the land banks of today have many features common to their predecessors.

In the rapid settlement of the West following the Civil War, farm problems were many and the solution of cheap money, or at least more adequate credit services, often was advocated. The Granger Movement, the Free Silver Movement, National Greenback Party, Farmers Alliance, and Populist Party, all proposed solving the farmers credit problems through currency inflation rather than through more soundly based schemes. The National Banking Act, passed in 1863, was designed to serve the needs of the growing industrial and commercial economy, but it was disappointing to farmers because it expressly prohibited national banks from investing in farm mortgages, and most non-mortgage credit was limited to 60- to 90-day borrowing.

By the turn of the century, the "Homestead" era was near an end and there was little cheap land available even in the West. Not only was acquisition of a farm more costly, but more money was needed to improve farms, to buy equipment and to operate. Tenancy was increasing at a rate that concerned many people. Mortgage credit with which to buy land or make improvements was limited and unsatisfactory. Seldom was a mortgage written for more than five years, and interest rates of eight percent and 10 percent were common. Often a commission of five percent was charged to renew the mortgage. At times, the lender was unwilling or unable to renew and the farmer, being unable to pay his debt in full, was faced with loss of his farm through foreclosure.

Men and Commissions

A succession of events in the new century laid the groundwork for emergence of the pioneer in cooperative credit for United States agriculture. First, the Country Life Commission was appointed in 1908 by President Theodore Roosevelt and headed by Liberty Hyde Bailey, Dean of the College of Agriculture at Cornell University. Dean Bailey was a horticulturist by training, but he had keen insight and an interest in the total spectrum of agriculture and rural life. As one of his large contributions to research and teaching in agriculture, he emphasized and helped develop the survey method to supplement research as a means of finding a sound basis for programs of action. He especially valued the views of farm people themselves about their problems and what should be done about them.

These characteristics made Dean Bailey an ideal man to head the Commission of seven men, others of whom were agricultural leaders of their time. The Commission sent out a questionnaire to half a million people and received more than a hundred thousand replies. During November and December, 1908, members of the Commission held 30 public hearings that were attended by thousands of people from 40 states and territories. The report of the Commission was made in 1909 as Senate Document 705 of the 60th Congress. It contained many recommendations for the improvement of life in rural areas, most of which were implemented over the years by action programs.

With respect to credit, the Commission found a "lack of any adequate system of agricultural credit, whereby a farmer may readily secure loans on fair terms." It further stated that "a method of cooperative credit would undoubtedly prove of great service. . . . The present banking systems tend to take the money out of the open country and to loan it in town, or to town and town-centered interests." Considerable momentum was given to the movement for agricultural credit reform by the brief but meaningful statements in the Commission's report.

A National Monetary Commission was appointed by President Roosevelt in 1909 to study general banking conditions. It included a brief report on the Landschaft system of mortgage credit for farmers through their own cooperative associations that had been in operation in Germany as early as 1769. American ambassadors to several European countries were asked by President Taft in 1912 to investigate the rural credit systems of these countries.

Myron T. Herrick, United States Ambassador to France 1912–14, performed an outstanding service in this respect. He had a keen interest in cooperative credit growing out of 28 years' connection with the Cleveland, Ohio, Society for Savings, one of the largest and most successful mutual savings banks in the country at that time. He was designated by President Taft to receive these reports made on rural credits by our ambassadors, and to combine them in a general report. This report was a scholarly treatise of great assistance to those trying to develop an appropriate credit system for our farmers. With the collaboration of R. Ingalls, Ambassador Herrick used this material as the basis for an excellent book, *Rural Credits—Land and Cooperative,* first published by D. Appleton & Co. in 1914. It was widely used at the time, and is still recognized as an outstanding work on rural credit systems of Europe.

David Lubin, a California merchant of considerable vision and imagination who had suggested founding the International Institute of Agriculture at Rome and who was first United States delegate to the Institute, may have played a role which is not generally recognized. Before going to Rome, he had demonstrated interest in problems of rural finance. One bit of evidence was his article, "Credit for Farmers," that appeared in *Bankers Magazine* in 1910. He thought that cooperative groups of farmers should be formed to pool their individual assets into negotiable bonds that might be marketed through a national corporation. While serving in Rome, Lubin studied the Landschaft system of Germany and the agricultural credit programs of some other European countries. In April 1912, he returned from Rome and participated in the meeting of the Southern Commercial Congress at Nashville, Tenn., where he explained some systems of cooperative credit with which he had become familiar in European countries. The delegates to this Congress must have been much impressed for they passed a resolution asking that a commission be appointed of two men from each state to go to Europe and study farm credit systems there. This was a crucial point in the movement for a rural credit system in the United States. It marked the beginning of an action program.

David Lubin played a significant role in the work of both the American Commission on Agricultural Cooperation in Europe, that resulted from the Nashville resolution, and the United States Commission appointed in 1913 by President Wilson under an Act of Congress. This is attested by the following quotation from the joint report the two Commissions made to Congress in early 1914:

> The American Commission on Agricultural Cooperation in Europe was assembled under the auspices of The Southern Commercial Congress and was composed of delegates from different states as well as representatives of important associations. Seven delegates, representing four Provinces of the Dominion of Canada, were a part of the American Commission, and cooperated in every possible way in the studies and business of the Commission.

The American Commission, sponsored by the Southern Commercial Congress, without doubt prompted Congress to make provision for the United States Commission to which President Wilson appointed the following as members:

United States Senator Duncan U. Fletcher, of Florida.
United States Senator Thomas P. Gore, of Oklahoma.
Congressman Ralph W. Moss, of the fifth district of Indiana.
Colonel Harvie Jordan, planter, of Atlanta, Georgia.
Dr. John Lee Coulter, agricultural expert of the Census Bureau, Washington, D. C.
Dr. Kenyon L. Butterfield, President of the Massachusetts Agricultural College, Amherst, Massachusetts.
Dr. Clarence J. Owens, Managing Director of the Southern Commercial Congress, Washington, D. C.

Differing Philosophies and Legislative Proposals

The work of these two commissions that cooperated in the European credit study for three months in mid-1913, and submitted to Congress both separate and joint reports in early 1914, provided the foundation on which the specialized credit system for United States farmers was built. That the members of the two commissions were representative of differing points of view on the question of the best approach to solving agricultural credit problems is attested by the reports themselves and by legislation proposed. In the 63rd Congress, 30 bills and two joint resolutions were introduced in the Senate; and 68 bills, eight joint resolutions and two committee resolutions were introduced in the House, all proposing agricultural credit legislation. Each of them involved one or a combination of three quite different philosophies.

One of the groups believed that the government should organize farm mortgage banks similar to the national banks. They would be privately owned and managed with their operations supervised by the federal government. They would be privileged to issue bonds supported by farm mortgages. The supporters of this viewpoint believed that private capital and initiative represented the proper approach to the farm mortgage problem. They stressed the importance of competition and the profit motive as essential to sound business practice. The success of such banks in some European countries was cited as a further justification.

A second group proposed to organize a system based on cooperative principles. They believed that to leave the problem in the hands of private mortgage banks would not serve the farmer borrowers' interests. They, in turn, pointed to the successful experience of foreign cooperative credit societies. They believed it would be necessary at the outset for the government to give some financial assistance.

The third group recommended direct loans to farmers by the federal government through an agency to be established in the U. S. Treasury Department. Their principal arguments seemed to be that the federal government would be best able to obtain loan funds on terms most favorable to farmers. It is interesting to note that the general farm organizations supported this approach.

Debates by the advocates of these three points of view were long and extended. Many compromises were proposed and rejected. Nearly 2½ years later a compromise bill drawn up by a joint conference committee passed both Houses of Congress, and on July 17, 1916, was signed by President Wilson as the Federal Farm Loan Act.

The following statement from House Committee Report No. 630, May 8, 1916, is significant:

> The bill reported, therefore, whatever its obligations to successful foreign systems, provides for a *distinctively American system* of rural credits and endeavors to embody . . . . the best thought which the thorough discussions of the past years have developed with reference to rural credits legislation.

The Compromise—Two Systems

The basic compromise in this legislation involved provision for both privately financed joint stock Land Banks, and cooperatively organized Federal Land Banks. Both were to be supervised by a Farm Loan Bureau established in the Treasury Department. Some supporters of the cooperative system doubted it could succeed in competition with the private joint stock system. The cooperative system required the farmers to make a stock investment equal to five percent of his loan. No stock investment was required of the other. The Federal Land Banks were restricted to loans of $10,000 or less, while no restriction on size of loan was imposed on the joint stock Land Bank. Truly it seemed the cards were stacked against the cooperative system.

No one individual seems to stand out as an exceptional leader in the Congress during this rather prolonged legislative controversy. Senator Fletcher who served as Chairman of the United States Commission, was joint author with Congressman Moss, Vice Chairman of the Commission, of identical bills introduced in both Houses on January 14, 1914, advocating the private, or joint stock land bank approach. A few months later, Senator Hollis and Congressman Bulkley introduced identical bills in both Houses that called for a cooperative farm credit system. Since no one of the Members of Congress who participated in the farm credit legislation appears to have made particularly outstanding contributions, we turn our attention to some of the individuals who were most effective in their appearance before Congressional committees, or in later efforts that resulted in building a successful farm credit system.

One of these was C. W. Thompson, an economist from the University of Minnesota who came to the United States Department of Agriculture in 1913 as "Specialist in Rural Organization." He had a particular interest in credit for agriculture, perhaps inspired by the comprehensive study of the subject made by the State Bureau of Labor in Minnesota and reported in 1895. His first major effort was directed to a study that would give a detailed picture of the volume, terms, and conditions of credit used by farmers. In early December of that year, he made a preliminary report on this study to a subcommittee on Rural Credits of the House Committee on Banking and Currency. His later reports of findings from these studies before the committees of the Congress in 1915 and 1916 provided the most authentic information about farm mortgage credit needs on which the Farm Loan Act of 1916 was based.

This pioneer agricultural credit system was to be administered by the bipartisan Federal Farm Loan Board composed of four members appointed by the President with the advice and consent of the Senate, together with the Secretary of the Treasury as Chairman of the Board. In commenting on the early years of the system, E. H. Thomson who for 25 years was President of the Federal Land Bank of Springfield, beginning in 1919, made this statement in a historical memorandum written in 1964:

> First, the selection of the members of the Federal Farm Loan Board was most fortunate. Governor Norris, who was the first chairman, was a banker and a financier of wide experience. Judge Charles E. Lobdell was a lawyer in Kansas and had wide experience in the farm mortgage field especially in the whole midwestern area. Herbert Quick was with the Curtis Publishing Company and brought to the Board wide experience in publicity and public relations. Capt. W. S. A. Smith of Sioux City, Iowa, was a conservative Scotsman familiar with agriculture and with commerce. These four men of diversified background had much to do with the sound organization and development in the early years of the system. Men of any less ability could easily have started the Land Bank System in some unfortunate lines of endeavor. It was also fortunate that the Farm Loan Act provided for a bipartisan board which, under the changing administrations common in this country, was good.

Federal Land Banks Establish Pattern

With World War I in progress, this was not an opportune time to launch the first lending program of any kind to be sponsored by the federal government. Many problems were encountered. The privately-owned joint stock Land Banks were generally not a success and eventually all were liquidated. The cooperatively organized Federal Land Banks, with special assistance from the government during the Great Depression of the 1930s, survived and are an outstanding success. We, therefore, turn our attention to important elements underlying their success and which were followed in most respects in establishing the other parts of the cooperative Farm Credit system.

The law provided that the federal government would charter these banks and supervise them. The original capital was furnished by the government, but provision was made that as each farmer borrowed from the system, he must invest in its capital structure and that eventually the government investment would be replaced by farmers' investment. Since 1947, all 12 Federal Land Banks of the United States and the local associations through which they make loans have been completely owned by their farmer-borrowers.

Another important element in this pattern involves the source of loan funds. From the beginning of the system, loan funds came from the sale of the system's own securities to the investing public, rather than from the United States Treasury. These Farm Credit securities are not an obligation of the United States Government, and they are sold in the money market in competition with a great variety of securities. Their reputation has been so good over the years that they typically have sold to yield an interest return a little above United States Treasury securities of comparable term.

The matter of control is a significant feature of the system which represents a highly decentralized operation. Although it is supervised by the federal government through the Farm Credit Administration, control largely rests with elected farmer-directors on district Farm Credit bank and local association boards. Most credit decisions are made by the association loan committee made up of two or more board members and the manager they employ. Because loan funds come from the investing public, loans must be soundly made which means that ability of the borrower to repay is very important. Interest charged the farmer-borrower is limited to the bank's cost of loan funds plus its cost of operating, including some addition to reserves. Thus, the farmer borrows at cost from his credit cooperative.

Critical periods bring into being new institutions. Following the sharp agricultural depression of 1920 and 1921, the inadequacy of the Federal Reserve System to meet the already increasing short-term credit needs of farmers was re-emphasized. This led in 1923 to the passage of the Agricultural Credits Act creating 12 Federal Intermediate Credit Banks with territories coterminous with, and with the same officers and directors as the 12 Federal Land Banks. Purpose of these banks was to discount short- and intermediate-term agricultural paper for commercial banks, agricultural credit corporations, livestock loan companies, and farmer cooperatives.

Although the credit banks were successful, only a limited number of farmers had access to them through the privately capitalized credit institutions. In the early 1930s, the short- and intermediate-term credit situation became very acute. In 1933, Congress established the production credit system which provided for local cooperative associations that farmers could join and thereby obtain access to the services of the credit banks. These Production Credit Associations, as they are called, have proven to be an outstanding success and all but three of the 471 in operation in 1966 were completely owned by their farmer borrowers.

The third member of the cooperative Farm Credit team is the Banks for Cooperatives established by Congress in 1933, with one located in each of the 12 Farm Credit Districts, plus the Central Bank in Washington, D. C. They make loans only to farmer cooperative associations. They have been outstandingly successful and have for years provided approximately 60 percent of all the funds borrowed by farmer cooperatives. Some of the banks have retired their government capital and all of them expect to achieve this goal by 1970.

Also created by Act of Congress in 1933 was the Farm Credit Administration, an agency charged with the responsibility of supervising, giving leadership to, and rendering certain services for the district banks and associations that make up the operating parts of the system.

Test by the Great Depression

The Federal Land Banks probably rendered their most notable service to United States agriculture in the period 1933–35 when they enabled hundreds of thousands of farm families to avoid foreclosure and loss of their farms. As a result of the Great Depression nearly all credit had disappeared from rural areas. Many lenders needed their money and pressed farmers for payment. Tax delinquency on farms was widespread, and many county governments were practically broke. Bold action was needed so Congress passed the Emergency Farm Mortgage Act in May, 1933. It strengthened the capital structure of the Land Banks so they could carry their own delinquent borrowers. Even more importantly, it made additional loan funds available from the banks themselves and made them agents for the newly-created Land Bank Commissioner emergency loans. Another provision of the Act made "normal value" rather than the then current depressed value of farms the basis for making loans.

Henry Morganthau, first governor of the newly-created Farm Credit Administration, William I. Myers, his deputy who soon was to succeed him as governor, and Albert S. Goss who became Land Bank Commissioner on July 1, 1933, vigorously pressed officials of the 12 Land Banks to rapidly expand their staffs and to make loans to distressed farmers. Loan applications came to the 12 banks so fast they had to increase their appraisal force from 210 in May to more than 5,000 by November. In May, 1933, the 12 banks loaned little more than $2 million. The peak month in 1934 they loaned $150 million. In the three most active years of the refinancing program, the Land Banks received applications for loans on nearly half of all the mortgaged farms in the country. In this period, they loaned more than they had loaned in the first 16 years of their existence, a total of more than $2 billion in about 760,000 loans. This accomplishment was possible only by prolonged, dedicated overtime service on the part of thousands of employees.

Albert S. Goss—Outstanding Pioneer

Because of the important role he played in this gigantic refinancing program and a number of other significant contributions he made, Albert S. Goss deserves special recognition as a Land Bank Pioneer. He was a farmer and farm leader in both Oregon and Washington. As a member of the farm credit committee of the Washington State Grange, he visited the nation's capital on behalf of the pending land bank legislation in 1916. He helped organize one of the early National Farm Loan Associations in his home state, became its President and later its Secretary-Treasurer. He was an appointed director on the board of the Spokane District Federal Land Bank from 1927 until he was appointed by President Roosevelt as Land Bank Commissioner with headquarters in Washington, D. C. in 1933. Mr. Goss spent considerable time in Washington in the early months of 1933 helping draft legislation that created the Production Credit System as well as the Emergency Farm Mortgage Act. He was instrumental in having incorporated in this legislation provision for basing land bank loans on normal value.

Mr. Goss accepted as a great personal challenge the saving of farms from foreclosure during the depression. Although a devoted family man, it is reported that he ate but one evening meal at home the first year he was Land Bank Commissioner. His day began at the normal hour but through this time of stress, he seldom left his office before 10 p.m. or even midnight.

In that part of the country between the Mississippi River and the Rocky Mountains, serious drouth occurred during much of the 1930s, compounding farmers' income problems caused by the depression. Mr. Goss strove to develop and have the banks adopt collection policies that would not impair the ability of delinquent borrowers to succeed in the future, while still protecting the financial integrity of the Land Banks. A variety of loan treatments were developed and many of them used during this period of distress. Simple extensions were augmented by deferments of principal, reamortization, variable payment and other payment plans to enable deserving farm families to span periods of low income.

Mr. Goss was personally responsible for development of the so-called "Personal Standard Test," to which a borrower must conform to be eligible for one of the special loan treatments. Indeed, still today a

Land Bank borrower will not be subjected to foreclosure of his mortgage if he meets this test:

1. Is doing his honest best.
2. Is applying the proceeds of production, over and above necessary living and operating expenses, to the payment of primary obligations (taxes and loan installments).
3. Is taking proper care of the property.
4. Is capable of working his way out of his existing burden of debt.

No sooner had the peak of the farm mortgage refinancing passed than Mr. Goss gave emphasis to rehabilitating and strengthening the National Farm Loan Associations (now called Land Bank Associations) because he believed them to be an essential part of a cooperative system. Because the Farm Loan Act permitted ten successful Land Bank borrowers to form an association, literally thousands of small, inefficient associations were chartered. By 1935, there still were more than 5,000 of them in existence, most in poor financial condition and with weak, part-time managers. Some people in the system advocated abandoning the associations and having each bank service its loans and make new ones through field offices manned by bank employees. Mr. Goss opposed this and encouraged the banks to undertake educational programs and to systematically bring about mergers of associations with overlapping territories and grouping the business of two or more associations in one office so the volume would be sufficient to enable employment of a competent full-time secretary-treasurer (since 1959 legally designated "manager"). That this program succeeded is evidenced by the fact that today only a few more than 700 Land Bank Associations, averaging more than two full-time employees per office, serve the entire country.

Threat to the Cooperative Credit System

Effective July 1, 1939, the Farm Credit Administration ceased to be an independent agency by executive order of the President that transferred it to the Department of Agriculture. Soon after, a movement was afoot, with considerable support within the Department of Agriculture, to abolish essential cooperative features of the Land Bank System. The plan was to enable the banks and associations through government subsidy to refund to borrowers their five percent stock investment and to substitute a nominal membership fee. Land Bank bonds would be fully guaranteed as to both principal and interest by the federal government. Early in 1940, legislation incorporating these and other features were introduced in both Houses of Congress (S. 3509 and H.R. 8748). Mr. Goss, still Land Bank Commissioner, opposed this legislation. His opposition was primarily responsible for his forced resignation in June, 1940.

From the outside, Mr. Goss was in a much better position to oppose. With strong support from the National Grange, the American Farm Bureau Federation, and the National Council of Farmer Cooperatives, this legislation and subsequent legislation with somewhat the same objective was defeated. Had the Land Banks been converted to government-owned lending institutions, one may be certain there would have been no program later for permitting the Banks for Cooperatives or the federal Intermediate Credit Banks to become farmer-owned. It seems unlikely that even the Production Credit Associations would have become farmer-owned. Mr. Goss did indeed do more than any other individual to preserve the cooperative credit system for United States farmers.

For one other important contribution to the cooperative Farm Credit System Mr. Goss deserves credit. He was convinced that the Farm Credit Administration must be an independent agency of the government if it was to supervise a cooperative credit system, obtaining its loan funds in the money market. So the same time he opposed doing away with the cooperative features of the system, he advocated returning Farm Credit Administration to independent agency status. It was his belief also that it should be under the jurisdiction of a policy-making board. When he became Master of the National Grange in 1941, he was made chairman of a Joint Farm Credit Committee of farm organizations that worked toward this objective. This and the independent agency objective was achieved when the Farm Credit Act of 1953 became effective in December of that year. Unfortunately, Mr. Goss did not live to experience the realization of this dream. On October 25, 1950, after speaking on an agricultural subject to the famed annual Herald-Tribune Forum in New York City, he collapsed and died of a heart attack.

As a memoriam to Albert Goss, one of his former associates in the Farm Credit Administration wrote the following tribute soon after his passing:

> Here was a man who had devoted his entire adult life to the service of his fellowman and by his sincerity, his devotion to his ideals, and his wide knowledge of farm and financial problems, has already become almost a legendary figure. It is impossible to measure the effect of his life and his works except to say that his philosophy of cooperative credit is today reflected in the workings

of the Federal Land Bank System, and the present position of agriculture in our national economy is to an unknown extent attributable to his knowledge, his unflinching integrity, and the dedication of his life to the betterment of his country.

We have lost a good friend in Albert Goss, a wise counselor on whom we could always depend for sage advice, and a man who in his own words "walked humbly in the sight of God."

Fifty Years of Service

As the Federal Land Banks make plans for national recognition of their 50th anniversary in 1967, it seems appropriate to briefly summarize here their major contributions to the agriculture of the United States. Already we have pointed out their great service in preventing perhaps a million farms from loss to their owners by foreclosure in the 1930s. This was a spectacular but transitory accomplishment. Their greatest contribution, no doubt, was pioneering a mechanism by which farmers might continuously pool their credit and market it advantageously in the money centers of the country. Their success in doing this opened the way for the Intermediate Credit Banks and the Banks for Cooperatives to do the same. Permanent channels were established for correcting the traditional credit shortage in rural areas.

Out of the efforts of the Land Bank pioneers came a complete credit service for farmers and their cooperatives. This cooperative system has grown rapidly since the mid-50's. In 1966 it loaned farmers and their cooperatives $8 billion. This was approximately 14 percent of the short- and intermediate-term credit, and 20 percent of the farm mortgage credit used by farmers. For years the Banks for Cooperatives have provided some 60 percent of all the credit used by farmer cooperative associations. They have, in addition, assisted with the organization and business-like operation of thousands of cooperatives. For more than 30 years they have been a dominant factor in the growth and development of farmer cooperatives. Credit has played an important role in enabling farmers to take advantage of modern technology and to achieve their near-miracles of abundant agricultural production of recent years. The general availability of dependable sources of credit have enabled great numbers of farm families to participate in the agricultural revolution rather than to make it the province of a few corporate giants.

The Federal Land Banks and their associations, the Federal Intermediate Credit Banks, the Production Credit Associations, and the Banks for Cooperatives have made a significant, direct contribution by their dependable, specialized lending. Perhaps an even larger contribution over the years has been the influence of their presence on other lenders. Not only have they brought reasonable interest rates, but they have provided standards for loan terms generally that have been fashioned to the farmers' needs. All farmers who have used credit, therefore, have benefitted directly or indirectly from this great cooperative Farm Credit System that emerged 50 years ago from the dreams of pioneer farm leaders.

The Authors

Martin A. Abrahamsen, Deputy Administrator of Farmer Cooperative Service, previously served that Agency as Chief of the Farm Supplies Branch and Director of the Purchasing Division. Born in Wisconsin in 1908, he taught vocational agriculture in that state and completed his Master's and Ph.D. degrees in Agricultural Economics at the University of Wisconsin. He spent 13 years at West Virginia University and North Carolina State University in teaching and research in agricultural marketing and cooperation. He is co-editor of *Readings in Agricultural Cooperation,* a widely used college reference text, and author of some 220 bulletins, reports, and other publications relating to agricultural marketing and cooperative subjects.

Erma Angevine is director of women's activities and coordinator of meetings for the National Rural Electric Cooperative Association in Washington, D. C. She was on the staff of the *Cooperative Consumer* and assistant editor of *Cooperative News Service,* published by the Cooperative League of the U.S.A. in Chicago. She was graduated from Friends University and studied at the University of Kansas, Kansas City, and University of Chicago. In 1959 she wrote *In League With The Future,* giving personal sketches of the 129 men and women who served as directors of the Cooperative League from 1916 to 1959.

John C. Bagwell is a native of Laurens County, S. C. He received a B.S. degree in Agriculture from Clemson College in 1925, an M.S. in psychology from the University of North Carolina in 1927, an LL.B. degree from the University of Kentucky in 1932 and an S.J.D. degree (Doctor of Juridical Science) from the University of Michigan in 1933. He joined the legal staff of the Farm Credit Administration in 1933 and transferred to the legal staff of the Department of Agriculture in 1935. He served as General Counsel of the Farm Credit Administration from 1954 to 1961, and has been General Counsel of the Department of Agriculture since 1961.

Hayes Beall is Director of Peace Corps Cooperative Projects for the Cooperative League of the U.S.A., and was Director of its Educational Services, 1951–63. He is author of *Member Educational Manual for Cooperatives* (1961); Executive Secretary, Association for Cooperative Education; Editor, *Cooperative Education;* and was President of Council of National Organizations for Adult Education. During a two-year assignment in Europe he studied cooperative education in six countries. He has known E. R. Bowen for more than 30 years.

C. H. Becker was General Manager of Illinois Farm Supply Company from 1941 until the fall of 1962 when it was merged into FS Services, Inc. Since then he has served as Executive Vice President and General Manager of the merged organization which has doubled in size during the past four years, now encompassing three states and four farmer cooperatives. He entered the system 10 years earlier in 1931 as a local manager. He and

Fred Herndon were close associates over a period of 24 years. They worked harmoniously and well together throughout the full time and were close friends as well as business associates.

James LeRoy Bender, better known as Roy Bender, was born in Kansas in 1893. He was reared on a farm and educated in Oklahoma schools. In 1926, he became Manager of Farmers Cooperative Elevator Company, Douglas, Okla. In 1929 he was elected Executive Secretary of Farmers Cooperative Grain Dealers Association of Oklahoma, Enid, Okla., and he continued as Executive Officer until retirement in 1960. He now serves as Cooperative Consultant.

Merle E. Betts was born on a farm in Iowa (1922). He holds B.S., M.S. and Ph.D. degrees from Iowa State. In 1953, he joined the staff of the Farm Credit Banks of Omaha as Director of Information. Later the position was broadened to include research and management training activities for the Federal Land Bank, Federal Intermediate Credit Bank, and Omaha Bank for Cooperatives. His writings include the editing of a textbook, *Financing Farm and Ranch Activities,* and numerous articles on credit and cooperatives for farm publications. He is now Secretary of the Omaha Bank for Cooperatives.

Wendell C. Binkley was born in Fulton, Ky., on November 19, 1914. He graduated *summa cum laude* from the University of Kentucky in 1939 with a B.S. degree in Agriculture. He received the M.S. degree from the same institution in 1942. He had further graduate training at the University of Kentucky and at Vanderbilt University in 1951–52. During World War II he spent four years in training work at Fort Bragg, Ga. After World War II he was for five years engaged on an intensive approach to extension education work with farmer cooperatives for the University of Kentucky. He then joined the resident staff of the Department of Agricultural Economics of the University and has since engaged in research and teaching, primarily in the field of agricultural cooperation. In the fall of 1964 he and Glenn S. Hedlund of Cornell University made a study of cooperative education in India under the auspices of the Ford Foundation. In 1964–65 he took leave of absence to do management consultation work for the National Rural Electric Cooperative Association. Mr. Binkley is especially interested in youth education and serves on the Youth Education Committee of the American Institute of Cooperation.

C. W. Bowles is presently board secretary for Plains Cotton Cooperative Association, Lubbock, Tex. He came up through the Texas Extension Service, as County Agent, District Agent, and finally as Cooperative Marketing Specialist. After 16 years in Extension, he served 15 years as Secretary and Vice President of the Houston Bank for Cooperatives. He has written several basic bulletins on cooperative principles, organization, and procedures. He edits the *Cotton Cooperative Commentator,* his association's house organ.

Gordon H. Busboom has been Executive Secretary of the Nebraska Cooperative Council since 1959. Previously he taught vocational agriculture and distributive education in Nebraska high schools. He received a Bachelor of Science degree from the University of Nebraska in 1953 and has taken graduate work at Colorado State University. He is a member of the board of directors of the National Council of Farmer Cooperatives, serves on two national committees of the American Institute of Cooperation, and on the Agriculture Committee of the Lincoln Chamber of Commerce.

Gordon Cameron, President of the three Farm Credit Banks of Springfield, Mass., is a Middle Westerner come East. Born in Missouri, a graduate of the University of Kansas, he received his MBA degree from the Harvard Graduate School of Business Administration in 1933. Except for military service in World War II, he has spent his business career with the Federal Land Bank of Springfield, the Federal Intermediate Credit Bank of Springfield, and the Springfield Bank for Cooperatives, which organizations he now heads. He has served on a number of national study committees for the Farm Credit System, especially those relating to the capitalization and management of the Banks. In addition he has interested himself in the early economic and agricultural history of the Northeast.

John D. Campbell was born near Chillicothe, Tex., but was raised in western Oklahoma. He completed a B.S. degree at Oklahoma State University and farmed cotton for 14 years. Then he returned to OSU for an M.S. degree. He was employed for nine years as cooperative agent and economist on cotton at OSU, and then worked for Arkansas University for four years. He has been with Farmer Cooperative Service since 1956 working on problems relating to cooperative cotton marketing.

Wallace J. Campbell was born in Montana and graduated with a B.S. Degree from the University of Oregon in 1932. He received a Master's Degree from that school in 1934, and served as an Assistant in its Department of Sociology from 1932–34. Since 1964 he has served as President of the Foundation for Cooperative Housing. From 1960 to 1964 he was first, Director of Public Affairs and later, Vice President, Administrative Assistant to the President, Nationwide Insurance Company. From 1934 to 1960 he was on the staff of the Cooperative League of the U.S.A., serving in such capacities as Assistant to the General Secretary and Director of its New York and Washington offices. Mr. Campbell was a member of the organizing committee of CARE and he has served as its Vice President since 1958. Among his publications are: *Here Is Tomorrow,* and (with Jerry Voorhis) *The Morale of Democracy.*

Harry B. Carroll was born in Kansas City, Mo., in 1885. He attended public schools in St. Paul, Minn., and graduated from the University of Minnesota in 1909, with a B.S. in agriculture. After eight years of farming in the state of Washington, he served for 17 years as County Agricultural

Extension Agent at Bellingham, Wash. During the next eight years he was Administrative Assistant of the Washington State Extension Service and Washington State Conservationist. He was Executive Secretary of the Washington State Council of Farmer Cooperatives from 1945 to 1959. He helped organize many cooperatives in Washington—among them, the Western Farmers Association in 1917. He has known Harry J. Beernink intimately for some 50 years.

William M. Corwin was born in Michigan in 1912. He spent most of his early life in West Virginia and graduated from West Virginia University in 1932 with an A.B. in Journalism. After a year as a reporter for the Clarksburg (W. Va.) Exponent, he worked for a year in the Public Relations Department of the Monongahela Power Company. He joined the Information Department of Southern States Cooperative, Richmond, Va., in 1944 and became Director of Publications in 1946, and Director of Information— Publications Service in 1947, the position he now holds. Mr. Corwin is well known for his work as a writer and editor. He has served as President of the National Cooperative Editorial Association and of the Advertising Council of Cooperatives. He is now a member of the Public Relations Committee of the National Council of Farmers Cooperatives. He has known W. G. Wysor intimately for more than 20 years.

Paul T. DeVore, a native of Minnesota, spent several years on an eastern Montana wheat farm prior to attending the University of Montana where he obtained a B.A. degree in journalism. After 17 years as an agricultural reporter on daily papers, as Associate Editor of the *Montana Farmer-Stockman,* and as Assistant General Agricultural Development Agent of the Great Northern Railway in St. Paul, he became Director of Information for the Farm Credit Banks of Spokane in 1943. He is currently President of the Spokane Public Relations Council.

Davis Douthit has been connected with the Office of Public Relations of the Nationwide Insurance Companies, Columbus, Ohio, since 1951. He was born in Decatur, Ill., on January 24, 1904, and was graduated from Millikin University there in 1929. After two years as a reporter on *The Decatur Review,* he spent seven years as a city desk rewrite man and foreign news copy editor for the *Chicago Tribune.* From 1938 to 1951 he was on the staff and served as Editor of the *Midland Cooperator,* membership publication of Midland Cooperatives, Inc. (Minneapolis). He joined Nationwide's public relations staff 15 years ago.

John W. Dysart was born in Iowa and grew up on a dairy farm in Northern Minnesota. He graduated from the University of Minnesota with a B.S. Degree in Agricultural Education. For 10 years as a county agricultural extension agent he worked closely with the cooperatives. In 1947 he became Director of Public Relations for Land O'Lakes Creameries, Inc., Minneapolis. As part of this work he is Editor of the *Land O'Lakes News.*

John E. Eidam, President of the Omaha Bank for Cooperatives since 1955, grew up on a farm in Nebraska. After serving on the management team of Westcentral Cooperative Grain Company, he was on the legal staff of the Omaha Bank for Cooperatives from 1933 to 1948. He is known internationally for his work with credit unions, having served as President of the Credit Union National Association in 1949–50. Mr. Eidam is presently Secretary-Treasurer of the American Institute of Cooperation, and Chairman of its Finance Committee. He is a member of the Dean's Advisory Committee of the University of Nebraska College of Agriculture, and he was recently honored by being named a charter member of the Order of the Tower at the University of Omaha.

Henry E. Erdman—see biography pp. 160–164.

J. W. Fanning, Vice President for Services, University of Georgia, has been associated with agriculture for most of his professional career. He served as County Agent, Special Agent in Marketing, Extension Economist and Chairman of the Division of Agricultural Economics of the University of Georgia. He organized and directed the Institute of Community and Area Development, a service program of the University giving emphasis and providing assistance to a new Georgia and its fast developing rural-urban communities. Mr. Fanning has worked closely with Georgia cooperatives in his positions of teaching, research, and extension. He is a great admirer of M. C. Gay and has supported and assisted him in his broad program of community and state service.

Gilbert C. Fite was raised on a farm in South Dakota. He graduated from the University of South Dakota and received his M.A. there in 1942. His Ph.D., from the University of Missouri, was granted in 1945. Since September, 1945, he has been a member of the History Department at the University of Oklahoma where he has specialized in American economic and agricultural history. In 1960–61 he was President of the Agricultural History Society. His publications include many articles in the field of agricultural history, plus a number of books. The latter include *Peter Norbeck: Prairie Statesman* (1948); *George N. Peek and the Fight for Farm Parity* (1954); *An Economic History of the United States* (1959 and 1965); *Farm to Factory: A History of the Consumers Cooperative Association* (1965); and *The Farmer's Frontier, 1865–1900* (1966).

Herbert C. Fledderjohn, upon graduation from Indiana University in 1931, joined the staff of Central States Grain Association. He transferred to the Accounting Department of the Indiana Farm Bureau Cooperative Association in 1932, and served successively as an Educational Assistant, Field Auditor, Editor of the cooperative paper, Director of Distribution and, finally, as Assistant General Manager. In 1934, he accompanied I. H. Hull as a member of the first Cooperative League tour of Europe. He resigned his post with IFBCA in 1963 to become Director of the American Friends

Service Committee Project in cooperative development in Amman, Jordan. Herb returned to the United States in July, 1965, to become President of the International Cooperative Development Association (ICDA), a federation of U.S. cooperatives concerned with assisting in the development of cooperatives in the less developed countries. As a Quaker, he is active in the affairs of the American Friends Service Committee.

Raymond L. Fox was born (1914) in Illinois. While in high school he became one of the charter members of the Future Farmers of America. He graduated from the University of Illinois with majors in Animal Husbandry and Agricultural Economics. He was employed by Armour and Company in production, sales, and public relations work in the 1930's. He then worked for the Producers Livestock Marketing Association, National Stockyards, Ill., until 1942 when he served four years in the U.S. Air Force. He joined the Livestock and Wool Branch of the Farmer Cooperative Service in 1946. He succeeded C. G. Randell as Chief of this branch in 1962, having worked with him intimately for some 15 years. He is the author of an FCA Bulletin, *The Marketability of Meat-Type Hogs,* and many other publications relating to cooperative livestock marketing.

Kelsey B. Gardner—See Biography, pp. 172–177.

M. C. Gay—See Biography, pp. 188–190.

Anne L. Gessner, a native of Illinois and graduate of the University of Wisconsin, joined the Farm Credit Administration in 1934. Her early publications dealt with labor-management relations in cooperative food processing plants and possibilities for cooperatives in fruit and vegetable freezing. When Farmer Cooperative Service was formed in 1953, she became Chief of its History and Statistics Branch and was responsible for the annual publication *Statistics of Farmer Cooperatives,* which is widely distributed in the United States and foreign countries. She also wrote publications dealing with integrated operations in petroleum, feed, and dairy cooperatives. After 31 years of government service, she retired in July, 1965, to enjoy cultural activities.

Jack Hackethorn has been Public Relations Director of the Missouri Farmers Association since 1950. Following graduation from the School of Journalism of the University of Missouri, he worked as a news photographer in Washington, D. C. These were the early Roosevelt years and he helped cover the 1936 election campaign. Later he worked on the *Detroit Free Press* and the *St. Louis Post Dispatch.* He served in the Navy during World War II.

Harold Hamil is senior vice-president of Farmland Industries, Inc., (formerly Consumers Cooperative Association), Kansas City, Mo. A native of Colorado, he earned his bachelor's degree at Hastings, Nebr., College, with a major in English. He worked on newspapers in Nebraska, and for three years he was director of the School of Journalism of the University of Nebraska. He spent a year with the Associated Press in New York City, and for seven years was editorial writer on the St. Louis, Mo., *Star-Times*. Hamil has been with CCA since 1951 and has been identified with the public relations, member relations, and educational programs of this organization. He is Editor of CCA's membership publication, *The Cooperative Consumer*.

Robert Handschin, economist for Farmers Union Grain Terminal Association, St. Paul, Minnesota, since August 1943, has been closely associated with M. W. Thatcher since 1939. Born in St. Paul in 1911, Handschin grew up at the University of Illinois where his father began the work in agricultural economics and helped form the Illinois Agricultural Association. After graduating from the University in mathematics, Handschin took graduate work in economics and rural sociology and worked on rural research projects. He has long been interested in the history of farm organizations and cooperatives.

Willis H. Hayes, Vice President and Secretary of the Federal Land Bank and the Federal Intermediate Credit Bank of Springfield has been closely associated with the credit needs of Northeast farmers and their cooperatives since 1940, except for three years in the Navy as a Lieutenant. Born in Hartford, Conn., he was graduated from the University of Connecticut in 1937 with a B.S. in agricultural education and dairy husbandry. Prior to entering the field of farm credit, he was a teacher of vocational agriculture in New York state from 1937 to 1940.

Tom J. Hefter is Public Relations Director of CUNA International, Inc., formerly the Credit Union National Association (CUNA). Previous to his appointment as Director, he had served as Assistant Director and News Manager. He is a graduate of the University of Wisconsin Journalism School. Hefter is the present Chairman of the Public Relations Committee of the Cooperative League of the U.S.A.

James Hill, Jr., was born on a wheat farm in Oregon. "My early education was at a country school house. Charles Baker walked three miles, but I only walked a mile." Later he graduated from Pendleton, Ore., high school and attended Whitman College. "Just as I was beginning to develop into a good 'mule-skinner,' the tractor came on the farm scene and destroyed my interest in farming. From Whitman College I went to Harvard Graduate School of Business Administration. Upon completion of my education in 1932, I returned to Pendleton and took a job with Pendleton Grain Growers, Inc., a small grain cooperative organized in 1930. I have been here ever since." The Pendleton Grain Growers has grown appreciably under Mr. Hill's direction, for he became its Manager in 1932. It now serves some 2,000 members and has an annual business volume of $21 million. Mr. Hill is President of Pacific Supply Cooperative, Portland, Ore.

Kenneth Hinshaw is a Washington rancher's son who won the national 4-H Club leadership award in 1926—an award sponsored by Horace Moses, one of the founders of the Eastern States Farmers' Exchange. When young Hinshaw graduated from Washington State University in journalism in 1928, Moses was instrumental in bringing him East to work for Eastern States. Hinshaw became editor of the *Eastern States Cooperator* in 1930, and his editorial career reached its climax in 1962 when he received the Cooperative Editorial Association's top honor, the Klinefelter Award. Hinshaw "invented" the Cooperative Information Service Fair which has become an important feature of the annual meetings of the National Council of Farmer Cooperatives. With John H. Davis, he authored *Farmer in a Business Suit*, the book that helped introduce the agribusiness concept of agricultural economics.

W. Gifford Hoag is Chief of Information Services for the Farm Credit Administration. Since 1934 he has been associated with that agency. He was born (1909) and raised in New York state, and received B.S. and M.A. degrees from Cornell University, where he developed his interest in agricultural economics and journalism. He has thus known W. I. Myers as a student, employee, and friend, for over 35 years. He has been active in a wide variety of cooperative organizations and at present is President of the Board of Trustees of Group Health Association, a prepaid, comprehensive, user-owned and controlled health plan with 57,000 participants. He is also Treasurer of Greenbelt Consumer Services—the largest cooperative of its kind in the nation. In 1965, Mr. Hoag received the Klinefelter Award for his contributions to cooperative journalism.

French M. Hyre, Chief, Farm Services Branch, Farmer Cooperative Service, was born at Frenchton, W. Va., March 31, 1902. He holds a B.S. degree in Agricultural Economics from West Virginia University, 1929, and an M.S. degree in Agricultural Economics from Cornell University, 1932. His professional experience includes work in agricultural extension, research, and teaching; also a year with the Federal Farm Board, Washington, D. C.; a year with the Agricultural Adjustment Administration, U.S.D.A., Washington, D. C.; and 31 years with the Farmer Cooperative Service and its predecessor organization, the Cooperative Research and Service Division of the Farm Credit Administration. Mr. Hyre succeeded Dr. Victor N. Valgren as Head of the Insurance Section, CR&S Division, FCA, in 1943 and has been in charge of the Agency's program of research, service and education with farm business service cooperatives since that date.

Joe Jenness was born in California in 1900. As a field representative for the Rural Electrification Administration in the 40's, he aided in the development of electric cooperatives in Kansas, Colorado, and Wyoming. Before joining REA, he administered the Central Ohio District of the National Youth Administration, engaged in training thousands of boys and girls for jobs in war production plants. He served as Executive Secretary of the Kansas Electric Cooperative 1951–56, and as Assistant General

Manager, and as a Legislative Consultant of the National Rural Electric Cooperative Association from 1956 until his retirement in June, 1966.

Adolph Ladru Jensen, Professor of Corporation Law at the University of Utah since 1932, was born at Ephraim, Utah on April 14, 1896. After receiving his AB Degree from Brigham Young University, he studied at the University of California where he received the AM Degree in 1924 and JD Degree in 1925. He was admitted to the bar of California in 1925. Before joining the University of Utah as Associate Professor of Law in 1926, he was General Counsel of the Farmers Grain Cooperative, Ogden, Utah. As Consultant in Legal Education of the American Institute of Cooperation, 1945-50, and Chairman of the Committee on Classification and Terminology of Cooperative Corporation Law of the American Bar Association, 1947-1952, he made significant contributions to better understanding of cooperatives in corporation law. He was a major contributor and editor of *Cooperative Corporate Association Law and Accounting—1950,* published by the American Institute of Cooperation. His voluminous writings include: "Failures of Farmers' Cooperatives," (with Raymond W. Miller) in *Harvard Business Review,* winter, 1947; and the "Cooperative Marketing Corporation," in *Law and Contemporary Problems* of Duke University School of Law, summer, 1948.

Alyce Lowrie Jewett is a native of California. Majoring in animal husbandry she received a B.S. Degree with highest honors from the University of California at Davis in 1931. Mrs. Jewett was the first student of the College of Agriculture of that institution to be elected to Phi Beta Kappa. She completed her Master's Degree at the Giannini Foundation where she studied cooperatives under Dr. Henry E. Erdman. Mrs. Jewett then joined the staff of the Department of Agricultural Economics at Davis and later did graduate work for a year at Harvard University. Returning to California she joined the staff of the Farm Security Administration. In 1945, she was appointed analyst for Poultry Producers of Central California. She remained with that organization for 10 years most of the time as Administrative Assistant to the Manager. For 18 months she held the position of Director of Information for the Agricultural Council (cooperative) of California, and for a number of years she served as Public Affairs Officer for the University of California at Davis. She is the senior author of a well known book, *Agricultural Cooperatives: Strength in Unity.*

John Bryan Jones graduated from Texas A & M in 1926, with a B.S. degree in Agricultural Administration. He then began his cooperative career as a Loan Inspector for Texas Cotton Growers Finance Corporation, a wholly-owned subsidiary of Texas Farm Bureau Cotton Cooperative. In 1931 he helped to organize, coined the name, and served as the first Manager of the Production Credit Corporation of El Paso, a wholly-owned subsidiary of Southwestern Irrigated Cotton Growers Association. When the Houston Bank for Cooperatives was organized, Jones became Secretary.

He later served as Secretary-Treasurer and Vice President and Treasurer of that Bank before he became General Manager of Texsun Citrus Exchange. He has been on the staff of the Baltimore Bank for Cooperatives since January 1, 1943, and is now Vice-President and Secretary.

Erick Kendall Managing Editor, Midland Cooperatives, Inc. Publications, Minneapolis, Minn., was born in Finland (1908). He came to the U.S. at age 15, and has worked for cooperatives, and particularly cooperative newspapers, since 1930, as circulation manager, advertising manager, editor and manager of information services. He was one of the founders of a cooperative youth movement in the northern North Central States in the 1930's. He made a lecture tour of Colombia, South America in 1948, and was the representative of the International Cooperative Alliance to the first Western Hemispheric Technical Conference on Cooperative Development, sponsored by the International Labor Office in Mexico City, 1955. He is a former director and past president of the Cooperative Editorial Association of America.

Joseph G. Knapp was born in Loveland, Colo., on November 22, 1900. His college work was done at Colorado State University, University of Illinois, University of Nebraska, University of Chicago, and Stanford University. He holds B.S. and M.A. degrees from the University of Nebraska, and a Ph. D. from Stanford University. He served on the staff of the Brookings Institution, Washington, D. C., 1926–29 and 1945–46, and as an associate professor at North Carolina State University, 1929–34. He was head of the Cooperative Purchasing Section of the Cooperative Research and Service Division of the Farm Credit Administration, 1934–1948, and its Associate Chief, 1948–53. He was Administrator of the Farmer Cooperative Service in the U.S. Department of Agriculture from December, 1953, to July, 1966. He is the author of five books and many bulletins, reports, and articles relating to agricultural marketing and agricultural cooperation. Titles of his books are: *The Cooperative Marketing of Livestock* (with Edwin G. Nourse), 1931; *The Hard Winter Wheat Pools—An Experiment in Agricultural Marketing Integration*, 1933; *Stokdyk, Architect of Cooperation*, 1953; *Seeds That Grew, A History of the Cooperative Grange League Federation Exchange*, 1960; and *Farmers in Business—Studies in Cooperative Enterprise*, 1963.

E. Fred Koller is a professor in the Department of Agricultural Economics, University of Minnesota. He teaches and does research in the fields of agricultural cooperation, dairy marketing, and agricultural finance. He has authored and co-authored dozens of bulletins, pamphlets, chapters in books, and articles in technical and professional journals. Dr. Koller has served on many state, regional, and national research committees in the areas of marketing and cooperation. He spent one year with the National Bureau of Economic Research (New York) on a project entitled "Financing of Farmers Cooperatives in the United States." Dr. Koller was born in Barron County, Wis., in 1907. He graduated from Augustana College in Sioux Falls, S. D., and has M.A. and Ph.D. degrees from the University of Minnesota.

Grace H. Larsen is Associate Specialist in the Experiment Station and on the Giannini Foundation, University of California, Berkeley. She obtained her doctorate in American History from Columbia University, New York. She formerly taught history at Rutgers University, Swarthmore College, and Bryn Mawr College. During the past decade, she has been associated with Dr. Henry E. Erdman on research projects in cooperation and has published a number of articles relating to cooperative developments in California. She is co-author with Dr. Erdman of *Revolving Finance in Agricultural Cooperatives* (1965). They are presently collaborating on a history of agricultural cooperatives in California.

Joseph Douglas Lawrence was born in Roanoke, Va., in 1895. He attended High School at Florence, S. C., and received his college education at the University of Virginia. He is a Certified Public Accountant (Georgia and Iowa). In World War I he was a Private, Sergeant, and Second Lieutenant. He was in combat in Belgium and Meuse-Argonne, and was awarded the Crox de Guerre and the 29th Division Citation. After serving as Business Analyst for the Federal Farm Board he became Deputy Commissioner of the Farm Credit Administration in charge of operational development for the Banks for Cooperatives. After two years as Treasurer and Controller for the Consumers Cooperative Association, Kansas City, he returned to the Farm Credit Administration in 1947 as Director of Finance and Accounts. He served as Deputy Governor and Director of Cooperative Bank Services prior to becoming President of the Columbia Bank for Cooperatives. After retirement in 1961 he engaged in cooperative bank development work in Latin America and Southeast Asia. He is now farming near Columbia, S. C. "J. D." worked at close range with S. D. Sanders for many years.

Roy W. Lennartson is Associate Administrator of the Consumer and Marketing Service (formerly the Agricultural Marketing Service), United States Department of Agriculture, Washington, D. C. Mr. Lennartson was reared on a farm in northern Minnesota, and is a graduate of the University of Maryland. He joined the Department of Agriculture in 1936 with the Farm Credit Administration. After a period of service with the Army (1942–1945) he returned to the Department as Assistant Director of the Poultry Branch, Production and Marketing Administration. In 1951 he was named Assistant Administrator for Marketing with that Agency. In late 1953, Mr. Lennartson was named Deputy Administrator in the newly organized Agricultural Marketing Service, which position he held until 1962 when he was appointed Associate Administrator of the Agency.

John T. Lesley has been General Manager of the Florida Citrus Exchange, Tampa, since 1951. He was born in Florida (1910), and was educated at Riverside Military Academy, the University of Florida, and Southern College. He is a Director of the Central Bank for Cooperatives, Washington, D. C., a member of the National Agricultural Research Advisory Committee, and is an officer or member in many agricultural and business organizations. For many years he has been interested in foreign markets for United States products, and he is presently President of the U. S. Agricultural Export Corporation. He has traveled throughout Western Europe, and in the Middle East, Japan, Southeast Asia, the Caribbean countries, and South America.

Adrian H. Lindsay was born in Ohio in 1897. He was granted a B.S. at the University of Illinois in 1922, an M.S. at Iowa State University in 1923, and a Ph.D. from Iowa State in 1929. He taught Economics and Business Administration at Auburn, Ala., and at Iowa State University prior to coming to the Department of Agricultural Economics of the University of Massachusetts in 1929. He was made Head of the Department in 1935. He retired in 1959 as Emeritus Professor and Department Head. Dr. Lindsay taught the course in Cooperative Principles for 20 years, and for 15 years was a director of the New England Institute of Cooperation.

M. G. Mann, Jr. is Editor of Publications and Director of Education for Carolinas Cotton Growers Association and FCX, Inc., of Raleigh, N. C. The publications include *Carolina Co-operator*, a monthly magazine and *The FCX Patron*, a monthly tabloid newspaper. He has served the two cooperatives in the past as Director of Advertising, Director of Information, as well as Director of Visual Aids (movies, slide films, etc.) He was educated at Hargrave Military Academy, North Carolina State University, and Randolph-Macon College.

Albert E. Mercker feels an indebtedness to Mr. Rule, for inspiration, know-how, and ability to get the facts. He was with the U. S. Department of Agriculture for 36 years and worked on problems of the fresh fruit and vegetable industry. In 1948, he received an honorary degree of Doctor of Laws from the University of Maine for distinguished service to the potato industry. In 1963, he was honored with a certificate of merit by the Agricultural Marketing Association at the 50th anniversary of the establishment of an organized marketing service in the U. S. Department of Agriculture, as one of the 50 outstanding agricultural marketing men in the United States.

J. Franklin Nix was born on a corn, cotton, and truck farm 46 years ago in West Tennessee where he spent his youthful years until he entered the University of Tennessee. His college education was interrupted by four years in the United States Navy. He received three battle stars for duty in the Arctic Ocean, the Pacific Ocean, and the Mediterranean Sea. He re-entered the university and was graduated in June, 1946. He then taught vocational agriculture in Tennessee for one year before joining the Feed Department of Tennessee Farmers Cooperative in 1947. In March,

1954, Mr. Nix was named general manager of Tennessee Farmers Cooperative. In September, 1964, Mr. Nix was elected president of National Cooperatives, Inc., of Albert Lea, Minn. Mr. Nix is also a director of the American Institute of Cooperation, and serves as this organization's Tennessee finance chairman.

Richard Phillips is Vice President of Agri Research, Inc., (Manhattan, Kansas). He was born in Iowa in 1923, and grew up on a farm. He holds B.S. and Ph.D. degrees from Iowa State University. From 1943–1946 he was Aerial Navigator with the U.S. Navy Air Corps. From 1950–1962 he was Professor of Agricultural Economics at Iowa State University. From 1962–1965 he was Research Director of Agri Research, Inc. He is the author or co-author of many technical bulletins and articles dealing with agricultural marketing and related fields, and a 660-page textbook, *Managing for Greater Returns in Grain, Feed and Other Retail Businesses Serving Agriculture* (1957). He wrote both his M.S. and Ph.D. theses under Professor Frank Robotka.

Don H. Phipps is Manager of Northwest Wholesale Incorporated, having worked in the Washington fruit industry most of his life. He is a graduate of Washington State University, School of Agriculture, 1929. He was President of the Washington State Council of Farmer Cooperatives, 1962–63, and has served as a Director of Farm Credit Banks of Spokane since 1958, and as a Director of the Central Bank for Cooperatives since 1962. He is a past board member of the National Council of Farmer Cooperatives. He is also a past Vice-President of the National Council of Young Men's Christian Associations, and the past President of the Northwest Area of YMCA's.

Warren A. Ranney grew up in the Mohawk Valley dairy region of New York state, in the area where Herkimer County cheese originated. He lived both in the rural village of Mohawk and on a nearby 150-acre dairy farm. He entered Cornell in 1925 and started working part-time for GLF in 1926. He graduated with a B.S. degree, class of 1929. His early jobs in GLF were in advertising and promotion, with numerous assignments from H. E. Babcock. Later he became a Promotion Manager, Director of Education, Director of Industry Relations and, in 1957, he assumed his present job (continued in Agway Inc.) as Director of Public Relations.

Ewell Paul Roy is Professor of Agricultural Economics and Agribusiness at Louisiana State University, and Secretary of the Louisiana Council of Farmer Cooeratives. He is a native of Louisiana and received the B.S., M.S., and Ph.D. from Louisiana State University. His professional work is in cooperation, poultry and egg marketing, and contract farming. He has helped organize over 30 farmer co-ops in Louisiana, and served five years as President of a million dollar credit union. He has authored two books: *Contract Farming, USA* and *Cooperatives: Today and Tomorrow*.

Theodore Saloutos is a professor of history and former chairman of the History Department at the University of California at Los Angeles. A student of farmer organizations, cooperatives and protest movements, he is the author of *Farmer Movements in the South, Agricultural Discontent in the Middle West* (in collaboration with John D. Hicks), *They Remember America,* and *The Greeks in the United States.* A holder of senior Fulbright Research Grants to the University of Athens in 1952–1953 and again in 1966–1967, a visiting Fulbright Lecturer to the University of Freiburg in Breisgau in 1959–1960, a former president of the Agricultural History Society, and a Guggenheim Fellow, he is currently engaged in writing a history of The New Deal and the Farmer.

Charles Richard (Jerry) Sayre got his nickname from an Illinois farm mule named Jerry. With an early education in public schools of Edgar County, Ill., Sayre earned B.S. and M.S. degrees in Agriculture and Agricultural Economics, University of Illinois, and M.A. and Ph.D. degrees in Economics from Harvard University. Farm management research in the Bureau of Agricultural Economics, U.S.D.A., was followed by a World War II tour as a Naval officer. After a brief return to farm management research were tenures as Superintendent, Delta Branch Experiment Station, Stoneville, Miss.; Head, Cotton and Other Fiber Crops and Diseases, Bureau of Plant Industry, U.S.D.A., Beltsville, Md.; President and Managing Director, Delta and Pine Land Company, Scott, Miss.; and President and General Manager, Staple Cotton Cooperative Association, Greenwood, Miss. At 52, Sayre has numerous business and civic responsibilities, including board membership with Central Bank for Cooperatives. He served as a member of the National Agricultural Advisory Commission, 1960–65.

Marvin A. Schaars was born on January 15, 1902, at Merrill, Wis., where he received his public school education. He received his B.S. (1924), M.S. (1927) and Ph.D. (1932) from the University of Wisconsin. He was a Social Science Research Fellow at Harvard University in 1928–29. He joined the staff of the Department of Agricultural Economics at the University of Wisconsin in 1924 and was chairman of this department, 1955–60. As Professor, he teaches courses in Agricultural Marketing and Cooperation, and conducts research in agricultural marketing and farmer cooperation. He also performs agricultural extension work in the same subjects. He has served as visiting professor at North Carolina State University (1949), Utah State University (1951), and University of Minnesota (1961). With Professor Henry Bakken, he is the author of the well-known text, *Economics of Cooperative Marketing.* He has published many bulletins, circulars, special reports, and articles in journals on agricultural marketing and cooperation. He is a member of the following scholastic societies: Alpha Zeta, Phi Kappa Phi, and Delphi Phi Epsilon. He is a Rotarian, director of the University book store, and director of a Madison bank.

Claud L. Scroggs is Director of Economic Research, Southern States Cooperative, Inc., Richmond, Va., a position he has held since 1958. He

earned his doctorate as an agricultural economist at North Carolina State University. He has been closely associated with cooperatives as a researcher and a teacher, having held positions with the Farmer Cooperative Service, U.S. Department of Agriculture, and the Department of Agricultural Economics of the University of Tennessee. He is co-editor, with Martin A. Abrahamsen, of *Agricultural Cooperation—Selected Readings,* 1957. He has been a long-time student of the Common Market, and in 1963 he was the seminar leader for a group of agricultural and business leaders in a study tour of the EEC countries.

Oren R. Shelley came to the St. Paul Bank for Cooperatives as a business analyst in 1942 after earning a Bachelor's and Master's degree from the University of Minnesota, where he majored in Agricultural Economics. He was born and raised on a farm in south central Minnesota. In 1944, he accepted a commission in the Navy as a Lieutenant. Upon his release in 1946 he returned to the bank as a business analyst. He was elected Secretary in 1950, and is currently Vice President. In addition to his major duties in connection with loan committee activities, Mr. Shelley's responsibilities include new business development, and member education and public relations.

Miss Helen J. Smith was born and raised on her parents' Dairymen's League farm near Fillmore, N.Y. She is a graduate of Fillmore Central School, received her bachelor's degree in Home Economics from Buffalo State Teachers' College, and her master's degree from Syracuse University. After teaching homemaking in the Cato-Meridian Central School at Cato, N.Y., she became Supervisor of Home Economics Education at Mansfield State Teachers' College, Pa. She then taught home economics at Palmyra-Macedon Central School, and later became Supervisor of Secondary Testing and Instruction in that junior-senior high school. The position of Home Service Supervisor for the Dairymen's League Cooperative Association was assumed in September, 1963. She is an advisor to New York State Council of Rural Women, and a member of American Home Economics Association and National Education Association.

Homer G. Smith, President of the Central Bank for Cooperatives, Washington, D. C., since January 1, 1956, began his career in the Farm Credit Administration as a Land Bank Examiner in 1934. In 1936, he became a Field Accounting Supervisor with the Production Credit Division. He rose in successive steps to the position of Assistant Deputy Director of Short-Term Credit Service. Prior to his work with the Banks for Cooperatives, he was engaged in coordinating and supervising the financial management and operations of the 12 production credit corporations and 488 production credit associations. For his initiative and leadership in developing operating improvements, Mr. Smith received a U.S.D.A. Superior Service Award in 1947.

Bruce V. Snow was born and raised in the potato farming areas of Long Island. He went to work for the Dairymen's League as a field reporter-photographer on the *Dairymen's League News* following graduation in 1949 from Syracuse University, School of Journalism. He subsequently became Associate Editor, Editor, Assistant Manager of Public Relations, and then Manager of Public Relations for the League. He is Chairman of the Public Relations Advisory Committee of the National Council of Farmer Cooperatives, a member of the Public Relations Society of America, Advertising Club of New York, the National Agricultural Relations Council, and an associate member of the American Agricultural Editors' Association.

Gordon Sprague, Economist for Land O'Lakes Creameries, Inc., Minneapolis, Minn., was born on a farm in southern Minnesota where he grew up and later attended the University of Minnesota. His attendance at the University of Minnesota was interrupted by World War I after which he returned to college and later worked for 17 years in the U.S.D.A., part of which time was with the Division of Cooperative Marketing. After World War II he left the Department and went to work for the Western Condensing Company at Appleton, Wis., where he worked for 11 years. In 1956, he joined the staff of Land O'Lakes Creameries, Inc., where he has continued until the present time.

Beryle Stanton is Editor, *News for Farmer Cooperatives,* a monthly magazine published by Farmer Cooperative Service, U.S.D.A. As head of the Service's cooperative information work she has studied cooperatives and their growth for over two decades. Mrs. Stanton has been President of the Federal Editors Association, an organization of government information people, and Secretary and on the board of the Cooperative Editorial Association, a group made up of staffs of membership publications of cooperatives in the United States and Canada. In 1966, she received its H. E. Klinefelter Award for contributions to cooperative journalism. Mrs. Stanton was born in Kansas and attended Kansas State University, Manhattan, Kans.

Thomas H. Steichen, who succeeded Emil A. Syftestad as General Manager of the Farmers Union Central Exchange, was born and raised on a 160-acre general farm near Watertown, S. D. He was educated in Watertown schools, including its business college, and cooperative schools sponsored by the Northern States Cooperative League and the Central Exchange. Starting his cooperative career as Manager of the New Richmond, Wis., Farmers Union Cooperative Oil Company, he became a Central Exchange employee on April 15, 1936, in the credit department. He was appointed Assistant Credit Manager in 1938, Credit Manager, 1951; Assistant General Manager, 1955; and General Manager on July 19, 1957. In addition to his management duties, he is President, Northwest Cooperative Mills; General Manager, Cenex Pipeline Company; General Manager and Executive Vice President, Cenex, Inc.

Milo K. Swanton has been a farmer all his life, owning and operating the farm he first rented in 1919. His education began in a one-room rural school and continued through graduation from the University of Wisconsin. His agricultural cooperative career began in 1919 as local Secretary of the American Society of Equity. In 1922, he led in organizing the Madison Milk Producers Cooperative Association and became that organization's first President. He helped in organizing the Wisconsin Cooperative Tobacco Pool and the Southern Wisconsin Breeders Cooperative. As Executive Secretary of the Wisconsin Council of Agriculture Cooperative from 1937 until his retirement in 1964, Milo K. Swanton worked on a broad scale for farmer cooperatives in Wisconsin and nationally.

George H. Thomson has been Director of Information and Education, Producers Livestock Association, Columbus, Ohio, since 1947. He is a native of Spearfish, S. D., and a graduate with a Journalism major of the University of Nebraska. After serving on the staff of South Dakota State University, Brookings, he was from 1936 to 1947 with the Information Division and Governor's Office, Farm Credit Administration, Washington, D. C. He is presently Field Editor of the *National Live Stock Producer,* Chicago; Producers' Editor of the *Buckeye Farm News;* and Radio Market Broadcaster, WRFD.

Glenn W. Thompson is Membership and Public Relations Director of Midland Cooperatives, Inc. He was born and raised on a farm in Indiana, and graduated from Wabash College in 1926. After graduate work at Indiana University and high school teaching, he joined the Indiana Farm Bureau Cooperative in 1933. He joined Midland's staff in 1936. He is a director of Minnesota Association of Cooperatives and Minnesota Consumers League, and has served on the Minneapolis Board of Education.

Robert B. Tootell was reared on his parents' homestead in central Montana. A graduate of Montana State College, he later spent much of his professional career there as an instructor in economics, as the first Extension Land Economist in the U. S., and later as State Director of Cooperative Extension work. He was Extension Director also in Washington State for a brief period. Tootell earned an M.S. degree in Agricultural Economics from the University of California in 1931, an M.P.A. degree from Harvard University, and was awarded an honorary LL.D degree from Montana State in 1956. He spent 10 years with the Federal Land Bank of Spokane beginning in 1934. After 10 years away in Land-Grant College work, he returned to the cooperative Farm Credit system in early 1954 as Governor of the Farm Credit Administration, in which position he is still serving in 1966.

Orion Ulrey has been with the Department of Agricultural Economics at Michigan State University since 1928. He was raised on a farm in Clark County, Ill., and received his B.S. in Agriculture at the University of Illinois in 1923. He was granted the Ph.D. in Agricultural Economics at

Cornell University, 1934. He studied cooperatives in Western Europe and Scandinavia in the 30's, and was a Fulbright teacher, University of Peshawar, Pakistan, 1954–55. He also served as a social scientist, University of Missouri AID team, Ranchi Agricultural College, India, 1958–62. He investigated the role of cooperatives and training programs in patterns of rural development in African, Asian, and East European countries during the summer of 1963. He initiated student cooperatives and a credit union at Michigan State.

Lloyd L. Ullyot, President of the St. Paul Bank for Cooperatives, was born and reared at Clark, S. D., was graduated from South Dakota State University. He took graduate work at the University of Minnesota, and was on the staff of the Department of Agricultural Economics until 1934 when he joined the staff of the St. Paul Bank for Cooperatives as a business analyst. Elected Treasurer of the bank in 1942, he then served as Vice President and Treasurer from 1954 until his election as President of the bank in November, 1958. Mr. Ullyot also presently serves as Chairman of the Presidents' Committee for the Farm Credit Banks of St. Paul.

J. Kenneth Ward has been President of the Louisville Bank for Cooperatives since 1952, and Chairman of the Presidents' Committee of the Farm Credit Banks of Louisville since March, 1959. He joined the staff of the Louisville Bank for Cooperatives in 1936, after 12 years in the Accounting and Auditing Department of the Indiana Farm Bureau Cooperative Association. He has known Marvin Briggs for nearly 40 years.

Francis R. Wilcox, now President of the National Council of Farmer Cooperatives, was born in Utah in 1900. He graduated from Utah State University and took graduate work at the University of California. After several years as a farm management and marketing specialist at the University of California, and two years with the U.S.D.A., in charge of marketing agreements work, he joined Sunkist as Treasurer. He became Assistant General Manager under Mr. Armstrong in 1941, and succeeded him as Manager in 1957. He retired from Sunkist in 1964.

Leslie E. Woodcock was born in Wilson, N. Y., in 1893. He received his B.A. and M.A. degrees from the University of Rochester, with majors in sociology and economics. He was one of the little group of intellectuals who organized Consumers Cooperative Services, New York City, and was its Secretary, 1921–30. He became Manager of Eastern Cooperatives, in 1931, and held that position until he resigned in 1950. He has been Permanent Representative of International Cooperative Alliance to United Nations Economic and Social Council since 1950, and ICA Observer at UN headquarters. Currently he is a member of the Executive Board of the American Country Life Association and was President of that organization during 1949–51.

Index

American Milling Co.,—G. L. F. part-
nership, 313
American Society of Equity, 15–16, 209,
295, 297, 497, 498
Andrews, Stanley, quoted as to Robin
Hood, 238
Angevine, Erma—
biography of, 563
Parker, Florence E.—A Beacon
Light, 379–382
Armstrong, Paul S.—
review of Farmer Cooperative service
work, 34–35
Sunkist Salesman, 30–35
Arnold, Carl Raymond—
*Farmers Build Their Own Production
Credit System*, 37
The Molder of the Production Credit
System, 36–38
standards for credit agency officers,
362
Arnold, Mary Ellicott—
Creative Urban Worker, 39–41
work with James Peter Warbasse, 40
Associated Cooperatives, 187
Association of Washington Industries,
Harry Beernink active in, 58
Auditing Service, provided Wisconsin
co-ops, 298
Authors, of biographical sketches, 563–
580

Babcock, Howard Edward—
A Renaissance Man, 42–49
first secretary, builder of G.L.F., 46–
48
influenced by frustrating circumstances of farm life, 42–44
succeeded 1937, by James A.
McConnell, 310
work with James A. McConnell,
312–313
Bagwell, John C.—
biography of, 563
Hulbert, Lyman S.—Cooperative
Lawyer, 243–247
Bailey, Liberty Hyde, headed first
Country Life Commission, 550

Baker, Charles F.—
An Enthusiastic Cooperator, 50–54
created Pacific Supply Cooperative,
52–54
Walla Walla Wheat Plan, 51
Banks for Cooperatives—
See Farm Credit.
Beall, Hayes—
biography of, 563
Bowen, Eugene R.—Converted Ad-
vocate, 79–83
Becker, C. H.—
biography of, 563
Herndon, Fred E.—Sagacious
Leader, 198–201
Beernink, H. J.—
creation, activities with Washington
Cooperative Egg & Poultry
Assn., 56–58
Mr. Egg Co-op, 55–58
Bender, James LeRoy—
biography of, 564
Puckett, Edward Newton, He Never
Turned Back, 414–418
Benjamin, Roland N.—
built Pa. Farm Bureau Cooperative
Assn., 59–64
"The Chief," 59–64
unusual partnership with H. S.
Agster, 60
Benson, Ezra Taft, 34, 194
Bergengren, Roy F.—
Credit Union Crusader, 65–70
helped create, administered CUNA,
66–70
quoted on contributions to credit
unions of E. A. Filene, 168–169
Betts, Merle E.—
biography of, 564
Peterson, Henry C.—From Covered
Wagon to Co-op Leader, 395–
398
Bingham, Charles A., first Secretary,
Michigan Farm Bureau, 99
Bingham, Robert Worth—
Co-operative Marketing Act, 73
defended by Sapiro, 452
Cooperative Marketing plan for to-
bacco, 71, 72–73, 152